Management Consulting Today and Tomorrow

This new edition gathers more than 22 experts to outline the theory behind consulting, providing insight into change processes and management issues in the field. The business of consulting has grown faster than most other businesses, due not only to increased demand by clients, but also to the innovative capabilities of numerous consulting firms as they develop new services.

Divided into six parts, the book introduces readers to the consulting industry, addressing the major practice areas, contexts, and implementations of the field. Significant updates detail the effect of the economic troubles between 2004 and 2010 and then 2010 and now; analyze the market response to consulting in recent years; and provide a more thorough understanding of how consulting is applied in the different areas of a business, such as operations, marketing, and finance. Introductions written by the editors offer further insight into the themes and learning goals of each section, helping readers to recognize the elements of a successful consultation, and utilize their new skill set. The text concludes with a look at the future of consulting with regards to ethics standards and how strong manager-client relationships contribute to financial growth. Readers will also learn how the developing field of entrepreneurship creates new economic structures and job opportunities.

Practitioners, consultants, clients, faculty, and students of business and management will learn not only how to consult, but also gain the skills needed to adapt to and lead organizational change, giving them a competitive edge when they enter the field.

Flemming Poulfelt is Professor of Management and Strategy and Vice Dean at Copenhagen Business School, Denmark.

Thomas H. Olson is Professor of Clinical Management and Organization at University of Southern California-Los Angeles, U.S.A.

"This book is both timely and excellent. It meets a need to significantly improve our understanding of what is effective, cutting-edge consulting to business and covers the key issues of consulting in a brilliant way: appropriately eclectic and broad, but focused on what is essential to know. This will have a strong impact!"

Peter Lorange, *Lorange Institute of Business Zurich, Switzerland*

"For this book, Poulfelt and Olson have assembled a veritable 'who's who' in the world of management and organizational consultants, including themselves. One could not ask for better coverage: comprehensive and broad yet with depth and very current. I know of no better compendium on today's consulting world."

W. Warner Burke, *Columbia University, USA*

"When Larry Greiner published his seminal work on 'Consulting to Management' some 35 years ago, he laid the groundwork to a deeper understanding of a practice which has been growing exponentially since. The new and updated edition builds on his heritage and provides an impressive kaleidoscope which constitutes today's diverse universe of management consulting. An indispensable companion for consultants and their clients alike!"

Roland Deiser, *Claremont Graduate University, USA*

"The business of management consultancy has been changing over the last 30 years. The business grew economically, the skills of the consultants developed further, the roles of consultants became more differentiated, and the firms were better managed. This book covers a complete set of issues on management consultancy compiled by well-known and experienced professionals in this field. The group of editors and authors has succeeded in collecting relevant theory, experience, and practices to describe the state-of-the-art of the sector."

Leon de Caluwe, *Vrije Universiteit, The Netherlands*

"In this newest edition, like the original Greiner and Poulfelt edition, Poulfelt and Olson have designed a book that can be used for my own consulting work or in the classroom where wannabe consultants are yearning for the most current consulting knowledge. Students demand cases, challenges, and insights from the shrouded world of consulting – these authors offer it all with real world learnings."

Therese Yaeger, *Benedictine University, USA*

Management Consulting Today and Tomorrow
Perspectives and Advice from Leading Experts

Second Edition

Edited by Flemming Poulfelt
Thomas H. Olson

Routledge
Taylor & Francis Group
NEW YORK AND LONDON

Second edition published 2018
by Routledge
711 Third Avenue, New York, NY 10017

and by Routledge
2 Park Square, Milton Park, Abingdon, Oxon OX14 4RN

*Routledge is an imprint of the Taylor & Francis Group,
an informa business*

© 2018 Taylor & Francis

The right of Flemming Poulfelt and Thomas H. Olson to be identified as the authors of the editorial material, and of the authors for their individual chapters, has been asserted in accordance with sections 77 and 78 of the Copyright, Designs and Patents Act 1988.

All rights reserved. No part of this book may be reprinted or reproduced or utilised in any form or by any electronic, mechanical, or other means, now known or hereafter invented, including photocopying and recording, or in any information storage or retrieval system, without permission in writing from the publishers.

Trademark notice: Product or corporate names may be trademarks or registered trademarks, and are used only for identification and explanation without intent to infringe.

Library of Congress Cataloging-in-Publication Data
A catalog record for this book has been requested

ISBN: 978-1-138-12427-1 (hbk)
ISBN: 978-1-138-12428-8 (pbk)
ISBN: 978-1-315-64829-3 (ebk)

Typeset in Sabon
by Apex CoVantage, LLC

Contents

Contributors   xi

PART I
Consulting Industry, Skills, and Professionalism   1

    Introduction   1

1 The Changing Global Consulting Industry   5
    FLEMMING POULFELT AND THOMAS H. OLSON, UPDATED FROM
    FLEMMING POULFELT, ARVIND BHAMBRI, AND LARRY GREINER

    A Return to Consulting's Heyday 5
    The Global Financial Meltdown 6
    Back on Track 6
    What Lies Ahead? 11
    After the Burst of the Bubble 13
    History in Brief 16
    Enduring Trends and Client Needs 23
    Responses of Consulting Firms to Marketing Trends 26
    Industry Restructuring 31
    Role Restructuring 32
    More Questions than Answers 33

2 Professionalism in Consulting   37
    DAVID MAISTER

    Forging Attitudes 38
    Skills with Clients 41
    Integrity at the Core 42

vi Contents

    Problems of Enforcement 46
    The Real Bottom Line 49

3 The Marketing and Selling of Consulting Services   51
    ROBERT DUBOFF AND PETER R. GIULIONI

    The Challenge 52
    Where to Start? 53
    Achieving the Right Balance 54
    Keys to Effectiveness 56
    Compensation and Rewards 64
    Relationship Marketing 65
    Advertising, Public Relations, and Media Management 66
    Other Approaches 68
    Solo Practitioners and Small Firms 68
    Future Needs and Challenges 69

PART II
Major Practice Areas in Consulting   71

    Introduction   71

4 IT Management Consulting: The Industry and Profession   75
    MICHAEL A. MISCHE

    1.0 Introduction 75
    2.0 Evolution of IT and IT Consulting 77
    3.0 Defining the IT Industry 91
    4.0 Defining IT Management Consulting 97
    5.0 Future of IT Management Consulting 111
    6.0 Conclusion 115

5 Strategy and Organization Consulting   118
    DAVID A. NADLER AND ADRIAN J. SLYWOTZKY

    Before 1960: The Primacy of Intuition and Judgment 119
    1960–2000: Sequential Consulting, Divergent Disciplines 119
    From Business Policy to Value Creation Models 121
    Organization Consulting: From the Individual to the Enterprise 126
    Requirements for Organization Consultants 131
    Change Management Consulting 131
    An Aging Model 133
    Concurrent and Integrated Enterprise Design 135
    Implications for Consulting 137

6 Trust-Based Selling of Consulting Services 141
CHARLES H. GREEN

The Paradox of Consulting Sales 141
The Alternative: A Trust-Based Approach to Selling Consulting Services 144
Building a Consulting Firm That Sells on Trust 152

7 Operations Management Consulting 155
RICHARD B. CHASE, K. RAVI KUMAR, AND PETER R. GIULIONI

Who Are Today's Operations Consultants? 157
The Five Ps of Operations Management 158
Key Concepts for OM Consultants 160
Different Contexts for OM Consulting 162
Analytical Tools of Operations Consultants 166
Practical Problems Facing OM Consultants 168
Future Issues for OM Consulting 169
The Challenge and Reward of OM Consulting 173

8 Human Resources Consulting: 2016 175
GERALD E. LEDFORD JR. WITH EDWARD E. LAWLER III
AND SUSAN MOHRMAN

Definitions 175
Market Size and Characteristics 176
Types of HR Consulting 177
Types of HR Consultants 178
Buyers of HR Consulting Services 180
An Overview of the HR Consulting Field 180
Conclusion 182

PART III
Consulting in Different Contexts 183

Introduction 183

9 Consulting to CEOs and Boards 187
MARK B. NADLER AND DAVID A. NADLER

Consulting to CEOs 188
Consulting to the Board 198
Consulting to Both the CEO and the Board 206
Know Thyself and Thy Client 207

Contents

10 Consulting on the Global Stage   209
MATTHEW C. HEIM

Introduction 209
Pre-Engagement Considerations 210
Putting the Global Consulting Approach to Work 220
The Global Consulting Experience 226

11 Public Sector Consulting   228
THOMAS H. OLSON

1. *What Is Public Sector Consulting? 228*
2. *Process for U.S. Federal Government Consulting – Contractor/Client Roles, Relationships, Rules, Regulations and Request for Proposals 233*
3. *The Role of the Consultant/Contractor Vis-à-Vis Competitor Clients/Customers – Prior, During and After the RFP 238*
4. *Responding to Request for Proposals 241*
5. *The Top Government Consultants/Contractors/Key Competitors/Products and Services/Linkages via M&As 248*
6. *The Future of Public Sector Consulting 253*
Appendix 1 – Federal Acquisition Regulation 255
Appendix A – Lockheed Martin Major Consulting/Production Contracts 259
Appendix B – Boeing Acquisition of Rockwell International Major Consulting/Production Contracts as Described in a Federal Trade Commission Article at the Time of the Acquisition 260
Appendix C – Northrup Grumman Acquisition of TRW Major Consulting/Production Contracts and Short History of TRW 261
Appendix D – Details of the Raytheon Merger with Hughes 263
Appendix E – Details of the Leidos Holdings/SAIC Consulting Services 268

PART IV
Implementation in Consulting   271

Introduction   271

12 Intervention Strategies in Management Consulting   273
TOM CUMMINGS

Key Dimensions in Consulting Interventions 274
Four Alternative Intervention Strategies 280
Implications for Consultants, Clients, and the Profession 289

13 Consulting to Integrate Mergers and Acquisitions 294
ANTHONY F. BUONO

Dynamics of M&A Consulting 295
Common Integration Issues 301
Intervention Strategies and Techniques 306
The Future of M&A Consulting 314

14 Business Transformation and Innovation Consulting 319
MATTHEW C. HEIM

Introduction 319
Business Transformation Defined 320
Consulting Roles in Business Transformation 321
Transformational Leadership 323
Collaboration and Innovation 333
The Business Transformation Consulting Experience 335

PART V
Managing and Growing the Consulting Firm 339

Introduction 339

15 Managing Growth Stages in Consulting Firms 341
LARRY GREINER AND JAMES MALERNEE

Growth Stages and Crises 344
Stage I: Exploring the Market for Growth Opportunities 346
Stage II: Focusing on a Specialized Market Niche 350
Stage III: Diversifying into Multiple Offices and Related Services 353
Stage IV: Institutionalizing into a One-Firm Firm 356
Fifth Stage and Resulting Crisis? 360
Developmental Leadership 361

16 High-Performance Consulting Firms 365
JAY W. LORSCH

Strategy, Goals, and People Success Factors 365
Leadership and Partnership Behavior 371
The Firm's Culture: Cause and Consequences 375
Alignment and Firm Size 376

17 Knowledge Management in Consulting 379
MICHAEL A. MISCHE

1.0 Introduction 379
2.0 Competing on Knowledge 389
3.0 Learning and Knowledge Transfer in Management Consulting 394
4.0 Knowledge Management Systems in Consulting 398
5.0 Conclusion: Thinking About the Future of Knowledge 402

PART VI
Looking Ahead at Management Consulting 407

Introduction 407

18 Ethics and the Trusted Advisor 411
CHARLES H. GREEN

Ethics, Virtues, and Values 411
How Do Trusted Advisors Behave? 412
How Can We Create Ethical Firms of Trusted Advisors? 416
Evaluating Success as a Trusted Advisor and as an Ethical Firm 420

19 Consulting in Entrepreneurship: Essential Foundations for Consultants 423
RICKIE A. MOORE

The Entrepreneurial Revolution 424
Creation or Discovery? Are Business Opportunities Created or Discovered? 426
The Entrepreneurial Journey 426
Dynamic Value Creation in Entrepreneurship 428
Evolution of Roles and Skillsets 430
The Entrepreneurial Mindset 430
Innovation and Disruptions – Evolution and Revolution 431
Implications for Consultants 432

Literature on Management Consulting 437
Index 441

Contributors

Arvind Bhambri is Associate Professor of Management and Organization at the Marshall School, University of Southern California, where he specializes in strategic change, competitive strategy, global business development, and leadership. He is co-author of three books and more than 30 articles and cases.

Anthony F. Buono is a Professor of Management and Sociology at Bentley University. He has written and edited nineteen books, and is editor of the *Research in Management Consulting* book series. Dr. Buono is a two-time past Chair of the Academy of Management's Management Consulting Division. His research and consulting interests include the management consulting industry, organizational change, and mergers and acquisitions.

Richard B. Chase is Professor of Operations Management at the Marshall School, University of Southern California. He has written and lectured extensively on the subject of service design. His textbook, *Operations Management for Competitive Advantage* (with R. Jacobs and N. Aquilano) 9th ed., has been among the most widely adopted textbooks in the field for over 35 years.

Tom Cummings is Professor and Chair of the Department of Management and Organization at the Marshall School of Business, University of Southern California. He has authored/co-authored 23 books, and was the 61st President of the Academy of Management. His major research and consulting interests include designing high-performing organizations and managing strategic change.

Robert Duboff is a Lecturer and Executive-in-Residence at The Carroll School of Management at Boston College. He was a line consultant for over two decades with Mercer Management Consulting, serving a client base that featured professional service firms. He then served as Director of Marketing for Ernst & Young.

Peter R. Giulioni is an Associate Professor in the SMO Department and Assistant Dean for Nanyang Business School's Graduate Studies Career

1 The Changing Global Consulting Industry

Flemming Poulfelt and Thomas H. Olson, updated from Flemming Poulfelt, Arvind Bhambri, and Larry Greiner

The Changing Global Consulting Industry was the headline of the chapter on the consulting industry when the book was published originally. Yet the title seems even more relevant to Private Sector, as well as Public Sector, consulting in 2016, as these Sectors are once again undergoing major transformation. In hindsight, we might conclude that consulting is permanently in a state of transition. In fact it *needs* to be, if a firm wants to present itself as a professional advisor to businesses and Public Sector organizations facing their own need to evolve and change. So it is fitting that consulting firms and practitioners describe themselves as being embedded and engaged in a continuous change process. As we noted in the first edition, "It is not the strongest of the species that survive, not the most intelligent, but the one most responsive to change" (Darwin). This observation is just as valid today.

Our original mapping of the industry and its major challenges still has relevance too, although the context now differs from that of the big market shock at the turn of the millennium – the bursting of the dotcom bubble, 2001 bankruptcy of Enron and ensuing recession, compounded by 9/11/2001, implosion of Arthur Andersen in 2002, and increasing global unrest. All of this hurt the consulting industry across sectors for years, creating a turbulent time of fluctuating revenues and profits. It wasn't until around 2004–2005 that the industry started to recover: as late as 2003 a consulting magazine cited the continued wait for a market upturn.

But what has been happening since then? What has been the experience of the industry over the last decade, and what are some of the challenges consultancy firms are facing today? The following provides an update.

A Return to Consulting's Heyday

The turbulence experienced by the consulting industry following the economic recession in the early decade of this century wasn't wholly negative: firms became crisper and clearer in the way they ran their organizations.

For example, efficiency had been on the agenda, followed by new development in service offerings to clients. The industry took off again, seeing new high growth rates and an increase in employment. In 2006 and ensuing years consulting business boomed across sectors once more, and many firms assumed something of a 'walk on the water' attitude. Growth rates were back to double digits (around 10 percent), new services such as real outsourcing were being introduced, intensive price competition persisted, IT heated up again, and classic services thrived as buzzwords lost credibility. Optimism largely dominated until early 2008 when signs of economic malaise began to appear, as the financial sector started to overheat.

The Global Financial Meltdown

On October 9, 2007, the Dow Jones Industrial Average set a record by closing at 14,047. A year later, it had plunged to just above 8,000, having dropped by 21 percent in the first nine days of October 2008. Major stock markets in other countries had plunged alongside the Dow. Credit markets were nearing paralysis. Companies began to lay off workers in droves and were forced to put off capital investments. Individual consumers were being denied loans for mortgages and college tuition. After the nine-day US stock market plunge, the head of the International Monetary Fund (IMF) had some sobering words, warning that "Intensifying solvency concerns about a number of the largest US-based and European financial institutions [had] pushed the global financial system to the brink of systemic meltdown" ("IMF").

The explicit trigger was the collapse of the investment bank Lehman Brothers, which filed for bankruptcy on September 15, 2008, initiating a cascade effect across Wall Street and other financial institutions around the world. The ripples were felt across most markets, including the Public Sector. Everyone was hurting. Before long, booming consulting markets turned to doom.

The implications for consulting were tremendous as clients started to cut back. Firms found themselves having to lay people off again, as they took their foot off the accelerator.

The road to recovery would be a long one.

Back on Track

Turning the consulting business around again took time, due to the industry's dependence on the recovery processes in other markets. But slowly it adapted to the 'new normal', fueling positive growth rates, although on a lower level compared to 'the good old days'.

Taking stock of the consulting industry in the year of 2016 provides the following picture:

Good Times Return

Although not quite enjoying a booming market, consulting has been growing on a healthy trajectory compared to many other industries. On average, the Private Sector consulting industry has seen growth rates in the 5–10 percent range, though with geographical and discipline-related variations. For the Public Sector, and with major synergies and client needs, the grow rate has outstripped the Private Sector for particularly the major companies. This led to the splitting of Private and Public Sector services – with a most notable being the historically older Booz Allen Hamilton. The most recent estimates for revenue in Public Sector note that the US alone spends approximately 600 billion dollars on one of its major clients – quite a large pool of monies for contractors and the Public Sector Consulting / Contactor Industry.

Paradoxically, demand has been going up, yet fees have not. So firms have not been able to rely on the old model of pushing up rates once business picks up; the market's ability to sustain price hikes can no longer be assumed. For the Public Sector, performance metrics have grown as more the basis for compensation. For the Private Sector, this may well be a result of central procurement departments' greater involvement, despite consultancy's associations with knowledge skills and the emphasis on people and relationships. Seemingly this now has less bearing on decision-making processes, which are increasingly based on securing greater value for less money.

Another increasingly common theme being seen in many consulting markets is a rise in tender processes, especially in the Public Sector. In many countries this is an explicit part of the public procurement for tasks above a certain scope.

Commoditization Continues

Private Sector consulting firms have commonly struggled to find the right balance between tailoring a solution to the client versus delivering standardized off-the-shelf solutions. To some degree we have seen a trend towards greater commoditization of services, over developing unique solutions for clients. This might be due to the pressures on pricing, but it could be argued that it also reflects the relatively low rate of innovation in consulting. For Public Sector consulting companies, these businesses have become more reliant on customization – especially with the very large contracts being awarded to 10 or so consulting companies with each company needing to 'compete' for task work and revenue.

Revised Business Models

Some would argue that the fundamental Private Sector business model in consulting has not changed in more than 100 years. While there might be a ring of truth about this, new business models have evolved over time. In their *HBR* article in 2013, Clayton Christensen et al. suggest there are three models – the first a more classic approach, the others new modes of doing consulting business based on other foundations:

Solution shop, as seen at McKinsey, Bain, BCG, IDEO:

a) Structured to diagnose and solve problems whose scope is undefined;
b) Delivers value primarily through the consultant's judgment rather than through repeatable processes;
c) Customers pay high prices in the form of fee-for-service.

Value-added process business, as seen with Motista, Salesforce.com, McKinsey Solution:

a) Structured to address problems of defined scope with standard processes;
b) Processes are usually repeatable and controllable;
c) Customers pay for output only.

Facilitated Network, as exemplified by OpenIDEO, CEB, Gerson, Lehrman Group, Eden McCallum, Byg:

a) Structured to enable the exchange of products, services;
b) Customer pays fees to the network, which in turn pays the service provider.

There is some refreshing of service models in the consulting industry, then – and indeed the illustrations above are not the only manifestations. A further consideration – whether the new models will have major impact on fee structures – remains an open question, as the introduction of fee structures based more around value, for instance, has been a slow process up to now.

The Business Model of the Public Sector remains RFP driven. This said, and per Ashton Carter in the most recent very few years, the challenges of consulting in the Public Sector in 2016 requires significant challenges in moving 'the model' to be more innovation adaptive and collaborative and much quicker to 'navigate' in the 'contracting process'.

Digital Transformation Has Legs

Digitalization or digital transformation is a preoccupation for many companies, now. The explosion of digital consulting in recent years is a response to this and reflects the value that consultants are perceived to offer here. After all, at the heart of digital transformation ambitions is the ability to drive innovation through technology and new systems, to accelerate and generate new business, by changing the way companies do things. This could not be truer of both the Private and Public Sectors. As a result, IT consulting has become a rapid growth area – not just for traditional Private Sector IT-based consultancies but for this Sector's strategy and operational management consulting firms which now offer comprehensive 'digital transformation' services. For the Private Sector, with significant events involving terrorism and intelligence, the access and utilization of digital data and processes have become ever more relevant and important as well as a substantive revenue source.

M&A Activity & Market Consolidation

M&A activities have not returned to previous levels within the Private Sector as, for example, those seen during the dotcom period. However, M&A has been significant in the Public Sector.

Within each Sector a few notable M&As have taken place.

One example in the Private Sector is Deloitte's acquisition of Monitor in 2012. This followed the separation of Deloitte into six separate entities as a function of the Enron debacle and collapse of Arthur Andersen. Although Monitor's 1,200 employees was a drop in Deloitte's ocean of 200,000, Deloitte improved its position in strategy practice, to compete with McKinsey-tier firms (the MBB firms = McKinsey, Bain & BCG). It's possible that the reason for the sale from the seller's side was an attempt to survive the mid-sized consultancy tier.

For the Public Sector Consulting Contractors, the composition of the most dominant consulting companies has remained more the same (as is the case for the Private Sector). Still, there have been major changes. And the most significant of these changes that occurred in the Public Sector was the acquisition by Northrop Grumman of TRW. This then followed with the move of NG Headquarters from Los Angeles to the Washington, D.C., area.

Additionally, Huntington Ingalls Industries (HII) was founded in 2008 as part of the Northrop Grumman Company principally to focus on the US Navy as the client. However, HII then separated from Northrop Grumman and became a separate corporation in 2011.

Further, Hewlett Packard (HP) moved to create HP's (more Public Sector) consulting arm as Hewlett Packard Enterprises in November 2015. This was, essentially simultaneously, accompanied by Computer Sciences Corporation's (CSC) 'spin off' of its Public Sector business and the acquisition of SRA, creating CSRA in November 2015, as well. Additionally, of major changes, a last to be mentioned here is that Leidos became a joint 'spin-off' of Science Applications International Corporation (SAIC) and is a US Public Sector Company headquartered in Reston, Virginia, that provides a variety of consulting services.

Client Professionalism

There is no doubt that both Private and Public Sector clients have become much more 'savvy' professional buyers and users of consultants over the years. Large companies and agencies / organizations, in particular, with extensive experience of using consultants, have found ways to systematize their dealings with consulting firms, formulating explicit policies for when and how to engage them and how to streamline historically more complex and time-consuming processes. However, there are still many companies and agencies reluctant to invite consultants into their operations, for fear of running up charges based on a ticking clock or meter, a perception the Private Sector industry hasn't quite shaken off and the Public Sector works to make more efficient while maintaining effectiveness and quality.

Entrepreneurialism

For the Private Sector, consultants have not made as much 'entry' and impact – largely due to entrepreneurialism being 'earlier in the live cycle' stage of development (Greiner, Evolution and Revolution HBR article from 1972). For the Public Sector, consultants have made more impact with becoming part of large and 'open' contracts that are granted in which multiple contractors are 'preapproved'. This, then and in-turn, allows Public Sector consultants to 'move' more quickly and innovatively to seek out (as by submitting legally approved position 'statements' and the like) to advance the identification of 'needs'.

All said, the use of entrepreneur consultants in both the Private and Public Sectors has been relatively underutilized. Nonetheless, the use of more equity-based-ownership entrepreneurialism by consultants in the Private Sector may well lead to more value creation–like consulting (a la Bain Capital) long into the future. This should then build more successful development of entrepreneurs into viable and valuable companies.

It's Still About Value Creation

A key issue in consulting has always been how much value consultants offer their clients, and how to make value creation more visible. This has been the case for decades within the Private Sector. And it has become much more the case in the most recent decades for the Public Sector – especially since major changes away from fixed-price contacting took place.

In the Private Sector, Bain made a smart move in this area by highlighting the observation that its clients outperform the market at a rate of 4:1, measured against S&P 500 Index companies (http://www.bain.com/about/client-results/index.aspx). And in the Public Sector, more and more engagements are value-based as well – particularly for larger production programs.

Analyses have shown that consultants typically add value in three ways:

- They provide specialist knowledge that helps clients take better decisions.

- Their experience in project delivery helps clients execute their plans more effectively and efficiently.
- The skills of individual consultants improve the capability and team work of managers in client organizations.

More specifically, UK analysis (2010) showed that the average value consultants add to their clients is 10 times the fees paid! This means that in most cases the return on consulting makes for a highly profitable business case. No wonder consultants are working on the basis of the Return on Consulting (RoC) – although making the formula visible in practice can be trickier.

What Lies Ahead?

As we look ahead, consulting firms are facing what have been called 'wicked' problems, i.e. those problems that are difficult or impossible to solve because of incomplete, contradictory and / or changing requirements which may be hard to recognize (Grinth, 2008).

However, this is consultants' *tour de force*: navigating turbulent waters. And there are no indications that this pattern will change. 'Transformation' will always be the quest, then, whether for the client, or for consultants.

But what are the issues consultants and their firms should watch out for? We can point to five clear ones that lie ahead:

Accelerating the Innovation Cycle

With the speed, volatility, and need for continuous renewal and reinvention, clients need consultants to increase the effort and resources they allocate to innovation and development. Per Ashton Carter, this is key to new initiatives in the Public Sector. This could be by developing new services and offerings, by developing the professionals themselves, by cooperating with the clients in new ways, and by experimenting (especially with new and innovative processes in the Public Sector) to a greater degree. If failures are good indicators of success (being prepared to experiment increases the risk that some ventures will fail), consultants could do with generating some more. As Churchill once said, "Success is not final, failure is not fatal: it is the courage to continue that counts."

Anticipating & Driving Disruption

Disruption has become a buzzword, not only in consulting language and rhetoric but also more generally in business. Consultants can help their clients in three ways here. First, they can act as advisors, to stimulate a client to be more disruptive in its behavior and in developing new business models and so on. Secondly, consultants can support their clients by helping them to avoid being disrupted. Third, they themselves can act as disruptors by introducing new services, offerings, or business models. So developing a disruptor's mindset might be a useful priority for consulting firms.

Accommodating the Need for Simplicity

Running a business has become a complex undertaking in the modern age. Growing legislative requirements are another example of what businesses must contend with, and a common source of complaint. But *internal* complexity doesn't make business any easier, either. Although information technology is championed as a vehicle to make systems and processes more efficient and smooth, often the opposite is true. So consultants have an opportunity to help by helping clients simplify their IT estates and business processes.

Thinking Global, Acting Local

Under pressure at home following the financial crisis, many consulting firms looked for new markets outside their national domain or overseas. However, for many it has not been an easy ride, as working in other contexts and cultures can be more challenging than expected. This has become even more substantively problematic for major Public Sector consulting firms that are straddled with more security of information and processes requirements.

But the global perspective is still an important driver for many consulting firms – not only as a business growth initiative, but also as a mindset. To succeed internationally, consultants need to blend global vision and strategy with local considerations, i.e. 'think global, act local' (often shortened to the rather clumsy term, 'glocal').

Leading Practices

Most consulting firms will have upgraded their leadership skills over the years and refreshed their approach to managing their practices. However, running a professional services firm can present its own challenges, when most professionals have been hired for their ability to tackle challenging client assignments. But experience shows that if a consulting firm is well managed, this has a positive impact not just on profitability but also on the caliber of person the firm is able to recruit. This is because professionals want to be employed somewhere where assignments are challenging and rewarding, and where they feel appreciated, and will be nurtured and developed.

Leadership investment and prioritization should also be high on the agenda for consulting firms into the future. This is particularly the case within the Public Sector. Given the aggregation as of 2016, the seven largest Public Sector consultants / contractors with the US across the world markets remained essentially the same: Lockheed Martin (LMC), Boeing, Raytheon, General

Dynamics (GD), Northrop Grumman (NGC), Leidos Holdings (w SAIC – two separate companies now), and Huntington Ingalls Industries (HII).

Of course, there are other major and large (in terms of revenue and employees) consulting firms to the Public Sector that cross over into the Private Sector. These include: Accenture, BAE, Booz Allen Hamilton Inc., (now split in two separate companies), Computer Sciences Corporation (CSC), General Electric, HP (Enterprise Services – Hewlett Packard Enterprise as of November 2015), International Business Machines (IBM), SRA International, Inc., Unisys Corporation, and AECOM that acquired URS Corporation in October 2014. While these are but a few of the literal tens of 100,000s of businesses that provide Public and Private Sector consulting, these businesses are widely recognized and significant and are the focus of this text book. And, therefore, these consultants will be referenced and used as representative examples of engagements and programs about which more information is available and known.

Summing up: the future will therefore belong to those consulting firms and professionals that can appreciate the past but are not bound to it; to those who anticipate emerging trends; and who can run faster, work more flexibly and efficiently, and add more value than their competitors. It's a race that will require a lot of foresight, stamina, and clever tactics.

Bibliography

Christensen, C.M., Wang, D. & Bever, D. van. Consulting on the Cusp of Disruption. *Harvard Business Review*. October 2013.

Grinth, Keith (2008). Wicked Problems and Clumsy Solutions: The Role of Leadership. *Clinical Leader*, Volume I Number II.

'IMF in Global "Meltdown" Warning,' *BBC News*, October 12, 2008.

Management Consulting Association, 2010 and 2016.

http://www.bain.com/about/client-results/index.aspx

After the Burst of the Bubble

For over four decades leading up to 2000 and the new millennium, the management consulting industry experienced explosive and continuous growth, approximating an increase of 15 to 20 percent per year. Profit margins also increased dramatically, due to larger projects, better leverage ratios between partners and staff, and diversification into new services, such as outsourcing. Total revenues of the global industry are now moving toward $150 billion, and the worldwide number of consultants is close to 1 million, including both those who work in large and small firms, as well as solo practitioners. Few other industries in history have experienced such sustained growth and financial success for so long a period of time.

This impressive record of growth and financial success is only an indication of the consulting industry's deeper and wider impact around the world. Over the years, the industry's many firms and consultants have made significant worldwide contributions to management knowhow and, in so

Consulting Insights Trianz, Inc.–Succeeding in the New Era

During this discontinuous shift in the consulting industry, Trianz is a consulting firm that has achieved triple digit growth to become a respected player in its information technology niche. Trianz helps clients to reinvent business processes across the entire value chain, using the Internet as the medium for achieving leverage in the chain. Trianz provides a full-service outsourcing infrastructure in the United States and India, supported by a team of professional consultants capable in strategic and value chain analysis.

To begin our assessment of the industry's future, we must first establish an historical perspective for the industry. In doing so, we will identify earlier trends and issues that still face firms and consultants today. As we move along, we will point out what are likely to be the changing needs of clients and how consulting firms will have to change their strategies to meet these needs. Without this broadened perspective, consulting firms can easily misjudge where they are in the unfolding dynamics of the industry. Hanging on to past practices and strategies will likely become a recipe for future disaster.

History in Brief

In a 1998 article in the *Journal of Management Consulting*, Staffan Canback made an interesting observation with reference to the experience curve in consulting services. He wrote:

> If the experience curve applies in consulting services, then it may be noteworthy that approximately 80 percent of all consulting experience was generated in the last 17 years, and only 20 percent in the period from 1886 (when Arthur D. Little started the first consulting firm) to 1980.[1]

With further accumulated experience since Canback's article, we can reasonably conclude that, in this 115+ year-old industry, more than 90 percent of all experience has been generated in the last 20 years.

What are the factors that stimulated growth in the 1980s and 1990s and made the industry fundamentally different in both quantity and quality from the preceding years? What can we conclude about this growth that may influence client needs and consulting practices over the next few decades? As Exhibit 1.1 shows, changing business issues and opportunities facing clients have led to new management techniques and concepts, which in turn have changed the offerings of consulting firms.

Before 1950

Prior to 1950, most consulting firms focused on efficiency and technical issues in manufacturing. The first consulting firm was Arthur D. Little

(ADL), founded in 1886 (and filed for bankruptcy protection in 2002). ADL grew out of a research laboratory, and it continued to maintain links with its technical roots for several decades, long after its management consulting accounted for a majority of its revenues. ADL's ascendancy occurred in the

Exhibit 1.1 The Historical Developments of Consulting

Phases	Time	Firms	Management Issues
1. Origins of consulting	Before 1900	Fayol, Taylor	Birth of scientific management
2. The engineering epoch	1900–1925	Arthur D. Little	Scientific management, work design
3. Birth of personnel and HR	1925–	Hay, Towers Perrin	Human relations, compensation
4. Emergence of the generalist approach	1930	McKinsey, Booz Allen, PA	General management
5. Internationalization/ reentrance of engineering	1950	Cresap	Operations management (OR, OM)
6. Rise of computer consultants, conglomerates	1960	The Big 8 Accounting Firms	Performance measurement, electronic data processing, portfolio management
7. Business strategy	1970	BCG, Bain	Planning, organization structure, marketing, competitive advantage
8. Restructuring and effectiveness	1980	March & McLennan, Saatchi & Saatchi, KPMG, Ernst & Young	Excellence, culture, M&A, globalization
9. Information technology and reengineering	1990	Accenture, PwC, Monitor, IBM Consulting Services	Internet leadership, change, Y2K, BPR, ERP
10. E-Business and value chain	2000	Cap Gemini/ E&Y, IBM Global Services	Outsourcing, transformation, networks, alliances

maturing period of scientific management, whose origins go back to Frederick Taylor[2] and Henri Fayol[3] in the early 1990s.

In the first half of the 20th century, most of the consulting firms were founded either with specific customer opportunities in hand, such as Booz Allen Hamilton with the US government, or with a specific functional specialization, such as Towers Perrin in compensation and human resources. For the most part, this early imprinting led to a lasting impact on both firms. Thus, even today Booz Allen continues to retain significant federal business, and Towers Perrin is still known for its major presence in human resources consulting.

Following World War II, the focus of management consulting turned to designing, improving, and systematizing the internal functioning of client organizations and the marketing of products. Specific emphasis was given to designing divisional structures, formal budgeting, performance evaluation, strategic planning systems, goal setting, compensation schemes, and other such performance improvement techniques. Advertising and sales force management were major issues in marketing. Most consulting firms chose to specialize only in a narrow range of needs as expressed by clients.

In the 1960s, a dramatic and discontinuous shift occurred in the scope and complexity of management consulting. Client companies were growing rapidly through diversification and creating the first conglomerates, and the novelty of international competition was fast becoming a reality. In this changing environment, companies asked consultants for help on pressing strategic questions about which business they should be in and how they should internationalize themselves. This was the stage where the elite strategy consulting firms, such as BCG, became household names.

1960–1980

McKinsey & Co. had existed as a generalist firm for almost four decades (since 1925) when Bruce Henderson founded the Boston Consulting Group (BCG) in 1963. Henderson pioneered the marketable idea of strategy consulting based on expert analysis of a client's competitive situation. BCG differentiated itself through promoting new strategy concepts, notably the Experience Curve and the Growth/Share Matrix. The accelerating popularity of these concepts began to establish the credibility of consulting firms as developers of intellectual capital and led to a two-way, synergistic relationship between business schools and consulting firms. The top strategy consulting firms became the first job choice of MBAs, an advantageous recruiting position that certain elite firms like McKinsey and BCG continue to maintain to this day.

During the 1960s nontraditional players began to enter the consulting industry, but often with mixed results. A negative example was Citibank acquiring Cresap, McCormack & Paget, and then divesting it to preserve the consulting firm's independence. Eventually, Towers Perrin acquired Cresap. The high visibility of top strategy consulting firms in the 1960s also attracted attention from the Big 8 accounting firms, which had long established auditing and tax relationships with many large Fortune 500 companies. Without exception, these accounting firms all launched management consulting services, which promised higher fees and margins than yielded by their auditing services. For the most part, the consulting divisions of the accounting firms were not able to penetrate the elite strategy market. However, with a larger employee base and lower fees than the strategy boutiques, they gravitated toward operations consulting and information technology.

1980–2000

By the end of 1980, the stage was set for the golden era of management consulting, which evolved around information technology and global expansion. Consulting firms grew in the 1980s and 1990s through both organic means by developing new practices in-house and also rapidly by mergers and acquisitions. This was also the era of global growth for US consulting firms as they moved out around the world to capture over 80 percent of the world consulting market.

At the same time, the accounting firms made many mergers and acquisitions in order to achieve greater scale and leverage in their auditing and consulting practices. Thus, we saw PMI (Peat Marwick International) merge with KMG (Klynveld Main Goerdeler) in 1987 to become KPMG; Deloitte merged with Touche Ross in 1989 and turned into Deloitte & Touche; Ernst & Whinney with Arthur Young in 1989 to become Ernst & Young; and Price Waterhouse with Coopers & Lybrand in 1998, turning into PricewaterhouseCoopers. In addition, numerous small- and medium-sized consultancies were acquired by larger firms during this same period, such as the French company Sogetti in 1991 acquiring both the MAC Group, which was founded as a faculty-based general management consulting firm, and United Research, an operations consulting firm. These latter acquisitions were merged to form the core of Gemini Consulting.

Attracted by the consulting industry's growth and high profitability, several nontraditional companies also attempted to enter the industry through high profile acquisitions. Saatchi & Saatchi was one of the first companies to articulate the concept of 'one-stop-shopping' for professional services. Their acquisitions included Petersen in litigation consulting and Hay in human resources and compensation consulting, along with other companies in market research and financial services. The results of Saatchi's acquisition strategy proved disastrous; most of the acquired consulting firms were later sold back to their original sellers for a fraction of the price paid just a few years earlier. Marsh & McLennan, from insurance, was more successful in moving into consulting with the acquisition of Mercer and several other professional services firms.

By the 1990s, the main driver for acquisitions appeared to shift toward providing integrated IT solutions under one roof, which in turn led to EDS acquiring A.T. Kearney and to CSC acquiring Index. These combinations were not deterred, even though some consulting acquisitions by non-consulting firms resulted in serious incompatibilities. By far the largest growth during this period occurred among the information system providers. Driven by the increasing interdependence of information technology and strategy, these firms helped clients to formulate an information strategy, and then to design and install the appropriate IT infrastructure, all of which is further discussed in Chapter 4, *Information Technology Consulting*.

During the late 1990s, many of the IT consultancies diversified into outsourcing, which subsequently became a major growth driver. As clients began outsourcing their entire IT departments to consultants, this attracted hardware and software firms like IBM and EDS. In the marketing of outsourcing, the consultant's value-added proposition is that of shifting assets to the consultant so the client's balance sheet is improved, and the client can focus on its core business.

Firms in the IT segment included IBM Global Services, which is now the largest consulting firm in the world, Electronic Data Systems (EDS), Accenture, Deloitte Consulting, and Cap Gemini Ernst & Young (CGE&Y). Their primary consulting focus, other than outsourcing, is on providing a wide range of IT services, including: 1) the assessment of a client's IT infrastructure; 2) the development of appropriate systems and software; 3) the integration of incompatible technology; 4) the redesign of business processes; 5) the purchase and installation of appropriate hardware; and 6) change management and training of employees. Among the many services provided by these firms, strategy analysis is a relatively small segment, and even it is usually conducted with an IT emphasis.

2000 into the Storm

As Exhibit 1.2 shows, in 2001–2002, the 10 largest consulting firms recorded approximately $52 billion in revenues (about 42 percent of the total market), up from less than $2 billion in 1980. This suggests an industry that is increasingly dominated by a few large firms, primarily IT-oriented firms. Only two generalist firms, McKinsey and Mercer Consulting, appear in the top 10 in revenues. The IT firms remain at the top even if we discount their revenues by 20 to 40 percent derived from outsourcing.

If we break down total revenues into separate practice areas, Exhibit 1.3 reveals that, in 2001–2002, the 10 largest consulting firms accounted for approximately $9.8 billion in revenue for the strategy practice area; the

Exhibit 1.2 The 10 Largest Global Management Consulting Firms, 2001–2002

	Revenues (US$/b)	Number of Consultants	Estimated Market Share (%)
IBM	$10.8	50,000	8.6
Accenture	9.5	63,000	7.6
Cap Gemini Ernst & Young	5.9	31,500	4.7
Deloitte Consulting	5.6	26,000	4.5
PricewaterhouseCoopers Consulting	5.5	32,000	4.4
CSC	3.6	15,500	2.9
McKinsey & Co.	3.3	8,400	2.6
EDS (inc. A.T. Kearny)	2.9	8,900	2.3
KPMG Consulting	2.7	7,500	2.1
Mercer Consulting Group	2.2	11,700	1.8
Total	$52.0	254,500	41.5

Source: *Management Consultant International*, June 2002

10 largest information technology practices for $27.6 billion; the 10 largest human resources consulting practices for $9.2 billion; and the 10 largest operations consulting practices for $9.9 billion. As one can see, the IT segment is about three times larger than each of the remaining services, all of which are at about the same level.

Interestingly, in Exhibit 1.3, 22 different firms compose the top 10 across the four practice areas, which indicates some degree of cross-specialization, since the table would require 40 firms if it was 'pure' specialization with no overlap across practice areas. However, only two firms, Accenture and PwC (now IBM), have been successful in broadly diversifying themselves across all four categories, although we suspect that much of this coverage is closely related to IT activities. As for profitability, the economics clearly favor the strategy consulting firms over the IT consultants. The top strategy consulting firms average about $450,000 in revenues per consultant per year, which compares to approximately $200,000 in IT-based consultancies. The profits per strategy consultant are considerably higher than in IT firms. Although Accenture is approximately eight times bigger than McKinsey in total number of employees, it is only three times larger in total revenues. However, the IT firms clearly lead in total revenues and total profits because of their much greater size.

Exhibit 1.3 The Top 10 Revenue Firms in Four Practice Areas

Strategy	2001	IT	2001	HR	2001	Operations	2001
1. Deloitte Consulting	$1.7	IBM	$8.6	Mercer Consulting Group	$1.9	Accenture	$2.5
2. McKinsey & Co.	1.6	PwC	3.2	Accenture	1.2	CGE&Y	1.4
3. Accenture	1.4	Deloitte	2.8	D&T—Human Capital	1.2	PwC	1.1
4. BCG	0.9	Accenture	2.6	Towers Perrin	1.1	IBM	1.1
5. CGE&Y	0.9	EDS	2.6	Watson Wyatt	1.0	McKinsey & Co.	0.9
6. CSC	0.8	CSC	2.1	Aon Consulting	0.9	Deloitte Consulting	0.8
7. PwC	0.7	KPMG	1.8	PwC	0.5	CSC	0.7
8. Bain & Co.	0.7	CGE&Y	1.6	Hewitt Associates	0.5	EDS/A. T. Kearney	0.6
9. Booz Allen Hamilton	0.6	Atos	1.2	Buck Consultants	0.5	Booz Allen Hamilton	0.5
10. EDS/A. T. Kearney	0.5	T-Systems	1.1	Andersen	0.4	Getronics	0.3
TOTAL	$9.8		$27.6		$9.2		$9.9

All numbers are in billion dollars
Source: *Consultant News*, 2002

Exhibit 1.3 also suggests that human resources consulting is a highly specialized field where the IT firms are not so dominating. However, this practice area is also more IT-focused in its development (see Chapter 8 on *Human Resources Management*). Apparently, the fastest growing part of human resources consulting lies not in its historical work on HR strategy and compensation but in arranging for the outsourcing of a client's back-office HR functions. In these arrangements, some or all of a client's entire payroll, benefits, and training programs are transferred to an outsourcing partner.

Enduring Trends and Client Needs

The current period of industry turmoil provides an opportunity for consulting firms to examine the underlying forces shaping the future needs of clients. Being able to meet these needs will determine the consulting winners in the future. Firms need to avoid the easy assumption that their growth is assured by client growth. Today, many clients aren't growing, or they are turning away from consultants to rely on their own staff professionals for help. So it is important to begin with prospective clients to see what is on their minds – this is where all consulting firms should start their analyses as they reexamine their future business strategies.

We detect five major trends affecting client needs, all of which arose over the past decade and are likely to continue into the future. Consulting firms must tune their service offerings to these trends.

1. Keeping up with the pace of change. All industries have increasingly had to cope with ever shortening product life cycles. Although some industries, such as personal computers and consumer electronics, have long operated with cycles of less than a year, even traditional, long life cycle companies like aircraft engines and airplane manufacturers are now greatly reducing their cycle times for competitive reasons. In addition, many potential clients are facing other threatening shifts that limit long-term thinking, such as new nontraditional competitors, deregulation, and technological shifts – all of which create uncertainty and cause companies to rethink their strategic positions and reinvent themselves more frequently.

Discontinuous change requires new strategic concepts, which is the province of strategy consultants. Not surprisingly, new and proprietary strategy concepts and tools have become a major basis for achieving differentiation among the offerings of consulting firms (see Chapter 5, *Strategy and Organization Consulting*). In the future, consulting firms that focus their strategies and skills on helping clients with issues of speed to market, whether it is in operations or in marketing, will likely receive a favorable audience.

2. Continuously reducing costs. Operational efficiency and cost containment have become necessary for corporate survival (see Chapter 7, *Operations Management Consulting*). As a result, companies are seriously reevaluating their mix of operating activities, and many are deciding to outsource activities that are not part of their core competency. For the most part, these outsourced functions include backoffice departments concerned with logistics, data processing, human resources transactions, and sometimes even the complete manufacturing of products.

This trend toward reconfiguring a company's value chain is leading to considerable growth in consulting. Consultants are undertaking large projects to help companies assess and reengineer their activity mix, assisting them in deciding what their core competencies are, and what activities should be outsourced. In addition, consulting firms are becoming primary outsourcing and infrastructure providers to their clients. This is opening up an entirely new and sizeable revenue stream with a reliable cash flow, in contrast to a tradition of sporadic payments by clients.

3. Accelerating product and market development. As companies face maturing markets and intense competition in their home bases, they are actively seeking new products and redesigning old ones. In this effort, tradition-bound companies often lack creativity within their organization cultures, and so they look to consultants for outside help. This requires consultants to study customers' needs and competing products and to work closely with a client's R&D, marketing, and product designers, as illustrated in Chapter 6, *Trust-Based Selling of Consulting Services*.

In addition, there are now major international openings in nontraditional markets, including China, India, and Eastern Europe. With limited experience in these markets and abundant horror stories of failed ventures, client companies are seeking assistance from consultants with offices abroad. Not surprisingly, McKinsey's office in India became its fastest growing, most profitable office in the late 1990s.

4. Coping with discontinuous technology shifts. Many experts argue that science and technology are driving the economics of business and product development. Moving from central mainframes to client servers and distributed computing, from intra-networks to EDI and then to Web-based collaboration, many companies have found that information technology is not just an implementation tool but a key driver of business strategy. Most companies have learned painfully that the impact of information technology has been pervasive throughout society, causing them to rethink strategically the state of their product lines, asset utilization, and likely future markets.

This need has in turn reopened debates such as "What should be owned versus outsourced?" and "Where in the value chain should we add value?" Indeed, companies like Dell have become industry leaders because of their ability to outsource almost their entire value chain, and thereby construct a new business model based on tight coordination with outsiders. On the other hand, Nokia outsources very little of its operations relative to its competition, and yet it remains successful through the extensive use of IT for coordinating internal production and logistics.

The emergence of industry leaders with nontraditional business models, such as Dell, has made it a business imperative for companies to reexamine the fundamentals of their business models. For example, entrenched competitors like General Motors and Ford have come together to form a joint venture, Covisint, to create and manage common e-commerce platforms for procurement. Similarly, the largest consumer packaged goods companies have joined to form Transora. In both cases, a major portion of the initial budget of these new ventures went to consulting firms who helped to set up the joint venture.

5. Meeting the global imperative. As we shall see in Chapter 10, *Consulting on the Global Stage*, consulting firms of all sizes, in order to prosper in the future, are positioning themselves to handle the globalization of industries and companies. Large consulting firms will need to locate themselves overseas at many sites, and smaller ones will have to join with larger consulting firms to assist clients in addressing issues of globalization. Consultants have long recognized that their clients will require at some point a global presence and perspective. However, many consulting firms choose to globalize only after following an existing client overseas. More proactive consulting firms have decided to internationalize before their clients so as to exploit new markets abroad. For example, a US firm choosing Japan can begin to serve back-home clients but also local companies in Japan. Research also supports a commonly held belief among large potential clients that consulting firms must be international in order to qualify as a leading-edge player.

Moving abroad may also be a matter of survival. In a 1990 report from ACME, it was noted that North American consulting firms had experienced a continuing drop in revenues attributable to domestic operations to 81 percent of total revenues, with predictions of a further drop to 67 percent in 2000.[4] Similar shifts have been observed in Europe. According to *Consultants News* in 2002, the breakdown of total worldwide consulting revenues is as follows: 56.6 percent North America, 34.5 percent Europe, Latin America 1.4 percent, Asia Pacific 5.6 percent, and rest of world 2 percent.[5] These numbers indicate that, although consulting is popularly regarded as a global industry, 90 percent of the market remains concentrated in North America and Europe. Interestingly, Asia trails far behind with only 5.6 percent, which not only indicates an opportunity, but also a difficult challenge to penetrate.

All 50 leading global consultancies now occupy offices spread around the world. A majority have expanded abroad through mergers, acquisitions, joint-ventures, and alliances. Today, many firms are focusing on Asia, especially China (see Consulting Firms in China). However, some have also closed offices or operations during this same period due to the recession and an inability to manage operations in a different culture. For example, both CSC Index and Gemini closed down in Japan after several years of frustration and lack of success.

Responses of Consulting Firms to Marketing Trends

In this section, we give our opinions about how consulting firms are adjusting to the new competitive world facing them. These adjustments represent the transformation currently taking place in the consulting industry.

Consulting Insights Consulting Firms in China

Is China the next big growth market? In 2002, BearingPoint was the largest international consulting practice in China with about 350 consultants in four offices and two more soon to open. Its main clients include Beijing Airport Group, China Construction Bank, Samsung, BMW, and China Mobile. The consulting market in China is growing about 50 percent per year. Other firms present include: McKinsey with 180 consultants and $20 million revenue, A. T. Kearney with 70 consultants and $6 million, and Accenture with 160 consultants and $4 million. Also present are Mercer, Monitor, BCG and Roland Berger. The largest domestic firm is HANPU (51 percent owned by China's Legend Computers) in IT consulting with 400 consultants. Clients of these firms include multinationals trying to become profitable in China, large SOEs (state-owned enterprises) required by government and WTO entry to restructure to become private and profitable (telecom, aerospace, energy, banking), and government ministries attempting to become more effective and less bureaucratic.

Key issues include strategy (planning, implementation, change), marketing (branding, advertising, channels), and operations management (organization, goal setting, incentives, control systems). Barriers include lack of understanding among Chinese managers about value and use of consultants. International consulting firms face difficulty in understanding Chinese enterprises and government and being price competitive. Local Chinese consulting firms, numbering only three over 90 consultants, lack sophistication and credibility but possess strong local knowledge.

From detached experts to involved partner

Traditionally, consulting firms have promoted themselves as experts who possess superior analytic capabilities and tools. Thus, a BCG consultant would apply its Growth-Share Matrix in a way that a client company's staff could not do. Moreover, the client's competitors were at a presumed disadvantage because they did not have access to the consultant's model and talent in using it. Over time, however, clients have gradually become disillusioned with the difficulties, if not impossibility, of implementing many of their consultant's abstract conclusions and recommendations.

In response, more and more consultants are becoming involved in implementation and change management. These topics will be further explored in

Chapters 12, 13, and 14 (*Intervention Strategies in Management Consulting*, *Consulting to Integrate Mergers and Acquisitions*, and *Business Transformation and Innovation Consulting*).

The value of a consulting engagement has moved from an emphasis on expert analysis to greater involvement in a client's operations, so as to directly influence the results. Consequently, the role of the consultant is changing from one that relies on expert knowledge to one of collaborating with clients to implement action plans. Some consulting firms even stake their fees and advertising on promised results. Bain, for example, tracks the increase in the share prices of its clients and is known to proclaim, "Our clients outperform the market 3 to 1."

Several large IT firms measure their success on the basis of successful implementation of new information systems. And McKinsey now considers itself successful if it has built in-house client capabilities to solve its own problems the next time around. It remains a moot question as to how far firms should go with the depth of their involvement and promises to clients before possibly losing their objectivity. Clearly, safeguards have to be built and the litigious consequences also weighed.

From advisory services to outsourcing revenues

A press release from *Top-Consultant.com* on October 20, 2002 highlights where the growth opportunities are in today's consulting environment when they state:

> The thousands of consultants that have faced redundancy in the last 12 months would be bemused to hear the industry fared well in 2001. The reality is that traditional consulting suffered while a strategic push into outsourcing has allowed consultancies to cushion the fall.

In the same report, *Top-Consultant* notes: "The U.K. consulting sector enjoyed revenue growth of 17% in 2001, according to figures released this week by the Management Consultancies Association (MCA). However, this favorable picture was largely thanks to 50% growth in outsourcing revenues."

This last quote highlights the fact that underlying the recent growth of the consulting industry is the outsourcing market. In 2001–2002, the six largest consulting firms in terms of total revenues were all firms with strong positions in outsourcing, e.g., IBM, Accenture, PwC, Deloitte Consulting, EDS, and CSC. All types of noncore activities are being considered by clients for outsourcing, from supplier management to routine human resources transactions such as signing up for benefit plans. Many efficiencies can be achieved, as well as self-service through Web-enabled systems.

However, this growth in outsourcing is not without its issues of concern. Clients can lose control over certain operations, leaving themselves vulnerable to the quality of the outsourcing firm. For the consulting firms, there is the potential conflict of interest question: how can IT consulting firms provide objective consulting at the same time it is actively managing major business functions for the same clients? Some industry critics have recommended that once a client becomes an outsourcing client, all consulting should cease for that client.

From conservative professionals to aggressive marketers

As consulting firms move to increase their competitiveness, they are making big investments in marketing to differentiate themselves, including branding efforts, increased advertising, dedicated sales forces, innovative incentive contracts, books with gurus, free seminars, and even low-priced consulting as a loss leader (see Chapter 3, *The Marketing and Selling of Consulting Services*). Direct advertising, once a 'no-no', is now fairly commonplace; Accenture, for example, spends in excess of $50 million on advertising.

Consulting firms are also turning to indirect forms of marketing, using investments in intellectual capital as a strategic differentiator. Many of the leading firms have funded so-called centers of excellence, as well as research in collaboration with academic scholars to produce books and frameworks to enhance the firm's reputation for intellectual leadership. Large firms now offer their own quarterly journals, electronic newsletters, newsy Web sites, and other publications.

From go-it-alone firms to networks

The management consulting industry is slowly developing from stand-alone firms to new organizational forms involving the combination of firms into networks and alliances. The most serious are the alliances between IT consulting firms and their vendors. Accenture with Hewlett-Packard, and SAP with several big IT consultancies, are just two examples. All outsourcing contracts clearly involve outside partners where control and commitment remain somewhat tenuous.

Another type of nonoutsourcing network is a 'loose' one representing various combinations of partners such as locally owned franchises operating under one brand name, while others promote themselves as a large 'alliance' in order to appear bigger in the eyes of potential clients. Most networks are unstable over the long term, so some firms have moved to acquire their former partners, such as IBM Global Services buying PwC Consulting in 2002. Learning how to manage oneself and the other partners in an alliance is a new challenge where a collaborative give-and-take attitude must be the norm.

From private firms to public ownership

The question of what legal form is the most suitable ownership structure – private partnership or public ownership – has been on the agenda of firms for many years. Mostly, consulting firms, especially the general management ones, have long believed in the partnership model. Some earlier attempts to go public have been failures. For example, Booz Allen endured a disastrous period as a publicly owned company in the 1970s. PA Consulting Group went public in the late 1970s, but in the early 1990s, they were close to bankruptcy. Also the Swedish firm, Indevo, in its public offering during the 1980s fell short of its expected outcome from being listed.

One explanation for these negative experiences is offered by Rodenhauser in his newsletter *Inside Consulting*: "The bottom line of going public is that it only works with good management, sustainable business enterprise systems and scalable pricing models for those systems. Very few firms can measure up to all three factors."[6]

Today, several publicly listed consulting firms are selling well below their offering prices. Ernst & Young has sold its consulting business to CAP Gemini, which is quoted on the Paris Stock Exchange, but not fairing well in market value. KPMG Consulting in the US is now listed on the New York Stock Exchange and has changed its name to BearingPoint, Inc., but it is also down by more than half from its opening IPO price.

Just what will happen in the future is problematic, with much depending on the stock market. Consulting firms would like access to capital that a public listing can bring; it also provides a way to put a clear valuation on the firm, enabling them to reward partners and eventually cash them out. A significant deterrent, though, is the potential for an erratic stock market, as well as continuous pressure from financial analysts for quarterly improvement.

We doubt that the large private general management firms will eventually go public, but most of the IT firms will, if not already, because their capital requirements for outsourcing equipment are much larger than private partnerships can provide. Small- and medium-sized firms don't have the same option of going public unless they are acquired by larger, publicly owned companies.

As for the effects on the firms that go public, many questions remain unanswered. There will be governance questions, conflict-of-interest questions, and public scrutiny questions. We do believe that those firms that go public will be driven by market pressure to grow faster in revenues and profits and to expand their operations further into non-consulting services. And what will be the effects on the 'partnership mentality' and traditional spirit of collegiality when the stock market drops precipitously and a partner's net worth is depleted?

From single projects to long-term relationships

In the 1960s and 1970s, consulting was typically thought of as a single, discrete project where the consultants arrived, performed their study, made their recommendations, and left, moving on to the next interesting client. It was Bain that pioneered the art of relationship consulting when it promised exclusivity to a client, rejecting projects from other companies in the same industry. Then the IT companies, with their very large multi-million dollar projects, began to set up offices within clients, staying as long as five years and perhaps longer if they assumed an outsourcing contract.

Today, the general norm in many consulting firms is to strive for long-term relationships with clients – estimates are that at least 60 percent of current consulting revenues originate from existing or former clients. The benefits for the consultants are that it reduces marketing costs and startup time in getting acquainted, and the benefits for the client are that they are dealing with a known quantity. The essential elements of trust and credibility are already established.

Despite the potential for conflicts of interest and even litigation if projects go wrong, we believe that consulting firms will continue to pursue long-term relationships with clients, and they will develop new services and products to assure the continuation of this relationship.

From 'loose' confederations to 'tight' professional leadership

Given the current market slowdown and the intensity of competition, consulting firms are increasingly being challenged to manage themselves more effectively and professionally. In particular, those firms that are publicly listed are also feeling strong pressure from analysts and boards to increase their performance. Previously, many consulting firms were managed more as a loose confederation of partners, led by a Managing Partner who was often elected, either formally or informally by popularity and political power. Many of the 'best practice' attributes that these firms recommended to clients – clear, focused strategy, well aligned organization structure, pay for performance, etc. – were frequently lacking within the consulting firm itself.

For the many Managing Partners with 'laissez-faire' styles, it was rather easy to manage loosely, so long as growth was abundant, thereby providing for high compensation, while hiding lots of mistakes. As a close observer, J. A. Moynihan of PA Consulting, commented, "Most consulting firms are very badly managed. They wouldn't survive a day if they had to compete with GE or whomever."[7]

Today we find more firms carefully scrutinizing the selection of their future CEOs. They want 'take charge' leaders who are well schooled in professional management and who know how to motivate and move firms in a coherent strategic direction. For these new leaders, difficult choices await them on their strategic agenda, including making acquisitions, developing innovative marketing programs, going public, forming alliances, creating Web opportunities, and developing the intellectual capital of the firm. In addition, performance standards need to become clearer and rewards more closely tied to performance. These new leaders must come out of their offices to articulate the firm's future strategy and encourage a unified effort in implementation, which is further discussed in Chapter 15,

Managing Growth Stages in Consulting Firms and in Chapter 16, *High-Performance Consulting Firms.*

Industry Restructuring

The emerging profile among consulting firms is one of large, multiservice businesses using aggressive consumer marketing techniques, forming alliances, and displaying a willingness to enter non-consulting businesses. Most of these firms' new services, such as outsourcing, require large infusions of capital investment and substantial sales volume in order to achieve scale and efficient operations. This trend, therefore, suggests fundamental implications for the emerging structure of the industry, which in many ways is witnessing the creation of mega-enterprises where management consulting may only become a subsidiary division of a multi-service holding company.

In a provocative book titled *The Rule of Three*, Sheth and Sisodia propose an intriguing thesis on industry maturity, supported by case studies from many industries, arguing that "naturally occurring competitive forces, if allowed to operate without excessive government intervention, will create consistent structures across nearly all mature markets."[8] They conclude that every industry will inevitably form a core, or inner circle, of three major players who are full-line generalists, surrounded by niche companies that are product or market specialists. They also caution that professional services firms have been slow to reach a level of structural maturity because the combination of ownership and management in professional services creates "emotional attachment and inhibits purely efficiency-driven economic decision-making."

We believe that the time is coming when the "Rule of Three" will likely emerge in the consulting industry, composed most probably of IBM, Accenture, and one of either CGE&Y or Deloitte Consulting. The big gorilla here is IBM after its recent growth in Global Services and its acquisition of PWC for only $3.5 billion. The goals of these firms are directed toward achieving large-scale market dominance, and already they are the biggest in total revenues.

Other technology hardware firms, such as HP, Cisco, and Oracle, are likely to increase their acquisitions of smaller consulting firms once their stock prices recover and they are able to use their market value for acquisitions. The equipment makers and software providers, like HP and Microsoft, realize that consulting services are a necessary complement to the sales of their other products. For these firms, consulting might be used as a 'loss leader' in hopes of landing bigger dollar contracts in hardware and outsourcing.

We suspect that the general management consulting firms, though far behind in the acquisition game, will also consolidate, with McKinsey, Mercer Consulting Group, and Booz Allen likely becoming the major players, swallowing up the likes of BCG, Monitor, Bain, and Towers Perrin.

The net result over the next 10 years may be an industry that divides itself into two different industries composed of 'infrastructure providers', such as IBM and Accenture, and 'problem solvers', such as McKinsey and Mercer. Each segment might have three dominant players surrounded by a number of market and / or product specialists.

Thinking further out, will General Management merge with IT? The increasing trend among clients is toward internalizing their intellectual value-added activities while outsourcing back-end systems, and assets suggest that the consulting industry may become one large market with three core IT / Infrastructure companies in the center and all other firms acting as specialists around the periphery.

For the future, there are not only emerging opportunities but also profound questions to be raised about the current direction of the consulting industry. Clearly, a major transformation is occurring, not only in the industry but within firms. This will result in major changes that create not only challenging identity questions for firms but perhaps a split in the industry between firms that are problem solvers and those that are service providers.

Role Restructuring

Until recently, the use of knowledge and tools for advanced analysis was very much the captive domain of consulting firms and business schools. Thus, it was assumed that BCG understood the experience curve better than others; that Monitor understood the value chain more than others; and that Strategos led in its understanding of core competencies. However, experienced MBAs and former consultants now permeate all levels and functions of client organizations. Thus, management knowledge and techniques are widely disseminated and available, especially analytical concepts, techniques, and best practices.

These changes have altered the relative balance of expertise and power between consultants and clients. Increasingly, clients are using consultants to supplement their own thinking rather than to supplant it. We believe that clients will do less intellectual outsourcing (i.e., strategic planning) while continuing to increase operations outsourcing (i.e., infrastructure and back-office) over the next decade. This bodes well for the IT folks, but not so well for the general management consultants. Many clients will increasingly become reluctant to turn over intellectual control to consultants; instead, they will want to stay heavily involved in the analytical and implementation process, to the point where the consultant needs to become more a facilitator than an expert diagnostician.

Another role change is occurring in the traditional definition of a professional consultant as a specialist observer giving independent and expert advice. Deviating from this definition are the IT-oriented firms, which are developing a broad array of non-consulting services, such as outsourcing, facilities management, interim turnaround management, and IT software and hardware tools. Because of profit pressures, many consulting firms seem willing to take on new services, products, and ventures that may or may not have much to do with consulting.

As a result, industry critics are asking if consulting firms have forgotten their heritage as independent observers who restrain themselves from over involvement in those management situations where there can be conflicts of interest. This concern obviously applies to the IT-oriented consulting firms; however, we note this retort by a senior executive at IBM Global Services, "We are not independent – but we are objective. What we do is in our customer's best interest."

Thus, today's consultants are taking on a broad set of diverse roles and agendas – acting as sparring partners in connection with strategic development, as recruiters of new CEOs, as advisors in merger cases, as facilitators in management development, as arbitrators in settling alliance conflicts, as consultants to government, and as managers and operators of IT outsourcing operations. Some of these specialized roles and issues are discussed in Chapter 9, *Consulting to CEOs and Boards,* and Chapter 11, *Public Sector Consultation.*

More Questions than Answers

Historically, the consulting industry has been an influential player in shaping the evolution of a variety of industries and public agencies. In doing so, it has provided useful intellectual frameworks for rethinking business strategies; it has helped to design innovative organizations, systems, and processes; and it has been a translator of academic concepts into techniques for industries to use. Now, it is becoming a partner in streamlining its value-chains through the design and management of outsourced functions, information infrastructure, and physical assets. As consultants provide these new services, the consulting industry is being transformed into a business of enormous size and global scale with a wide array of services.

This transformation process raises many serious questions for reflection and debate within consulting firms and the profession at large.

Consulting vs. Non-consulting

We need to ask what constitutes and should be defined as management consulting in the future? For example, is outsourcing a consulting function? On the surface, it is not, but one might argue that it is a form of implementation resulting from an earlier consulting study. We prefer the more traditional definition that consulting involves the independent study of a client issue, and often times with assistance in implementation, but not with taking over the managerial function. We do not object to consulting firms building other divisions that do outsourcing and other businesses, but the 'firewall' needs to be stronger than what existed previously in accounting firms between auditing and consulting.

We predict this issue of potential conflict will gain considerable public scrutiny and attention in the future, and that consulting firms will have to do more to indicate separation of their problem solving and infrastructure support services, such as legally setting up separate companies, probably under different boards and perhaps with restrictions on the amount of combined consulting and non-consulting services that can be performed for a single client. If firms don't make headway on this issue, there is likely to be legislation.

This brings us to a related issue concerning the tendency of many consulting firms to aggregate their non-consulting revenues into their total consulting revenues. We believe this practice misleads the public, competitors, and potential clients. Professional associations and trade publications concerned with the consulting industry, as well as financial analysts and FASB, can perform a valuable service by asking for financial reports that make a clear distinction between consulting and non-consulting revenues and profits.

Ethics vs. Pressure for Results

Consulting firms in the future are likely to face public challenges to their credibility, ethics, and governance. We, therefore, need to ask what are the appropriate standards of professionalism that consultants should adhere to in their relationships with clients? This is a difficult challenge considering that consulting is a highly competitive industry with little or no barriers to entry. Most industry-wide attempts at certifying consultants have been weak at best. We prefer that firms themselves take charge of this issue through their selection and training methods. A few firms already do an outstanding job of extensive training in ethics, but this training should be mandatory for all consultants across all firms. Clear written policies are necessary, and performance reviews should include the degree of professionalism exhibited by consultants on projects. In addition, responsibility for monitoring a firm's professionalism should be assigned to a key partner at the highest level of the organization. Any signs of an individual breaching firm policies should result in immediate termination.

Education vs. On the Job

Most consultants really learn to be consultants on the job, which is not saying much for a profession that earns its living from being on the leading edge. Despite business schools being the spawning ground for most consultants, few schools provide explicit training in consultant skills, and they continually overlook issues of professionalism and ethics (see Chapter 2, *Professionalism in Consulting*). These schools need first to understand that training managers in the functional disciplines is not by itself sufficient preparation for consulting, which requires many other skills ranging from proposal writing to interviewing methods, to reducing complex analyses to communicable insights, and to persuading reluctant clients to make difficult changes. Every MBA program should sponsor at least one course on consulting, and hopefully consulting firms will be supportive and involved in this effort. Also, business schools (and even consulting firms) have been slow to support research on consulting and consultants. We still know very little about the actual behavior of 'good' consultants on the job and why certain projects succeed or fail; these issues are further discussed in Chapter 19, *Consulting in Entrepreneurship*.

Links between universities and consulting firms will no doubt intensify as consultants search for new frameworks for viewing client problems, and for new techniques that facilitate change and implementation. There will also be extensive contact on the computing science side as information technology advances. In addition, some firms will develop exclusive agreements with 'gurus' from the universities to advise them internally, as well as showing them off in their marketing and before clients. More books and articles are likely to be written by consultants and internal staff working in well-funded R&D departments, as illustrated in Chapter 17, *Creating and Sharing Knowledge in Consulting*.

Analysis vs. Facilitation Billing

The essence of consulting firms rests in their intellectual capital, which is reflected in their branded conceptual frameworks, proprietary software, and skills of their consultants. However, many clients have become much more sophisticated in their management knowledge and skills, making them competitive with their consultants, if not resistant to consulting help. It is, therefore, likely that consulting firms will need to develop new skills at facilitating behavioral processes where the consultants act more as a facilitators than as expert problem solvers.

Because these facilitative efforts will involve less consultant time, this will change the traditional billing formula based on hours and days. A strategic planning engagement that previously took hundreds of hours might now take only 100 hours in holding a series of retreats. Another example that is already reducing time as a billing factor is online forms of consulting, as discussed in Chapter 18, *Will Consulting Go Online?* Clearly, new billing concepts will have to evolve, and we predict these will be based on some subjective judgment of the value of results to be derived for the client.

Diversity vs. Homogeneity

To date, many large consulting firms are international in their operations, yet they still retain much of their home-country character in their internal cultures. Given that many pundits predict that this current century will be the Asia / China / India century and not the American or Western century, what will this mean for consulting firms and their consultant skills? A much more diverse consulting workforce will be needed.

Perhaps in conflict with this future market direction toward the Far East is the movement of many large Western consulting firms, especially the IT-oriented ones, toward standardized services. How can they strike a balance between standardized versus customized services in order to meet the needs of diverse clients? This question raises the issue of whether *Fordism (assembly line consulting)* will take over or will the industry develop new concepts that allow for individualized types of services with a personal consulting touch? Our hunch is that the business strategies of IT-oriented firms will focus on selling to large multinationals with homogeneous needs across all their operations; global general management firms with greater flexibility will opt to establish relationships with or acquire local or regional specialty firms that can tailor-make strategies to regional clients. Small 'boutique' consulting firms with specialized practices limited to single countries will likely become acquisition targets by larger firms acting to diversify their services. Small local and regional consulting firms will continue to take on smaller clients nearby, and they will emphasize personal service and lower fees.

These complex and potentially divisive issues will preoccupy tomorrow's consulting firm managements, if not already today's leadership. Their strategic responses will determine who will survive in the new millennium. As Charles Darwin pointed out about 150 years ago, "It is not the strongest of the species that survives, not the most intelligent, but the one most responsive to change." This book addresses many of the key change issues facing these firms.

Notes to the Chapter

1 Staffan Canback, "The Logic of Management Consulting (Part One)," *Journal of Management Consulting*, 10, no. 2 (1998): 1–8.
2 Frederick W. Taylor, *Principles of Scientific Management* (New York: Harper & Brothers, 1911).
3 Henri Fayol, *Administration Industrielle et Générale* (Paris: Dunod, 1916), translated in *General and Industrial Management* (London: Pitman, 1949).
4 J. E. Kielly, *Global Outreach in Management Consulting 1990: The State of the Profession* (New York: Kennedy Publications, 1990).
5 Consultant News (2002). Personal communication with Flemming Poulfelt.
6 T. Rodenhouser, *Inside Consulting* Newsletter (2000).
7 M. Skapinker, "Counting the Cost of Going Public," *Financial Times* (UK), (July 5, 2000).
8 Jagdish Sheth and Rajendra Sisodia, *The Rule of Three: Surviving and Thriving in Competitive Markets* (New York: Free Press, 2002).

2 Professionalism in Consulting

David Maister

Like many profound ideas, "professionalism" is an ambiguous concept used to refer to a wide range of attitudes, skills, values, and behaviors. For example, if one asks people what it means to refer to a consultant as "really professional," one hears a variety of replies. A really professional consultant, I am told:

- gets involved
- doesn't just stick to the assigned role
- reaches out for responsibility
- does whatever it takes to get the job done
- is a team player
- is observant
- is honest
- is loyal
- really listens to the clients' needs
- takes pride in his or her work
- shows a commitment to quality
- shows initiative

This list indicates some of the differences between a "really professional" consultant and an ordinary consultant. It reveals that a high level of professionalism doesn't stop with a foundation of technical qualifications and analytical skills. In addition to these basic attributes, the right *attitudes* and *behavior* must also be in place, and these become the distinguishing factors for achieving real professionalism. My former business manager, Julie MacDonald O'Leary, said it best: "Professional is not a title you claim for yourself; it's an adjective you hope other people will apply to you. You have to earn it."[1]

"You have to earn it" may not be a bad way to summarize what professionalism is really all about. It means deserving the rewards you wish to gain from others by being dedicated to serving their interests, as part of an implied bargain. Professionalism implies that you do not focus only on the immediate transaction, but you care about your relationship with the person with whom you are working. It means you can be trusted to put your clients' interests first, can be depended upon to do what you say you will do, and will not consistently act for short-term personal gain. Professionals make decisions using principles of appropriate behavior, not just short-term expediency.

Significant efforts have been made, and continue to be made, to "professionalize" consulting by promoting the use of the CMC—Certified Management Consultant—qualification. However, professionalism is not about qualifications and certification. Having an MBA from a name school or official recognition from a trade association or certifying body might say something about your *knowledge,* but these pieces of paper are unlikely to be predictive of your *attitudes* and *behaviors,* and maybe not even your *skills.* No formal qualification will ever provide complete assurance to the buyer that the provider will act appropriately, even if equipped with the required skills.

Forging Attitudes

The B-School Problem

It is not clear how consciously business schools, even those with special programs on consulting, set out to forge the appropriate attitudes for consulting. Through oversight or neglect, they may even sometimes create inappropriate behaviors. For example, many professional schools, whether in law, business, or medicine, work hard to create a sense in their students that they are an elite, the "best and the brightest." This can breed an arrogance that later shows up (no matter how unintentionally) as pompous, patronizing, condescending behavior when dealing with clients. "You are the person with the problem; I am the trained expert, so shut up and do what I say." Only in recent years have medical schools begun to provide programs to fight this socialization, and few business or law schools have anything substantive in this area.

Some schools have attempted to tackle the difference between knowledge and skill by building real or simulated consulting projects into the curriculum, but few, if any, are consciously designed to provide a critical examination of the consulting experience, by debriefing and exploring issues such as (a) what does it feel like to be a client?; (b) what is the difference between being an expert (providing answers) and being a skilled advisor (helping the client solve his or her own problem)?; (c) what is the consultant's role when members of the client organization are at odds or in disagreement?

Yet the need is readily apparent to each of us whenever we contemplate our own experiences as buyers of professional services. In working with professionals, I frequently ask them to tell me what they dislike about having to deal, as a client, with other professionals such as doctors, accountants, lawyers, interior designers, and, yes, management consultants. The list I am given of how people are treated as clients by these professionals is remarkably similar, regardless of the profession being discussed. Professionals ("those guys") I am told:

- Are pompous, patronizing, condescending, and arrogant
- Don't listen
- Treat me like a job, not a person
- Don't explain what they're doing and why
- Don't like to be asked questions or challenged
- Leave me out of the loop and take over my issue
- Tell me what they think I must do, instead of giving me options
- Are more interested in my money than me
- Ignore my feelings and treat the issues as purely technical
- Apply standard solutions and approaches; don't make me feel as if they are customizing to my needs
- Don't act as if they care about me

Test this list against your own experience as a patient or client with professionals. Does it sound familiar? What should be obvious about this list is that many, if not all, of the behaviors reported as missing are the very ones we would use to describe someone as a real professional. Note, however, that none are technical in nature, and all relate, one way or the other, to the provider's attitude toward dealing with the client.

A business-school education does little to help students distinguish between the "consultant as expert" (I can solve your problem) and consultant as helpful advisor (I can facilitate your decision-making process, and help you make your decisions).[2] Successfully conveying an attitude of trying to *help* (as opposed to being *right*) is a prerequisite for all consulting work. Without the ability to earn a client's trust, clients will not listen to content expertise.

Few consultants report that they have been trained in these human interactive skills. Their entire education in schools and in firms has been about logic, rationality, and intellect; little, if any, experiential learning was provided to them on how to earn trust, win influence, and establish relationships. Many do not want to engage in the interpersonal, social, and emotional activities that being a "trusted advisor" requires. Many consultants consciously avoid anything that smacks of intimacy with their clients, and rush to return to the "high ground" of detached, logical analysis where they feel most comfortable.

Further attitude problems, perhaps unconsciously, can be formed from the educational experience itself. In case study intensive programs, the student is invited to stand as the "outsider" and form judgments on the solution of business problems. This can breed an attitude of detachment or disengagement, a view that logical, rational, intellectual analysis is the primary virtue, and that emotions, passions, and interpersonal dynamics are relevant only as subject matter to be studied and likely of secondary importance in consulting unless one is a "behavioral" consultant. At no time does the student receive the message that immersing oneself in the messy human dynamics of a business situation is a requirement to find constructive solutions.

This problem is accentuated by other social conditioning absorbed in business schools about what business is about and what management involves. In one school of my acquaintance, hardly a single case study was examined without someone saying something like, "This company is not in business to make widgets, it's in business to make money," thereby dismissing any need to feel passionately involved in the product, the customers, or the employees. For better or for worse, such attitudes will influence the future consultant's view of what is important in his or her profession and inevitably send the wrong signals to clients.

Firm Weaknesses

The socialization that takes place in consulting firms varies immensely. Firms often develop their own cultures of what they think is "professionalism" and consciously or unconsciously socialize their employees into their specific definition of the term. They use the term constantly in their hiring and in proposals to prospective clients.

These varying definitions of professionalism differ immensely from firm to firm. For example, some firms emphasize "implementation" as the key to their professionalism, while others stress that their value is added by providing a "big picture" review. Is one of these strategies more "professional" than the other? Clearly not. It would be wrong to conclude that, for example, one must be involved in implementation or to give the big picture to be deemed fully professional. The underlying issue is really one of integrity. Is the firm consistent in what it claims to be and do? Does it deliver on what it claims to provide? In essence, the issue is whether or not the firm has (and lives by) a clear ideology of high standards.

Some firms with a clear ideology, such as McKinsey, go out of their way to indoctrinate new hires into their value system (their way of doing things): concrete positions on the role of the consultant, the appropriate way to work with clients, and the attitudes expected of all consultants. Of course, what makes this formal indoctrination "stick" is whether or not the attitudes preached are, in fact, the ones that the young consultant sees modeled every day by the more experienced people in the firm.

Other firms such as the Boston Consulting Group and Bain also have a reputation for articulating clear, consistent, firm-wide positions on what they consider the role of a consultant to be (an ideology) to which all members of the firm are expected to adhere. Naturally, these definitions are not identical, firm-to-firm, but all serve the role of communication and forming a set of attitudes that are *required* by the firm. Whether or not the firm provides formal training or documentation is of lesser importance than the fact that there is a clear role model that all recruits are expected to emulate, and that the culture is strong enough to rein in instances of noncompliance.

However, many firms, particularly those that provide widely varying services to widely different marketplaces, experience a harder time in conveying a clear, unambiguous view of the consultant's role. In addition, many firms do not have a firm-wide ideology on this point. For these firms, which are probably in the majority, there is no enforced, common approach to working with clients. Individuals are socialized not through formal indoctrination, but informally and randomly by the specific individuals they happen to work with. Little or no attempt is made to discuss formally the consultant's role, and the attitudes it requires. As a consequence, the concept of professionalism is left ambiguous and, almost certainly, randomly implemented.

Skills with Clients

An effective consultant who wishes to become "fully professional" must develop a long list of skills. While many firms train their people in such things as presentations, written communications, proposal writing, and selling, a much smaller percentage actually teach their people about how to work with a client. Client service training, where it exists, is spotty and is usually an after thought. Almost none of it is taught in business schools.

Again, there are singular exceptions. Not surprisingly, McKinsey, with its reputation for making a heavy investment in training, is one of the shining examples. Formal programs of "influence skills," taught by psychologists, are required and reinforced by a second or third consultant sitting in on client meetings to observe and debrief the interactions. Such activities take place in other firms, but few have such an organized approach that is clearly signaled and is mandatory for skill development, rather than one that is optional and idiosyncratic.

Other skills are required as a consultant develops. Paul Glen, in his book *Leading Geeks*,[3] lists, among others, the following competencies needed by an IT professional:

- Ability to manage client relationships
- Ability to manage technical teams
- Ability to play positive politics

- Ability to help expand client relationships
- Ability to work through others and make them productive
- Ability to manage ambiguity
- Ability to manage time horizons
- Ability to manage client relationships

To this fairly familiar list one could add a number of skills that most consultants wish they had mastered earlier in their careers:

- How to earn other people's trust and confidence
- How to earn, deserve, and thereby nuture a relationship with a client
- How to give advice without being assertive or patronizing
- How to deal with conflicts among client personnel
- How to manage meetings
- How to supervise others so they want to work for you again
- How to get the best out of those in support or administrative roles
- How to get someone in a more senior role to want to help you
- How to receive work delegated to you so you know what you're supposed to be doing
- If, when, and how to say "no" to a senior person or client
- Getting feedback from others, inside and outside, in a timely manner and form you can use

All of these are learnable skills (some are even teachable), and all are components of what I mean by the term "a fully skilled professional." Some of these are commonly contained in the typical firm's training program; a remarkable number of these skills are not.

Integrity at the Core

Integrity is usually taken to be central to the idea of professionalism. But what, precisely, does integrity mean? Consider the following list of statements, each taken from the mission or values statement of a real consulting firm:

- We always put the clients' interests first, ahead of our own.
- If a client wants to pay us to do things that we think aren't in his or her best interests, we'll turn the work down.
- If we have even the smallest doubt that we can't do this work to excellence, we'll turn the work away.
- We never lie, misrepresent, or exaggerate, in any way, to anyone, under any circumstances.
- We stand by our work. If clients don't like our work, we refuse to take their money.

- If a client treats our people badly, or with a lack of respect, we'll walk away from that client.
- We will fire any employee who fails to treat others (at any level) with respect and dignity.

How many firms do you know that could meet all these standards? If you think the standards are too tough to be realistic, how would you change them? Do you think a firm that lived by these rules would flourish financially or die? What else do you think belongs on the integrity rules list? Every firm (and individual consultant) should reflect on the above questions.

The key point is that integrity cannot be judged by what you advocate, only by that which you always do. A claim to integrity is only meaningful if it includes this follow-up statement:

> We treat our espoused values as nonnegotiable minimum standards, and counsel anyone who is not in compliance with them. If, after counseling, the person does not or cannot get into compliance with our values, we will help them find alternative employment.

One of the readers of my Web site, where I first posted this statement, responded as follows:

> No firm meets all these tests. Putting the clients' interests first, ahead of our own is difficult to rationalize in public corporations. The commonly held guideline for behavior (maximize shareholder value) inevitably leads to a violation in spirit of this principle. Leaders are willing to deceive (if not outright lie) to anyone producing a "drag coefficient" on revenue, including customers. Can (should) this change? I don't think that adherence to strict integrity rules would actively constrain a firm's performance. However, the traits that lead to violations may lead to disadvantages down the road (e.g., lying can work in the short term, but not the long term.)

Another reader of my Web site posed the following question:

> Do you think many professional firms are compromising their integrity in favor of money? The more competitive their environment and the larger their firm, it seems the pressure to maintain or increase revenue is just too great. Are professionals in such firms, just high-paid technicians, if the driving force from the firm is to make money even if this means risking its reputation?

As these cynical comments show, there clearly are those firms out there that send a clear message to their people: "It's about the money, stupid: do whatever it takes." I have experienced firsthand those consulting clients who create such pressure to meet short-term financial goals that their people are led into faking orders, padding bills, neglecting client service, and psychologically beating their staff to a pulp. In fact, if you read the gossipy bulletin boards on the Internet about consulting firms, you can easily conclude that such behavior is more common than not.

Integrity Pays Off

It is difficult to prove with hard science, but my twenty years of watching consulting firms leads me to believe that, in consulting, you can't get away with a lack of integrity or ethics for long. I'd risk the generalization that those consulting firms that have, over the years, vigorously enforced values, standards, and principles will also have achieved the best brand names and the highest profits.

In my book *Practice What You Preach*,[4] I surveyed 5,500 people in 139 professional firm offices in thirteen countries, posing seventy-four culture questions, as well as obtaining three years' worth of financial performance data. Using both stepwise regression and structural equation modeling (path analysis), I discovered that the answers to only *nine* questions accounted for more than 50 percent of all financial performance differences between and among these 139 businesses.

- Client satisfaction is a top priority at our company.
- We have no room for those who put their personal agenda ahead of the interests of the clients or the office.
- Those who contribute the most to the overall success of the office are the most highly rewarded.
- Management gets the best work out of everybody in the office.
- Around here you are required, not just encouraged, to learn and develop new skills.
- We invest a significant amount of time in things that will pay off in the future.
- People within our office always treat others with respect.
- The quality of supervision on client projects is uniformly high.
- The quality of the professionals in our office is as high as can be expected.

The firms that succeeded financially were not those that preached these standards (nearly every firm does) but those whose staff, top to bottom, agreed that they were the principles on which their firm actually operated. What's notable about this list is how familiar it is. All it says is that the firms making the most money are those who are actually living up to familiar standards that everyone preaches. The message is that you can make more money when you behave and enforce standards, not when you superficially advocate them or merely post them on a bulletin board or company Web site.

Whether or not a consulting firm actually has the necessary standards of professionalism is proven by whether or not there are consequences for noncompliance. If a firm has a partner who does not treat others with respect, that partner must be counseled, and if the counseling doesn't work, then that partner must be fired. If the firm is prepared to go that far, it can, in my opinion, be called truly professional and will likely make more money.

Origins of Failure

If all this evidence is valid, why then is excessively risky short-term behavior reported to be so common in business in general, and even in many consulting firms? Why do we keep hearing of managers "forcing" their people into behaviors that, at their kindest, can be described as "cutting corners," and at their worst, as unethical?

The most important point to make is that you don't have to be unethical to be dumb. As my questioner put it, consulting firms are doing things to make short-term profits that put their reputation at risk. That's not necessarily a lack of integrity; it's just stupidity. And, at some level, it's even understandable stupidity. A slightly compromised reputation might hurt you tomorrow, or the day after that, but, hey, that's the future, and you wouldn't believe the discount rate we apply to profits in the future compared to today! (And we'll have a year or two to make up for it, won't we? And maybe the clients will forget that we weren't that great two years ago!) Call this the *short-termism* excuse.

There are others too. I have sat in strategy meetings where firm leaders acknowledge the future cost of compromising reputation, but argue that, by the time it hurts the firm, they will have made their pile and cashed out. These people aren't really short-termers; they're just *selfish* and *greedy*.

Then there are consulting firm leaders who don't really believe their own mission statements, vision, values, and strategy. They say that they believe a reputation for excellence is worth its weight in gold, but they are not willing to actually put the proposition to the test. For example, how many firms that preach dedication to outstanding client service are also willing to give an unconditional client satisfaction guarantee? Not many! These people are not being excessively short-term thinkers: They are cynics and unbelievers. They don't really think that building or sustaining a reputation is worth sacrificing any amount of short-term cash.

Another pathology that occurs among a firm's leaders who are not short-term thinkers, greedy, or cynical, is that they are scared and lack courage.

They would really like to stick with the firm's strategy and standards and not accept a short-term hit, but they are frightened to take such a risk, either because they think their partners will rise up and revolt, which is actually quite possible, or, if they are publicly held, that Wall Street will take out a substantial chunk of their market value.

A final group of consulting firms with low standards engages in short-term compromises and acts of expediency because they actually don't have ambition. To accept a short-term adverse consequence, you've got to have a passionately held ambition to get somewhere. Otherwise, why would you make sacrifices? Yet many firm leaders are more concerned about "not messing up" than they are about "going for the gold."

So what have you got to be as a person to "do the right thing?" You have to have integrity, *and* really believe in your strategy, mission, and values, *and* have a dream, fervently desired, *and* have the patience and courage to bet on the long term, and resist palpable pressure from the constituencies you serve, *and* be willing to accept the short-term consequences of your actions. This all takes a level of self-discipline that few of us measure up to in our everyday behavior. I guess that's why it's not common. And I guess that's why they call it professionalism.

Problems of Enforcement

If you really want to obtain the commercial benefits from any strategy, you must put in a system that forces you to execute that strategy. The tragedy of many consulting firms, and the source of their lack of professionalism, is that they have not put in place systems to enforce accountability for standards.

As an example of one that has, consider EDS, the computer services giant. They have a Web-based project management system that records everything about the project—when the next due dates are, what has been done, what's on time, what's delayed, and how much of the budget has been spent and accumulated. Here is the key point: This information is entirely accessible to the client! At any time, the client can log in and see where his or her project stands, with budget, due dates, deliveries, etc. They ask their clients to log in every two weeks to indicate on a simple scale of one to four their level of satisfaction with the client project so far. The chairman of this multi-billion dollar company logs in every day and can see client feedback from every client for the entire company, and that is the first thing he does every day.

What's impressive about EDS is not the technology but the willingness to be held inescapably accountable to high standards. Many consulting firms haven't even got a decent internal project management system, let alone one to which they would give access to clients. Most firms have a mission statement that declares a commitment to client satisfaction and client service.

But how many have a feedback system where they regularly ask clients, at the end of every transaction, how happy they are with the work? Only a few! How many publish those results with the names of the relevant partner to everybody in the firm? Even fewer! Instead, what exists in most firms is a frequently espoused belief that client service is very important, yet a refusal in their actual behavior to accept accountability for it.

Firms typically leave it up to the individual and his or her self-discipline to accomplish high standards of professionalism, but that usually doesn't do the job. If there is no system that keeps people honest about performing up to standard, you don't get the benefits. The key, if you really want to make something happen, is don't leave it to self-discipline. If you really want to make something happen, create an external discipline. And if you don't want to try that hard, and if you don't want to be held strictly accountable, then fine, move on to something else. But if you can't find anything you're prepared to actually commit to, then recognize that you're probably never going to be anything other than no worse than anybody else.

The Upside

Imagine a world where every junior member of the firm says, "In this firm, one thing you can bank on is that you will be superbly supervised on every transaction. It is a matter of professional principle with us. We don't do work unless we supervise it superbly." (Note that this was one of the nine profit predictors in my statistical study). What commercial benefits would come to that consulting firm if it were true that supervision was always done superbly?

First, from the firm's point of view, there would be less wasted time and rework, and the firm would experience lower write-offs and higher realization. You could obtain better economic leverage because people would feel more confident delegating work to trained people. Second, the firm would spread skills faster and the firm would do a better job of retaining people.

Clients, on the other hand, will notice a higher level of quality and therefore might feel less fee sensitive, knowing that they had found someone who always supervised the work well. This is terribly scary, because maybe that might mean they also notice when the work is not supervised superbly.

If, as a senior partner, I knew that every junior consultant had been supervised superbly since the day they joined the firm, I might actually trust these young people and delegate more to them. Whereas, if I am living in a normal consulting firm where excellence in supervision happens only sporadically, then it's quite logical never to delegate because the juniors are untrained, unguided missiles.

This list of benefits for both firms and clients can be obtained by diligent, enforced adherence to a high standard of project supervision. But here is the issue: Why are many consulting firms not getting these benefits despite everything they promise to new recruits about the importance of quality, professional pride, and great work environments? Why does the average consulting firm not enforce this standard? Because they can get away without doing it!

Many consulting firms fail to meet the high standards of professionalism, not because they do not believe in them and advocate them, but because they fail to enforce them. It's not an issue of being "unprofessional" or unethical. It's simply a matter of the difference between the true pursuit of excellence and the acceptance of mere competence. They have wonderful standards of quality that are preached. But they will forgive any partner who does not do this, as long as he does not go to the opposite extreme and do something ugly—sexual harassment or get us sued. Competence ("Don't mess up") is not the same as professionalism ("uncompromisingly high standards").

Partners' Failed Leadership

If you go to the typical consulting firm today and ask, "What percentage of your partners would put hand-on-heart to say they regularly read every issue of their main client's trade magazine? Not all your clients, just your main client?" I can report from experience that, around the world, the answer is sadly in single digits. Yet we all know that clients like for their consultants to show an interest in their business. So let me ask again: "Do you act as if you care about your clients?" In the typical consulting firm, the honest answer is, "We believe that we should care, but we frequently don't act that way."

I often talk about meeting three kinds of partners in consulting firms: *dynamos, cruisers* and *losers*. This, by the way, is not different people; rather it is all of us at different stages in our lives. A *dynamo* is somebody who is always acting like they have a career. In addition to taking care of this year, every year they are doing something to bring about their personal future. Every year they're always saying, "Where do I want to go next, and what do I do today to make that happen?"

The *cruisers* (by definition, not *losers*) are a very important category that includes the majority of partners. They are good, solid citizens, coming in each week to make the sausages. They come in next month and they make the sausages. They come in next year and they make the sausages. And everybody knows those sausages are fabulous. The quality is there. The hard work is there, but that person isn't actually going anywhere. He's acting like he's got a job, but if you said, "Where do you want to go next with your career? What kind of transactions do you want to be doing three years from now?" he'd say, "Sausages!" He has no particular desire to advance his professional career.

At some stage in your life, you're probably a *loser*. The usual reasons: divorce, alcoholism, cocaine, manic depression, the kids have been arrested again. Things happen. If you're lucky, you deal with it and recover; if you're unlucky, you get stuck.

In the typical consulting firm, I am told by firms around the world, the percentage of partners in those three categories is about 15 percent *dynamos*, 75 percent *cruisers*, 10 percent *losers*. If that's the makeup of the typical partnership in the typical consulting firm, only 15 percent of the partners are trying to get somewhere, but the large majority is just coasting along while making sausages day after day. Is that professionalism?

If my estimate is accurate, firms should not waste their time doing strategic planning. Because strategic planning in that environment is like trying to figure out which way shall we point the thundering herd when the herd isn't thundering. The issue is not direction or strategy. The issue is do they or do they not have the appetite to go somewhere, and to accomplish it with high standards of professionalism?

We, therefore, come to the key choice if you're considering a firm to join as a partner: Which gang do you want to belong to? The tolerant firm says, "If you want to cruise, that's okay. Not only is it acceptable, but it's actually the overwhelming norm here," just like in many consulting firms. Or you might want to join a firm where they say, "The rule here is you've got to be learning and growing, or otherwise you're not meeting your requirements as a partner. It's something we have a right to expect of each other, that we are all continually learning and growing." Notice there's an option here for firm leaders to confront and decide. The choice is do you want to set forth and enforce a high standard in your partnership agreement?

The Real Bottom Line

The lessons should be clear. You get the benefit of that which you actually do, not that which you encourage. Ultimately, professionalism goes beyond attitudes, knowledge, and skills and is about dependable, reliable, consistent behavior. You may believe in something, know how to do it, and be skilled at doing it. But unless you can be relied upon to actually do it (unfailingly), then you cannot hope to develop a reputation for professionalism.

The way you make money in consulting is not to be good at managing the money. The way you get money is to decide how you want to compete—whether it be quick delivery at McDonald's or fabulous cooking for some cuisine connoisseur—and then enforce the standards appropriately for that choice though superb leadership. The money is an outcome of how high your standards are and what you do about them. He or she who lives to the highest standards—in other words, is most professional—wins.

Notes

1 David H. Maister, *True Professionalism* (New York: Free Press, 1997).
2 David H. Maister, Charles H. Green, Robert M. Galford, *The Trusted Advisor* (New York: Free Press, 2000).
3 Paul Glen, *Leading Geeks* (San Francisco, CA: Jossey-Bass, 2002).
4 David H. Maister, *Practice What You Preach* (New York: Free Press, 2001).

3 The Marketing and Selling of Consulting Services

Robert Duboff and Peter R. Giulioni

Successful consulting businesses require deep domain knowledge and talented consulting resources combined with both effective marketing and exceptional sales, all of which must be closely aligned and made consistent with timely delivery of professional services to expectant clients. Seemingly effective marketing matched with poorly executed sales dooms a firm's ability to deliver in the marketplace and eventually leads to revenues too low to justify added investments in marketing. Successful sales efforts backed by marginal or sub-standard marketing leads to an overworked and often frustrated sales force and wasted marketing resources. Both will be further compromised by project deliverables and services that don't measure up to client expectations set by marketing and/or sales resulting in dissatisfied client stakeholders and a damaged reputation in the marketplace.

The need for consistency between marketing and sales should be obvious, but there is often overlap and confusion between these two key functions. The demarcation between them is usually blurry at best and is often indistinct in many professional services firms, regardless of size or location. Often this is compounded by the fact that many of today's consultants want to be perceived as trusted advisors and to avoid looking like salesmen. After all, most consultants want to serve clients, not sell. Many times they will use euphemisms such as "business development" or "thought leadership" instead of acknowledging the need to do marketing and selling at the front end of each consulting engagement. The romanticized notion of consulting carries the legacy belief or assumption that good consultants should be able to produce revenues without ever asking for the business and certainly without such unseemly acts as advertising.

Borrowing Duboff's working definition, marketing for consulting firms includes all indirect activities aimed at attracting a broad market segment composed of many potential buyers, such as a particular industry segment (financial services, FMCG, public sector, media and entertainment, etc.), while sales usually encompass all direct activities designed to secure one or more specific client engagements.

Even today in some of the most respected global firms you may encounter debate or even confusion about which activities are marketing, and which are sales. We all can agree on the importance of driving towards strategic agreement within a firm so that marketing and sales strategies are consistent and set (and often revised depending upon changing market conditions) correctly for the target market(s) and client(s).

Typically, marketing is handled by a small group of staff professionals, occasionally augmented by contract outsiders, combining market research, advertising, public relations, speeches, and publications. Sales are frequently the exclusive domain of senior line resources (partners, principals, directors, senior managers, etc.), the most successful of whom are often referred to as the firm's "rainmakers" and are highly compensated and often promoted. Sales techniques are numerous and are usually no different in consulting firms from other professional services enterprises. In between marketing and sales lie the murky waters of firm employees working in sales support and client proposal development. For our purposes, these practitioners are better thought of as part of the sales process than as marketers.

Solo practitioners and owners of boutique firms, of course, must play all marketing and sales roles, although some use outsiders such as wholesalers and brokers for marketing assistance.

The Challenge

Consulting is one of the most intangible of all professional services, depending on individuals or teams often engaged primarily in words, ideas, and strategies. Furthermore, although consultants like to call the business a "profession," almost anyone can call themselves a "consultant." Until recently there was no set training, expertise, or regulatory body to certify an individual as a qualified consultant.

All of this makes actual differentiation difficult, if not impossible, for any firm or individual consultant to assert a true difference from other firms or individuals.

To make the marketing and selling of consulting services even more difficult, the fundamental tool of pricing frequently remains outside the control of those directly engaged in marketing and selling. While consulting services marketers often are given leeway to create positioning, themes, brochures, and the like, they are rarely involved in pricing. The firm's CFO, CEO, or the entire partner senior management team annually set daily rates or hourly fees that then become the basis for the pricing portions of client proposals.

Most client proposals rely on a model of pricing based on estimates of hours or days multiplied by a rate per consultant or consultants with the expertise and experience needed to deliver the services. The changing nature of the marketplace and sophistication level of clients drove many senior consultants responsible for pricing to shift to other models (e.g., stock in lieu of dollars or agreements in which the consulting firm shared in future returns or in savings created, etc.).

These incentive-based arrangements can become problematic because they alter the consultant-client relationship by threatening the independence, if not the objectivity, of the consultant(s) and the consulting firm. A more equitable alternative for establishing the project fees would be to define and agree upon the near and long-term value to client created by the consultant's work. Using the agreed upon value as the basis for pricing, a consulting engagement on the surface appears to be the fairest and most logical approach; reaching agreement on the value is often a project unto itself.

Where to Start?

What are marketers and salespeople to say when asked why a potential client should hire their firm? This largely depends on the stage of a potential engagement, which exists along a continuum.

Exhibit 3.1 describes the all-important process of converting non-clients or prospect into clients, and then extending the existing consulting relationship through the sale of additional work. Using this perspective, the early stage objectives (target selection, awareness building, and establishing qualifications) are primarily the marketers' domains with sales professionals often participating and contributing but following the lead of the firm's marketers. Sales professionals begin to take over leadership of the effort from marketing at the point where demonstrating expertise and qualifications turns toward setting specific expectations about what the firm is qualified to perform for that client prospect.

Exhibit 3.1 Stages in Consulting Services Marketing and Sales Cycle

Objective	Sales and Marketing Focus
Selection	Marketing: Market sizing, competitive analysis, profitability analysis (for clients)
Awareness	Marketing: Name recognition
Qualifications	Marketing: Positioning Sales and marketing: Setting expectations
Selection	Sales
Building a long-term relationship(s)	Marketing: Information dissemination (e.g., newsletter); thought leadership Sales: Customizing and personalization

Note too, that after an initial sale and successfully completed project, marketing has a role in working to develop and maintain a long-term relationship with the client through various media, some tailored to the specific client and others broadly distributed to many clients, such as newsletters.

Most seasoned and successful consultants would agree that the first stage, selection, is the most important and, along with establishing differentiation, the most difficult. Selection requires the combination of economic foresight as to which types of clients can be served profitably, competitive insight as to which types of clients can be sold successfully, and understanding of the marketplace to develop a realistic understanding of the value of the firm's services to the client.

Even when this is done well, consultants need to practice great discipline to avoid the temptation to try to be all things to all clients and pursue prospective clients who do not fit the desired target profile. They also need even more discipline to abandon a client relationship that has proven unprofitable or otherwise undesirable. Firms who have taken the time and practiced the discipline to objectively analyze their client portfolio typically find that up to one third of all existing client relationships are historically unprofitable. Yet, senior partners in firm leadership roles still find it hard to "weed out" clients in the vain hope that over time unprofitable clients will once again become profitable, or because partners serving those clients have become too comfortable with the client relationships.

Achieving the Right Balance

While the marketing and sales functions each have a distinct role, consulting firms struggle with their relative priorities, service offerings, budgets, changing market demands, and allocation of scarce consulting resources. Typically, rather simplistic judgments are made, such as marketing budgets being set as a percent of last year's revenues based on the assumptions that client demands are fixed, the economy is stable, and the marketplace will always increase.

Marketing by its very nature is a forward-looking function where the objective is to sustain current revenues while laying the groundwork to build future revenues. So, logically, if revenues are flat or even worse, declining, more marketing fuel is needed for the firm to grow. So the prevalent percent-of-past-revenues model allocates fewer funds when revenues are declining, a strategic disaster in the making.

A potentially useful way to consider these trade-off decisions is to use a classic consultant's two by two matrix – what Dubhoff refers to as the Sales and Marketing Matrix – depicted below in Exhibit 3.2.

The first step is to compute or estimate the raw numbers in each of the four quadrants. It will be necessary to find these numbers through marketing research and interviews with line consultants and hopefully

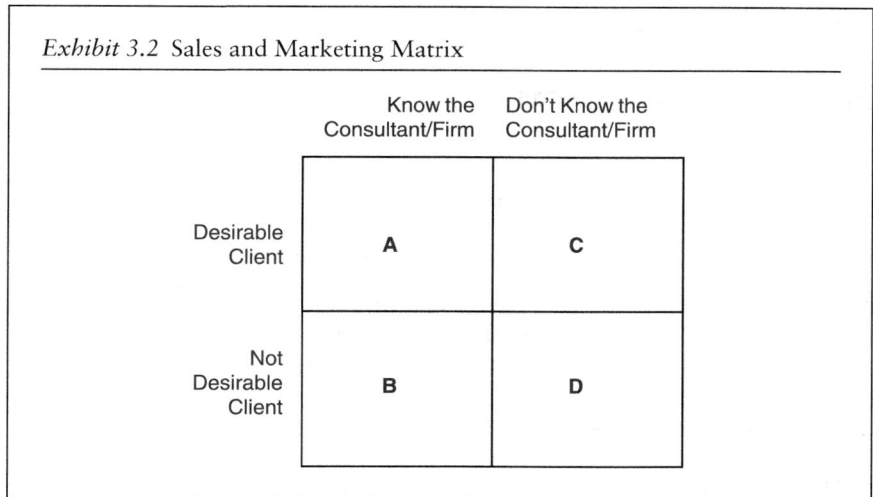

Exhibit 3.2 Sales and Marketing Matrix

existing and potential clients. Focus should obviously be on those prospects (or for that matter, existing clients) in quadrants A and C, while rapidly discontinuing any expenditure(s) directed primarily at prospects and existing clients in quadrants B and D. A key number for determining a marketing emphasis can be found in quadrant C – how many desirable prospects or existing clients are there who don't really know the full range of services offered by the firm?

Sometimes, this is a relatively manageable number, such as when the consulting firm is targeting CEOs in a specific industry and in a specific geography, e.g., Oil & Gas CEOs in ASEAN. The number doesn't necessarily dictate the marketing strategy, but a comparison of quadrant C to quadrant A can help inform the firm about who to target and in what way.

The issue for quadrant A is to employ sales techniques focused on and customized to the individual target(s). On the other hand, quadrant C requires marketing's tools, whether designed for name/brand awareness or to present the firm's qualifications for consulting to clients in certain industries. Quadrant C's numbers could be in the hundreds, and, therefore, an efficient allocation of marketing time, talent, and treasure will be required. In this case, advertising in a business magazine, industry trade journal, or even one or more inflight magazines on geographically key airlines, and publishing white papers targeting the specific industry/industries or function(s), or participating in industry conferences are all potential alternatives. If the number is relatively small, advertising would not be a good choice; perhaps a better choice would include a personal email campaign including an attachment describing the firm's intellectual capital, marketplace success, or recent white paper.

Keys to Effectiveness

Even the most rational priority setting and budgeting does not ensure successful marketing and sales. While there are any number of ways to achieve effectiveness, we believe there are five major underlying and essential pathways to driving effectiveness.

Key 1: Marketing and Sales Must Link to the Firm's Strategy

Years ago, David Maister suggested that there are two main types of professional service firms – hunters and farmers.[1] The hunter culture is characterized by a sales driven/dominated culture where each partner, principal, or director acts as a separate entrepreneur, out selling and defining the work to be performed and often leading the project him or herself.

These "hunter" firms are usually not bound together by any cohesive set of principles proscribed to guide the entire firm's consultants; central discipline is often lacking. Farmers on the other hand – and here many of the top tier firms like BCG, EY, Bain, Strategy 8, and McKinsey are striking examples – are characterized more by a core philosophy that is enforced across all geographies and all practices. It is the collective image, reputation, consistent quality of consultants, and team effort of the firms that attract clients. There are numerous examples at these firms where adhering to principle overrode short-term revenue opportunities. Although both hunting and farming cultures do operate successfully in the global marketplace, the philosophies normally don't work well together in the same firm since the hunting ethos would undermine the discipline that defines a farmer type firm.

Too often today, companies try to market their way to success. Frequently, businesses launch or change and then relaunch advertising campaigns, logos, and the like in a new "branding initiative," but at its core, these approaches will not work if they are not based on the firm's underlying business model and business strategy. Deloitte Consulting's failed transition to Braxton, and PwC Consulting's short-lived pivot to Monday (immediately prior to its sale to IBM) in the early 2000s, and more recently the massive restructuring of Infosys Consulting, were visible examples of this phenomenon, but even these ill-fated attempts to market oneself to success have done little to discourage others from making similar mistakes. Launching a Marketing Initiative within the Firm (Exhibit 3.3) gives an example of how one should go about developing a new marketing initiative within a professional services firm.

No one is quite sure how branding started. Historically of course, artisans and ranch owners had two purposes for brands – to signify ownership/authorship and to emphasize quality, or, at least, consistency. Over time, the meanings have become blurred and even confused. "Brand" is often used when "brand name" or "name" is what is meant, and the term

Exhibit 3.3 Consulting Insights: Launching a Marketing Initiative within the Firm

---

The key to launching an effective professional services firm's branding campaign is making a connection between what services and value the firm's consultants can consistently deliver with what potential, current, and future clients demand. The best first step is to develop a fact-base understanding of the current market (clients, prospects, employees, and competitors), then to line them up with how these prospects fit with trends (both recognized and anticipated) in the marketplace.

Next, review this information with the firm's leadership and secure their commitment to the investment of time, talent, and treasure needed to move the firm towards its new marketing strategies. Often the immediate "next step" is planning to hold one or more strategy meetings with the firm's key principals to sift through the key data and discuss implications for new marketing strategies. It is advisable (some would say imperative) to have an outside and objective third party to facilitate the discussion, capture the essence of the discussions, and offer unbiased counsel.

A typical agenda for these meetings might include:

Pre-Meeting Preparations
- Pre-read research on the market (e.g., market research, articles, etc.), firm and competitor data (e.g., market share, key clients), and client information (e.g., profitability, satisfaction, retention)
- Kick-off dinner with speaker (a visionary or commentator on the industry) and call-to-action by firm leaders

Day #1
- Small group discussions to determine likely trends and shifts in market relevant to the firm's future
- Panel moderated by the 3rd party facilitator, of senior client representatives and/or senior leadership from key prospects to give their perspective
- Diagnosis or "post-mortem" of recent client defections and proposal loses
- Plenary session to review a few proposed alternative marketing scenarios
- Discuss proposed scenarios to consider if the firm can deliver on what is needed to meet what is demanded by the changing/evolving marketplace
- Proposed actions to close gaps between delivery capability and what's expected in the marketplace
- Working dinner

Day #2
- Presentation from teams on specific action steps, including time-line, "owners," budget implications, internal feedback mechanisms, and resources needed
- Debate/discussion/agreement and commitment regarding next steps including time-lines and "owners"
- Adjourn

"brand equity" is associated with financial concepts so as to convey an impression that having a brand automatically adds value. Not surprisingly, branding has also been used by proponents of advertising to suggest that this marketing technique is best at building name recognition over time such that customers and clients will be willing to be loyal to that brand and even pay a premium price.

Promoting a brand not linked to an underlying strategy translates into meaningless marketing. Promoting a brand promise that is not consistently delivered translates into a marketing mismatch. Marketing and strategy must be aligned and yet even then, without solid consistent execution, the venture will fail.

A brand only has a meaning if there is consistency. For years now, every Apple product has characteristics that make it uniquely Apple; Gucci, L'Oréal, MBZ, Nike, Starbucks, Disney, Universal Studies, and even many universities (Stanford, Wharton, INSEAD, Chicago Booth, Kellogg, etc.) have succeeded in establishing themselves as a unique brand. Branding is relatively easy – albeit not inexpensive – for products but more problematic for professional services. Hotels strive to offer a consistent guest experience at their properties, and those who have challenges doing this have the weakest brands and, by default, businesses.

A US-based domestic carrier, Southwest Airlines, is recognized by many as one of the most consistent airlines by far with its branding strategy, signifying low price, and frequent departures, while Singapore Airlines represents a more "up-scale" international travel experience, with frequent departures and higher prices, but all of the frills the seasoned travel has come to expect. Many other airlines, both domestic and international, struggle with the consistency issue because of their diverse offerings, which are often the result of trying to be all things to all travelers. Brand strength requires consistency in both delivery and execution. Consulting firms should not market a brand unless they can deliver on it.

In summary, a firm that is a hunter should likely avoid explicit branding and attempt to market itself in other ways (e.g., build up the reputation of individual senior consultants and thought-leadership) while investing in a robust sales support function, while firms that have adopted the farmer culture can more easily use branding tactics to promote the firm's reputation.

Key 2: Link Internal and External Communications

Internal communications to consultants and staff are just as important as external communications for implementing effective marketing and sales. This is true for any professional service where the delivery depends so heavily on human motivation and skill, and where every client expects to be and often should be treated as unique. If communications about the firm's strategy, marketing, and sales are not in alignment, prospective clients are likely to question the firm's credibility and lose interest in engaging with the firm. Over time, non-aligned and inconsistent communications lead to damaged credibility and diminished reputation.

Internal marketing is not only vital to keep employees informed about the firm's current strategies and policies, but also, if done skillfully, to help employees feel included in, aware of, and committed to the "big picture" of the firm. As with any business, employees' views of the enterprise are shaped by the information they receive and the day-to-day behaviors of management/leadership. Effective internal marketing, which includes recruitment brochures, new hire orientation programs, newsletters, emails, blogs, events, training, regular performance management conversations, and visits by senior partners to offices and project sites can augment compensation programs and other tangible benefits to create greater loyalty among staff members.

One best practice, for example, is EY's *The Daily Connection*, a cleverly written set of two to three daily news blurbs of relevance distributed daily to thousands of employees. Those who want more information on a topic (e.g., a new voluntary benefit or particular EY report) can click on an imbedded link for details. While employees can opt out of *The Daily Connection*, over the years, less than 1 percent have done so.

Close alignment between internal and external messaging creates a positive effect on potential recruits who can access the firm's websites and any number of blogs, as well as personal and professional networks to learn more about what is going on inside the firm. On the other hand, when alignment is poor or mixed messages are given, these same candidates may well perceive the firm as not having its act together – or worse yet, being disingenuous.

Unfortunately, even in this time of instant global communications, many firms still do not actively reconcile their external recruiting messaging with their internal outreach to current employees. These different firm functions behave as though since they have different stakeholders, they can go their separate ways. Certain information is, of course, germane only to potential new employees; but there is little justification for sending employees, candidates, and alumni a host of separate messages about the firm from different departments. In today's connected world, clients, prospects, undergrad and MBA students, experienced hire candidates, and employees can and often do readily gain access to the same information. It should be apparent to all that ours is now an instantly connected and highly transparent world requiring consistent messaging and brand meaning.

A disastrous example of poor messaging alignment occurred several years ago when a communique from the New York–based advertising firm of Saatchi & Saatchi to its investors touted its rapid growth through acquisitions and soaring profits. The firm's current and prospective clients gained access to this information and complained both privately and publicly, and demanded lower fees, because in their view, Saatchi's profits seemed exorbitant. The agency soon experienced a temporary decline in revenue. An example of a very real lesson in aligned messaging for a premier advertising firm.

The point is to focus on the internal stakeholders and be sure that messages are consistent both inside and outside the firm. In this regard, while the firm's ads designed for clients and prospects may or may not gain public attention, employees will definitely see them and react. If the messages do not ring true to employees, they will lose confidence in their firm's leadership. In fact, the best practice is to test all potential external communications on people within the firm first. After external testing as well, all employees are notified about the communication before the ad appears or is distributed to current and prospective clients.

Today's employee is tomorrow's alumnus and potential client. Aligned messaging and communications build credibility – the key and necessary ingredient to effective marketing and sales. If recipients don't believe what you say, it doesn't matter how often, how cleverly, or how loudly you say it.

Key 3: Understand Buyer Values

Any professional services firm needs to know the buying criteria that clients will use to select or reject its proposals. The term "buyer values" comes from Michael Porter's work where, as many readers know, he describes two viable ways to compete within any industry[2]. You can be a "low cost" leader, which affords the luxury of being the lowest priced while still having a good chance of achieving sales and profits through volume. Price will always be a factor with most, if not all, buyers of professional services.

However, the second option is to differentiate, but you must differentiate on a dimension that buyers will value sufficiently to pay a premium – either price or time or both. This allows the consultant to sell services for a price point above the low cost provider.

In spite of its usefulness, many marketers frequently ignore Porter's theory and seem willing to assert almost anything that appears to have been generally attractive to clients in the past. They forget about whether the proclaimed virtue holds real value to the current buyer. Investing the time and energy into finding out about buyer values is not easy, but it is necessary.

While successful sales and marketing are predominately arts, it is foolish not to use whatever information is available or can be secured. The best way is through marketing research, and Exhibit 3.4 gives a brief summary of a solid research process.

Exhibit 3.4 Marketing Research Steps

Step 1	Summarize what is currently known (or thought to be known) about the relevant buyers.
Step 2	Through discussions with line partners, principals, and project leaders, generate one or more hypotheses about buyer values.
Step 3	Set up an internal senior level steering committee to oversee and drive the research, which, with Step 2, will help ensure that the results will be used.
Step 4	Conduct qualitative research (such as focus groups, client surveys, third-party research, etc.) with buyers to explore and refine initial hypotheses and if needed, develop new ones.
Step 5	Conduct a survey of potential buyers. This will require at least 100 interviews with any given target level (e.g., CFOs, IT Directors, entrepreneurs, etc.). Once the questionnaire is developed and tested, it can be administered by face-to-face, telephone, Skype, or on-line.
Step 6	Conduct analysis guided by the hypotheses that pinpoints in rank order those buyer values that can drive the initial selection and long-term retention decisions. The research must also detail current potential client perceptions about the firm's credibility for delivering on the valued dimension(s).

It is critical that the results of market research be presented and discussed at the highest levels of the firm so that resulting recommendations are accepted by firm leadership and will be implemented across the firm.

While it would be nice to identify a single universal client buyer value on which the firm has a leading reputation, this rarely happens. More typical is to locate a set of attributes that is valued by many clients (current and potential), and supported by people within the firm, too. Then, assuming the marketplace has confidence in the firm's abilities in this area, the firm can emphasize the attributes internally and communicate them externally.

Needless to say, it is folly to simply begin asserting attributes if the firm's line consultants are not able or willing to deliver them. Many consulting firms under-utilize market research despite its use in one of the most successful strategies in the history of professional consulting. In the early 1990s, Victor E. Millar, a senior partner of Arthur Andersen & Company (one of the most successful of what at the time were called the "Big 8" firms), launched research into buyer values for all three of the firm's divisions – audit, tax, and consulting. Up to that point, Millar had helped drive Andersen & Company's consulting business to a market leadership position. His research revealed how buyer values were distinctly different in selecting an audit firm compared to hiring a consulting firm. This insight (and his instinctive understanding of *Key 1: Marketing and Sales Must Link to the Firm's Strategy*, above) led to the strategic split of Andersen Consulting (a new brand name at the time) from Arthur Andersen. And as we all know, Andersen Consulting rebranded itself as Accenture shortly thereafter.

The power of research extends to other arenas as well. Professional services firms can survey their client-facing resources to develop strategies to engender client and employee loyalty. There are also advanced research techniques to aid in identifying trends and looming changes in the marketplace.

It is also imperative to use research techniques to garner objective feedback from clients about past marketing campaigns and each sales effort. Too often firms spend thousands of dollars and hundreds of man-hours on a proposal but make no systematic inquiry into why the engagement was won or lost.

If the consulting principals who are directly involved in the proposal process also make the inquiry, the potential client will invariably and politely reply that the proposed fees were "too high." However when a less personal and independently hired research firm makes the same inquiry, far more useful insights are likely to be gained. It may come down to seemingly minor points such as some clients prefer to receive materials in advance of a presentation and others don't. Some like to know the key points before hearing details; others prefer the reverse order. In a similar vein, "blind" follow-up satisfaction surveys are needed to learn if delivered performance matches the marketing and sales claims made earlier in engaging with a client. The book *Market Research Matters*[3] contains many useful points for those interested.

Key 4: Match Expectations and Performance

Again, David Maister's work provides a useful framework, depicted in Exhibit 3.5, for discussing various types of consulting that can be delivered to meet a client's needs and expectations.

It is important in staffing and pricing that client and consultant agree about what is being sought. In fact, most unsuccessful projects probably were doomed by lack of mutual understanding as to what the client really wanted from the consultant. Consultants like to believe the clients want their brainpower and don't really care about how the job is staffed, akin to pure strategist. However, it may be that the client merely wants some temporary help (or staff augmentation) to gather some information to which it will later apply its own brainpower in analyzing the data. This kind of mismatch helps to explain a variety of client misunderstandings and complaints about overpriced consulting or off-target reports.

The matrix is also helpful in explaining why consulting is so hard to market and sell. Each firm has a variety of services and sometimes even some products to sell. At the "product" end, it might be proprietary software or an off-the-shelf training solution, while at the other end it could be the

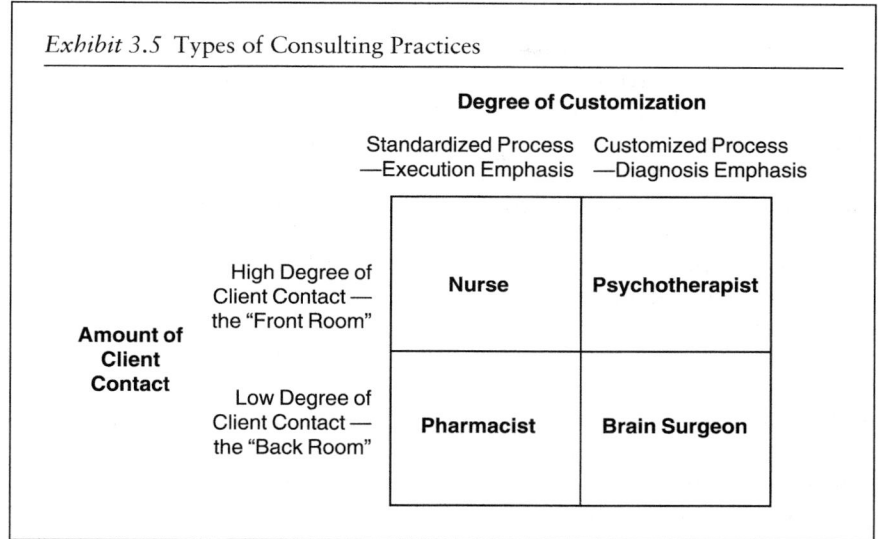

Exhibit 3.5 Types of Consulting Practices

design of a unique business strategy requiring extensive data gathering and analysis. Fees can range from a few thousand to millions of dollars.

To prevent serious misunderstandings, consultants need to perform a great deal of upfront work carefully reviewing the client's business case for undertaking the project and in-depth interviewing of the client about its needs and expectations. Then some basic fundamentals take over as a written proposal becomes essential for clearly stating the client's needs from the consultant's viewpoint, as well as laying out in concrete terms the consultant's views on deliverables, benefits, resources, schedule including progress check-points, and finally the fees. The consultant also needs to review this proposal carefully with the client before work begins, and then return to it frequently in meetings with the client to assess progress. It may be that the original agreement will have to be amended using a previously agreed upon change order process or in extreme cases, renegotiated, but this should happen before a project goes too far in the wrong direction. These are simple common sense fundamentals, but often a determining factor in client satisfaction or lack thereof.

Key 5: Monitor and Measure

The only way to deal with the variety of challenges and complexity in the marketing and selling of consulting is to relentlessly monitor and measure each of the many tactics used. Isolating the impact of any single tactic or even any single strategy is difficult.

The key is to follow the admonition of Len Lodish in his classic book *The Advertising and Promotion Challenge*, where he opts for being "generally right" instead of "precisely wrong."[4] At a minimum, sales should conduct a win/loss analysis based on an objective third-party debriefing after each major sales pursuit. Marketing should also conduct a survey each year, both internally and externally, to assess progress on major objectives (e.g., current client satisfaction or prospective client awareness for the firm's services).

At the firm-wide level, the firm's leadership should accept and agree upon key measures of marketing and sales accomplishment. If surveys are not credible to senior management, then other additional measures should be planned and used; for example, the firm's CEO might contact people he or she respects who have been previous targets of the firm's marketers. However, even if the CEO doesn't fully embrace the existing measures, the marketers and sales leaders can still use this information for themselves as self-guidance for improvement. It is difficult to improve at any activity if you don't measure the results and determine if improvement is needed.

While the measurement of sales results can be fairly straightforward in terms of wins and losses, the assessment of marketing programs is far more complicated and usually more qualitative in its measurement.

Some possible approaches include:

- How many new clients were attracted by marketing (won/lost interviews can show the impact of positioning, marketing events, etc.), and what is their projected lifetime value,
- How many current clients were positively influenced by a marketing campaign, and what is their (increased) lifetime value to the firm,
- Growth in customer/client total lifetime value that might be attributed to marketing due to more positive attitudes toward the firm,
- Changes in how clients/recruits/alumni feel about the firm consistent with marketing campaigns, etc.

It is important to consistently implement and adjust measures that are tailored to the firm's specific activities. Remember not to fall into the trap of measuring marketing progress in merely terms of sales results alone; that unitary measure can be very misleading about marketing's success or failure. The real purpose of marketing should be to focus on a longer time horizon and to create broader effects on the market in general.

Compensation and Rewards

Different consulting firms handle this issue differently. Firms with a hunter orientation recognize partners and principals who produce the most business. If a hunter identifies a less effective business developer within the firm, even if a very effective service delivery resource, he or she will probably fire that individual or, at the very least, never promote him or her.

The farmer orientation will reverse the emphasis and be willing to let go of a poor consultant or disruptive citizen regardless of selling ability. Of course, in a large firm, an underlying issue is whether or not the management can accurately identify which people are skilled at either marketing or selling. Scorekeeping on revenue generation alone is a thorny subject, and even the most sophisticated systems can be misleading if the only basis is annual gross revenue produced while overlooking profitability for each client.

Another troubling issue is the potential trade-off of work sold versus quality of work delivered. "Quality" is very difficult to assess because the delivered service is intangible, depending on client perception and other factors outside the control of the consultants.

A third difficulty for professional services firms lies in ascertaining who really sold what. Sales are usually a team activity, and the most senior partner or principal is not always the deal closer. Win/loss analyses and client satisfaction surveys can help management assess performance in general, but allocating specific rewards to individuals is a subjective process and does not always recognize or produce the best consultancy.

Most of today's successful professional services firms emphasize both individual and team rewards, while occasionally placing more emphasis on the latter. The criteria used should include multiple measures, such as revenues, profitability, quality, contribution to the longevity of the client relationship, and overall client satisfaction.

Ethics, although sometimes overlooked, should also be a component. Has the consultant done the work professionally and in accord with the firm's values? Too often, firms ignore this issue. Overlooking ethical violations can be debilitating and alienating to junior people who are more likely to witness violations of ethical policy. The best companies plot both ethical and economic performance.

Relationship Marketing

Often, consultants fail to practice relationship marketing well. This is especially disturbing because in the case of current clients they are usually the easiest and most cost-effective to sell additional services. Instead, in many firms, rewards and budgets tend to emphasize the acquisition of new clients. Somehow, developing a new client relationship is regarded as a more noteworthy sign of sales success than add-on selling to an existing client. For those few wise firms that value deepening relationships with current clients, a number of strategies are employed. Incentives are carefully designed to reward retaining a client and increasing revenues. Sales teams and senior partner or principal rainmakers are assigned to existing clients instead of aligning them only against new prospects. It also means entertaining and visiting clients when there is no new project on the table. Intellectual capital is developed for existing client issues, not just designed to attract new clients. Consultants who are best at building relationships follow a process based on their understanding of how they have previously succeeded in developing long-term, profitable relationships. They are able to identify clients with this potential and then know how best to serve them.

Those firms that have implemented effective client relationships follow a defined process with steps like these:

- Designate the clients to target for long-term investment
- They should be profitable now and likely to be so in the future
- Solid chemistry already exists between the client and the firm, as well as the client and relationship manager
- Client culture is open to loyalty to professional services providers
- Focus on building loyalty, while trying to maintain the relationship
- Strategize what the client needs and which individual consultant resources might work well with the client
- Ensure that the client knows you are qualified to deliver the services needed
- Reward loyalty by providing intellectual capital
- Visit often, especially when no new work is in the offering
- Develop an ongoing engagement and communications plan
- Systematically prioritize efforts and continuously measure effectiveness

Loyalty is also built at the interpersonal level through "chemistry" between consultant and client. David Maister and Jag Sheth have separately written extensively on how individual consultants can best become "trusted advisors" and cultivate lasting relationships. It may be "old school" networking ties that gain an introduction, but the relationship continues only if the client finds it easy to talk with the consultant and, more importantly, values the consultant's advice and ability to serve as a wise sounding board. Years of experience, emotional and cultural intelligence, and lack of ego create these kinds of skillful consultants.

Advertising, Public Relations, and Media Management

Over the past decade, Accenture (formerly Andersen Consulting) has demonstrated that consistent advertising can significantly help a firm establish a strong brand image. When still Andersen Consulting, Accenture embarked on its program in the early 1990s and has stuck with its campaign, designed initially to differentiate Andersen Consulting from the firm's other business lines. But its real goal was to be compared with IBM, and they succeeded, eventually separating completely from the accounting business and becoming the largest consulting firm in the world.

Andersen's success at brand building stood the firm well when it changed its name to Accenture. Teresa Poggenpohl is an author as well as Partner and Managing Director of Global Image at Accenture, and one of the

Accenture marketing professionals to have been involved with the firm's advertising since its inception.

She credited several factors for Accenture's long-term success[5]:

1   Each stage "informed the next." All the learning from Andersen Consulting's decade plus of advertising was applied to the launch of Accenture. The company was able to design a new name and initiate successful advertising within 147 days of learning they would need to change.
2   Accenture has taken a "consumer marketing approach to professional services." It was the first in its category to use advertising, as well as to use market research, to understand buyers and measure results. Perhaps most importantly, they have "employed the strategy of continuous investment" in the brand. Often competitors will use a burst of advertising to create "a spike in results" and then "spend the next eighteen months doing nothing, completely eliminating any gains they had made." Accenture annually invests in advertising in countries across the world.
3   There is also strong "commitment from incredible leadership partners" willing to make the necessary investment in advertising, even though image advertising is difficult to link directly to sales.

We "measure literally everything," but Poggenpohl acknowledges that image advertising cannot really be proven. Advertising does not work for all firms, particularly where discipline and strategy to give meaning to brand image is lacking and/or when senior management has little commitment to advertising. The rewards are there, since numerous research studies across industries show that the larger spenders over time are granted a perception of leadership. Interestingly, only a few firms have pursued advertising with a long-term goal of building their reputations and brand names.

An alternative route to marketing that is less expensive and more in keeping with what consultants like to do is through promoting their intellectual capital. One of the PR masters in the industry is Pat Pollino of Mercer Management Consulting. He and Mercer have a three-prong strategy:

- "Source" articles in which Mercer experts are quoted,
- Placing articles written by Mercer professions, and
- Prominent mentions in articles about the strategy consulting industry.

This is the path taken by McKinsey, as it publishes its own journal. The *McKinsey Quarterly* supports speech-making opportunities for its principal-level consultants and sponsors an annual prize for the best article in the *Harvard Business Review*. McKinsey's emphasis on its intellectual capital allows the firm to establish itself on the leading edge in management thought, which is appealing to many clients.

Other firms, which are normally smaller in scope and scale, use techniques like consultant-authored books on important issues to attract clients.

These can be highly effective in establishing the author's point-of-view, and many books have launched consulting growth. It is clear that a best seller with a strong message, such as Champy and Hammer's *Reengineering the Corporation*,[6] Slywotsky's *Value Migration*,[7] Kotter and Cohen's *Heart of Change*,[8] and Reeves's *Your Strategy Needs a Strategy*,[9] among others, all helped greatly to increase their respective firms' revenues.

Other Approaches

Another popular marketing technique is sponsorships, which straddle marketing and sales. Often the decision to sponsor an event or a professional sports team or individuals such as golf professionals or race car drivers is as much to entertain clients and recruits as it is to gain brand recognition or differentiation. Some firms also rely on pro bono work to garner positive press for their citizenship and, not incidentally, make connections at a senior level to produce leads for gaining future business. For example, as Bain and BCG expanded geographically years ago, they offered "free" studies to a few mayors of large cities, knowing this would lead to interviews with CEOs on the projects.

A relatively new strategy is to hire a "professional" sales force to overcome the frequent problem of good consultants not being good salespeople. Only a few firms have done this with the scale necessary to allow salespeople to feel comfortable within the firm and to give them enough staff to be successful. EY and Mercer HR have both gained some revenue growth from a sales group. The cultures in both of these firms are rather self-effacing, sufficiently so that line partners readily accept the possibility that sales professionals are able to market and sell a service even when these salespeople have not been consultants themselves.

Solo Practitioners and Small Firms

Much of the thinking in this chapter applies to all professional services firms. However, the size of a firm does make a difference in marketing and selling. If a rainmaker at a large firm has a bad year or two, success of the other partners or principals can keep the firm growing. But when there are only one or a few partners, this luxury rarely exists. The solo consultant is constantly caught in the "do-sell" cycle, alternating back and forth between delivery and selling – a cycle that can be highly inefficient and exhausting. This requires added discipline from the solo consultant to ensure making a certain number of calls/emails/visits each week to prospects for future work. Careful monitoring of progress through the steps in Exhibit 3.4 is also critical, in order to make sure there are sufficient numbers at each stage to produce sufficient numbers of clients in the future.

It is also vital for solo practitioners to recognize their own strengths and weaknesses. If they are strong closers, able to sell well, but weak at marketing, they should consider hiring others to help produce leads (through advertising, PR, ghost writing, and/or telemarketing/prospecting). In the reverse instance of being weak at sales, they might hire a sales representative or join an alliance with other solos or brokers who are good at selling projects where they need help. Finally, solo or small firms should measure and monitor their marketing and sales efforts just like the larger firms to allow for self-reflection, analysis, and improvement.

Future Needs and Challenges

The marketing and sales functions in consulting firms have clearly become more diverse and complicated in their approaches. Some have moved more aggressively to advertising; others have engaged a professional sales force or aligned with brokers. In addition, the economics of book publishing have changed to make it possible for many consultants to publish books such that many large firms have multiple authors on staff. The proliferation of the Internet and advanced computer capabilities has also made available new marketing and sales techniques. On another challenging front, ethical concerns will continue to preoccupy senior leaders of most firms, including their marketing staffs.

They need to ask if their firm's marketing and sales are accurately and candidly describing what the firm is able to deliver. In an era where neither marketers nor consultants are above reproach, this is a serious challenge. The firm's marketing leaders must think twice before exaggerating benefits that can't be delivered. It is unethical to promise what one can't deliver, but even if this remains a moot question, a mismatch will be created that will inevitably cause lower credibility and a short-lived "one and done" relationship.

As more consulting firms go public, they will need to become highly sophisticated in communicating to a new set of audiences (analysts, shareholders, etc.). Historically, consultants have remained largely "invisible" and not worried about their communications to legislators or to the general public. Certainly, publicly traded firms will have to focus their communications on multiple stakeholders. In the wake of the Enron meltdown and the collapse of Arthur Andersen, even privately owned professional services firms will need to constantly manage their public image.

At the same time, the proliferation of web-based content will require new skills allowing firms to disseminate intellectual capital in highly efficient and more customized ways than in the recent past.

Many firms now provide access to their on-line journals and publications to anyone who registers. Users can then order updates on whatever topics they select. Many major professional services firms use their websites to accommodate real-time questions and answers, combining instant messages and live-chat capabilities.

All of these occurrences have made marketing and sales a far more vibrant part of the professional services industry, while establishing these functions in the front lines of an industry struggling amid unsettling economic conditions. For the foreseeable future, it will take strong and creative marketing and sales efforts for firms to remain competitive.

Notes

1 David Maister, *Managing the Professional Service Firm* (New York: Free Press, 1993).
2 Michael Porter actually lists alternatives but focus (e.g., on an industry) can be viewed as an aspect of differentiation. *Competitive Strategy* (New York: Free Press, 1980).
3 Robert Duboff and James Spaeth, *Market Research Matters* (Wiley, 1999).
4 Leonard Lodish, *The Advertising and Promotion Challenge* (Oxford: Oxford University Press, 1986).
5 Interview with Teresa Poggenpohl, July 9, 2002.
6 Michael Hammer and James A. Champy, *Reengineering the Corporation* (New York: HarperBusiness, 1993).
7 Adrian J. Slywotsky, *Value Migration* (Boston: Harvard Business School Press, 1996).
8 John Kotter and Dan Cohen, *Heart of Change* (Boston: Harvard Business School Press, 2002).
9 Martin Reeves and Knut Haanaes, *Your Strategy Needs a Strategy* (Boston: Harvard Business School Press, 2015).

Additional Bibliography on Marketing Consulting

On Marketing ROI:

Ambler, Jim. *Marketing and the Bottom Line* (Financial Times/Prentice Hall, 2000).
Jensen, Bill. *Simplicity* (Cambridge, MA: Perseus Books, 2000).
Kotler, Philip, Thomas Hayes, and Paul Bloom. *Marketing Professional Services, Second Edition* (Paramus, NJ: Prentice Hall Press, 2000).
Schiemann, William, and John H. Lingle. *Bullseye* (New York: Free Press, 1999).

On becoming a trusted advisor:

Maister, David H., Charles H. Green, and Robert M. Galford. *The Trusted Advisor* (New York: Free Press, 2000).
Sheth, Jagdish, and Andrew Sobel. *Clients for Life* (New York: Simon & Schuster, 2000).

Part II
Major Practice Areas in Consulting

4	IT Management Consulting: The Industry and Profession (MICHAEL A. MISCHE, UNIVERSITY OF SOUTHERN CALIFORNIA)	75
5	Strategy and Organization Consulting (DAVID NADLER, MERCER DELTA ORGANIZATIONAL CONSULTING, AND ADRIAN J. SLYWOTZKY, MERCER MANAGEMENT CONSULTING)	118
6	Trust-Based Selling of Consulting Services (CHARLES H. GREEN, CEO TRUSTED ADVISORS)	141
7	Operations Management Consulting (RICHARD B. CHASE, K. RAVI KUMAR, UNIVERSITY OF SOUTHERN CALIFORNIA, AS UPDATED AND PETER R. GIULIONI, UNIVERSITY OF SOUTHERN CALIFORNIA)	155
8	Human Resources Consulting: 2016 (GERALD LEDFORD WITH EDWARD LAWLER AND SUSAN MOHRMAN, UNIVERSITY OF SOUTHERN CALIFORNIA)	175

Introduction

This section focuses on the five major practice areas of consulting that are dominant today and likely will be well into the future: 1) Information Management (commonly Information Technology – IT) consulting, 2) Strategy and Organization consulting, 3) Trust Based Selling (historically, Marketing) consulting, 4) Operations Management consulting, and 5) Human Resources consulting. These five areas comprise approximately 90 percent of the total consulting market, with approximately 40 percent in the IM/IT area, 16 percent in strategy, 10 percent in marketing consulting, 10 percent in operations management, and 14 percent in human resources.

Clients hire consultants for their leading-edge knowledge and ability to solve problems within each of the five major practice areas. Knowledge within each area is constantly changing, as are the issues that clients face.

The beginning consultant is usually challenged to become an expert in only one of these five areas. But as one gains consulting experience and rises to senior levels, it is important to become more aware of all five fields because each greatly affects the other in the client's situation. Clients expect a breadth of awareness from their senior consultants in determining how specific recommendations will fit with the rest of their business.

Information Management/Information Technology consulting is the largest and most expansive area within the industry today. In Chapter 4, "IT Management Consulting: The Industry and Profession," the author provides a review of IM (IT) consulting and its development over time and into the future. The remarkable growth of IM/IT consulting has passed from an era of information systems used for simple financial reporting to today's conduct of e-business. As a result, IM/IT has become a source of competitive advantage for the firm, as well as an efficiency tool. It has also become a basis for outsourcing, which is now a major generator of revenues for consulting firms. The competitive dynamics have also changed as large computer hardware and software firms, e.g., Oracle, IBM, and HP, have moved in on the consulting industry to become major players. We see in this chapter how this IM/IT evolution and revolution took, and is taking, place, and what it portends for the future with the advancement of the Internet and social media and other upcoming opportunities.

Another major practice area of consulting is concerned with "Strategy and Organization Consulting," which is covered in Chapter 5. Here the authors examine the evolving relationship between these two disciplines over the years. In the early writings of Peter Drucker, these fields were indistinguishable, but they separated in the 1960s with the advent of new economic models for strategic planning, such as BCG's Growth Share Matrix. In contrast, the organizational discipline became dominated by psychologists with motivational models and sociologists with structural models. Only in recent decades, according to the authors, have the two areas been "rejoined" as an integrated response for coping with fast-moving markets and the dynamics of hyper-competition.

While Marketing has been a classic discipline in consulting for years, it is changing significantly with more focus on building trust relationships as well as with the continuing advancement of social media technology and electronic channels of distribution and communication to customers. In Chapter 6, "Trust-Based Selling of Consulting Services," marketing is discussed in the context of "selling" from a trust perspective. For example, many new client opportunities are developed for selling via the building of trust and trustful relationships. These opportunities give the marketing consultant powerful new social based tools and problem-solving services to bring to clients. In addition, the chapter highlights various types of trust selling. It concludes by identifying a number of trends lasting into the future that will affect the trust-based marketing consultant to the building of nurturing lifetime customer relationships.

Operations Management consulting is the oldest practice area, going back to Frederick Taylor and the utility of the stopwatch in measuring worker productivity. Although often overlooked, operations management remains a thriving domain for consultants. Clients are continually concerned about the efficiency and quality of their production processes. Chapter 7, "Operations Management Consulting," discusses how OM consultants go about their jobs, attacking major operational issues in a variety of contexts that make each project different, such as in companies with multiple plants versus those with only one plant. The effective OM consultant needs to understand these varying contexts because they often require unique solutions, not cookie-cutter programs that advocate best practices derived from entirely different situations. The chapter also covers major concepts used in OM consulting, from supply chain management to mass customization. It concludes with predictions about the future issues facing tomorrow's OM consultants.

Chapter 8 on "Human Resources Consulting" takes a provocative stance in arguing that HR consulting has gone, and continues to go, through a major transformation caused by information technology. Much of the HR function in companies has for years been involved in routine transactions involving benefits, payroll, EEO, and policy communication. Now, much of these routine operations can be performed through the company intranet or even completely outsourced to a consulting firm. The chapter discusses several alternative approaches to automation, from "do it yourself" to complete outsourcing. The chapter recognizes a variety of different roles that have emerged for HR consultants, ranging from acting as HR strategy consultants to outsourcing managers. Consulting firms are also being challenged as to whether they should specialize in a narrow HR niche or adopt a broader range of "one stop" HR services. All of these challenges offer significant opportunities, though HR consulting must be prepared to embrace the new IT reality.

4 IT Management Consulting
The Industry and Profession
Michael A. Mische

1.0 Introduction

This chapter examines **IT management consulting** and how the IT industry and IT consulting have evolved to create essential components of the consulting profession and global economy. For the management consultant, this is an important chapter not only because IT is so pervasive and essential to our daily lives and the operations of a contemporary enterprise, but because it defines and differentiates the services of an IT *management* consultant from other IT service providers.

This chapter discusses the evolution, role, and services of the IT management consultant, the competitive dynamics among IT management consultants, the factors that drive IT consulting service demand, what services IT consultants provide, how IT consultants help their clients, the IT consulting process and how the IT management consultant delivers services, and the competitive and economic factors that drive IT management consulting.

This chapter is organized into six sections:

1.0 Introduction
2.0 Evolution of IT and IT Consulting

    2.1 History of IT and IT Consulting
    2.2 Seven Decades of Transformation

3.0 Defining the IT Industry

    3.1 Description and Definition of the IT Industry
    3.2 Industry Size and Dimension
    3.3 Major Markets and Segments for IT Expenditures
    3.4 Competitive Dynamics of the IT Industry

4.0 Defining IT Management Consulting

    4.1 The IT Management Consultant
    4.2 IT Management Consulting Firms
    4.3 Competitive Dynamics Among the Strategic IT Consulting Firms
    4.4 IT Consulting Services

76 Michael A. Mische

5.0 Future of IT Management Consulting
    5.1 Future IT Consulting Services
    5.2 Future of IT Service Delivery Models
6.0 Conclusion

The chapter contains 11 exhibits in support of the topics and subjects. Additionally, there are over 38 endnotes and footnotes that guide the reader to the sources used in this chapter and additional materials and resources. The list of exhibits include:

Number	Title
4.1	Evolution of IT and IT Consulting
4.2	Evolution of IT Consulting Services
4.3	Percentage Change in U.S. Corporate Profits Correlate to U.S. GDP
4.4	Percentage Change in U.S. Corporate Profits to the Percentage in IT Spending
4.5	Distribution of IT Purchases by Primary Segment
4.6	Distribution of IT Spending by Function/Technology
4.7	Distribution of IT Spending on Services and Technologies by Category
4.8	Total Estimated IT Spending on Goods, Services, and Staffing – U.S. Only
4.9	Strategic IT Management Consulting Firms' Typical IT Consulting Service Offerings
4.10	Management Consulting IT Consulting Primary and Specialty Service Offerings
4.11	Emerging Technologies and Their Potentially Disruptive Impact on Industry and Consulting Services

At the completion of this chapter the reader should have a thorough understanding of IT and the role and importance of the IT management consultant, the IT management consulting process, the differences and distinctions between IT consultants and contractors, the types of services that IT management consultants provide, and the primary drivers of the IT industry and the demand for IT management consulting services.

5.0 KEY WORDS

    Artificial Intelligence (AI)
    Virtual Reality (VR)
    ENIAC
    Technology Enabled Living (TEL)
    Firm of the Future (FOF)

ERP
MRP
MRP-II
IT Consultant
IT Evolution
Virtual Service Provider
Integrated Service Provider
Displacement

2.0 Evolution of IT and IT Consulting

2.1 History of IT and IT Consulting

Few things in life, other than perhaps pondering the origin of the universe, can be as interesting and exciting as a computer. And nothing, perhaps other than science and medicine, can be as professionally challenging and satisfying as getting a computer to improve the lives of people. With just a few clicks, billions of instructions can be performed in less than a second; knowledge is created, accessed, and shared; billions of dollars can be transferred; lives can be saved; the human experience transformed; and communications that once took days, weeks, and even years can be performed virtually instantaneously. With technology, distances collapse and time moves more quickly and efficiently. Cultures, businesses, economies, and today, even planets are interconnected in unseen ways that only a generation ago were science fiction.

Computing technology is not new. Computing aids, such as the Tally Stick and abacus, can be traced back to at least 2400 BC. Undoubtedly, there had to be some enterprising "management consultant" back then advising paying clients how to best use them!

Electronic computing technology has its early heritage in World War II and was born out of necessity. In 1943, the U.K. built and implemented the "Colossus" to help break the secret communication codes of Nazi Germany.[1] Similarly, from 1943 to 1946, in the U.S., and in the basement of a building at the University of Pennsylvania, the ENIAC was born.[2] At 50 tons and with 18,000 vacuum tubes, the ENIAC filled 1,800 square feet of space, and consumed over 200 kilowatts of electrical power, which was enough to power several homes at time. However, ENIAC was an electronic, programmable computer that could perform 5,000 arithmetic (simple addition and subtraction) calculations per second! The concept of the computer was proved.

From weighing more than 50 tons and requiring some 1,800 square feet to technology that is smaller and as light as a postage stamp, computer technology has become ubiquitous. Today, the information technology (IT) industry is so pervasive and complex that it's difficult, if not impossible, to

78 Michael A. Mische

separate IT from our daily lives. Indeed, the IT industry is so omnipresent and diverse that it is difficult to accurately define and measure. Is a microchip implanted in a person IT or healthcare? Is software used in automotive braking, suspension, and drivetrains included in IT industry estimates, or is it part of the automotive sector estimates?

As technology continues to change, so have management consultants. Where once consultants predominantly performed technical and scientific services and confined their efforts to data centers in secured locations, today IT consultants are deeply integrated in business processes and participate in C-suite decisions.

2.2 Seven Decades of Transformation

To better appreciate how IT has become so pervasive and critical to the service offerings and service delivery capabilities of a management consulting firm, it's useful to first understand how what was once called "scientific data processing" moved to become data processing, to Management Information Systems (MIS) and IT. IT has now evolved into the digital economy, the digital enterprise, the Internet of Things (IoT), cyber-business, cyber-life and to *Technology Enabled Life* (TEL). To fully appreciate today's IT management consulting industry, let's examine how IT evolved and the IT consulting changed. Exhibit 4.1 and Exhibit 4.2 summarize the evolution of IT and the IT consulting industry, as well as some of the pertinent IT consulting services that evolved and emerged throughout the 1940 to 2015 period.

- **The 1940s: The Birth of the Modern Computer**

"Modern" computer technology dates back to the 1940s and World War II. Financed by the U.S. Army to help calculate artillery firing and improve accuracy and developed at University of Pennsylvania by J. Presper Eckert and John Mauchly, the ENIAC became the first electronic data processing device, or computer, capable of mass manipulation of data and calculations at what was then amazing speeds. These early machines were dedicated to scientific applications and the war effort. Made of vacuum tubes that generated enormous amounts of heat, ENIAC computers used miles of wire, consumed vast amounts of energy, and filled rooms the sizes of most homes. But, these precursors of today's computers were effective enough to prove a concept and launch an industry. Even in these early years, the power and potential of the technology were unknown, or certainly, under-anticipated. In fact, IBM founder and president Thomas J. Watson[3] is purportedly to have commented, "I think there is a world market for maybe five computers."[4] Although there is no substantial proof that Mr. Watson really ever said those words, at the time, he might have been very well correct about the fledging technology that was primitive, unproven for commercial use, and costly.

During this period, IT consulting, if indeed we can call it that, was largely confined to research and development efforts related to inventing computers, proving computers, and making computers work. As IT had not found its way into mainstream business applications, consulting firms such as McKinsey and AT Kearney, as well as the major accounting firms, had not developed any specific competencies or consulting services in IT.

- **The 1950s: Creating an Industry and the Dawn of the Mainframe**

It's been said that in the 1950s, the Big-3 G's dominated the world: General Eisenhower, General Motors, and General Electric. But the 1950s also ushered in two other major events: Baby Boomers and the first major commercialization of IT and with that, the emergence of IBM[5] and UNIVAC.[6] UNIVAC which stands for "Universal Automatic Computer" was the product of the Eckert-Mauchly Company, which was later acquired by Remington Rand, then Sperry and ultimatley, UNISYS.

The 1950s also marked the second generation (2-gen) of computers. In the early part of the 1950s, computing technology was still forming, the engineering was still exploratory, and the idea, although proved, had yet to create any critical mass. But the 1950s were a decade of great interest. The Cold War was heating up, UFO sightings were almost a daily occurrence, and the space race and nuclear arms race were daily conversations around water-coolers in most homes and offices in the United States. The B-52 was placed into operation, missile defense systems such as the Nike Hercules and Nike Zeus were deployed, ICBMs were fitted into nuclear submarines, and NASA was formed. All of these events created a healthy appetite for research and development and computing technologies.

Building off the "proof of concept" of the 1940s in computing for defense and scientific applications, IBM also launched an ambitious program to bring computing into mainstream business. Although early computers were largely dedicated to defense and scientific applications, as technologies evolved for those markets, transference of portions of that technology to the private sector began. Early (1950s) applications for these technologies included the U.S. Census Bureau, U.S. Army, New York University, Westinghouse and the Nuclear Energy Commission.

The early 2-gen computers were based on vacuum tubes, hard wires, magnetic storage, and highly specialized machine languages. The introduction of the magnetic drum memory device by ERA-Remington Rand provided a basis for mass storage and memory management. With a growing infrastructure of devices and some rudimentary software, IBM's 701 and later its 1400 series of computers would soon find a market, at least for scientific applications in business.

IBM's late decade 7000 series of computers would be revolutionary in the sense that it was based on transistors and not vacuum tubes. In particular, computing power advanced at exponential rates. By the mid-1960s IBM's 7094 series of computers, which were used to support the Nike Air Defense System, could perform over 250,000 calculations per second. But the architectures and engineering for these 2-gen systems were relatively inflexible, highly specialized, and built for "mission specific" purposes. The circuitry, operating systems, computational power, data base architectures, and communication networks were highly complex and, of course, primitive by today's standards. Networks were "captive" and proprietary, while databases had no resemblance to those of today. What business needed was a more open and growth flexible architecture.

In a bold decision, and one that would be a landmark in computing technology, IBM launched an internal research and development program to build more flexible computers that would have mass appeal. Led by the now legendary engineer Gene Amdahl,[7] IBM initiated a journey to create what would become in 1964 the IBM 360[8] mainframe.

With the commercialization of the technology came the need for consulting services that could help organizations *understand* how to best use the technology. Hence, the rudiments of the IT consulting profession were founded during this period. As computing was entirely mainframe based and IBM had a reputation for impeccable technical service, the early IT consultants were generally trained on IBM mainframe computing principles and in the development of "in-house" custom applications to support mostly administrative computing needs. Exhibit 4.1 illustrates the six phases of IT and IT consulting throughout the years.

- **Phase 1.0: The 1950s – Birth of the Industry**

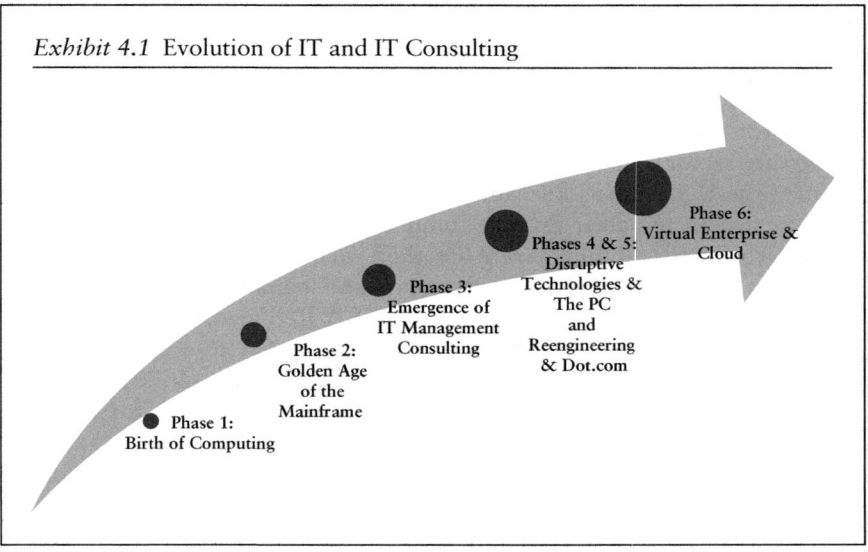

Exhibit 4.1 Evolution of IT and IT Consulting

During the 1950s the rudiments of the IT consulting profession were formed and tended to concentrate in two practice areas:

- Technical consulting services
- Scientific application services

With the escalation of the Cold War, the 1950's were a decade of economic expansion largely fueled by infrastructure and defense spending. IT was essential to the defense of the "Free World" and military spending helped to accelerate engineering advancements and the use of electronic data processing. With this technology came the need for a new generation of management consultants. Consequently, the management consulting industry experienced growth largely attributed to demand pull from clients for its services.

- Phase 2.0: The 1960s – The Golden Age of the Mainframe: The IBM 370

During the 1960s the IT consulting profession began to formalize and create specialty practices areas:

- Hardware selection
- Application software development
- Implementation services

The 1960s represented a decade of social turbulence and technological change. From the election of a young president, to landing on the moon, the 1960s saw great social change, great sadness, and the *Golden Age of the Mainframe*. The computing technology of the 1960s had its lineage in the mid-1950s, when IBM initiated a project to radically change the way computers operated with the IBM 360 program. IBM's investment of over $5.0 billion resulted in a new mainframe computer named the IBM 360. The IBM 360 provided the basic design and "DNA" for advanced computing and the computers today. Interchangeable parts, cooling systems, and integrated semiconductor technology replaced transistors and vacuum tubes. Where only a decade earlier a computer could perform 5,000 calculations per second, the IBM 360 could support over 34,000. The IBM 360 was cheaper, faster, and more powerful. All of which became the design tenants of computers today.

Actual computing, that is the processing of data, was generally done in large, homogeneous batches. The predisposition to "computing" and processing large quantities of data and the supporting of largely administrative functions, made the organizational placement of "data processing" natural for accounting and finance. Consequently, it was common practice to find data processing under the direction of the controller or chief financial officer.

Throughout the 1960s computing technology advanced and the market for computers grew. In 1965, Gordon E. Moore[9] published his seminal paper, "Cramming More Components onto Integrated Circuits," which established "Moore's Law" of computing and computing power.[10] Indeed, it was during the launch and marketing of IBM's 360 series that IBM began the design for its new 370 series of mainframes that would appear in 1970 and set more performance landmarks.

During the 1960s, the use of data processing began to propagate to other business functions and areas of the enterprise. The propagation of technology created the need for specialized consulting services, especially in administrative and manufacturing functions. While Japanese manufacturers such as Toyota, implemented much of W. Edwards Deming's[11] theories and practices on quality and production, Joseph Orlicky,[12] in 1964, developed what would become known as Manufacturing Resource Planning (MRP).[13] MRP is the precursor of and foundation for MRP-II, which would emerge in the 1970s. Much of the concepts and functional integration of MRP and MRP-II would ultimately evolve to find their way to what is now Enterprise Resource Planning (ERP).

IBM's success with its 360 architecture was a double-edged sword. By 1969, IBM was squarely in the crosshairs of the U.S. Justice Department and the target of anti-trust action that would last 13 long tortuous years, cost hundreds of million of dollars, and, to many, set the innovation back by years.[14]

The solidification of the mainframe as a computing platform for business and the appearance of more business specific software applications provided a great impetus for IT consulting services. It was during this period that specialized IT consulting firms were founded and/or gained momentum, and the larger accounting firms that composed the "Big-8" began to amass IT competencies. The combination of these factors formalized IT consulting as a practice within the consulting industry.

- **Phase 3.0: The 1970s – Emergence of IT Management Consulting and Packaged Software**

If the 1960s were the Golden Age of the Mainframe, the 1970s were the dawn and establishment of the software business. By 1970, IBM's headquarters in Armonk, New York, became the center of the computing universe and the standard from which all technology was measured. IT represented a new industry and new business opportunities. It was in the 1970s, in California and in a place called the Silicon Valley that unknown companies such as Apple, Cisco, Intel and Oracle would emerge to disrupt and destroy the dominance of IBM.

The introduction of the IBM 370 in 1970 set the stage for technologies that we use today and created the opportunity for the ever-enterprising management consultant to create professional services targeted to both the public and private sectors. With speeds five times faster than the 360 and integrated circuits for memory and virtual memory capabilities, computing technology, operating systems, and data management methods of the IBM 370 all took a major leap on the technology curve. The IBM 370 architecture made it possible for multi-tasking, concurrent computing for multi-users (customers), and the processing of vast amounts of data. As most companies were organized around functions and hierarchical in form, concepts for application, data, and enterprise "integration" were still primitive and decades away. Most application software was custom written specifically for a particular application or set of applications and dedicated data. The construct for a universally defined and accessible database was yet to be commercialized and reports, data analysis, and any manipulation of data required specialized programming skills.

Virtually every major company, at least in the U.S., had some type of mainframe computing capacity, and virtually every major electronics company entered the IT industry with their own computer offerings. Although IBM dominated the mainframe market, other companies, such as Honeywell, GE, Hewlett-Packard, Amdahl, Burroughs, Siemens, NCR, Hitachi, NEC, Phillips, RCA, Westinghouse, and Boston-based Digital Equipment, produced or offered mainframe products. The computer industry was in a hyper-growth state, enormously attractive and fiercely competitive. Computer designs and engineering were accelerating, and technology and software were becoming more powerful, sophisticated, and reliable.

With the proliferation of mainframe computing technology and the growth in computer usage came more and more functional specific software. General marketplace application software products were being built and sold commercially by application suppliers. Companies such as McCormack and Dodge, Computer Associates, Computer Sciences Corporation, Automatic Data Processing, Oracle, and others began to appear. These companies created and marketed function specific software applications designed to improve operational efficiencies, reduce errors, and generate more accurate and timely management reports. Under Oliver Wight, MRP became MRP-II and by the mid-1970s, over 700 companies had adopted the concepts of MRP and many were using some type of MRP related software.[15]

However, the software still "followed" the general design and distribution of functions within the organization. That is, the software was highly specialized to a specific function and generally designed as a vertical silo with little integration and multiple and duplicated data bases, most of which were isolated to their specific functions and, at best, randomly and partially synchronized.

Notwithstanding the success of IBM and the mainframe as the de facto standard in computing, in 1975, and far from IBM's Armonk, New York, headquarters and Digital Equipment's Boston home, there were obscure and little known players and new technologies lurking far off the grid, and well under the radar of the mainstream technology giants.

84 *Michael A. Mische*

The 1970s also marked a decade of major coalescence for IT consulting, as many of the top consulting firms such as Arthur Andersen,[16] Price Waterhouse,[17] and Peat, Marwick & Mitchell began to supply IT as a core service offering for their clients.[18]

It was during the 1970s, that more academic research and curricula in higher education were being developed for IT. As a consequence, a more formal profession began to be forged, consisting of higly trained and "degreed" technologists. New consulting companies such as EDS emerged with core competencies in IBM technology and a standard set of programming languages such as Assembler, CICS, COBOL, Fortran, and Basic were taught. As the technology and industry evolved, new techniques such as "Systems Development Lifecycle"[19] methods and "Data Modeling"[20] were introduced and became more popular as standard frameworks. IT management consulting, as a profession, began to embrace and deploy these formal and uniformly recognized methods, standards and practices.

During the **1970s** the IT consulting profession began to coalesce around professional standards and create more specialty practices areas such as:

- Application software selection
- Systems implementation
- MRP implementation
- Management reporting
- Early data base design and implementation
- Formalized SDLC and data modeling
- Early IT planning models

The 1970s ended with IT firmly established as a major and essential consulting competency and the emergence of the then Big-8 accounting firms and EDS as IT consulting thought leaders.

- **Phase 4.0: The 1980s – Disruption and the Personal Computer**

Perhaps no single decade in computing was, or will be, as exciting as the 1980s. The 1980s were the decade of political disruption and democratization. Madonna, Duran Duran, the launch of MTV, the appearance of celluar technology, and the dismantling of the Soviet Bloc set a dynamic social stage.

There was excitement in the air, and IT consulting was central to and a beneficiary of that excitement.

During the **1980s** the IT consulting profession expanded rapidly into practices areas such as:

- Enterprise resource planning
- Systems and data integration
- Functional automation
- Networked computing

- Client-server computing
- IT strategic planning
- IT performance and value
- Networking and wireless communications

Commencing in the early 1980s, IBM began mass-producing the IBM PC. The launch of the IBM PC was one the most successful product introductions up until that time. In one month, IBM produced over 241,000 PCs, or around 335 units an hour. IBM was churning out almost six PCs a minute!. IBM's commitment to the PC singularly proved the legitimization of the personal computer as a platform. It also singled the beginning of a long and painful decline for IBM that would ultimately require the need to dismantle its legacy business model and management practices and reposition the company for new challenges.[21] In the mid-1980s IBM changed some of its selling agreements to provide for the outright sale of mainframes. This significant change created prolific consequences as it disrupted the constant stream of recurring revenues that were associated with leasing.

Apple, Microsoft, and Oracle were all west coast companies with a technology *vision* and technologies that would eventually revolutionize computing and how technology companies, users and management consultants would all interact. These three seminal companies, and their founders, Steve Jobs,[22] Bill Gates,[23] and Larry Ellison,[24] would ultimately create technologies that changed lives. The power of the computer that was once the exclusive domain of the mainframe and held captive by only those technically trained was now at the fingertips of the individual user. With Apple and Microsoft, the capabilities of computing would be dispersed and the power of the software placed into the hands of individual, non-technical users. In Oracle, the notion that data was strategic and individual data elements were or could be related to many other elements soon found not only technical endorsement, but also user excitement and rapid adoption. With the launching relational data base technologies, the promise of gaining insights and competitive advantages through "Big Data" analysis was a reality.

The appearance of the Apple Macintosh in January 1984 and its iconic unveiling in a Super Bowl Sunday TV commercial cleverly and metaphorically played off of IBM as "Big Brother" from George Orwell's *1984*.[25] With a female athlete hurtling a hammer at a talking face, Apple marked a systemic long-term transformation from data processing to information technology to ultimately what I have come to call *technology-enabled living (TEL)*. Simultaneously, technology was advancing to the point where computing power, as provided by client-servers, networked devices, the appearance of wireless communications and interconnectivity, all contributed to a rapid change in the computing landscape. IBM, which had enjoyed dominance since the 1960s, now found itself confronted with a different landscape and new competitors who were faster, more innovative and more aggressive. Were IBM enjoyed size, this new breed of technology provider was agile, revolutionary and 'cool'. The shift hit IBM squarely on its P&L and Balance Sheet. The mainframe computer, which represented 50 percent of IBM's revenues and somewhere between 70 to 80 percent of its profits, was being displaced by newer technologies.

With the appearance and growing use of desktop computing technologies, business functions began a long-journey of linkage and integration with other business processes and common data and supporting application. Benchmarking, 'best practices,' extended enterprise concepts and EDI, stimulated firms, such Andersen Consulting (Accenture). As American and European industry struggled to keep pace with the Japanese, CEOs turned to IT to provide competitive advantage. Consequently, the growth was precipitated by a number of factors, including:

- A more literate and computer enabled user.
- Ease of use and understanding of computers.
- Greater use of applications to support business processes and functions.
- A movement towards greater business function and application integration.
- A shift from sequential and indexed data to relational databases with flexible structures.
- The need for data repositories, rationalized architectures, standard query languages, and easy accessibility to support data analytics and advanced management reporting.
- Increasing expenditures on IT by organizations and ever expanding deployment of technologies in the workforce and for private use.

With Apple's Macintosh and Microsoft's suite of PC-based software, the basic tools of the management consultant also under went a profound transformation, as well as the *process* of rendering management consulting services. Speed, efficiency, access to data and applications, desktop publishing, and now advanced data analytics and instantaneous communications became common tools of the management consultant. The adoption and application of these tools to the consulting process significantly altered the dynamics of how consultants worked and the relationship between client and consultant. A significant example was how clients and consultants could more effectively communicate and collaborate on work products, issues and research.

Not surprisingly, as organizations spent more and more of their financial resources on IT-based solutions and consulting services, IT began to generate greater interst and visibility in the C-suite. As With IT absorbing a greater share of organization's budget, senior business leadership began to become active and more discriminating with respect to what IT was used, how IT was used, and whether IT should be treated as operational process, tactical need or strategic asset. What soon followed were passionate arguments about IT in the boardrooms of many organizations. The higher profile and level of interest ushered in a fourth service offering in strategic planning for IT. Firms such as KPMG's Nolan-Norton[26] began to interpret the trends and implications of IT for C-suite members and apply planning discipline to help form the C-suite's perspective and use of IT for straetgic purposes and competitive in their enterprises.

- Phase 5.0: The 1990s – Reengineering, The Internet, Dot.com, and Y2K

The 1980s might have been the decade of IT excitement, but the 1990s will best be remembered as the decade of President Bill Clinton and political scandal, the Internet, the era of the dot.com, and mass migrations to standardized ERP and CRM product offerings. Technology became more simple to use and less expensive to obtain, use, and support. The Internet created a major shift (and rift) in the IT world. With a PC, Internet connection, and some software, a business could be started. Companies such as Amazon were formed and launched. What followed were major disruptions to industries such as retail banking, travel, entertainment, specialty retailing, and many others.

During the 1990s the IT consulting profession expanded rapidly into practices areas such as:

- Enterprise-wide solutions
- Customer relationship
- Internet and interconnectivity
- E-commerce
- E-business
- Business process reengineering
- Sales force automation
- Website design and hosting
- Client-server computing
- Y2K

But the 1990s were also a transformative decade of tough economic times for most U.S. businesses. Commenciing in the 1970s, U.S. competitiveness as a world industrial power had experienced al long and systemic decline The quality and value of U.S. products, especially in the automative, consumer appliances and electronics sectors seemed to have been abandoned for lowest cost an highest profit strategies. As provided in Michael Moore's 1989 film, '*Roger & Me*,' nowhere were the effects of that strategy more exemplified than the U.S. automotive industry.* Foreign competition, especially from Japan and Germany, wrecked havoc for most U.S. manufacturers. The recognition for operational change drove an urgency for more creative and value generating technology applications. Digital Equipment and new upstarts such as Compaq and Dell were competing and winning

---

*https://en.wikipedia.org/wiki/Roger_%26_Me

88 *Michael A. Mische*

against IBM. In IBM's Armonk, New York, headquarters the company had cut 40,000 jobs. In 1991, IBM's revenues plummeted by 60 percent, earnings dropped by over $2.8 billion, or 146 percent from the prior year, and it incurred a $3.7 billion restructuring charge. Dell Computer, which had its beginnings in a dormitory room at the University of Texas, had now displaced IBM as a had now become a supplier of choice for many business and public sector buyers.[27]

For much of the 1990's and certainly towards the end of the twenth century, IT consulting grew at double digits. The rapid growth of the Internet, together with the proliferation of wireless communications, created companies such as Google and fueled the need for infrastructure providers such as AT&T, Cisco, EMC, and Verizon. Larger firms, such as Accenture and the Big-6 (now Big-4) accounting firms, capitalized on the intersection of Business Process Reengineering (BPR) and enterprise application software solutions (ERP) provided by companies such as Oracle and SAP. Smaller, specialty firms sprang up to create websites and e-commerce on the Internet. And many firms capitalized on the fears of Y2K and the possibility that software would implode and cause airplanes to fall out of sky, traffic to stop and appliances to malfunction at the stroke of midnight. But, alas, the decade ended on a relatively quiet note.

- **Phase 6.0: 2000–2015 – Virtual Enterprise and Cloud Computing**

With Y2K safely behind, the IT industry and IT consulting were poised for explosive growth in the new millennium. However, what followed were a series of major events that would force unplanned adjustments to the IT industry and IT management consulting.

- In March 2000, the stock market experienced a major adjustment to the technology sector in what would become known as the "dot.com bust." In a matter of days, billions of dollars were drained or wiped out. In response, companies slashed their IT budgets and the use of consultants.
- On September 11, 2001, the terrorist attacks on the U.S. created tremendous disruption to business and uncertainty in the private sector. The uncertainty further adversely affected the management consulting but also amplified the need for cyber-security and the expanded use of IT for homeland security purposes.
- In March 2002, the U.S. launched military action against Iraq and Afghanistan, and entered the longest military engagement in U.S. history.
- Commencing in late 2006 and culminating with the collapse of Lehmann Brothers in 2008 and continuing into 2016, the U.S. experienced its worst economic performance since the Great Depression (1929 to 1939). Known as the "Great Recession" the consulting industry slowed and actually contracted for several years, before beginning a recovery in 2012.

- The uncertainty in the political and economic environments amplified the surplus of management consultants relative to client demand. In response, many professionals who had consulting experience were forced to leave the profession to find more stable positions in industry. The over capacity in consulting, combined with the political and economic environment and trained consultants exiting the profession allowed more organizations to build their own internal consulting-like competencies. Given the industry dynamics and pressures, consolidation of the consulting industry was inevitable.

World political and domestic economic events shaped the IT management consulting industry. Consequently, for the better part of the 2000 to 2015 period, IT management consultants spent increasingly greater proportions of their time and talents on services such as: cyber-security, risk identification and mitigation. M&A related IT issues, enterprise integration, and more creative IT-enabled business models.

As the need for more innovative strategies for business expanded, new software for "customer facing" and insights were offered. These new strategies and technologies stimulated the demand for consulting services in customer relationship management, sales force automation, mobile device applications, and data analytics were developed. The management consulting profession responded with new services and specializations. Throughout the 2000s the IT profession evolved its services to include capabiliites in business functions such as automated call centers and advanced and remote customer services and diagnostics. For example, from its initial years of commercialization in the late 1980s, the Philippines, India, and U.S. have dominated the outsourcing industry that employs about 4.0 million people in the U.S.[28]

During the 2000–2015 period, there has been some consolidation of the IT consulting and a corresponding profession expanded rapidly into practices areas such as:

- Strategic use of IT
- Social media and networking
- IT deployment and management
- Cloud-based computing
- Software as a Service (SaaS)
- Infrastructure as a Service (IaaS)
- Cyber security
- Risk mitigation
- Due diligence for IT
- Call centers
- Specialized outsourcing (business processes and functions)
- Business process transformation
- Enterprise-wide standardization

Exhibit 4.2 summarizes the evolution of IT and IT consulting services and begs the question: What's the future hold? That is the subject of section 5.0 of this chapter.

Exhibit 4.2 Evolution of IT Consulting Services

2000 to 2015

- Strategic use of IT
- Social media and networking
- IT deployment and management
- Cloud-based computing
- Software as a Service (SaaS)
- Infrastructure as a Service (IaaS)
- Cyber security
- Risk mitigation
- Due diligence for IT
- Call centers
- Specialized outsourcing (business processes and functions)
- Business process transformation
- Enterprise-wide standardization

1990s

- Enterprise-wide solutions
- Customer relationship
- Internet and interconnectivity
- E-commerce
- E-business
- Business process reengineering
- Sales force automation
- Website design and hosting
- Client-server computing
- Y2K

1980s

- Enterprise resource planning
- Systems and data integration
- Functional automation
- Networked computing
- Client-server computing
- IT strategic planning
- IT performance and value
- Networking and wireless communications

1970s

- Application software selection
- Systems implementation
- MRP implementation
- Management reporting
- Early data base design and implementation
- Formalized SDLC and data modeling
- Early IT planning models

1960s

- Hardware selection
- Application software development
- Implementation services

1950s

- Technical consulting services
- Scientific application services

3.0 Defining the IT Industry

3.1 Description and Definition of the IT Industry

There is little question as to the significance and dominance of IT as an industry and its impact on GDP and employment. IT today is integral to virtually all aspects of our lives. In a modern society, technology controls everything from simple water and air temperatures in washers and driers, to sophisticated robotic surgeries, to automobiles, to space flight.

From its early stages, the IT industry has, quite naturally, been defined by technologies that it invents and markets.

- In the 1940s, the IT industry structure was relatively easy to characterize: it was composed of inventors of computing technology hardware.
- In the 1950s the industry structure consisted primarily of two types of providers: (1) Hardware producers such as IBM, and (2) Technical programmers.
- With the rapid growth in mainframe computing, the 1960s and 1970s saw the formation of two new segments: (3) Application software providers, and (4) IT consultants.
- The appearance of the personal computer in the 1980s created a disruptive effect and set the stage for the dot.com era of the 1990s and the "Internet of Things" of today.

Some IT research firms have four classifications as primary groups; some have more. This chapter organizes the overall U.S. IT industry into <u>seven</u> primary categories. These categories represent IT products, manufacturers, software, technologies, and services and include:

1. Technology providers such as Apple, Hewlett-Packard, and IBM.
2. Communication providers such as Verizon and AT&T.
3. Infrastructure providers such as Cisco and EMC.
4. Enterprise solutions providers such as Oracle and SAP.
5. Internet-based knowledge, content and data providers such as, Google, YouTube, and Yahoo.
6. E-commerce providers such as eBay, Ababa, and Priceline.
7. IT consulting service providers such as Accenture.

Notwithstanding the classification for purposes of this chapter, there are crossovers, overlaps, and inherent imprecisions in the assignments of a particular technology provider or supplier to a specific category. For example, almost all suppliers provide "support and maintenance" services.

3.2 Industry Size and Dimension

In advanced economies, such the United States, IT expenditures are a significant component of GDP and private and public sector spending. Measuring an industry as large, diverse, and ubiquitous as IT is not without its challenges. There is some consistency among research firms as to what exactly should be and is included in the definition and measurements for the IT industry; however there is no universally defined and accepted method for representing actual economic dimensions of the industry or IT-related services. Consequently, various research firms have defined and measured the industry somewhat differently. For example, three of the most widely recognized research firms have published the following estimates:

- Gartner]Inc. estimates worldwide IT spending for 2015/16 to be around $3.4 trillion dollars and $1.23 trillion in the U.S. with growth to $3.8 trillion by 2020.[29]
- IDC Research estimates worldwide IT spending for 2015 to be around $2.5 trillion with an increase to $2.8 trillion dollars in 2019.[30]
- Forrester Research estimates U.S.-based IT spending for 2016 to be $1.453 trillion.[31]

The disparities in the spending estimates can be attributed to several factors; chief among those is how each researcher defines the industry and the methods that each uses to collect and assess data. Various researchers and data collection efforts will use different definitions for IT spending, what is included or excluded in IT spending, whether fiscal or calendar years are used, how data collection is validated, the responsiveness and quality of the

IT Management Consulting 93

data sources, categories for the types of services to be included/excluded, interpretation, and many other factors. All of these methods and assumptions affect how the industry is measured and reported.

Spending for IT is somewhat cyclical, but not volatile, and moves with relative consistency with changes in U.S. GDP. The primary influences that have a direct influence on IT spending include: (1) Major or disruptive shifts and changes in technology, (2) Corporate profits and free cash flows, (3) Severity of competitive threats and the need to respond, (4) CEO sentiment, and (5) Legislative mandates and regulatory changes. In the U.S. corporate profits are directly correlated with changes in the GDP, hence, IT spending closely follows corporate profits. **Exhibit 4.3** below summarizes the relationship between the percentage change in U.S. corporate profits and the percentage change in the U.S. GDP.

Corporate profits, along with CEO sentiments about future economic conditions, are a key driver in IT spending. Summarized in **Exhibit 4.4** below is the percentage change in U.S. corporate profits as compared to the percentage in IT spending in the U.S. for the 2007 to 2020 (estimated) period. The dramatic downward shift in spending in IT for the 2014 to 2016 period can be attributed to many factors, chief among which are: the lagging of the "catch-up" effect in IT spending from prior years, the "build-out" of enterprise-wide solutions for most organizations, and CEO trepidation related to risk to the U.S. economy, unemployment, and uncertainty surrounding the U.S. presidential election.

Exhibit 4.3 Percentage Change in U.S. Corporate Profits Correlate to U.S. GDP

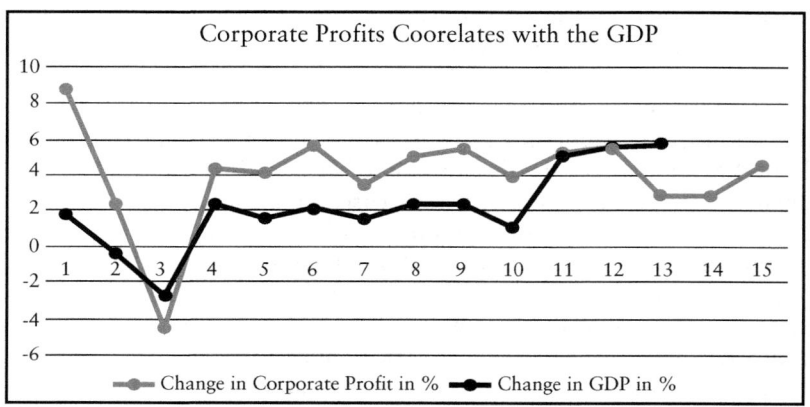

IBIS World http://clients1.ibisworld.com.libproxy2.usc.edu/reports/us/industry/keystatistics.aspx?entid=1415

Exhibit 4.4 Percentage Change in U.S. Corporate Profits to the Percentage in IT Spending

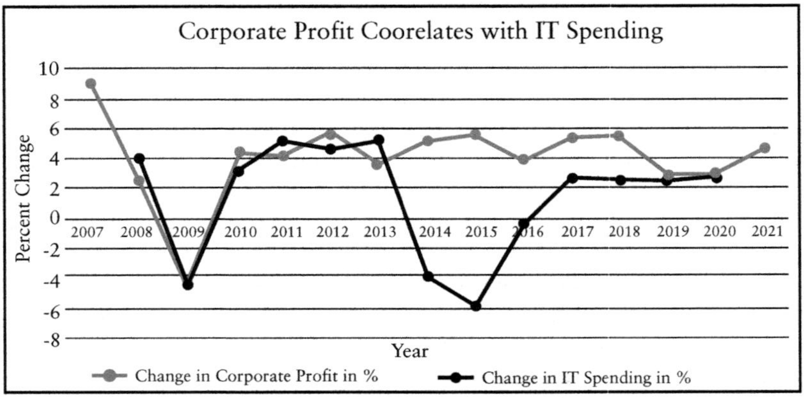

```
Corporate Profit Coorelates with IT Spending
```
[Chart showing Change in Corporate Profit in % and Change in IT Spending in % from 2007 to 2021, Percent Change on y-axis ranging from -8 to 10]

IBIS World http://clients1.ibisworld.com.libproxy2.usc.edu/reports/us/industry/keystatistics.aspx?entid=1415

3.3 Major Markets and Segments for IT Expenditures

Spending estimates by market sectors or segments vary among research firms. According to Gartner Inc. the four largest segments of technology spending include: banking, manufacturing, communications, and government.[32] The research firm, Gartner, Inc. estimates that these four segments collectively represent 67.5 percent of the total estimated worldwide expenditures for IT. Alternatively, Forrester Research estimates the largest IT spending organizations as: government, finance and insurance, business services, and media and entertainment. Based on a composite of various estimates, the United States and Canada represent the greatest concentration for spending at over $1.5 trillion, or 44 percent.[33] In the U.S., federal government spending for 2016 is estimated to be around $80 billion.[34] **Exhibit 4.5** summarizes the distribution of IT spending by primary market segment/customer based on Forrester Reasearch information.

Buyer values, that is, the motivations for selecting and deploying a particular technology, differ among segments. Some buyers are early adopters of technology; others prefer to wait until a stable or dominant technology becomes de-facto. All buyers of technology, however, must consume and use infrastructure technologies to support network computing, communications, email, Internet, E-commerce, cloud-based computing, and other Life Enabled Technologies. Depending where an organization resides on the "technology curve" and its use and deployment of technology will vary somewhat within an industry. As scope, scale, and profitability grow, in general, so does IT spending and embedment within the organization. **Exhibit 4.6** depicts the distribution of IT spending by primary application based on Forrester recommendations.

IT Management Consulting

Exhibit 4.5 Distribution of IT Purchases by Primary Segment

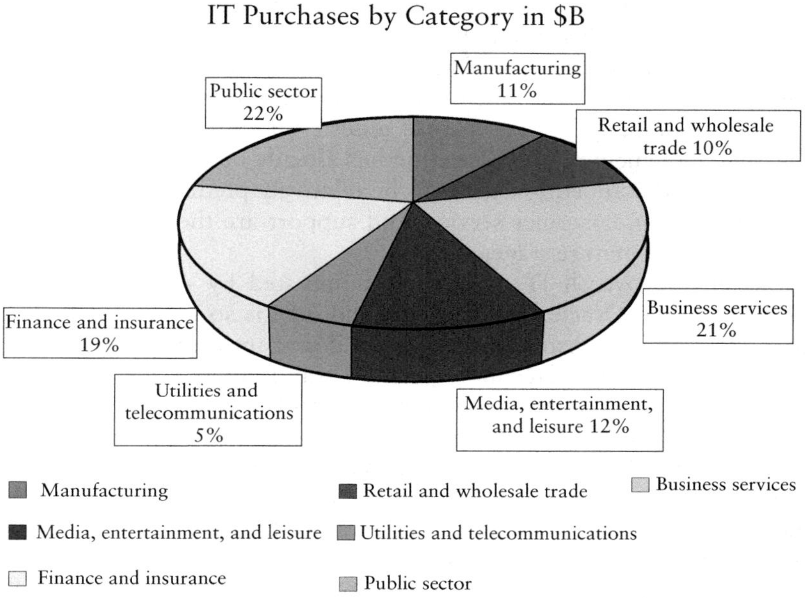

IT Purchases by Category in $B

- Manufacturing 11%
- Retail and wholesale trade 10%
- Business services 21%
- Media, entertainment, and leisure 12%
- Utilities and telecommunications 5%
- Finance and insurance 19%
- Public sector 22%

Legend:
- Manufacturing
- Retail and wholesale trade
- Business services
- Media, entertainment, and leisure
- Utilities and telecommunications
- Finance and insurance
- Public sector

Forrester – https://www.forrester.com/report/2016+US+Tech+Budgets+The+Outlook+For+Tech+Spending+Overall+And+By+Industry/-/E-RES121248#figure8

Exhibit 4.6 Distribution of IT Spending by Function/Technology

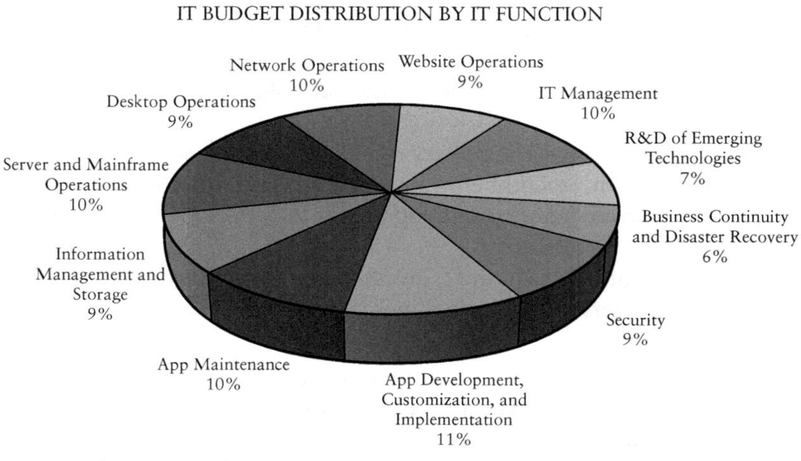

IT BUDGET DISTRIBUTION BY IT FUNCTION

- Network Operations 10%
- Website Operations 9%
- IT Management 10%
- R&D of Emerging Technologies 7%
- Business Continuity and Disaster Recovery 6%
- Security 9%
- App Development, Customization, and Implementation 11%
- App Maintenance 10%
- Information Management and Storage 9%
- Server and Mainframe Operations 10%
- Desktop Operations 9%

Forrester–https://www.forrester.com/report/YearEnd+2013+IT+Budget+Benchmarks/-/E-RES104963#figure1

3.4 Competitive Dynamics of the IT Industry

Consistent with most other industries, the evolution of the IT industry follows the traditional industry life cycle. However, unlike many other industries, the IT industry has been subjected to rapid development, disruptive technologies, and accelerated adoption and adaptation. Overall, the IT industry is mature with a growth rate ranging between 2 percent and 3.2 percent, annually.[35] As a mature industry, innovation by the leaders tends to be incremental, differentiation has already been established among the leaders, and competition tends to be relatively predictable. Pricing and service packaging, customer service, and support are the general basics of competing in the mature stage.

Although the overall IT industry is dominated by Apple, IBM, Intel, Hewlett-Packard, Oracle, and SAP, the industry is so large and extensive that concentration is dispersed among the dominant firms. Thus, although there are dominant firms, technologies, and brands, there is no single firm or company that has a concentration of powers and dominance over the entire spectrum of IT and the IT consulting industry.

Make no mistake, the competitive dynamics of the IT industry are ruthless and unforgiving. Companies such as Compaq, NCR, Digital Equipment, and Burroughs, were and UNIVAC once the darlings of Wall Street investors, are now merely footnotes to the history of the computer industry. Notwithstanding the constant possibility of disruptive technologies, the IT industry is best characterized:

1. Highly competitive at the enterprise level and buyer bargaining powers are high.
2. High switching costs make incumbent technologies difficult to displace and supplier powers increase.
3. Highly segmented with respect to the application of technologies; thus depending on the technology, application of the technology, and buyer, powers can shift rapidly.
4. Highly specialized and specific to the technology; the supplier has bargaining powers.
5. Competition among IT suppliers for hardware and software is intense, but dissipates with incumbent longevity. In this situation, the buyer has bargaining powers over competing technology providers, but not necessarily over the incumbent.
6. Cost, benefit, and return on IT investments become increasingly important as IT budgets expand, thus increasing buyer bargaining powers.

To compete effectively in this environment, management consulting firms must be able to effectively span the technical nuances of highly sophisticated technologies, navigate the C-suite, understand the implementation risks and issues, and perhaps above all else, prove value.

4.0 Defining IT Management Consulting

4.1 The IT Management Consultant

With the proliferation of IT, it's little wonder that IT consultants are virtually everywhere, figuratively and literally, and come in all sorts of varieties. For example:

- What were once predominantly hardware companies, such as IBM and Hewlett Packard, now have a significant percentage of their annual revenues generated from services. Are IBM and Hewlett-Packard IT consulting firms?
- Similarly, what were once application software companies, today report considerable growth and revenues from solution service offerings, such integrated suites of software products. Are Oracle and SAP consulting firms?
- Traditional IT consulting service firms such as Accenture have moved into IT-related services such as third-party processing and call centers. Are call centers consulting services?
- One could easily argue that Google with its query search, intelligence capabilities, and responses is a "virtual" consulting firm and as such, provides virtual IT consulting services. Is Google a management consultant . . . after all Google provides research services?

So who are the IT management consultants? Well, like much in life, it depends on who you ask, how you ask them, when you ask them, and how the question is framed. For purposes of this chapter and for purposes of bringing some order and perspective to the IT management consulting industry, I offer the following definition of IT management consulting and an IT management consultant:

Definition of IT Management Consultant

IT management consulting is the process of providing independent, objective, and professional advisory services, on a fee for service basis, to assist clients plan, select, deploy, utilize, and leverage technology for strategic, operational, organizational, and competitive advantage and financial value.

In this definition, I purposely use the adjectives "professional," "objective," and "independent" as primary descriptors of IT *management* consulting. The incorporation of these terms is essential for a general defintion of management consulting and for differentiating a management consultant from an employee who may be functioning as an internal consultant, a contractor or 1099 employee and an analyst. Professional IT management consultants are distinct from contractors, analysts, employees, and academicians in three significant ways:

1. IT management consultants, as defined in this chapter, are formally trained in the consulting process and in delivering services to their clients.
2. As a professional management consultant, they are trained to a certain standard of practice and performance, and they operate within a recognized and legally enforceable code of professional ethics, such as the AICPA Code of Professional Conduct.[36]
3. As a professional management consultant they are independent and objective with respect to their methods of work and any technology, software, architectures, vendors, or suppliers.
4. With formal training and a deep appreciation for how IT can contribute to the competitiveness of a business, IT management consultants interact not only with specialized IT talent and resources of the client, but also interact throughout the organization and especially with members of the C-suite.
5. Professional consultants are compensated on a fee for service basis and those fees generally reflect the talent, competencies, training and value propositoin of the consultant.

In contrast, a contractor, although she or he may be highly qualified and experienced, is generally hired to perform a particular set of tasks as an external resource, or "contract employee," and usually under the direct or quasi-direction of the employer. Contractors may possess deep subject matter expertise in certain technologies, but those technologies may not necessarily be in the best interest of the client. Hence, irrespective of their credentials and qualifications, they may not be in a position to maintain objectivity and independence, especially if their individual financial interests are involved.

For the remainder of this chapter IT management consulting is discussed within this definitional framework and context.

4.2 IT Management Consulting Firms

As indicated earlier, there were probably management consultants back in the day of the Tally Stick and abacus. There might have even been consulting firms! But for our purposes, we can trace modern era management consulting to the 1920s and 1930s in the United States with firms such as AT Kearney, McKinsey, Peat, Marwick & Mitchell, and Price Waterhouse.

It was not until the commercialization of the computer in the 1950s by IBM that mainstream management consulting firms began to create IT consulting practices (service lines). Commencing in the mid-1950s, gaining momentum and critical mass in the 1960s, and solidifying itself as a recognized and an essential professional service offering in the 1970s, IT consulting has grown to be a significant and essential capability for consultants and any consulting firm.

With the commercialization of the Internet in the 1990s, the dot.com era, and mass migrations to standard ERP and CRM product offerings, many different types of IT consulting firms emerged. During the 1970s and 1980s, application software firms began offering packaged solutions for business functions such as accounting, manufacturing (MRP and MRP-II), point of sale (POS), inventory and supply chain, and other systems. The appearance of these highly specialized systems stimulated the need for management consultants who not only understood technology, but how technology could be employed and deployed to the better of the enterprise. Firms such as Price Waterhouse (now PWC), Peat, Marwick & Mitchell (now KPMG), Electronic Data Systems (EDS), Deloitte, Haskins & Sells (now Deloitte & Touche), Computer Associates, and others formed consulting services that proved to be in high demand and their IT service offerings, highly lucrative. Other firms, such as McKinsey, Bain, and BCG, were generally late adopters of IT consulting practices, and comparatively have a considerably lesser presence in IT consulting.[37]

IT consulting firms span the spectrum from one-person shops specializing in website designs, to specialty firms that concentrate on certain technologies and software offerings, to the entrepreneurial "app" developers, to mega-sized, one-stop firms such as Accenture that provide enterprise-wide solutions. With over 377,000 employees and 2016 annual revenues of approximately $32 billion, Accenture dwarfs all other consulting firms and is capable of addressing virtually any IT problem and service need.[38]

IT has neutralized many advantages associated with location and size. Essential competitive attributes, such as operational excellence, organizational agility, knowledge and customer relations, data analytics, AI, and virtual reality are inseparable from IT and thus, management consulting. In the digital world, IT may not be a core competency or main service line for some of the prominent consulting firms, but it's abundantly clear that a major consulting firm cannot compete effectively without an appreciation, profound awareness, and working knowledge of how IT affects the behavior, valuation, competitiveness, and performance of a client.

Determining the size of the IT management consulting profession and industry is exceedingly difficult. The enormity of the IT industry creates as equally large and complex IT consulting opportunities. Depending on the consulting firm or the market research firm and its methodology, the number of IT consulting firms ranges from the hundreds to thousands and the number of people employed range from hundreds of thousands to over 1 million. Not surprisingly, revenues estimates for the profession range from several hundred million to billions of dollars. **Exhibit 4.7** below provides a summary of top research services with respect to their estimates as to the size of the IT *consulting* market.

However, these estimates may or may not include spending for IT enabled processes such as business transformation, data analytics, and extended enterprise business models. A factor to always consider is that IT tends to employ many independent contractors[39] and "situational workers," as well as those who are fulltime employees of major consulting firms. Some estimates may include IT call centers as consulting services; others may not. Some sources might include specialty markets and consulting practices such as healthcare, supply chain, enterprise architecture planning, and outsourcing in their estimates; others may not. Sizing issues with respect to number of employees, revenues, etc. are created by various definitional inclusions, or exclusions.

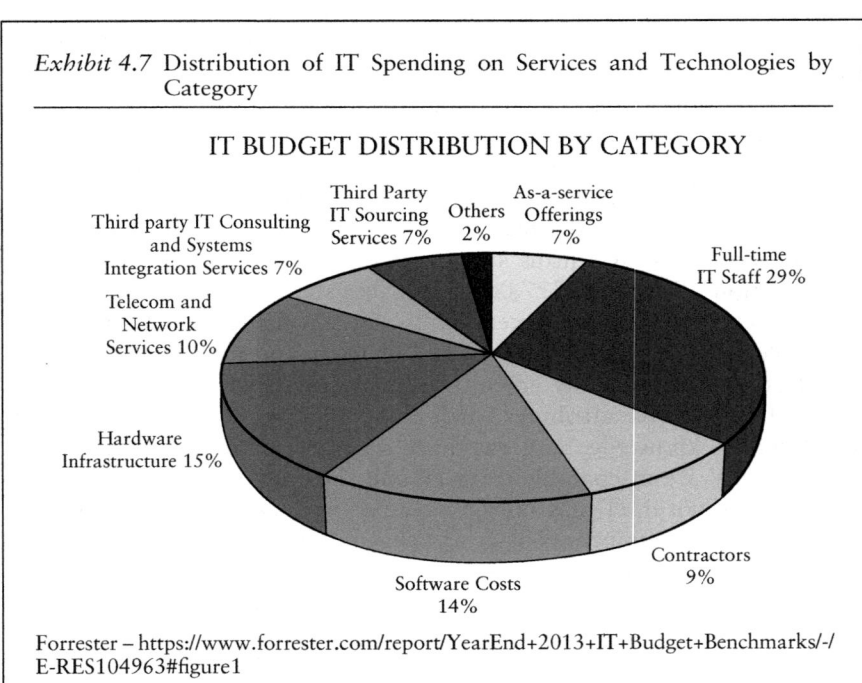

Exhibit 4.7 Distribution of IT Spending on Services and Technologies by Category

IT BUDGET DISTRIBUTION BY CATEGORY

Third party IT Consulting and Systems Integration Services 7%
Third Party IT Sourcing Services 7%
Others 2%
As-a-service Offerings 7%
Full-time IT Staff 29%
Telecom and Network Services 10%
Hardware Infrastructure 15%
Software Costs 14%
Contractors 9%

Forrester – https://www.forrester.com/report/YearEnd+2013+IT+Budget+Benchmarks/-/E-RES104963#figure1

For example, "systems integration" project spending as reported by a company or reported as a service by a consulting firm may include new spending for infrastructure as part of the overall integration process; other companies and firms may not. In the absence of a single or unifying measurement of IT consulting, understanding and estimating revenues, number of employees or even what or how consultants are differentiated from contractors is subject to individual interpretation. **Exhibit 4.8** provides another representation of IT spending by category. It is worthwhile noting that "IT consulting services" may be associated with all of those categories. Hence the challenge of accurately estimating IT consulting revenues . . . suffice it say that IT revenues are *large*.

Adding to the challenges of determining size and importance of IT consulting as a service line or practice is that many firms such as KPMG, PwC, McKinsey, and Deloitte are *privately owned* and therefore do not publish financial statements or data for public use. Thus, estimating the revenues generated from IT consulting and the various sizes and services of these privately owned firms is subject to individual interpretation, discretion, and, at best, intelligent approximation.

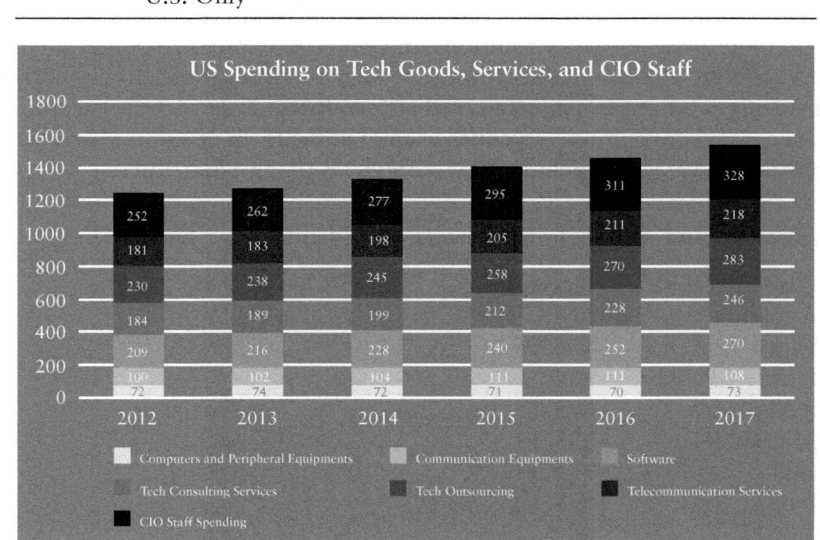

Exhibit 4.8 Total Estimated IT Spending on Goods, Services, and Staffing – U.S. Only

Forrester – https://www.forrester.com/report/US+Tech+Market+Outlook+For+2016+And+2017+Cloud+And+Business+Caution+Will+Slow+Growth/-/E-RES126966

Once considered to be the exclusive domain of the technical expert and IT consulting was not within the lofty thinking of traditional *management* consultant. After all, computers were in the basements of buildings and far from the C-suite that management consultants roamed. As IT became more endemic and de rigueur to the operations of the enterprise, IT management consultants began to design IT services that offered a *business value proposition*. These services appealed to the business acumen of the C-suite and included strategic themes such as: IT strategy for competitive benefit, IT deployment, and how to best use IT to differentiate the enterprise and gain cost advantage. Ultimately, the IT management consulting profession evolved to represent the confluence of business, strategic, operational, organizational and technology planning, and thinking. Today, IT consulting has a distinct *management* orientation and a prominent position in the C-suite.

IT consulting firms can be best described within the context of our definition of an IT management consultant. Based on that definition, four primary types of IT management consulting firms dominant the industry:

1 Technology and Application Software Providers.

Description. Technology and application software providers include those firms whose primary source of revenue is attributed to technology offerings (hardware, infra-structure software) and application software providers (enterprise software solutions and other integrated packages). These firms generate a considerable portion of their revenues through the marketing, selling, and implementation of their products. These products, in turn, can generate "consulting" revenues usually in the form of solutions services. **Firms in this category include: IBM, Oracle, SAP, and Symantec.**

Technology and Application Software Providers[40]

Firm	Revenues
Apple	$233.70
Samsung	$167.90
Hewlett-Packard	$103
IBM	$93.40
Microsoft	$93.30
Dell	$59.00
Intel	$55.4
Cisco	$48
Oracle	$38.80
EMC	$24.40
SAP	$23.30
Symantec	$6.60
VMware	$6.04

2 Strategic IT Consulting Providers.

Description. Strategic IT consulting providers best align with the definition in this chapter of IT consultants. Strategic IT consulting firms can provide an extensive range of IT management consulting services such as: digital enterprise strategic planning, enterprise IT planning, data analytics, software and technology assessment and selection, project management, IT deployment, business process integration, and many other services. These firms generate the majority of their revenues through direct fees for consulting services (fee for service model) and not through the marketing and selling of their proprietary products. **Firms in this category include:**

Strategic IT Consulting Firms[41]

Firm	Revenues
Accenture	$32.8B
Cap Gemini	$14B
Cognizant	$10.3B
Infosys	$8.7B
TATA Consultancy	$15.1B
KPMG	(1)
PwC	(1)
Deloitte & Touche	(1)
Ernest & Young	(1)
BCG	(1)
Bain	(1)
McKinsey	(1)
AT Kearney	(1)

(1) Revenues Not Available

3 IT Research Providers.

Description. IT research providers are those organizations that specialize in the publication of IT-related research, data, surveys, estimates, and prognostications. These firms produce the majority of their revenues through subscription fees, selling of research, and tailored offerings such as seminars, methodologies, and educational programs. As these firms can also engage in directed research as a result of a particular client need, they can also generate "consulting fees." **Firms in this category include:**

IT Research Firms[42]

Firm	Revenues
Gartner	$2.62B
IBIS	$39M
Forrester	$314M

4 **Specialized IT Service Providers.**

Description. Specialized IT service providers are those firms that have deep expertise and resources in a particular area of technology, such as: cyber-security, technology, application, suite of applications, programming languages, integration, deployment, cloud-solutions/migration, data analytic tools, etc. This category can also include firms with extensive skills in digital enterprise design, Iaas, SaaS, SDS, data base design, data migration, etc. **Firms in this category include:**

Specialized IT Service Providers[43]

Firm	Revenues
Cap Gemini	$14B
Cognizant	$10.3B
Infosys	$8.7B
Tata Consultancy	$15.1B
Mindtree	$700M
HCL Technologies	$1.6B

The expansiveness of the IT consulting industry creates the opportunity and need for crossover in specializations and classification among the above four categories. At any time and for any reporting period, a firm classified in one category may generate sufficient revenue to launch into another or appear to be dominant in another. In reality, there are many other types of IT consultants and firms. For example, there are many small, "boutique" consulting firms specializing in technical services, website design and hosting, disaster recovery planning, cyber-security, IT license compliance and fee auditing, call center operations, etc. Undoubtedly, there are countless numbers of independent contractors and sole practitioners, one-person companies small companies, or members of networks. For the remainder of this chapter, our emphasis will be on the services and practices as provided by the *Strategic IT Consulting Providers* as defined and classified above.

4.3 Competitive Dynamics Among the Strategic IT Consulting Firms

Firms that have high levels of specialized services, such as IT strategic planning, without correspondingly deep technical capabilities, are at a competitive disadvantage compared to full service firms such as Accenture. However, firms that have significant reputations and skills in a particular IT service, such as risk assessment and mitigation, will naturally have a competitive advantage, if indeed the client has a very specific and well-defined need.

In general, clients select an IT management consultant based on a number of factors, the most significant include:

- Social pedigree of the firm including, credentials, reputation, and history.[44]
- Practice specialization and expertise.
- Reputation and stature in the industry.
- Technical expertise and industry expertise.
- Past experience and or relationship.
- Perceived fees paid versus value delivered relation.

Competitive dynamics among the top IT management consulting firms is best characterized as *severe*. Rivalry among the firms is intense and with the supply of consulting hours easily exceeding the demand of client hours, competition among the firms is tremendous. Firms compete aggressively for the same clients and projects. In general:

- Firms that have scale and breadth of service offerings have a distinct advantage over those firms that do not.
- Firms that can successfully demonstrate deep technical expertise in digital enterprise modeling, data analytics and transformational integration that integrate business process, organizational compression, and data analytics have an advantage over those firms that do not.
- Firms that can demonstrate the ability to assemble and mass deep technical, industry, and strategic skills on a project team have an advantage over those with only limited resources and depth.
- Firms that can demonstrate experience and a command of technologies such as computing platforms, networks, applications, topographies, enterprise models, and how to best optimize the financial and strategic returns on IT spending are in a superior position to those firms that cannot.

4.4 IT Consulting Services

As a profession, IT consulting has evolved based on the prevailing technology. The permutations and combinations of services offered by IT consulting firms have changed with the technology. Contemporary IT consulting services span the spectrum of business needs and *is* the point of confluence between technology capabilities, business functions, analytical process, and decision-making. With such diversity in service offerings and specializations, it's no wonder that it is growing more difficult to define IT consulting services and segregate those services from business models, business functions, and the daily and strategic management of the enterprise. As a consequence, the IT consulting "universe" is enormous, complex, varied, and constantly evolving.

Despite the complexity and constant state of change, contemporary IT consulting services that the top IT firms, as in those identified as "Strategic IT Consulting Firms," provide can be arranged into 12 basic categories. Within each category are many different sub-sets and specializations of services. As summarized in **Exhibit 4.9** below, these service offerings span a broad range but are reflective of the confluence of business needs, the state of technology, analytical needs, and managerial decision-making.

Depending on the breadth and size of the IT consulting firm, its consulting capabilities, and experience, the composition of the above services will differ. Some firms, such as Accenture, Deloitte, and TATA Consultancy, will provide the complete spectrum of offerings, while firms such as McKinsey and Bain, which are considerably smaller, may provide only a few services or services that are significantly limited in scope on a comparative basis. Each of the services has a number of sub-services/specialty services as depicted in Exhibit 4.10 below.

Exhibit 4.9 Strategic IT Management Consulting Firms' Typical IT Consulting Service Offerings

1. Application Selection, Development, and Deployment
2. Digital Enterprise Modeling and Enablement
3. Cyber Services: Security, Technology, and Protection
4. Due Diligence for IT
5. IT Organizational Performance and Effectiveness
6. Due Diligence, Integration Assessments, and Risk Mitigation for M&A
7. Organizational Agility and Effectiveness
8. Outsourcing
9. Project Management and Risk Mitigation
10. Specialized Services for Various Enterprise Software Solutions and Products
11. Strategic Planning for Technology
12. Strategic Technologies such as, Data Analytics, Virtual Reality and Artifical Intelligence
13. Systems and Data Integration and Rationalization
14. Technology Deployment
15. Technology Enabled Business Processes (TEBP)

Exhibit 4.10 Management Consulting IT Consulting Primary and Specialty Service Offerings

Strategic Planning for Technology
    Business Intelligence and Data Analytics
    Competitive Positioning and Adaptation of Technology
    Transformative Business Models
    Cyber-Security
    Infrastructure Computing and Network Technology
    Operational Technology
    Strategic Technology

Strategic Technologies
    Virtual Reality and Artifical Intelligence (AI)
    Internet of Things (IoT)
    Data Analytics
    Digital Enterprise
    Integrated (All-in-One) Enterprise
    AI and Embedded Intelligence
    Self-Learning Systems

Application Development and Deployment
    Creation
    Selection
    Integration
    Deployment
    SaaS (Software as a Service) and Cloud-Based Technology

Technology Deployment
    Core Technologies
    Architecture
    Infrastructure Technology
        Network Design and Topography
        Deployment
    IaaS (Infrastructure as a Service) and Cloud-Based Technology

Technology Enabled Business Processes (TEBP)
    Automated Customer Interactions
    Assembly Line Integration

Digital Enterprise Design and Deployment
    Process Automation
    Process Integration and Compression

Intelligent Systems, AI, and Analytics
CRM and Sales Force
Cyber Services
Cyber-Security
Application and Data Security
Technology Security
Data Acquisition
Data Design
Data Base Design and Implementation
Data Accessibility and Reporting
Data Analytics
Organizational Effectiveness and Performance
Collaborative Work Environments
Multi-Cultural Team Effectiveness
Virtual Team Enablement and Effectiveness
Knowledge Capture, Management, and Learning
Knowledge Dissemination
Information Management
Project Management and Risk Mitigation
Project Planning
Project Management
Project Assessment and Variance Analysis
Project Status Reporting
Project and Contract Administration
Project Management Office
Program Management
Program Management Office
Outsourcing
Data Center Operations
IT Customer Support and Operations
Network Operations
Application Development, Programming, and Maintenance
Specialized Business Functions and Operations
  Customer Support (External Customers)
  Call Center Operations
  IT User Training and Support
Cyber Security: Technology and Data Security, Integrity, and Protection
Risk Assessment and Risk Mitigation Services

Cyber Threat Assessment
Vulnerability Assessment
Disaster Recovery Planning
Enterprise Records Keeping
Essential Enterprise Data (EED)
Cyber Security Design, Testing, and Implementation

M & A and IT
Software Verification
Software Deployment
Enterprise Effectiveness
Integration Risk Assessment
IT Organizational Rationalization
IT Spending and Investment Analysis
Restrictions & Usage
Cyber-security
Network Design & Integrity
Data Bases
Degree of Functional Integration
Level of Process Automation & Integration
Internal Controls
Budgets & Costs
Outsourcing Arrangements

Due Diligence for IT
Auditing License Compliance, Versions, and Usage
Auditing License Fees
Application Installations and Deployment
Data Residency and Deployment
Redundancy and Outdated Systems
Infra-Structure Composition and Longevity
Auditing of Service Contractors and Consultants
Project Management Effectiveness
Application Development Processes and Effectiveness
Risk Assessment for IT and Digital Enterprise

IT Organizational Performance and Effectiveness
Configuration Planning and Management
Contribution to Business Effectiveness
Contribution to Strategic Goals and Position
IT Effectiveness, Cost Performance, Benefit, and Value
Customer/User Support Effectiveness and Responsiveness Comparative Performance Metrics

Specialized Services for Various Enterprise Software Solutions, Technologies, and Products

Oracle
SAP
Salesforce
E-commerce
Website Services
Search Engines Facilities (SEF)

Exhibit 4.11 Emerging Technologies and Their Potentially Disruptive Impact on Industry and Consulting Services

Industry	Possible Impact: 30% to 40% Displacement/Reduction in Employment from 2016 Levels
Automotive:	Job displacement due to more manufacturing and factory automation.
Banking:	Job displacement (continued) due to expanded use of automation and availability of alternative funding sources for mortgages, lending, and investing.
Transportation:	Job displacement due to driverless cars and automated trains and subways.
Fast Food:	Job displacement due to increased wage costs and the use of automated ordering systems.
Casual Dining:	Job displacement due to increased wage costs and use of kiosks and tablets.
Travel:	Job displacement (continued) due to automated booking services.
Entertainment:	Job displacement due to increased on-demand capabilities and content.
Healthcare:	Job displacement due to increased use of virtual medicine, remote diagnostic services (telehealthcare), walk-in and self-diagnostics, and automated care for certain symptoms, injuries, and diseases.
Pharmacy:	Job displacement due to automated dispensing and delivery of medications with interactive drug checking.
Education:	Job displacement due to the continued and expanded use of on-line education, virtual reality, experiential learning experiences, and just in time instruction.
Delivery and Moving:	Job displacement due to robotics, automated packing, and automated delivery services.

Industry	Possible Impact: 30% to 40% Displacement/Reduction in Employment from 2016 Levels
Warehousing:	Job displacement due to automated lines, picking and packing, and direct shipping models.
Harbor Freight:	Job displacement due to embedded RF technologies linked to robotics for the loading and unloading of freight containers.
Public Utilities:	Job displacement due to expanded use of automated consumption tracking, bill payment, and service initiation and termination technologies.
Public Service:	Job displacement due to automation demands by the public for faster, more reliable, and responsive services.

5.0 Future of IT Management Consulting

5.1 Future IT Consulting Services

There is little debate that IT consulting services will continue to evolve in response to advances in technology and ever-changing client needs. However, for any consultancy, there are five significant issues that must be addressed: (1) What services will the IT consulting firm of the future offer (2) What service model will be most effective in delivering those services, (3) What services are clients demanding today, (4) What services will clients need in the future?, and (5) How will consultants justify fees and prove the value of delivering those services?

The seminal services related to enterprise solutions, digital enterprise models, process automation, and organizational integration will most likely remain core service offerings of the IT management consulting firm. However, the successful firms of the future will be building additional capabilities designed around three primary strategic themes: (1) advancing the competitiveness of their clients, (2) responding to societal requirements, and (3) exploiting emerging and potentially disrupting technologies. To realize those three themes, it will be essential for IT management consulting firms to develop, acquire, or enhance their service capabilities in five straetgic areas:

- **Organizational Compression Integration.** IT is compressing and integrating business models and processes. Consequently, the deployment of technology has a displacement effect on employees and staffing. Industries such as travel, banking, and food and beverage have seen the effects of displacement from technology. Kiosks, automated teller machines, tablets, and mobile apps are replacing activities that have been traditionally labor intensive or of lower intellectual content. AI-based applications will facilitate decision-making, selection, and service levels, thus linking data with real-time performance and service delivery. The IT management consulting firm that can elevate its service offerings in organizational integration and assisting clients to better navigate the displacement effect will have distinct advantages over those that do not.

- **Digital Enterprise Business Model and Transformation.** Digital enterprise models have been used in various forms for well over a decade. However, the degree to which the organization is "digital" and the level of digital integration vary considerably. Digital enterprise business forms offer inherently great mobility, agility, and abilities to react to changes in the organization's landscape and internal capabilities. Designing and effectively helping organizations navigate to a digital enterprise model requires the IT consultant to provide services that go far beyond technology. These services will expand into technology-enabled living (TEL) where the enterprise behaves and reacts more uniformly and quickly to external stimuli and competitive threats. Inherent to the digital enterprise is the Internet of Things (IoT) and the progressive connectivity of devices, applications, data, and networks. Ultimately, the digital enterprise will evolve into a "neural network" of processes, AI-based rules, and human interactions designed to anticipate, react, and integrate at unprecedented speed. The IT consulting firm that can strategically position its clients for TEL will render valuable services as compared to those that do not have comparable services.

- **Virtual Reality (VR).** VR will play an increasing role in the digital enterprise and in the organization's ability to compete, train, anticipate customer needs, and perform operations at the highest levels. IT management consultants who help clients introduce and deploy VR to simulate actual events, experience the customer before engaging the customer, simulate business operations before actually implementing new processes, transfer knowledge, and reduce errors through training will be in a superior position to capture and retain clients to those consulting firms that do not have VR services and capabilities. The creation of advanced VR capabilities will also change the way IT consultants address and develop interventions and solutions for their clients. Firms utilizing VR will be able to simulate their recommendations and client reactions *before* presenting them to the client. This will be a fundamental shift in the service delivery model of IT consultants and those firms that have such capabilities and internal resources will have a distinct competitive advantage over those firms that do not.

- **Self-Learning Systems (SLS).** SLS differs from AI-based applications in that SLS are those systems that have the ability to learn as they process. SLS-based applications have the ability to learn, anticipate, perform, and correct themselves as they process data, stimuli, or input. The deployment of SLS will not only position the client for greater competitiveness through organizational compression, but will fundamentally change the way IT consultants interact and deliver services to their clients.

- **Intelligent Data Analytics (IDA).** IDA combines data analytics with the capabilities of SLS. The elite IT management consulting firms will develop, acquire, and enhance their capacity to build intelligent enterprises through the design and implementation of IDA. IT management consulting firms that can incorporate strategic analysis with the power of data analytics and SLS will be able to generate significant demand for their services and capabilities.

Thinking about how technology will change our lives and behaviors has always been fascinating. As a young boy, I was captivated by "Hal, the computer" in Stanley Kubrick's *2001: A Space Odyssey*. Much of what "Hal" did in that movie is being done today.

The fact is that technology changes things and has an impact on jobs, education, and industries. Thinking about the 'State of Technology' and the future impact of technology on employment and industries creates a financial and employment picture that is well worth the attention of policymakers and educators. **Exhibit 4.11** summarizes some of the industries and jobs that may be most affected by technology.

Technology has both an accretive and displacement effect on employment. Clearly, technology enhances productivity and leverages processes, but in the quest for doing more faster and with less cost, human beings are displaced from jobs. The positions, jobs, trades and professions depicted in Exhibit 4.11 are all considered to be vulnerable to major disruption and displacement by technology. In general, we can expect displacements and reductions in employment levels in these positions and jobs ranging between thirty percent (30%) to forty percent (40%) over the next ten years.

However, the potential for displacement is not restricted to industry. The consulting profession is not immune from the disruptive influences of technology. Indeed, technology has and will continue to change how consultants deliver services and how clients perceive the need for services. The consulting professional will continue to grow, but in different ways and with different talents and competencies. Thus, we can expect continued consolidation in consulting and volatility in employment levels.

5.2 Future of IT Service Delivery Models

Advancements in technology has driven the growth of IT consulting services and the services that consultants perform and deliver. When a significant technological breakthrough occurs or a disruptive technology enters the market, consultants quickly respond with services. When regulatory changes impact operations and systems, consultants configure services to help clients respond and continue their processes and businesses. This pattern of technology driven change and response will undoubtedly continue. Given the nature of change and technology's impact on consultants and consulting firms, the profession is confronted with the challenge of creating and successfully operating what I call "firm of the future" (FoF). As we consider the future of IT consulting and IT consulting firms, four primary business and service delivery models begin to emerge:

- **The Virtual Service Provider (VSP).** Advances in technology, automated software, Self-learning Systems, highly integrated networks, and access to data will enable a virtual service delivery model for consulting. This model, which is used today, will continue to evolve to expand in its offerings and efficacy. Consultants must be able to provide these services remotely, while supporting the efforts and needs of their clients. For example, in medicine, the VSP will link specialists in major hospitals with general practitioners in rural areas using virtual reality and data analytics to render more responsive health care services. Other examples might include driverless technologies and on demand job training.
- **Integrated Service Provider (ISP).** These are and will remain top firms in the Strategic IT Service Provider category of firms. The ISP firm will continue to be the focal point of critical mass for services, capabilities, and talent for the IT management consulting professional. This form of organization will dominate the IT consulting landscape with a comprehensive suite of service offerings and sufficient funds to invest in R&D. Look for these firms to enhance their relationships with the specialty firms, such as Oracle and SAP, in the areas of concurrent design and development, process integration, and digital enterprise initiatives.
- **Facilitated Network Provider (FNP).** Clayton Christensen predicts a disaggregation of the management consulting industry and with it, the emergence of the FNP.[45] The FNP model is neither new nor unique to consulting. The FNP works similar to the building and construction industry where a general contractor will have overall control and coordination for a project, but will utilize highly specialized skill sets and competencies. Although in theory this form of organization has some implicitly appealing attributes, concerns related to quality assurance, legal liability, collaboration, intellectual property rights, and resource management can exponentially add to the complexity and perhaps even

to costs of the project. This organizational design and service delivery model will have only a limited role in IT service delivery.
- **Specialty Service Provider (SSP).** Specialty firms for cyber-security, e-commerce, enterprise solutions, knowledge management, and large solutions providers will continue to provide mission-specific technology solutions. Mega-firms, such as Oracle and SAP, will continue to dominate this space along with VMware. The mega-firms will force further consolidation in the specialty firms as they acquire smaller firms for incremental market share and customers and move to acquire technologies and ideas.

6.0 Conclusion

At the onset of this chapter I began with writing, "nothing could possibly be as exciting as a computer." I'm sure that many chuckled at the thought . . . I certainly did and still do. But as this is the completion of the chapter, I stand more confident in that statement. Computers are and will continue to become omnipresent in our lives, business, governments, and health. Time, space, distance, culture, language, and social class are all made smaller, and sometimes eliminated, by technology. In the age of technology-enabled living our challenge is not how to build the technology. We know how to do that and we will continue to do it. No, I think the challenge is something different.

The role and responsibilities of the IT management consultant will evolve with the technology and must address an important challenge:

> *How do we continue to invent, deploy, and optimize technology for the better of the organization, but also for the better of the environment and those species living on the planet?*

What a wonderful challenge and what an exciting time it is to be an IT management consultant.

Notes

1 See https://en.wikipedia.org/wiki/Colossus_computer.
2 See https://en.wikipedia.org/wiki/ENIAC.
3 See https://en.wikipedia.org/wiki/Thomas_J._Watson.
4 See http://ifaq.wap.org/computers/famousquotes.html.
5 Various. For a nice summary, see http://www.theatlantic.com/technology/archive/2011/06/ibms-first-100-years-a-heavily-illustrated-timeline/240502/.
6 See https://en.wikipedia.org/wiki/UNIVAC.
7 See https://en.wikipedia.org/wiki/Gene_Amdahl.
8 See https://en.wikipedia.org/wiki/IBM_System/360.
9 See https://en.wikipedia.org/wiki/Gordon_Moore.
10 See http://www.cs.utexas.edu/~fussell/courses/cs352h/papers/moore.pdf.

11 See https://en.wikipedia.org/wiki/W._Edwards_Deming.
12 See Orlicky, Joseph. *Materials Requirements Planning: The New Way of Life in Production and Inventory Management.* New York: McGraw-Hill, 1975. ISBN-13: 978-0071755634.
13 See https://en.wikipedia.org/wiki/Material_requirements_planning.
14 See https://www.justice.gov/atr/case-document/united-states-memorandum-1969-case.
15 See https://en.wikipedia.org/wiki/Material_requirements_planning.
16 See https://en.wikipedia.org/wiki/Arthur_Andersen.
17 See https://en.wikipedia.org/wiki/PricewaterhouseCoopers.
18 See https://en.wikipedia.org/wiki/KPMG.
19 See https://en.wikipedia.org/wiki/Systems_development_life_cycle.
20 See James Martin (1933–2013) for a discussion of early leaders in data modeling, systems analysis, and application development at: https://en.wikipedia.org/wiki/James_Martin_(author).
21 See Applegate, Lynda M. and Collins, Elizabeth. "IBM's Decade of Transformation: Turnaround to Growth." Harvard Business School Press. April 2005, revised, July 8, 2009. (Product # 805130).
22 See Steve Jobs (1954–2010) https://en.wikipedia.org/wiki/Steve_Jobs *and*, Steve Wozniak https://en.wikipedia.org/wiki/Steve_Wozniak.
23 See https://en.wikipedia.org/wiki/Bill_Gates.
24 See https://en.wikipedia.org/wiki/Larry_Ellison.
25 See https://www.youtube.com/watch?v=axSnW-ygU5g.
26 KPMG acquired Nolan Norton in 1987.
27 HBS Case.
28 http://cds.frost.com.libproxy1.usc.edu/p/67359/#!/ppt/c?id=K0B8-01-00-00-00&hq=call%20centers.
29 See http://www.informationweek.com/strategic-cio/digital-business/gartner-it-spending-will-top-$35-trillion-in-2016/d/d-id/1323962.
30 See https://www.idc.com/getdoc.jsp?containerId=prUS41006516.
31 See https://www.forrester.com/report/2016+US+Tech+Budgets+The+Outlook+For+Tech+Spending+Overall+And+By+Industry/-/E-RES121248.
32 See http://www.gartner.com/newsroom/id/3135718.
33 Source: Author.
34 See http://www.gao.gov/assets/680/677436.pdf.
35 Author calculation based on various sources.
36 See AICP Code of Professional Conduct, https://www.aicpa.org/interestareas/forensicandvaluation/resources/standards/downloadabledocuments/sscs.pdf.
37 On a comparative basis with firms such as Accenture, Deloitte and PwC.
38 https://newsroom.accenture.com/fact-sheet/
39 Independent contractors are routinely referred to as "1099" non-employees.
40 Complied by author. See also http://fortune.com/2015/06/13/fortune-500-tech/ *and* https://en.wikipedia.org/wiki/List_of_the_largest_information_technology_companies.
41 Complied by author. See also https://en.wikipedia.org/wiki/List_of_the_largest_software_companies.
42 Complied by author. See also https://en.wikipedia.org/wiki/List_of_largest_Internet_companies.

43 Complied by author. See also https://en.wikipedia.org/wiki/List_of_IT_consulting_firms.
44 Rivera, Lauren A. *Pedigree: How Elite Students Get Elite Jobs*. Princeton, NJ: Princeton University Press, 2016. ISBN: 9780691155623.
45 See Christensen, Clayton M.; Wang, Dina; van Bever, Derek. "Consulting on the Cusp of Disruption." Harvard Business School Press. October 2013. https://hbr.org/2013/10/consulting-on-the-cusp-of-disruption.

5 Strategy and Organization Consulting

David A. Nadler and Adrian J. Slywotzky

Since its earliest days, management consulting has rested squarely on the twin pillars of strategy and organization. In the beginning, the two concepts were practically indivisible; the same practitioners consulted in both areas. Those were simpler times. Over the past four decades, the increasing complexity of business organizations has given rise to two very different—and very separate—consulting disciplines, each rooted in very different methodologies, knowledge bases, and delivery models, and each achieving a remarkable level of sophistication. But nothing stays the same.

For a host of reasons—the increasingly global nature of business, massively accelerated product life cycles, the growing frequency of major discontinuities in the marketplace—we are witnessing a fundamental shift in the way many clients require consulting services about strategy and organization. Despite its intellectual elegance, the consulting model we've all come to accept—a highly compartmentalized process of strategy development followed by organization design followed by implementation—is quickly losing its relevance and value.

Companies no longer have the luxury of dealing with issues of strategy and organization either separately or sequentially. They need to understand that strategy and organization consulting work happens in parallel and have a reciprocal influence on each other; they must deal with the fact that strategic change begins the moment one starts discussing a new strategy or organization structure, and it has to happen faster than ever before.

Our goal in this chapter is to describe how we got where we are today, where we believe we're headed, and what this implies for the profession of management consulting. We will trace through history how current concepts about strategy and organization have evolved. Many of the older concepts are still useful when supplemented with current thinking. On the other hand, too many consultants are still using outdated concepts that they learned years ago. Most important, the client context under which these concepts are used is dramatically different today.

Before 1960: The Primacy of Intuition and Judgment

Management consulting has always mirrored and been shaped by the way managers think about their jobs and their organizations. The real roots of modern consulting were planted in a much simpler time, when the prevailing model of industrial companies basically involved figuring out how to systematize a process for churning out the highest possible volume of products at the lowest possible cost.

The early consulting pioneers (for example, Marvin Bower, 1966, and Peter Drucker, 1946) generally thought of strategy and organization as almost indistinguishable. From the 1930s through the early 1960s, their consulting model consisted of experienced practitioners incrementally adding to the intuition and judgment of senior managers. Consultants would begin by helping clients think about their business, both in terms of planning the strategy and organizing the work. Then consultants would turn their focus to execution, advising on staffing, and methods of controlling and directing the work, all with the goal of improved performance.

As one looks at this early model of consulting through a modern lens (see Exhibit 5.1), three deficiencies are worth pointing out. First, it's startling to note the absence of focus on the influence of the external environment. In contemporary terms, it was a "closed system." The emphasis was on the internal workings of each organization, rather than on its interaction with the larger business environment. In part, that reflected the comparatively stable times in which this model was used.

That leads to the second issue: This was not a model built for speed. Compared with today, product life cycles in the first half of the 20th century were nearly generational. You could easily get by producing essentially the same products in basically the same ways, with only occasional incremental improvements, for ten or fifteen years.

The final issue speaks to the nature of the value consultants brought to their assignments. The best that consultants had to offer was their experience, insight, and analytical abilities. Generally speaking, consultants on strategy and organization brought little in the way of formalized concepts, conceptual models, transferable tools, or a body of knowledge that we would describe today as intellectual capital. Instead, it was a model that relied on the wisdom and judgment of each individual consultant, backed up by the analysis of more junior associates.

1960–2000: Sequential Consulting, Divergent Disciplines

The modern era of strategy and organization consulting really began in the 1960s and 70s, when the extended post-war era finally came to an end. During

Exhibit 5.1 Early Consulting Model

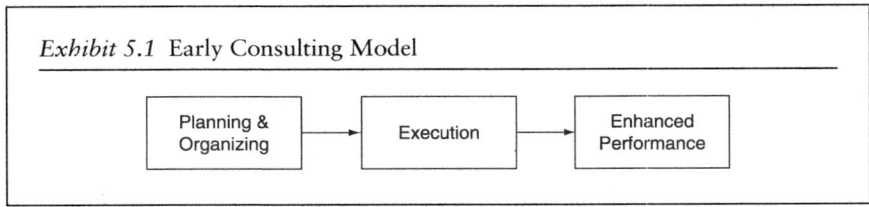

that turbulent era, U.S. companies confronted a new set of challenges: foreign competition, domestic deregulation, market fragmentation, and the inevitable exhaustion of pent-up consumer demand that had for so long made it so easy to sell so much to so many.

As time went on, good managers realized they needed new and sophisticated strategies involving technology, distribution, and marketing—a whole host of specialized approaches that hadn't been necessary in the past. So the search was on for consultants who could help managers attack each specific issue with a scientific, disciplined, and specialized approach. This was a dramatic departure from the days of the intuitive wise men who would consult on everything. Managers wanted strategy consultants to help them with strategy. At the next stage, there was a widely accepted assumption that "strategy dictated structure," so for the next phase of work, they turned to the organization design consultants. And when they were finished, it was time for the change management consultants. The result: a steadfastly sequential, highly compartmentalized approach to consulting (see Exhibit 5.2). The same process might be repeated every five years or so, as senior managers came and went, and the environment experienced periodic change.

This model of executive behavior—and of management consulting—became and still remains pervasive today. To a great extent, it was fueled not just by the needs of companies but by an explosion of research and writing within each discipline at major business schools. As a result, the major consulting firms capitalized on this trend toward specialization and built separate practice areas in each discipline. The result was a historic shift from the early model of general, intuitive management consulting into three distinct, scientifically rigorous consulting disciplines, each with its own tools, methodologies, models, and vocabularies.

Broadly speaking—and we'll describe this evolution shortly in more detail—the general management consultants migrated toward strategy. Thanks in large part to the work of such thought leaders as Bruce Henderson, founder of the Boston Consulting Group (BCG), and Igor Ansoff at Carnegie, the 1960s brought a series of conceptual breakthroughs, an unprecedented degree of intellectual rigor, and a whole new set of methodologies. During this same period, a burst of creative activity at the nation's top business schools laid the groundwork for an emerging

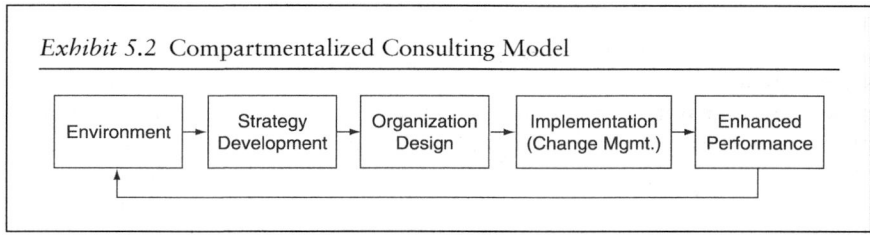

Exhibit 5.2 Compartmentalized Consulting Model

discipline in organizational consulting that focused on integrating the formal structures and processes of the organization with the human side of the enterprise.

As the consulting disciplines diverged along very different paths, it became increasingly difficult for the strategy and organization types to integrate their work. They came from different academic roots and viewed the organization from very different vantage points. Modern strategy consulting emerged from economics, while organization consulting found its roots in psychology—two inherently uncongenial disciplines. Moreover, strategists viewed their work as a "top-down" proposition centering on senior leaders who put their stamp on the strategy and announced it to the organization. Conversely, organization work, with its initial focus on individual and small group behavior, started with group dynamics and then looked upward at the organization. It was virtually impossible to connect strategy and organization consulting until both began seeing potential in joint activity at the top of the enterprise—something that didn't happen until the 1990s.

Those are the broad outlines of the consulting model that has prevailed for the past two decades. In order to understand the threats to this model's continued viability, it's important to step back and fully understand the specific ways in which strategy, organization, and change management consulting developed.

From Business Policy to Value Creation Models

Up until the 1960s, only a few companies—most notably, the General Motors of Alfred P. Sloan—practiced what would today be called "strategy." Even when practiced, the word itself was rarely used; executives spoke instead of "business policy" or "planning," and most firms made strategic decisions on an *ad hoc* basis, guided more by instinct and tradition than by empirically driven, methodology-based analysis.

In the 1960s, Bruce Henderson (Boston Consulting Group, 1968) produced the first major breakthrough in the field of business strategy. Trained as an engineer, Henderson became intrigued by the question of why the unit cost of products varied so greatly among suppliers, even those using seemingly identical equipment and processes. His work uncovered what is now a familiar notion: the concept of the "price experience curve." Later, quantitative research and modeling under the rubric of the Profit Impact of Market Strategy, or PIMS, showed that Henderson's E-Curve was virtually a universal phenomenon and that higher market share meant higher profits.

Henderson's work also led to a method of strategic resource allocation called the Growth Share Matrix. In the 1970s, state-of-the-art strategic thinking was based on the economic logic of "get as big as you can as fast as you can." Increased market share would let you build bigger factories, reduce your costs, improve your products, and open up an ever-widening advantage over your competition. During the 1980s, GE's success with its formula of participating only in businesses where it was number one or number two in market share illustrated the logic of this low-cost-producer class of strategies.

The Porter Breakthroughs

The next major breakthrough was Michael Porter's work at the Harvard Business School. In his book *Competitive Strategy* (1980), Porter broadened the focus from market share by describing the so-called Five Forces that determined any company's strategic effectiveness (supplier power, barriers to entry, threat of substitutes, buyer power, and degree of rivalry). For Porter, strategic thinking demanded awareness of the threats and opportunities posed by each of the Five Forces, and a winning strategy had to take all of them into account.

In his book *Competitive Advantage* (1986), Porter popularized another key concept (one that was already being used within a number of strategy firms) with his description of the *value chain*. Porter showed that any business can be modeled as a chain of value-creating activities, beginning with inbound logistics and including operations, outbound logistics, marketing and sales, and service. By analyzing how this generic value chain operates in a specific business, managers can discover a range of strategic options involving how to optimize the process flows, determine which steps to outsource or eliminate, and streamline linkages among the remaining steps.

As a result of Porter's work, there were now three different competitive strategic alternatives for managers to consider. First, the Hendersonian low-cost, market-share strategy still was relevant. Second, Porter added the differentiation strategy (maximizing the relevant differences between a firm and its immediate competitors); and third, the niche strategy (identifying a defensible niche market relatively immune to external cost and competitive pressures). This three-alternative system may be considered the classic formulation of strategy. And for a while it worked.

The Classic Models Falter

But changes in the business environment gradually forced practitioners and theorists to reconsider the simplicity of the Henderson-Porter models. During the late 1980s and early 1990s, market value was increasingly seen as a crucial determinant of company success. As the decade progressed, market value and sales volume were seen to diverge more and more. The implication was that the rules of business were changing—that such widely accepted corollaries as "Get market share and the profit will follow" were no longer as reliable as they had been.

At the heart of this new strategic problem was the emergence of so-called "no-profit zones": businesses in which companies were apparently *unable* to earn a profit, no matter the size of the market share they controlled. The concept of no-profit zones emerged in the early 1990s because of a variety of changes in the business environment. These included:

- Global over-capacity in many product categories;
- An increase in customer power, thanks to broader global competition among suppliers and increased availability of information about alternatives;
- Improved capabilities for imitating any product or service offering, including an expansion of global manufacturing capacities and reduced transportation costs;
- Venture capital funding of new competitors unburdened by old business models and assets.

Due to these and other pressures, more and more businesses, from airlines and D-RAMS to consumer banking and electronics, were unfortunately transformed into no-profit zones.

Business Design Innovation

As a result, the 1990s caused management practitioners and thinkers to consider a new range of strategic issues. A company's products, technology, quality, and efficiency all remained important, but even more important was its business model. In response, a new strategic discipline known as *business design innovation* emerged.

In our view, a company's business design includes five strategic elements:

- Customer selection—Who are my customers, and why do I choose to serve them rather than any others?
- Unique value proposition—Why do my customers buy from me?
- Value capture—How do I retain, as profit, a portion of the value I deliver to customers?

- Strategic control—How do I protect my profits from competitor imitation and customer power?
- Scope—What activities in the value chain must I engage in to remain customer-relevant, to generate high profits, and to create strategic control?

During the 1990s, business design innovation increasingly became the key to strategic effectiveness. Businesses with traditional designs became less relevant and lost value, while companies that developed new business designs better suited to changing conditions captured growing shares of profit. This phenomenon, whereby value shifted from firms like Sears, American Airlines, Compaq, U.S. Steel, and IBM to firms like Wal-Mart, Southwest Airlines, Dell, Nucor, and Microsoft, became known as value migration (Slywotzky and Morrison 1998; Slywotzky 1996).

Value-Driven Business Design—The Current Framework

Strategy consultants have developed a variety of models to assist clients' pursuit of value, which is the theme of much strategy consulting today. As an illustration, we'll briefly describe our own consulting approach, which we call Value-Driven Business Design (see Exhibit 5.3).

Value-Driven Business Design is about strategic choices. It involves understanding the opportunities to create value in the marketplace and then making the choices that enable a business to address the customer's most important priorities and capture a return for shareholders. The choices must be aligned with where customers and competitors are going

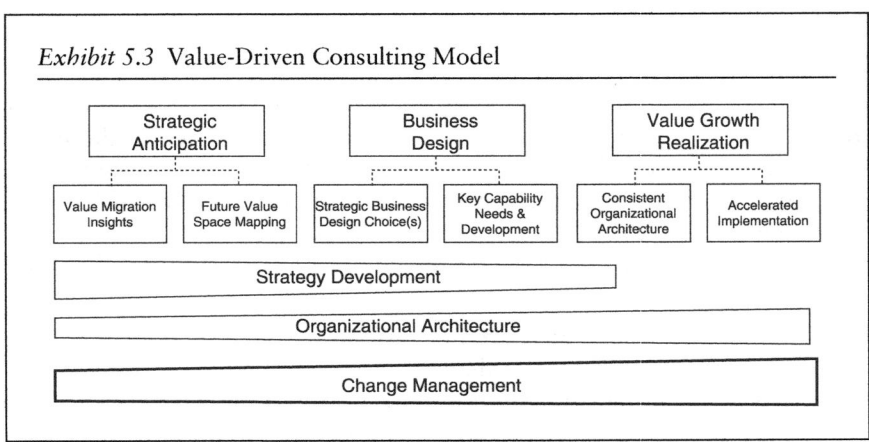

Exhibit 5.3 Value-Driven Consulting Model

to be in the future. And the choices must be internally consistent and mutually reinforcing. Typically, the Value-Driven Business Design process consists of six phases.

1. Value migration insights. Most companies that create significant growth in shareholder value do so by acting on insights that change the rules of competitive advantage in their industry. So the first step in the process is to help clients break through the barrier of incremental thinking by engaging in exercises that help them redefine their competition, anticipate where future value will emerge, and consider which business designs might best exploit that value opportunity.

2. Future value space mapping. The next step is to use sophisticated interview and analysis methodologies to determine how customers and competitors are likely to react to a client's innovative value growth initiatives, which, in turn, makes it possible to determine where potential revenue and profit opportunities might exist in the future.

3. Strategic business design choices. The next step is to define one or more business designs that will create high utility for customers and high value for shareholders. It is often possible to identify multiple opportunities and business design options; and from those, they need to select the best.

4. Key capability needs and development. New business design choices often create the most value when they are driven by an understanding of a future value space, rather than by an organization's current competencies. So the next phase is to identify and start filling the gaps between the organization's existing capabilities and those required by the new business design.

5. Consistent organizational systems. By an overwhelming margin, senior managers believe that internal barriers are the primary cause of strategy failures. To pave the way for successful strategy implementation, it is essential to develop a plan to redesign those aspects of the organization that are inconsistent with the new direction.

6. Accelerated implementation. To create high value growth, new business designs must be implemented rapidly. A year's delay in launching a new business design can easily have a serious negative impact on value. In the current environment of hyper-competition and technological change, accelerated implementation of the business design is crucial.

Looking Ahead

One final thought regarding strategy consulting. In the model we just described, you will see a forewarning of our previously stated premise that strategy, organization, and change management consulting are now converging, both for dynamic competitive reasons and in part because they were neither as distinct nor as sequential as we have portrayed them in the past.

126 Nadler and Slywotzky

The last three of the six steps in the Value-Driven Business Design model, involving organizational capabilities, organizational "systems," and the process of implementation, mark a clear move from pure "strategy" work into both organizational consulting and change management. Now, as we move into our discussion of these other fields of consulting, we'll see that the boundaries delineating all three have become increasingly porous in today's business environment.

Organization Consulting: From the Individual to the Enterprise

In contrast with strategy consulting, organization consulting's historical roots were primarily academic. With foundations in behavioral science—the confluence of psychology, social psychology, and sociology—organization consulting was largely divorced from the work of the large management consulting firms, which were firmly rooted in the disciplines of engineering and economics. More specifically, organization consulting can trace its intellectual roots to four sources.

The first source stems from the famous Hawthorne studies (Roethlisberger and Dickson 1939; Homans 1941). Their work, for the first time, applied rigorous methodologies to the study of human behavior in organizations and formed the basis of the hugely influential organizational behavior group at the Harvard Business School. Ultimately, this work proved to be the source of entirely new perspectives about systems in organizations.

The second source involved work in the new area of small group dynamics. Beginning with the work of Kurt Lewin at the Massachusetts Institute of Technology, then later at the University of Michigan and the National Training Laboratories (NTL), this area of study led to the development of the concept of organization development. Building on the pioneering work of Chris Argyris (1962), Ed Schein (1973), Douglas MacGregor (1960), and Warren Bennis (1966), among other notable figures, this work focused on issues of leadership, culture, and team behavior and grew aggressively during the 1960s and 1970s.

The third important source was "organization design." Rooted in the work of Lawrence and Lorsch (1967), it formed the basis of work in the 1970s and 1980s by Jay Galbraith (1973), David Nadler, and Michael Tushman (1987, 1998). Organization design involved a systematic and behavioral-based approach to designing an organization's formal structures, systems, and processes.

The final ingredient was open systems theory, drawing off biological theory and finding its industrial roots in the Hawthorne work of Henderson and his colleagues. By the 1960s, researchers at Harvard and Michigan were beginning to explore the similarities between naturally occurring systems and human organizations. However, it wasn't until the mid-1970s that systems theory found wide acceptance among students of organizations. Its first published appearance was Harold Leavitt's *Star Diagram* (1964), and further refined by Jay Galbraith at MIT. At Columbia, Nadler and Tushman (1979, 1980), building on the work of earlier theorists (Katz and Kahn 1966; Lorsch and Sheldon 1972; Seiler 1967), were developing their own model based on systems theory. This outpouring of work in the early and mid-1970s marked a major milestone in the development of organization design, focusing on the integration of technical systems with social dynamics—the organization's "hardware" and "software."

By the early 1990s, there was a convergence of thought around the notion of "fit models," which integrated the various emerging views of organization design:

Open systems. In sharp contrast with early models, the new models emphasized the organization as an interactive entity, influencing and influenced by environmental factors;

Organizational dynamics. Traditional models were static, involving a snap-shot in time of formal structures and systems. They failed to reflect the reality that organizations change over time or to demonstrate the ways in which those changes are triggered or the impact they have;

Integration of hardware and software. An emerging view that neither formal structures nor social interactions exist in a vacuum;

Organizational diagnosis. Reflecting increasing scientific rigor, the models underscored the need to collect and analyze valid data as a precursor to diagnosing organizational problems;

Concepts of change management. These models also embraced the emerging approaches to managing large-scale change, touching upon the implementation phase that had long been considered beyond the purview of traditional organization design.

As we said, a variety of useful models was developed and came into wide use in the 1980s and 1990s. As an illustration, we'll describe the Congruence Model of Organizational Behavior (Nadler & Tushman 1980, 1998), which we and others continue to use as a core organizational consulting tool (see Exhibit 5.4).

The Congruence Model describes the organization as a system that draws input from both internal and external sources, employs a strategy to translate its vision into a set of decisions about where and how to compete, and provides a transformation process that combines the technical and social components of the organization to convert input into output. The model's power lies in its ability to help clients understand the components of their organization and the relationship of one component to another.

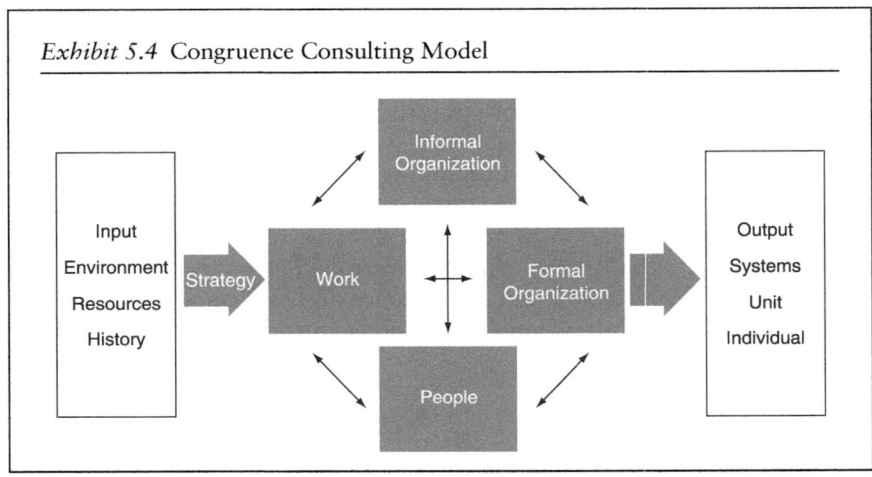

Exhibit 5.4 Congruence Consulting Model

From Input to Output

The three sources of input for the organizational system each affect the organization in different ways.

1. **Environment:** Every organization exists within—and is influenced by—a larger environment involving conditions (political, economic, technological, etc.) and constituencies (customers, investors, lenders, regulators, etc.). The environment creates demands and opportunities while imposing constraints on the organization's ability to meet both.
2. **Resources:** The full range of accessible assets—employees, technology, capital, and information.
3. **History:** Landmark events in an organization's past strongly influence its current behavior in terms of strategic decisions, culture, values, and responses to crises.

Like other contemporary models, the congruence model acknowledges the importance of strategy. Every organization must select the optimal alternatives for creating and sustaining value by deciding which business to be in and how to configure their resources in response to opportunities, threats, and constraints in the external environment. The goal is to produce the optimal "output." In this context, the term output describes not only the organization's ability to create products and services but also to achieve certain levels of individual and group performance.

The Organizational Transformation Process

The heart of the model is the transformation process, which draws upon the input implicit in the environment, resources, and history to produce a set of outputs. This process is shaped by four key components that make up each organization:

1. **The work:** The inherent activity engaged in by the organization and its people. Any analysis from a design perspective must focus first on the nature of the tasks to be performed and the inherent requirements of those tasks in the context of strategy.
2. **The people:** What knowledge and skills do they bring to their work? What are their preferences, perceptions, and expectations about their relationship with the organization?
3. **The formal organizational arrangements:** The pattern of structures, systems, and processes that define and coordinate how roles are defined and work gets done.
4. **The informal organization:** The unwritten processes, practices, and political relationships that embody the organization's values, beliefs, and behavioral norms.

The Concept of "Fit" and Resulting Output

So far, we've been describing the components of an organizational system. But the model is more than a list or a chart; its real value is that it helps us understand how the components interact to produce a result. The underlying hypothesis is that tighter alignment leads to greater congruence and better performance. Indeed, the congruence model suggests that the interaction between each set of organizational components is more important than the components themselves.

For years, the field of organization design attempted to align all of these elements by using formal organization structure as the linking mechanism. As a result, we saw the growth of different structural forms—functional, product, geographic, and matrix—each intended to link the major elements under different conditions faced by a company in its markets and with its given technology and business strategy.

In normal times, the job of managers was that of constantly fine-tuning the formal structure and systems to maintain alignment of the key elements. However, when the environment shifted substantially, organizations were required to undergo radical change. During these periods, simply maintaining the alignment of the organizational components through the formal structure is not only insufficient, but likely dangerous. These situations call for discontinuous change, which sometimes involves the profound overhaul of most, if not all, of the organizational components (Nadler 1998; Nadler, Shaw, and Walton 1994).

For example, the Internet and the alternative of outsourcing has caused major disturbances in how organizations should be designed and managed. We now see the birth of "virtual" organizations where major functions, such as information technology and manufacturing, are being outsourced (see Exhibit 5.5). This change has required management to manage in a more "horizontal" way through alliances and partnerships, often connected together through the Internet and software systems—and personal relationships. In these situations, decisions have to be negotiated with partners, not simply announced to subordinates, as in prior models.

Formal structure obviously has serious limitations in a world where change is a constant phenomenon. Organizations must now seek new internal arrangements that are more flexible and resilient, thereby shifting emphasis from structure to the informal culture and the quality of leadership and employees throughout the organization. In the Internet world, many employees are working out of sight from their supervisors, thereby requiring new forms of leadership, motivation, and control. Autonomous work teams are being formed and empowered to react quickly. Spans of control are widening, placing a premium on self-management, the selection of self-starting employees, and the use of online knowledge sharing in place of formal training.

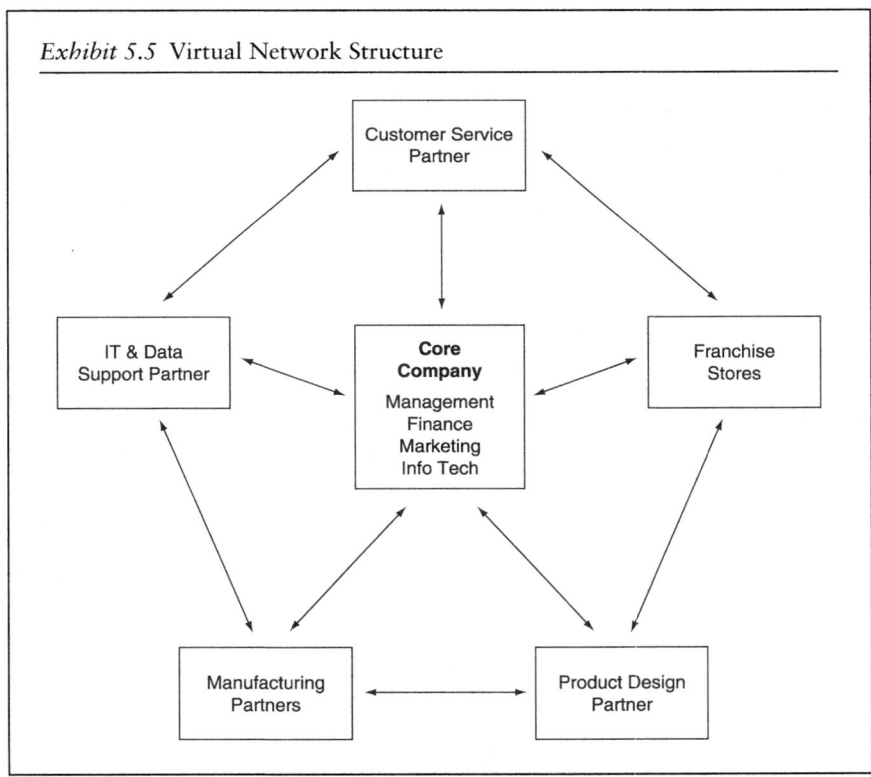

Exhibit 5.5 Virtual Network Structure

Requirements for Organization Consultants

As organization consulting developed to embrace concepts such as the congruence model, the skills and strategies required to successfully consult in this area have evolved as well.

First, while early practitioners tended to be psychologists largely concerned with individual and small group behavior, today's consultants must understand the organization as a complex system, including both technical systems and social dynamics, and one that both influences and is influenced by the strategy. It is no longer sufficient to think about business strategy and human behavior as separate, isolated, and unrelated phenomena.

Second, rigorous diagnosis has become a mandatory prelude to organization consulting. However, in contrast with the initial market research that often sets the stage for strategy consulting, much of the essential information about how an organization functions can only be found within the client organization itself. So consultants need to understand how to use the diagnostic process as a lever for engaging the client and, hopefully, increasing the client's understanding of the issues at hand and its ownership of results incurred under its management.

Third, consultants who think of organizational performance in terms of "fit" understand that the solutions will take a variety of forms involving both the organizational hardware (e.g., structure and systems) and software (e.g., culture and leadership). It is insufficient for a seasoned practitioner to deal exclusively with one side of the organization or the other.

Finally, significant and sustainable organizational change succeeds only if critical groups and individuals feel genuine commitment to, and ownership of, the changes about to take place. For consultants, that places a premium not on passive recommendations, but on engaging interventions that actively involve clients in their own design process.

Change Management Consulting

The origins of change management consulting were closely associated with the development organization consulting. Because organization consulting involved a broad range of changes involving both the technical and social dimensions of the organization, its implementation required special attention to the human dynamics of change. Strategy consulting did not move toward change management issues until much later, since early strategy projects focused mainly on a very small group of very senior leaders.

The discipline of change management had its earliest roots in academic experiments on changing individual behavior, and later, on group behavior.

By the 1960s, academics were also serving as consultants focusing on changing organizational behavior in companies, largely through the medium of training programs, such as the *Managerial Grid* (Blake and Mouton 1964) and sensitivity training. Early on, these efforts became known as "organization development programs," a term that later gave way to "change management" in the late 1980s. The watershed work in this area was Dick Beckhard's book, *Organizational Transitions* (1977), in which he proposed the simple but powerful idea that successful change requires a set of deliberate actions that move an organization from its *Current State* through a turbulent and often perilous *Transition State* in order to reach the desired *Future State*.

Many similar models of change have been developed over the years, which propose a series of phases beginning with the arousal of the need for change, through introducing the required changes via formal and informal means, and finally reinforcing these changes to assure a lasting result. More recently, models of change focused on CEOs and their attempts at strategic change have been offered, which again involve a series of specific phases but with additional attention to surrounding conditions in the organization and environment that facilitate or impede the change sequence (Greiner, Cummings, and Bhambri 2003).

Building on the Beckhard approach of phases, we have developed in our practice a set of concepts about change and intervention that has formed the basis for our consulting over the past two decades (Nadler 1982; Nadler, Shaw, and Walton 1994; Nadler 1998). In our experience, successful change requires leaders to address certain issues:

Power: Major change raises concerns about a significant redistribution of power within the organization, leading to an upsurge in unproductive and often harmful political activity;

Anxiety: The uncertainty and lack of information that often accompany major change fuel anxiety which, in turn, diminishes individual and organizational performance; and

Control: The very prospect of impending change loosens management's control, as widespread uncertainty dulls both the fear of punishment and the hope of reward.

Consequently, any successful change strategy must address those issues by:

- Shaping the political dynamics in ways that generate support;
- Motivating constructive behavior and providing ways for people to participate in planning their future; and
- Managing the transition with the structures, processes, and resources needed to maintain performance during the interim period.

Over time, we have also developed our own list of "best practices" (see Exhibit 5.6) for managing successful transitions.

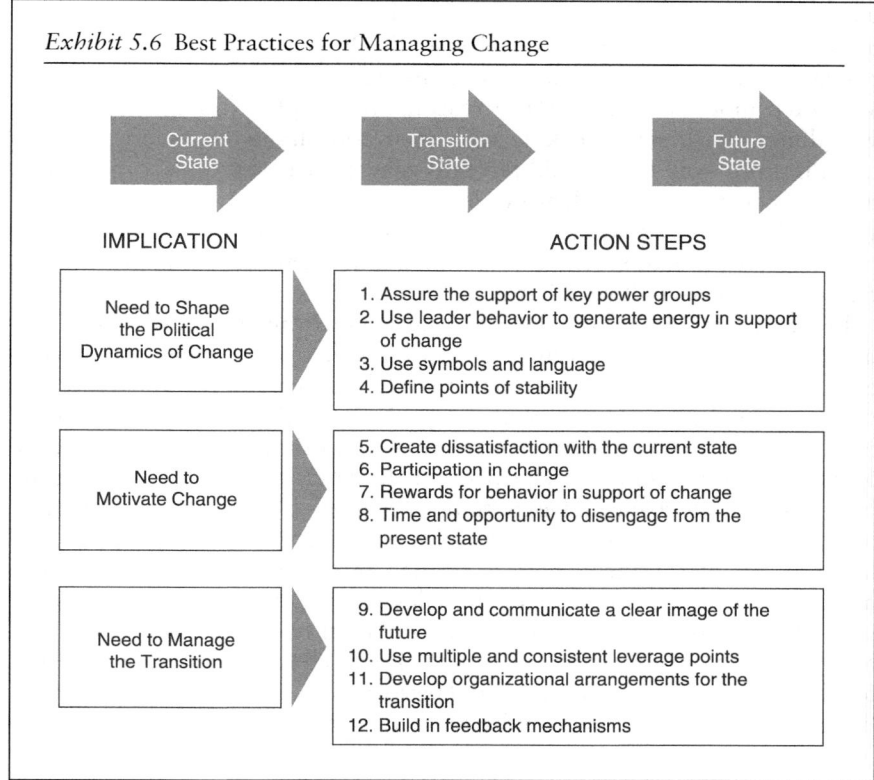

Exhibit 5.6 Best Practices for Managing Change

An Aging Model

The sequential consulting model that reflected the evolution of strategy, organization, and change management as highly compartmentalized disciplines firmly took hold in the 1980s and 1990s. To a large extent, it worked—and in many situations, still does.

But as the 1990s drew to a close, we started to see some cracks in the model. We're not suggesting that the current model is bad; in fact, it's intellectually right, and in a perfect world, would point the way to successful consulting. But it has two major flaws: It is ill suited to the pace and intensity of change in the modern marketplace, and it fails to recognize the inherently messy ways in which consulting plays out in real-life situations.

Adapting to the Changing Marketplace

To be successful, consulting must enable companies to keep pace with the demands of the marketplace—and ideally, to stay one step ahead. The early consulting model that had its roots in the years following World War I worked just fine in an era when product life cycles were measured in decades. Similarly, the current model was ideally suited for a world of five-to-ten-year product life cycles. For example, companies might easily take six to ten months to work out a reasonably complex strategy. Once that was done, they'd start working with their consultants on redesigning the organization—and that would typically take anywhere from six months to a year. Then came the implementation phase, and by the time that kicked in, you might have been at this for close to three years. And that was all right, because you still had seven years remaining of a ten-year cycle in which to reap the benefits of all your hard work.

In a growing number of industries, that same arithmetic doesn't work any more. On average, product life cycles last less than six years; in some cases, especially high technology products, the cycle is closer to one to two years.

The second issue is the nature of change. You could pursue a more leisurely pace in a world of incremental change. Your competitors might figure out how to make a product faster or cheaper, but the fundamental basis of competition really hadn't changed. Discontinuous change—a sharp, dramatic change in the marketplace or the nature of competition—was rare. In the 1950s, you might find a Sears, General Motors, or IBM introducing new technology or a new business model that changed the rules of the game, but it didn't happen often. In the past decade, in contrast, more than two dozen companies created that kind of seismic impact (e.g., Dell and eBay). A drawn-out process for shifting strategy, organization, and performance, rather than costing some business while catching up, could actually cost the entire business.

Fallacy of Sequential Processes

The second problem with the current consulting model is that it still embraces the traditional wisdom that "structure follows strategy." That might have been true at a time when most changes in strategy were really nothing more than refinements of an existing business model; you tinkered with the strategy, then you tinkered with the organization to make it fit the strategy.

Today, strategy and organization are interdependent. Strategic work starts with a lot of "what if" questions. A company's existing organization—who is sitting around the table, in what roles, and bringing which skills, experience, knowledge, and perspectives to the discussion—will inevitably shape the conversation and influence the company's ability to assess a broad range of strategic alternatives. For example, if you happen to be a slide rule company trying to figure out if it's time to make the big leap into calculators, and if everybody sitting around the table is a life-long slide-rule expert who doesn't know the first thing about electrons or circuit boards, the discussion will inevitably turn to how to build a better slide rule.

By the same token, we've seen CEOs come up with brilliant strategies—visionary, far-reaching plans that were just what the company needed—but they quickly realized that they had neither the right people nor the right structures and processes nor the right culture to begin implementing it right away. So even though, in a pure sense, Strategy A might be the right way to go, the CEO had to settle for Strategy B or C as an interim option while getting on with the work of building an organization capable of executing Strategy A.

In other words, strategy and organization are inseparable, no matter what the model suggests. In the real world, it's impossible to work on one without talking about the other. The realities of the organization will lead to a set of rational or irrational strategic choices and will probably have an even greater influence than the realities of the marketplace on a company's future direction.

Finally, just as strategy and organization happen in parallel, rather than in sequence, the reality is that change management doesn't fit neatly into a separate, clearly delineated third step in the model. For better or worse, as soon as you begin working on strategy, the process of change is underway. The moment you begin talking about the strategy and what kind of organization will be required to achieve it, you inevitably start asking, "How are we going to make this happen? How do we get from here to there?"

If we're honest, we have to acknowledge that the iterative nature of strategy, organization, and change was always true, even if it didn't fit the neat model used by consultants and expected by clients. Handled sequentially, the process ignored the fact that the dynamics of change had already been triggered by the initial strategy and organization work.

Concurrent and Integrated Enterprise Design

In light of the inherent and increasingly serious weaknesses in the sequential consulting model, which unfortunately is still quite popular, we believe a new model is imperative (see Exhibit 5.7). What we have in mind is actually

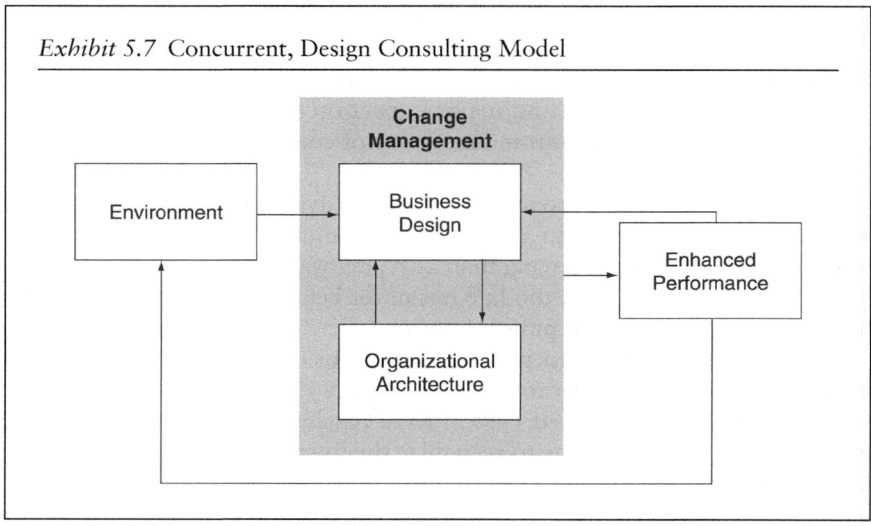

Exhibit 5.7 Concurrent, Design Consulting Model

a new version of the earliest model, combining our now-rigorous disciplines of strategy, organization, and change management consulting into a concurrent, reciprocal consulting process.

This new approach, which we call concurrent, dynamic enterprise design, is like the shift from batch to parallel processing. Rather than continuing to impose the intellectual straightjacket of a sequential, compartmentalized model, it acknowledges that consulting on strategy, organization, and change management is like trying to solve a set of simultaneous equations. The moment you solve for one variable, you change all the other equations. Here's how we envision the new model:

It begins with an aggressive, proactive approach to the environment. Companies frequently put off developing a new strategy until developments in the outside environment are absolutely clear; however, this approach can prove fatal in today's fast moving world. Therefore, they need concepts such as strategic anticipation and value migration to help them understand proactively what's happening in the marketplace and its implications for their value proposition.

It involves an integrated, iterative approach to strategy and organization. It recognizes that the earlier assumption of "strategy drives structure" is only half the equation, because the shape of the organization also drives critical thinking about strategic alternatives. Neither issue can be worked in isolation; instead, both must be considered inside the envelope of change management, because how you get "from here to there" will shape, and is shaped by, both strategic objectives and organizational capabilities.

This is a model in which the feedback loops are more pronounced and immediate than in the past. Within the organization, the impact of strategy, organization, and change upon one another is significant and swift, which is why we talk about the iterative nature of the model. Interestingly, greatly enhanced performance resulting from this model can also have a sudden and major impact on the external environment, causing major disruptions in the nature of competition.

We believe this new approach—concurrent, dynamic enterprise design—is an appropriate response to a business environment that is more complex, less forgiving, and faster moving than anything we have experienced before. The cost of doing too little, too late has never been higher, and the markets have never been quicker to punish failure.

It also recognizes and incorporates the various consulting disciplines that have developed along separate but not entirely different paths. Strategists such as Ghoshal and Bartlett (1997) have reached beyond the traditional boundaries of their discipline to recognize the importance of the human side of the organization. Organization consultants such as Nadler and Tushman (1997) have made a strong case for incorporating strategy into any

Strategy and Organization Consulting 137

discussion of organizational issues. And organization design's relatively recent shift in focus from individuals and small groups to change driven from the top has created a shared perspective with strategists regarding enterprise-level consulting.

In essence, the disciplines have begun talking to each other, making it easier and more efficient to solve issues iteratively rather than proceeding all the way down one road before starting on the next. And it is the iterative, concurrent nature of consulting that is really the key to this model. If we can employ it successfully, we can make it possible for clients to successfully design and deploy complex, discontinuous change in a fraction of the time previously consumed in sequential consulting assignments while engaging in incremental change. In short, this is all about enabling organizations to move at least as fast as their markets.

Implications for Consulting

The ability to understand the environment, anticipate change, select business models that capture value, to design and create organizations capable of implementing those models—and to do all of that quickly, concurrently, and continuously—is the task of management in the modern era. That's simply the way it is. So, regardless of the consulting models each of us might hold dear, our job is to accommodate to our clients' needs.

The clear imperative is a faster, fully integrated approach to consulting. That's easier said than done; if it were simple, more of us would be doing it already. Nevertheless, just as our clients must periodically revamp a long-cherished business model, so must we.

This new mode of consulting is still in its earliest stages. More experience will give us a clearer idea of how best to deliver it and what obstacles stand in our way. But we have some preliminary thoughts on the implications—some troubling, some exciting, and all of them challenging for consulting firms and practitioners.

1   Increasingly, clients will be looking to consultants for help in the form of fully integrated, multi-disciplinary teams that can help them work their range of strategic and organizational issues concurrently. The Holy Grail for consulting firms will be the true integration of the consulting disciplines, starting with intellectual capital and tools specifically designed to weave together the various processes and continuing through the coordinated delivery of various consultative services. Thus far, no one has truly cracked the code of how to accomplish all of that, given the inherently different delivery models.

2   Although we envision a need for increased integration of consulting capabilities, we are not suggesting a return to the original model of the consultant as generalist. To the contrary, there's a growing need for people who bring deep knowledge in the areas of strategy, organization,

and change management. What we will need, however, are consultants who are conversant in all three disciplines so they can work seamlessly with consultants from other disciplines.

3. As strategy work becomes more closely integrated into organization design and change management, it will be necessary to involve more people in the client organization in order to build broader participation and ownership. The shift from imparting expertise to building ownership might well require a fundamental shift in delivery models from strategy consulting's traditional "study/recommend" mode toward the "teach and facilitate" mode more common among organization consultants (to use the appropriate terminology discussed by Tom Cummings in Chapter 12). Indeed, we may need to rethink the highly leveraged, case team approach favored by strategy consulting firms and move instead toward a more dynamic model that features senior consultants collaborating and interacting closely with their clients as they work together as peers to solve complex strategy and organization issues simultaneously. The previous model of lengthy data gathering and analysis controlled completely by the consultant, which resulted in high fees, is likely on the wane. And so would be the formula of charging by the hour.

4. Organization consultants, for their part, will have to develop much more streamlined processes for designing organizations to suit particular strategies. The best consulting firms, for years, have eschewed the idea of off-the-shelf designs, and rightly so. But if they're to work concurrently with the strategy consultants in a fast-moving process, they can't start with a blank sheet each time; it simply takes too long. It might well become necessary to start thinking more in terms of a limited set of design alternatives that might be optimal for certain business models—an approach that will require considerable research and analysis in the very near future. Similarly, change management consultants will have to find ways to build understanding and buy-in faster than ever before. They'll have to employ new participative approaches—smarter use of large group interventions, for instance, or more creative use of information technology to involve people—in order to accelerate the speed of change.

5. If our view is correct—that many organizations now experience almost constant change—then we should reevaluate exactly how we provide value to clients and what we charge for it, because it's hard to imagine any of them wanting us to endlessly hang around gathering data and working on new strategies and organization designs. Instead, we need to arm our clients with the tools and methodologies to handle incremental change on their own, while providing more intense, specialized support during periods of discontinuous change.

6. At the end of the day, we must be ready to sell our services in whatever configuration our clients want to buy them. For the foreseeable future,

some clients will be hesitant to buy a fully integrated package of consulting services from a single firm. So it's essential that we continue to maintain the modularity of our offerings even as we pursue our efforts to integrate our expertise.

As we said at the outset, we seem to be coming full circle with the convergence of strategy and organization consulting. But this time, there are profound differences. We're looking at the reintegration of disciplines based on science and experience rather than intuition. We're operating in a very different time, and with the benefit of decades of experience and highly sophisticated concepts and tools. The question now is whether we can successfully apply some of these tools to our own businesses and recreate our consulting models to help our clients meet their own compelling challenges.

References

Ansoff, I. 1965. *Corporate Strategy*. New York: McGraw-Hill.
Argyris, C. 1962. *Interpersonal Competence and Organizational Effectiveness*. Homewood, IL: Dow-Jones-Irwin.
Beckhard, R. 1977. *Organizational Transitions: Managing Complex Change*. 2d ed. Reading, MA: Addison-Wesley.
Bennis, W. 1966. *Changing Organizations*. New York: McGraw-Hill.
Blake, R., and J. Mouton. 1964. *The Managerial Grid*. Houston, TX: Gulf Publishing.
Boston Consulting Group. 1968. *Perspectives on Experience*. Boston: The Boston Consulting Group.
Bower, M. 1966. *The Will to Manage: Corporate Success Through Programmed Management*. New York: McGraw-Hill.
Drucker, P. 1946. *Concept of the Corporation*. New York: John Day.
Galbraith, J.R. 1973. *Designing Complex Organizations*. Reading, MA: Addison-Wesley.
Ghoshal, S., and C.A. Bartlett. 1997. *The Individualized Corporation: A Fundamentally New Approach to Management*. New York: HarperCollins.
Greiner, L., T. Cummings, and A. Bhambri. 2003. 4-D Theory of Strategic Transformation: When New CEOs Succeed and Fail. *Organization Dynamics*, 32 (1): 1–16.
Homans, G.C. 1941. *The Western Electric Researchers*. National Research Council Report. New York: Reinhold.
Katz, D., and R.L. Khan. 1978. *The Social Psychology of Organizations*. 2d ed. New York: Wiley.
Lawrence, P.R., and J.W. Lorsch. 1967. *Organization and Environment: Managing Differentiation and Integration*. Homewood, IL: Richard D. Irwin.
Lorsch, J.W., and A. Sheldon. 1972. *The Individual in the Organization: A Systems View*, in J.W. Lorsch, and P.R. Lawrence, eds. *Managing Group and Intergroup Relations*. Homewood, IL: Irwin-Dorsey.
Leavitt, H. 1964. *Managerial Psychology: An Introduction to Individuals, Pairs, and Groups in Organizations*, 2d ed. Chicago: University of Chicago Press.
MacGregor, D. 1960. *The Human Side of Enterprise*. New York: McGraw-Hill.

Nadler, D. A. 1982. *Implementing Organizational Change*, in D. A. Nadler, M. L. Tushman, and N. G. Hatvan, eds. *Managing Organizations*. Boston: Little, Brown.

Nadler, D. A. 1998. *Champions of Change: How CEOs and Their Companies Are Mastering the Skills of Radical Change*. San Francisco: Jossey-Bass Publishers.

Nadler, D. A., and M. L. Tushman. 1979. *A Congruence Model for Diagnosing Organizational Behavior*, in D. Kolb, I. Rubin, and J. McIntyre. *Organizational Psychology: A Book of Readings*, 3d ed. Englewood Cliffs, NJ: Prentice Hall.

Nadler, D. A., and M. L. Tushman. 1980. Frameworks for Organization Behavior. *Organizational Dynamics*, Autumn.

Nadler, D. A., and M. L. Tushman. 1987. *Strategic Organizational Design*. New York: Scott Foresman.

Nadler, D. A., and M. L. Tushman. 1997. *Competing by Design: The Power of Organizational Architecture*. New York: Oxford University Press.

Nadler, D. A., R. B. Shaw, and E. A. Walton. 1994. *Discontinuous Change: Leading Organizational Transformation*. San Francisco: Jossey-Bass Publishers.

Porter, M. E. 1980. *Competitive Strategy*. New York: Free Press.

Porter, M. E. 1986. *Competitive Advantage*. New York: Free Press.

Roethlisberger F., and W. Dickson. 1939. *Management and the Worker*. Cambridge: Cambridge University Press.

Schein, E. H. 1973. *Process Consultation*. Reading, MA: Addison-Wesley.

Seiler, J. A. 1967. *Systems Analysis in Organizational Behavior*. Homewood, IL.: Irwin-Dorsey.

Slywotzky, A. J. 1996. *Value Migration*. Boston: Harvard Business School Press.

Slywotzky, A. J., and D. J. Morrison. 1998. *The Profit Zone: How Strategic Business Design Will Lead You to Tomorrow's Profits*. New York: Three Rivers Press.

6 Trust-Based Selling of Consulting Services

Charles H. Green

The words "trust" and "sales" are not often found in the same sentence. This is particularly true within intangible services – especially consulting services.

Consultants, it can fairly be said, walk around with a barely subconscious antipathy to sales. Most people join the profession out of love for the subject matter in question, as well as a desire to be a subject matter expert.

Few if any of them joined in order to be a salesperson; yet ironically, if they are successful, most end up having to sell. The self-image of a "salesperson" is uncomfortable for consultants, who are largely intellectual overachievers, not the most socially at-ease, and who were attracted to their profession for the expertise-based meritocracy it promised. The thought of being chosen for reasons other than palpably visible expertise is discomforting to them.

The Paradox of Consulting Sales

Yet this is precisely what happens. Since consultants are chosen to access expertise by those who, by definition, lack their levels of expertise, the process is inherently an exercise in trust. Given the complexity of issues, the asymmetry of expertise, and the ambiguity of outcomes, the most effective relationship between client and consultant would seem to be one of acknowledged mutual trust.

And yet the process by which buyer and seller meet is rife with attempts to mitigate, or even deny, this fundamental role of trust. In its place, we see inherently competitive models; processes grafted from other industries; approaches to sales issues rooted in mistrust; and misguided efforts to elevate expertise beyond its inherent value. These processes and approaches show up in sales-related areas as diverse as positioning, pricing, objection handling, presenting, closing, lead qualification, cross-selling, and proposal writing.

This paper will suggest that the most natural and effective relationship during the sales and business development process (as well as later, during project delivery) is rooted in mutual trust. I will map out in detailed areas where this approach can be developed.

Consulting vs. Industry at Large – Basic Differences in Sales

Consultants are as exposed to general sales literature as are other business professionals. Such literature tends to be driven by consumer models and basic industry models, e.g. the AIDA model of Awareness, Interest, Desire, Action,[1] Miller Heiman's[2] buyer/influencer model (Economic buyer, technical buyer, influencer, coach), or Salesforce.com's[3] ubiquitous sequential process model built on the traditional sales "funnel" (lead generation, lead qualification, presentation, proposal, negotiation).

These consumer and general industry models differ from consulting in six notable ways.

- *Seller as agent.* Buying a candy bar (or a car) is relatively seamless: the consumer sees an ad, forms a desire, gets information, and makes a decision. The decision about which store or dealer to visit is relatively unimportant. By contrast, the "right consultant" is a much bigger issue.
- *Buyer-seller relationship.* The strategic view of most business relationships is still anchored in 1970s strategists like Michael Porter[4] – at root, a relationship of competition. Of Porter's famed Five Forces, two of them – customers and suppliers – are viewed explicitly as competitors.

The relationship of "competitor" works on many dimensions for complex industrial businesses like GE, but it is anathema to a consulting firm to conceive of a client in those terms. Nonetheless – no doubt in part because consulting firms *teach* concepts like Porter's Five Forces – they have drunk their own Kool Aid and have come to view their own relationships as rooted in competition rather than collaboration.

- *Shared expertise.* Buying janitorial supplies or car fleets is largely non-mysterious; buyer and seller share a common language about a common area of expertise. By contrast, the asymmetry of expertise makes consultants, like physicians, masters of their domains.
- *Size and riskiness of purchase.* Even buying a plane (Boeing vs. Airbus) is an exercise in rational low-risk-modeling. By contrast, the impact of a successful vs. non-successful consulting engagement is difficult to analyze, and subject to widely varying risk profiles.
- *Two step buying process.* Unlike the linear traditional sales-side "funnel" model would suggest, the buying of consulting services is done in two distinct steps by most clients – screening, and selection.[5]

The screening phase ("round up the usual suspects") is a rational one, often delegated to juniors, pegged on spreadsheets, and discussed in terms of data. Often discussions narrow the field down to two or three, who get to do the "dog and pony show."

The selection process is quite the opposite. It is personal – literally so, in the case of presentations. Selection decisions are made viscerally (though often communicated, or "rationalized," in terms of data).

Screening is done with the brain; selection with the heart. This explains why the low consulting firm bidder rarely wins, yet price is nearly always given as a rationale to the losing firm(s).

Arguably the greatest selling mistake consultants make is to think they're still in the *screening* process when they're in fact in the *selection* process. A job candidate knows not to recite his resume at the job interview; but a consulting firm will insist on opening the presentation with 5–10 slides "about our firm." It is antithetical to trust at precisely the point in the buying process when trust is most valuable.

- *Role of expertise in buying.* Expertise in the screening process is a necessary condition – in fact, it is typically a major criterion, even the only criterion. But expertise is *not* a *sufficient* condition for the *selection* process.

What clients want in the selection phase is a sense that the consultant understands them, respects them, and has their best interests at heart. Clients want to feel that both the risks of purchase and of asymmetry of expertise are mitigated by the trustworthiness of the consultant.

Quantitative results of the TQ Trust Quotient Self Assessment,[6] based on the Trust Equation (70,000 takers), have shown that the power of the two "soft skills" factors – Intimacy and Other-Orientation – are statistically more powerful determinants of trust than the two "hard skills" factors – Credibility and Reliability.

Broadly speaking, the extant sales models from non-consulting industries do not reflect these differing aspects of the consulting industry. That alone suggests the need for a different approach.

Self-Sabotaging Consultants and Clients

Yet it is worse still. Consultants (and their clients) are complicit in an elaborate psychological self-deception that keeps them from fully recognizing the differences between selling consulting services and selling all else. The heart of that self-deception is *the belief that the consultant's main role is effective and efficient delivery of expertise from consultant to client.*

This false belief shows up in the first encounter, when the client says, "So, tell me about your firm." The consultant – drenched in his expertise-and-content-based view of the world – takes the client's question literally, and proceeds to talk, almost always for too long, about himself, his firm, and his expertise. It is not the client's fault – the client has no training in buying, and is asking an open-ended question hoping to gain information that might inform her decision; instead, she gets a resume dump.

David Maister once said, "The problem is never what the client said it was in the first meeting."[7] This insight reflects the true locus of value-adding in consulting. It does *not* come about in the form of answering questions (the usual way "expertise" is evaluated); it comes about in the joint formation of hypotheses, which then results in an agreed-upon problem definition.

A parallel insight was raised in a 2005 conversation[8] with Neil Rackham,[9] author of SPIN Selling,[10] when he was asked to define the "biggest single problem in sales":

The most pervasive and hardest sales problem? Premature solutions. The mistaken belief that the sooner they can begin solving the problem, the more effective they will be.

This rush to solve the problem isn't unique to consulting – but it's enabled by the nature of the consulting business (clients typically presenting problems, rather than requesting solutions) and the nature of consultants (who have been hired, trained, promoted, and incented precisely for their ability to solve problems).

In sum: the consulting industry's approach to sales too frequently draws on inappropriate models based on other industries. This is exacerbated by consultants' (and clients') expertise-centric views of the nature of consulting.

The Alternative: A Trust-Based Approach to Selling Consulting Services

The alternative approach is both simple and yet comprehensive: focus more on the selection phase of sales, focus more on the interpersonal components of trust, and redefine the consultant-client relationship.

I will focus on what happens to eight aspects of sales when it is built from trust – positioning, pricing, proposal writing, handling objections, giving "the pitch," networking, closing, and lead management. First, however, it's helpful to define what a trust-based client/consultant relationship looks like.

Redefining Client Relationships from Trust

There are four trust principles[11] which – when followed during all client relationships,[12] during both the sales process and results delivery processes – serve to create trust-based relationships. Those principles are:

1 A focus on client interests *first*, in all interactions.
2 An instinct for collaborative, not competitive, relationships.
3 A focus on the long-term relationship rather than the short-term transaction.
4 A default to transparency, except when to do so would be illegal or harmful.

Trust-Based Selling of Consulting Services   145

It is these principles, applied to the eight tactical components of sales, which begin to show the granular and distinct implications of the trust approach.

Positioning with Trust

Many consultants are enamored of value propositions or of branding. Each of those has its place, but only in the screening process – they are each mostly irrelevant in the selection process, which is heavily about personal trust.

This issue gets triggered when consultants hear an early sales call question like, "So, tell us in a nutshell – why should we buy from you?" It is often phrased combatively and skeptically, which only reinforces the consultant's tendency to reach for the firm's expertise, or its "value proposition."

In fact, it's better answered with trust, by using the four trust principles. For example:

Q. *Why should we buy from you?*

A. Good question. And to be clear, at this early stage – I'm not even sure that you *should* buy from us. We know a few things about you, have a few hypotheses – but we haven't had a chance to test them out with you, much less find out your concerns and issues.

In our experience, the clients who *do* end up buying from us tend to be focused on [business process design] issues rather than [vertical industry expertise] themes, to take one example. And, they tend to have strengths in marketing.

Those who do *not* end up buying from us frequently go with a more industry-based competitor; some of them also have weaker marketing departments.

The biggest differentiator, then, seems to be the relative importance to you of vertical market experience vs. functional marketing capability. That's clearly what we should focus on in talking together, so that you end up making the best decision.

And by the way – the last thing that *we* want is for you to make the wrong decision. Because then we have to end up delivering and knowing we're not the best choice for you. I've been there once or twice, and I don't want to ever do it again – it's embarrassing! We really want to do right by you, and have you choose us only for the right reasons.

So – does that help? And shall we then talk about industry focus and marketing?

How Trust Alters Pricing

Most consultants (and most clients) view pricing as a zero-sum game, to be played close to the vest, and with a thinly-veiled undercurrent of challenge.

The prototypical price question – "Why is your price so high?" – is phrased in a passive-aggressive manner. The prototypical answer is defensive – "It's not really so high . . . it's high because . . . it's worth it because . . ." and so forth.

Applying the trust principles changes everything.

- Focusing on client-first means we check our ego at the door and lead with, "Help me understand. . . ."
- Focusing on collaboration means we drive for a win-win answer, one that feels fair to both.
- Focusing on relationships not transactions means "fair" has to stand the test of time.
- Focusing on transparency means you have no hesitation in sharing information with the client.

Put them together and you have:

Q. *Why is your price so high?*
A. Well, help me understand what you mean by that. Because in my experience, "high price" can mean any one of four different things.

- It can mean it's higher than you expected, and you're dismayed.
- It can mean it's over your budget, and that's a problem.
- It can mean it's 20% higher than what you heard from a competitor, and you're concerned about fairness.
- It can mean you just never accept price quotes at face value and prefer to bargain as a matter of principle.

Now, some of those we can maybe help with by sharing information and detail, and some maybe not. Let's dig into it together and see. But please start by helping me understand the nature of your concern.

Handling Objections from Trust

One of the assumptions uncritically taken by consultants from the non-consulting world of sales is the approach to "handling objections." Typically "objection handling" is voiced similarly to "snake-handling," i.e. an inherently dangerous under-taking, with a few proprietary "tips and tricks" designed to foil the dangerous attempts of the snake to bite the handler.

The metaphor is revealing. But confronting it with the trust principles changes the metaphor. The "objection" is not a problem – it is simply a form of engagement. The real enemy is not "objection," it is disengagement.

The problematic nature of the "objection" is entirely within our heads. The right answer has to be collaborative, not oppositional. And a key approach is to be completely transparent, rather than give in to the desire to hide one's tricks from the other.

Conventional sales wisdom calls for "answering" the objection, then re-testing ("So, with that out of the way, are you ready to buy? And would you like the videotape or the live version of the program?"). From a trust perspective, this is pushy, presumptive, and operating from the salesperson's timeframe – not the client's.

The trust-based answer would sound more like:

> Um, let me think out loud with you about that . . . You're saying you're concerned about the effect on the morale of the sales support organization? Help me know a bit more how that would play out, will you? Like, what would trigger it? And what would that mean downstream? . . .
>
> Well, it sounds like we can address the technology part of that, but I'm not sure we can do a better job than you on the communications end of it . . . maybe that's something we work together on? I'm also happy for us to get together with one past client of ours in particular who might shed some insight. . . .
>
> How're you feeling about this? I'm guessing we'll need to bring Lucille into this on your end too, wouldn't we? Are we ready to raise it with her yet? Or shall you and I work it some more?

Giving the "Pitch"

The concept of the "pitch" is another unfortunate metaphor taken from the more competitive approaches to selling. The purpose of the "pitch" is to blow one past the batter, "strike him out," or "throw them a curve they can't hit." Also known as the "dog and pony show," the "beauty contest," and "the orals," they all carry with them a sense of tension and of a contested event. None of these metaphors fit well a trust-based approach to sales.

The biggest single failure of "pitches" is to continue operating in the screening mode, when in fact the "pitch" is the embodiment of the select mode. Almost all pitches lead off with a section on firm qualifications – and it is almost always a mistake. Your qualifications are what *got* you the pitch – put it in the leave-behind material pile and get on with the pitch.

The second biggest mistake in pitches is violating the first and fourth trust principles by refusing to directly answer a direct question. When a client asks you a direct question, you must answer it directly (client focus first) and precisely (transparency). Don't say, "We'll get to that in the last section" – just go there.

When a client asks questions during a pitch, consultants invariably hear them as questions about expertise: but their answers are far more revealing about trust. Consider these two answers:

Q. *What experience do you have in the legal services industry?*
A1. We've done a lot of solid work for law firms, including some research on legal services, as well as interacting with some legal services issues through law firm projects. I can get you a list of client names that can attest to our abilities in the legal arena.
A2. We did a small job for LexisNexis in 2012. Law is our #4 industry sector; two of our five law firm clients used us in legal services marketing.

The first answer assumes the client cares mainly about the particular answer (they may, they may not), and tries to massage the question. The second answer not only gives more information in fewer words, but demonstrates respect – both by answering the question straightforwardly, and by letting the client choose whether they want more – or not.

The message: ask us a direct question, you'll get a direct, no-spin-control answer.

The Role of Closing

The concept of "closing" goes all the way back to peddlers in the 19th century in the US.[13] It is still around today in automobile sales, with the line "there are no be-backs," meaning if the customer says they'll be back, they won't. Hence the pressure to "close."

Very few retail customers enjoy being "closed," so it's something of a mystery why the concept still shows up in B2B sales. In any case, it has no valid role in a trust-based approach to selling for consultancies.

The concept of "closing" implies the primacy of the consultant's need to sell over the importance of the client's needs about buying – it thus violates the first and the second trust principles (client first, and collaboration).

But it goes more deeply. The acronym ABC (Always be Closing), originally part of the respected Xerox Sales program, is entirely built around the seller's efficiency. It is a reminder to the seller that time spent on a no-sale is time wasted; hence, the need to proactively push things along.

But consulting clients, almost without exception, do not appreciate being "pushed along," any more than consultants do. It immediately raises questions of self-focus (see principle 1), and of short-term focus (principle 3).

From a trust perspective, the only good time for a client to close a deal is when it makes sense *for the client* to close the deal. That doesn't mean a consultant can't ask a genuinely trust-based question about what timing is best for the client – but to ask it that way is about the client, not about closing. The concept is rooted in high self-orientation – the antithesis of trust.

Lead Qualification

Lead management, as usually presented, is similar to closing in that it is primarily aimed at the seller's sales efficiency. In particular, the idea of "lead qualification" is pushed by sales managers. The ability to measure the "age" of a lead and the pace at which it is pushed through the sales "funnel" is a key feature of CRM systems, and consulting firms buy into the concept along with their B2B clientele.

Lead qualification, posed this way, implies that the value of the client to the seller can be reduced not only to the particular lead in question, but to the time value of that lead. It also ignores marketing impact. This is an extremely narrow view of client value.

Trust principle three reminds consultants that the value of a client lies in the long-term relationship, not the short-term transaction. Envision a client encountering two consultants in the sales phase. The client notices that one is willing to spend an extra half hour on the phone, suggest some referrals, and offer to send some extra information, even when there is no obvious pay off – while the other consultant seems eager to get off the phone when it sounds like there's no immediate sale.

The impact on the client is clear: when that client *does* have a real lead in hand, he or she is going to the first consultant. In effect, the first consultant was willing to invest in marketing, while the second consultant was constrained by a transactional view of sales.

Cross-Selling from Trust

Repeat business for consulting firms is vastly more profitable than new-client business, because the cost of sales is multiples higher with new clients.[14] One of the most profitable sources of new sales for a consulting firm is a variation on repeat business – cross-selling, or the sale of existing or new services to an existing or new client buyer *within* an existing-client organization.

Cross-selling of consulting services is successful in spite of itself: most consulting firms vastly under-perform their potential, for one simple reason. They think that the scarce resource is the subject matter expertise.

For example, consider consultant Jo and client Gerry. One day it occurs to Jo that Gerry might benefit from speaking to Jo's colleague, Jenna, over in the supply chain practice of Jo's consulting firm.

Typically, Jo will say to Gerry, "Hey Gerry – it occurs to me you might benefit from a chat with our supply chain practice. I know someone, Jenna, over there. How about I give you each other's business cards?"

The odds of Gerry and Jenna actually talking in this scenario are not high – and the reason is trust. Specifically:

- Jenna doesn't trust that Jo knows enough to make a smart referral.
- Gerry doesn't trust that Jo knows enough to recommend Jenna.
- And even Jo may not be sure about trusting Jenna with Jo's client.

And yet, all pretend that the introduction makes sense – because Jenna has some expertise that presumably Gerry needs.

The answer is to treat the relationship, not the expertise, as the precious resource. The solution is for Jo to invest in time – first with Gerry, then with Jenna – so that in each case Jo feels just knowledgeable enough to ask useful and intelligent questions. And when Jenna and Gerry actually meet, Jo will be there as well – to ensure that both parties feel taken care of, and have an "out" should things not feel right.

The Role of Proposal Writing

In my experience, less experienced clients are more likely to insist on a detailed RFP-driven process,[15] culminating in a proposal. This is against their own best interest, as the sales process is an invaluable opportunity for a client to gain insight from consultants – and for free! Yet they are driven by fear – the fear of the consultant's command of the expertise, and of being "taken" by an all-knowing "expert."

The best proposal is in fact a meeting, followed up with a (very) short email stating little more than, "As we discussed, summary attached, please call me about changes, and if none, sign below."

The point is that the written word is far more useful when summarizing prior conversations than when substituting for them long-distance. Proposals get used, in some measure, to:

- be draft contracts
- show off expertise
- offer an approach
- offer a workplan
- provide a basis for comparative decision-making by the client
- provide the basis for a productive meeting.

In almost all cases, the value of the proposal is enhanced if it is intended from the outset as the basis for a meeting – in which case, it is often better prepared as a presentation than as a document. In fact, if the client insists on receiving *only* written proposals and refuses the suggestion to have an open, value-adding proposal meeting, then it is probable that you have either:

- a wired proposal process – someone else has the job already, or
- an overly fearful client, for whom an inability to engage is an early warning sign of relationship troubles to come.

Clients and consultants have legitimate needs to exchange resumes, project plans, references, and past experience. But these are not the "guts" of a proposal, and should always be relegated to the "attachment" part of a document. The real "guts" of a proposal – and the reason why it should almost always be done in conjunction with a meeting – lies in problem definition.

The key role of problem definition in consulting sales. It is worth re-quoting Maister's line, "The problem is never what the client said it was in the first meeting." The point is not that clients are ignorant. The key point is that *the process of joint problem identification is the locus of value-adding in the project.*

The consultant reading this paper can easily think of examples where a key meeting resulted in an ah-ha moment, a meeting of minds, a shared agreement between consultant and client that "Yes, *this* is the issue we've got to nail down."

It is in that moment that the client gains confidence the consultant *really understands* the issue; and, given that understanding, the client also gains confidence that the consultant can deliver. It is also in that moment that the consultant actually *gets* the sale, even if it's not said out loud. Such moments constitute the end of the selection process (and the beginning of the justification process, characterized by a reversion to rational thinking, aka rationalization).

To put that another way: it is the success of *problem definition* that triggers the buying decision.

This points to yet another misconception by consultants about value: they think value comes via delivery. But in a real sense, value is provided to the client in problem definition: and the sale is, in a validly emotional way, the "reward" for having served up that definitional value.

After all – why would a client buy from anyone *except* the firm that helped them to develop that problem definition? They wouldn't.

The role of proposals in problem definition. I am discussing this point in the proposal section because you cannot easily create that "moment" from afar, in the form of a written document. It is like knitting with boxing gloves on, from across the room, via levers and pulleys.

And yet, consultants and clients alike are seduced to try and do so, for dozens of reasons. Because that's how it's done in the telecomm business; that's what the sales books say; that's the client's purchasing process; the client doesn't want to feel pressured. And so on.

Much of the "art" of consulting lies in making clients feel comfortable discussing ambiguity; and much of the skill at the art comes from consultants themselves feeling comfortable with ambiguity. Until clients and consultants can feel comfortable openly discussing hypotheses, value, and risks, the discussion will lack trust.

In many ways, trust-based relationships follow the Rules of Romance, as spelled out in *The Trusted Advisor*.[16] The rules of romance are not rules of proposal writing, they are rules of engagement. The trust principles help guide those interactions – particularly the principles of client first, collaboration, and transparency. Trust is personal; consulting is about people; selling consulting services is an extremely personal process that transcends written proposals.

Building a Consulting Firm That Sells on Trust

Consulting firms are first and foremost collections of individuals. The beliefs and values of the firm's consultants have the biggest impact on the firm's trust-based approach to selling.

Consultants who believe the purpose of selling is to make the sale are self-focused – not client-focused. A client-focused consultant believes the purpose of selling is to *earn the right to improve the client*. Such a consultant is not attached to outcome, but at the same time trusts that continually operate that way will in fact produce greater sales. (That belief also solves the "fear-of-sales" problem in consulting – it means the only difference between sales and delivery is the simple act of getting paid. This reduces the fear considerably.)

Getting consultants to believe such things is not done by treating them as rational maximizers of economic self-worth. Behavioral metrics and financial incentives are ineluctably perverse in the context of consulting firms, where there are so many thousands of variables and ways to subvert intentions.

The far better way to scale in a firm of people (herding cats) is through values. Values in turn are best inculcated through language, and through example (think about how children are raised, or not raised, ethically). It is important to have stated values, and it is more critical than in most areas of business that leaders Walk the Talk. Nothing shrieks hypocrisy more than people who say "trust me" but who themselves never trust others.

When clients do come to trust consultants, a number of positive results come about. The sales cycle is shorter. Pricing resistance is lower. Decisions are made faster. Small errors are forgiven. Information is more forthcoming. Secrets are shared. Contracts are shorter, but more easily revised for contingencies. Follow-on work is much greater, driving higher retention rates, higher consultant utilization, and higher profitability.

Moreover, all those benefits are win-win – the clients are every bit as well-off with trust-based relationships as are the consultants. These benefits are clear to all, on discussion: why, then, don't they pan out more often?

The answer, I think, is short-term, self-centered fear. The antidote is a heavy dose of collaboration, transparency, and other-focus, and a long-term perspective – delivered mainly by leaders who are willing to lead by example.

Notes

1 First attributed to Elias St. Elmo Lewis, by Edward Strong, in *The Psychology of Selling and Advertising*, 1925. https://en.wikipedia.org/wiki/E._St._Elmo_Lewis.

2. See for example *The New Strategic Selling*, Miller, Tuleja, Heiman et al., Grand Central Publishing, New York, 2005.
3. Salesforce.com "Sales Process Map: A step by step guide to reach prospects, qualify leads and close deals," https://www.salesforce.com/assets/pdf/misc/EB_sales_process.pdf.
4. See *Competitive Strategy: Techniques for Analyzing Industries and Competitors*, Free Press, New York, 1980.
5. *Managing the Professional Services Firm*, David Maister, Simon & Schuster, New York, 1993.
6. White Paper "Think Expertise Will Make You Trusted? Think Again," Charles Green, Sandra Styer, Bob Bowers, 2014 http://trustedadvisor.com/public/files/pdf/2010_TA_Whitepaper_Think_Again_Special.pdf.
7. David Maister, conversation with Charles H. Green, c. May 2003.
8. Interview with Neil Rackham, Leesburg VA, c. April 2005.
9. See bio of Neil Rackham, http://neilrackham.com/.
10. *SPIN Selling*, McGraw-Hill, 1998.
11. *Trust-Based Selling*, Charles H. Green, McGraw-Hill, New York, 2005.
12. One of the implications of using the same principles during sales as during delivery is that the distinction between sales and project delivery falls away: the "right thing" to do is always the same thing, "closing" becomes a trivial event, and the idea of sales can finally be incorporated into the much more comfortable ideology of client service overall – a shift which many consultants find very comforting.
13. *Birth of a Salesman: The Transformation of Selling in America*, Walter Friedman, First Harvard University Press, Cambridge, 2004.
14. See for example "Putting the Service-Profit Chain to Work," HBR, Heskett, Jones, Loveman, Sasser, Schlesinger, July–August 2008. In my own work with The MAC Group, I estimated cost of sales for new clients at four to seven times that for existing clients.
15. I am leaving aside government and non-profit clients, who for completely separate and valid reasons have no choice in the matter but to go for competitive bidding processes.
16. *The Trusted Advisor*, Maister, Galford, Green, Free Press, New York, 2001; Chapter 5.

Bibliography

Birth of a Salesman: The Transformation of Selling in America, Walter Friedman, First Harvard University Press, Cambridge, 2004.
Competitive Strategy: Techniques for Analyzing Industries and Competitors, Free Press, New York, 1980.
Managing the Professional Services Firm, David Maister, Simon & Schuster, New York, 1993.
The New Strategic Selling, Miller, Tuleja, Heiman et al., Grand Central Publishing, New York, 2005.
The Psychology of Selling and Advertising, 1925. https://en.wikipedia.org/wiki/E._St._Elmo_Lewis.
"Putting the Service-Profit Chain to Work," *Harvard Business Review*, Heskett, Jones, Loveman, Sasser, Schlesinger, July–August 2008.

"Sales Process Map: A step by step guide to reach prospects, qualify leads and close deals," https://www.salesforce.com/assets/pdf/misc/EB_sales_process.pdf.
SPIN Selling, Neil Rackham, McGraw-Hill, New York, 1998.
Trust-Based Selling, Charles H. Green, McGraw-Hill, New York, 2005.
The Trusted Advisor, Maister, Galford, Green, Free Press, New York, 2001; Chapter 5.

7 Operations Management Consulting

Richard B. Chase, K. Ravi Kumar and Peter R. Giulioni

Operations Management (OM) consulting is often overlooked in today's discussions about what is "hot" in professional services and management consulting; instead, more attention is paid in the media and at business schools to the romance and rewards of strategy consulting, closely followed by IT consulting. According to Gartner's 2015 Market Share Analysis Report, globally spending on management consultants has grown to USD $125.2 billion in 2014, up 6.1 percent from 2013. The same report indicates that the market for operations management services is estimated to be worth around USD $70 billion, making it, together with Financial Advisory, the largest segment in the industry.

Despite the cyclic nature of the consulting marketplace, well respected operations consultants normally remain in high demand by global clients. The reasons for this demand include: increased market and profit pressures on clients to reduce costs; usually resulting the need to reengineer core processes and eliminate those processes that are no longer considered core; continued globalization requiring advice on setting up and effectively managing operations in foreign markets; outsourcing options and ultimately decisions relative to current operations; and the need for real-time information to better guide global operations.

What Is OM Consulting?

Many people think OM consulting is only concerned with technical matters, machinery, and engineering. In other words, an OM consultant should have a degree in engineering in one hand and a stopwatch in the other. In reality far more MBAs than engineers are employed in operations consulting, and much of their work is performed in service-oriented companies that exist and thrive without plants and machinery.

Operations consulting deals with advising and normally assisting clients in developing and implementing operations strategies and improving systems that affect the production, delivery, and after-service of a product or service. It can often play a central role in the formulation and implementation of a company's overall business strategy, especially where operations can be a source of competitive advantage or an efficient deliverer of goods and services—or both!

Treacy and Wiersema[1] suggest that market leadership can be attained in one of three ways: (1) product leadership, (2) operational excellence, or (3) customer intimacy. Each of these strategies normally calls for unique operations capabilities. The operations consultant must be able to assist client management in understanding these requirements, and then be able to define the most effective combination of technology, systems, processes, and people to execute the business strategy. See the sidebar for two examples of potential OM consulting issues.

Consulting Insights—Examples of OM Problems

Waste reduction: In October 2014, the *Business Insider* reported that every year US consumers and retail outlets throw away up to one-third of all the food produced—133 billion pounds of food—and the grocery industry is responsible for tossing 10 percent of that food. The industry has inherent wasteful practices that include overstocking of inventories of products that do not sell well and understocking products that do. They also include inefficient performance due to poor coordination of various partners in the value chain, namely, manufacturers, wholesalers, distributors, and logistics service providers. Operations consultants are called in to identify best practices and innovative ways in which remedies to such large-scale inefficiencies can be implemented.

Logistics: This area encompasses the various activities of freight transportation, inventories, warehousing, etc. According to an *International Student* report, in 2011, nearly USD $1.3 trillion was spent in the US transportation and logistics industry, which made up approximately 8.5 percent of the Gross Domestic Product. With the current focus on redefining and restructuring supply chains, which deal with the integration of suppliers to final customer(s), the scope for operations consulting in this area alone is enormous, and the task daunting for companies seeking competitive advantage. For example, in the mid-2000s Boeing's much anticipated new 787 commercial airliners originally scheduled to enter service in May 2008 weren't getting finished quickly enough. When it finally went into service in October 2011, Boeing blamed the fact that they wanted to rapidly change the assembly process and the supply chain simultaneously—and too quickly—leading to disastrous results and an over three-year delay.

Historical Foundations

Modern OM traces it roots back to industrial engineering, as pioneered by Frederick W. Taylor, H.L. Gantt, and Frank and Lillian Gilbreth. It was Taylor, "the father of scientific management," who devised a philosophy and system of production management at the turn of the century. His book, *The Principles of Scientific Management* (1911),[2] converted what had been an art into a systematic, teachable approach to the study and design of work—Taylor's book was the *In Search of Excellence*[3] of its day, and it became a best seller even in Japan.

H.L. Gantt, the developer of the bar chart, worked with shipbuilders during World War I to improve the scheduling and refitting of liberty ships. Frank Gilbreth developed the principles of motion study, which became part of the consultant's tool kit, and his spouse Lillian developed the application of basic psychology to work design. The industrial model for operations processes was the assembly line design implemented by Henry Ford and his engineers. From the 1920s until the 1960s, OM became synonymous with factory management; during WWII, we often associate the name of Henry Kaiser with applying factory production techniques to shipbuilding and after the war to producing home construction in the US on a mass scale.

The 1970s and 1980s saw a broader and more holistic view emerge of operations management, mainly through the widespread application of Materials Requirements Planning (MRP), Just-in-Time (JIT), and Total Quality Management (TQM) systems. These approaches recognized the need to view all parts of a production system holistically and as being interrelated.

Who Are Today's Operations Consultants?

Operations consultants range from the neighbor down the street who used to work for General Electric and who is now a sole practitioner, to multi-billion-dollar global professional services firms, like Deloitte Consulting, PwC, EY, KPMG, IBM, Accenture, Tata Consulting, or Infosys. Each, in their own way, supports the needs of clients in terms of improving operations efficiency and effectiveness.

Multi-Service Operations Consultants

Firms like those mentioned above are large consulting businesses offering a wide range of operations consulting services. Their menu of operations and consulting skills includes operations strategy, manufacturing operations, logistics, sales-operations planning, channel, configuration, talent, and service management. They also take on a large amount of outsourcing activities from clients in the area of logistics and support service.

Specialized Operations Consultants

Here we find McKinsey, BCG, and Bain focusing on operations strategy, PRTM (now a part of PwC) for supply chain, Aon/Rath & Strong (a subsidiary of Aon Consulting) for Six Sigma, PROS for revenue management software, along with such industry-focused firms as SAIC for government and aviation, and Food Consultants Group for the food industry. Each of these consulting companies positions themself as best-in-class for a narrow portion of the market serving the particular needs of their clients.

Independent Operations Consultants

Many small consulting firms, sometimes just individuals, draw on their operating experience from large companies to service the needs of small and medium-size companies in their particular locale or region.

These clients usually cannot afford the fees of large consulting firms; moreover, clients probably feel more comfortable working with a local consultant who can give them a lot of personal attention. These consultants usually seek to build a long-term relationship with the owner-manager, serving as a confidant and advisor on operations issues.

Internal Consulting Groups

Some large diversified companies have invested in their own internal staff to become consultants serving line managers in efforts to improve the operational effectiveness of various business units. The newly popular process view of business has created the need for cross-functional consulting teams to address and rationalize the effectiveness of large parts of the value chain, such as order-fulfillment and customer service. Apple, Google, General Electric, Bank of America, Citi, and American Express are acknowledged exponents of this approach. GE for example developed a large cadre of internal consultants who work throughout various GE operations while using Six Sigma methods to improve quality.

The Five Ps of Operations Management

It is important for consultants to understand the objectives under which the operations function is normally measured against in most companies. Obviously, the most commonly known objectives are the cost and quality of producing products and services. But over the years, we have seen additional priorities assuming importance, such as speed (e.g., time-to-market in new product development and response to sales opportunities) and flexibility (e.g., responsiveness to customization requests, timing, and mode of delivery). For those companies that want to draw closer to customers in services, the quality of a company's services, such as field and sales support, call centers, and order status, have become a way to differentiate oneself in the marketplace.

With these objectives in mind, one needs to turn to the key building blocks of operational plans. Exhibit 7.1 provides a useful lens for considering five key focal areas in operations management, which overall is concerned with managing the inputs through transformation to outputs and including even the servicing of outputs. The five Ps represent five specific and interrelated concepts that consultants often address in their analyses and recommendations when attempting to create strong and integrated operations management systems and practices.

Manufacturing Versus Services Operations

In operations consulting, the five Ps take on a different character depending on whether one is looking mainly at manufacturing products or delivering services. Manufacturing operations deals with transforming material inputs into physical product outputs. This transformation process can be described as a two-way interaction between technology and the production worker. In theory, the variability that enters the process is highly controllable as one standardizes the material inputs, rationalizes the worker's job, and automates the process. The focus is on inanimate objects, which means that much of manufacturing OM consulting is devoted to figuring out how to produce, move, store, and distribute physical objects in the most efficient

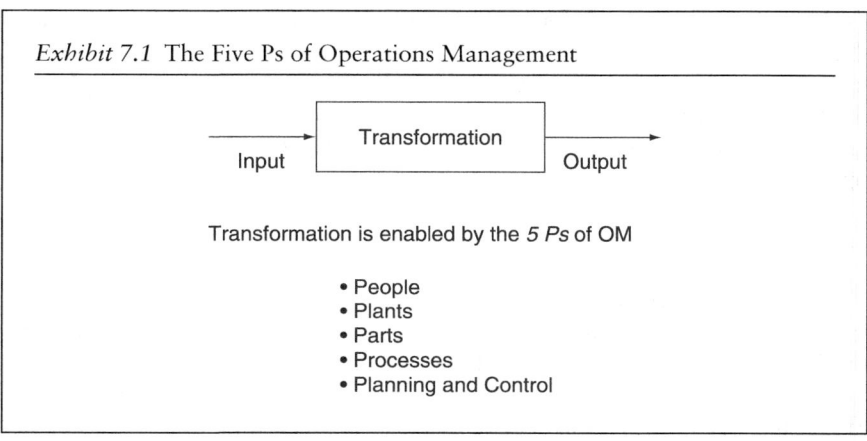

Exhibit 7.1 The Five Ps of Operations Management

manner. This challenge implies that the skill set of manufacturing consultants lies heavily in materials management and factory technologies.

For services OM, we must add a big C—for Customer—to the five Ps list. The addition of the customer creates a three-way interaction between the technology through which the service is carried out, the service provider, and the customer. The service process is thus both a production process and an experiential process. The experience element puts service quality in the eye of the beholder (the customer!), which also creates difficulties in measuring service performance. What works well in providing one kind of service may prove disastrous in another. For example, consuming a restaurant meal in less than half an hour may be exactly what you want at a fast-food outlet, but such brevity in eating would be totally unacceptable at an expensive French restaurant.

OM consultants need to understand that the quality of work is not the same as the quality of service. For example, an auto dealership may do good work on your car, but it may take a week too long to get the job done. Also, contributing to the variability issue is the service person's attitude and demeanor, which may vary from day-to-day or even minute-by-minute.[4] Additionally, services often take the form of cycles of encounters involving face-to-face, telephone, electronic, on-line, and mail interactions. Each of these encounters may call for different skills on the part of the services workforce. Finally, the service encounter is really just the tip of the iceberg—successful performance is also the result of "back-office" support functions (e.g., shipping, delivery, and invoicing). In total, these features mean that the service OM consultant's skill set will have to include an understanding of consumer behavior, as well as the blocking and tackling side of operations process design.

Key Concepts for OM Consultants

Today's operations consultants need to be armed with fundamental ideas that are the bedrock of sound practices in operations management. The following concepts are widely used to illuminate operational issues, be they in the US or other parts of the world. In-depth knowledge about each concept can help the OM consultant deal with many of the problems encountered in operations management.

Total Quality Management

The general history of Total Quality Management (TQM) is well known: Its renaissance began in Japan with the auto industry, and it spread to the United States at the urging of the quality gurus—Deming, Juran, and Crosby.[5] An integral part of TQM is the recognition that the organization's ability to provide high quality products or to deliver high quality services is dependent on the quality of its management.

Operations executives (and consultants) need to be educated to view quality improvement as a continuous never-ending process, and that the goal should be one of preventing quality problems, rather than solving them later when customers complain. A strong management will implement sophisticated improvement approaches, such as Six Sigma[6] quality, which signifies a level of quality that allows for less than three to four defects per million operations.

Supply Chain Management

Since the mid-1990s, the concept of "supply chain management" has come to the forefront, acknowledging the fact that materials management extends beyond the four walls of the factory to include suppliers upstream and distributors and retailers downstream. This concept has also become central in the teaching of operations management in most universities. Its objective is to move goods and services as expeditiously as possible across the broad chain from raw materials supplier to the end-user/customer. A thorough study by consultants is required of the entire chain, including identification of those processes that can best be performed by the client and those that should be performed by others. There is also a need for a supportive IT network system to enable the management of the overall process.

Lean Operations

A fundamental concept underlying much of the practice of OM is the philosophy of "lean" operations. With origins in JIT and TQM, this framework approaches operations with a view to eliminate "waste" and improve productivity. To do this, "waste" is identified as any non-value adding activity, with value typically being defined from the end-user or customer's perspective. Thus, the problems in moving a part from one place to another or in machine downtime (be it due to breakdown or for setup activities) need to be investigated and eliminated where possible. Ideas such as cellular workflows, setup time reduction, and preventative maintenance are standard ways to drive waste out of the system.

Theory of Constraints

A key construct that emerged at the same time as "lean" operations was one of prioritization, meaning all work areas and resources are not equally important! This viewpoint is articulated in the "theory of constraints,"[7] which focuses on managing one's way through both required and unnecessary bottlenecks (those barriers that constrict the outflow of goods and services). These bottlenecks affect volume throughout and lead-time of products in the queue; hence, there can be major effects on revenue and cash inflow to the company.

Focused Operations

A fundamental concept that relates to operations strategy is that of focusing the appropriate resources on the target market. The notion of focus is that operations processes should be chosen to fit the market conditions for the product in terms of specific volume and variety required. For example, assembly lines are more suited to high product volumes and low product variety, while those operations configurations based on flexible cells or machine functionality are more suited to low product volume and higher product diversity.

Prior to the 1970s, a common belief among non-operations senior management, particularly in discrete parts manufacturing companies, was that operations labor and machines should be used to produce whatever products, in whatever quantities, at whatever timeframes, in whatever quality, and at whatever cost was needed to satisfy customers!

International competition, not just from the Asia but from many European manufacturers as well, demonstrated the importance of not trying to be all things to all people.

Mass Customization

Finally, the inexorable push towards getting the best of both worlds is achieved through mass customization, which couples higher price margins from custom products with standardized production. This typically occurs through the design of products or services where a few key attributes are chosen to be customized, usually occurring at the tail end of the production process. This gives the opportunity to produce the product in a very efficient cost-effective manner, while also achieving higher profit margins.

Furthermore, customization can be done through involving the eventual customer, both spatially and temporally—thus, the addition of value is de-linked from typical factories, and labor costs are often reduced. As a simple example, a cafeteria prepares food in a standardized manner but places the food out for customers to make their own selections as they pass through the line.

Customers can also be involved before the production process begins, such as occurs when a new car purchaser orders a car in advance on-line, indicating the desired options. In the highly automated Audi plants, each car platform passing down the line includes a small box with a computer program representing the customer's chosen design features, and the robots at each station perform according to this program.

Different Contexts for OM Consulting

The set of operations problems facing clients today vary considerably by the context in which they occur. Exhibit 7.2 presents a useful framework for classifying four different contexts that raise different OM issues centering

Exhibit 7.2 Classification of Operations Challenges

	Domestic	Global
Single Facility	Configuration Issues (A)	Configuration and Communication Issues (B)
Multiple Facilities	Configuration and Coordination Issues (C)	Configuration, Coordination, and Communication Issues (D)

around two key dimensions: (1) the number of operations facilities involved from single to multiple, and (2) the geographical scope covered from domestic to global.

Clearly, the complexity of OM problems increases from single facility to multiple facilities, and from domestic to global spread. As the number of facilities increases, the coordination between them poses a significant problem, and similarly, the larger the spread in geography, the greater the communication difficulties involving language, culture, and local regulations/customs.

Single Facility/Domestic Issues

The typical problems facing consultants with clients in quadrant **A** are generally concerned with productivity and quality improvements. One way that these companies get into operational trouble is that they become a victim of their own success. Their products/services do so well in the local marketplace that their managements have only one goal in mind—to expand existing capacity in the same plant as fast as possible to keep up with demand. When this happens, procedures are trampled on, recruiting is haphazard, quality becomes variable, and the entire operation is stressed. A myriad of problems get embedded into the operations, and these issues last even after demand slows down.

Frequently, local demand is not as great as predicted to fill increased capacity; a better decision would have been to expand geographically to open a second factory in a new market.

Another challenge that frequently arises in this rapid growth scenario is the resulting large increase in inventories of raw material, work-in-process, and finished goods. This asset intensity starts to compromise profit and cash-flow performance, and even worse, it starts to impede production throughout and worker efficiency. Wrong product in the wrong place in the wrong quantity! Operations consultants typically will benchmark the operations to highlight the gap in performance between this company and best-in-class performance. Then, they will identify the sources of the problems, focusing on supply-demand coordination and its alignment with the planning process. The consultants in this case may propose new planning methods that sometimes are pilot tested before moving to full implementation.

This is also a chance to apply the philosophy of just-in-time and total quality management to see if more improvements can be made in productivity and quality. The OM consultant can check to determine whether the level of vertical integration in the company is too high, compared to best-in-class, and, if so, can then suggest outsourcing options. Finally, issues such as procurement and supplier management processes may also be audited to identify improvement potential.

Single Facility/Global Issues

For a company located in quadrant **B**, all of the challenges mentioned for quadrant **A** are applicable, plus even more! When facilities are in a foreign location, a variety of new issues arises pertaining to language, culture, local customs, and government regulations. For example, consider a US consumer household retailer who is expanding by opening additional retailing facilities in several Asian cities. The retailer's first instinct is to replicate its success in the United States by structuring its new facilities (layout, shelving, light fixtures, cash registers, parking lot, etc.) in exactly the same way.

However, many problems can arise. Besides the issue of managing procurement of goods that cater to local taste, the retailer may run into trouble if it tries to implement a just-in-time delivery model for replenishment. The availability of reliable logistics service providers can be questionable, especially if the overall infrastructure is lacking and the availability of large container-load trucks (as used in the United States) is difficult to predict. The company may also get into difficulty trying to outsource services such as food services, housekeeping, information services, etc.

Finally, the type of service culture needed in the US may be impossible to implement given the nature and customs of the local people. Thus, the consultants (and eventually the client company) will have to adjust their US-based notions of TQM, JIT, outsourcing, and lean operations to fit these other cultures.

Multiple Facilities/Domestic Issues

As companies expand and grow their businesses geographically, the natural tendency is to launch more new facilities, even if they are just stocking points—the case of a company in quadrant C. Sometimes when the business is not growing, there is a tendency for labor intensive companies to move centers of operations elsewhere in search of low-cost labor. Yet another rationale is to escape tough environmental rules and regulations that some countries impose. As soon as more facilities are added, the efficient configuration of the various facilities and their coordination becomes critically important.

Consider the case of a growing manufacturer who, due to pressures of customer service, decided to increase the number of regional distribution centers around the country or region. Clearly, while delivery was expected to improve, the inventory intensity also increased. As a result, as time went on, there was an increase in product variety, which greatly increased the amount of financial investment in inventory. Even worse, the delivery service performance began to decline!

Consultants are often called into situations like this to sort out the interfaces between manufacturing and the various distribution facilities. For example, how many stocking points should there be? Should the client company install a Distribution Requirements Planning system to mimic a pull-system of inventory planning while coordinating manufacturing supply and distribution demand? Should all the slow-moving items be stocked in only one facility, with the fast-moving items assigned to the remaining facilities? Should there be inventory pooling that allows for centralization of some stock and then use delivery via local courier service(s)? Should the client company outsource the transportation function or have their own trucks do the distribution?

Operations consultants utilize a variety of techniques to model the ideal functioning of a multi-facility system and then advise their clients on using principles of supply chain management and lean operations.

Multiple Facilities/Global Issues

When one adds the global dimension on top of a large number of facilities, the severity of problems increases dramatically—this is a multinational company in quadrant D. With trade barriers continuing to fall dramatically, the availability of financing globally, and the WTO enhancing the globalization of business, many new international opportunities are facing companies. Each must decide on what types of customers to serve, what suppliers to select, and where their own value-adding facilities should be located.

Consider the case example of a PC company, which uses partners from Asia and the United States to produce standard parts for their notebooks, LCD monitors, and hard drives. They also rely on suppliers such as Intel and Microsoft for supplying various components, and Chinese, Japanese, and Korean manufacturers to produce memory chips. The client company does all the final assembly in the US to customer order. Clearly, the company cannot increase inventories since product obsolescence will decimate the value of stocks. Time to market is also essential since competition is severe and customers remain fickle. Worst of all, the challenge of managing new product launches with myriads of suppliers located globally is extremely difficult because a small glitch can account for failure to deliver and a multi-million-dollar loss.

Operations consultants are called in to the company to resolve an internal debate between those who advocate a process focus (i.e., an assembly plant served by central manufacturers and outsourcers) and those who subscribe to a product focus (i.e., all the processes to make the product are self-contained in the plant).

For the OM consultants, the following questions (among others!) are on the client's agenda:

- Should a global production center produce all of a particular component for global demand in order to take advantage of economies of scale?
- Should there be assembly lines in each marketplace to customize products for that local market?
- With multiple stocking points in various countries, how does one optimize the level of inventories in the supply chain?
- What processes/products should the company produce internally and which ones should they outsource?
- How does one drive each of the facilities to be "best-in-class"?
- How should new product development be coordinated when design, component manufacturing, final assembly, and key customers are spread out across a variety of locations?
- What kind of software solution(s) should the client company use, such as collaborative forecasting, product data management, supply chain design and optimization, or enterprise resource planning, in order to connect their far-flung operations and to effectively plan, schedule, and execute efficient operations?

When the OM consultant considers the entire value chain (suppliers, alliance partners, channel) as the total unit of analysis in seeking performance improvements, one can imagine the explosion of consulting work in the global operations management area.

Analytical Tools of Operations Consultants

The operations consultant's tool kit consists of a wide variety of assessment tools, such as gap analysis, plant audits/tours, benchmarking, process analysis, capacity analysis, simulation, and optimization modeling.

Gap Analysis is commonly used to assess a client's performance relative to the expectations of its customers, or relative to the performance of its competitors along key dimensions. An example is shown above in Exhibit 7.3. Portraying data in this graphic form can be useful in gaining the client's attention and understanding of the OM issues involved.

Full Manufacturing Audits are a major undertaking, entailing measurement of all aspects of the production facility and processes, as well as support activities such as maintenance and inventory stock keeping.

Plant Tours, on the other hand, are usually much less detailed and can be done in a half day. The purpose of the tour is to get a general understanding of the manufacturing process before focusing on a particular problem area. The rapid plant assessment (RPA) tour,[8] which was created by a professor at Michigan, enables a consulting team to determine the "leanness" of a plant in just thirty minutes. Sample questions/inquiries include: Are ratings for customer satisfaction and product quality displayed? Is the plant laid out in continuous product line flows rather than shops?

Benchmarking as a process is well understood, and now consulting firms are incorporating write-ups of their benchmarking efforts in white papers to advertise the value of their services to potential clients.

Process Analysis and **Capacity Analysis** are basic to operations consulting. Process Analysis deals with improving each step of a process by changing the way it is done or eliminating it if it doesn't add value to the product or service. It may entail something as minor as eliminating a wasted motion in an assembly operation or something as major as transferring parts directly

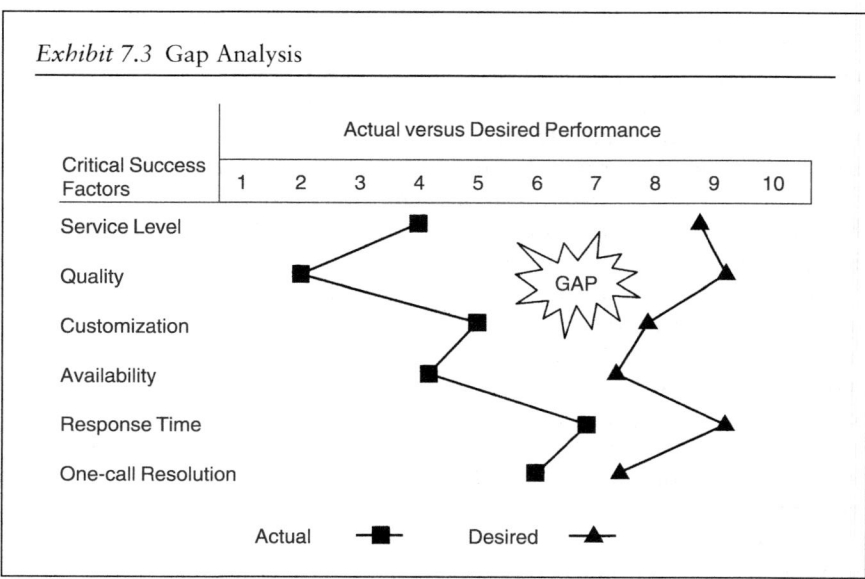

Exhibit 7.3 Gap Analysis

from the receiving dock to the assembly line rather than placing them temporarily in a stockroom.

Capacity Analysis deals with matching resource capabilities to production demand requirements over a specific period of time. It might focus on plant sizing in manufacturing or workforce staffing levels in services. Interestingly, process and capacity analysis are both low tech compared to recent developments in other analytical tools of simulation modeling and optimization modeling. Simple flowcharts and spreadsheet models are about all that are needed for capacity analysis; in contrast, the major consulting firms have developed sophisticated and often proprietary software tools for simulation analysis.

Practical Problems Facing OM Consultants

One of the practical problems facing operations consultants is that their clients demand quick results and their work is usually easily measurable. If there isn't an improvement in output, cost, quality, or flexibility as a result of the consultant's recommendations, the engagement is likely to be viewed as unsuccessful. The client demand for quick results often drives operations consultants to pick low hanging fruit, even if it is better to spend time on tougher problems. In an attempt to address client fears about accomplishing specific results over the long haul, some consulting firms offer service or performance guarantees. For instance, some major firms allow clients to choose from a menu of performance measurement options. For example, if the consultants do not cut lead time by x percent, clients can choose from among such options as refunds or gratis overtime consultant work to achieve the agreed upon results.

A second practical problem is the complexity of data gathering. Production reports, for example, are often highly idiosyncratic and poorly designed, having evolved from a time when the business was young. A case in point is the experience of one of the authors who was working with a major computer manufacturer that sold advanced production control packages while itself relying on homegrown desktop programs to track its own production. Even when various reports within a client's operations are state-of-the-art, the consultant must still figure out how to reconcile those that use different time periods or units of measure or both.

Similarly, problems arise when key information systems don't generate across-the-board performance data. Today's standard ERP systems, for example, provide detailed information on materials flow, forecast accuracy, and schedule performance but some don't provide Cost of Quality (COQ) reports. All of this calls for the consultant to possess the ability to ask the right question, at the right time, using a collaborative tone and tenor, and the tenacity to follow through to create a coherent picture of a system's strengths and weaknesses.

Sometimes, key clues to solving a production problem may lie in simple documents. For example, every assembly station in a plant has a "parts short list" that identifies the part or component which was unavailable for the production run that day and had to be rush-ordered from upstream operations. An analysis of this list could indicate whether parts were short due to quality problems or scheduling issues or again, both.

A third practical problem is that productivity improvements traditionally generate worker resistance. Of course, all consulting efforts normally lead to changes in some aspect of a client's business, but none has a stronger internal impact than changing the procedures by which work is done. It is no surprise that even a sophisticated workforce will feel threatened by operations consultants. This fear often translates, for instance, into foot dragging by a shop floor supervisor assigned to help the consultants gain access to data or to arrange interviews with appropriate operations personnel.

Finally, there is the challenge of working with other links in the supply chain. If the focus is on a factory, the OM consultant often has to establish a good relationship with suppliers upstream and distributors and retailers downstream because supply chain members can be a valuable source of insight into how a client's processes might be modified and ultimately improved.

Future Issues for OM Consulting

We predict several trends will continue to impact the market and skill-set of operations consultants for the foreseeable future.

Service Encounter Design

Although services are projected to constitute roughly 82–83 percent of GDP in the US, and about the same percentage of employment, the most pervasive of all business processes—the service encounter between customer and employee—is still approached in a highly unscientific fashion.[9] Most operations consultants' tool sets contain sophisticated simulations of waiting lines and call centers but are wholly inadequate in even the rudiments of service psychology.

Proper service design requires not only an understanding of the basic concepts of service quality (e.g., measurement, recovery planning, critical incident analysis) but also sophisticated psychological concepts flowing from behavioral decision theory. Here close attention needs to be paid to how customers perceive the passage of time and recall the flow of events that make up their service experience.[10] This continued need for behavioral expertise creates a major opportunity for future consulting in services operations.

What is striking to us is how little attention is paid in the operations consulting community to understanding what is already known about best practices in service encounters that accompany the core services of retailing, health care, education, etc. Consultants would be wise to take a page from the casino Harrah's book in going about achieving service excellence in a commoditize industry.

> **Consulting Insights—On Service**
>
> In late 1998 Harrah's, and many of the other original Las Vegas hotels and casinos, was facing a big problem—given the company's aging, undistinguished Las Vegas hotel and run-of-the-mill casino facilities, how could it compete with the architectural splendor of its competitors on the Vegas Strip?
>
> Of course, they could invest millions in an effort to create their own Bellagio, Paris, or Caesar's Palace, but at best about all they could do was just catch up. In analyzing the situation, a new management team headed by its then CEO, Gary Loveman, hit upon a novel idea for the gaming industry—how about competing based on *service?* Why service? Analysis showed that what was important from a service standpoint to gamblers was not having to wait in lines, as well as employee friendliness and helpfulness.
>
> Making sure that the customer doesn't have to wait for service to check in to the hotel, to get chips, or to get into the restaurants signals to customers that the company respects the value of their time. Even today, if you win a jackpot at Harrah's, you'll have someone there to help within ninety seconds. To further reduce waiting, Harrah's invested heavily in self-service technology, such as "players' cards" so guests can avoid waiting in line at the cashier's cage.
>
> Friendliness and helpfulness create a pleasant overall experience even when losing money. Employees are encouraged to talk to guests and are measured internally by supervisors and externally by mystery shoppers as a part of their "Spotlight on Success" program. Each department supervisor continues to communicate the message at the start of each shift to reinforce elements of Harrah's service culture— senior management do the same on a daily basis. To reward good service, Harrah's introduced a bonus program in which every employee receives a bonus for each quarter in which the measured level of service goes up by 3 percent or more.
>
> After crunching data, taking surveys, and conducting focus groups, Harrah's management initially discovered that gamblers who were more satisfied with their service experience also increased their gaming expenditures by 10 percent and that those who were extremely satisfied increased their gaming expenditures by 24 percent! The results of these efforts are high levels of customer loyalty and profitability that remain the envy of the industry![11]

Outsourcing and Virtual Integration

The restructuring of companies to focus resources on core competencies often turns to alliances and outsourcing partners to replace low priority activities, and this movement is creating a wealth of opportunities for operations consulting firms. For example, Accenture, while acting as a supplier of logistics services to firms, will contract with suppliers, warehouses, trucking, shipping, etc., and then manage the whole process for clients.

Another service that operations consulting companies have been trying to provide is the disposal of excess inventories in companies. Rather than sell it to liquidators at a drastically reduced price or go through the arduous process of selling through on-line outlets, consulting companies are offering liquidation services to their preferred clients.

Another common phenomenon involves consulting firms using their own personnel to staff such previously untouchable core positions as Purchasing Manager or Logistics Manager. In a similar vein, consultants may actually take on management roles for extended periods to help implement their solutions from an engagement and also help on recruiting and training of their replacements.

Global Supply Chains

As economies become more global and value-adding activities are spread across the world, the need for operations consultants to be capable in dealing with the global supply chain is becoming extremely important. For example, with the shift of so much manufacturing to China, India, and emerging Asian economies, clients now need for their operations consultants to deal with government regulations, state-owned suppliers, and be able to converse in a multitude of other languages.

Today's successful consulting firms are increasingly employing a multicultural workforce that can deal in many aspects of a client's value chain, which may stretch across several countries and continents. This means that the clients, like external consultants, need to understand the work environments, culture, and business practices in countries all over the world, so they can make rational business decisions.

Privatization/Deregulation

The worldwide movement toward market economies has created significant trading opportunities in Russia, China, and India as well as Eastern Europe, Latin America, and throughout ASEAN. Indeed, these countries and the companies located there have rushed to globalize their economies and restructure their companies to compete in the world economy.

Operations consultants can play a major role in helping to transform large state-owned companies to compete in the private-sector economy.

For example, as India continues to privatize its telecommunication industry, the government needs to know the best ways to structure the ensuing industry, how to set up regulatory structures, how to allow multinationals to enter into the marketplace, and also how to revamp state-owned companies.

This also includes work at the firm level where changes will be needed in operations infrastructure, workforce policies, and technology adoption so that these firms can compete in deregulated environments against multi-nationals.

Real-Time Technology

Information technology has changed the nature and scope of operations in most companies. In the last half of the 20th century, multi-nationals could possibly take from thirty to sixty days to close their accounting books at fiscal year-end. They needed that much time to figure out where inventories were located around the world.

Today, information technologies (e.g., Internet, client server architecture, global databases, ERP software, CRM software) have made information available and possible anywhere, anytime, and on any device (computer, telephone, PDA, etc.). This information revolution offers operations consultants many opportunities to determine how clients can better manage in a real-time environment.

It is quite reasonable to expect that innovative consulting companies will develop war-room versions of operations monitoring and make full use of "real-time" performance measures.

This also applies to companies leveraging technology to more effectively drive customer satisfaction. Samuel Greengard writes in his June 2014 online article "How to Provide World-Class Customer Service for Baseline," "A basic tenant of business has always been to keep the customer satisfied. Yet, over the last decade, the task has become infinitely more complicated as consumer expectations have grown and a mind-bending array of technologies and channels have entered the picture. . . ."

In his article Greengard quotes Scott Clarke, head of digital customer experience at Capgemini: "Customers are more sophisticated and demanding," says Clarke, "they want to interact with companies on their own terms, through the channel of their choice and with the device of their choice. This is forcing businesses to adapt."

Greengard goes on to say, "Not surprisingly, this new era of customer service is redefining relationships, including those between business and IT. As a growing array of technologies and processes intersect—and the connection points with customers grow—organizations must confront these challenges and construct a framework that fully supports the digital age. . . ."

The opportunities for the technologically savvy OM consulting firm appear endless.

Mass Customization in Services

The historic approach in services operations has been to: 1) find a successful concept; 2) standardize the service; and 3) scale up by franchising or stamping out the standard format globally. A classic and successful example of this approach is Wal-Mart—so successful that it opened more than 400 new stores in 2003. However, while this cookie cutter approach has worked in the past, it is in many ways close to running its course as more customers turn to on-line purchasing platforms for many of their day-to-day purchases.

There will be an increasing need for consulting firms to design systems for mass customization that apply to both the manufacturing and service sectors. With the advent of real-time information systems and the Internet, data about individual customers are being gathered in large quantities.

Data-mining techniques followed by decision support systems can allow services to customize many features that are important to customers and still standardize back-office activities to gain scale economies. Early on McKinsey published a report on what was then a new method called micro-market modeling, which uses local customer segmentation, operational analysis, and financial evaluation to customize services offered in different geographic locations.

The Challenge and Reward of OM Consulting

The moral for OM consultants is that to be successful, you actually have to make positive visible changes with a measurable impact on performance. More than any other consultant, you have to make recommendations that result in real improvements in the physical aspects of a manufacturing process or in the subjective experience of customers in services.

Even in high-level operations strategy consulting, there is pressure for the rubber to meet the road, whether in strategizing about supply chains, facility location, or technology choice. The visibility of OM consulting contrasts with other types of consulting where results are hard to see and measure. This is the challenge and the reward of operations consulting.

Notes

1 Treacy, M. and F. Wiersema, *The Discipline of Market Leaders* (Reading, MA: Addison Wesley, 1997).
2 Taylor, F.W., *The Principles of Scientific Management* (New York: Harper & Bros., 1911).
3 Peters, T.J., and R.H. Wasserman, *In Search of Excellence* (New York: Warner Books, 1984).
4 Pugh, S.D., J. Dietz, J.W. Wiley, and S.M. Brooks, "Driving Service Effectiveness Through Employee-Customer Linkages," *The Academy of Management Executive*, 16, no. 4 (2002): 73–85.

5 For a discussion of the Quality gurus and current TQM practices, see Chase, R. B., N. J. Aquilano, and R. F. Jacobs, *Operations Management for Competitive Advantage*, 9th ed. (Burr Ridge, IL: McGraw-Hill/Irwin, 2000): 258–289.
6 George, M. L., *Lean Six Sigma: Combining Six Sigma Quality with Lean Speed* (New York: McGraw-Hill, 2002).
7 The Theory of Constraints was developed by Eliyahu Goldratt and is part of the tool kit of virtually all manufacturing OM consultants. See: Goldratt, E. M., and J. Cox, *The Goal: A Process of Ongoing Improvement* (New York: North River Press, 1986).
8 Goodson, R. E., "Read a Plant-Fast," *Harvard Business Review*, 80, no. 5 (May 2002): 105–113. Also look at: Upton, D., and S. Macadam, "Why (and How) to Take a Plant Tour," *Harvard Business Review* (May–June 1997): 97–106.
9 A recent call to arms on this issue is presented in: Bowen, D. E., and R. Hallowell, "Suppose We Took Service Seriously? An Introduction to the Special Issue," *The Academy of Management Executive*, 16, no. 4 (2002): 69–72.
10 Chase, R. B., and S. Dasu, "Want to Perfect Your Company's Service? Use Behavioral Science," *Harvard Business Review* (June 2001): 79–84.
11 Gary, L., "Simplify and Execute: Words to Live By in Times of Turbulence: How Harrah's Bet on Loyalty Paid Off," *Harvard Management Update* (January 2003); and personal conversations with Gary Loveman (CEO) and John Bruns (Corporate Director of Customer Satisfaction Assurance) at Harrah's.

8 Human Resources Consulting: 2016

Gerald E. Ledford Jr. with Edward E. Lawler III and Susan Mohrman

The field of human resources (HR) consulting is large, extremely diverse, and highly dynamic. This chapter provides a view of the HR consulting marketplace and the types of individuals and consulting firms that occupy it, as well as the organizational actors who purchase and consume HR consulting services. It includes a discussion of different types of HR consulting services, the types of consultants who work in each area, the buyers and users of consulting services, and the scope and potential business impact of each type. The business of HR consulting has evolved rapidly and has become a major determinant of how consulting services are delivered and how people are managed in organizations.

Definitions

Human resources management is concerned with the structures, practices, and processes for managing people in an organization. It includes but is broader than the typical personnel processes that the HR department manages, such as talent acquisition, rewards, performance management, and learning and development. It also includes human resource strategy, the technology for managing HR processes, organization design and change, and other areas of practice that concern structures and process for managing people.

HR consulting involves providing expert advice and services on human resource management issues. Here we are primarily concerned with consulting services that take the form of projects that result in organizational decisions about HR strategies, policies, practices, and systems. HR consulting services can be and are provided by solo consultants and by large firms with thousands of employees, consulting projects can last from a few days to years, and projects may have a very narrow or very broad scope.

Our consideration of HR consulting will omit "guru consulting," an activity that is highly visible and lucrative for a few individual practitioners but very different from other HR consulting. We know of no studies or data about this market segment, but it is certainly tiny in size relative to the overall HR consulting market, despite its prominence. In this market, a handful of individuals who are prominent enough to be considered gurus command daily speaking fees that may exceed the annual income of many HR consultants. Gurus include professional speakers, personalities, authors, and professors who espouse a "hot," provocative point of view on an HR-related topic. Guru consulting is fundamentally different from other types of consulting in that its unit of service is the presentation, not a project that helps an organization to make specific decisions, create new processes, or design and implement changes. Indeed, gurus often have no experience or interest in guiding organizational action related to their topics. In the guru market, inspiration and entertainment are more important than action.

Market Size and Characteristics

There are a few studies of the HR consulting market; most notable are the Barnes Reports (2015) and IBISWorld (2016). These studies give a rough sense of the size and characteristics of the market, although none provides a complete perspective on HR consulting. Therefore, the available market data somewhat understate the size of the market, the number of practitioners, and the types of projects that HR consultants do. Also missing is good growth data, although there is little doubt that the market has grown significantly since our 2005 chapter was written.

Barnes Reports (2015) does not define HR consulting, but it lists major sub-industries (which also are not defined) as HR consulting services, compensation and benefits planning, incentive or award program consultants, employment agencies, labor and union relations consultants, personnel management consultants, programmed instruction service, and training and development consultants. This perspective focuses on only some of the segments that we see as important in HR consulting. It does cover most of the key issues that HR executives report their functions spend their time on (Lawler and Boudreau, 2015). The HR consulting market for just these segments is very large.

Barnes Reports (2015) indicates that the HR consulting U.S. market alone will be $24.5 billion in 2016. Some 16,608 firms employ 24,541 people (an average of only 3.8 per establishment), and both the number of firms and employment are down significantly since 2012 (both down 28%). Barnes Reports offers some interesting global data. The U.S. market is by far the largest market. The five next largest based on sales in U.S. dollars are somewhat surprising: China ($18.9 billion), Japan ($9.7 billion), Germany ($6.1 billion), and Brazil ($4.1 billion). China and India employ the most HR consultants, with 493,000 and 403,000 respectively, and they are the only countries that employ more than the U.S.

Using a somewhat different and much broader construction of the HR consulting market, IBISWorld (2016) indicates that the U.S. HR consulting market generates $22.7 billion in revenue, $2.2 billion in profit (for an average margin of almost 10%). It reports that industry growth has been faster than the growth of the overall economy but is slowing. The report indicates that an astounding 43,765 enterprises in the industry employ 182,904 people, up from employment of 141,268 (30%) in just the previous five years. This indicates that the average consulting firm employs four people. Average wages in the industry were $73,602 in 2016. Given that the compensation of senior consultants and principals in major firms is several times that amount, the median wage must be far lower.

IBISWorld (2016) focuses on personnel services in its report but includes other segments as well. Major market segments in its study are compensation and benefits (42% of total revenue), HR management consulting (34%), actuarial consulting (11%), and "other" (13%). Compensation and benefits is the largest, but executive, employee, and sales compensation and benefits have different practitioners, different buyers, different goals, and different business cycles. HR management consulting includes consulting on personnel programs and services, including supervision, training, performance management, and employee assessments. Actuarial consulting assesses risks and is used in creating various kinds of insurance programs, benefits, and financial programs. "Other" includes consulting on business strategies, custom computer applications, executive search, and advice on corporate restructuring.

IBISWorld (2016) characterizes the HR consulting market today as mature because it has revenue growth approximating the rate of the economy, accelerating merger and acquisition activity, established technology and process, market acceptance of its products, and rationalization of low margin products and brands. Consolidation clearly is occurring, and relatively large firms are emerging. For example, in 2010, Aon Consulting Worldwide merged with Hewitt Associates to form Aon Hewitt. Also in 2010, Towers Perrin merged with Watson Wyatt, and the combined entity merged with Willis to create Willis Towers Watson. More recently, executive recruiter Korn Ferry acquired Hay Associates.

The differences in the data between the Barnes Reports and IBISWorld reflect the different segments of the market that they cover. Barnes focuses more on the lower margin segments traditionally associated with personnel services, while the IBISWorld data includes other, higher margin, growing segments such as HR strategy consulting and some HR technology work. This difference is reflected not only in the size of the market reported, but also in the overall growth of the HR consulting market reported in the two studies.

Types of HR Consulting

There are seven major streams of HR consulting: human capital strategy, HR technology, organization design, organizational change, HR process reengineering, HR outsourcing, and HR program design and execution.

Human capital strategy involves developing an HR strategy that supports, enables, and influences the business strategy of a particular organization. A classic strategy issue is the decision about whether to "make, buy, or rent" (hire and train new employees, hire trained employees from elsewhere, or outsource) particular types of employees that are essential to the business strategy.

HR technology consulting involves helping an organization choose the best technology solutions and implementing technology to assist with tasks such as tracking employee work hours, managing payroll, and assisting with other HR transactional processes. Organization design helps organizations create the structures and processes that support their business strategies. A classic problem is determining whether a functional structure, a business unit structure, matrix, or some more complex structure is the best fit for the organization's needs. Organization change is variously called organization development, change management, and organizational effectiveness, and involves helping management to manage major changes in the organization. For example, consultants may help manage the process of integrating the employees into an acquired company or help management learn to behave in a less cumbersome, bureaucratic manner. HR process reengineering involves helping the organization redesign its work processes to increase effectiveness, reduce costs, and/or increase work quality. This may include changing work designs, communication patterns, reporting relationships, and information systems.

HR outsourcing involves hiring outside vendors to provide services. Typically this involves outsourcing routine, transactional processes such as payroll or retirement plan administration, but in rare cases can involve outsourcing of the entire HR function. Finally, HR program design and execution entails designing and operating programs that are part of one or more HR processes, such as talent acquisition, compensation, benefits, learning and development, careers, or succession planning.

Types of HR Consultants

The traditional HR consultancies still play a major role in HR consulting. Large firms in this space include Aon Hewitt, Willis Towers Watson, Mercer (part of Marsh McLennan), and the Hay Group (now part of Korn Ferry). IBISWorld (2016) indicates that Aon Hewitt has a 10 percent share, Willis Towers Watson has a 4.8 percent share, and Marsh & McLennan (including Mercer and other firms) has a 4.4 percent share. These firms are able to handle multi-million dollar assignments from the largest global companies, can deploy large teams to staff projects, and can offer services in every segment of the market. There are innumerable mid-sized, small, and tiny firms that handle HR consulting assignments, usually specializing in a very limited number of areas of HR. For example, there are dozens of firms that only assist in the management of employee recognition programs, including providing merchandise services and gift cards that are used in these programs.

The major accounting firms, including PWC, Deloitte, Ernst & Young, and KPMG, have human resource consulting practices. Over the years, these firms have built large human resource consultancies, divested them when regulators viewed such consulting as constituting a conflict of interest with their core accounting services, and rebuilt their human resource consulting operations when the regulatory climate became more favorable.

Many of the major strategy consulting firms, including McKinsey, Booz Allen Hamilton, and Bain & Company, offer HR consulting services, often called "human capital consulting." The strategy firms have built, downsized, and rebuilt their human resource consulting practices over the years as market demand has waxed and waned. Several firms operate at the intersection of strategy, operations, IT, and outsourcing, including Accenture, Capgemini, and AT Kearny. Their offerings always have included some type of HR consulting expertise due to the people issues involved in their specialties. Finally, a wide variety of large firms with other primary businesses also do some HR consulting, including information technology firms such as IBM, outsourcing vendors such as ADP, "best practice research" firm CEB, and executive search firm Korn Ferry (largely through the Hay Group).

Firms with a primary consulting business outside of the HR consulting industry, such as McKinsey, tend to specialize their work rather than to develop a comprehensive HR consulting offering. For example, the strategy firms gravitate to human capital strategy and organization design consulting. IT-oriented firms tend to offer HR technology consulting and organizational change consulting, because systematic change management is a core process in technology implementation. Operations firms tend to offer HR technology, change management, and process reengineering solutions. The accounting firms, especially Deloitte and PWC, come closest to rivaling the HR consulting firms in providing services for most or all types of HR consulting, although different firms concentrate on different areas. For example, Deloitte has an especially prominent HR technology implementation business.

Although we have emphasized large brand-name consulting firms in illustrating the types of firms in the marketplace, small firms perform a great deal of HR consulting. IBISWorld indicates that there are almost 44,000 U.S. consultancies in this space, most of them very small. Perhaps the major reason for this is that there are very low barriers to entry in HR consulting. Licenses and other formal credentials are required only in a few specialized areas, little capital investment is required for most types of HR consulting, and there is relatively little government regulation of the industry.

The HR consulting industry is mature with few new products and services, and competition among HR consulting firms is intense. The largest, global firms tend to give most of their consulting assignments to the largest consultancies, which have the manpower and global footprint to meet the requirements of such firms. Smaller organizations tend to be more price-sensitive, and are more likely to employ smaller and mid-sized HR consulting firms. However, there is considerable overlap between size segments, and large clients sometimes use small consulting firms, and small clients sometimes use large consultancies.

Buyers of HR Consulting Services

There is a distinction in the marketing of consulting services between the financial buyer and user buyers. The financial buyer, quite simply, is the person or group with the funding to purchase consulting services. In the case of HR services, the corporate or business unit executives outside of HR often are the financial buyer and the HR department must rely on these executives for final approval of some or all projects. The larger the project scope and cost, the more likely it is that the financial buyer will be outside the HR function. Some types of projects are typically funded by a financial buyer from outside of HR, including major HR technology projects, large organization design projects, process reengineering, and outsourcing projects.

User buyers are those who deal with consultants day-to-day in program development and ultimately use the services that the consultants provide. User buyers can include HR managers, line managers, the information technology function, and other groups. User buyers typically influence the process of purchasing consulting services by shaping project specifications, and their assistance may be essential to the success of the project.

We know of no data on who the buyers of HR services are, but it is clear that many types of HR consulting services are provided by firms from outside the traditional HR consulting market. HR consulting firms tend to be dominant in HR program design and execution and HR process outsourcing, but other types of consulting firms are able to use their access to buyers from outside the HR function to gain business in all other types of consulting services. Overall, the more visible the project is to the executive suite, the higher the price tag, and the more risk to the organization the project presents, the more likely it is that other types of consultancies will have a significant market share.

An Overview of the HR Consulting Field

Table 8.1 provides a summary of the major segments of the HR consulting market, the types of consultants who do the most work in each segment, as well as the primary financial buyers, user buyers, project scope, and potential business impact in each area. Our characterizations of potential project impact may be controversial in some quarters. We believe that the rows near the top of the figure are more likely to represent large projects with a large potential business impact than are those at the bottom of the chart. That is precisely why the financial and user buyers are more likely to be in

Table 8.1 Major Types of HR Consulting

Type of Consulting	Project Example	Type of Consultants	Primary Client(s)	User Buyers	Typical Project Scope	Maximum Business Impact
Human Capital Strategy	Whether to "make, buy, or rent" talent	Strategy, HR, accounting	Top executives, CHRO	Business managers, HR	Small to large	Very large
HR Technology	Implementation of Workday HR suite	IT, HR, accounting	Top executives, CHRO	IT, HR, management, employees	Large to huge	Very large
Organization Design	Fix the way our network organization works	Organization design, strategy, HR, accounting	Top executives	Business managers, HR	Moderate to large	Very large
Organization Change	Help with integration of an acquired company	Change management, HR, IT, accounting	Top executives, business managers	Top executives, business managers	Small to large	Large
HR Process Improvement or Reengineering	Streamline workflow, reduce cost of talent acquisition	Strategy, HR, accounting, IT, organization design	HR	HR, business managers, IT	Moderate to large	Moderate
HR Outsourcing	Vendor servicing of retirement plans	HR, IT, specialized outsourcers	Top executives (large-scale), HR (smaller scale)	HR, managers	Moderate to very large	Very large
HR Program Design and Execution	Create a new incentive plan	HR, accounting	Executives, HR, Managers	HR, managers	Small to moderate	Moderate

the executive suite for assignments in these segments, and why the price tags for projects in the top rows of the figure are, on average, much higher than for projects in the bottom rows. Most multi-million dollar consulting assignments are outside of HR program design and execution, although there certainly are projects of that size in the HR program design and execution segment. The risk and impact of decisions to outsource HR services, change an organization's design, or adopt a new HR technology platform or a new human capital strategy is likely to be far greater than for the typical HR program change.

Projects in any of the market segments can have an important impact on business results. For example, one of the authors of this chapter was part of a team that helped a Fortune 100 firm overhaul its sales rewards program, and an internal study by the client company indicated that the project had a return on investment of over $100 million from higher sales and reduced turnover of top sales performers. However, most HR program design and execution projects are smaller in scope and impact and do not attract much visibility with senior executives.

Our primary conclusion is that HR consulting firms do not provide most HR consulting services, and most buyers of HR consulting services are not part of the HR function. This is particularly true for projects in market segments that are likely to have the greatest cost, risk, and value-added potential for the client organization. Further, there is no reason to believe this will change in the next decade.

Conclusion

As lot has changed in the last decade with respect to how HR consulting is delivered and what is delivered, but it remains true that HR consulting is inseparable from the future of the HR function in organizations. It is changing and will continue to change. Thus, the next decade is likely to see many changes in the HR consulting world. They are likely to include major changes in technology, strategy, and the offerings of consulting firms.

References

Barnes Reports. (2015) *Worldwide Industry & Market Outlook*. Bonita Springs, FL: Barnes Reports.

IBISWorld (2016). *IBISWorld Industry Report 54161b: HR Consulting in the US*. Los Angeles, CA: IBISWorld.

Lawler, E. E., and Boudreau, J. W. (2015). *Global Trends in Human Resource Management: A Twenty-Year Analysis*. Palo Alto, CA: Stanford University Press.

Part III
Consulting in Different Contexts

9 Consulting to CEOs and Boards (MARK B. NADLER AND DAVID A. NADLER, MERCER DELTA CONSULTING)	187
10 Consulting on the Global Stage (MATTHEW C. HEIM, INNO 360)	209
11 Public Sector Consulting (THOMAS H. OLSON, UNIVERSITY OF SOUTHERN CALIFORNIA)	228

Introduction

Management consulting is "contextually bound"—or in plainer words, "one size doesn't fit all." The challenge facing every consultant is to strike a balance between relying on the generalizations inherent to many consulting concepts and models, while also ensuring relevance and adaptation of unique solutions to specific client situations. In many ways, every client is special and different, yet the astute consultant cannot start over each time. Rather, an intermediate ground advocates that the consultant be aware of certain broad classifications of contexts, such as financial services versus high-tech manufacturing, where certain patterns of client behavior and consulting issues can be anticipated.

This section highlights three important contexts among the many that exist in management consulting—the CEO and boardroom consulting, global consulting, and public sector consulting. We selected these three major areas because they have become much more relevant and important and perhaps even dominant today and likely to continue to do so into the future. Not covered here, but still very important, is the uniqueness of certain industries, such as pharmaceuticals, communications, high technology, retailing, and so forth. Also not recognized here is the varying size of organizations where some clients may be smaller entrepreneurial ventures while others are vast holding/more global companies. We have drawn the line rather arbitrarily around our chosen three practice areas, which have been, and may be, lesser known or experienced by many consultants. We hope their coverage will alert the reader to be broadly sensitive to all contexts and to be more alert to the kinds of issues—economic, organizational, or technological—that will likely be encountered.

Chapter 9, on "Consulting to CEOs and Boards" provides us with an inside look at many of the issues facing these CEOs and Boards as each grapples to be more effective. The chapter points out the powerful advantages of having a CEO as a client yet warns us that this client requires a form of consulting unlike most other kinds of consulting. Most consultants are not prepared for consulting at this level. Many new pressures face CEOs today that were not present five to ten years ago. These new pressures involve needing to deal with more strident stakeholders to winning over an entire workforce in achieving a more shared commitment to major changes in strategy and organization. There are also stages to a CEO's tenure, with each stage presenting unique problems and solutions. The chapter concludes by closely examining Boards and the need for them to become a team, not a loosely connected group. It also considers the complex relationship between the CEO and the Board and how the consultant can sometimes assist both parties but runs the risk of becoming trapped in the middle of a complex political context.

Another important context for consulting is clearly the global arena, which is covered in Chapter 10 on "Consulting on the Global Stage." Most companies today, including small ones, find themselves doing much more business on an international basis, and frequently they need assistance in dealing with complex issues arising from different cultures, economies, and political systems. This chapter presents the *Global Consulting Approach Model* as a platform to describe how to conceptualize a global consulting project for a client. Each of the six elements of the *Global Consulting Approach Model* represents a separate dimension to consider for each and every consulting project. The six elements involve local markets and customers, local skills and practices, local cultural nuances, local law and regulations, global and local supply chain, and global client organization.

Chapter 11, on "Public Sector Consulting," explores a third context—federal, state, and local government. The focus is on the federal government as a rapidly changing and growing sector—though one in which private sector trained consultants often have little if any training and/or experience.

The public sector has grown considerably in the past decades and has become a significant market for consulting and contactor firms. The author makes clear that consulting in the public sector requires a special understanding and sensitivity on the part of consultants to the multi-purposes of government and the cumbersome bureaucracy and contracting process that affects business development—particularly due to significant differences driven in government contract acquisition.

The author observes that differences with government vs. business consulting services typically evolve about what or how professional services are "requested" and managed. Examples of differences (that need to be understood) by consultants new to the public sector are topics relating to: government requests for proposals (RFPs) of services, understanding and responding to specific requirements (in the RFP) involved in proposing contracts for services, the role of government "intermediaries" (typically known as "Contract Officers"), transparency in the bidding and feedback on proposals, etc. Further, individual/organizational privacy and other rights and issues will differ depending on variations in law under which the business and/or government is legislated. These topics (including the contractual requirements of Federal Acquisition Regulation—FAR, etc.) are discussed in more detail in this chapter.

The author further observes that while the private sector is made up of entities that are not owned or run by government, the public sector is made up of entities that are owned and run by government (federal, state, and municipal in the US with variations to these distinctions depending on country). The consulting/contractor businesses that provide the bulk of these public sector consulting services and contracts are, therefore, the focus of this chapter. The chapter concludes by observing that public sector consultants will be continually challenged by ever increasing complexity and response time. This will, in turn, make consulting in the public sector quite demanding and rife with opportunity.

9 Consulting to CEOs and Boards

Mark B. Nadler and David A. Nadler

Chief Executive Officers and boards of directors have long availed themselves of a wide array of advisory services, particularly in specialized technical areas such as law, finance and executive compensation. But in recent decades, that interest among CEOs and, more recently, boards of directors, has expanded into relatively new areas focusing on both individual and organizational effectiveness. As the role of both the CEO and the board has changed dramatically, so too has the role of the senior, trusted advisor in both the C-suite and the boardroom.

For consultants, the change is rooted in two closely related developments in corporate governance – most specifically, but not exclusively, in the U.S. The first, dating back to the 1990s, was the gradual disappearance of the traditional "imperial CEO" model of corporate governance, where nearly all real power resided with a single individual who held the titles of both CEO and chairman of the board. Starting at about the same time – and then turbocharged by the powerful backlash against the corporate scandals of the early 2000s and the financial crash of 2008 – there has been an accelerating rise in the power of the board of directors. Responding to both regulatory and marketplace pressures, boards are becoming more active and engaged, less subservient to management and more directly accountable to shareholders. The result has been an historic shift in the balance of power at the top of the organization, with enormous implications for those of us who consult to leaders at that level.

Our intent in this chapter is to provide a perspective on the special nature of consulting to CEOs and boards. Although our focus is on consulting in the context of the U.S., much of what we have to say is likely to apply to corporations based abroad, as well. While there are significant differences across geographies in the roles of both CEOs and boards, there are some fundamental similarities in the dynamics involved in working at the top of the organization.

We also hope to dissipate some of the mystery that seems to enshroud consulting at this level. To be sure, relatively few of the many thousands of management consultants have personal experience with what goes on behind the closed doors of the CEO's office or in the inner sanctum of the boardroom. The consultation that takes place in these obscure venues, by its very nature, is highly sensitive and absolutely confidential, leading to a variety of misconceptions about the nature of the work and relationships between consultants and senior executives. As we'll describe in this chapter, the reality can be incredibly challenging, risky and rewarding – but at the end of the day, it's like any other kind of consulting: if you're not producing substantive results, you're not invited back.

Consulting to CEOs

The key to consulting to CEOs – regardless of the kind of company they lead – is to understand the world in which they operate. It is a world like no other. For years, the financial press and entertainment media have popularized a simplistic stereotype of an all-powerful "celebrity CEO" – a Steven Jobs or Mark Zuckerberg – who dreams big dreams, barks precise orders and then sits back and watches everyone leap to obey.

Nothing could be further from the truth.

In reality, the CEO sits at the center of a universe of stakeholders, both internal and external, who constantly try to impose difficult and often conflicting agendas (see Exhibit 9.1). Each set of stakeholders has its own expectations, interests and standards for judging the CEO's performance. The CEO must constantly weigh the importance of these stakeholders and the legitimacy of their demands, and then balance them against his or her own vision, strategy and goals.

The exact nature and relative importance of stakeholder groups will vary, depending upon the company's corporate structure (e.g., public, private, family-owned, private equity portfolio, etc.), its stage of growth and the state of the business.[1] But these constituencies are always present in some form, and generally are categorized as either internal or external stakeholders. The external stakeholders include the *value chain constituencies* – customers, suppliers, strategic partners and the financial community. There are also external *social* constituencies – which often exert demands that conflict with those of the value chain constituencies – including government agencies, regulators, the press, interest groups, local communities and society at large. Internally, the CEO deals with several stakeholder *employee* groups who, again, can impose conflicting demands – the executive team, middle management, unions and various employee groups. The final stakeholder group, which encompasses both internal and external constituencies, is the *shareholder investor*, ranging from what has emerged as the CEO's most important stakeholder – the board of directors – to the wide variety of shareholders ranging from huge institutional investors, hedge funds and day traders to employees and retirees.

Exhibit 9.1 The CEO's Universe of Stakeholders

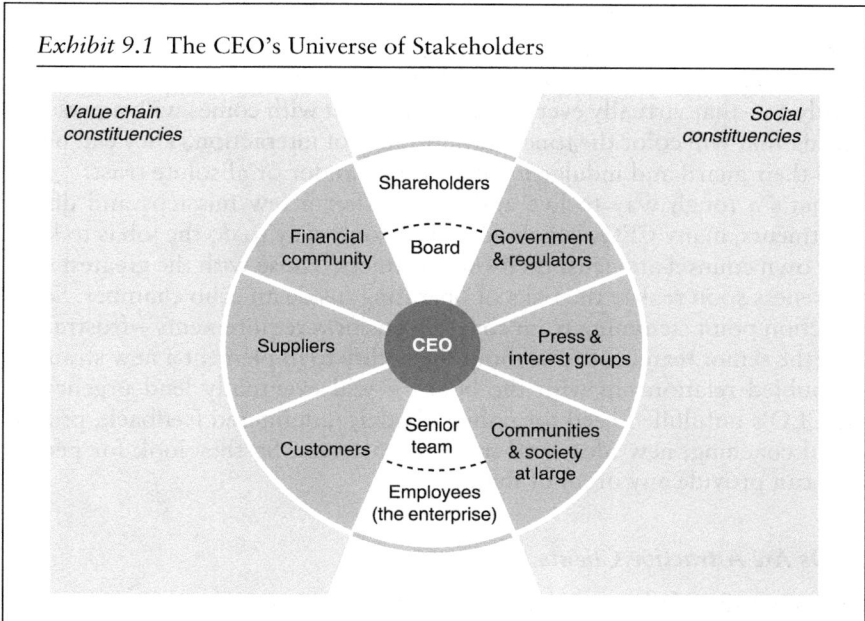

The one aspect of the CEO's job that makes it so unique is that he or she is the only individual in the entire organization who is in direct contact with – and personally held accountable by – the full universe of stakeholders. No one else in the organization has a job that comes close in terms of scope of responsibility and complexity of major decisions.

Today's CEO is also required to fill a wide array of roles – ambassador and chief spokesman to the outside world, chief strategist, leading deal-maker, articulator of the corporate vision, role model for the company values, cultivator of top talent, leader of the senior team and, in about 39 percent of U.S. public companies, chairman of the board. On a daily basis, the CEO, more than anyone else, must deal with the demands and expectations of multiple constituencies. They are surrounded by people seeking access, attention and approval in pursuit of all sorts of personal and institutional agendas. And CEOs are acutely aware that any misstep can dramatically increase the chances of failure.

One other factor defines the CEO's world: the timeworn yet accurate cliché that "it's lonely at the top." Anyone who has worked closely with CEOs can attest to their sense of isolation. They have no peers inside the organization, and few on the outside who they can talk to with complete confidentiality. Rarely can they step out from behind the desk, even for a few moments, and share their deepest concerns with anyone in the company. As one new CEO admitted, "The thing that is the greatest surprise to me in this job is the intense and profound loneliness." They are convinced – and rightly so – that virtually every person they meet with comes with a personal agenda that will color the tone and substance of interaction. They can never drop their guard and indulge in either total candor or absolute trust.

That's a tough way to live and work. After a few missteps and disappointments, many CEOs conclude that the only way to do the job is to keep their own counsel and trust their own instincts. Those with the greatest self-awareness soon realize the risks of operating inside an echo chamber. Some inflection point stemming from concrete business requirements – frustration with the senior team, concern about the ability to implement a new strategy, a troubled relationship with the board – will eventually lend urgency to the CEO's unfulfilled need for unbiased advice, unfiltered feedback, professional coaching, new ideas and fresh perspectives. So they look for people who can provide any or all of that.

CEOs Are Attractive Clients

Let's state the obvious: many consultants seek CEO clients for the status it confers. Consulting to the top of the client organization implies you are at the top of your own profession. In large consulting firms, having CEO clients not only elevates you to an elite status within your own company, but also positions you as the ultimate "owner" of the relationship with the client organization and all that implies in terms of overseeing the sales and delivery strategy – and the associated fees.

But for many of us, the primary attraction is the actual work. We are drawn by the inherent importance and complexity of the issues, the unique cast of characters we'll deal with and the professional challenge to help a client solve some of the knottiest problems imaginable. There's an undeniable vicarious thrill in being personally involved – even from the sidelines – in decisions that shape a company's future. And if we're honest with ourselves, we'll admit to the personal satisfaction that comes from having these important, powerful, sometimes charismatic leaders turn to us for guidance. It would be both silly and dishonest to discount the personal and professional gratification that often comes from consulting at this level.

Perhaps most importantly, consulting directly to CEOs offers the greatest opportunity for providing real value to client organizations. While others in the organization have vital roles to play, the CEO is the ultimate driver of transformative, sustainable, enterprise-wide change. As frustrating as the CEO's job might be, only he or she has access to all the levers for implementing major changes – the ability to shape the strategy, the organization structure, the culture and the talent. The CEO enjoys more degrees of freedom for taking broad action than any other leader in the organization; he or she is the final decision maker and the ultimate arbiter of all appeals.

Consequently, CEOs are in greater need of outside advice than just about anyone in the organization. They have no peers in the organization, no internal aide whose advice isn't colored by some agenda. Every CEO can benefit from the advice and counsel of an experienced, objective, dispassionate professional whose only agenda should be to enhance the CEO's effectiveness and, by extension, the organization's success.

What kind of consulting a CEO needs often depends on what stage they're at in their tenure. In very general terms, we have observed four fairly distinct phases in a CEO's tenure when different kinds of consultation tend to be most appropriate[2]:

Perplexed new CEO. As soon as a newly appointed, first-time CEO finishes celebrating the good news, they inevitably pause and ask themselves, "OK – now what? How do I get started, and what should I do first?" Depending upon the circumstances – whether they've been promoted internally or recruited externally, whether the company is on an even keel or reeling from a crisis, whether it was a planned or emergency succession, whether they're an industry veteran or newcomer – the new CEO will require help on any number of fronts. Perhaps more than anything, the new CEO needs a safe place to acknowledge concerns, test out ideas or simply talk through frustrations – all without feeding the rumor mill or sending misleading signals to the financial markets.

Frustrated sophomore CEO. Entering the second year in office, the CEO has a clear strategy and detailed plan of action, but not much is actually happening. A few years ago, the second-year CEO of a large pharmaceutical company complained to us that he felt like he was on the bridge of a large ship, busily manipulating all the controls and then finding that none of them were attached to anything. It's a common frustration among sophomore CEOs, as they personally experience the countless internal barriers to setting an organization of any complexity on a new course. Many decide they need to look outside the organization for help in overcoming the forces of inertia and re-energizing their initial agenda.

Worried mid-term CEO. Given the volatility of today's business environment, every CEO can expect to experience at least one major crisis – and probably more – that will require radical, large-scale organizational change. It might result from new forms of competition, disruptive technologies or shifts in public policy. Whatever the cause, the organization has to find fundamentally new ways of doing business. Many CEOs seek outside help in thinking through the top-level strategy for designing, managing and sustaining change on that scale.

Reflective late-term CEO. While recent trends in governance have shifted the dominant role in executive succession from the CEO to the board, the CEO still has a critical role to play in terms of managing the identification and development of potential successors. In reality, as we've described elsewhere, CEO succession is one of the most politically and personally sensitive topics that any board and CEO will ever have to deal with.[3] It often benefits from the involvement of an outside advisor who can help the CEO and the board understand their particular roles, design the process and initiate meaningful, if often difficult, conversations.

A special case: Understanding the CEO's "Second Act." Boards will sometimes select a new CEO who seems particularly well qualified to handle a major crisis or execute a new strategy, such as a merger, downsizing or geographic expansion, which will fundamentally reshape the business. The problem comes once the CEO has successfully completed that specific mission – "Act One" – and then faces the challenge of leading an Act Two which often requires a distinctly different set of capabilities. In fact, the more specifically the CEO's skills match the particular demands of Act One, the greater the risk that he or she lacks the experience or skills required in Act Two. At that point, the CEO needs to understand whether the emerging job profile is something he or she can – or even wants to – do, or whether it's in everyone's best interests to start thinking about a successor. That kind of candid self-appraisal often benefits from the help of an outside advisor.

Understanding the Spectrum of Consulting Roles

A new consulting engagement with a CEO starts with a very specific problem. CEOs do not tell their head of HR to go find them an all-purpose senior trusted advisor; as one of our colleagues used to say, "The CEO didn't hire you because he's looking for a new best friend." The consultant's ability to grow that initial work into a comprehensive, long-term relationship is shaped by two factors: the actual content of the work they're engaged in, and the behavioral approach the consultant employs to engage the CEO with the content. In other words, every outside advisor is interacting with the CEO along two key dimensions, represented as the vertical and horizontal axes in Exhibit 9.2.

- **Ideas versus Actions:** Does the advisor bring fresh perspectives, information on best practices or a new "Big Idea"? Or is he or she helping the CEO to identify specific actions to take in order to address a specific issue? Is the consultant focusing on the "what" or the "how"?
- **Prescriptive versus Facilitative:** Does the advisor recommend a specific decision, or does he or she view his or her role as helping the client to identify a range of alternatives and providing a process through which the client can make the most appropriate choice?

The work of every consultant, specialist and advisor to CEOs combines some mix of these two dimensions. Their interplay suggests that most CEO-level consulting falls into one or more of these six roles:

- **Technician:** Highly prescriptive about specific actions the CEO should take (e.g., crisis communications, legal strategies for handling specific litigation.)

- **Guru:** Also highly prescriptive, but with focus on concepts or ideas at an abstract level, rather than specific actions.
- **Content Expert:** Somewhat prescriptive, offering advice and opinions on areas in which the consultant specializes, such as leadership, strategy or organization change.
- **Process Facilitator:** Brings participative skills and approach to help clients identify their problems and create their own solutions.
- **Coach:** A pure facilitation role focusing on the client's personal development rather than on broader organizational issues.
- **Sage:** A rare and unique role where the advisor brings new ideas but interacts in a facilitative manner to help the CEO think through significant issues. This role usually occurs in combination with one or more of the other roles.

Of course, these categories are somewhat arbitrary. As consulting relationships extend over time, they become increasingly complex; distinctions grow fuzzy; roles merge. And that's our point; consulting relationships, like any other relationships, are dynamic and complicated. Those that succeed inevitably change, deepen and grow over the course of the CEO's tenure.

With that in mind, we offer two observations regarding these relationships:

First, successful, long-term advisors can start in almost any of the roles, but invariably end up combining two or more roles. Less effective consultants tend to get stuck where they started, both in terms of their content domain and delivery approach.

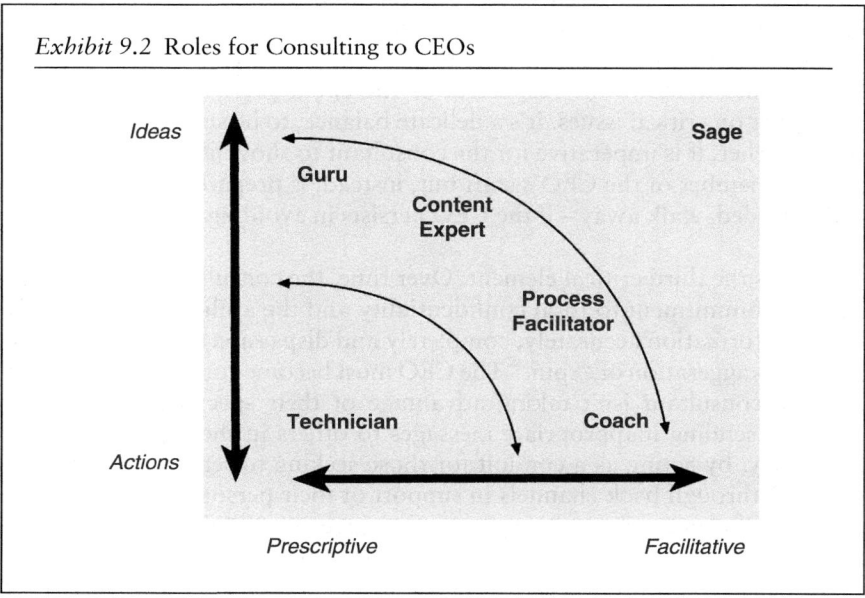

Exhibit 9.2 Roles for Consulting to CEOs

Second, in addition to specific roles, the successful consultant ultimately assumes the role of "trusted advisor." In their insightful book, *The Trusted Advisor*,[4] Maister, Green and Galford suggest that trustworthiness results from the interplay of four key components: credibility, reliability, intimacy and, the one to be wary of, self-orientation. It's an interesting way of defining a complex relationship; as the term "trusted advisor" continues to gain currency, there will undoubtedly be others. But the underlying idea is right: technical expertise, in the absence of a trusting relationship, will result in seriously diminished opportunities for impact. So it is important to understand how these rare relationships are developed and sustained over time.

Developing the CEO Relationship

It's important to remember that the role of "trusted advisor" is the goal, not the starting point, of a CEO consulting relationship. The relationship almost always begins with a very specific assignment to help with a particular problem. If the relationship progresses well, the focus gradually expands into a broader role encompassing a much wider range of issues. The relationship must evolve naturally; consultants who walk into the room for the first time and immediately attempt to create an artificial "trusted advisor" relationship are doomed to failure.

Our own experience suggests that several elements are critical to building this relationship – a list not too dissimilar from that suggested by *The Trusted Advisor*.[5] First and foremost, the relationship must be built on a foundation of substantive, *high-quality work* and beneficial advice. It doesn't matter how terrific the personal chemistry may be between the consultant and the CEO if the work doesn't add value and the advice doesn't make sense.

The second critical element goes to the *tone* of the engagement process; the consultant should be respectful of the client yet willing to confront him or her on critical issues. It's a delicate balance, to be sure. But as we suggested earlier, it is imperative for the consultant to show he or she is not just another member of the CEO's staff but, instead, is prepared to push back – and if needed, walk away – if the CEO persists in avoiding an issue or ignoring data.

Trust is the third critical element. Over time, the consultant must demonstrate a commitment to total confidentiality and the ability to consistently deliver information accurately, completely and dispassionately, without distortion, exaggeration or "spin." The CEO must become completely confident that the consultant isn't taking advantage of their special relationship – either by sending inappropriate messages to others in the organization or, conversely, by acting as a conduit for those seeking to send information to the CEO through back channels in support of their personal agendas.

The final element is *positive personal engagement*. In essence, this is the corollary of the first element. Without substantive, value-added work and advice, the relationship goes nowhere; yet, as a client once observed, "If

I don't enjoy the personal relationship, it doesn't matter how smart you are – I won't keep working with you." Personal chemistry is critical to the trusted advisor relationship.

Process Determines Content

While there are certainly similarities between the process of consulting to CEOs and to other executives, there are also important differences. For example, asking questions rather than providing answers – frequently a useful approach – takes on particular importance with CEOs. By nature, many CEOs tend to be more oriented toward action than introspection. Their role demands the ability to evaluate a situation, make a decision and move on, rather than spending much time on reflection or second-guessing. The consultant is uniquely positioned to provide the CEO with a safe space in which to step back and reflect privately and confidentially on concerns, doubts and sources of anxiety about impending business decisions. The simple question, "What's keeping you up at night?" may sound trite, but it's amazing how often it elicits a revealing response.

The process of consulting to CEOs emphasizes discussion over detailed explanation and authoritative conclusions. Its greatest value lies in the informal give and take, not formal presentations. That's an important and often difficult hurdle for some consultants to overcome; many have become accustomed to marching into any client meeting armed with a thick, carefully rehearsed Power Point presentation. That's the last thing a CEO wants to see in a private meeting, where they have neither the time, interest nor attention span to sit through a detailed data dump.

Certainly, there are situations – generally, in group settings – where the CEO will want to see data presented in a formal way. Nor does the idea of an informal, private discussion diminish in any way the importance of careful preparation, which includes bringing vital data to the meeting but "keeping it in your back pocket," introducing it only if and when it is appropriate. Most importantly, these meetings must be tailored to the CEO's schedule, energy and priorities, and the consultant must have the flexibility to use whatever time is available in the most beneficial way. A good deal of value that the consultant may provide comes from structuring information so as to give a fresh viewpoint; the consultant provides a cognitive "frame" to structure significant information in ways that are informative, insightful and meaningful to the client. Effective consultants go beyond gathering data; they help the CEO to translate data into knowledge, and knowledge into action.

Sometimes the most important service the consultant provides is to simply listen. CEOs are constantly grappling with issues and problems that can't be discussed candidly with anyone in the organization. Like any of us, they sometimes need an outlet to just vent anger, frustration or anxiety. The consultant should understand that sometimes the best way to help is to simply listen, because the CEO isn't really looking for advice – just a safe audience.

Dilemmas in Consulting to CEOs

Consulting to CEOs not only requires some unique processes, it also presents some very distinct dilemmas:

- **Insulation:** Research shows that over the course of their tenures, most CEOs tend to become more isolated.[6] Early on, they reach out to the organization and develop multiple sources of information. As time passes, and as they become more comfortable in their jobs and more wary about the information they receive, they gradually limit the number of subordinates they rely on for information. (It's interesting to note that most modern U.S. presidents have followed that same pattern of relying on a steadily shrinking circle of trusted aides as their tenure proceeds, usually to their detriment.) We've found that consultants must be wary of duplicating that pattern. All too often, in the latter stages of the relationship, consultants restrict their interactions to the CEO and perhaps one or two other senior executives, which severely limits their ability to provide the CEO with objective and varied perspectives. Realizing that CEOs are constantly constricting their sources of information, consultants must consciously maintain or even expand their own.
- **Clientship:** In the most challenging relationships, CEO consultants often face an incredibly difficult question: who is the real client – the individual or the organization? The simplistic answer is this: by helping the CEO perform effectively, the consultant is providing value to the entire enterprise. That can easily become a rationalization for continuing work which, by all rights, should end. But sometimes, it becomes painfully evident that the CEO is simply unable or unwilling to provide the kind of leadership the organization needs, and no amount of coaching or advice will help. Consequently, is there some point at which the consultant should conclude that the organization would be better off with a different CEO? There is no easy answer; it's important to recognize that it's a perplexing dilemma that comes with the territory. One approach we've taken is to deliberately ask the CEO whether they honestly believe they are capable of doing what needs to be done – or even want to. Needless to say, these are incredibly difficult conversations; they sometimes border on cathartic. However, more than once, a CEO has ended up acknowledging that they're just not the right person to take the company where it needs to go. Others have not gone as well, and we have – with great regret – terminated our relationship with the CEO and the organization rather than collude in sustaining the perception that festering issues are being resolved. It is one of the most perplexing dilemmas a consultant can face, but at some point, you need to decide whether your CEO client has the capacity to do the job – and if the answer is "no," to candidly ask yourself what is motivating you to avoid calling the question.

- **Influence Balance:** CEO consultants engage in an endless balancing act to counter the risk of being perceived by the organization as having either too much or too little influence. If you're perceived as having insufficient influence, it becomes difficult to get on people's calendars, to get invited to the right meetings and to be privy to necessary information. On the other hand, consultants can sometimes be perceived as a kind of Svengali, the mysterious figure behind the curtain who is really pulling all the strings – a role people properly resent and deal with by either avoiding or undermining the consultant. It can be enormously damaging to both the organization and to the CEO if people interacting with the consultant aren't sure who they're really dealing with. Will everything they say be repeated to the CEO? And conversely, is feedback or advice from the consultant actually originating with the CEO? Lack of clarity can do immense damage, which requires that CEO consultants must constantly guard against abusing their special relationship.
- **Backstairs Channel:** As mentioned previously, some people who perceive a close relationship between the consultant and the CEO will try to use the consultant as a conduit to the executive office. The consultant must be careful to maintain relationships with others in the organization without being used as a tool for advancing other people's agendas.
- **Over-Identification:** It's inevitable, over time, that a close association with the CEO will color the consultant's own views. That's a natural consequence of being privy to information that others don't have; you begin to tell yourself, "If they only knew what the CEO knows (and what I know), they'd understand his decision." It's essential not to become so close to the CEO that your perspective becomes indistinguishable – in other words, you can't "go native." At that point, the consultant simply mirrors rather than challenges the CEO's thinking, and stops adding value.
- **Inflated Ego:** Some CEO consultants tend to forget that they are consultants, not CEOs. They get carried away with their own sense of influence, power and access. They become insufferably arrogant; they forget that they're in the room to give advice, not to make decisions. Another variant of this is frequent dropping of the CEO's name, which can easily become perceived as transparent self-enhancement. The ego-inflated consultant becomes intoxicated as a result of closeness to "the throne."
- **Assessing People:** As the relationship develops, it's inevitable for the CEO to occasionally seek the consultant's assessment of particular people in the organization. That is a dangerous path to go down; it's risky, even irresponsible, for the consultant to offer off-the-cuff assessments based on limited interactions and incomplete data. And if word gets out that the consultant is the source of assessments, the consultant's dealings with other executives become tainted by fear and suspicion. The consultant's role needs to be made clear; if executives are to be assessed, the consultant can help assure a fair and objective process, most likely involving other professionals.

Clearly, the relationship between the trusted advisor and the CEO is a risky one. To be successful, and to provide real value to the client, the consultant must bring to the table a rare combination of content knowledge and process skills. It is a role that requires maturity, confidence, keen intellect and emotional insight. It is not for everyone; for a great many consultants, it's simply not the kind of consulting they're comfortable with, nor does it involve the kinds of technical expertise or personal interaction they enjoy. But for those who do consult successfully at this level, there is great satisfaction in the ability to have substantial impact by influencing the direction and performance of entire organizations.

Consulting to the Board

The role of corporate boards – and the job of consultants who work with them – has changed much more dramatically in recent years than that of CEOs and their consultants. In some ways, we've all been finding our way through new territory. Just as the engagement, influence and accountability of boards have been evolving at an unexpectedly rapid pace, so too have the challenges for board consultants.

Prior to the 1990s, U.S. boards served largely as cosmetic appendages to the corporate governance structure. The real power in each company almost always rested with a single individual, who held the titles of both CEO and chairman of the board. Typically, boards met infrequently in highly ritualistic settings. Their role was to fulfill a bare minimum of statutory responsibilities without interfering in the real business of managing the enterprise.

Then came the corporate scandals of the early 2000s, provoking an historic backlash in the form of Sarbanes-Oxley legislation and revised New York Stock Exchange and NASDAQ listing requirements, all aimed at substantially increasing the independence and accountability of boards. Those reforms accelerated governance reform, but not enough; the financial crash of 2008 was precipitated, in large part, by irresponsible risk-taking enabled by lax board oversight. That second wave of scandals brought its own legislative reaction in 2010 – the Dodd-Frank rules, which led the way to even stricter oversight and opened the door to greater shareholder access to board elections.

Faster than almost anyone had anticipated, U.S. boards have been passing through several general phases in less than 20 years:

- Passive Observers: The traditional U.S. board – passive, disengaged, largely ceremonial and generally willing to defer to the CEO who had selected them;
- Active Monitors: Bowing to pressure from regulators, politicians, the press and the public, boards began focusing on management compliance with basic legal and financial requirements;

- Active Collaborators: More engaged boards began viewing themselves as partners with the CEO, seeking to contribute substantive value to the organization rather than simply overseeing compliance;
- Activist Boards: We're already beginning to see signs of this latest stage, the emergence of activist boards as a corollary to activist shareholders. We're not sure we would go quite so far as to describe them as *Boards That Lead*, as Ram Charan, Dennis Carey and Michael Useem entitled their excellent book,[7] but boards are clearly assuming an unprecedented role in demanding constant management attention to shareholder value. This will inevitably fuel sharp debates regarding the conflicting priorities of short-term versus long-term value creation.

Along with growing attention to what boards should do, there is heightened scrutiny of how well they do it. At the most basic level, boards are beginning to periodically evaluate not only their formal structures and work processes, but also – and perhaps even more importantly – the dynamics of how they interact to make decisions, resolve conflict and fulfill their responsibilities. Adding to the complexity is the still evolving practice of individual director performance evaluation, the highly sensitive, last remaining element of governance reform yet to win wide acceptance.

Accordingly, we've seen the gradual emergence since the early 2000s of a specialized field of consulting to boards beyond the legal, financial and executive compensation advice they've long received. And many aspects of this new consulting are significantly different than the approach to CEO consulting discussed up to this point.

Content of Board Consulting

The first requirement for consultants who work with boards is to understand exactly what it is that boards are supposed to do – no easy task in itself. At the most basic level, according to the respected legal handbook *Liability of Corporate Officers and Directors*,[8] public company boards are responsible for a few very specific responsibilities, including approval of major corporate actions (such as mergers, acquisitions, divestitures, stock splits, etc.); oversight of the performance of the chief executive, including hiring, firing and setting compensation; ensuring effective audit procedures; and monitoring the company's compliance with legal and financial regulations and standards.

For a more specific picture of what boards actually do, consider the 2015–2016 Public Company Governance Survey by the National Association of Corporate Directors,[9] in which directors listed 20 different activities on which their boards spend the most time. Those at the top of the list (in descending order):

- Strategic planning and oversight
- Corporate performance and evaluation

- Corporate growth/restructuring (e.g., M&A)
- Financial oversight/internal controls
- CEO succession
- Risk oversight
- Executive talent management and leadership development
- Regulatory compliance

The list goes on, and includes important topics such as CEO evaluation and compensation as well as others involving the board itself, such as succession planning and director evaluation. But those top eight encompass the issues that take up the bulk of the board's time.

The Board's Unique Process Issues

With the expansion of the board's influence, accountability and scope of engagement, there has been a growing realization that the board's internal dynamics – the ways in which its members engage with each other and with senior management in the exercise of their duties – constitute a critical component of board performance and effectiveness, and for two key reasons.

The first is that in legal proceedings, the courts have established the so-called "business judgment rule" as a legal defense that can be invoked by directors in liability cases. Recognizing that judges and courts are not necessarily qualified to second-guess the correctness of complex business decisions, the courts have chosen instead to focus on a boards' decision-making processes. Special attention is being given to whether the board acted with the corporation's best interests in mind, was well informed, acted within the bounds of the law and avoided conflicts of interest.[10, 11]

Second, the growing demand that boards become more aggressive and engaged implies that boards are expected to do "real work," a sharp departure from the distinctly undemanding activity that formerly went on in boardrooms. In the past, boards were merely disparate groups of individuals who gathered four times a year to formally approve management's stack of recommendations and then adjourn for cocktails and a nice meal. The question of how well the board performed was largely irrelevant. Now, boards face mounting expectations to provide independent oversight and "credible challenge" to management, to exercise disciplined oversight of risk management, to communicate as necessary with key stakeholders – the list goes on and on, making it clear that today's boards are expected to roll up their sleeves and do "real work" in ways their predecessors never imagined.

Consultants quickly concluded that the answer was for boards to shape up and become high performing teams. The problem is that boards didn't need to "up their game" – they needed to change it. The traditional U.S. board wasn't just a poorly performing team; in fact, it was the antithesis of an effective team, in terms of its structure, composition, culture, leadership

Exhibit 9.3 Differences Between Boards and Teams

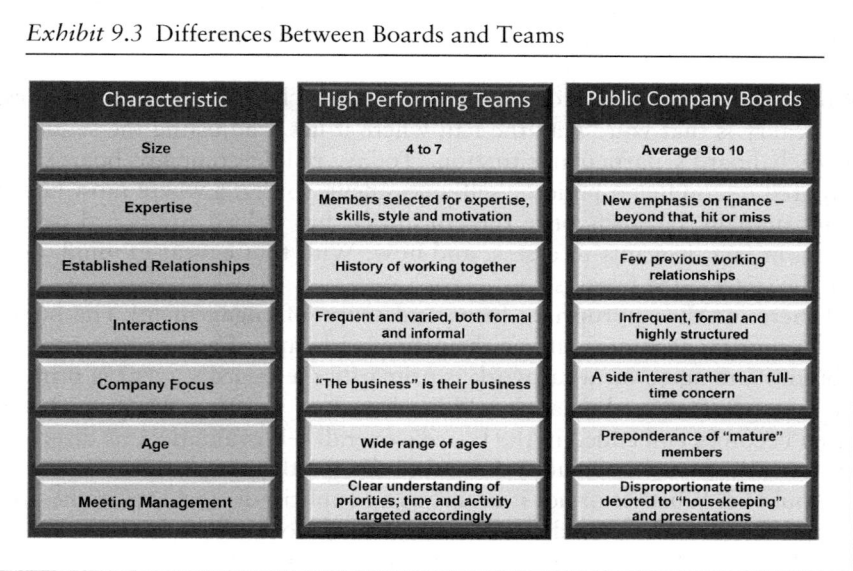

and work processes. Unlike typical high performance teams normally found within organizations, the traditional board had unique legal obligations, met briefly and infrequently, was composed of members who rarely brought much relevant skill or experience to the table and involved ambiguous power relationships among immensely influential people who rarely interacted with each other outside of formal meetings.

Thus, for board consultants, the central question is this: exactly how does a board go about transforming itself from a ritualistic appendage to a real team? How does it strike the proper balance between a do-nothing rubber-stamp and an out-of-control mob eager to assume management's rightful duties or fire the CEO at the first sign of trouble? How do you create a board that is truly effective – one that not only meets its minimum legal obligations but also becomes a source of added value to the company? The good news is that an increasing number of boards are becoming serious about finding the answers to those questions.

The Blueprint for Building Boards

Over the years, we have developed a board-building process which includes elements relevant to every board.[12] As the process begins, the consultant must help the board to focus on two key questions:

- How do you determine the "gap" between your current and desired performance?

- What specific actions should you take, in what sequence, over what period of time, in order to truly become a high performing team?

While we can suggest a logical sequence to the board building activities, the reality is that you "play the ball where it lies," adjusting the sequence to each board's particular situation. Today, public company boards are required to conduct a periodic self-assessment, so that's where most board work actually begins – once the consultant has helped the board decide what, in fact, it wants to assess, and how. With that caveat in mind, here are the steps in the process:

Determine the appropriate focus and scope of engagement: The board and senior management survey the entire landscape of governance responsibilities and agree on what work is primarily the board's, what is primarily management's and what should be shared. In practice, this critical step often becomes embedded in the board's overall self-evaluation, as directors measure the board's actual performance against their expectations of what it should be. Whether or not it occurs as an explicit, distinct step in the process, the consultant should never lose sight of its overall importance.

Take stock: Ideally, the evaluation should examine the performance of the full board, its committees and its individual members. In the best cases, it combines some sort of survey and confidential interview process with observation of meetings, analysis of key materials (agendas, minutes and the board information packet) and benchmarking against relevant best practices by other boards.

Ensure effective board composition: Two elements of composition are essential to high performance. The first is ensuring that the directors bring the right mix of skills and experience, given the nature of the business and its strategic challenges. The second is making sure that directors consistently meet the board's performance standards, and putting in place a process for replacing those who don't – a politically sensitive process which is now euphemistically referred to as "refreshment."

Evaluate board work processes: This crucial area includes an examination of very detailed issues involving how the board actually goes about its work. It includes matters such as the board's committee structure; the size and meeting frequency of the full board; the process for developing agendas for both regular and special meetings to ensure appropriate time is allocated to the right topics; and board access to timely, useful information from management as well as information from a variety of sources other than top management.

Evaluate board leadership: There are two central issues here. The first is the structure of board leadership; in other words, if there is an executive chairman (which could be the current or former CEO), is the lead director playing an active and effective role in representing the interests of the independent directors, who now must constitute the majority on public company boards? The other issue is the quality of leadership in terms of

Exhibit 9.4 Board Building Process

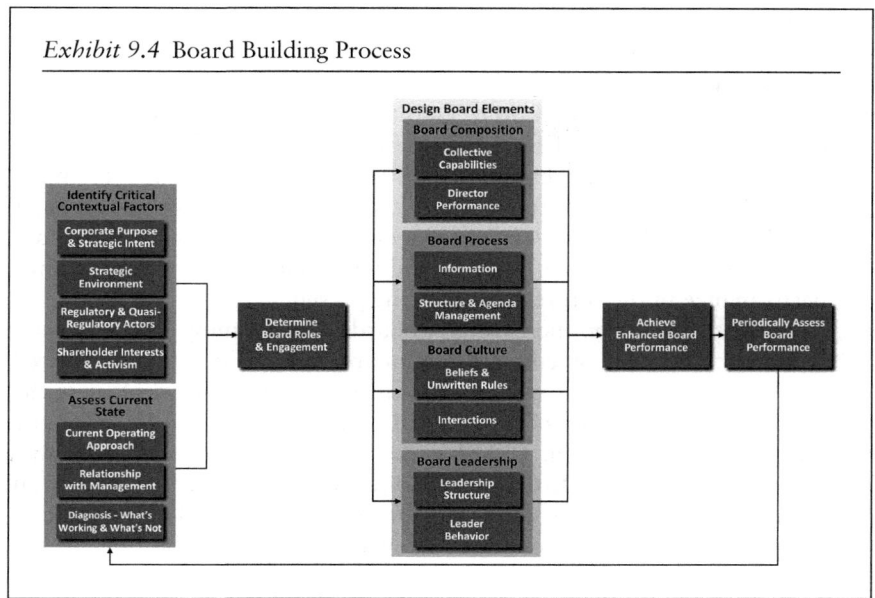

communication, meeting and agenda management, and the setting of a tone for dealing with board members, management, shareholders, regulators and other stakeholders.

Evaluate the board's culture: It's important to get the right people doing the right work using the right processes; but without the right culture, the other three won't matter. This is perhaps the biggest challenge for board leaders: to reshape a deeply entrenched, traditional culture of passivity, deference to management and excessive formality into a culture that encourages independence, constructive dissent, broad participation, unfettered openness and spirited inquiry. The burden falls squarely on the shoulder of board leaders; no one else can set the tone and encourage the desired behavior and values.

Understand the potential for value creation: If the board has successfully mastered the requirements up to this point, then ideally the outcome will be engagement that adds value to the organization. Beyond the area of audit and financial reporting, which has been the primary focus of the recent governance reforms, there are four areas where the board is uniquely positioned to add significant value to the overall quality of an organization's governance.

- *Corporate strategy.* Many directors believe that the development and oversight of corporate strategy is one of the board's most critical functions, but it's also an area where they believe they've been least effective. A high-performing board, through its collective experience, expertise

and rigorous questioning, can add immense value to management's thinking. Ineffective boards either rubber stamp management's plans or, conversely, get far too involved in the details.
- *CEO performance evaluation.* Traditionally, the board mainly relied on lagging indicators of financial performance to determine the CEO's compensation. But an effective evaluation process should do much more. Although it needs to recognize the importance of the financials, it should also evaluate the CEO's leadership based on outcomes that are directly within his or her control, and will influence the organization's performance in the future as well as the present.
- *Executive succession.* Increasingly, boards are assuming a greater and, in many cases, even preeminent role in an area traditionally dominated by the CEO. While there is an important role for the CEO, it is the directors – all or most of whom will still be overseeing the company long after the incumbent CEO has departed – who must own the succession process and ultimate decision. Nevertheless, this remains an incredibly sensitive area where the interplay of personal emotions and corporate politics often muddies the waters and blurs the roles of the CEO and the board.[13]
- *Risk assessment and crisis management.* The board is uniquely positioned not only to oversee a rigorous process for assessing risk and planning for crises, but also to take center stage when the CEO is the focal point of a crisis. That situation can arise for a host of reasons, as we have seen in recent years; the most obvious involve the CEO's sudden inability to perform the job, due to either legal or health issues. The board is suddenly thrust into a role of quickly replacing the CEO on an emergency basis, stabilizing the organization and reassuring key stakeholders.

Implications for Consulting to Boards

Working with boards on the kinds of issues we've just described involves some of the most rewarding and challenging work consultants can do. In many ways, consultation on board work process and dynamics – as opposed to technical advice on legal and financial matters – is still evolving as a specialized practice. Nevertheless, some overarching implications are already becoming clear.

Not everyone gets to do this: The ability to be perceived as a trusted advisor in the boardroom requires a combination of experience, content mastery, professional stature and personal attributes – including a degree of maturity, even gravitas. Engagements come almost exclusively through personal referrals; directors are generally guided by endorsements from other directors. What is less obvious is that a great many boards prefer working with small boutiques, or even sole practitioners, rather than with the "board practice" of large consulting firms. Directors are extremely wary of consultants who use board work as a "loss leader," an underpriced foot in the door of the organization which will hopefully lead to much larger, long-term, high margin projects elsewhere in the company. Many prefer to work with a consultant who is there to work with the board, not to keep trying to sell them something else.

It requires unusual combination of both expert and facilitative consulting: At the very least, consultants need a comprehensive understanding of corporate governance and the ability to develop a strong point of view regarding the effectiveness of the board and its members by drawing upon personal experience, observation, interpretation of feedback and knowledge of best practices. At the same time, it requires the ability to design and deliver the work – including the methodology for gathering data and the process for sharing findings and recommendations – in ways that will build the support of the leadership and the engagement of the members.

It involves a balance between firm principles and flexible application: Directors are put off by consultants who dogmatically insist upon a specific approach. Consultants should be flexible, while at the same time being clear about how far they're willing to go in accommodating those boards – and there are many – who are simply looking for the easiest, cheapest and least intrusive way to complete their required evaluations. For example, while we urge our clients to use a combination of both a confidential survey and in-depth interviews to obtain the most robust feedback, we've certainly been willing to forgo the survey, if asked. However, we have steadfastly refused to do the opposite – to drop the interviews and merely administer a survey – because we would be unwilling to stand behind the quality of that woefully incomplete feedback. The challenge for each consultant is to understand what's negotiable.

It demands an awareness of the multiple audiences for the work: Much of the work produced by a consultant for a CEO remains absolutely confidential; in some cases, a carefully edited version might be shared with other top executives, or members of the board. In contrast, board consultants must keep in mind that their work product will be seen not only by the entire board, but by others, as well – most notably, government regulators, who tend to pore over every word and sometimes read more into the text than was ever intended. There's also growing interest among shareholders in having the board report not only on the process used in its evaluation, but on actions resulting from it. The bottom line for consultants is to assume that everything in a written report is discoverable, which requires that you take special pains to avoid ambiguity, exaggeration, sloppy handling of data or unsupported observations. It also means being very deliberate in determining what to include in written reports versus what material to communicate orally in confidential discussions or board executive sessions.

It requires a clear understanding of who is the client: As we discussed earlier, this only becomes an issue for CEO consultants in the most extreme cases where you believe the organization is ill-served by your client continuing in office. It's different for board consultants, who from the outset have both an immediate client – the board – as well as the ultimate clients, the shareholders. After all, the point of the work is to determine how effectively the board is serving the shareholders' interests, and how it might do that better. By its very nature – particularly in cases where a comprehensive assessment is being sought precisely because there's a suspicion that major change is required – the consultant's work is likely to result in changes that displease some of the immediate clients. For example, nearly half of our board assessments have been followed either immediately, or in very short order, by the resignation or removal of the chairman or lead director. At one major financial institution, where we were hired specifically to help the board address some serious composition problems, the board experienced 80 percent turnover among its 10 independent directors over the next three and a half years, far beyond the normal average of one change per year. If the consultant is brought in because change is necessary, then it is inevitable that at least some of the clients will end up displeased, to put it mildly – and that can include the specific individuals responsible for hiring you in the first place.

Consulting to Both the CEO and the Board

Through the 1980s and 1990s, and even into the early 2000s, it wasn't unusual to consult to a CEO for years without spending any significant time thinking about the board; it simply wasn't much of a factor. For consultants (not to mention for CEOs, as well) things were much simpler, from a governance standpoint: through most of those years, somewhere around 85 percent of U.S. public companies were led by a single individual who held the titles of both CEO and chairman of the board. If the consultant worked with both the board and the CEO, the client was almost always the same person.

Jump ahead a decade and a half, and the situation has changed much faster than any of us had anticipated in the early 2000s. The U.S. model was quickly shifting to look like the U.K.'s. By 2015, the CEO and chairman roles were shared by a single person at only around 39 percent of U.S. public companies, and just 37 percent of private companies.[14] That statistic graphically illustrates the rapidly changing relationship between the CEO and the board.

From the consultant's perspective, we experienced that change first hand, and perhaps most dramatically, in consultation regarding CEO succession. Through the 1980s and 1990s, our client for that work was almost always the CEO; the board's involvement came at the very end, and generally involved a pro forma approval of the CEO's hand-picked successor. But since the mid-2000s, the client for this work is almost always the board, which owns the process and the final decision. The CEO still has an important role to play – but figuring out exactly what that is in each situation has become one of the more challenging aspects of succession consulting.

Overall, this changing relationship and shifting balance of power between CEOs and boards create major implications for consultants who consult to both:

Beware the inherent conflict of interest: Having both the CEO and the board as clients, at the same time, is more likely than not to result in a conflict of interest. In the past, a good relationship with the CEO might become an entrée to work with that company's board. Today, boards and CEOs tend to want their "own" consultants; they don't want to worry about whether information or conversations are being shared inappropriately, and they certainly don't want the consultant to have any reservations about whose interests are uppermost in his mind when the CEO and the board have a major difference of opinion. Attempting to consult to both the CEO and board is a recipe for disaster.

You can't consult to either without understanding both: While we don't believe you can have both the CEO and the board of the same company as clients at the same time, we do believe that it's almost impossible to consult effectively to either a CEO or a board without consulting experience in both the boardroom and the C-suite. Both roles – the CEO and the board – are so thoroughly intertwined that an effective consultant must bring to the table holistic understanding of governance. In areas such as risk oversight, succession, strategy, talent development and stakeholder relations, to name just a few – consultation involves helping the parties working out their respective roles, in relation to each other. There's no way for the consultant to do that without understanding what the issue looks like from both sides of the table.

Be prepared to play the role of honest broker: Sometimes the greatest service you can provide is to help bring both parties to the table to discuss things they've been avoiding for years – often, due to mistaken assumptions about the other party's motives or priorities. In other cases, it helps to act as an intermediary between the board and the CEO, until they've reached a point where they're ready to deal with each other constructively. Each situation is unique, and they all require the consultant to do much, much more than sit in the background and whisper into someone's ear.

Know Thyself and Thy Client

Consulting to the senior-level figures in corporate governance offers enormous opportunities, both for consultants and their clients, yet this unique role presents serious questions and significant risks. It is no place for amateurs or rookies; only the most talented and experienced consultants are likely to succeed, while drawing upon a wealth of personal experience and a deep reservoir of confidence, courage, empathy and integrity. Beyond that, consultants who try to swim in these deep waters must possess an unusual degree of self-awareness and self-confidence, meaning they must understand their personal strengths and weaknesses and be exceptionally clear about the kinds of technical expertise, content knowledge and intervention steps that will work best, both for themselves and for their demanding clients.

Notes

1 David A. Nadler and Janet L. Spencer. *Executive Teams*. (San Francisco: Jossey-Bass, Inc., 1998.)
2 David A. Nadler and Mark B. Nadler. *Champions of Change*. (San Francisco: Jossey-Bass, Inc. 1998.)
3 Mark B. Nadler in *Boardroom Realities*, edited by Jay A. Conger. (San Francisco: John Wiley & Sons, 2009.)
4 David H. Maister, Charles H. Green, and Robert M. Galford. *The Trusted Advisor*. (New York: The Free Press, 2000.)
5 Maister *et al.*
6 Sydney Finkelstein and Donald C. Hambrick. *Strategic Leadership: Top Executives and Their Effects on Organizations*. (Mason, OH: South-Western College Publishing, 1996.)
7 Ram Charan, Dennis Carey, and Michael Useem. *Boards That Lead*. (Boston: Harvard Business School Publishing, 2014.)
8 William E. Kepper and Dan A. Bailey. *Liability of Corporate Officers and Directors*. (Charlottesville, VA: The Michie Co., 1998.)
9 National Association of Corporate Directors. *2016–2017 Public Company Governance Survey*. (Washington, D.C.: NACD, 2016.)
10 Jay A. Conger, Edward E. Lawler, III, and David L. Finegold. *Corporate Boards: Strategies for Adding Value at the Top*. (San Francisco: Jossey-Bass, Inc., 2001.)
11 Jay W. Lorsch and Elizabeth Maclver. *Pawns or Potentates: The Realities of America's Corporate Boards*. (Boston: Harvard Business School Publishing, 1989.)
12 David A. Nadler, Beverly A. Behan, and Mark B. Nadler. *Building Better Boards*. (San Francisco: Jossey-Bass Publishers, 2006.)
13 Mark B. Nadler in *Handbook of Corporate Governance*, edited by Richard LeBlanc. (New York: John Wiley & Sons, 2016.)
14 NACD Survey.

10 Consulting on the Global Stage

Matthew C. Heim

Introduction

Global consulting can vary dramatically from regional or nation-wide consulting engagements, and adopting the right approach can save both consultant and client significant time, rework, and money. Global companies present a higher degree of complexity – not only because of their diverse organizational structures, but also because of the legal, regulatory, cultural, and other variances within each country. When a consultant engages with a client that has organizational entities in scope that are in multiple countries, having foreknowledge of the possible implications will not only better support the engagement, but will also add a great deal of credibility to the consultant. Consulting practices develop their intellectual capital in the form of systems and methodologies, but rarely take into consideration the ramifications of a global scope. In this chapter we will focus primarily on the challenges that should be taken into account before planning the global engagement approach, thus fostering a higher potential for customer satisfaction and engagement success.

I have personally spent over 16 years of my life living abroad, and over 30 years working with global companies on six continents. After a stint of simultaneous work and study in Germany, I began my consulting career in the tech sector, then transitioning to strategic services. After returning to my home in the United States, I continued working with client companies around the world. The experience of full immersion into another country's social and business cultures is incomparable. I have experienced many challenges, successes, and incredible insights that I wouldn't have experienced if I had chosen to work only in the US. These insights and experiences have had a great deal to do with the person I am today and have had a significant impact on my consulting career over the years. Having to shift the gears of perception when flying from South Africa to Germany, then on to the United Arab Emirates all in one week is an experience that most people may never have. In the consulting industry, this type of experience only adds to our flexibility, adaptability, and overall awareness that is a crucial part of any successful consultant's make-up.

You too can have the experience of facilitating a merger, which incorporates new entities in Tokyo and Mumbai into the newly designated headquarters in the United Kingdom. You too may become the lead consulting manager on a global information systems implementation in France, Hong Kong, Jakarta, and Sao Paulo. You may be asked to participate in the rollout of a new strategic innovation management program to locations in New York, Frankfurt, Seoul, and Sydney. Either of these experiences on their own would prove to be transformative and shed new insights that will forever change your consulting career. When planning new engagements that will touch upon other countries, your mind will automatically reach back to those memories of foreign business and cultural nuances you had to face, and you'll find yourself integrating that valuable knowledge and awareness into the next project.

This chapter will not serve as a substitute for the actual experience of living and working abroad, but it will afford you many of the perspectives from those who have, and prepare you for the exciting journey that lies ahead. In this chapter you will be provided with a global consulting framework that can be integrated into your work abroad. While describing the various elements of this framework, I have included several real-life experiences that will help bring you closer to that situation. After reading this chapter, you should be better prepared to take the journey that millions have taken before you, and return a more rounded and fulfilled person and consultant.

Pre-Engagement Considerations

Immediately after the client articulates the project goals and objectives, and before project planning or even proposal writing begins, the consultant must systematically develop an understanding of the possible global aspects of the engagement that may require specialized resources and skills to successfully complete the tasks at hand. If not properly understood and anticipated, these implications could cause significant complications in the midst of the engagement, force the consultant to assume the costs of the unforeseen resources and increases in scope, and in the worst case, it could lead to complete project failure.

Global engagements can vary, from a complete reorganization of the company, to an information systems implementation within a specific business unit or function. Global engagements may also include the rollout of special programs or initiatives within a single department, such as Human Resources, that impact many different business units or entities around the world. With each global engagement also comes a unique set of local requirements to be considered. The Global Consulting Approach outlined below will be discussed throughout this chapter to provide the knowledge and understanding necessary to deliver a highly successful global engagement, regardless of the scope.

Figure 10.1 The Global Consulting Approach

Global client organization

It is a given that understanding the client's organizational structure and geographic distribution are necessary pre requisites to launching an engagement, but this may also reveal new opportunities to add value, beyond the scope of the project. Some companies experience both organic growth and growth through acquisition over time, gradually ending up with a geographically oriented structure that no longer makes sense from a sales, production, distribution, or supply chain perspective, or overall cost perspective. Inquiring about the geographical structure and its origins will likely reveal whether or not they were strategically placed, or ended up in that location as the result of a previous acquisition, or because the facility originated in that location to serve a local market, but is no longer the optimal location under the new strategic direction.

Understanding the relationships among the various organizational entities and locations will help the consultant to determine the directional flows of process, information, goods, and services, both internally and externally. For example, if the consultant is part of a global Enterprise Resource Planning (ERP) system rollout, this knowledge is necessary to ensure the right transactions, approvals, and reporting are being executed at the right place and time, regardless of time zone, language, and other geographical challenges. Seamless integration between Sales, Production, Services, Procurement, Materials Management, Finance, and HR is the ultimate goal. However, often times the consultant will notice that information and processes are siloed in companies that have outgrown their old accounting and information systems, and by recognizing these silos beforehand, significant value can be added if the new systems are designed with enterprise-wide transparency and real-time access in mind.

Developing a complete understanding of the client's corporate-wide process flow and organization in its most simplistic form will help to set the stage for a deeper understanding of how these processes flow across geographies and business units. The sample high-level enterprise-wide process flow diagram below can be used to seed that understanding.

After mapping the enterprise-wide process flow at its highest level (see above), the consultant can then begin to ask where each of the major functional activities occur (i.e. in which country, in which facility, etc.). Following "high-level" mapping, the consultant can follow with drilling down into the details of each major process area. This high-level starting point will quickly bring the consultant to a complete and global understanding of the flow of information, materials, and goods across the global enterprise.

Companies that have had the opportunity to take a more strategic approach to their organizational placement may place their manufacturing or other facilities in a country or region for a specific reason. These reasons can range from labor cost savings, supply chain access, resource availability, and customer proximity. All of these factors should be considered and leveraged in the global rollout approach, so as to avoid creating new challenges and unnecessary barriers where strategic geographical placement has already been achieved.

Understanding the client's local skills, education levels, and workforce demographics can also provide insight into the potential nuances or challenges of service delivery. Some locations are chosen because of lower labor costs, and finding local managers who understand the objectives of the work at hand can be difficult. After the fall of the Iron Curtain, a Western consulting team was sent to former East Germany to integrate the strategy, organization, and processes of the East German Railroad into the Deutsche Bahn (West Germany's modern commercial rail system), and when the consultants began to engage the local workers, they quickly realized that all of the prior workers who had any experience or education had fled to the West, in fears that East Germany would close it borders again. The remaining

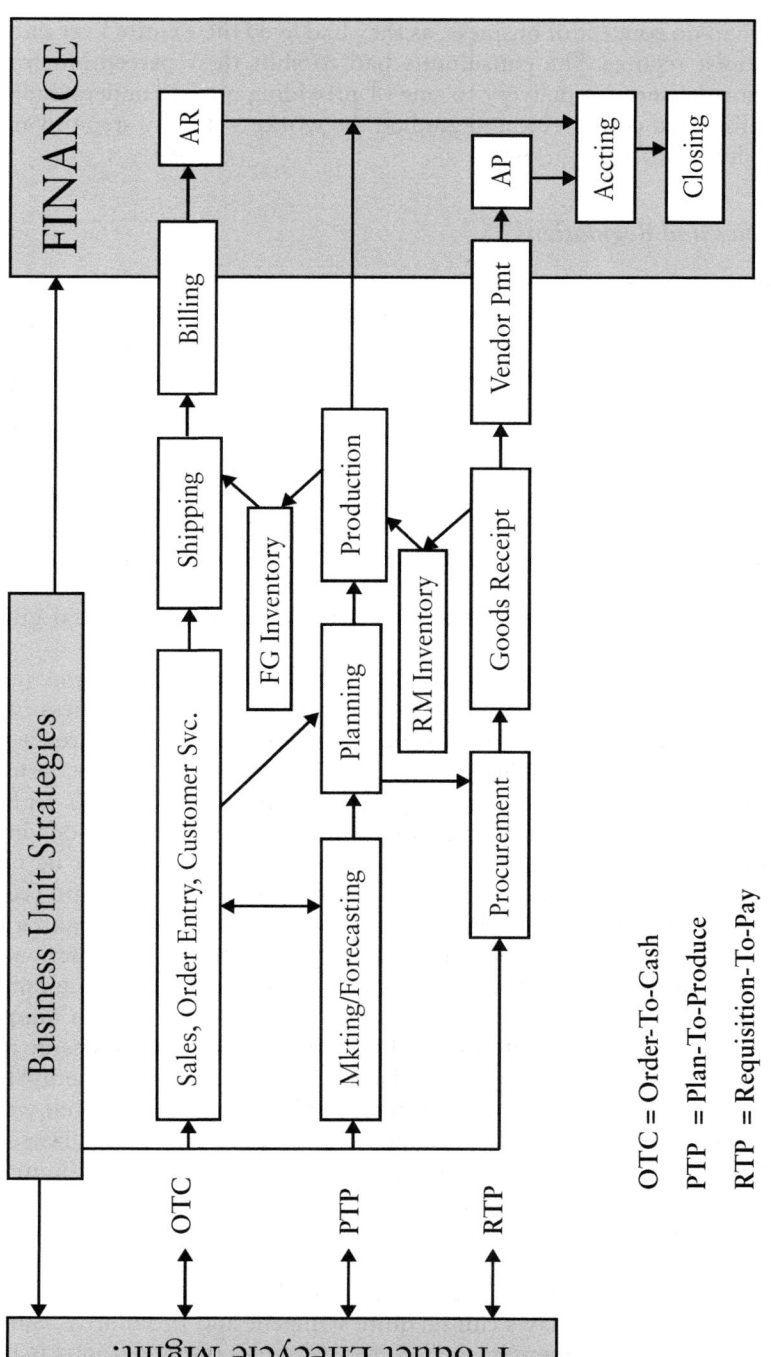

Figure 10.2 Sample Enterprise Process Flow Depiction

workers had no concept of business, as they had lived their entire lives under a communist regime. The consultants had to shift their perception from that of normal services delivery to one of providing a basic understanding of capitalism and commerce, and guiding the workers step-by-step towards basic business process.

Local Laws and Regulations

Each country and region comes with its own set of laws, regulations, statutes, and rules – both written and unwritten. In order to attain success in any global engagement, these requirements must be understood and integrated into the plan for each location impacted. Financial regulations, reporting requirements, and local tax codes are the most common examples, and compliance is typically ensured by the client's financial organization, although a consultant implementing a financial accounting system or process must also have an understanding of these local regulations. Human resource laws, like financial regulations, are also country and region specific, and must be considered with any personnel or personnel process changes. In some countries these HR regulations can be very complex, for example, preventing employees from being terminated, and requiring adherence to local guild laws for skilled workers.

Manufacturing laws differ in each country and economic region (e.g. European Union) and may preclude a company from doing business in a given region if certain standards are not met. For example, adherence to the ISO 9000 family of quality assurance standards is required in certain regions and countries, which not only affects manufacturing facilities within the region, but also companies that wish to send manufactured goods into that region. There are also quality and safety standards that must be met in certain countries for specific products, such as TÜV (the German Technical Inspection Association, which ensures product safety with regards to human beings and the environment) and OSHA (Occupational Safety and Health Association, which ensures employee safety in manufacturing facilities). Product designations and labeling requirements are also often unique to specific countries, and must be considered where applicable, to ensure the proper value recognition is assigned to the product. Examples are EnergyStar ratings for appliance efficiency and Organic certification for foods that were generated without the use of chemical pesticides, herbicides, or fertilizers.

A relatively new set of laws that continues to evolve in many countries are data protection laws. These laws prevent the storage of certain information (varying from country to country) and often catch systems integrators and developers off guard when trying to introduce their software product or network in a country that enforces such laws, like Canada and the European Union, where such laws can be quite stringent and prohibitive. Small systems and web developers in the US, for example, often run into issues in Europe and Canada, when setting up systems and networks that store personal information of employees and other network participants, forcing them to make costly changes after the fact. Having an understanding of these, and other local laws and regulations, will not only prevent major rework, but also prepare the product for global scalability.

Local Consulting Skills and Practices

The concept of "consulting" can show up in different ways. For example, there are independent consultants, small boutique consulting firms, and large international consulting firms. There are also "internal" consultants who work for large companies, and "customer success" or "customer engineering" consultants who work for software and systems companies, responsible for the successful implementation and adoption of their products.

Regardless of the size, structure, and purpose of the consulting entity, careful consideration must be given to the resources and skills needed for successful service delivery in other countries. While this may be an obvious consideration for independent consultants and smaller boutique firms, even larger multinational firms must consider local skill set requirements. For example if a client engagement with a company in Japan requires consultants be on site at a manufacturing facility in Brazil, the firm must determine whether or not they have consultants with the skills needed (e.g. industry, technical, process skills) within the proximity of that facility. If not, they must decide whether to ship them in from another country or to partner with a local firm that possesses the required skill set. Both quality and cost-effectiveness are to be considered with any such decision, and early determination can prevent quality issues and eroding profit margins on these types of global engagements.

On most global engagements the client's local skills and capabilities should be taken into consideration. As a rule of thumb, the client's Human Resources department should be brought into the planning and implementation phases of a project, to ensure the appropriate reward systems are in place to motivate the workers for the additional workload that they will be carrying during the implementation phase, and then see that the proper metrics and key performance indicators are designed into the new processes at both the department and individual levels. If the local facility has specific regulatory requirements (e.g. pharmaceutical or medical device manufacturing facilities), then working with the client's Regulatory and Validation team can help to avoid costly mistakes with the introduction of new processes and systems in these facilities. And in some cases, the client's Regulatory and Validation team may require consulting support from advisors who are familiar with the regulatory requirements of that location, and the newly proposed changes and systems.

Local Markets and Customers

A thorough assessment of a client's markets and customers in each region will help the consultant to identify new opportunities – especially where such consulting engagements involve product placement, distribution, sales process optimization, or Internet sales. Global markets present a higher degree of complexity, yet they can provide a much higher return if leveraged properly. Again, as we have seen, many successful regional organizations evolve, only to attain moderately effective global results because they have held on to the structure they started with. It is often necessary to question the organizational structure, in association with the customer base and markets it is selling to, to determine if it is achieving optimal market penetration and sales results.

With the assessment of each business unit, it is a good idea to look at the low hanging fruit. In other words, does the unit have full local market penetration? The answer may not always be so obvious. Some businesses originally create their products for a single B2B customer or a specific geographic location. A good example is the thin film solar panels manufactured in the US. For the first five years these panels were being manufactured, they were virtually impossible to find in the US, as they were all being sent to Germany, where large volume contracts and high demand made it easy to ignore other markets – even the local US market. Alternatively, a product may have optimal penetration locally and be missing a significant opportunity on a global scale. While going global can result in high growth and return, it has also been known to take down highly successful companies who launch an unsuccessful and often incomplete global push, where overseas market, legal, and cultural considerations were ignored.

Since the advance of the Internet we have seen small garage start-ups quickly spring into major competitors to larger, well-established companies. This space has since become highly competitive, where consumer expectations shift every year due to unprecedented content provider innovations (e.g. Amazon, Alibaba, and Netflix). While this may sound intimidating, Internet market growth continues to grow each year, opening new territory – especially for companies offering unique products and services. The Internet is also an effective vehicle for quickly growing a small regional company into a national or international contender. Understanding the local and global markets and market opportunities, both physically and virtually, can provide significant insight and advantage to the consulting engagement when taken into consideration with other attributes of the Global Consulting Approach.

Global and Local Supply Chain

Uncontrolled and non-strategic organizational growth can not only lead to costly distribution of products and services, it can also lead to major supply chain cost overruns. When assessing the client's global supply chain, the consultant must fully understand the choices made in support of certain suppliers. Certain materials may have a unique feature that provides product differentiation and superiority, and replacing them with less expensive, inferior material may lead to deterioration of the end product. Some suppliers that may appear to be superior may have less than desirable distribution capabilities that would cause work and delivery disruptions. For the consultant, making an uninformed supplier recommendation could lead to the loss of credibility with the client.

Often times a business will choose material supply based on cost – even if it is sourced from another country, when the same material is also available locally. Other companies choose their supply based on locality; for example, more and more food chains select their food sources locally, to support local economies and to bolster their image in local communities. Some automobile manufacturers do the same; for example, Nissan boasts that some of their vehicles are designed, sourced, and built in the USA, even though they are a Japanese company. This lends them credibility within the local US markets with buyers who are concerned about domestic jobs and the economy, and in some cases, allows companies to charge a premium price for their products.

In those cases where more costly supply sources are not justified, significant cost saving opportunities may be found. Some companies, over time, neglect to assess their supplier costs, and this complacency ends up eroding their profits with higher material costs than necessary. This can often be remedied through supply chain consolidation or by implementing vendor selection processes that require competitive bidding and due diligence. These selection processes can become quite complex, depending on the type of relationship required with the vendor. For example, some vendors not only provide basic materials, they may also offer research and development and testing services to the client, co-developing new products, and offering joint go-to-market services. Understanding the intricacies of the client's supply chain relationships and choices can not only help consultants reveal new cost saving and value generation opportunities, but also help them understand where and when to leave things as they are.

Local Cultural Nuances

One of the most important considerations in the Global Consulting Approach is culture. While it may be more difficult to justify direct cost savings or revenue success, the development of trust and credibility with the client is vital. It has been demonstrated in customer surveys again and again that trust, credibility, and relationship are some of the most important drivers of engagement success and repeat business with the client. Ignoring the important cultural nuances of our clients can lead to an immediate loss of credibility and trust. On the other hand, demonstrating some knowledge and appreciation for the local culture can add credibility, develop a deeper level of trust, and enhance the overall relationship with the client.

An example of the benefits of cultural openness can be explained through an actual event where a group of US and European based consulting managers was invited to participate in an evening event of karaoke by their hosts – managers from a global Korean consumer electronics company. One of the consulting managers thought that the idea was frivolous, and chose not to join the group. While the managers who attended the event that evening ended up having a good time, bonding with their client counterparts, the other manager was unheeded throughout the rest of the engagement by the client managers, and eventually had to be replaced – even though he had a stellar performance record before that engagement. The manager who chose not to attend failed to understand the informal aspects of the culture that could open the door to the "shadow system," where informal communications can often reveal much more than the "legitimate system," or formal communication channels.

Language is perhaps the most important aspect of local culture. Understanding the local language is like holding the key of understanding to that culture. Multinational engagements can be conducted in a single language, but developing a deeper, more sustainable relationship with the client may require an understanding of the client's language. People are more likely to express themselves at a deeper level when they can speak in their native tongue, and they are more likely to articulate their specific views about decisions that need to be made during the engagement. Missing these key client insights can lead to major disruptions in the transformation process, if the client is not prepared to accept the change at hand. Knowledge of the local

Table 10.1 Cultural Nuance

Cultural Nuance	Explanation
Use of language and metaphor	The choice of certain terms or metaphors should be carefully considered for each country where they are applied. Terminology used in training manuals, presentations, etc. can carry different meanings and should be reviewed by someone native in that culture before rolling out to a broader population.
Participation in local rituals and events	All countries have their own cultural rituals, and knowing when to participate (or when not to participate) can help break the formal barriers that exist in many countries.
Product or company fit and acceptance	Some products may not be a good fit in certain areas because of cultural beliefs. Discount "big box" stores, for example, are a poor fit in countries like Korea and Japan, where shopping habits differ from those in the West.
Bowing rituals in Asia	Some Asian countries use bowing as a greeting instead of handshakes. Knowing how far to bow, based on your position and the position of the person being bowed to, defines social and hierarchical position, and trying to shake hands while bowing can cause confusion.

Cultural Nuance	Explanation
Food and drink choices and eating habits	Asking for pork or alcohol in Middle Eastern countries, or beef in parts of India, can surprise, or even offend the host. It is important not to laugh at unusual food choices made by the host, as this may also offend. In some cultures where bread is used, in place of a fork, to pick up food on a plate, it is a good idea not to use the left hand.
Inter gender communications and gesturing	Interactions between men and women in certain cultures often carry strict rules. In Muslim countries, it is a good practice for a man not to extend the hand for a handshake, but rather, wait to see if the woman extends her hand first. Slightly bowing with the right hand on the heart is often a more acceptable approach.
Management authoritative behavior	Some cultures do not accept a consensus approach like, for example, in the US. US managers will often fail in foreign cultures because of this approach. In some cultures, it is expected that the manager will use a more autocratic approach, and not doing so may cause the manager to lose respect and credibility in that culture.
User Interface (UI) considerations	In software design, the user interface will often use metaphors, images, etc. to convey purpose. Some metaphors or images can be offensive, or cause confusion in some cultures. When rolling out a system to other countries, the impact of these metaphors should be carefully considered and vetted prior to implementation.
Formal vs. informal language	Some languages (e.g. German, French, and Spanish) have both a formal and informal use. Communicating using the informal (i.e. familiar) language can be offensive if using the informal is not mutually agreed upon. Over time, one may be invited to use the familiar form of the language, which may be followed by a local ritual.

language, therefore, should be a key consideration in the placement of consultants on a multinational project.

When working in an unfamiliar culture, dropping our ethnocentricities, and being aware of our own cultural biases can open us up to new opportunities to learn about our clients and help us form more sustaining relationships. While there may be thousands of cultural nuances to be considered when consulting in foreign countries, the table below exemplifies just a few to make a point.

Having not been exposed to a culture beforehand, a consultant cannot anticipate all of the local nuances and expectations. However, being more observant and open minded can lead to great success when working in unfamiliar countries. The more exposure consultants have to working abroad, the more culture-sensitive and adaptable they will likely become, and such exposure will become a significant asset to any global consulting practice.

Putting the Global Consulting Approach to Work

The best way to explain the integration of the Global Consulting Approach into existing methodologies is to do so through example. Below are several examples of global consulting scenarios using the Global Consulting Approach – the first being an acquisition of a multinational company, the second scenario describes a global information systems rollout, and the third describes the transformation of a national state-run enterprise to a global business. All three scenarios are designed to demonstrate the integration of the Global Consulting Approach in different scenarios.

Multinational Acquisition

Multinational acquisitions occur for many different reasons and look different in every case. If a client acquires a company or spin-off that is physically located in several different countries, the new locations can not only serve as a new source of revenue and distribution for the acquiring company, parts of the acquired entity can also be leveraged to better position the new company globally, in ways that neither company individually could have achieved on its own. As the integration of the two companies is being planned, understanding these new opportunities can return a much higher value than originally anticipated.

Consulting firms that have resources in the locations of the newly acquired entities will have a significant advantage. Ensuring the proper resources are in place for process, organization, financial, and IT integration can expedite the completion of the integration significantly. Local consulting resources must also have an understanding of the local laws and regulatory constraints. If, for example, local manufacturing facilities will be leveraged for new business development opportunities in other countries, the company and consultant must ensure the incorporation of those countries' regulatory requirements as well.

A good practice to ensure that the new organization (i.e. the combined acquiring and acquired entities) can optimize its global footprint is to conduct an organizational simulation. In doing so, the consultant virtually assembles the combined organizational entities as if they were already merged, and asks a series of "what-if" questions. These questions would explore various market potential scenarios, using all existing locations and facilities to determine the best distribution of resources. Simulation scenarios should explore sales, distribution, production, administrative, and supply chain allocations on a global scale, combining and separating resources as needed to achieve the most optimal outcome, while considering time, revenue, and cost factors associated with each change. Scenarios could also include the utilization of existing third-party resources, including supply chain and partnership entities, as well as new partnerships that could serve as a bridge to introducing the company's goods and services into the new country.

Cultural nuances of each geography should be carefully considered with each change caused by the acquisition. Business transformation efforts can vary dramatically, depending on the local culture. In some cultures workers are more conditioned to go with any changes the company imposes, where in other cultures, a forced change can be detrimental, if the workers' voices are not included in the planning process. The acquiring company must consider its own cultural biases when moving into new regions before imposing changes that could affect its local workers, suppliers, and customers.

When integrating a foreign entity into the new organization, there may exist a great deal of what is known as the "FUD" factor (Fear, Uncertainty, and Doubt). Workers in the acquired business may be anxious about the business practices of the new company, and fear their positions changing, or worse yet – their jobs. Some may have been through a failed acquisition before and wonder how long it will take for this one to follow the same fate. How to handle these situations will differ dramatically from country to country, and choosing the wrong approach can be detrimental to the success of the project.

In North America, for example, the incorporation of a new company into the new structure would require lots of empathy, collaboration, and consensus-oriented communication with the newly acquired organization to successfully bring the acquired entity on board with worker buy-in. However, in other parts of the world, structure, conviction, and absolute authority would present a more effective approach. In fact, using the empathetic, consensus-based approach (perceived as too soft in some cultures) may cause confusion, or cause workers to lose respect for the new management team, potentially leading to worker descent, lack of buy-in, and even failure. Knowing the various management styles and workplace cultures in each country can help create the optimal global integration approach.

Global Information Systems Rollout

There are many different types of information and accounting systems, and nearly every department of every global company uses them to capture, process, and disseminate information within the department and to other entities inside and outside the organization. The one thing that each system has in common is that in nearly every case, the system implementation and rollout is conducted either by or with consultants. Consultants not only bring the unique skills needed to effectively implement the systems, but also to ensure the complimentary processes are in place, as well as organizational awareness and training. In other words, on a global scale, the task requires much more than technical skills to ensure success.

Global information systems rollouts require much forethought before implementation – much of which has to do with the organizational structure and the impacts of change at each location. The different locations involved can create issues and barriers as a result of time zone differences, products, disparate processes, and local buy-in. Some key systemic organizational questions must be considered, which could impact the planning, cost, resource allocations, and even the overall success of the rollout. The following questions are a few examples of the many that need to be asked, depending on the structure of the target organization:

- Who is responsible for capturing the system inputs, and where are they located?
- Who is responsible for preparing the system inputs, and where are they located?
- Does the system automatically disseminate and make transparent all information needed throughout the company? If not, who is responsible for disseminating the system outputs, and at where are they located?
- Who needs to receive the system outputs, reports, or alerts, and where are they located?
- Who else could be affected by the information captured, processed, or disseminated by the system and its users, and where are they located?
- Do local time zones interfere with the effective timing of information flow, and if so, where would these time gaps originate?

Information systems and implementation engagements can be impacted by local laws, reporting requirements, regulatory constraints, and other statutory requirements. Once the scope of the implementation is defined, each location must be closely assessed to determine whether or not they require specific data restrictions, configuration requirements, or reporting formats. Regulations regarding financial and human capital management are perhaps the most common, and are usually accounted for in most off-the-shelf systems. But other requirements may not be so obvious and can cause major delays to the rollout effort if not addressed beforehand.

Data protection laws do not exist in some countries, yet in others these laws can be quite restrictive and must be adhered to in order to prevent the untimely shutting down of the system. Europe and Canada have the most restrictive laws, and most globally deployed information systems vendors provide for these regional requirements. However, in some cases, systems are custom designed for a unique company and use, and the developer may not be aware of the country-specific requirements. If consultants wish not to lose credibility, they must anticipate these requirements beforehand and advise both client and developer accordingly to avoid potentially costly mistakes.

When the organizational and change impact assessments have been made, and local laws and regulations are understood in the context of the information system rollout, it is time to begin planning for the resources to be deployed. Functional consultants, such as financial, materials management, and sales-distribution experts, can be assigned for specific configuration and process requirements, as well as technical resources to support the infrastructure development needs. In some cases, specialists will be required to tackle regulatory and other needs, depending on the product, industry, and location. Resources will be allocated to the various locations in scope, and coordinated by the engagement partner or manager to navigate the global complexities and ensure proper communication and integration across all location-specific teams.

With systems implementations, culture is not always the first thing that comes to mind when planning the engagement. However, with global systems rollouts, there is much to be considered to ensure successful buy-in at each location. While language may not play a highly significant role in the system and technical configuration phases, other project-related activities do require close consideration of these often obscure success factors. For example, change management is a key component to large-scale system rollouts, and native language comprehension is necessary to be able to understand and capture user inputs during the design phase, and to properly establish communication plans and discussion points to ensure enterprise-wide buy-in.

Consultants will often hold business "town hall" meetings and "brown bag sessions" to present the changes forthcoming, solicit design inputs and foster future user support and buy-in. The ability to effectively facilitate, and understand the sometimes subtle feedback coming from these user forums requires a total command of the local language. Training design and curriculum may also be impacted by local culture and language comprehension. Understanding the local language and culture, including acceptable idioms and metaphors, is a critical success factor in any enterprise-wide system implementation effort. In training, cases and "what-if" scenarios are often used to exemplify a specific workplace situation. Without clear articulation during these training sessions, the consultant can confuse the client, causing process and system failures, as well as lack of user buy-in.

Transforming a State-Run Enterprise into a Global Company

This scenario exemplifies the many enterprises that have, and continue to be, spun off of national state-controlled enterprises previously run under non-capitalist economic structure. In the past 35 years we have seen many countries shift from extreme nationalist or communist ideologies into a more democratic and capitalist-based system. After the collapse of the Soviet Union, we saw many countries struggle to shift their government structures and state-run enterprises to a more open ideology. During these changes many smaller businesses were left behind, but larger enterprises were often privatized, allowing the new government to establish a foothold in a new economy. It was in the state's interest to retain as much revenue-generating business as possible to ensure that employment and a steady tax revenue stream would carry the new government.

We saw how quickly new Russian oil companies like Lukoil and Gazprom were formed to replace the old Soviet-run enterprise. In fact, these companies formed so quickly under a new society that lacked regulation, that corruption filled the vacuum, leading to decades of problems that dramatically impacted the national economy. In modern-day China we see the emergence of large global companies like Haier and Sinopec emerge, building out their global presence, and even acquiring Western companies and spin-offs to establish a dominant global presence.

In the transformation of these, and the many other like businesses under diminishing authoritarian states, the biggest challenge is the compatibility of business practices – or better stated, the lack of business practices. If a regime change happens quickly, like in the former Soviet Union or East Germany, there will always be a period of chaos, until the local government is able to establish new laws, regulations, and oversight committees to ensure appropriate and ethical business practices. In places where economic changes occur more gradually, like in China, there tends to be an ongoing struggle within the government to try to maintain control over the company, while at the same time, attempting to be a viable contender in the global marketplace. In either case, consultant beware!

This type of business transformation experience is not for those who require a lot of structure in order to be successful. In fact, it requires a great degree of flexibility and change aptitude. For a consultant walking into an enterprise that does not have clear business practices (i.e. like those we learn in business school), no individual business skills, rapidly changing laws and regulatory requirements, no identifiable local market or customer base, and a rapidly dissolving local supply chain, this can be enough to cause a consultant to choose another profession. On the other hand, it can be one of the most rewarding, memorable, and beneficial growth opportunities that can be leveraged as part of a highly valued consulting experience portfolio. Through a slightly different lens, the Global Consulting Approach can be just as useful in these situations as in other, more standard applications of the model.

In the case of the state-run enterprise transformation, the organization must be assessed in a more unconventional method. Spending time assessing as-is organizational structures and process flows can be a futile exercise. Focusing more on the assets and product or service strengths will shed light on the future possibilities for the enterprise. Mapping existing business practices won't work, merely because they likely don't exist. Focusing more on the raw potential of the organization, and using more of a greenfield approach (i.e. like starting a new business that has significantly large assets), will yield higher results, and prevent the organization from trying to hold onto an unrealistic system that simply will not work in today's global economy. The enterprise, in these cases, should be treated like a corporate acquisition that is being dismantled and reconstructed into another, more successful business. The only difference is that there is no acquiring business in this case, and that new structure must be invented.

Local business laws like we know them may not exist, per se, but other, more restrictive laws and regulations may be in place. These laws can slow down the transformation process, and add significant resources and cost to the engagement. These laws can range from those protecting the worker (i.e. the derivative of old guild laws), to those requiring unusual transparency, allowing the State, for example, to see all of the inner workings of the company. In situations where the local government is undergoing vast and rapid change, the same can be expected in new laws and regulations being imposed on the evolving business.

Assessing a company's local markets and customer base can be a bit daunting and often requires a great deal of imagination in these cases – simply because they may not exist today. However, these types of economies often undergo a period of rapid growth after opening up to the global marketplace (e.g. India, Viet Nam, China), and the sudden emergence of a blossoming middle class is the result – a middle class that is desperate to buy goods and services it has long heard about in other countries. While these markets cannot be ignored, other regional opportunities should be addressed as well, providing a safety net of diverse market options, in case the local economy experiences the classic "boom-bust" phenomenon, where the economy explodes, then slows to a snail's pace as it normalizes with the rest of the global economy over time.

The state-run enterprise transformation will, in most cases, benefit greatly with a total reassessment of its supply chain. In these cases, the previous lack of business regulation along with the limited access to suppliers often shows itself in poor quality materials and limited or frequently disrupted supply, which must be addressed before a global launch. If not addressed in a timely manner the business, and its products, can quickly find itself with a reputation of poor quality across the global marketplace. Establishing the right supply chain can prevent the disruption of production and prevent significant costs in product returns – or worse yet, loss of customers. Since the local business would not have had much choice in the selection of its prior supply chain, educating the client on supply chain best practices (e.g. supplier vetting, selection and management, cost models, consolidation practices, etc.) will help ensure the sustained success of the new organization.

In newly emerging economies, the most educated and capable workers are the ones most likely to leave the country for more promising horizons in well-established countries and economies. The remaining workforce in these situations may be steeped with a deep sense of fear, resentment, and lack of confidence. Working with the workforce in these business transformation situations requires much empathy, attention, and patience. Consultants used to working with highly educated and experienced people in other global companies are in for a much different experience. Treating the client workers with impatience and superiority will only cause problems and can jeopardize the engagement. Understanding the situation, showing compassion for the workforce, and patiently establishing programs that will raise their understanding and awareness will go a long way, while offering the consultants a unique experience to add to their global resume.

The Global Consulting Experience

Consulting on a global scale can be highly rewarding, and in some cases, it can even be a transformative experience. A person's entire perspective changes after they have had the opportunity to work abroad, engaging with foreign business clients and mingling with local cultures. We learn a lot about ourselves, becoming more aware of who we are from the perspective of others outside of our own culture, resulting in tremendous growth and awareness. These personal insights, along with the learning that we gain through international exposure, can serve us well for many reasons. As consultants, many of our client counterparts are from other countries. Being able to connect with their common experiences can only enrich the relationship and build trust. Credibility is also established with both the consultant's organization and its clients, when a person has been exposed to other countries' business practices, regulatory structures, and cultural nuances.

I have used many of my own experiences, and those of my colleagues, with whom I worked so closely, and learned so much, to craft the messages in this chapter. You may never have to convert a Communist-run enterprise into a global company, or you may never have to integrate processes and systems across six continents. As a consultant, however, you will very likely have to go abroad to lead or contribute to a global engagement in a culture that is so very different from your own, and that is when I hope you will be able to remain a step ahead of the challenges that will come, and leave that engagement with a new, positive experience.

In the meantime, try to imagine yourself in either one of the aforementioned global consulting scenarios, and think how you would respond to the different behaviors and beliefs of the local client personnel, unforeseen restrictions and challenges, and the vast cultural differences. Would you be prepared to drop your personal biases and ethnocentricities (which we all have), and open your mind to a new experience and way of doing things? Would you be prepared to connect with those who think and, in many cases, act differently than you in a very different business environment? Opportunities for global consulting continue to become more and more available, and if you are up for the challenge, it shouldn't be too difficult for you to find such an experience. Understanding the considerations and approach described in this chapter will help you to anticipate and navigate some of the known challenges, and in some cases, to avoid the unknown challenges that often arise in global consulting.

As global consultants, we tend to build networks that are very rich, carrying with them a high utility when seeking new business development and partnership opportunities, or even future employment. Businesses tend to view global work experience as a valuable asset, and this experience increases our own hiring potential and the likelihood of being promoted in a consulting firm. But most important is the fun and excitement of going into another culture, and experiencing the differences in both work and play. It rounds us out as individuals, and makes our own lives that much more exciting and meaningful.

Chapter Bibliography

1. Axtell, Roger E. *Do's and Taboos Around the World*. White Plains, NY: Parker Pen Company, 1993.
2. Ball, Donald and Michael Geringer. *International Business: The Challenge of Global Competition, 13th Edition*. New York: McGraw-Hill Education, 2012.
3. Barabasi, Albert L. *Linked*. New York: Penguin Plume, 2003.
4. Beniger, James R. *The Control Revolution: Technological and Economic Origins of the Information Society*. Cambridge, MA: Harvard University Press, 1986.
5. Collins, James and Jerry Porras. *Built to Last*. New York: Harper Business Books, 1997.
6. Daneke, Gregory. "Coming Full Circle: On the Return of Systems Thinking to Strategic Management." *Journal of Business and Management* (Fall 1994): 8–33.
7. Debenham, Lucy. "Etiquette in the United Arab Emirates." Travel Etiquette Website, January, 2016.
8. Dresser, Norine. *Multicultural Manners: Essential Rules of Etiquette for the 21st Century, 1st Edition*. Hoboken, NJ: Wiley & Sons, 2005.
9. Drucker, Peter. "Long Range Planning." *Management Science* (1959, Vol. 5): 3.
10. Heim, Matthew C. *Breaking the Musashi Code: Transcending Competition through Visionary Strategy*. Sonoma, CA: Visionary Partnership Press, 2007.
11. Hill, Charles W.L. *International Business: Competing in the Global Marketplace*. New York: McGraw-Hill, 2014.
12. Morrison, Terri and Wayne A. Conway. *Kiss, Bow or Shake Hands: Asia – How to do Business in 12 Asian Countries*. Avon, MA: Adams Media, 2007.
13. Oshry, Barry. *Seeing Systems: Unlocking the Mysteries of Organizational Life*. San Francisco: Barrett Koehler, 1995.
14. Porter, Michael E. *Competitive Strategy*. New York: The Free Press, 1980.
15. Rosenbloom, Arthur. *Due Diligence for Global Deal Making: The Definitive Guide to Cross-Border Mergers and Acquisitions, Joint Ventures, Financings, and Strategic Alliances*. Princeton, NJ: Bloomberg Press, 2002.
16. Rumelt, Richard P., Dan E. Schendel, and David J. Teece. *Fundamental Issues in Strategy*. Boston: Harvard Business School Press, 1994.
17. Singh, J.V. "McKinsey's Managing Director Rajat Gupta on Leading a Knowledge-Based Global Consulting Organization." *Academy of Management* (May 1, 2001, Vol. 15, No. 2): 34–44.
18. Soofi, A. and Yuqin Zhang. *Global Mergers & Acquisitions: Combining Companies Across Borders*. New York: Business Expert Press, 2014.
19. Stacey, Ralph. *Complexity and Creativity in Organizations*. San Francisco: Barrett Koehler, 1996.
20. Teece, David. "Economic Analysis and Strategic Management." Glenn R. Carrol and David Vogel, eds. *Strategy and Organization: A West Coast Perspective*. Boston: Pittman, 1984.

11 Public Sector Consulting

Thomas H. Olson

1. What Is Public Sector Consulting?

1.a. Public Sector as Compared/Contrasted with Private Sector

Public Sector (Government) Consulting is the aggregate of all professional services provided to governmental organizations as a part of a country's overall economy. The Public Sector constituency is made up of all persons in the country; the purpose of the Public Sector is to provide for the general public. Organizations that are not government, but businesses, are not Public Sector. For the Private Sector (businesses), the economic purpose is to generate profits for its constituency – the owners of the business. Different from Private Sector services, Public Sector services are essentially benefiting all of the country or a 'greater good'. Public Sector services are generally funded through taxation. This is contrasted with the Private Sector that is essentially made up of privately owned entities (independents, families, stockholders of corporations, etc.) that benefit those owners. In the US, these privately owned entities – both 'for profit' and 'non-profit' – are not part of any government. For discussion of organization forms, see Daft (2012).

While the bulk of this textbook focuses on Private Sector Consulting, this chapter will focus on Public Sector Consulting and Contracting. As an additional comment to Public and Private Sectors, there is a third sector of Consulting Services within countries, the Volunteer/Charity Sector. And as the Charity Sector is relatively small (and typically calls on significant numbers of volunteers) as compared to the Public Sector and Private Sectors, it is not nearly as large a sector for professional consulting services.

Professional consulting services provided in the Public vs. Private Sector are similar, as well as different. Similarities in government and business services include providing professional advice (thought/ideas), diagnoses/problem solving (data/assessment) and/or implementation/production/sustainment contracts (make/do something / operate and maintain something). Differences with government vs. business consulting services typically evolve about what or how professional services are 'requested' and managed. Examples of differences that need to be understood by consultants new to the Public Sector are topics relating to: government requests for proposals (RFPs) of services, understanding and responding to specific requirements (in the RFP) involved in proposing contracts for services, the role of government 'intermediaries' (typically known as a 'Contract Officers'), transparency in the bidding and feedback on proposals, etc. Further, individual/organizational privacy and other rights and issues will differ depending on variations in the law under which the business and/or government is legislated. These topics, including the contractual requirements of Federal Acquisition Regulation (FAR), are discussed in more detail later in this chapter.

In summary, the Private Sector is made up of entities that are not owned or run by government. And the Public Sector is made up of entities that are owned and run by government (federal, state and municipal in the US with variations to these distinctions depending on country). The consulting/contractor businesses that provide the bulk of these Public Sector consulting services and contracts will, therefore, be the focus of this chapter. Private Sector companies provide consulting services to Public Sector customers. Reference for additional comment: *Oxford Handbook of Management Consulting*, especially, "Part 5: Consultants and Their Clients".

1.b. Public Sector: United States vs. International

1.b.i. Consulting Contractors to the US Federal Government vs. Other Countries

There are essentially two (2) complex questions here:

1. How do US-based (individual and company/firm) consultants/contractors provide services in the US vs. internationally – especially with every country having differences in procedures, rules, law, etc.?
2. How do non-US-based (individual and company/firm) consultants/contractors provide services in the US (and then, relatively, in their own country)?

Collectively, responses to these questions regarding domestic vs. international 'presence' and competition are complicated and complex – making this a 'fascinating topic' for discussion. For domestic consultants/contractors – such as Lockheed Martin Corp (LMC), Boeing and Northrop Grumman Corp (NGC) – they do, indeed, provide services and products not only domestically but to other countries as well. However, there are some domestic US companies for which it may not be 'true' that they provide international services. As an example, this may be well exemplified by consultants/contractors such as Scitor Corporation (now owned by SAIC) that specialize in the 'Intel world'. Scitor may well be limited to domestic to best maintain security related to its services and technologies. As an example of the complexity of Public Sector services across borders, Scitor Corporation states on May 16, 2016, on its home page the following:

> Scitor's world-class workforce is comprised of professionals from broadly diversified backgrounds such as former military, government and intelligence officers, business leaders from wide-ranging industries, multi-disciplinary scientists, mathematicians, information and financial analysts, and all disciplines of engineers. We collaborate with customers and across our business areas to support all phases of complex systems and programs – from initial concept and requirements definition, to acquisition, development and deployment, to operations and maintenance.

Conversely for internationall based consultants/contractors, some of these, such as BAE, are not United States based/owned. And as such, they operate in the United States via subsidiary and/or align with United States Companies in order to bid on some US Contracts.

Please reference the BAE case in *Contemporary Consultant's Experts Casebook* (Greiner, Olson & Poulfelt 2010) for insight regarding this issue.

US companies with US Public Sector business must be aware of and comply with applicable export regulations and laws. Further, companies such as Hewlett Packard Enterprise (now a separate company from HP Inc.) and IBM in the Public Sector do provide services to other countries. And these consultants/contractors tailor what they provide to the United States Government and foreign customers based on the fact that they are international. For example, one well known consultant/contractor provides *defensive* cyber for the US Government, but does not provide *offensive* cyber. Generalizing, this would be the case for other companies dealing in the international arena.

1.b.ii. Effects of Consulting/Contracting 'Globalization'

Given the economies of countries becoming ever more global in reach and affect, it is important to note that the array of all consulting, Private and Public, services has become more similar across the developed countries of the world. In this regard, while Public Sector consulting varies from country to country, most developed countries provide Public Sector services that involve education, health care, the interior/infrastructure (roads, waterways, etc.), the law (enforcement, prison systems, etc.), the military and other 'service domains'. In the United States, the Federal Government organization of services is attained via different Cabinet Level Departments (Education, Defense, Health and Welfare, Interior, Justice, etc.). And it is to these Departments that most of the money spent on Public Sector Consulting occurs.

It is important to observe that there are significant and potential issues related to non-US (individual and company/firm) consultants/contractors working in the US with Public Sector. The obvious issues involve any and all of those factors that relate to working with Classified, Secret and Top Secret information and technology of Public Sector clients. It is the foremost requirement to safeguard information and the 'flow/access to' that information. And given that non-US citizenship persons/consultants cannot be vetted for US security clearances, the issue is patently clear. This is a principal reason that non-US citizen consultants/contractors are limited. Blend this issue with heightened issues of international terrorism and other adverse threatening acts shrink access by non-US consultants to the Public Sector as well.

Non-US (individual and company/firm) consultants/contractors (based outside of the US) to the Public Sector are limited not only in the kind of work they can be 'allowed' to pursue. Other limits have to deal with not being allowed contact with a broad variety of persons and clients (such as intelligence agencies) and more. The limitations for non-US (individual and company/firm) consultants are in place to protect the security and best interests of the US. And these interests are best protected by limiting access by non-US citizens to non-sensitive and non-classified information and technologies and requiring specific clearances that must be attained via vigorous and thorough vetting/investigation.

There same issues are present with US companies working internationally – though with a reverse focus. The most relevant issues involve international clients' concerns that parallel those that the US has for non-US consultants regarding their home country's Classified, Secret and Top Secret information and technology. The obvious concern of protection of our consultants in countries where there is higher potential or history of terrorism and other dangers (kidnapping, coercion, etc.) is clear as well. As is commonly understood, the protection of US consultants having rich, sensitive or classified information or technology is paramount. And given the responsibilities of US consultants to keep secure their 'knowledge and processes' abroad, the protection of information and technology are paramount here, too. Export laws restrict even the carrying of electronic devices that have held potentially sensitive information related to the Federal Government outside of the United States.

1.c. *Brief Observation of Public Sector Distinction/Separation in US – Federal vs. SLED (State, Local, and Educational)*

In the US, the Public Sectors/governmental bodies are built from the local (town/city) to county to state to federal levels. At essentially each of the levels there exist Public Sector services for defense (law enforcement), education, health care, interior (roads and rivers), legal (judicial courts, jails/prisons) and so on. States and municipalities contract for services such as infrastructure construction and maintenance and information technology in a manner similar to that of the Federal Government, but using state and local government laws and policies. Additionally, state and local educational institutions follow their own processes for hiring and managing contractors and consultants, adhering to applicable federal law.

Suffice it to observe, there has been continual debate in the US as to what Public Sector activities should be or need to be provided at each governmental level. As changes in Public Sector law and resulting services are driven by the legislative and legal branches of the government bodies at all levels in the US, these changes become the basis for the establishment of, or changes to, new and/or different Public Sector law and resulting services and solutions. Ultimately, it is the US federal level legislature and (Federal and Supreme) courts that determine the 'boundaries' for Public Sector activities.

Among the most important matters for the entire US, as well as most countries of the world, is the US Federal Government mandate to provide for the overall defense of the US as well as for coordination and oversight of all other public services. It is most relevant to observe here that in addition to the Federal Debt and Social Security that the largest amount spent federally in the US are those monies related to Defense and GSA (General Services Administration).

1.d. Context – Industry Size and Major Companies Providing Consulting/Production Services

As we know, and per the US budgeting and spending processes, every year the US government budgets and apportions vast amounts of money, billions of dollars, in many Public Sectors. As mentioned earlier, some of the major Public Sectors include defense/infrastructure, general services, the National Debt, social security and health care. And according to the census of 2015, the federal government has spent over 4 trillion dollars in these Sectors with a significant amount of that budgeting and spending being allocated to contracts that were 'bid'/negotiated with private consulting/contracting businesses. It is these private consulting/contractor businesses that have a long and involved and, some pundits observe, complicated relationship with the US government – with many engaging in first and/or primary contracting essentially starting just after World War II. It is these private consulting/contracting businesses, and their consulting relationship with the Public Sector Federal Government in the US, that will be the focus of this chapter.

1.e. Public Sector Consultants by Size – Seven Largest

As of 2016, the seven largest consultants/contractors with the US government were: Lockheed Martin (LMC), Boeing, Raytheon, General

Dynamics (GD), Northrop Grumman (NGC), Leidos Holdings (w SAIC – two separate companies now) and Huntington Ingalls Industries (HII). Other major and large (in terms of revenue and employees) consulting firms to the Public Sector included: Accenture, BAE, Booz Allen Hamilton Inc., Computer Sciences Corporation (CSC), General Electric, HP (Enterprise Services – Hewlett Packard Enterprise as of November, 2015), International Business Machines (IBM), SRA International, Inc. (see next sentence), Unisys Corporation and AECOM, which acquired URS Corporation in October, 2014. Regarding CSC and SRA, it should be noted that CSC 'spun off' its Public Sector business and acquired SRA, creating CSRA in November, 2015; this was called a merger, though financially, it was more an acquisition. While these are but a few of the literally tens of hundreds of thousands of businesses that provide Public Sector consulting, these businesses are widely recognized and significant. And, therefore, these consultants will be referenced and provided for representative examples of engagements and programs about which more information is available and known.

Further, it is well known that these companies are associated with the defense industry and general and other services' Public Sectors. They are significant consultants and contractors thereto. In this regard, it is to be noted that the US spends approximately 600 billion dollars on its military every year – quite a large pool of monies for contractors and Public Sector Consulting/Contactor Industry.

In a subsequent section, there is a brief discussion of each of the seven largest companies. These discussions will provide the reader an overview of the history and the current condition of each primary contractor company and Public Sector Consulting domain as a whole.

2. Process for U.S. Federal Government Consulting – Contractor/Client Roles, Relationships, Rules, Regulations and Request for Proposals

2.a. 'Building the Client Relationship' in Advance to Help 'Shape' Requirements and Process

Let us be very clear – consultants/contractors build relationships with existing and potential clients. This is very similar to the strategic positioning of the consultant to the client as in the Private Sector (Greiner and Cummings 2009).

This said, there are specific 'can dos' and 'no can dos' regarding the consultant-client relationship in the Public Sector. This is especially so regarding the necessity to learn (so as to assist a client) how to 'put together' a prospective RFP's requirements (or other work) in advance of a formal announcement.

One particularly important 'can do' is to build and know (and some would say, influence) the customer in advance of any (especially major expenses incurred for) formal RFPs. This 'process' is often described as investing in 'customer intimacy'. The logic and rationale are obvious . . . the more the consultant knows the client's needs and motives and choice processes, etc., the better the consultant can positively (while legally) influence the 'shaping' of RFPs and key factors therein.

Traditional methods for Public Sector consultants/contractors to build and influence 'the client relationship' and knowledge of the consultant/contractor are to be involved and participate in and with the same professional organizations as clients. Some of these professional organizations include the Armed Forces Communications & Electronics Association (AFCEA), the National Defense Industry Association (NDIA) and many more. Relationship building and exchange of information in the professional organization setting can be formal, such as presentations at conferences, or informal, such as one-on-one or small group discussions at a luncheon.

As for 'no can dos', one particularly important 'not allowed' (that is strictly forbidden for a consultant/contractor to do) is to overtly or covertly specifically define requirements for the client on which the consultant/contractor would actually be bidding. Specifically defining requirements is not allowed to be provided to clients by the consultants/contractors in advance of any other consultant's/contractor's knowledge. As should seem clear, this would be a very 'slippery slope'. This kind of influence is not allowed no matter how small or large the RFP requirement.

The above said, it is allowed for consultants/contractors to build relationships with client decision-makers that allow (all) the consultants/contractors to make presentations, deliver unsolicited papers and have conversations to help 'shape' requirements by means of suggestions to the government client. And a methodology used most often involves consultants/contractors employing marketing and/or sales organizations (Business Development executives/managers/staff) that focus on current and potential customers. Public Sector Business Development is central (as it is in the Private Sector) to the building of client relationships, influencing client needs and ultimately, the RFP content. As with the Private Sector, a most vexing decision for the consultant/contractor is regarding how many dollars to commit to spend on marketing/sales and 'customer intimacy'. Strategic marketing decisions need to be made by the consultant/contractor regarding government markets and customers to pursue, indirect and direct expenditures for Professional Association participation, advertising, marketing (print/on-line) directed to the Public Sector in general and/or on more specific Cabinet level 'organizations', programs, processes, etc. Additionally, it should be noted that the major Consulting/Contractor Firms have formal lobbying organizations within Business Development/Marketing or Public Affairs.

2.b. *'Winning' Proposals Are Key to Public Sector Consulting*

The Public Sector consultant/contractor must identify client needs and develop business largely via 'the **Federal Acquisition Regulation (FAR)** Process'. Essentially, this requires consultants to not only understand how to identify client requirements but to build proposals that would be designed to meet all of the requirement elements for the client. These client requirement elements are presented in what is known as a Request for Proposal (RFP) that is 'issued' by the Public Sector clients.

The 'building of proposals' by consultants is most often a labor intensive process that involves significant expenditures in development costs to identify client needs and build responding proposals. For larger contract awards (in the millions or more) in the Public Sector, 'the proposal process' is sophisticated and complex. There are most often hundreds – if not thousands – of requirements. And the consultant's proposal must specifically address each requirement.

A simple 'failure' of not responding to literally any one requirement can result in not having an entire proposal considered – let alone having it not compete and, therefore, not be considered for award. It is paramount, as in the Private Sector, that Public Sector contractors understand clients'/customers' 'wants, wishes and needs'. This said, it is central to 'capturing' Public Sector contracts that consultants ensure that each proposal is built to each and every stated requirement and all evaluation criteria. It is equally important to 'capturing' contracts that each proposal provides details of what the consultant/contractor is committing to do and provides many specific examples of past successes. Key personnel can be, and usually are, very important to identify as well (and consistent with Private Sector consulting). In today's competitive marketplace, 'low price' (although not always lowest price) is essentially mandatory. Specific requirements/elements that 'govern' the 'proposal/acquisition process' are the following:

2.b.i.   Federal Acquisition Regulation (FAR)

REFERENCE RESEARCH HERE FROM HTTPS://WWW.ACQUISITION.GOV/ – LATEST REFERENCE APRIL, 2016, INCLUDING HTTPS://EN.WIKIPEDIA.ORG/WIKI/FEDERAL_ACQUISITION_REGULATION

(Reference footnotes are provided in Appendix 1.)

> The **Federal Acquisition Regulation (FAR)** is the principal set of rules in the Federal Acquisition Regulations System. The FAR System governs the "acquisition process" by which executive agencies of the United States federal government acquire (i.e., purchase or lease) goods and services by contract with appropriated funds.[1,2,3] The process consists of three phases:[4]
>
> 1   Need recognition and acquisition planning;
> 2   Contract formation; and
> 3   Contract administration.
>
> The FAR System regulates the activities of government personnel in carrying out that process. The FAR System is codified at Title 48, Chapter 1

of the Code of Federal Regulations. These requirements can be found in the Code of Federal Regulations at 48 C.F.R. 31.

While nearly all federal government executive agencies are required to comply with the FAR, some executive agencies are exempt (e.g., the Federal Aviation Administration[5,6] and the U.S. Mint.[7,8] In those cases, the agency promulgates its own specific procurement rules.[9,10] The remainder of the FAR System consists mostly of sets of regulations issued by executive agencies of the federal government of the United States to supplement the FAR.[11]

The specific elements of the FAR include the following 'contents' as quoted from the reference noted: Purpose, Procedure, Authority, Structure and Supplements. These elements are found in Appendix 1.

2.b.ii. Competition in Contracting Act of 1984

REFERENCE RESEARCH HERE FROM HTTPS://INTERACT.GSA.GOV/BLOG/COMPETITION-CONTRACTING-ACT-CICA OR WIKIPEDIA

Transparency in competition for the US government is a cornerstone of the 'winning' Public Sector work. In addition to needing to follow the FAR System, it is necessary to follow 'additional regulations' as set forth in The Competition in Contracting Act (CICA) of 1984. It is the CICA, as issued as Public Law 98–369 (98 stat, 1175 et seq.), that authorizes the use of "general solicitations" or Broad Agency Announcements (BAAs). It is these solicitations and announcements that provide a foundation for 'basic' proposals – where in it is stated that the use of general solicitations is limited by the CICA to "basic research proposals". Additionally, it is stated that Contracts awarded under these general solicitations must meet the "full and open" (transparent) competition requirements of CICA.

2.b.iii. Broad Agency Announcements (BAA)

REFERENCE RESEARCH HERE FROM HTTPS://EN.WIKIPEDIA.ORG/WIKI/BROAD_AGENCY_ANNOUNCEMENT; REQUESTS FOR INFORMATION (RFIs); REQUESTS FOR PROPOSALS (RFPs)

Further, to the 'proposal/acquisition process', the Broad Agency Announcement (BAA) is a competitive solicitation procedure used to obtain proposals for basic and applied research and that part of development not related to the development of a specific system or hardware procurement. The BAA is described in FAR 6.102, "Use of Competitive Procedures", and FAR 35.016, "Broad Agency Announcements".

Basic Authority is as cited above for the CICA. The type of research solicited under a BAA attempts to increase knowledge in science and/or to advance the state of the art as compared to practical application of knowledge.

2.c. After 'Winning' a Public Sector Consulting Contract . . . 'Next Steps' . . . to Commence a Consulting/Contracting Engagement

In today's environment, first, the consulting contractor needs to wait through the 'protest stage'. It is 'post winning' that 'non-winning' consultants can contest the 'award'. This is typically called a 'protest'.

This occurs often and can/does delay the commencement of the engagement by potentially months and months. Non-winning businesses must weigh the pros and cons of submitting a protest. The non-winning company must have a substantiated claim that the evaluation criteria was not followed, or evidence of unfair competition. Protests can be expensive and often require the use of outside counsel. Protests are allowed and have become a norm in Public Sector contracting; the procuring office cannot retaliate against a company for a protest. But sometimes a protest leaves a less-than-positive image of the protesting company. As in the Private Sector, companies need to consider their overall business reputation and the impact of that reputation on future potential business opportunities.

Following this 'protest stage', the typical 'next steps' include i. Client meetings, ii. 'Kick-off' discussions, and iii. Documentation of expectations. These meetings/discussions are pursued to best assure that the contract clearly defines what is expected. This said, some contracts allow for negotiation and elements of the contract 'award' can be 'realigned/restructured'. Further, some contracts may – by intent – be vague to allow for more flexibility. And, if working on a fixed price, this can be an issue. Consulting Contractors (essentially always) want the engagement to be a win/win so a 'management of expectations' is pursued without it 'looking' as such. This is where having a Program Manager and management team with the ability to have 'trust of customer' while keeping 'contract limitations' in mind is very valuable and important. Please reference Charles H. Green's chapters (Chapters 6 and 18) of this textbook.

Additionally, what the consultant contractor 'is allowed' to do vis-à-vis its relationship with Contract Officers varies broadly (for contracts that the Consultant/Contractor has 'won'). In some cases, only Contracts Specialists and Managers from the consultant/contractor companies are allowed to contact/speak with Government Contracting Officers. Yet in other contract RFP/circumstances, other Public Sector clients allow sales, marketing and Program Managers to have contact with Government Contracting Officers.

Table 11.1 Government Fiscal Year 2016 Socioeconomic Goals

Goal Category	Goal %
Small Business	23%
Small Disadvantaged Business	5%
Women Owned	5%
Service Disabled Veteran Owned	3%
Certified HUBZone Small Business	3%

2.d. Small Business Administration and Socioeconomic Requirements

REFERENCE FROM: HTTP://SMALLBUSINESS.DATA.GOV/ PROVIDES THE SB DASHBOARD

The US Federal Government has set socioeconomic goals to assist small businesses, service-disabled veteran-owned businesses, women-owned businesses and HUBZone (Historically Underutilized Business Zone) businesses grow and thrive. US Federal Agencies generally adopt these goals or set their own goals that vary slightly from the federal goals. Government Contracting Officers usually attach small business goals to contracts awarded to large businesses in accordance with the FAR. In some contracts, goals are set as a percentage of business subcontracted; in other contracts, small business requirements are set as a percentage of total revenue. Large prime contractors must often include in their proposal a plan describing the extent of participation of small businesses. Small businesses that are awarded a contract as a prime contractor in response to an RFP achieve small business goals without having to subcontract.

3. The Role of the Consultant/Contractor Vis-à-Vis Competitor Clients/Customers – Prior, During and After the RFP

3.a. 'Winning' the Contract Vis-à-Vis Your Competitors

Consultants/Contractors must know not only their own strengths and weaknesses but the strengths and weaknesses of their competition as well. Consultants/Contractors must also know what the customer client's 'hot buttons' are – typically, quality, time to complete and cost – and how to 'address' these in the Consultant's/Contractor's Proposal to the Client RFP. If all of what the Consultants/Contractors perceive as 'hot buttons' are not included in evaluation criteria, there is substantive argument (and strongly suggested) that the Consultants/Contractors write the Public Sector RFP Contracting Officer, and others available to inquire as to evaluation criteria. This said, it is too late to do this after a RFP is released. This can only be accomplished if a draft RFP is released. Draft RFPs are often released with the request and expectation of input from industry. It is highly suggested that Consultant/Contractors spend the time to read and comment on draft RFPs for this reason. Consultant/Contractors can also make suggestions prior to RFP release that will impact acquisition in other ways: contract type, timing of responses, technological feasibility WRT timeline, etc.

In regard to the above for the Consultants/Contractors it is equally significant to keep in mind 'ghost' or offer hot button 'solutions' in building the Consultant's/Contractor's proposal. Consultants/Contractors often argue that the BEST 'approach' is to know the customer well (enough) to help the customer shape his/her requirements without going to the point of writing requirements. Warnings are in order; Consultants/Contractors need to avoid even the appearance of a potential conflict of interest. Getting too close to the client can lead to a contractor's proposal being 'excluded' from consideration and evaluation due to 'being overly conflicted' and thereby excluded from the competition . . . (OR competitor can protest saying that you helped to write requirements).

3.b. Key Points to Be Known/Considered When Consultants Build Proposals

The consultant contractor must build its Proposal to *ALL of the requirement elements of the RFP* as specifically as possible. *Not responding to any one requirement can result in not having a Proposal considered – let alone having it compete and be considered for award.* It is paramount, as in the Private Sector, that Public Sector contractors understand customers' 'wants and needs', yet make sure that the Proposal is built to stated evaluation criteria. It is equally paramount to provide details of what the contractor is going to do and provide examples of past successes. Key personnel can be, and usually are, very important. In today's competitive marketplace, 'low price' (although not always lowest price) is very important.

Bear in mind that the consultant/contractor must 'decide' on which RFPs it will dedicate professionals' time regarding proposals at least in two regards. The first has to do with 'pre-RFP' commitments the consultant makes regarding assigning resources and time to 'search' for qualified opportunities and RFPs on which the consultant could have interest and capability to respond. The second has to do with the actual preparation of a proposal to each of the selected RFPs. Each of these require time and money that the consultant/contractor must be willing to spend to review possibilities and then to construct proposals responding to requirements of RFPs.

3.c. Growth in Company/Client's Size – Especially Number of Employees, Geographic Presence, Client Mix and Revenue/Profitability

It goes without saying that size is a significant factor in the Public Sector. This is particularly true for the very large (billion-dollar) production consultant contracts.

The sheer number of employees, global distribution of people, economic size (cash flow/simple magnitude of money for Business Development and R&D), etc. are critical. Further, it is obvious over the past years that growth by M&A has been substantive and 'changed the landscape' of the major Public Sector consultants/contractors. Specific examples include the largest firms, especially Boeing (with Rockwell – albeit for Rockwell Collins that is still prominent, especially after acquiring part of ARINC December 2013), Lockheed Martin and Northrop Grumman (with TRW and Litton). These examples reflect some of the major 'aggregation' that has occurred with the Public Sector consultants/contractors.

Of course, there has been organic (vs. M&A) growth, although mergers and acquisitions have been the largest source of growth in the relatively 'flat' Public Sector market. Some additional changes involving 'spin-offs' (as with SAIC and Huntington Ingalls Industries – HII) have been significant to the Public Sector.

3.c.i. Knowing the Client/Customer IS Key to Growth

A key element – if not most important – is 'Knowing the Client'. As mentioned earlier in this chapter, this is often referred to 'customer intimacy' in the Public Sector. Knowing the client is critical to 'winning' work and growth. This is essentially no different than consulting in the Private Sector. The more we know of a client's/customer's 'make-up', the better. Typical strategic analyses are very relevant here. (Please see the "Strategy and Organization Consulting" chapter as a reference.) Suffice it to observe that any/all variety of factors including client motivation, financial condition, strategy, organization, etc. are important to know and understand. Especially important are the factors: technical and 'mission' requirements, risk tolerance and cost/price sensitivity. These are significant to building 'the best knowledge' of the client, and, therefore, to the 'winning' of work.

3.c.ii. Following 'the Proposal Process' – A 'Must' to Grow Business

As mentioned earlier, a key to growing business as a consultant is 'Influencing' the client in ways that are acceptable. This translates to appropriately responding as a means of providing feedback and suggestions to potential government customers. Further, writing and providing 'white papers' (thought/idea 'papers' with applicable research, etc.) to the client (with marking of proprietary when applicable) is also prudent for the consultant to legally do. The consultant must bear in mind that asking questions of the client is acceptable though must be done with the knowledge that the client (government) is legally responsible to provide equal access (to all consultants). This legal requirement can, and does, at times equal no access to all. Government acquisition of services typically reaches a point in the acquisition cycle in which consultants/contractors no longer have access to the decision maker and must communicate with the government solely through the warranted Contracting Officer. The Contracting Officer will then make questions and answers available to all potential responders. Growing revenue, etc. does require the consultant to influence to be competitive.

4. Responding to Request for Proposals

4.a. Propose to Stated Requirements and Evaluation Criteria

As stated earlier, it is critical that each response to an RFP address each and every contract parameter/element/requirement. This is significant as the client Public Sector government agency will be contractually bound by each of these requirements to what is submitted by and agreed to by the consultant/contractor. It is imperative that the 'full set' of all requirements be addressed as specifically in detail as possible. This is the 'heart' of the response process.

4.b. Pricing the Proposal in the Detail as Per the Client RFP

In today's environment, cost/price is the central parameter for contract award. For the reader not familiar with Public Sector terminology: Price is cost + fee (profit) to the government. Cost is often considered to be labor + materials + 'wrap' without fee, where 'wrap' is overheard, fringe, G&A, material handling fee in whatever manner the company applies these. For cost + contracts, all is disclosed to the government. Usually in firm fixed price, the government sees one total price inclusive of everything . . . and there are multiple versions between these.

Of course, and in addition to cost/price, there are quality and time-to-perform requirements as well as other factors that include contributions to improve and/or develop new technology(ies)/patents and the like. Without a competitive cost/price bid, it is not likely that a consultant/contractor proposal will be seriously considered. As mentioned, there are some mitigating circumstances that involve unique 'solutions' to meet requirements. These unique solutions may involve significant/break-through new technology(ies) and/or process(es) or the like that may be 'just developed' or 'new' (as proprietary or licensed intellectual property) to one of the competitive consultants/contractors.

For those interested in understanding more of the 'costing' methodologies, please refer to the Cost Accounting Standards (CAS) and the FAR (part 30 as well as Wikipedia's CAS description). Additionally, and an element of costing are other factors related to performance. In many years past, decades ago, most consulting/contractor agreements were 'actual' cost plus fee. And over time theses 'sky's-the-limit', actual costing contracts disappeared due to the fact that the higher the cost of the program, the higher the revenue and profit for the consultant/contractor. This contracting methodology does not incentivize cost savings, but is still used in some developmental programs. Most cost plus type programs were replaced by fixed costing/pricing agreements – often with incentives-for-performance if certain target indices were met. For the consulting professional pursuing more knowledge here, it is suggested that those interested seek additional information from FAR as well as determinations as to whether all federal contracting must be CAS compliant.

4.c. Consultant/Client Contract Awards and Protests – Trends Toward Low Price Services

Section 2.c. presents an introduction to and discussion of awards and protests. For US Federal Government contracts, Contractor/Consultant protests are handled by the US Government Accountability Office (GAO). GAO provides information related to the protest process (timelines, regulations and guidelines) as well as questions and answers on its web-site: http://www.gao.gov/legal/bid-protests/our-process and http://www.gao.gov/legal/bid-protests/faqs.

4.d. Proposal Outline/Contracting Process within the Public Sector – '9 Step Model'

The following is a prototype Proposal Outline, the *'9 Step Model'*, to follow to assure best proposal results. This is a recommended 'Step by Step' reference to 'build' a proposal for all Public Sector (as well as Private Sector) consultants/contractors.

> Please recognize and note that this is a Copy written Document identified as "Developing Successful Consulting Proposals" and presented/referenced at several Annual Meetings of the National Academy of Management. The title of this reference Document is: "Developing Successful Consulting Proposals", Thomas H. Olson. The *'9 Step Model'* follows.

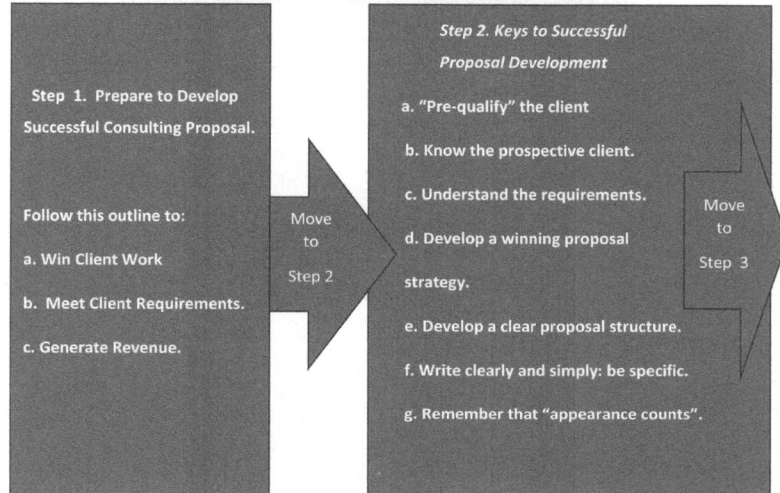
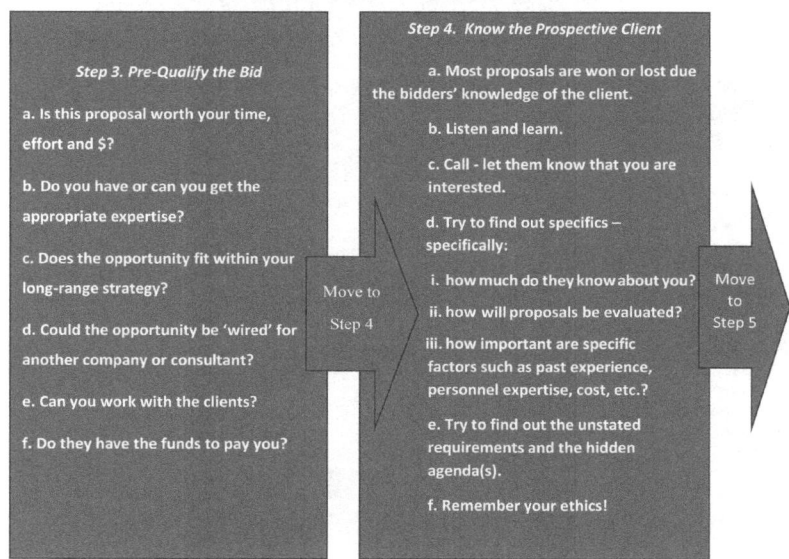

Figure 11.1 Prototype Proposal Outline

© Copyright and Proprietary Document. May not be copied or reproduced, in whole or in part, without the written consent of the author Thomas H. Olson.

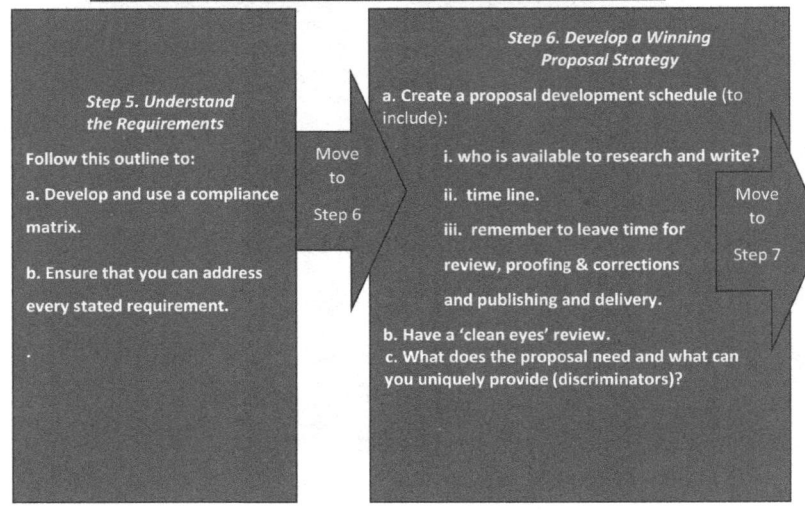

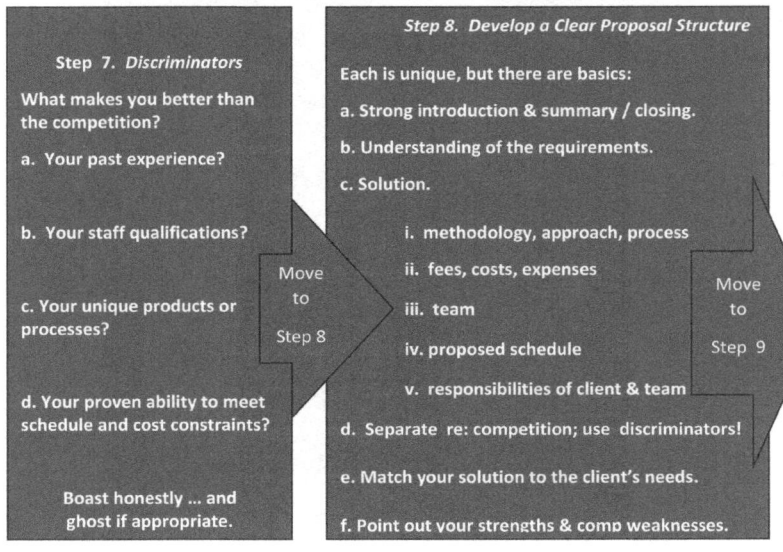

Figure 11.1 Continued

Prototype Proposal Outline

9 Step Model with 3 Reference Exhibits – Step 9

Remember - Writing Style and Appearance Count

a. Substantiate your claims
b. Emphasize customer benefits
c. Be clear & straightforward — vague proposals are confusing
d. Skip the fancy stuff (reverse type, too many fonts or artsy styles)
e. Use graphics for simpler illustration — describe the relationship between data and strategy
f. Use action language and action caption

Prototype Proposal Outline

9 Step Model – 3 Reference Exhibits follow below

Figure 11.1 Continued

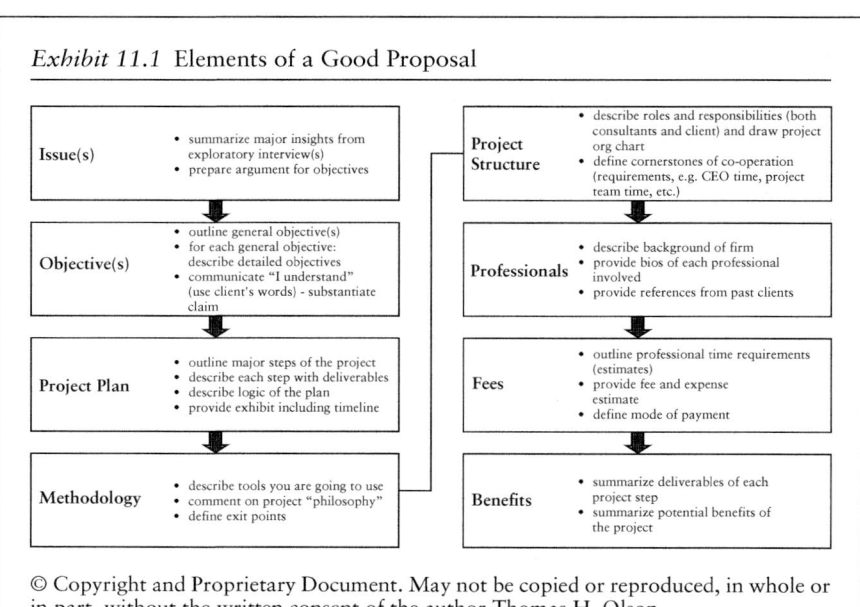

Exhibit 11.1 Elements of a Good Proposal

© Copyright and Proprietary Document. May not be copied or reproduced, in whole or in part, without the written consent of the author Thomas H. Olson.

It is critical that each of the 3 Reference Exhibits be followed and completed for each proposal prepared and submitted. The Public Sector (as with the Private Sector) client will specifically look for each of these.

To assure the best presentation and submission and to leverage the evaluation of the proposal, each of these 3 Reference Exhibits needs to be completed in detail and specific to the requirements of the RFP. Make your best effort to create the best of each of the Reference Exhibits!

To this end:

1 It is significant and essentially critical that the 'Proposal Team' follow the "Elements of a Good Proposal".
2 Further, each Proposal Team needs to prepare a substantive 'Project Plan'.
3 And, additionally, each Proposal Team needs to prepare a thoughtful and detailed numeric estimate of all 'Staffing/Workload' in the form of at least one 'Master Chart'.

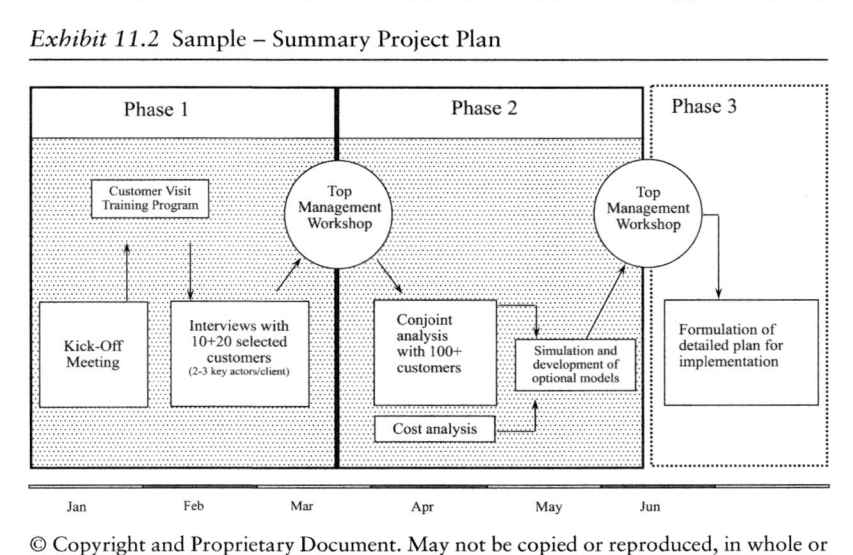

Exhibit 11.2 Sample – Summary Project Plan

© Copyright and Proprietary Document. May not be copied or reproduced, in whole or in part, without the written consent of the author Thomas H. Olson.

Exhibit 11.3 Sample – Staffing/Workload Chart

Project Staff: Phases/Activities below:	1	2	3	4	5	6	7	8	9	10	11	12	Total
Analysis & Diagnosis		2	10	10	5	10	5		3	5			50
Strategy Design	4	4	4	4	2	4			1				23
Business Planning	5		15	20		18	15		1	5	15		94
Align Organization		10	10	10	10					7	5		52
Executive Search				2	6	2		10				5	25
Implementation Actions		3	7	12	12	4	5		2		5		50
Training / Development	2	3		2					8				15
Project Management		3	24										27
Account Management	4												4
Final Report												10	10
Total Days	15	25	70	60	35	38	25	10	15	17	25	15	350

© Copyright and Proprietary Document. May not be copied or reproduced, in whole or in part, without the written consent of the author Thomas H. Olson

5. The Top Government Consultants/Contractors/Key Competitors/Products and Services/Linkages via M&As

Lockheed Martin: Lockheed Martin Corporation (LMC) is the largest contractor of the US Federal Government and the largest aerospace and Defense Company in the world. However, LMC did not become the biggest contractor until 1995 when Lockheed and Martin Marietta merged.

Some suggest that The Lockheed Company was founded in 1912 by Allan Loughead, and it was operated mainly as a company that manufactured float planes for commercial airlines. The history of Lockheed Martin (http://www.lockheedmartin.com/us/100years.htm) states that Allan and Malcolm Loughead founded the Alco Hydro-Aeroplane Co. in December, 1912, and Glenn Martin founded the Glenn L. Martin Company in August 1912. Alco Hydro-Aeroplane was renamed Lockheed Aircraft Co., and later merged with Martin. From the Lockheed Martin's Timeline page, it seems that Loughead was changed to Lockheed in 1920 (http://www.lockheedmartin.com/us/100years/timeline.html).

With the onset of World War II, Lockheed began its close association with the US military by producing the twin engine P-38 fighters, the only fighter plane for the US Air Force during the War. In 1945, Lockheed designed the P-80 Shooting Star, the first American jet aircraft to enter operational service. During the Cold War, Lockheed also accomplished great achievements such as the SR-71 Blackbird and the F-117A Nighthawk stealth fighter – the first jet capable of flying at more than three times the speed of sound (Amir). In the 1990s, the Lockheed Corporation expanded with the acquisition of some aircraft elements of General Dynamics and gained the production of F-16 fighter, too. This was a significant acquisition as the F-16 was an aircraft sought globally by ally countries to the US, and Lockheed generated substantive revenue and profitability from the F-16. In 1995 the Lockheed Company merged with the Martin Marietta Company (one of the most well-known Ballistic missile producers) to become the largest defense corporation in the world. This became the Lockheed Martin that we know today.

Since 2000, Lockheed Martin has focused on the production of stealth fighters such as F-22 and F-35. Particular to the F-35s, Lockheed Martin is expecting to sell more than 3,000 of these aircraft to multiple nations in the now global marketplace. Additionally, LMC generates large revenues from the Space and Missile Systems Centers and has become 'big-in-space' – satellites and launch vehicles – as well (particularly with the US Air Force & NASA).

Since the late 1990s, the Lockheed Martin Company has administered a number of US government contracts. The contracts are all 'consulted by' the I&TS, which is a subsidiary of Lockheed Martin that mainly deals with negotiating contracts with the US government and its respective Agencies/Departments. For informational technology (I&TS), LMC provides professional consulting services regarding the manner in which information is efficiently delivered, clearly understood and effectively secured. Additionally, the I&TS also does considerable actual consulting with the government that generates significant revenues and profitability largely related to products/services for the Department of Defense/branches of the military. One of the most notable achievements 'outside of the DoD' is a 10-year contract with the FAA re: operating the Automated Flight Service Station (in 2005). And one of the most notable military contracts was the design and production of the B-2, a stealth two-billion-dollar bomber having the ability to penetrate other countries' defense systems. For additional discussion of specific consulting programs/efforts, please reference Appendix A to this chapter.

Boeing: The Boeing Company is the second largest contractor of the US government only behind Lockheed Martin. The company was founded in 1811 by William Boeing, and, as most know, Boeing is major designer and producer of military (as well as commercial) aircraft. A first major military aircraft for the Boeing Company was the development of the B-10 bomber. This was followed by continuous work crafting and creating many other applied and surveillance aircraft for the next decades – particularly to WWII. After World War II, Boeing expanded more of its efforts to missiles and commercial aircraft for the growing commercial airline market. Further, in the 1960s, Boeing was awarded with the Minuteman Intercontinental Ballistic Missiles contract still used today. In addition to the missile market, Boeing also contracted for the installation of missile bases and the maintenance support systems. In the 1970s and 1980s, Boeing designed and produced significant numbers of commercial aircraft for the airlines. These aircraft included the Boeing 737, 747, 767 and 777 (Amir). The most notable aircraft may well be the Boeing 747 as it was the largest commercial aircraft until the Airbus A380 in 2009. During this period of time, Boeing also worked on the design and production of aircraft for the US Air Force – most notably, bomber aircraft, such as B-52 and B1-B (Rockwell International before being acquired by Boeing). In the new centuries, Boeing specifically worked on the design and production line of 787, which is a new commercial aircraft that's expect to take over the role of its 747 (Amir). As of 2016, Boeing has customers in 145 countries, employees in 60 nations and offices in 26 US states.

Boeing is currently the largest aerospace and commercial airplane company in the world and the second largest defense corporation behind Lockheed Martin. A major contributor to building the size of Boeing was its acquisition of Rockwell International's Aerospace and Defense businesses in the late 1990s – though not including Rockwell Collins headquartered in Cedar Rapids and acquired by ARINC in 2013. For additional discussion of Rockwell International specific consulting programs/efforts and a discussion of the Boeing Company's acquisition of Rockwell International's Aerospace and Defense businesses, please reference Appendix B to this chapter.

Northrop Grumman: The Northrop Grumman Company (NGC) is another contractor of the US Government that was based in Los Angeles, CA, and recently relocated to Falls Church, VA. This company began as two separate businesses, Northrop and Grumman. Most notable for Northrop Grumman in recent decades is the design and production of the B-2 bomber and significant consulting to the US government as exemplified by Government-wide Acquisition Contracts such as GSA's ANSWER, MILLENIA and ALLIANT contracts. Specific to the Northrop Company and its early years, Northrop was noted for its work in design and production of the F-5 tiger fighter in the 1950s and 1960s. This was a very 'successful' program for Northrop in that this aircraft was produced in many versions and was contracted and sold to all the NATO countries. Further, and as stated earlier, the B-2 Stealth bomber entered service in 1993 and was expected to be produced for the US Air Force over the ensuing next 15 years. However, due to the high costs of B-2 ($2 billion per aircraft), the Pentagon restricted its purchases to 21 aircraft. This aircraft remains one of the most 'high tech' weapons of the US DoD – with substantive development based on significant IT and other Northrop Grumman consulting. The Grumman Company was established in the 1950s, and it had little relationship to the US government until the beginning of the 1970s. It was in 1970 that Grumman received a contract to build the air superiority fighter F-14 Tomcat. This aircraft soon became the most advanced and the costliest fighter at that time. Another notable Grumman aircraft was the A-6 'intruder attack' jet that was the first aircraft to be designed specifically for airborne early surveillance. The F-14 and A-6 were mass produced in the 1970s and 1980s for the US Navy. As time passed into the 1990s, the Grumman Company merged with Northrop in 1994. After 1995, Northrop Grumman focused on the design of applied radar systems for the military. In addition, Northrop Grumman continued to grow through the acquisition of the Litton Company. Litton was originally founded by Tex Thornton and Roy Ash in Beverly Hills, CA, in the 1950s as a competitor of RW (TRW). Over time Litton grew to become the largest production firm of non-nuclear ships for the US Navy for which Litton designed, built and overhauled warships of the US government. Some notable ships produced by Litton/Northrop Grumman included the Nimitz class super-carrier and the Virginia class nuclear attack submarine (Weiss). In 2011 Northrop Grumman 'spun off' Huntington Ingalls (ship builders) to maintain numerous contracts for US Navy ships and radar. Recent news observes that Northrop Grumman has just received the contract to design the next generation stealth bomber for the Air Force.

As known in the Public Sector, Northrop Grumman most recently acquired TRW. TRW began as RW, founded in 1953, to compete with Litton. It is with some irony that both Litton and TRW are now part of Northrop Grumman. Regarding TRW, it was founded as RW by two former engineers with Hughes Aircraft (missile) Company: Simon Ramo & Dean Woolridge. These two began their business to compete with Hughes.

And, over time, RW merged with Thompson to become TRW, and TRW then was acquired by Northrop Grumman just a few years ago.

For additional discussion of TRW-specific consulting programs/efforts and a discussion of the Northrop Grumman acquisition of TRW businesses, please reference Appendix C to this chapter.

General Dynamics: The General Dynamics (GD) Company (now Corporation) was founded in 1899 as an 'electric boat' company. As of 2012, GD became the world's 5th largest defense consultant/contractor based on revenues ("Defense"). GD currently has 4 primary consultant/contractor businesses, including Aerospace, Combat Systems, Information Systems and Marine Systems (reference wiki for additional information).

In history, and particularly during the two World Wars, the company mainly produced submarines and surface ships for the US Navy. As can be easily understood, General Dynamics was operating a 'full capacity' business during wartime. And following WWII, the company began its design and development of the F-111 bomber to replace the aging B-52 fleet. Unfortunately, the GD design turned out to be unsuccessful, and the utility of F-111 as a replacement for the B-52 greatly diminished. During the Cold War era, the company also designed numerous types of warships including the Los Angeles class submarines with some 62 conveyed to the US Navy by early 1990s. Another huge success for General Dynamics was the F-16 aircraft with GD producing more than 4,000 for the US as well as US allies. The F-16 became the largest program of General Dynamics, and it became known as one of the most successful military projects since 1945. After the Cold War ended, GD sold its aircraft production to Lockheed Martin and its Space system to McDonnel Dougal. Having divided itself of its aviation holdings, GD concentrated on land and sea products. However, in 1999, GD purchased Gulfstream Aerospace to reenter the airframe business. In the 21st century, GD purchased the defensive division of General Motors, and it is now a major supplier of armored vehicles of all types, including the M1 Abrams, LAV 25, and a variety of land systems. As of 2016, despite a number of budget cuts by the Federal Government, General Dynamics remains one of the biggest contractors for the Department of Defense.

Raytheon: The Raytheon Company was established in 1922 and was headquartered in Waltham, MA. In the early years, Raytheon was essentially an electrical company. It produced a large amount of rectifier and power equipment for the general public of the United States. During World War II, Raytheon received contracts from the federal government to build magnetron, a specialized microwave generating electron tube that markedly improved the capability of radar to detect enemy planes (Press). During WWII, Raytheon manufactured 80 percent of the magnetrons and also pioneered the production of ship radar system. During the Cold War, Raytheon began its development of guided missiles. In 1950, its Lark missile became the first such weapon to destroy a target aircraft in flight. Raytheon then received military contracts to develop the air-to-air Sparrow and ground-to-air Hawk missiles – projects that received more support due to the Korean War. In later decades it remained a major producer of missiles, among them the Patriot antimissile missile and the air-to-air Phoenix missile. In 1980, Raytheon acquired Beech Aircraft Corporation and started its business jets business. The company continued to thrive in the 1990s and the 2000s with numerous contracts being signed each year.

Raytheon merged with Hughes Electronics' Defense Business in 1997. For additional discussion of Hughes's specific consulting programs/efforts and a discussion of the Raytheon acquisition of Hughes businesses, please reference Appendix D to this chapter.

As of 2011, Raytheon employed over 70,000 people worldwide and had markets in more than 80 countries around the world. Looking forward, Raytheon states its plans to remain committed to its current markets and produce more communication system and satellite components for the US military.

Leidos Holdings (SAIC): Leidos is a joint 'spin-off' of Science Applications International Corporation (SAIC) and is a US Defense Company headquartered in Reston, VA, that provides a variety of consulting services. Leidos (SAIC) is most often referred to as SAIC. The brief most current history of Leidos is as follows:

> Leidos Holdings, Inc. (Leidos), incorporated on August 12, 2005, is a holding company. Leidos is described primarily as an applied technology company. The Company, through its subsidiary, Leidos, Inc., is engaged in delivering solutions and services that leverage data analytics, systems integration and cybersecurity across three markets: national security, health and engineering. Its services are provided to agencies of the United States Department of Defense (DoD), the intelligence community, the United States Department of Homeland Security (DHS) and other United States Government civil agencies, state and local government agencies, foreign governments and customers across a range of commercial markets. The Company operates in segments: National Security Solutions (NSS); Health and Engineering (HES), and Corporate and other. (http://www.reuters.com/finance/stocks/company Profile?symbol=LDOS.N)

For additional discussion of Leidos / SAIC's specific consulting programs/ efforts and a discussion of the Leidos acquisition of SAIC businesses, please reference Appendix E to this chapter.

Huntington Ingalls Industries (HII): Compared to the other contractors, Huntington Ingalls Industries doesn't have a long history. It was founded in 2008 as part of the Northrop Grumman Company to build warships for the US Navy. However, it separated from Northrop Grumman and became a separate corporation in 2011. Despite the fact that this is a young company, it serves an important role for the Department of Defense. HII is the sole designer, builder and refueler of nuclear powered aircraft carriers of the United States. Additionally, 70 percent of the navy fleet was built by Huntington Ingalls. HII is headquartered in Newport News, VA, and the Newport News Shipbuilding is the largest shipbuilding complex in the world. Some of the major projects of HII including the Gerald Ford class aircraft carriers and Virginia class nuclear submarines. Both classes of warships are crucial in the fact that they are the future of the US Navy Strike group. As of early 2016, HII's current order backlog amounts to 224 billion dollars. It's likely that Huntington Ingalls Industries will remain the largest contractor of the US Navy for quite a long time.

6. The Future of Public Sector Consulting

As described by Ashton B. Carter, PhD, (25th Secretary of Defense), significant challenges lie ahead regarding issues of accelerating technology growth and how quickly the Public Sector can respond. These challenges, coupled with ever more changes – particularly related to complexity and response time – will make consulting in the Public Sector quite demanding and rife with opportunity. This will involve greater and greater needs to build (and perform to) proposals to address most urgent needs as quickly as possible. See, for example, http://www.defense.gov/About-DoD/Biographies/Biography-View/Article/602689.

For Secretary Carter and all within the Public Sector leadership style and thinking – as representatively described by Bennis and Hughes – is significant to advance Public Sector consulting and contracting process. It is new leadership 'modeling' that is significantly required to improve the quality and response time of Public Sector consultants to contracting opportunities.

Particular efforts into the future will have to do with two principal sets of elements. The first set of elements are process related – especially speed to respond to identified need with excellent quality and capability. The second set of elements will require more and greater developed applications of more and more specialty knowledge and expertise – as, for example, and is particularly relevant in the ever growing non-traditional/terrorist 'warfare' global environment in which we all exist.

More and more leadership of the kind as described by Bennis in *Judgment: How Great Leaders Make Winning Calls* will become more and more critical. The Public Sector is a future high-growth market by essentially every consultant's estimation. And great leadership and innovation with security are critical to best addressing advanced challenges in a difficult world marketplace. Reference for additional comment and insight: Christensen, Wang and Van Bever 2013.

Bibliography

"Ashton B. Carter", http://www.defense.gov/About-DoD/Biographies/Biography-View/Article/602689, accessed June, 2016.
Bennis, W. *On Becoming a Leader, 3rd edition.* Perseus Books Group, 2009.
Bennis, W. with Biederman, P. Ward. *Still Surprised: A Memoir of a Life in Leadership.* San Francisco, CA. Jossey-Bass, 2010.
Bennis, W. with Tichy, N. *Judgment: How Great Leaders Make Winning Calls,* New York. 2009.
Christensen, C., Wang, D. and Van Bever, D., "Consulting on the Cusp of Disruption", *Harvard Business Review,* October 2013.
Cummings, T. and Worley, C. *Organization Development and Change,* 10th edition. Stamford, CT. Cengage Learning, 2015.
Daft, R. *Organization Theory and Design.* Stamford, CT. Cengage Learning, 2012.
"Defense News Top 100 for 2012". *Defense News,* July 22, 2013.
Greiner, L. and Cummings, T. *Dynamic Strategy Making: A Real-Time Approach for the 21st Century Leader.* San Francisco, CA. Jossey-Bass, 2009.
Greiner, L., Olson, T. and Poulfelt, F. *Contemporary Consultant's Experts Casebook.* Routledge, 2010.
Hughes, M. *The Leadership of Organizational Change.* New York. Routledge, 2016.
International Directory of Company Histories, Vol. 40. St. James Press, 2001.
Kipping, M. and Clark, T. "Part 5: Consultants and Their Clients". *Oxford Handbook of Management Consulting.* Oxford, UK. Oxford University Press, 2012.
"Lockheed Martin Corporation". *Encyclopædia Britannica Online.* Encyclopædia Britannica Inc., 2016. Web. 01 Apr. 2016.
"Northrop Grumman Corporation". *Encyclopædia Britannica Online.* Encyclopædia Britannica Inc., 2016. Web. 01 Apr. 2016.
Olson, Thomas H. "Consulting – Teaching Professional Practice Is Not Enough", National Academy of Management, Montreal, August 2010.
Olson, Thomas H. "Developing Successful Consulting Proposals, an outline to apply w significant elements", Academy of Management (several Annual Meetings).
Olson, Thomas H. "Variations on the Design and Teaching of Management Consulting – Discipline Discussion and Analysis without Practice Are Not Sufficient", National Academy of Management, Boston, August 2012.
Olson, Thomas H. with Greiner, L. and Poulfelt, F. *Management Consulting Today and Tomorrow Casebook.* Routledge, 2009/10.
Olson, Thomas H. with Greiner, L. and Poulfelt, F. *Management Consulting Today and Tomorrow Casebook Practitioners Notes.* Routledge, 2009/10.
"Raytheon Company". *Encyclopædia Britannica. Encyclopædia Britannica Online.* Encyclopædia Britannica Inc., 2016. Web. 03 Apr. 2016.
https://en.wikipedia.org/wiki/TRW_Inc http://fas.org/man/company/docs/970116-raytheon.html
http://fas.org/nuke/guide/usa/bomber/b-2.htm
http://fas.org/man/company/docs/970116-raytheon.html
https://www.ftc.gov/news-events/press-releases/1996/12/boeing-company-settle-charges-rockwell-acquisition
http://www.lockheedmartin.com/us/100years.htm.
http://www.lockheedmartin.com/us/100years/timeline.html

http://www.reuters.com/finance/stocks/companyProfile?symbol=LDOS.N
http://www.scitorcorporation.com/the-scitor-story

Federal Acquisition Regulation (FAR) References:

REFERENCE RESEARCH HERE FROM https://www.acquisition.gov/ – latest reference April, 2016, including https://en.wikipedia.org/wiki/Federal_Acquisition_Regulation

1. ^ [b] 48 C.F.R. 1.101.
2. ^ 48 C.F.R. 1.104.
3. ^ 48 C.F.R. 2.101 (see definitions of 'acquisition', 'contract' and 'executive agency').
4. ^ 48 C.F.R. 2.101 (see definition of 'acquisition').
5. ^ 49 U.S.C. § 40110(d)(2); Department of Transportation and Related Agencies Appropriations Act for FY1996, Pub.L. 104–50, § 348, 109 Stat. 460–61 (Nov. 15, 1995).
6. ^ 48 C.F.R. 1201.104(d).
7. ^ 31 U.S.C. § 5136.
8. ^ 48 C.F.R. 1001.104.
9. ^ E.g., the Federal Aviation Administration (FAA) Acquisition Management System (AMS).
10. ^ Federal Aviation Administration Life Cycle Acquisition Management System, 61 FR 15155 (April 4, 1996).
11. ^ 48 C.F.R. 1.101.
12. ^ 48 C.F.R. 1.101 (2012).
13. ^ 48 C.F.R. 1.102 (2012).
14. ^ 48 C.F.R. 52.101(e) (2012).
15. ^ See *Davies Precision Machining, Inc. v. U.S.*, 35 Fed. Cl. 651 (1995).
16. ^ Pub.L. 93–400 and Title 41 of the United States Code, Chapter 7.
17. ^ 41 U.S.C. § 421(c)(1).
18. ^ 41 U.S.C. § 405.
19. ^ 48 CFR Table of Contents, vol. 1 p. 1 (2010).
20. ^ 48 CFR 1 Table of Contents, vol. 1 p. 3–4 (2010).
21. ^ 48 CFR 1 Table of Contents, vol. 2. p. 3 (2010).
22. ^ 48 C.F.R. 1.105–2 (2012).
23. ^ 48 C.F.R. 1.303.

Appendix 1 – Federal Acquisition Regulation

"Purpose: The purpose of the FAR is to provide "uniform policies and procedures for acquisition."[12] Among its guiding principles is to have an acquisition system that satisfies customer's needs in terms of cost, quality, and timeliness; minimize administrative operating costs; conduct business with integrity, fairness, and openness; and fulfill other public policy objectives.[13]

Procedure: When a federal government agency issues a solicitation, it will specify the applicable FAR provisions, which may be numerous. In order to be awarded a contract, an offeror must either comply with the provisions, demonstrate that it will be able to comply with them at the time of award, or claim an exemption from them. As an example, Part 30 (Cost Accounting Standards Administration) allows for small businesses to be exempt from those requirements. If the offeror demonstrates that it meets the small business criteria, Part 30 does not apply.

The largest single part of the FAR is Part 52, which contains standard solicitation provisions and contract clauses. Solicitation provisions are certification requirements, notices, and instructions directed at firms that might be interested in competing for a specific contract. These provisions and clauses are of six types: (i) required solicitation provisions; (ii) required-when-applicable solicitation provisions; (iii) optional solicitation provisions; (iv) required contract clauses; (v) required-when-applicable contract clauses; and (vi) optional contract clauses."[14]

If the FAR requires that a clause be included in a government contract, but that clause is omitted, case law may provide that the missing clause is deemed to be included. This is known as the Christian Doctrine, which is based on the underlying principle that certain government regulations have the force and effect of law,[15] and government personnel may not deviate from the law without proper authorization. Prospective contractors are presumed to know the law, including the limits of the authority of government personnel. Thus, a mandatory clause that expresses a significant or deeply ingrained strand of public procurement policy will be incorporated into a Government contract by operation of law, even if the parties intentionally omitted it.

A contract award can be challenged and set aside if a protester can prove that either the contracting agency or the contract awardee did not comply with the requirements of the solicitation. A successful protest can result in reconsideration of the decision to award the contract or award of the contract to the protester in lieu of the original awardee. Even though a successful protester may not ultimately be awarded the contract, the government agency may have to pay the protester's bid and proposal costs.

Authority: The FAR was issued pursuant to the Office of Federal Procurement Policy Act of 1974.[16] Statutory authority to issue and maintain the FAR resides with the Secretary of Defense, the Administrator of General Services, and the Administrator of the National Aeronautics and Space Administration,[17] subject to the approval of the Administrator of Federal Procurement Policy.[18]

Structure: The Federal Acquisition Regulation is contained within Chapter 1 of Title 48 of the Code of Federal Regulations (CFR).[19] Chapter 1 is divided into Subchapters A–H, which encompass Parts 1–53. Chapter 1 appears in two volumes, with Subchapters A–G appearing in Volume 1 while Subchapter H occupies all of Volume 2.[20][21] The volumes are not formal subdivisions of Title 48, but refer instead to the fact that the FAR is printed by the Government Printing Office in two volumes for convenience.

The single most heavily regulated aspect of acquisition is contract pricing, which is addressed throughout the FAR, but especially in Subpart 15.4,

Parts 30 and 31, and Subparts 42.7, 42.8, and 42.17. A large part of the FAR, Subchapter D, describes various socio-economic programs, such as the various small business programs, purchases from foreign sources, and laws written to protect laborers and professionals working under government contracts.

The final three chapters of Title 48 (61, 63 and 99) establish the Civilian Board of Contract Appeals, the Department of Transportation Board of Contract Appeals, and the Cost Accounting Standards Board, respectively. The Armed Services Board of Contract Appeals has been established by charter within the Department of Defense.

The proper way to cite a regulation within the FAR is by part, subpart, section, subsection, without respect to chapter or subchapter.[22] For instance, the FAR rule on legislative lobbying costs is found at FAR Part 31, Section 205, Subsection 22 (cited as "FAR 31.205–22").

The table of contents, as of the edition published October 1, 2012, is as follows:[20][21]

In Volume 1:

- **Subchapter A:** General
  - Part 1. Federal Acquisition Regulations System
  - Part 2. Definitions of Words and Terms
  - Part 3. Improper Business Practices and Personal Conflicts of Interest
  - Part 4. Administrative Matters
- **Subchapter B:** Acquisition Planning
  - Part 5. Publicizing Contract Actions
  - Part 6. Competition Requirements
  - Part 7. Acquisition Planning
  - Part 8. Required Sources of Supplies and Services
  - Part 9. Contractor Qualifications
  - Part 10. Market Research
  - Part 11. Describing Agency Needs
  - Part 12. Acquisition of Commercial Items
- **Subchapter C:** Contracting Methods and Contract Types
  - Part 13. Simplified Acquisition Procedures
  - Part 14. Sealed Bidding
  - Part 15. Contracting by Negotiation
  - Part 16. Types of Contracts
  - Part 17. Special Contracting Methods
  - Part 18. Emergency Acquisitions
- **Subchapter D:** Socioeconomic Programs
  - Part 19. Small Business Programs
  - Parts 20–21. *Reserved*

- Part 22. Application of Labor Laws to Government Acquisitions
- Part 23. Environment, Energy and Water Efficiency, Renewable Energy Technologies, Occupational Safety, and Drug-Free Workplace
- Part 24. Protection of Privacy and Freedom of Information
- Part 25. Foreign Acquisition
- Part 26. Other Socioeconomic Programs

- **Subchapter E:** General Contracting Requirements
    - Part 27. Patents, Data, and Copyrights
    - Part 28. Bonds and Insurance
    - Part 29. Taxes
    - Part 30. Cost Accounting Standards Administration
    - Part 31. Contract Cost Principles and Procedures
    - Part 32. Contract Financing
    - Part 33. Protests, Disputes, and Appeals

- **Subchapter F:** Special Categories of Contracting
    - Part 34. Major System Acquisition
    - Part 35. Research and Development Contracting
    - Part 36. Construction and Architect-Engineer Contracts
    - Part 37. Service Contracting
    - Part 38. Federal Supply Schedule Contracting
    - Part 39. Acquisition of Information Technology
    - Part 40. *Reserved*
    - Part 41. Acquisition of Utility Services

- **Subchapter G:** Contract Management
    - Part 42. Contract Administration and Audit Services
    - Part 43. Contract Modifications
    - Part 44. Subcontracting Policies and Procedures
    - Part 45. Government Property
    - Part 46. Quality Assurance
    - Part 47. Transportation
    - Part 48. Value Engineering
    - Part 49. Termination of Contracts
    - Part 50. Extraordinary Contractual Actions and the Safety Act
    - Part 51. Use of Government Sources by Contractors

In Volume 2:

- **Subchapter H:** Clauses and Forms
    - Part 52. Solicitation Provisions and Contract Clauses
    - Part 53. Forms
    - Parts 54–99. *Reserved*

Public Sector Consultation 259

Supplements: As the original purpose of the FAR was to consolidate the numerous individual agency regulations into one comprehensive set of standards which would apply government-wide, the issuance of supplemental regulations is closely governed by the FAR. Nearly every major cabinet-level department (and many agencies below them) has issued such regulations, which often place further restrictions or requirements on contractors and contracting officers.

One of the best-known examples of an agency supplement is the Defense Federal Acquisition Regulation Supplement (DFARS), which is used by the Department of Defense. Chapter 2 is the Defense Federal Acquisition Regulation Supplement; Chapter 3 is the Department of Health and Human Services Acquisition Regulation; Chapter 4 is the Department of Agriculture's Acquisition Regulation; etc.

The required format for agency FAR supplements is to follow the basic FAR format.[23] To continue the example above, the supplemental DFARS section on legislative lobbying costs is DFARS Subpart 231, Section 205, Subsection 22 (cited as "DFARS 231.205–22").

Appendix A – Lockheed Martin Major Consulting/Production Contracts

Along with the B-52 and B-1B (see Boeing below), the B-2 provides the penetrating flexibility and effectiveness inherent in manned bombers. Its low-observable, or "stealth," characteristics give it the unique ability to penetrate an enemy's most sophisticated defenses and threaten its most valued, and heavily defended, targets. Its capability to penetrate air defenses and threaten effective retaliation provides an effective deterrent and combat force well into the 21st century.

The blending of low-observable technologies with high aerodynamic efficiency and large payload gives the B-2 important advantages over existing bombers. Its low-observability provides it greater freedom of action at high altitudes, thus increasing its range and a better field of view for the aircraft's sensors. Its unrefueled range is approximately 6,000 nautical miles (9,600 kilometers).

The B-2's low observability is derived from a combination of reduced infrared, acoustic, electromagnetic, visual and radar signatures. These signatures make it difficult for the sophisticated defensive systems to detect, track and engage the B-2. Many aspects of the low-observability process remain classified; however, the B-2's composite materials, special coatings and flying-wing design all contribute to its "stealthiness."

The B-2 has a crew of two pilots, an aircraft commander in the left seat and mission commander in the right, compared to the B-1B's crew of four and the B-52's crew of five.

The B-2 is intended to deliver gravity nuclear and conventional weapons, including precision-guided standoff weapons. An interim, precision-guided bomb capability called Global Positioning System (GPS) Aided Targeting System/GPS Aided Munition (GATS/GAM) is being tested and evaluated. Future configurations are planned for the B-2 to be capable of carrying and delivering the Joint Direct Attack Munition (JDAM) and Joint Air-to-Surface Standoff Missile.

B-2s, in a conventional role, staging from Whiteman AFB, MO; Diego Garcia; and Guam can cover the entire world with just one refueling. Six B-2s could execute an operation similar to the 1986 Libya raid but launch from the continental U.S. rather than Europe with a much smaller, more lethal, and more survivable force.

http://fas.org/nuke/guide/usa/bomber/b-2.htm

Appendix B − Boeing Acquisition of Rockwell International Major Consulting/Production Contracts as Described in a Federal Trade Commission Article at the Time of the Acquisition

December 5, 1996

The Boeing Company will settle Federal Trade Commission charges that its $3.025 billion acquisition of Rockwell International Corporation's Aerospace and Defense business would violate antitrust laws. The FTC charged that the proposed deal would violate antitrust laws by reducing competition in two markets: high altitude endurance unmanned air vehicles and space launch vehicles, including the Department of Defense's Evolved Expendable Launch Vehicle Program.

Boeing and Rockwell are two of the largest defense and space contractors in the U.S. In July 1996, Boeing proposed to buy Rockwell's Aerospace and Defense business. Boeing and Rockwell are members of the only two teams currently competing to develop high-altitude endurance unmanned air vehicles for the Department of Defense's Advance Research Projects Agency. Boeing, together with Lockheed Martin, is developing Tier III Minus, a stealthy, high-altitude endurance unmanned air vehicle, while Rockwell is supplying wings to a team headed up by Teledyne Ryan, which is developing Tier II Plus, a non-stealthy, high-altitude endurance unmanned air vehicle. According to the FTC complaint detailing the charges, the proposed acquisition would position Boeing as a member of both high-altitude endurance unmanned air vehicle teams and would likely lead to anticompetitive effects by allowing Boeing to increase the price of the components it is supplying or reduce its investment in technology and/or quality.

The terms of the proposed settlement, announced today for public comment, enable Teledyne Ryan, if it so chooses, to replace Rockwell, which will be owned by Boeing, as the Tier II Plus wing supplier without incurring any significant costs or risk. Under the proposed order, Boeing would be required to deliver to business locations designated by Teledyne Ryan, and at no cost to Teledyne Ryan, all of the assets needed to produce Tier II Plus wings, including the special tooling, special test equipment, engineering data and design data. The proposed order also prohibits Boeing from asserting or enforcing any proprietary rights in such equipment or data, or from holding Teledyne Ryan liable for any damages or costs resulting from the replacement of Boeing as the Tier II Plus wing supplier.

If Teledyne Ryan chooses to replace Boeing as the Tier II Plus wing supplier, the proposed order would further require Boeing to provide technical assistance, not to exceed four-man years over a one year period, at no cost to Teledyne Ryan, and would require Boeing to provide additional technical assistance through the duration of the upcoming Tier II Plus Phase II flight tests. The order also establishes a "firewall" between Boeing's Tier III Minus business and the Rockwell North American Aircraft Division that is currently providing Tier II Plus wings.

As a result of the proposed acquisition, Boeing would also be positioned as both a competitor in the market for space launch vehicles, including the Department of Defense's Evolved Expendable Launch Vehicle program, and a provider of space launch vehicle propulsion systems used by Boeing and its space launch vehicle competitors. Because space launch vehicle manufacturers provide a wide-range of proprietary information to their space launch vehicle propulsion system supplier, the FTC complaint alleges that Boeing's position as both supplier and competitor would allow it access to competitively sensitive, non-public information of its space launch vehicle competitors which could affect prices and reduce innovation and quality.

The agreement to settle the charges would forbid Boeing from making any space launch vehicle manufacturer's non-public information available to its launch vehicle division and would allow Boeing to use a competitor's proprietary, non-public information only in its capacity as a provider of launch vehicle propulsion systems.

https://www.ftc.gov/news-events/press-releases/1996/12/boeing-company-settle-charges-rockwell-acquisition

Appendix C – Northrup Grumman Acquisition of TRW Major Consulting/Production Contracts and Short History of TRW

TRW originated in 1901 with the Cleveland Cap Screw Company, founded by David Kurtz and four other Cleveland residents.[11] Their initial products were bolts with heads electrically welded to the shafts. In 1904, a welder named Charles E. Thompson adapted their process to making automobile engine valves,[11] and, by 1915, the company was the largest valve producer in America.[12] Charles Thompson was named General Manager of the company, which became Thompson Products in 1926.[13] Their experimental hollow sodium-cooled valves aided Charles Lindbergh's solo flight across the Atlantic.[12]

In 1937, Thompson Motor Products bought J.A. Drake and Sons (JADSON).[citation needed] The company made high performance valves that were used in many racing engines of the day, including the Miller Offy.[citation needed] Dale Drake (son of J.A. Drake) bought the Offy engine design with his partner Louis Meyer in 1946 and won the Indianapolis 500 twenty-seven times, more than any other engine design.

In 1950, Simon Ramo and Dean Wooldridge while working for Hughes Aircraft, led the development of the Falcon radar-guided missile, among other projects. They grew frustrated with Howard Hughes' management, and formed the Ramo-Wooldridge Corporation in September 1953,[13] with the financial support of Thompson Products.[2] The detonation of a thermonuclear bomb by the Soviet Union spurred Trevor Gardner to form the Teapot Committee in October 1953. Chaired by John von Neumann, its purpose was to study the development of ballistic missiles, including ICBMs. Ramo and Wooldridge were committee members, and Ramo-Wooldridge Corp. became the lead contractor of the resulting ICBM development effort, reporting to the United States Air Force.

With continued backing from Thompson Products, Ramo-Wooldridge diversified into computers and electronic components, funding Pacific Semiconductors in 1954.[14] They also produced scientific spacecraft such as Pioneer 1. Thompson Products and Ramo-Wooldridge merged in October 1958 to form Thompson Ramo Wooldridge Inc., unofficially known as "TRW".[13] In February 1959, Jimmy Doolittle became Chairman of the Board of Space Technology Laboratories (STL), the division which continued to support the Air Force ICBM efforts.[13]

Other aerospace companies challenged that TRW's Air Force advisory role granted it unfair access to its competitors' technology,[14] and in September 1959 the United States Congress issued a report recommending that STL be converted to a non-profit organization. With nearly half of STL's employees,[13] The Aerospace Corporation was formed in June 1960, which headed the Atlas conversion for Mercury, Titan conversion for Gemini, and provides ongoing systems engineering support for the United States government. The Air Force continued its ICBM work with TRW.[2]

During fiscal years 1961 through 1963, TRW produced 319,163 M14 rifles for the United States military.[citation needed]

Dean Wooldridge retired in January 1962[13] to become a professor at California Institute of Technology.[2] Simon Ramo became President of the Bunker-Ramo Corp in January 1964, a company jointly owned by TRW and Martin Marietta for the production of computers and computer monitors. Thompson Ramo Wooldridge officially became TRW Inc. in July 1965.[13] Free of anti-competitive restrictions, except regarding ICBM hardware, STL was renamed TRW Systems Group, also in July 1965.[13] The Credit Data group was formed in 1970[13] to compete with Dun & Bradstreet,[2] and ESL was acquired in 1978,[13] specializing in technical strategic reconnaissance. TRW Information Systems and Services Division (Credit Data) was spun off in 1996 to form Experian.[15] TRW acquired LucasVarity in 1999, then sold Lucas Diesel Systems to Delphi Automotive, and Lucas Aerospace (then called TRW Aeronautical Systems) to Goodrich Corporation.[16]

https://en.wikipedia.org/wiki/TRW_Inc

Appendix D – Details of the Raytheon Merger with Hughes

Raytheon Company
Corporate Communications
141 Spring Street
Lexington, MA 02173
617-860-2414

For Immediate Release

Raytheon Company and Hughes Electronics' Defense Business to Merge, Creating a $21 Billion Enterprise

Combination Creates a World Leader in Defense Electronics

New York, NY, January 16, 1997 — Raytheon Company announced today that it has entered into definitive agreements with Hughes Electronics Corporation to bring about the merger of the Hughes Electronics defense operations (Hughes Aircraft) and Raytheon. The combined company will be called Raytheon Company.

The transaction is valued at $9.5 billion, comprised of approximately $5.1 billion in common stock and $4.4 billion in debt. (See later discussion for the transaction specifics.)

On a 1996 pro-forma basis, the combined company will have revenues of approximately $21 billion, over $13 billion of which will be in defense electronics. The current backlog for the combined company will be approximately $23 billion, with defense electronics accounting for $18 billion. This transaction, coupled with the recently announced acquisition of the Texas Instruments defense business, will result in slight dilution to the earnings of the combined company in 1997, as compared to the earnings of Raytheon on a stand-alone basis for the same period. The transaction will be minimally accretive in 1998 and increasingly accretive thereafter. The transaction is expected to close by mid-year.

Dennis J. Picard, Raytheon's chairman and chief executive officer, said, "The people of Raytheon have always had the greatest respect for the technical expertise and management skills of the Hughes defense team. The combination of the Hughes and Raytheon defense businesses will create a unique technology company and a world leader in defense electronics.

Together, our combined businesses will have the critical mass needed to compete effectively in all of our global markets. Raytheon will now offer an even broader range of products and services to each of our customers, outstanding returns to our shareholders, and a more secure and promising future for our people.

"It is clear that the end of the Cold War, and the resulting decline in the U.S. defense procurement budget, have brought about fundamental changes to the defense industry requiring continued consolidation. The strategic combination of Raytheon, TI Defense, and Hughes Defense enables us to address those changes head-on and to grow in the best segment of the defense business—defense electronics.

"The substantial synergies inherent in the combined businesses will ensure that our revenue and profitability objectives will be met, and that resources will be made available to pursue new technology opportunities in defense as well as in our commercial businesses.

"In summary," Picard said, "we are truly creating another defense electronics powerhouse."

C. Michael Armstrong, chairman and chief executive officer of Hughes Electronics, said, "For Hughes Aircraft to remain competitive in a shrinking market, there was a need to increase its participation in the industry consolidation. Raytheon together with Hughes will create a much more competitive company that can better serve the defense market with leadership in systems and electronics."

John C. Weaver, president of Hughes Aircraft, said, "Our two companies have worked together successfully on several ventures in the past, such as the Standard Missile Company and Medium Extended Air Defense System (MEADS). That same spirit of cooperation will now propel us to greater growth and prosperity for our stakeholders than would have been possible individually." Weaver will report directly to Picard as the president of Raytheon Hughes Systems, which will operate as a division of the combined company.

Upon completion of this transaction, and closing of the acquisition of Texas Instruments' Defense Systems and Electronics Group, announced on Jan. 6, the combined company will have approximately 127,000 employees worldwide. Raytheon's headquarters will be based in Lexington, Mass.

In connection with the merger, C. Michael Armstrong; Charles H. Noski, currently vice chairman and chief financial officer of Hughes Electronics; and an independent director of GM to be named later, will be members of the Board of Directors of the combined company.

Hughes Aircraft Company

Hughes Aircraft, the Hughes Electronics' defense business, is expected to report 1996 revenues of approximately $6.3 billion (unaudited). It has *approximately* 40,000 employees, principally in the states of California, Arizona, Indiana, Texas, and Virginia.

Hughes is a premier supplier of advanced defense electronics systems and services, principally in Naval systems, airborne and ground-based radars, ground, air and ship-launched missiles, tactical communications, and training simulators and services. Hughes also supplies Air Traffic Control systems to the U.S. Federal Aviation Administration and to foreign governments, and is active in the fields of global positioning systems, infrared/electro-optics and Monolithic Microwave Integrated Circuits (MMIC).

In Naval systems, Hughes' programs include the MK48 ADCAP torpedo, the Phalanx Close-in Weapon System, UYQ-21 displays and Airborne Low-Frequency sonars. Hughes has also just been selected to provide state-of-the-art ship combat systems for the U.S. Navy's new LPD-17 assault landing ship.

In radar systems, Hughes provides the APG-series of airborne fire control radars for the F-15, F-18, and AV-8 Harrier. Ground-based radar programs include the TPQ-37 fire direction radar and the Ground Based Sensor.

Hughes' missile programs include Maverick, TOW, MEADS, Tomahawk, Stinger, RAM (Rolling Air Frame Missile), AMRAAM, Sparrow, Evolved SeaSparrow, Standard (as part of Standard Missile Company, a wholly owned Raytheon-Hughes subsidiary), and the new AIM-9X Sidewinder.

Hughes is also a provider of tactical communications and military radios, including the U.S. Army's Tactical Command and Control System, AFATADS (Advanced Field Artillery Tactical Data Systems) and a wide array of tactical radios. Hughes also provides trainers and simulators for helicopter and fixed-wing aircraft.

Raytheon Defense Electronics

Raytheon's defense electronics businesses include Raytheon Electronics Systems, Raytheon E-Systems and, prospectively, the Texas Instruments defense business, to be called Raytheon TI Systems upon completion of that transaction in the second quarter of 1997.

Raytheon Electronics Systems (RES) is a major provider of ground-based and shipboard radars, military communication systems, and naval combat control, sonar and mine hunting systems. RES is one of three teams selected for Phase II of the U.S. Navy/DARPA Arsenal Ship Program. RES missile systems include Patriot, Hawk, AMRAAM, Sidewinder, Standard, and Sparrow. RES is also a world leader in Air Traffic Control systems, having won over $1.6 billion in new radar and automation programs for the FAA and U.S. Air Force last year.

Raytheon E-Systems is a leader in defense systems integration and provides reconnaissance and surveillance; command, control, communications and intelligence systems; mass data collection, interpretation and dissemination;

specialized aircraft modification services, and ship-board and airborne countermeasures systems to a wide variety of customers worldwide.

Raytheon Service Company, a unit of Raytheon Engineers and Constructors, is one of the nation's leading government contractors, providing operations, maintenance, and technical services for many U.S. defense systems and agencies.

Raytheon TI Systems

Raytheon TI Systems brings to Raytheon significant positions in a number of major programs. TI is a leader in precision-guided munitions, with programs such as the Paveway laser-guided weapon system and the Joint Stand-Off Weapon (JSOW), a U.S. Navy/U.S. Air Force system for attacking high-value ground targets. The Javelin program is an anti-tank system for the U.S. Army. TI is a leader in Long Range Precision Strike programs, such as the High Speed Anti-Radiation Missile (HARM).

TI has strong positions in P-3 and S-3 ocean surveillance, F-22 airborne radars, and the LANTIRN terrain-following radar. TI produces electro-optics products, such as Forward-Looking InfraRed (FLIR) sensors deployed on the Bradley Fighting Vehicle, M-1 Tank, F-117 "Stealth" fighter, and the F-18 Hornet.

Raytheon's Diversified Commercial Strengths

Raytheon competes in a variety of commercial businesses, as well. Raytheon Engineers and Constructors is one of the largest engineering, construction, and operations and maintenance organizations in the world. Its markets include: fossil-fuel and nuclear power; petroleum and gas; polymers and chemicals, pharmaceuticals and biotechnology; metals, mining and light industry; food and consumer products, and pulp and paper, among others.

Raytheon Aircraft is the world leader in general aviation, offering the most extensive product line in the industry. Additionally, Raytheon Aircraft Company (RAC) provides special mission aircraft, aircraft maintenance services, target drones, and aircraft training systems to the military services. RAC won the 1995 competition for the multibillion-dollar, next-generation Joint Primary Aircraft Training System (JPATS) trainer for the U.S. Air Force and U.S. Navy.

Raytheon Appliances markets some of the finest brand names in appliances including Amana refrigerators, microwave ovens, cooking surfaces, and washer and dryers as well as Speed Queen, Huebsch, and UniMac commercial laundry equipment.

The transaction is subject to approval by Raytheon's stockholders, certain regulatory approvals (including Hart-Scott-Rodino antitrust review), approval by the holders of GM common stocks, and the receipt by GM of rulings from the Internal Revenue Service relating to certain federal income tax consequences of the transaction.

Transaction Summary

Hughes Aircraft will be spun off to the holders of GM's $1-2/3 and Class H common stocks in a transaction intended to be tax free. In connection with the spin-off and subsequent merger, two classes of common stock will be created: Class A common stock, which will be held by GM $1-2/3 and Class H stockholders after the spin-off and will be entirely held by the public; and Class B common stock.

Immediately following the spin-off of Hughes Aircraft, Raytheon and Hughes Aircraft will merge. In the merger, Raytheon stockholders will receive all of the Class B common stock of the combined company. The Class B common stock will represent approximately 70 percent of the equity of the combined company, and the Class A common stock will represent the remaining, approximately 30 percent.

The merger terms provide that Hughes Aircraft's total debt will be adjusted to reflect variations in the market price of Raytheon stock, subject to specified limits, so that the two components of value will total $9.5 billion so long as such market price is between $44.42 and $54.29 per share. The approximately $5.1 billion in common stock issued to the Class A stockholders is based upon the midpoint of this range. The balance of the $9.5 billion transaction value will be made up of approximately $4.4 billion in Hughes Aircraft debt.

In the election of directors to the combined company board, Class A common stock will have an 80.1 percent voting interest, and Class B common stock will have a 19.9 percent voting interest. The board of directors will have staggered terms for directors. Except as to voting rights for directors, each class will vote separately as to all other matters, and the Class A and Class B stock will have identical rights. In a merger, acquisition or any other type of reorganization, Class A and Class B common stock must receive the same consideration.

Background Information

Raytheon Company, headquartered in Lexington, Mass., is a $12 billion international, high-technology company with approximately 75,000 employees worldwide operating in four businesses: commercial and defense electronics, engineering and construction, aircraft, and major appliances.

Information about Raytheon and Hughes Electronics is located on the World Wide Web at http://www.raytheon.com, and http://www.hughes.com, respectively.

Statements which are not historical facts contained in this release are forward-looking statements that involve risks and uncertainties. These risks include, in addition to the specific uncertainties referenced in this release, the ability to realize anticipated cost efficiencies, the effect of market conditions, the impact of competitive products and pricing, and new product development. Further information regarding the factors that could cause actual results to differ from projected results can be found in Raytheon's reports filed with the SEC, including our Form 8-K filed today with the SEC formally disclosing the transactions referenced above and our Form 10-Q for the quarter ended September 29, 1996.

Media Contacts:
Robert Mc Wade
Blanche Necessary
Raytheon
617-860-2846
Dave Shea
Hughes Electronics
703-284-4245

http://fas.org/man/company/docs/970116-raytheon.html

Appendix E – Details of the Leidos Holdings/SAIC Consulting Services

National Security Solutions

National Security Solutions provides solutions and systems for air, land, sea, space and cyberspace for the United States intelligence community, the DoD, the military services, the DHS and government agencies of United States allies abroad. The Company's solutions deliver technology, large scale intelligence systems, command and control, data analytics, cybersecurity, logistics, and intelligence analysis and operations support to critical missions around the world. Its customers of National Security Solutions include national and military intelligence agencies, and other federal, civilian and commercial customers in the national security complex. The Company provides solutions for the arms control and the intelligence agencies and the DoD service arms, including the Defense Advanced Research Projects Agency (DARPA). This group focuses on distributed autonomous capabilities and systems, tying software and data capabilities together. It is a developer of the full spectrum Intelligence, Surveillance, and Reconnaissance (ISR) capability.

Leidos offers intelligence services and solutions. The Company provides systems development and operations support around the globe. The Company supports the army's migration of intelligence applications and infrastructure into the cloud and provides cloud computing architectures to the intelligence and the defense communities. The Company offers cybersecurity *solutions that detect and manage the sophisticated cyber threats. The Company's solutions include management systems to protect transmitted data, development tools to exploit cyber intelligence and programs to build situational awareness on military and intelligence networks. National Security Solutions represented 71% of total revenues for fiscal year ended January 30, 2015 (fiscal 2015).*

Health and Engineering

Leidos' Health and Engineering businesses' customers include the United States federal government, state and local governmental agencies, foreign governments and commercial enterprises in various industries. Its Health business provides services and solutions to commercial hospitals and the DoD, as well as conducting research and development for United States Government and Commercial enterprises in the life sciences field. Health and Engineering represented 29% of total revenues for fiscal 2015.

The Federal Health division develops and maintains an end-to-end Electronic Health Record (HER) system and numerous behavior health services (healthcare beyond the clinic) for the Department of Defense (DoD). Within the DoD, the Federal Health division serves the Defense Health Agency, which provides healthcare to active duty and retired military personnel and their dependents. It implements and optimizes EHR systems at commercial hospitals. In addition, it provides consulting services and operational support focused on initiatives, including health care legislation for Meaningful Use and ICD-10 transition, information technology (IT) strategy, revenue cycle management, accountable care transformation, risk management, technology infrastructure and project management.

The Company provides life science research and development support to the National Institute of Health, Army Medical Research community, commercial biotech companies and the Frederick National Laboratory for Cancer Research. The Company operates a range of research and development laboratories in the areas of genetics and genomics, proteins and proteomics, advanced biomedical computing and information technology, biopharmaceutical development and manufacturing, nanotechnology characterization and clinical trials management.

Leidos Engineering business leverages technology and skills in process engineering, engineering design and systems integration to create solutions for its customers. The Company carries out its engineering business in five areas: Process Industries Engineering, Security Products, Power Grid Engineering, Federal Environmental and Engineering and Transaction and Valuation Consulting.

Process Industries Engineering provides process industries engineering services and solutions to the United States market for capital improvement programs for clients across a number of industries, including mid-tier refineries and industrial companies. The Company provides security products, services and solutions that leverage its design, integration and process engineering technologies to build small footprint, minimally intrusive secure commerce systems for its customers. Its VACIS systems enable the rapid scanning of vehicles and cargo using patented technology that produces an image using a low radiation dose while using less space. Its Reveal line of explosive detection systems for checked airline baggage offers small, flexible systems that can be installed at airport check-in counters. It also has a line of radiation detection systems, which are used at ports, border crossings, and industrial facilities around the world, including ports and border crossings in the United States.

The Company provides power grid engineering services and solutions and offers smart grid as a service solution. The Company provides engineering and consulting to electric utilities and transmission companies. The Company also administers energy efficiency programs for states and utilities and provides an array of consulting services for utilities. The Federal Environmental and Engineering division provides consulting and engineering, primarily for the Department of Defense (DoD). The Company also has specialty consulting associated with specific environmental issues, such as underwater environmental issues, radiologic clean up, risk assessment training ranges and other specific needs. The Company also designs high-content facilities such as testing facilities and training centers. The Company provides transaction and asset valuation services for the power industry. The Company's customers are the lending institutions that require a comprehensive assessment of proposed projects for financing.

The Company competes with The Boeing Company, General Dynamics Corporation, Lockheed Martin Corporation, Northrop Grumman Corporation, BAE Systems plc, L-3 Communications Corporation, Raytheon Company, Booz Allen Hamilton Inc., Engility Holdings, Inc., CACI International Inc, ManTech International Corporation, Serco Group plc, SRA International, Inc., MITRE Corporation, Accenture plc, Computer Sciences Corporation, HP Enterprise Services, International Business Machines Corporation, Unisys Corporation, Jacobs Engineering Group, URS Corporation, KBR, Inc., CH2M Hill Companies Ltd., American Science and Engineering, Inc., OSI Systems, Inc., L-3 Communications Corporation, General Electric Company, Smiths Group plc, Agility Logistics Corp., Cerner Corporation, Epic Systems and Allscripts.

http://www.reuters.com/finance/stocks/companyProfile?symbol=LDOS.N

Part IV
Implementation in Consulting

12 Intervention Strategies in Management Consulting   273
    (TOM CUMMINGS, UNIVERSITY OF SOUTHERN CALIFORNIA)

13 Consulting to Integrate Mergers and Acquisitions   294
    (ANTHONY F. BUONO, BENTLEY UNIVERSITY)

14 Business Transformation and Innovation Consulting   319
    (MATTHEW C. HEIM, INNO360, INC.)

Introduction

From the client's perspective, the acid test of a consultant's value resides in achieving real improvement in performance. Otherwise, it is difficult for clients to justify their added investment in consulting. The inability of consulting firms to produce results can easily damage their reputation and cause prospective clients to shy away.

Unfortunately, too many clients have experienced projects that either fail or fall short of expectations. Not many years ago, and even in some cases today, this failure in implementation was blamed by consultants on the client because the consultants adhered to their expert role of only making recommendations while leaving implementation to the client.

However, the tide has clearly shifted over the past decade to place much more responsibility on consultants for producing results. Many consulting firms now employ intervention approaches that are designed to ensure ownership and commitment to change by the client's workforce, and they often stay longer into the implementation period. But these changes do not occur easily or naturally. Most clients prefer stability while adhering to past practices, and there are always senior executives who resist changes that threaten their power base.

Chapter 12, "Intervention Strategies in Management Consulting," argues that consultants often apply the wrong intervention approach to client situations. As a result, resistance arises and the change effort fails. The chapter goes on to describe four major intervention strategies from expert-based to process-based, each of which works only under certain conditions in the client situation. The challenge for the consultant is to understand the client's situation in-depth and to choose the appropriate intervention strategy. Unfortunately, it is not easily accomplished because consulting firms often have a "preferred" intervention approach (their own set of best practices) that they apply in most situations. The author makes a plea for greater flexibility in the consultant's choice of intervention strategies as they relate to certain conditions in the client firm.

Mergers and acquisitions, the subject of Chapter 13, "Consulting to Integrate Mergers and Acquisitions," covers another important change situation fraught with frequent failure. Two-thirds of all merger deals fall short of expectations, with half of those becoming outright failures. The chapter points out that most advisory work on current M&A transactions takes place before the deal is consummated, usually conducted by lawyers and bankers. However, a real need for consulting assistance exists, not only in the due diligence period but with the difficult problems of post-merger integration. The initial technical advisors often underestimate the subsequent post-merger implementation issues, which are the focus of this chapter. Highlighted are the barriers to integration, such as lack of preparation, divergent cultures, and disagreement among top managers about the goals of the merger.

The author suggests three consulting strategies (roles) that "evolve around three different but overlapping phases" to deal with these issues. These roles include: 1) pre-combination preliminary planning, 2) early integration implementation during combination, and 3) post-combination aftermath. Unfortunately, and despite performance of these three strategies, there is a high failure rate. This said, mergers and acquisitions will no doubt continue, and consultants will need to provide substantive pre-combination implementation as well as post-merger integration services. Assisting a client through organizational transformative change is one of the most demanding consulting tasks. This is a challenging requirement for the consultant as it requires a high level of innovation and leadership.

In Chapter 14, "Business Transformation and Innovation Consulting," the author posits for a new model of continuous change that requires a new leadership model. The chapter starts out with the definition of business transformation, and the integral role it plays with both corporate structure and the individual worker. The author continues with a discussion of the role of the consultant in a business transformation initiative and the various approaches used by consulting firms today. The chapter moves forward to explore the concept of transformational leadership and the transformational leadership model used to support continuous change. The author concludes with a discussion of the recent re-emergence of collaborative innovation and of the importance it carries in achieving and sustaining corporate growth.

12 Intervention Strategies in Management Consulting

Tom Cummings

Consulting firms typically describe their services in marketing brochures along dimensions having to do with specialized practice areas and the types of clients they serve, such as information systems in health-care businesses. Although these features help to explain what services the firm provides to what kinds of clients, they reveal relatively little about how the firm actually intervenes to provide these services. Intervention strategies are rarely advertised in management consulting but are left opaque and part of the "mystery" of the profession. Yet, I believe intervention strategies determine success in consulting outcomes.

Like all practical professions, management consulting faces persistent questions from researchers and critics of the profession about the efficacy of its applications. This is especially true when it comes to implementing proposed changes in organizations. Management consultants frequently discover that their recommendations, no matter how valid or relevant, make little if any impact on how their client organizations function. As a result, their advice fails to translate into real organization change. Explanations and excuses for this unfortunate execution gap between recommendations and implementation can come from consultants (e.g., no top management support to implement) and from the client (e.g., recommendations were impractical).[1]

The explanation for this gap lies in the way that consultants choose to intervene in organizations. They may use the wrong intervention approach for the problem at hand. Or the client may resist a recommended approach that indeed might work but which the client doesn't understand and therefore objects. Consulting firms are often wedded to their unique intervention approaches, the "XYZ firm way," regardless of the situation. And clients are often naive about what questions to ask regarding what types of interventions may or may not work in their organizations. As a result, they may buy the wrong intervention, only to learn too late about that mistake.

Greater knowledge about interventions is essential to consultants and clients alike for improving consulting practice and enhancing implementation success.[2] Consultants can benefit by knowing more clearly what kinds of interventions may or may not work under certain conditions. And perceptive clients can become more aware of the right questions to ask of

> **Case of Implementation Failure** – LEG Inc., a large multi-service consulting firm, is renowned for its advanced models and techniques for assessing and determining corporate strategy. Employing the brightest MBAs from mostly top-10 business schools, LEG has built a solid reputation for delivering the "goods" when it came to assessing clients and their markets and recommending appropriate strategies. Moreover, LEG responds rapidly to client needs. As one amazed customer remarked: "LEG is like the Army in Desert Storm. A dozen or more of them descended on us almost overnight, collecting data, crunching numbers, and making proposals." Unfortunately, LEG's approach to management consulting is increasingly coming under attack from critics who suggest that "good analyses and proposals" are not enough to achieve success. Rather, "execution" of corporate strategy is what matters. Indeed, the CEO of one of LEG's clients was recently cited in a popular business magazine as saying: "LEG did a good job for us. The market analysis was insightful and the recommended business strategy made sense. Where we ran into trouble was getting middle managers to buy into it. They just didn't seem to understand where we needed to go and what needed to done to get there. Perhaps this isn't LEG's fault, but they could have warned us. We wasted a large investment."

potential consultants about their intervention approaches before deciding to accept a specific proposal.

This chapter addresses both sides of the consulting relationship and shows how the nature of consulting interventions can affect outcomes, negatively or positively, in different situations. It presents a framework based on two key dimensions underlying most interventions, *delivery mode* and *content focus*. Delivery mode refers to how consulting is conducted (e.g., types of involvement) with the client, and content focus refers to the substance (e.g., theories and issues) being considered by the consultants. Then it describes how these two dimensions intersect in practice to give rise to four possible intervention strategies: expertise-based, organization-based, teaching-based, and process-based. Each strategy will be discussed for its strengths and weaknesses under certain conditions in a client's organization. The chapter concludes with broader implications for the future development of consultants, clients, and the consulting profession.

Key Dimensions in Consulting Interventions

As shown in Exhibit 12.1, the two dimensions of delivery mode and content focus lay behind the four basic intervention strategies in management

Intervention Strategies in Management Consulting 275

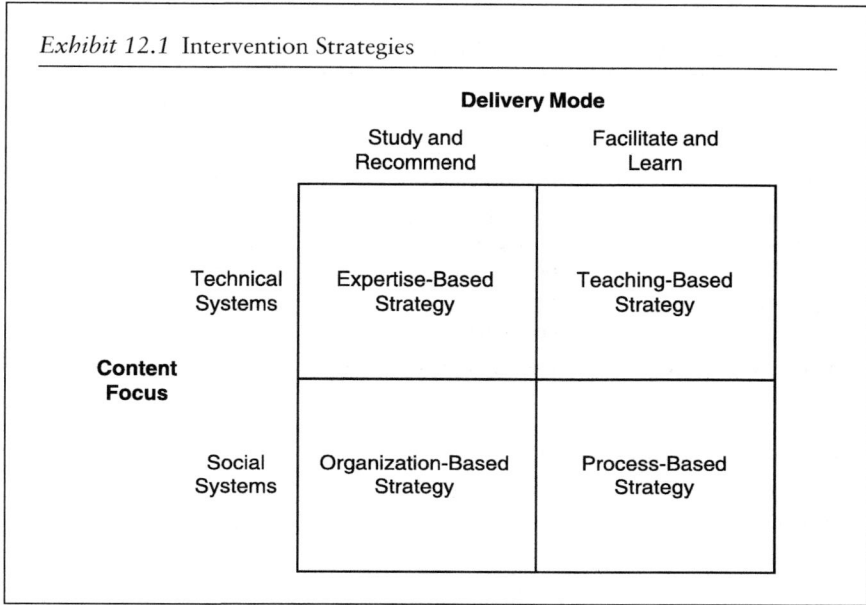

Exhibit 12.1 Intervention Strategies

consulting. The two dimensions in themselves provide useful insights into the assumptions and dynamics that underpin the intervention strategies.

Delivery Mode Dimension

The delivery mode in consulting represents a continuum with two different modes of delivery at each end, from *study and recommend* to *facilitate and learn* (see horizontal dimension in Exhibit 12.1). As these terms imply, the former mode involves analyzing the client's situation and proposing solutions; the latter mode emphasizes helping clients learn for themselves about how to improve their organizations. Similar distinctions made elsewhere in this book include describing consultants as "experts" versus "advisors" (Maister, Chapter 2); "prescriptive" versus "facilitative" consulting roles (Nadler and Slywotzky, Chapter 5); and in other literature, such as "consultant-centered" versus "client-centered" change processes.[3]

Exhibit 12.2 presents these two opposing delivery modes in terms of their history, basic assumptions, and other aspects that highlight their major differences.

Study and Recommend. This is the oldest and most prevalent delivery mode in management consulting. Consultants analyze clients' organizations and propose solutions to their problems. Its historical roots go back over seventy-five years to the rapid emergence of management consulting as a

Exhibit 12.2 Alternative Delivery Modes

	Study and Recommend	Facilitate and Learn
History	Engineering, ACME	Humanistic psychology
Assumptions about organization change	Empirical-rational process; change via persuosian	Normative-reeducative process; change via involvement
Underlying values	Effectiveness, efficiency	Collaboration, openness, trust
Major objectives	Getting it right	Increasing capacity of client to solve own problems
Consultant expertise	Discipline based	Clinical based
Role of consultant	Solution giver	Facilitator
Role of client	Solution implementer	Co-learner
Intensity and length of engagement	Arms length; periodic	High; continuous

profession following World War I. At the time, engineering was the most developed of the applied sciences with specific applications for business firms. Thus, its rational problem-solving approach heavily influenced how consulting services were delivered to management. Indeed, the profession's first society was called the Association of Consulting Management Engineers (ACME), which later changed its name to the Association of Management Consulting Firms (AMCF) as companies came to dominate the industry and other applied disciplines, such as accounting and economics, entered the field.

From its engineering origins, it is not surprising that the study and recommend mode treats organization change as an empirical-rational process. It assumes that managers are guided by reason and evidence and will use rational criteria to make decisions about changing the organization. Because the chief threat to rationality is ignorance or superstition, managers need objective empirical information to make good decisions. It is assumed that such so-called "facts" will persuade them to change.

Based on these assumptions, the study and recommend mode emphasizes hard data and bottom-line results. It values organization effectiveness and efficiency, with the goal of finding the right solution to a clearly defined management problem with profit-and-loss consequences.

This study and recommend mode tends to view management as a "science" where change is implemented via rational persuasion. Consultants study the client's situation to provide objective evidence about the causes of problems and give expert advice on what to do about them. To be successful, study and recommend consultants need to be seen by clients as objective experts. Thus, they work hard to differentiate themselves from clients. They act as detached solution givers and not involved implementers; they engage with clients in arms-length relationships where they meet only periodically.

To enhance their perceived expertise, consultants draw heavily on knowledge and methods from the academic business disciplines (e.g., finance and strategy), which provide them with analytical models and prescriptive solutions, such as Porter's Five Forces model or the BCG matrix. All this helps to assure, and reinforce the belief, that consultants are unbiased and professionally proficient. Such views are fundamental to the study and recommend delivery mode.

Facilitate and Learn. At the other end of the delivery mode continuum, the facilitate and learn mode focuses on helping clients learn how to improve their own organizations. It dates to the 1950s with the emergence of humanistic psychology and organization development and their applications to management consulting. Many corporate training programs eventually evolved out of this movement, such as Participative Management and the Managerial Grid. The facilitate and learn mode emphasizes the developmental nature of people and organizations. This approach assumes that the more developed an organization, the better able it is to solve its own problems and to improve itself. Thus, management consulting under this mode is concerned with transferring skills and knowledge to organizations so they can self-improve their capability to solve problems.

The facilitate and learn mode considers organization change as a normative re-educative process. It does not deny human rationality but assumes that in social contexts, people's behavior is heavily influenced by social norms and their commitment to them. For change to occur, people must modify norms and develop commitment to new ones. This cannot be accomplished by changes in the amount of information available and intellectual logic alone. It requires the active involvement of people in changing the attitudes, skills, and relationships underlying their behavior. Thus, people must participate in their own re-education and, thereby, change themselves if they are to change at all.

Given these assumptions, the facilitate and learn mode emphasizes learning and commitment to change. It values consulting relationships that promote collaboration, openness, and trust among participants, which in turn facilitate helping clients learn how to change and improve themselves. Facilitate and learn consultants instruct clients on how to change their organizations through active participation of employees in the change process itself. Therefore, consulting engagements tend to be highly intense and continuous. If clients are to grow and develop, they must transcend their natural dependency on consultants. This places a heavy demand on a consultant's clinical expertise and social acumen. The consultant must act more like a facilitator and trainer than an expert as clients develop their own competencies for implementing change and improvement.

Content Focus Dimension

The second key dimension that underlies most interventions concerns the content focus of a consulting engagement. This involves the substantive aspects of the client's organization that consultants address, such as corporate strategy, organization design, team decision-making, and employee motivation. It also includes the content of knowledge and methods brought to bear by the consultants, such as psychological theories, marketing models, and operations techniques.

Content focus differs enormously in management consulting and often serves as the basis for a firm to advertise its specialized knowledge and services in a particular practice area, such as human resources or information systems or strategy. Content focus falls along a continuum from *technical systems* to *social systems* (see vertical dimension in Exhibit 12.1). The former has to do with the strategy that client organizations use to gain competitive advantage and the organization design that structures the production and delivery of products and services, while the latter involves employee capabilities and the motivation and human relationships that occur among employees as they organize, coordinate, and control their efforts to make decisions and communicate with each other.[4] These two aspects of content focus are described further in Exhibit 12.3.

Technical Systems. Like the study and recommend delivery mode, the technical systems focus is the oldest and most pervasive content focus in management consulting. It dates back to Frederick Taylor's pioneering work in scientific management in the early 1900s, which emphasized efficiency at work through the analysis and redesign of jobs and work methods. Because organizations tended to be highly inefficient, the initial success of scientific management fueled widespread demand for such expertise. Thus, early management consulting concentrated on the technical side of organizations, primarily on the shop floor. Over time, this focus extended to organizations' marketing, administrative, and information functions, and more recently, to corporate strategy, supply chains, and strategic alliances.

Underlying the technical focus are certain assumptions about how to understand issues of concern to clients. It is assumed that there is a body of knowledge that can be drawn on by educated consultants from different disciplines. Such knowledge is viewed as applicable across situations. Thus, consultants intervene to apply general expertise and others' experience to different

Exhibit 12.3 Content Focus

	Technical Systems	Social Systems
History	Scientific management	Organization development
Primary emphasis	Solving problems correctly	Making things run smoother
Assumptions about the nature of organizations	Objective; independently measured	Subjective; socially constructed
Assumptions about knowledge utilization	General knowledge applies to specific situations	Local knowledge necessary
Action levers for change	Strategy, task structure, and business functions	Individuals, groups, and their relationships
Pertinent data	Manifest industry and competitors; client company; business functions	Latent leadership; decision making, communication, and problem solving processes; interpersonal relations, group process
Consultant selection criteria	Technical expertise and industry knowledge	Interpersonal competence
Consultant retention criteria	Demonstrable work and financial results	Trust

clients facing similar problems. Moreover, client organizations are treated as objective entities with their own properties and features. Therefore, consultants believe they can independently measure and analyze these features.

Based on these assumptions, the technical systems content focus addresses the more manifest or observable aspects of a client's problems. It emphasizes technical variables as action levers for improvement, including the client's strategy and organization design elements, such as structure, work design, information systems, and human resource practices.

Technically oriented consultants generally collect and analyze information about the organization's industry and competitors, its design elements, and how it achieves on various performance criteria. Based on that information, they apply technical knowledge and expertise to develop specific innovations for improving the organization. Thus, clients select management consultants for their strong technical expertise and knowledge of the client's industry. They often retain them again for demonstrating measurable improvements in client functioning and performance.

Social Systems. This content focus involves the human side of organizations, and it is rooted in the emergence of the knowledge fields of organization development in the 1950s, leadership change methods in the 1990s, and positive organizational scholarship in the 2000s. As organizations grew larger and more bureaucratic, they experienced a host of unintended social problems; members found it increasingly difficult to communicate both laterally and vertically, to resolve problems within and across groups, and to respond energetically to managerial directives. Also, consultants experienced growing resistance to the technical solutions offered to clients.

The field of organization development, drawing heavily on the disciplines of psychology and sociology, responded to these problems with a variety of interventions for improving social processes and overcoming resistance to change, such team-building, process consultation, and conflict management. In focusing on social content, management consultants placed heavy emphasis on resolving social ills and making things run smoother. They addressed social processes as the key to implementing organization change.

This content focus, supplemented by knowledge on leadership change and positive organizational scholarship, treats organizations from a subjective perspective, both in their design and in their evolution. Organizations are viewed as socially constructed out of employee intents, values, and perceptions. They involve members taking action and making sense out of this behavior, thereby creating shared meaning for organized activities. Thus, to understand organizations, it is necessary to see them as the members of the organization see them.

Subjective experiences play a key role in applying knowledge to organizations. Because member sense-making is unique in each organization, generalized knowledge must be adapted to fit specific organization contexts. So called "local knowledge" is essential to this adaptation process.

Given these views, the social systems focus treats individuals and groups as the key action levers for improving organizations, primarily through social processes having to do with employee development, leadership, decision making, and communication. Consultants typically spend considerable time with organization members to understand how they perceive those processes. Then, they apply their expertise to help make these social processes run smoother and more effectively. Clients tend to select management consultants having strong interpersonal competence and a belief that solutions lie within the members of the organization. They retain consultants they can trust and be open with during their contacts.

Four Alternative Intervention Strategies

The two underlying dimensions of interventions – delivery mode and content focus – interact in the real world to produce four basic intervention strategies for consultants (depicted earlier in Exhibit 12.1). I have labeled these four strategies as: *expertise-based, organization-based, teaching-based, and process-based*. In this section, I describe each strategy in some depth, exploring its strengths and weaknesses, and suggesting situations where each is likely to be more or less effective. Later in this chapter, I will consider how the four intervention strategies can be used in combination during certain types of consulting engagements and at different stages in a project.

Expertise-Based Strategy

This intervention strategy combines the study and recommend delivery mode with a content focus on technical systems. From its roots in engineering and scientific management, the expertise-based strategy has come to dominate management consulting. Today, it is used by most large consulting firms to intervene with clients.

The expertise-based strategy is relatively straightforward.[5] Consultants collect and analyze data about technical aspects of the client organization, such as its business strategy and organization design including structure, information systems, operations, and human resources. They then recommend specific solutions to client problems, such as a new global strategy, a decentralized structure, or a streamlined supply chain.

To be unbiased observers and advisors, expertise-based consultants clearly divide the consultant and client roles; the former is concerned with recommending while the latter with implementing. As experts, consultants work hard to show how their general technical knowledge applies to specific client situations.

A typical example of the expertise-based strategy involves a large management consulting firm that is hired to advise a company's top management team on possible changes in the firm's business strategy. Led by a seasoned engagement manager with experience in the client's industry, several consultants and analysts are assigned full time to the consulting project, which lasts from three to six months. They gather data on the client and its competitive environment, usually drawing on market research and industry dynamics. Based on this information and analysis, the consultants recommend specific changes to the client's business strategy. This is accomplished in a multi-media presentation to the top management team, backed by a written report containing supporting data. The consultants also might propose helping the client organization implement the proposed changes.

The expertise-based intervention strategy has a number of distinct strengths. It offers clients an objective and independent assessment of their situation, which can uncover problems and opportunities that clients have not addressed or considered. Expertise-based consultants bring new perspectives to clients; their knowledge of the client's industry and competitors will suggest best practices that clients can implement.

In recent years, expertise-based consultants have increasingly applied their capabilities to perform tasks or provide services that clients normally do themselves, particularly support functions such as accounting, human resource management, and information processing. This external capability provides clients with viable options to outsource tasks that are not part of their core competence and that consultants can do better and cheaper.

Perhaps the greatest strength of the expertise-based intervention strategy is that clients can easily understand it and defend its use to relevant stakeholders. Using experts to solve problems is generally considered normal and highly rational. In case of failure, clients can reliably blame consultants rather than themselves.

The expertise-based strategy also contains certain downsides, however. It is unlikely to lead to high levels of commitment to change, thus resulting in implementation problems. While expert consultants will brief the client occasionally on their progress, they typically do not involve the client in data gathering, analysis, and formulating recommendations. As a result, the client's employees may not support the proposed changes and may resist or even sabotage them.

The expertise-based strategy involves a division of labor where consultants analyze the client's situation and design improvements and the client implements them. This division can lead to differences in design criteria and change orientation between consultants and clients. Expertise-based consultants are likely to favor change programs with explicit schedules, goals, and change activities, while underplaying the ability of the client to implement the recommended change program. Moreover, consultants seek solutions with proven records of success and, consequently, rely on change programs that have worked well in other settings and that can be readily packaged and adopted by clients. These features are intended to assure that the consultants' expertise will be recognized and valued by clients and that the integrity of their recommendations will persist.

Clients, on the other hand, often prefer change programs that afford maximum freedom to modify and adjust the changes to fit their specific situation, including its culture, politics, and capabilities. They seek flexibility and local control over changes. These fundamental differences can lead to consulting reports that simply gather the proverbial dust on the CEO's book case, or that result in overt conflicts between consultants and clients.

Probably the most troublesome limitation of the expertise-based strategy is that it does little to improve the client's ability to improve itself. Expertise-based consulting is aimed primarily at solving client problems in a single engagement, not at providing managers and employees with the skills and knowledge necessary to analyze and solve future problems. Because the expertise to assess organizations and propose improvements resides with the consultants, clients tend to become dependent on them and see little need to gain such skills themselves.

Despite these inherent problems, the expertise-based intervention strategy is well suited to particular situations. It is especially relevant when client's problems are clearly defined, limited in scope, and require minimal amounts of organization change. In these settings, clients are likely to be clear about the "problem" but believe they do not have the knowledge or resources to understand and resolve it. Thus, they are likely to choose experts who meet their needs. The consultants can then apply their technical expertise without needing high levels of client involvement for implementation. Whether the client will then implement the recommendations remains problematic.

Organization-Based Strategy

This intervention strategy blends the study and recommended delivery mode with the content dimension focused on social systems. In dealing with the social side of organizations, organization-based consultants address client issues related to leadership, decision making, communication, power and politics, and interpersonal and group dynamics.[6]

Like the previous strategy, it is expert driven; consultants analyze and advise while clients implement change. Consultant expertise is generally rooted in the organizational behavior disciplines involving social relations, group process, and the like. Organization-based consultants seek to provide clients with the right solutions to their social problems, especially interventions that make things run smoother and more effectively.

Consultants applying the organization-based strategy typically look at organizations from a subjective viewpoint. They seek to understand client organizations as managers and employees see them, and thus employ diagnostic methods, such as interviews and surveys, that tap into members' perceptions.

Like expert consultants, organization-based consultants tend to regard organization change as a persuasion process supported by theory and evidence. To convince clients to change, they provide expert insights about members' subjective experience; they then draw on those interpretations to make skilled recommendations (e.g., new leadership styles and decision-making practices) for how clients can improve themselves. This application of external expertise to internal subjective data can change how clients view their situation; it can reveal new possibilities and show them how their local knowledge can inform change.

To make this work, organization-based consultants display a good deal of impartiality and empathy for the client's situation. They remain unbiased toward clients while establishing a close enough relationship with them to elicit relevant social data. Clearly, this is no easy task for even the best organization consultants.

An example of the organization-based strategy involves a mid-sized consulting firm that is hired to help a company understand and resolve persistent conflicts between members of the marketing and the product development departments who need to work closely together to meet customers' changing needs. A small team of experienced consultants is assigned to the project, and they negotiate a four-month contract to study the underlying causes of the conflict and make recommendations. The consultants collect and analyze data from members of both the marketing and the product development departments using focused interviews and a survey that measures several inter-group features that can lead to conflict between departments, such as differences in work styles, communication patterns, and performance goals. Based on the interview and survey results and their diagnosis, the consultants discover that the conflict between the two departments is caused mainly by differences in goal orientation, with marketing focused on gaining market share and product development aimed at product innovation. The consultants then recommend to the client in a formal report and oral presentation a joint goal-setting intervention with selected members from each department. The consultants also propose to facilitate the intervention for a specific time period and fee.

The organization-based intervention strategy has many of the same strengths and weaknesses as the expertise-based strategy. On the plus side, it provides an independent view of client organizations and can reveal problems and possibilities that clients have not considered. This is especially important when dealing with social issues, where clients are likely to be emotionally involved and may need an outside expert to help them sort things out.

On the negative side, the organization-based strategy can have problems with commitment to change and client dependency. Because clients are not generally involved in analyzing the organization or making proposals for change, they may not develop sufficient support to implement consultants' recommendations. Moreover, organizational change can be difficult and stressful, and clients may find it less painful to defend the status quo than to change it. Organization-based strategies, like expertise-based strategies, are particularly vulnerable to clients becoming excessively dependent on consultants to solve their problems. Because social expertise can be difficult to acquire, clients can overly rely on external experts to provide that skill and knowledge.

The application of organization-based intervention strategies is particularly appropriate in situations where clients recognize they have social problems yet do not have the expertise or resources to solve these problems themselves. It is also relevant when clients want to get an objective assessment of the social side of their organizations. Social audits, often called "cultural audits," are increasingly being used to supplement more common financial assessments. Finally, the organization-based strategy works well in situations where clients want experts to facilitate particular social interventions, such as team building and conflict resolution.

Teaching-Based Strategy

This intervention strategy is relatively new in management consulting. It is a combination of the facilitate and learn delivery mode with a content focus on technical systems.[7] Teaching-based approaches are responsive to the increasing need of organizations to adapt to environments that are changing rapidly and unpredictably. In these situations, organizations must continuously change themselves; this requires building the capability to change and improve into the organization itself so it becomes a core competence.

To help organizations accomplish this, teaching-based consultants impart knowledge and skills that get clients directly involved in analyzing and improving their organizations. When applied to technical content, teaching-based intervention strategies help managers and employees diagnose and change such organizational features as business strategy, organization structure, and information systems. Consulting engagements tend to be long and continuous; some consultants work as trainers while others work alongside clients as facilitators helping them learn skills and knowledge while they are changing their organization. Thus, clients become co-learners with consultants; they learn how to change their organization by doing it.

Teaching-based consultants typically have technical expertise in the content of their discipline, and some have facilitation skills as well. Some act more as teachers, while others act as internal on-the-job consultants. They apply clinical skills to facilitate client involvement and to help create the collaboration, openness, and trust that are essential to member learning.

What is unique about this approach to management consulting is that the consultants focus on the social dynamics related to designing and changing the technical side of the organization. In essence, social process is used to create technical content, such as formulating a new strategy and a new organization design to implement it.

Teaching-based consultants generally view organizations objectively, and they seek to impart knowledge and skills to client employees. They treat corporate strategy, structure, and business functions as subjects to learn about and also as key action levers for change. They help clients to analyze technical features and redesign them accordingly. General knowledge is applied to client organizations primarily through members learning how to tailor it to their setting. Clients typically select teaching-based consultants based on their technical expertise and clinical skills; they retain them based on how well they facilitate learning and how well the change process produces measurable results.

An example of the teaching-based strategy involves a pair of consultants with skills in corporate strategy and group dynamics who work with a senior executive team to develop and implement a new strategic direction for its firm. The consultants negotiate an initial six-month project that includes a series of off-site retreats where the team learns how to create strategy by doing it. Members learn how to conduct a SWOT analysis of their situation, determine a competitive logic for the business, set appropriate financial goals, determine guidelines for designing and managing the firm, and develop specific initiatives and action plans to implement the strategy. The consultants design the format and periodically present educational inputs to teach the team how to perform these strategy-setting tasks. The consultants also facilitate the process through which team members jointly carry out these tasks. Based on the success of this initial project, the consultants agree to work with the client team for several more months to help it implement the strategy. They teach the client's employees how to redesign the company and manage change. They help employees apply that knowledge to changing the company, and learn from those efforts how to improve it continuously. As the client gains skills and experience, the consultants play a less active role, returning periodically to help members assess overall progress of both the strategic changes and the learning process itself.

The teaching-based strategy has a number of strengths. Because clients are directly involved in diagnosing, redesigning, and changing their organization, they are likely to become more highly committed to implementing the changes. Such commitment is essential for transformational changes that involve most features and levels of the organization. Client involvement also increases the chances that consultants' content wisdom will be appropriate to the setting. Indeed, much of the learning is directed at helping clients translate general knowledge into situation-relevant structures, practices, and behaviors. This external vantage can also be helpful in coaching executives to develop leadership skills. Clients are likely to be less defensive about receiving feedback and direction about leadership behaviors from outside experts than from colleagues or bosses. Teaching-based consultants can provide executives with the psychological support that is needed for trying out new behaviors and learning from mistakes.

Probably the greatest strength of the teaching-based strategy is that clients learn how to change the organization, thus gaining the internal capability to change and improve it continuously. Paradoxically, successful teaching-based consultants work themselves out of a job.

A major downside of teaching-based interventions is the long time it generally takes to complete them. Clients must first gain rudimentary knowledge and skills to diagnose and redesign their organization. They must then spend time doing those activities and implementing the results, which can take one to two years or more. Clients may not have the time or persistence needed for teaching-based consulting; they may find it too long to meet their immediate needs.

Another problem stems from the fact that the teaching-based strategy is inherently more chaotic and uncertain than more common consulting interventions such as the expertise-based strategy. A teaching-based intervention typically involves multiple stakeholders who can have conflicting interests; because clients are involved in all stages of the intervention, it is difficult to predict how quickly they will learn and what direction they will take. These attributes of teaching-based consulting can be disturbing to clients, especially when they are used to dealing with more clearly defined, expert-driven consulting interventions.

Teaching-based interventions are ideally suited to organizations facing environments that are changing rapidly and unpredictably. To adapt to these conditions, organizations must continuously change and transform themselves, and teaching-based consulting can help them develop that capability. It can help clients gain the core competence to continually change and improve themselves; because such expertise is not easily imitated or acquired by organizations, it can provide a strong competitive advantage in turbulent environments.

The teaching-based strategy is especially applicable to organizations that must radically transform themselves from efficient bureaucracies into leaner, more flexible structures. To succeed, such large-scale change requires a great deal of member reeducation, commitment, and willingness to change. The client involvement intrinsic to teaching-based interventions can enable that to occur.

Process-Based Strategy

The last intervention strategy combines the facilitate and learn delivery mode with a content focus on social systems. From its origins in humanistic psychology and organization development, the process-based strategy has been used extensively in management consulting to help clients address social issues and acquire social expertise.[8] Expertise in process-based consulting is rooted in the clinical disciplines having to do with individual, group, and inter-group behavior. Consultants strongly value openness, trust, and collaboration among people and believe those values underlie healthy organizations that can perform well while satisfying members' needs.

This strategy views organizations as socially constructed and employs a normative-re-educative approach to change them. Organizational problems are addressed through the eyes of those who create them, and clients are directly involved in diagnosing and solving them. Process-based consulting tends to be highly intense and continuous. Social issues are often emotionally charged, and acquiring skills to understand and improve them can take considerable time.

Process-based consultants play a facilitative role. They work closely with clients to help them understand how their perceptions and behaviors contribute to social problems, such as inter-group conflicts, poor team problem solving, and mis-communication across managerial levels. Clients are taught how to apply their local knowledge to develop and implement appropriate solutions. They act as co-learners, making changes in their own behaviors while acquiring the skills and knowledge to make social processes work smoother and more effectively in the organization. Process-based consultants, for example, can help to resolve or mediate conflicts between members or work teams. In helping to resolve disputes, process consultants can teach members how to manage dysfunctional conflict in the future.

An example of process-based consulting would be a consultant who is hired to help a work team make faster, more effective decisions. The engagement starts with the consultant describing to the client what this strategy is all about, particularly the need for members to take ownership over their poor decision-making behaviors and be directly involved in learning how to improve them. Then, the consultant attends several team meetings where actual decisions are being made. Early in those meetings, she or he briefly presents members with a conceptual model explaining how teams function and what kinds of behaviors can contribute to effective and ineffective decision making. Then, based on that model, the consultant helps members periodically assess their decision-making behavior, which involves short assessment periods at the midpoint and end of each team meeting. Members are encouraged to lead these assessments, and based on them, to suggest and implement necessary changes. Over time, team members learn how to be better decision makers; they also learn how to assess and improve decision making in teams.

Process-based consulting is particularly strong at getting clients to own their social problems and to do something constructive about them. Like the teaching-based strategy, clients are directly involved in all phases of the consulting engagement and thus increase their commitment to solutions. Moreover, because those solutions derive from clients' local knowledge, they are clearly relevant to the situation.

Process-based consulting not only helps clients to solve particular social problems, it also provides them with the skills and knowledge to improve the social side of their organizations continually. Such social expertise provides a strong competitive advantage, especially in today's customer-driven organizations with lean, flexible structures.

The process-based strategy has certain downsides, however. It generally takes considerable time and effort, and clients are often not willing to commit sufficient resources to what they consider to be "soft" problems not directly related to bottom-line results. Because social problems are inherently emotional, clients may naturally feel uncomfortable with a consulting intervention that encourages them to confront and resolve such issues. They may find it easier and less stressful to turn to more expert-driven consulting, such as the organization-based strategy, for help. Process-based consulting focuses on social content and may ignore technical features of the organization that contribute to social problems, such as the organization structure, reward systems, and work designs. Unless these features are addressed, social problems may recur continually even with effective process-based consulting.

The process-based strategy is highly relevant to situations where clients have social problems and where those who are directly involved are willing to confront and resolve these problems. Such member commitment is essential for taking ownership over problems and developing relevant solutions. Process-based consulting also applies to settings where members want to gain the skills needed to address and improve social processes. Such expertise generally requires practice to acquire. Process-based consulting enables clients to learn by doing; they gain skills while learning to apply them to their own situation.

Implications for Consultants, Clients, and the Profession

The typology of four intervention strategies provides a broad overview of the major approaches used in management consulting today. It offers insights into how management consulting is applied to organizations and the likely results in different situations. The typology also suggests a number of implications for consultants, clients, and the consulting profession itself.

For Consultants

Management consultants generally specialize in a particular intervention strategy. They acquire expertise and experience in applying a strategy and, if successful, tend to repeat it with future clients. Specialization is a normal outgrowth of the evolution of the consulting profession and has certain advantages. As the problems facing organizations have become more complex, consultants have tended to focus on particular issues, clients, industries, and, of course, interventions. In all but a few large consulting firms, consultants do not have the broad expertise and experience to address the full range of client needs; specialization enables them to concentrate on a particular consulting niche and excel at it.

A major problem of specialization, however, is that it can lead to "intervention myopia." Consultants overlook important client features and dynamics that contribute to organization success, thus causing consulting failures despite consultants' best intent and effort. Consultants applying an expertise-based strategy, for example, are likely to ignore the social dynamics underlying technical problems; they are unlikely to see value in involving clients in the intervention process. Such neglect can result in excellent technical recommendations not being implemented. Conversely, consultants using a process-based strategy will probably ignore key technical issues underlying social problems; thus, the same social problems may recur regardless of effective process consultation.

These intervention failures could be lessened if management consultants had greater appreciation for intervention strategies other than ones they typically use. However, gaining this broader perspective is not an easy task. Consultants tend to be heavily invested in specific intervention strategies and are unlikely to consider alternatives unless there are compelling reasons to do so. Moreover, intervention strategies are generally reinforced with use and become habitual; consultants rarely question the assumptions and biases underlying them, and instead take their strategies for granted.

To overcome these problems, consultants might start with an explicit reevaluation of their favored intervention strategy, surfacing underlying assumptions about when it has worked and run into trouble. Then, these consultants could use their assessment as a baseline against which to compare other intervention strategies and to learn more about them. This effort at self-reflection can heighten awareness of critical blind spots in favored strategies and might reveal entirely new steps that would improve future interventions. For example, consultants might further choose to broaden their own expertise or to consider teaming with other consultants who have complementary skills and knowledge.

The typology of four strategies outlined in this chapter can help to guide this reevaluation by giving consultants more informed choices about alternative intervention strategies. It can also direct speculation about how consultants might combine the four strategies to complement each other and thereby achieve more powerful results, like in a multiplier effect.

Probably the easiest way is to blend two strategies that share a common dimension, such as broadening one's content focus from technical systems to include social systems while adhering to the same study and recommend delivery mode. In doing so, consultants would benefit from a different yet related content perspective under the same mode of delivery. Because both types of content share a study and recommend delivery mode, this shift does not involve such an enormous change in capabilities. An expertise-based consulting firm moving in this direction might then decide to hire organization-based consultants with advanced content knowledge about social systems.

A more difficult yet powerful way to combine strategies is where neither strategy shares a common dimension. Here, consultants would have to acquire an entirely different approach to consulting involving both a new content focus and a new delivery mode. For example, consultants using a study and recommend approach relying on technical systems content might attempt to broaden their approach to include both social systems content focus and the facilitate and learn delivery mode. This leap would require a drastic change in consultant skills and knowledge; so rather than learning the expertise themselves, consultants could form an alliance with or acquire a firm whose consultants subscribe to the other strategy.

While blending intervention strategies can take advantage of complementary perspectives, just how these combinations can be applied to specific client situations is still highly speculative. One plausible scenario, for example, might start with consultants using the expertise-based strategy to diagnose a client's technical systems content and make recommendations for change. Next, the consultants would apply the organization-based strategy to propose particular social systems processes needed to implement the technical changes. This could be followed with a process-based strategy where the consultants work directly with client members helping them to surface concerns about the change and reduce resistance. Finally, as employees gain social skills and become more involved in the change process, the consultants could apply a teaching-based strategy where new skills are taught to employees so they can cope better with the changes and lean how to implement them.

For Clients

Perspective clients can use the proposed typology of intervention strategies to make informed choices about management consultants. They need to first familiarize themselves with the strategies and the conditions under which they are more appropriate. Then, based on their consulting needs, clients can determine which of the strategies (or combination of them) best fits their situation. That information can then be used to choose a suitable consultant. For example, clients might interview consultants and ask pertinent questions about how they intervene with clients: What are their assumptions about organizations and change? What organization features and processes do they diagnose? What action levers do they employ? How do they measure success? What is their primary expertise? What role will they play, and what role do they expect clients to play?

Answers to these questions can provide added insight into a consultant's preferred intervention strategies. Such information can then be used to assess how well prospective consultants fit with the client's needs; it can also reveal limitations inherent to proposed strategies. Clients might, for example, select different kinds of consultants for different consulting needs; they might also employ them simultaneously or in a certain temporal order depending on how the situation evolves. Knowledge about different intervention strategies can help clients make these difficult choices.

For the Consulting Profession

The typology presented in this chapter raises important implications for the consulting profession, especially with regard to how consultants acquire competence at making interventions, and how the profession considers the value of different intervention strategies.

Management consultants generally gain skills and knowledge in only one of the strategies. The vast majority are trained in business schools, which strongly emphasize the study and recommend delivery mode with a focus on technical systems and occasionally on social content. Very little, if any, training is given in the teaching-based or process-based strategies.

This concentration of business schools on learning an expertise-based strategy of intervention is not surprising. It is what business schools do well, and it is the primary intervention strategy for the large consulting firms that do much of the hiring in the field. A smaller yet significant number of management consultants receive training in the helping professions, such as clinical psychology and social work, or in organization development. This education centers heavily on the facilitate and learn delivery mode with a focus on social systems; it prepares consultants for the process-based strategy of intervention.

Current training in the consulting profession contributes to a natural division in the field between hard-nosed, expertise-based consultants and softer, process-based consultants. Rather than perpetuate this schism, the typology proposed in this chapter strongly suggests that consultants will likely be more effective if they receive broader training that encompasses more than one intervention strategy. They do not necessarily need to become specialists in other strategies, but they should gain rudimentary skills and knowledge so they know how the strategies work under certain conditions. Such multi-strategy education should go a long way to overcoming the intervention myopia described previously. Management consultants might then begin to appreciate and may even practice the other strategies.

Like consulting education, the profession itself is split into different camps roughly along the lines of the intervention strategies described here. The dominant approach to management consulting is by far the expertise-based strategy. As shown in this chapter, these divisions are a natural outgrowth of the varied assumptions and practices that underlie the different strategies. Because the expertise-based strategy is so prevalent in the consulting profession, it is significantly more valued than the other strategies and, thus, is afforded a great deal more legitimacy. This not only perpetuates the intervention myopia and narrow training that permeates the profession, but worse, it makes it far more difficult for other strategies to draw talented recruits and clients.

The consulting profession appears to be on the "cusp of disruption,"[9] however, suggesting that its predominate delivery mode and content focus may come under increasing scrutiny and change. Faced with clients who want greater value, speed, and responsiveness, management consulting is gradually disaggregating into modular service providers. Examples of this trend include full-service consulting firms that restructure into specialized units that focus on a particular part of the consulting value chain; consultants who deliver their knowledge, methods, and analytics digitally and embed them in clients' information systems; third-party platforms that link freelance consultants to clients resulting in "uberification" of the consulting profession. All of these innovations suggest that the consulting profession may need to consider a broader array of intervention strategies than the traditional expertise-based strategy.

Hopefully, this chapter provides a useful framework for exploring different consulting intervention strategies and considering how they fit with consultants' and clients' emerging needs. It demonstrates the value and relevance of four intervention strategies and shows how none alone can succeed in all situations but that all are needed to satisfy a client's changing and varied needs, especially in today's fast-paced digital and global world.

Notes

1 Hughes, M. *The Leadership of Organizational Change*. New York: Routledge, 2016.
2 Mohrman, S. and Lawler, E. *Useful Research: Advancing Theory and Practice*. San Francisco: Berrett-Koehler Publishers, 2011.
3 Cummings, T. and Worley, C. *Organization development and change*, 10th ed. Stamford, CT: Cengage Learning, 2015.
4 Daft, R. *Organization Theory and Design*. Stamford, CT: Cengage Learning, 2012.
5 See, for example, "Part 5: Consultants and Their Clients" in Kipping, M. and Clark, T. *The Oxford Handbook of Management Consulting*. Oxford, UK: Oxford University Press, 2012.
6 See, for example, Silverman, M. (ed.). *The Consultant's Toolkit: High-Impact Questionnaires, Activities and How-to Guides for Diagnosing and Solving Client Problems*. New York, NY: McGraw-Hill, 2000.
7 See, for example, Greiner, L. and Cummings, T. *Dynamic Strategy Making: A Real-Time Approach for the 21st Century Leader*. San Francisco: Jossey-Bass, 2009.
8 See, for example, Schein, E. *Helping: How to Offer, Give, and Receive Help*. San Francisco: Berrett-Koehler Publishers, 2011.
9 Christensen, C., Wang, D. and van Bever, D. "Consulting on the Cusp of Disruption," *Harvard Business Review*, October 2013.

13 Consulting to Integrate Mergers and Acquisitions

Anthony F. Buono

A quick perusal of the business press suggests that, while merger and acquisition (M&A) activity continues to be running at a high point, many M&A deals, as demonstrated by the following illustrations, appear to be experiencing severe digestion pains.

- "ABC Corporation announced yesterday that quarterly earnings would miss Wall Street estimates because of weakness in its brokerage operations. ABC, which has posted erratic earnings during its struggles to integrate its operations after several acquisitions, reported another drop in earnings. . . ."
- "At its annual meeting last week, XYZ Company announced that it is jettisoning some of the most distinctive pieces that TargetCo brought to the merger in an attempt to reduce its exposure and regain its focus in the industry. . . ."

And on it goes.

The poor performance of combined firms continues to raise questions about the efficacy of mergers and acquisitions as a value creation strategy. While the criteria to evaluate the success of M&As vary considerably (e.g., share value, post-merger profitability, market share growth, R&D innovation and new products), it appears that roughly one-third of all M&As fail outright and another third fall well short of their operational, financial and strategic objectives.[1]

Echoing a 1985 cover story "Do Mergers Really Work?", a 2002 *Business Week* analysis (17 years later) concluded that both merging and acquiring companies continue to make the same mistakes, destroying shareholder value in the process.[2] Fast forward another 14 years and the picture remains unchanged – although expectations may continue to rise, post-M&A performance continues to disappoint, characterized as little more than a "crap shoot."[3] As a result, although there was a decline in overall M&A activity following the "great recession" (roughly 2007–2009), recent years have witnessed a resurgence of an M&A boom – juxtaposed with a significant wave of divestments and spin-offs.[4]

Dynamics of M&A Consulting

To a large degree, organizations use consultants during mergers and acquisitions for the same reasons that most companies use consultants – to draw on their unbiased analysis; to benchmark organizational processes against a range of best practices; to gain perspective and see the "big" picture; and to provide training and related implementation support.[5] The highly complex nature of the M&A process, however, leads client firms to seek out a broad range of consulting services that go well beyond those typically delivered by general management consulting firms. Typically merger deals are dominated by lawyers, investment bankers and accountants, and the need for management consulting is often left out until major problems emerge.

Transaction Advising versus Merger Integration Consulting

It is useful to distinguish between management consultants and transaction advisors.[6] Occasionally, the initial transaction advisors are actually management consultants hired by the firm to plan its acquisition strategy and then locate an acquisition target that fits with the proposed M&A strategy. More often, the transaction advisors involve financial and legal specialists who offer technical assistance leading up to the deal itself – a process typically characterized "from contact through contract." Clearly, the complexities associated with pre-deal decision-making (scouting for deals, due diligence assessments, forecasting value) and combination-related negotiations (which lead to general agreements on the value and details of the deal) are important determinants of M&A success.[7] For example, if an acquirer pays too much, it may never earn its money back. Clients rely on specialists who recommend how to proceed or turn back based on their expert advice. Large companies often run their own acquisition efforts and then bring in transaction advisors to consummate the deal.

These transaction experts (as well as the management teams themselves), however, often overlook, ignore or underestimate the problems of post-merger integration. This omission is understandable since the guiding assumption underlying much of their pre-deal work suggests that "if a deal is done well, the deal is done." Most transaction advisors are paid on a contingency fee basis tied to the value of the deal. So, while these advisors may strive to be objective and careful, it will come as no surprise that they often are fairly optimistic about the synergy prospects from the combined parties. Finally, most transaction advisors are hired to focus on narrow but complex technical issues rather than on broader strategic, cultural and political dynamics associated with the integration of two companies. Thus, they may lack perspective for anticipating what may turn out to be a major issue after the merger.

From a post-combination and integration perspective, this is where the real management and leadership challenges begin. Unlike the transaction advisor role where the advisor's judgment serves as the basis for a decision, merger consultants are called upon to help identify, frame and clarify issues, but they are not typically involved in the actual integration process. M&A integration decisions are best made by those executives intimately involved in the two organizations because they are the ones whose destinies are linked to the long-term success of the combined entity.

Merger integration consultants tend to embed their expertise in a process consultation mode. My experience suggests that the consultant's most effective interventions, rather than playing guru and "being right," evolve around what Maister and his associates refer to as the "trusted advisor."[8] This approach seeks to support and facilitate management in making their own decisions about integration.

An underlying dilemma, however, is that it takes time to become a "trusted advisor" in the eyes of a client. Given the frenetic pace that typically accompanies an M&A, consultants do not have much time or latitude to gain credibility. Instead, it is usually their past reputation that carries the most weight going in, and then the consultant must be quickly adept at bringing forth issues and helping management plan specific steps in the integration process. The initial skill and speed with which this is done often determines the consultant's fate and opportunities for a continuing relationship.

Throughout this process, it can be difficult to maintain the level of objectivity that, as consultants, we strive for. As much as we might not like to admit it, there is a certain element of excitement and gratification that comes from being part of the inner circle of advisors determining the fate of an organization.[9] Following months of preparatory work on building competency in acquisition integration, for example, I recall being part of a pre-acquisition working session with the senior-level integration team as the target of an impending acquisition was announced. As a buzz of excitement quickly spread through the room, I found myself getting caught up with the fervor – thinking "so that's who *we* are acquiring" – as the meeting turned to specific strategic and operational planning issues.

Thus, while much M&A consulting involves pre-merger financial and strategic analysis, along with deal support, this chapter will instead focus on post-merger issues of integration that are so often neglected. Our discussion will address the specific challenges that merger integration consultants face, and we will consider ways of dealing with these issues.

Integration Defined

Compared to the financial orientation of many past mergers and acquisitions, where being over-leveraged was the main risk, the recent M&A boom reflects deals that are more strategically driven. Today's deals are influenced by technological advances and R&D investment needs, the increased importance of accelerating speed to market, attempts to broaden geographical presence and the need to react to industry overcapacity and related global pressures for cost-cutting. A basic shift for acquirers has clearly occurred, moving away from purchasing any type of promising business to pursuing targets more closely related to their core business. The main risks associated with these latter-day M&As, therefore, have much more to do with concerns around assimilation and integration,[10] pressures that have created a vital need for highly focused, post-combination strategies and plans.

At the same time, we need to be clear about what the word "integration" means and implies. It does not mean that all acquired companies should be completely absorbed into the acquiring company and thereby cease to exist. Rather, there are degrees of integration. Some acquisitions, like those made by Johnson and Johnson, are left as freestanding entities retaining their former company names. However, they are brought on board in terms of strategic planning, operations budgeting, compensation and the cultural values specified in J&J's credo. On the other hand, if the acquisition is relatively small and its purpose is to fold its product line into the acquirer's existing product array, then the absorption is likely to be more complete. In either case, there are integration issues that, while different, can spell the difference between success and failure.

Lack of Preparation

There are many factors that account for the disappointing track record in M&A performance – from paying too much for a target company, to choosing the wrong partner, to misperceiving the potential synergies. However, the combination of misunderstood cultural differences and poorly conceived integration strategies is typically a potent factor contributing to failure.[11]

All too often, the reality is that the acquiring company's management is ill prepared to face the complex implementation dynamics once the deal is signed.[12] Studies indicate that even those firms that do develop systematic processes for selecting and dealing with acquisition targets, few actually operationalize and follow these plans.[13] Studies of M&A deals suggest that while acquirers typically had a fundamentally good strategy, there was an over-reliance on the financial model that drove the deal. As a result, poor integration planning and execution of the combination itself undermined the companies' ability to enhance shareholder value.[14] Similarly, other surveys of executives involved in M&A transactions indicate that over one-half of the respondents saw post-merger integration as the greatest failure risk and almost three-quarters felt far too little attention was focused on culture-related considerations during integration.[15]

No Single Best Strategy

Integrating two previously autonomous companies is an exceedingly complex and idiosyncratic process. Based on over 30 years of experience in studying and working with companies going through the M&A process, it has become very clear to me that such combinations are riddled with uncertainties, paradoxes and dilemmas. Although merger integration consultants do encounter some fairly common consulting challenges, regardless of the M&A assignment, several challenges are created by the unique characteristics of the specific M&A deal in question, and still others can easily emerge during the consulting assignment itself.

Yet, despite the reality that there are different types of mergers and acquisitions, we often group all M&As together.[16] The underlying hope, it seems, is that there is a core set of "best practice" strategies and tactics that will facilitate their success. But that hope is too general and idealistic! The strategy underlying a specific merger or acquisition dictates the unique aspects of the level of integration (financial, strategic, operational) necessary, the speed through which the integration should be achieved, and the ways in which the integration should be planned and implemented. Complete operational integration raises the most challenges and is clearly the most difficult to accomplish.

M&A Stages and Consulting Roles

As depicted in Exhibit 13.1, consulting roles during mergers and acquisitions evolve around three different but overlapping phases: (1) pre-combination preliminary planning, (2) early integration implementation during combination, and (3) post-combination aftermath.[17]

During the pre-combination preliminary planning phase, the consultant's interventions need to focus on ensuring that senior managers have a deeper understanding of and are clearly aligned with the strategic rationale for doing the deal. Emphasis should be placed on broadening the client's perspective and awareness of the need to include non-financial factors in the analysis (e.g., cultural factors, human resource capabilities, IT systems), and then to assist the client in assessing the implications for post-integration needs and outcomes. In essence, the focus should be on drawing out what it will take to make the merger or acquisition a success.

In the next stage of combination, early integration implementation efforts concentrate on the transition itself, drawing out ways to enhance inter-firm cooperation, bringing the two organizations together and working through merger syndrome-related problems and concerns, such as who will have which jobs and what the new organization structure will be.

Finally, during the post-combination aftermath period, the focus shifts toward tracking the combination, supporting ongoing integration initiatives and assessing and attempting to correct dysfunctional reactions and behaviors.

Although there are different foci within each of these three stages, the emphasis of consultants should be continuously placed on enhancing the capability of organizational members from both sides to: (1) clarify and understand the intent of the combination and the requirements for integrating the two companies; (2) deal with the anxieties and uncertainties that accompany the M&A process; and (3) refocus their energies on combination-related goals and objectives (see *Consulting Insights*).

Exhibit 13.1 Illustrative Merger and Acquisition Integration-Related Consulting Interventions

PRELIMINARY PLANNING *(Pre-Combination)*
- ◆ Strategy and selection
  - Vision casting and strategy setting
  - Inter-firm fit: Partner/target evaluation
  - Broadened due diligence foci (e.g., culture, HR practices, marketing, operating systems, IT)
  - Synergy and revenue enhancement analyses
- ◆ Announcement
  - Stakeholder analysis
  - Communication strategy: Internal and external
- ◆ Creation of integration plans
  - Level of integration analysis
  - Assessment of business and cultural impediments to integration success
  - Initial organization structure planning
  - Initial transition plans, selection of integration manager, and formation of integration teams
  - Key talent retention program(s)
- ◆ Focus on immediate feelings and concerns of organizational members
  - Stress reduction and merger sensitization workshops
  - Focus groups

EARLY INTEGRATION IMPLEMENTATION *(First 1–6 Months)*
- ◆ Enhance inter-firm cooperation
  - Orientation meetings and realistic M/A previews
  - Two-way communication (meetings, hotlines, newsletters)
  - Intergroup mirroring and teambuilding
- ◆ Focus on transition and integration
  - Transition teams and steering committee
  - Refine and implement integration plans
  - Focused reward systems (material and symbolic)
  - Focused use of organizational rituals
- ◆ Work through merger syndrome-related problems and concerns
  - Focus groups and survey feedback
  - Coach senior and middle management to model desired attitudes and behaviors

POST-COMBINATION AFTERMATH *(Next 6–18 Months)*
- ◆ Track the combination and support integration initiatives
  - Integration audits
  - Build capabilities
  - Exit interviews
  - Continued integration activities and transition-related rituals
- ◆ Assess and attempt to correct dysfunctional behaviors
  - Confrontation meetings and team building initiatives
  - Focus groups and survey feedback

Consulting Insights: The Focus of M&A Integration Consulting

An increasing number of consulting firms – from virtually all of the large consultancies to a broad array of smaller, boutique firms – offer merger and acquisition integration support. While the specific proprietary tools and approaches may vary, the essence of their offerings is essentially the same – to provide early planning and intervention to facilitate the combination of the two client organizations. As examples, Accenture emphasizes "strategic due diligence," focusing on creating an M&A portfolio strategy, with emphasis on operational due diligence and execution road maps, analyzing what will need to be accomplished during post-M&A integration to make the transaction a success. McKinsey & Co. stresses sources of future revenue growth, supported by strategic assessment and the need to identify and retain key talent that will enable the organization to meet those growth goals. The firm's recent focus is also on culture during integration. Bain & Company highlights the need for strategic due diligence and implementation planning, focusing on establishing the post-merger organizational structure, resolving back-office technology issues and maintaining "seamless customer interfaces" throughout the process. Willis Towers Watson (itself a merger between Towers Perrin, Watson Wyatt and Willis Group) emphasizes the alignment of human resource capabilities with merger-related goals and objectives, change management and communication strategies and determining an appropriate timeline and set of integration processes for the merger. Mercer stresses a strategic perspective on integration processes, suggesting "how you combine should be driven by why you combine." While the pace of mergers and acquisitions may ebb and flow over the years to come, as research by senior consultants from A.T. Kearney forecast, the continued consolidation of firms and industries is "unstoppable, . . . continuous and inevitable."

Ideally, the consultant's interventions should span all three stages. However, much M&A consulting is far more piecemeal and reactive, as different consultants are brought in to help resolve a particular problem that emerges in one aspect or another in the overall M&A process. In the pre-combination stage of preliminary planning, transaction advisors typically drive the process without the involvement of merger integration consultants. Unfortunately, merger integration consultants are often not brought in until problems arise late in the post-combination aftermath stage, long after the merger or acquisition has been consummated. At this point, clients often have unrealistic expectations about what can be accomplished from their consultants.

Temporal Constraints

Three time-related factors shape the challenges that consultants face when intervening in a merger or acquisition. The first set of issues is shaped by *when* the consultant is brought into the process. Consultants are faced with very different challenges depending on the stage of their intervention. Working with a client during the pre-combination preliminary planning phase (e.g., facilitating an initial integration planning assessment) is very different from intervening during the early integration implementation period (e.g., getting leaders to clarify strategic intent after the fact). All too often, merger consultants are only called in during the post-combination aftermath stage with the intent of "fixing" a particular problem (e.g., the exodus of key personnel).

The second time-related factor is whether the consulting assignment is a long-term engagement or an isolated, "hit-and-run" project. When working with two organizations over an extended period of time, it can be difficult to maintain an unbiased perspective vis-à-vis the two companies. I have found that it is all too easy – even at an unconscious level – to develop an allegiance to certain managers and one of the organizations. This can readily influence what you "see" and how you interpret different situations. On the other hand, in a short-term engagement, the consultant's problem becomes one of obtaining sufficient information about the details of the merger or acquisition. Everyone is very busy on many different sub-aspects of the merger, and it is very hard to track down a lot of data and opinions in a short time.

A third underlying problem facing consultants is that they are not around all the time, which makes it difficult to penetrate the aura of game-playing and veil of secrecy often surrounding the M&A process. As third parties, consultants may not be as intimately involved as may initially appear – even in long-term assignments. For example, in one of my engagements, I underscored that I should be kept involved in the decision process on an ongoing basis. But as the acquisition unfolded, however, I found that I was not privy to a host of key decisions taking place when I was absent – financial and operational – that created a very different context for what the organization was attempting to accomplish. It is difficult to carry out an accurate diagnosis and offer meaningful advice when operating from a partial understanding of what is happening.

Common Integration Issues

In some mergers and acquisitions, holding on to key people, especially technical talent or R&D expertise, is one of the keys to success. In another, the people in the target firm might be less important to retain, and the emphasis, for example, should be placed on integrating the information systems of both companies. In still another, if a company acquires a firm in the same industry due to excess capacity, key challenges include which operations to shut down, which employees to lay off and how to effectively resize the organization. Considering the different goals and outcomes associated with these disparate strategies, each of these combinations places different pressures and requirements on the integration process – and on consultants intervening in the system.

What Comprehensive Due Diligence Really Means

As part of the strategy and partner selection process, a key factor in successful pre-M&A integration is comprehensive due diligence. Clearly, financial, legal and regulatory analyses – in essence, risk assessment – dominate most due diligence efforts. Although financial projections typically accompany such assessments, the basic focus is usually placed on the history of the target firm more than its future potential.[18] Comprehensive due diligence, however, incorporates a much broader array of concerns, including sales and marketing strengths and weaknesses, human resource capabilities, supplier networks and commitments, and so forth. The key is that due diligence assessments should emerge from the future strategy and vision for the merger or acquisition.

The greatest challenge for management consultants in this area is related to the technical complexities involved in each dimension of due diligence assessment. Transaction advisors typically drive the process. For example, accountants focus on such tasks as the valuation of assets and liabilities, the tax consequences of the combination and fulfilling regulatory reporting requirements. Lawyers concentrate on jurisdiction and incorporation issues, securities law ramifications of structuring the deal, anti-trust concerns and so forth. The underlying assumption that consultants must challenge is that favorable judgments about financial, legal and regulatory aspects means that the strategic benefits of the merger will necessarily fall in line with the numbers. The reality of a merger or acquisition is often quite different from the M&A deal that exists in numbers and on paper.

The idea of comprehensive due diligence can be overwhelming because time pressures, legal restrictions and limited resources prevent organizations from fully following idealistic "best practices" recommendations. Consultants can, however, emphasize the importance of *strategic* due diligence by getting the acquirer to closely examine and clarify the strategic intent of the acquisition, and then to spell out all of the likely factors that have to fall into place to make the strategy happen in practice. Usually, a check list is required to prompt the acquirer to think of non-obvious criteria, such as the target company's talent pool, technical capabilities, its organization structure, cultural values and prevailing management philosophy toward decision making.

Capturing Merger-Related Synergies

Complexity in M&A integration revolves around the key strategic drivers rather than the size of the combination per se.[19] The strategic intent of the acquisition might be to reduce manufacturing and distribution costs, gain access to new customers or new markets or obtain technical talent or gain access to new technologies. Given the underlying objectives sought after, the strategic due diligence review should focus on the probability of attaining these desired synergies.

Recent studies by some of the major professional services firms, however, indicate that acquiring firms tends to fall well short of achieving desired synergies in such areas as growing market share, enhancing brand strength and reputation, and accessing talent capabilities and "know-how" in the target company.[20] Depending on the extent to which "softer," more intangible synergies are a driving factor (see Exhibit 13.2), the marketing and human sides of the integration process become increasingly critical.[21] While companies may have a relatively clear understanding of why they selected a particular acquisition target, there is usually significant uncertainty as to exactly *how* to capitalize on the intended synergies through integration.[22]

From a consulting perspective, it may seem to be relatively straightforward work to assess the extent to which tangible assets might be transferred from one firm to another. Yet, political dynamics, cultural overtones and general "win-lose" mentalities among M&A partners can readily complicate what might appear to be relatively clear-cut issues.

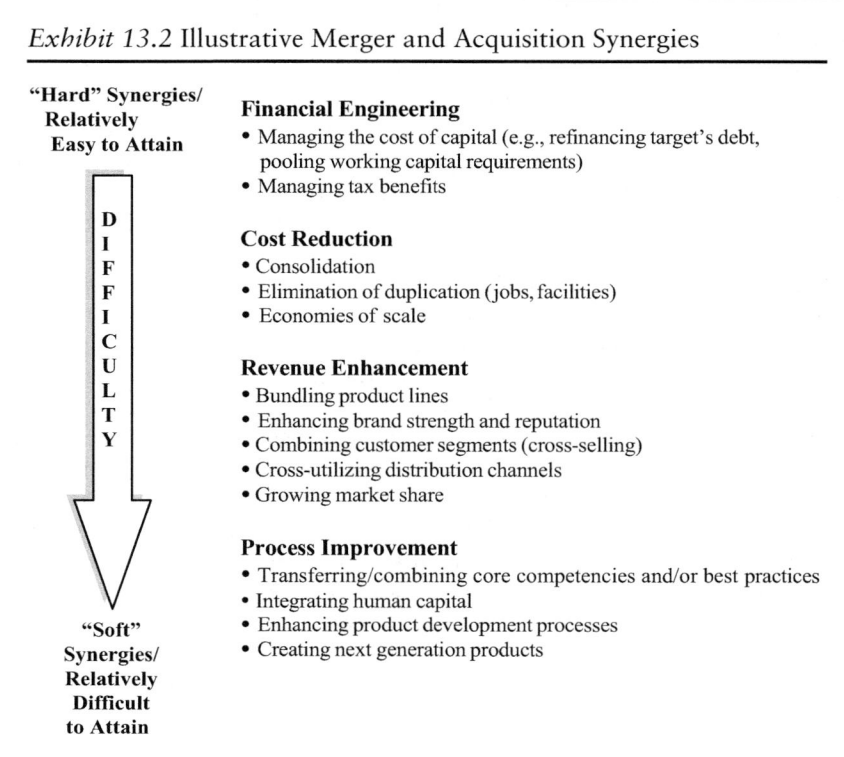

Exhibit 13.2 Illustrative Merger and Acquisition Synergies

"Hard" Synergies/ Relatively Easy to Attain

DIFFICULTY

"Soft" Synergies/ Relatively Difficult to Attain

Financial Engineering
- Managing the cost of capital (e.g., refinancing target's debt, pooling working capital requirements)
- Managing tax benefits

Cost Reduction
- Consolidation
- Elimination of duplication (jobs, facilities)
- Economies of scale

Revenue Enhancement
- Bundling product lines
- Enhancing brand strength and reputation
- Combining customer segments (cross-selling)
- Cross-utilizing distribution channels
- Growing market share

Process Improvement
- Transferring/combining core competencies and/or best practices
- Integrating human capital
- Enhancing product development processes
- Creating next generation products

USAir's acquisition of Piedmont Airlines provides a good illustration of these tendencies. Prior to the acquisition, USAir's reservation system and customer service were so poor that customers deemed the airline "Useless Air."[23] Yet, rather than engaging in an analysis of the relative disadvantages and costs associated with maintaining USAir's system compared to building on Piedmont's capabilities, which were noted to be much better, USAir's power politics prevented the combined airline from taking full advantage of potential operational synergies. Acquiring companies tend to impose their own systems on target firms rather than engage in a true joint diagnosis and analysis of the situation, a tendency that external consultants need to counteract.

Synergy-related challenges are particularly acute in those industries where intellectual capital is one of the determinants of organizational success. Ultimate M&A success in high technology companies, for example, can take years and successive generations of new products. In several of my consulting experiences, I have found that the lingering effects of previous mergers or acquisitions further exacerbate current combination integration efforts. Hewlett-Packard's acquisition of Compaq, for example, was complicated by Compaq's "hangover" from its acquisition of Digital Equipment Corporation. Within Compaq, organizational members still differentiated themselves as "Digital Classic" and "Compaq Classic" employees. Such stereotyping suggests that Compaq's acquisition of Digital was still not complete – which added a layer of complexity to H-P's acquisition of Compaq, a layer of complexity that further complicated the culture clashes between H-P and Compaq. These dynamics are, unfortunately, all too common as further illustrated by AOL's ongoing struggle with the highly politicized and turf-protecting culture of Time Warner, which culminated in one of the most prominent merger failures.[24]

Technology firms often believe that they can take the best of each other's businesses, and thereby generate end-to-end packages that will be attractive to a wider range of consumers. However, simply repackaging existing products and product lines is rarely sufficient. Rather it is the second and third generation products – through the innovation and creativity that a merged group of experts can create – that ultimately translates into long-term success. Thus, rather than simply acquiring patents, products or facilities, an underlying key to success lies in getting the talent in each organization to adopt a cooperative attitude and a willingness to collaborate on new products and processes. An early exodus of key personnel – "brains with legs" and "frogs in a wheelbarrow" (they can walk away or jump out at any time) as they are often referred[25] – can quickly create problems for the combined organization. The turnover and departure of key personnel following America Online's acquisition of Netscape, for example, delayed the scheduled release of Netscape's browser for two years, with similar difficulties created by the mass exodus of Nextel executives and middle managers in the wake of its acquisition by Sprint.[26]

Retaining Talent

Depending on the nature of the merger or acquisition and its underlying strategy, different levels of attention must be focused on the human element of the combination. Yet, even in those acquisitions where the strategic intent is to keep the target's core talent, it is crucial that these plans are made clear and explicit and announced as soon as possible. The uncertainty and anxiety that go along with being acquired can be debilitating and literally drain value from an acquisition.

As part of its diversification strategy, for example, SteelCo acquired a petrochemical company (Petro) and focused its initial energies on capturing short-term, financial gains.[27] Based on initial diversification planning, the positions of the technical experts, engineers and scientists at Petro were not threatened. In fact, SteelCo had mainly acquired the firm to secure the expertise of these technical employees. During the early integration implementation period, however, SteelCo's senior management focused on attaining immediate costs savings (the "hard" synergies depicted in Exhibit 13.2), consolidating basic functional areas and support groups – such as human resources, finance and legal. They never explicitly communicated their intended strategy to the organization or reached out to the target's technical core.

Petro's technical staff interpreted the changes and terminations in other sections of the company as "a sign of things to come" and began bailing out of the company. Even the scientists who were willing to "give SteelCo's management a chance" found themselves under significant pressure from colleagues and co-workers to exit the firm. By the time SteelCo realized what was happening, it found itself in control of the petrochemical company but without the core of technical professionals that made Petro a desirable acquisition target.

Consultants are often brought in at this point to help the organization "stop the hemorrhaging," but such efforts are frequently too little, too late.

Who Is the Client?

Inter-firm dynamics can also raise questions about who the "client" really is, as multiple parties jockey for position and attempt to exert their influence. While many of us might like to think that the "system" is our ultimate client, we are often faced with divided loyalties as parts of the system clash with each other. Our contact clients (i.e., the individual(s) who bring us into the organization) may be different from our primary clients (those who ultimately "own" the problem or issue). Similarly, our primary clients may also be different from our "intermediate" clients (the individuals or groups that we interview and interact with as part of the intervention).[28] Since the needs and expectations of each of these "clients" may be quite different, what we think we know about a client is, at best, a hypothesis that needs to be tested constantly.

Intervention Strategies and Techniques

The nature of possible consulting interventions in M&As varies widely, influenced by the specific task at hand, the intent of the merger or acquisition and the timing of when the consultant enters the process. Given the heightened anxieties, insecurity, mistrust and power dynamics that accompany the M&A process, intervening in one raises many unique challenges. It is hard to decipher real motives and deal with the inevitable conflicts that arise (e.g., creating collaboration versus undermining internal opposition, or ensuring objective analysis versus protecting vested interests).

Most useful prescriptions about the consulting process emphasize the need to develop rapport and a collaborative relationship with one's client. As in any large-scale change intervention, one of the basic challenges is to motivate employees to re-focus from their own self-interest to the collective interests of the combined entity. Earning the trust and confidence of organizational members in a merger environment, however, is quite challenging, as is generating valid data for understanding people's reactions about what is happening both to and around them.

In Exhibit 13.3, we see that goodwill and a cooperative spirit often characterize public exchanges at the deal announcement ceremony, with both parties emphasizing the promise of the merger or acquisition. But just under the surface, people are experiencing quite different feelings. Referred to by some observers as the *merger* syndrome,[29] these reactions reflect high levels of anxiety and stressful reactions. Heightened self-interest and preoccupation with the combination, culture clashes and restricted communication and crisis management orientations are all too commonplace realities. The result is a host of problems emerging at the individual and organizational level. Most client resistance stems from feelings of vulnerability and losing control.

As an M&A consultant, it is important to realize that organizational members tend to be very sensitive to literally everything around them, including the terminology used to describe the combination. The idea of a "merger," for example, is frequently stated and interpreted as a merger of "equals." Yet, in most instances, one of the merger partners is "far more equal" than the other. The reality is that most mergers are actually acquisitions. In merger after merger, for example, it is not uncommon for the majority of one of the partner's management teams to be terminated. If the intent is to assimilate one company into another, companies should resist the temptation to characterize the combination as a merger of equals. Perpetrating the ideal of "equals" only breeds confusion, contempt and mistrust on the part of those being acquired when expectations are not fulfilled – and M&A consultants can quickly be drawn into this turmoil.

Given these heightened emotions and reactions, people going through a merger or acquisition tend to be very guarded and are often less than forthcoming. They withhold or distort critical information when interacting with their M&A counterparts and related stakeholders – including consultants.

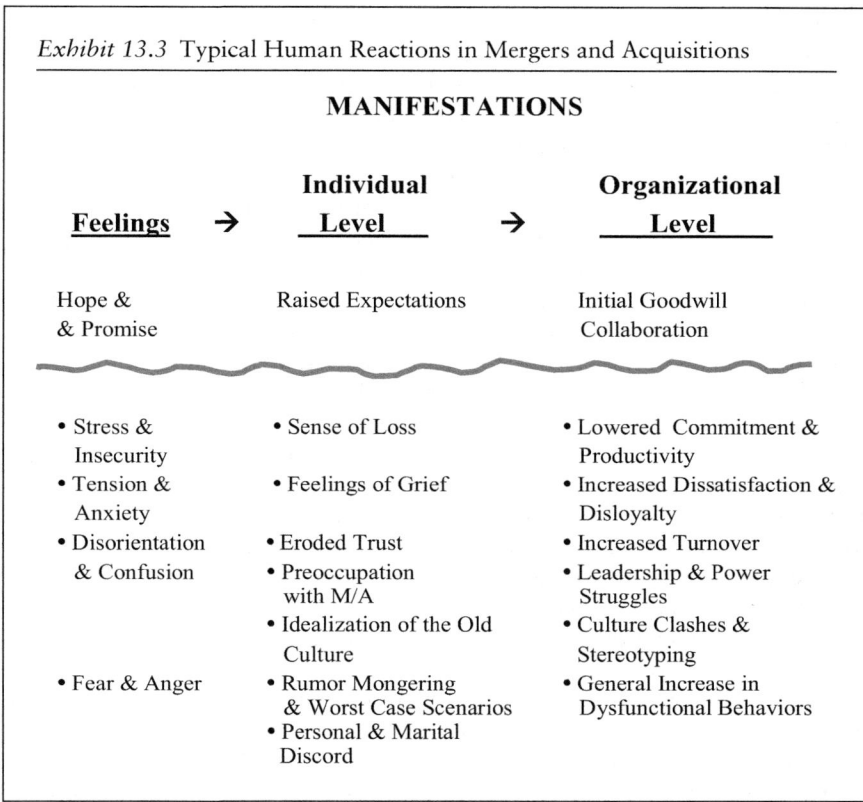

Exhibit 13.3 Typical Human Reactions in Mergers and Acquisitions

Even attempts to model authentic behavior on the part of the consultant – putting into words what you are experiencing as you work with a client, trying to build a base of trust and commitment – can be met with skepticism and even cynicism. A unique dilemma faced by consultants in this environment is that efforts to gain trust and commitment from one member of the two organizations can quickly create doubts and suspicions on the part of the other member. In essence, organizational members grapple with such concerns as whose "side" is the consultant really on, and whether the real client is that "other" organization.

Listening Deeply

As a way of dealing with this dilemma, a guiding approach that I have used throughout many types of interventions over the years is one of "listening deeply" to all parties affected by the intervention. This includes many discussions and interviews where I use my technical understanding of M&A dynamics and processes to get others to reflect on integration and implementation challenges that they are experiencing. In doing so, I try to assess and compare reactions and perceptions across organizational members; and then attempt to get individuals to listen to each other with greater attentiveness, compassion and understanding – especially on issues where there are strong differences of opinion.[30]

As objective third parties, consultants often meet with top executives and managers from different divisions or sides of the companies to discuss and assess their reactions – positive and negative – concerning the merger or acquisition and its future business prospects. As part of this interaction, I attempt to learn about the organization's cultural system, emotionally encompassing as much as possible in order to help describe and interpret it to its members. An underlying goal is to facilitate their understanding and knowledge about the breadth and depth of their own culture and its ramifications for the combination they are envisioning.

Within this listening and clarifying context, I often serve in a coaching capacity, helping the management team to understand the likely outcomes and reactions to various decisions and events. A key here is the extent to which the consultant can help the client to learn from his or her experiences and feelings, and then to build on these insights in adapting to the merger. An underlying challenge – especially when working with senior-level managers – is to get people who are far more action-oriented than introspective to engage in this reflective level of analysis.

Given the anxieties and political dynamics that are an inherent part of the M&A process, drawing these feelings out can be a challenge. Thus, in many instances, identifying what needs to happen may be relatively straightforward; working with the emotions of people across two organizations to actually make it happen is not.

Clarifying Strategic Intent

It is a given that the strategic rationale underlying the merger or acquisition in question should be fully understood by the senior management team. As such, consultants typically advise their clients that it is critical to fully think through their M&A strategy, understanding the risks as well as the potential benefits. Given the aura that permeates deal-making, however, there are times when actually accomplishing this task can be very difficult.

In one of my consulting engagements, for example, the CEO of an acquiring company and I decided that I should play a devil's advocate role during an acquisition-planning session with the firm's senior management team. I had previously undertaken a series of one-on-one interviews with each member of the team. Drawing on this information, the intent was to ensure that everyone fully understood the rationale underlying the acquisition and the potential difficulties involved. A key goal was to reach consensus on whether the firm should move forward with its acquisition plans.

During the planning session, I continually raised a series of questions and concerns, pushing each member of the team to clarify his or her thinking about the combination and what the company was trying to accomplish. The team ultimately reached consensus on the strategy and decided to move forward with their acquisition plans. In our debriefing discussion after the meeting, however, the CEO was furious, feeling that I was being overly negative and that I was attempting to lead the team to reject the acquisition. All of our pre-meeting talks about the irrational exuberance that often accompanies M&A game-playing and the need to step back for a critical look at the proposed acquisition were lost amid the CEO's emotional fervor to see the deal through.

Facilitating Integration Decisions

Merger and acquisition integration encompasses a broad array of change-related challenges, including: meshing operating systems; determining new roles and responsibilities; combining corporate functions and processes; setting priorities; enhancing cross-organization teamwork and collaboration; and forging a new organizational identity. All of this needs to be accomplished while maintaining sufficient flexibility to maneuver around inevitable roadblocks and barriers.[31] A general rule of thumb I have found is that the integration process typically takes more time and costs more than initially anticipated – a message that clients rarely want to hear.

Part of the consulting role in M&As is that of problem finder, bringing to the surface potential problems that can derail integration plans. This very activity, however, can create resistance, as already stressed-out organizational members are reluctant to take on what they see as yet another challenge. A related difficulty is that while integration planning is typically conducted at the highest corporate levels, its implementation is invariably a line responsibility. This essentially requires organizational members at all hierarchical levels to "think big" while "acting small," focusing on the details and implementation intricacies associated with successful combination.[32] Thus, one of the consultant's goals is to facilitate the problem-solving process and decision-making activities that are within each individual's and team's sphere of influence by providing a broader perspective on how different decisions relate to each other and to the overall integration challenge.

As a way of creating supportive conditions for M&A integration, I recommend that, as early as possible, organizational members should be provided with the basic knowledge they need to reduce change-related anxieties. This information should facilitate the ability of people to take care of personal and professional needs, identify with the merger or acquisition partner and accomplish job-related tasks. Thus, organizational members need information on roles and positions, compensation, reporting relationships, organizational policies and initial transition assessments and planning efforts.

Some common techniques that I use include: (1) holding orientation sessions and disseminating information packets; (2) get-acquainted "town meetings" with cross-organization and cross-function mixes of employees that allow people from the two organizations to meet and interact with each other; and (3) executive and top management visits to selected key sites to answer questions and "walk around," helping to more fully understand the merger partner or acquisition target. Such visits and appearances, however, must be carried out with sensitivity and caution. As one of the partners in a merger I worked on a few years ago lamented, "I felt little more than a used car, with the other management team kicking my tires."

Working with Integration Managers

One finding that has clearly emerged from studies of M&A activities is the importance of establishing a dedicated senior integration manager as early as possible. These individuals oversee merger integration teams and task forces, helping to create guidelines, metrics and accountability measures. They attempt to provide sufficient coordination so task forces do not go "off track" and that specific needs and details do not "slip through the cracks."

Integration managers should serve as internal consultants, helping to guide the M&A process on a daily basis, and serving as a conduit between the organization and its upper management.[33] Of course, this same person is usually a member of the acquirer team, and that can constrain how they might approach different situations and limit the willingness of organizational members to truly cooperate. Thus, in many instances, I have worked with these individuals as an external consultant, acting as a resource and sounding board for their decisions.

In working with integration managers, there is a distinct difference between the "on-stage" role that consultants often fill – operating more in public, open forums – and the "backstage," confidential roles involved in working intimately with a client.[34] As part of my "on-stage" role, for example, I often facilitate focus groups, conduct merger-syndrome workshops, and work with integration planning teams to discuss and analyze integration-related plans and activities. My role with integration managers, however, tends to reflect more of a "backstage" role, involving private conversations and exchanges. In these situations, I often engage in attachment-oriented behaviors – communicating empathy, respect and regard – the goal being to help the integration manager cope with the surrounding uncertainty by giving encouragement and comfort as well as practical assistance and technical guidance.

Over time, these interactions create the conditions for the consultant to become a "trusted advisor." An underlying dilemma, however, concerns how others perceive this role and relationship in the organization. Since much of the information involved in such "backstage" discussions can be very sensitive, people are often wary about being too open with the consultant, concerned about how far confidentiality might really extend. Thus, merger consultants must walk a fine line when working with integration managers. It is important to develop trust and close ties with them, while also attempting to maintain one's position of objectivity and openness to others in the organization.

Serving as Morale Auditor

Consultants can also serve as a "morale auditor," providing a basis for an organizational "health check" and focusing on helping employees better understand and manage merger-related stress. Of course, the idea that the human side of mergers and acquisitions must be attended to is not a novel idea. Yet, one of the frustrating realities of M&A consulting is that, in far too many instances, such "people issues" continue to be placed relatively low on the list of success measures, despite their eventual importance in driving the new business forward.

Most managers understand these dynamics on a cognitive level. A problem I've often faced, however, is that they are not prepared to deal with the emotional realities of the situation. Moreover, the romance of deal-making, coupled with impatience to get the deal done, often make it difficult for M&A consultants to be fully heard over the recommendations of transaction advisors. Thus, even when pre-combination transition planning teams are created, they continue to be disbanded too early. Communication plans about merger integration, which are often well intentioned and thoughtfully planned at first, quickly begin to deteriorate. Many of the insights that are generated through systematic assessments of acquisition targets or merger partners fall into a literal inter-organizational void due to time pressures and internal politics. It is far too easy for managers to get overwhelmed by the day-to-day pressures in a merger, with limited ability to step back and carefully think through next steps and action plans. Moreover, since a merger or acquisition is often seen as a one-time event, most managers think about getting them over with rather than attempting to understand how to do them better.[35]

Within this context, I find merger-syndrome workshops and focus groups to be very useful because they: (1) acknowledge the reality of peoples' fears, anxieties and uncertainties, (2) provide them with direction for M&A-related changes, and (3) prepare them for the stresses and tensions that accompany such transitions. It is important to ensure that the voice of the merger partner or acquisition target is clearly heard, allowing people to vent their feelings, concerns and frustrations. It is even more important, however, to use these activities as a bridge for people to let go and move on.

A key dimension of these workshops, which is often overlooked in their planning, is the need for an explicit link to priority "business" initiatives that reflect immediate, short-term results. Organizational members typically become increasingly focused inward, especially on "me issues," instead of on business-related activities, meeting the needs of customers and staying attuned to changes in the marketplace. Thus, as a way of building momentum for the merger or acquisition, it is useful for the participants to identify specific projects that could produce business results in 100 days or less. Focusing on these projects, cultural and psychological impediments can be identified, along with specific strategies for dealing with them. Successfully accomplishing these projects not only enhances operations but also begins to contribute to a new mindset as to how people view the combination.

Dealing with Culture

There is no other area of an M&A that is more frustrating for their consultants than culture change. But not every merger or acquisition necessarily requires the same cultural integration strategy. In some instances, and probably too often, the acquiring company will seek to totally integrate the target into its operations, including an attempt to assimilate the culture into its own. In others, firms may follow a cultural pluralism strategy, attempting to build on cultural differences in the target company. Ed Liddy, Chairman and CEO of Allstate, has noted that although his company has made a number of acquisitions they do not try to "Allstate-ize" all of them.[36] In some instances, Allstate completely integrates the target firm. In others, the strategy is to keep the acquired firm operationally separate, leaving it to rely on the unique characteristics – whether product, channels or key people – that made the company attractive in the first place.

Rather than trying to change an organization's culture – which can take years to accomplish – a key to successful integration focuses on significant behaviors and interactions instead. While organizational cultures often clash during a merger or acquisition, the cultures themselves are not the problem. Rather it is the relatively low level of understanding of how one's culture – and the culture of the merger partner or acquisition target – shapes and influences behavior.

The well-known example of Hewlett-Packard's "Stepford Wives" and Apollo Computer's "Hell's Angels" provides a good illustration.[37] When H-P initially acquired Apollo, its managers experienced difficulties integrating Apollo into its operations. It was easy to point to the distinctly different cultures of the two organizations as an intractable problem. An intergroup mirroring exercise during a consulting engagement, however, drew out the Stepford Wives-Hell's Angels analogy. Discussion centered on how members of the two organizations approached typical business challenges. Instead of attempting to change the cultures, the intervention focused on increasing mutual understanding about how the cultures of each organization had shaped their behavior. Once this became clear, greater mutual respect realized, and the focus turned to creating appropriate behaviors for how they could work together in the future, rather than trying to change their underlying values.

Hired by the Acquired Organizations

Despite the growing appreciation for the type of interventions discussed above, there are still numerous instances when consultants are contacted by the *acquired* firm rather than the acquiring company. The target firm is often in a difficult situation because of how it is being treated by the acquirer. Studies by the major professional services firms, for example, point to a number of common problems among unsuccessful acquirers. The mistakes centered around a failure to communicate even one-quarter of their integration activities to target company members and key stakeholders, the absence of a dedicated transition team in place and the lack of a clearly understood and supported strategy for the new entity.[38]

In these situations, consultants are faced with several unique challenges. I typically try to initiate an explicit strategy to increase open interaction between the firms (e.g., data-sharing strategies, joint action-planning and offsite team-building meetings). But I have found that target firm executives are often uneasy about initiating such efforts because of their secondary role in the acquisition. Since the acquiring firm did not undertake the initiative in the first place, these individuals are typically apprehensive about either (1) going to the parent company for guidance, or (2) having the acquirer find out that they have brought in a consultant to assist them with the change process.

While the prevailing view among many consultants is that long-lasting change will only occur when intervention begins at the top, there are some things that can be done at lower organizational levels. Of course, given these constraints, interventions focus more fully on facilitating coping strategies and adaptation. One of the most effective ways to assist organizational members in this process is by guiding them through a series of questions that help them come to terms with their situation and their spheres of control. The essence of these questions is to prompt employees to identify (1) the exact nature of their situation; (2) what it will take to resolve any problems and/or concerns; and (3) whether they currently have or might be able to generate sufficient resources to deal with these issues.[39] The objective is to enable individuals to distinguish between those aspects of their work environment that they can and cannot control, as well as alerting them to issues that they can manage through direct action, behavioral change or even a change in attitude.[40]

As organizational members concentrate on those areas where they are able to exert some influence, they can be encouraged to work constructively on possible solutions. When one set of issues is resolved, the next solvable problem often becomes more visible, encouraging organizational members to become more proactive in dealing with this issue. It is important to realize that in complex organizations such "small wins" do not necessarily connect in a neat, linear or sequential form, with each step reflecting a demonstrable movement toward a predetermined goal. This approach, however, can begin to develop momentum toward inter-firm cooperation and more positive attitudes.[41]

Clearly, there are limitations to this approach. One decision by the acquiring organization can quickly undermine what the target company and its members have attempted to do. Thus, in these instances, "helping" is limited to enhancing the ability of the client in the target firm to better handle their feelings of frustration and helplessness.

The Future of M&A Consulting

Merger and acquisition integration will remain an ongoing challenge for organizations – with each one having its own unique and idiosyncratic dimensions. Management consultants can play a valuable role in facilitating the complex process of successfully combining two previously autonomous organizations.

The overarching reason why firms enter into a merger or decide to acquire another company is the belief, albeit frequently naive, that the combination will allow the new entity to attain its strategic goals more quickly and less expensively than if the firm attempted to do it on its own. Yet, far too many M&A deals are dominated by the content of financial analysis, a focus on historical data rather than future sources of revenues and power plays that turn strategy into gamesmanship. Many companies still seem to meander through the post-combination integration process, literally paralyzed by the myriad dysfunctions that surround them.

Despite the poor performance and track record associated with merging and acquiring firms, future projections suggest that M&A activity will become more far-reaching and more complex than anything we have experienced thus far.[42] Many will take place across national boundaries and cultures. These deals will continue to be strategically driven, requiring a level of integration that makes key challenges as much cultural and psychological as they are financial and operational. A likely change is that merger integration consultants will share the table more frequently with transaction advisors earlier in the process of due diligence. Consulting engagements will become longer term, going beyond isolated interventions to focus more on the entire process of M&A planning and integration. It is clear that combination integration is an iterative process, not a one-time endeavor or a discrete stage of the deal that begins once the final documents are signed. Effective integration planning and implementation must begin earlier during the pre-combination preliminary planning stage and evolve to permeate the day-to-day realities of organizational life for both parties. Thus, from a consulting perspective, post-M&A integration will continue to become an increasingly important service.

Consulting to Integrate Mergers and Acquistions 315

One thing will not change. To achieve success, M&A consulting interventions will need to be guided by flexibility and openness, as consultants work closely with management teams during pre-combination preliminary planning, early integration implementation and post-combination aftermath stages. These efforts should focus on constantly tracking the combination, recalibrating plans as needed and facilitating the human dynamics associated with the change.

Notes

1 See, for example, R.W. Coff, "Human capital, shared expertise and the likelihood of impasse in corporate acquisitions," *Journal of Management*, 2002, 28 (1), 115–137; P.M. Elsass and J.F. Veiga, "Acculturation in acquired organizations: A force-field perspective," *Human Relations*, 1994, 47 (4), 431–453; and M. Lubatkin, "Mergers and the performance of the acquiring firm," *Academy of Management Review*, 1983, 8 (2), 218–225.
2 Compare the two *Business Week* cover stories: "Do Mergers Really Work?" June 3, 1985, and "The Merger Hangover: How Most Big Acquisitions Have Destroyed Shareholder Value," October 14, 2002.
3 C.M. Christensen, R. Alton, C. Rising and A. Waldeck, "The big idea: The new M&A playbook," *Harvard Business Review*, 2011, 89 (3), 48–57; R. Sher, "Why half of all M&A deals fail, and what you can do about it," *Forbes*, March 19, 2012 [retrieved from http://www.forbes.com/sites/forbesleadershipforum/2012/03/19/why-half-of-all-ma-deals-fail-and-what-you-can-do-about-it/#13a257bf20ae].
4 See "Establishing strategic guideposts for corporate buyers in the 21st century," *Mergers and Acquisitions*, 2001, 36 (5): 18–27; *OECD Business and Finance Outlook 2015* (Paris: OECD Publishing, 2015); and KPMG, *2015 M&A outlook survey report: The boom in back* [retrieved from www.kpmgsurvey-ma.com].
5 See A. Werr and H. Linnarsson, "Management consulting for client learning?: Clients' perceptions of learning in management consulting," in A.F. Buono (Ed.), *Developing knowledge and value in management consulting* (Greenwich, CT: Information Age Publishing, 2002), pp. 3–32; L.E. Greiner and R.O. Metzger, *Consulting to management* (Englewood Cliffs: Prentice-Hall, 1983); and M.G. Baaij, *An introduction to management consultancy* (London: Sage Publications, 2014).
6 See, for example, A.R. Lajoux, *The Art of M&A Integration* (New York: McGraw-Hill, 1998), pp. 49–53.
7 See, for example, R.G. Eccles, K.L. Lanes and T.C. Wilson, "Are you paying too much for that acquisition?" *Harvard Business Review*, 1999, 77 (4), 136–146; and M.N. Clemente and D.S. Greenspan, *Winning at Mergers and Acquisitions* (New York: Wiley, 1998).
8 See D.H. Maister, C.H. Green and R.M. Galford, *The Trusted Advisor*. (New York: Simon & Schuster, 2000).
9 David Nadler talks about a similar dynamic when consulting with CEOs and Boards of Directors in Chapter 9 in this volume.
10 A.F. Buono, "Technology transfer through acquisition," *Management Decision*, 1997, 35 (3), 194–204; D. Carey, "Lessons from master acquirers: A CEO roundtable on making mergers succeed," *Harvard Business Review*, 2000, 78 (3),

145–154; and P. Pritchett and R.D. Gilbreath, *Mergers: Growth in the Fast Lane* (Dallas: Pritchett & Associates, 1996).
11 A.F. Buono and J.L. Bowditch, *The Human Side of Mergers and Acquisitions: Managing Collisions between People, Cultures, and Organizations* (Washington, DC: Beard Books, 2003); and D. Kidd, "Who goes, who stays? Many mergers do not create the shareholder value expected of them," *Harvard Business Review*, 2001, 79 (1), 9.
12 A.F. Buono, J.W. Weiss and J.L. Bowditch, "Paradoxes in acquisition and merger consulting: Thoughts and recommendations," *Consultation: An International Journal*, 1989, 8 (3), 145–159.
13 See A.L. Velocci, "Merger experiences yield valuable lessons," *Aviation Week & Space Technology*, 2001, 154 (19), 80–81; and P. Haspeslagh & D.B. Jemison, *Managing Acquisitions: Creating Value through Corporate Renewal* (New York: Free Press, 1991).
14 Reported in *Mergers and Acquisitions*, "Establishing strategic guideposts"; see also G.K. Stahl and M.E. Mendenhall, *Mergers and Acquisitions: Managing Culture and Human Resources* (Stanford, CA: Stanford University Press, 2005).
15 M.M. Habeck, F. Kroger & M.R. Tram, *After the merger* (London: Financial Times/Prentice-Hall, 2000), pp. 3–5; and C. Deutsch and A. West, "A new generation of M&A: A McKinsey perspective on the opportunities and challenges," in *Perspectives on merger integration* (McKinsey & Company, June 2010) [retrieved from www.mckinsey.com/search.aspx?q=perspectives+on%20merger%20integration%202010].
16 For a thoughtful discussion of M&A strategies and their ramifications, see J.L. Bower, "Not all M&As are alike – and that matters," *Harvard Business Review*, 2001, 79 (2): 93–101.
17 Exhibit 13.1 has been influenced by a number of sources, including M.L. Marks, "How to Treat the Merger Syndrome," *Journal of Management Consulting*, 1988, 4 (3), 42–52; M.L. Marks and J. Cutcliffe, "Making mergers work," *Training and Development Journal*, 1988, 42 (4), 30–36; and Buono and Bowditch, *The Human Side of Mergers and Acquisitions*.
18 For a fuller discussion of the shortcomings of traditional due diligence efforts, see Clemente and Greenspan, *Winning at Mergers and Acquisitions*, Chapter 1.
19 Reported in *Mergers and Acquisitions*, "Establishing strategic guideposts for corporate buyers."
20 See J.A. Schmidt, "The correct spelling of M&A begins with HR," *HR Magazine*, 2001 (June), 102–108; and M.L. Feldman and M.F. Spratt, *Five Frogs on a Log: A CEO's Field Guide to Accelerating the Transition in Mergers, Acquisitions, and Gut Wrenching Change* (New York: HarperBusiness, 1999).
21 Exhibit 13.2 draws from R.G. Eccles, K.L. Lanes and T.C. Wilson, "Are you paying too much for that acquisition?" *Harvard Business Review*, 1999, 77 (4), 136–146; and R. Coff, "Human capital, shared expertise, and the likelihood of impasse in corporate acquisitions," *Journal of Management*, 2002, 28 (1), 115–137.
22 A good illustration of this can be found in P.H. Mirvis and M.L. Marks, "The human side of merger planning: Assessing and analyzing fit," *Human Resource Planning*, 1992, 15 (3), 69–92.
23 Reported in Marks, "Making mergers and acquisitions work" in A.F. Buono (Ed.), *Enhancing inter-firm networks and interorganizational strategies* (Greenwich, CT: Information Age Publishing), pp. 3–30.

24 See M. Dumon, "Biggest merger and acquisition disasters," Investopedia.com, retrieved June 17, 2008.
25 Reported in M.P. Ennen, "The war for talent: Physicians in management consulting," *Journal of the American Medical Association*, 2001, *285* (17), 22–52.
26 See Coff, "Human capital, shared expertise, and the likelihood of impasse in corporate acquisitions"; and Dumon, "Biggest merger and acquisition disasters."
27 This case is drawn from Buono and Bowditch, *The Human Side*, Chapter 8.
28 E. Schein, "Managerial consulting: Who is our client? Who should be our client?" Distinguished speaker presentation, Management Consulting Division, Academy of Management, Cincinnati, Ohio, August, 1996; see also E. Schein, "The concept of 'client' from a process consultation perspective: A guide for change agents," *Journal of Organizational Change Management*, 1997, *10* (3), 202–216.
29 See P.H. Mirvis and M.L. Marks, *Managing the Merger: Making It Work* (Englewood Cliffs, NJ: Prentice-Hall, 1992).
30 The discussion of listening deeply is based on A.F. Buono and A.J. Nurick, "Intervening in the Middle: Coping Strategies in Mergers and Acquisitions," *Human Resource Planning*, 1992, *15* (2), 19–33; and H.F. Stein, *Listening Deeply* (Boulder, CO: Westview Press, 1994).
31 For an in-depth discussion of these integration challenges see Buono and Bowditch, *The Human Side*; Clemente and Greenspan, *Winning at Mergers and Acquisitions*; and Haspeslagh and Jemison, *Managing Acquisitions*.
32 See Clemente and Greenspan, *Winning at Mergers and Acquisitions*; and Habeck, et al., *After the Merger* for a fuller discussion of these dynamics.
33 A good illustration can be found in R.N. Ashkenas and S.C. Francis, "Integration managers: Special leaders for special times," *Harvard Business Review*, 2000, *78* (6), 108–116. See also, A.F. Buono and K. Subbiah, "Internal consultants as change agents: Roles, responsibilities, and organizational change capacity," *Organization Development Journal*, 2014, *32* (2), 35–53.
34 The distinction between on-stage and backstage roles is drawn from P. Mirvis, "Midlife as a consultant," in P.J. Frost and M.S. Taylor (Eds.), *Rhythms of Academic Life* (Thousand Oaks, CA: Sage, 1996), pp. 361–369.
35 R.N. Ashkenas, L.J. DeMarco and S.C. Francis, "Making the deal real: How GE capital integrates acquisitions," *Harvard Business Review*, 1998, *76* (1), 5–15.
36 Reported in D. Carey, "Lessons from master acquirers," pp. 152.
37 A fuller discussion of the H-P/Apollo culture clash can be found in A.F. Buono and A.J. Nurick, "Intervening in the middle: Coping strategies in mergers and acquisitions," *Human Resource Planning*, 1992, *15* (2), 19–33; Mirvis and Marks, *Managing the Merger*; and T.L. Legare, "The human side of mergers and acquisitions: Understanding and managing human resource integration issues," *Human Resource Planning*, 1998, *21* (1): 32–41.
38 See Velocci, "Merger experiences yield valuable lessons"; Booz-Allen & Hamilton, "Merger integration: Delivering on the promise"; McKinsey & Company, "Perspectives on merger integration"; and KPMG, "Post merger people integration," KPMG, 2011.
39 See Buono and Nurick, "Intervening in the middle."
40 A good illustration of this dynamic can be found in M.L. Marks, *From Turmoil to Triumph: New Life after Mergers, Acquisitions, and Downsizing* (New York: Lexington Books, 1994), pp. 162–165.

41 This approach is an application of K. Weick, "Small wins: Redefining the scale of social problems," *American Psychologist*, 1984, *39* (1), 40–49.
42 For an intriguing assessment of the future of M&A activity, see "Merger outlook: You haven't seen anything yet" in Habeck, et al., *After the Merger*, pp. 1135–1140; KPMG, "U.S. executives on M&A: Fill speed ahead in 2016," KPMG, December, 2015; and Equitreg, "The global consulting mergers & acquisitions report 2015," Equitreg, May 2015.

14 Business Transformation and Innovation Consulting

Matthew C. Heim

Introduction

The world's business environment has changed dramatically in the past 30 years, as we see continuous business transformation slowly becoming the norm, rather than the exceptional change cycle that occurs every ten years or so after a business wakes up from a long period of dormancy. Corporate dormancy is a phenomenon that occurs just a few years after a business has gone through a major reorganization, when the effectiveness of that reorganization begins to wane, causing problems with product and service quality, loss of market share and profitability decline. Global business practices and technologies continue to evolve, and when the collective business community moves in a direction of increased efficiency, productivity and profitability, the effectiveness of those companies reluctant to change decreases in comparison. When a company begins to rest on its laurels, a collective lethargy begins to set in, where individuals and corporate entities naturally try to cling on to the structure they are used to, making it more difficult to change the longer that structure remains static.

Fostering an alternative solution to periodic stagnation, i.e., continuous change and transformation, can bring many benefits, and does not mean that a company has to invest large sums of money and implement major organizational, process and systems changes each year to remain competitive. It is more about creating a *culture* of change, uprooting individuals and corporate entities from the cycle of infrequent change and dormancy, and bringing forth a culture that maintains a continuous flow of value-based business enhancement initiatives, guided by a larger, continuously unfolding vision. Shifting to this new model of continuous change requires a new leadership model, which will be discussed at length throughout this chapter.

In the 1990s, and well into the first decade of the new millennium, corporations and their consultants launched monumental efforts to break down the silos of compartmentalized information, creating cross-functional processes that were more transparent and useful to other entities throughout the organization. Enterprise Resource Planning (ERP) systems became the norm, enabling the cross-enterprise flow of information, destroying those once dysfunctional business silos that kept managers from making informed decisions. Again, once these processes and systems were in place, we witnessed a new wave of corporate dormancy take place, leading up to the Great Recession in 2008. After 2008, companies realized that they couldn't remain stagnant, and the new era of collaborative innovation was born. Although "collaboration" and "innovation" are in the executive vernacular of nearly all companies today, each company has its own definition of these terms, and struggles to figure out how to integrate collaborative innovation sustainably across their existing corporate structures.

In this chapter, we will begin with the definition of business transformation, and the integral role it plays with both corporate structure and the individual worker. We will discuss the role of the consultant in a business transformation initiative, and the various approaches used by consulting firms today. We will then explore the concept of transformational leadership, and the transformational leadership model used to initiate and foster continuous change within the corporate structure. Finally, we will discuss the recent reemergence of collaborative innovation, and the importance it carries in achieving and sustaining corporate growth.

Business Transformation Defined

According to Wikipedia, the term "business transformation" is defined as follows:

> *Business transformation is about making fundamental changes in how business is conducted in order to help cope with a shift in market environment.*

In order to properly educate business leaders and consultants on the true nature of business transformation, we need a more robust definition. I offer the following definition in order to present a more unambiguous path towards true transformation:

> *Business transformation is the active alignment of corporate strategies, processes, technologies, people and partners under a meaningful vision, while fostering the attainment of innovative business goals and objectives on an iterative and continuous basis.*

The difference between these two definitions is that the first offers a conventional "business as usual" approach to change. It implies that if there is a shift in the market, then there needs to be a shift in the business. The latter definition implies the alignment of structural elements (i.e., strategies, process and technologies) along with people (i.e., the workforce) and partners (i.e., supply chain and other business partners) under a higher vision. If we fail to create a higher vision of what the company can become, we remain in a state of reactionary stasis, trying to play catch-up as long as the company can survive. Business transformation also requires the continuous birth and development of new innovative ideas that will help a company to *lead* in its markets, and not merely struggle to keep up. This completely changes the concept of strategic planning from what we know about it today.

Strategic planning has its roots in ancient times when armies would plan the capture or defeat of opposing forces. The concept of strategy hasn't hit the business world until well into the Industrial Age, when larger corporations developed new means of protecting their wealth and assets, while out maneuvering the competition. There are two fundamental flaws with the ways in which business strategy has evolved. First, it is primarily focused on competition. Second, strategic planning has been considered an activity that should take place every few years to reestablish the direction of the company.

We, as strategic business advisors, need to set our sights on a higher vision of what our clients' companies can become and what they can create from a position of market leadership. Furthermore, we need to understand and embrace a continuous, iterative strategic planning process whose lifecycle is more like a continuous spiraling of new ideas, rather than a single event followed by an implementation phase, and then long periods of stagnation. When strategic planning is conducted in an iterative, continuously unfolding fashion, innovation becomes deeply engrained into the heart of every business unit and department, and change becomes the norm, rather than the exception.

Consulting Roles in Business Transformation

Consultants play a crucial role in the business transformation process. They bring outside knowledge, process and insights to the client organization, as well as methodologies designed to transform the client's business. The consultant is a catalyst throughout the change process, and can be viewed as the outside expert coming in to show the company the way towards positive change, or to facilitate the extraction and harnessing of existing knowledge and insights from the client to form new strategies. Several different schools of thought exist that can each, in their own way, affect successful change in an organization.

Management Consulting Approach – Management Consulting (MC), also known as the "tell" approach, stems from a time prior to World War II, when firms were formed, combining accounting principles with engineering methodologies. Although the MC approach has recently declined in popularity, as contemporary consulting tends to focus more on client engagement and empowerment, there are still many consultants today who utilize this approach. Early management consultants were somewhat influenced by the earlier works of Frederick Taylor, but they eventually adopted a different philosophy, focusing more on the effective *organization* of their clients, rather than efficiency. Management consultants assume that there is a right way and a wrong way of doing business and help their clients to organize around their adopted command and control style organization structures. Often times after delivering a comprehensive and highly complex strategy to the client, these strategies are seldom adopted, because of two reasons. First, the consultant did not sufficiently solicit inputs, viewpoints and ideas from the client during the planning process, resulting in a lack of understanding and buy-in. Second, the consultant delivered the strategy with no follow-up action to see it through the implementation phases. While the strategy looked great on paper, there was no business transformation process that followed, and the strategy document ended up gathering dust on someone's shelf.

A few years after the end of World War II, a team of researchers in Scotland named Tom Burns and G.M. Stalker began to study companies that were once successful during the war effort, to see if and why they would survive and thrive after the war. They found that the vast majority of companies that were able to adapt to and survive in the post-war economy were less likely to have a rigid command and control structure. These surviving companies had a more flattened hierarchy and were more apt to change and adapt to new economic situations and drivers. These new insights, along with many other studies that followed, eventually gave birth to a completely new direction in the consulting industry.

Organizational Development Approach – Organizational Development (OD) consulting, also known as the "ask" approach, differs greatly from that of management consulting. OD consultants relinquish the role of the "expert" consultant and assume that the client has all of the answers needed to develop effective and sustainable strategies. The OD consultant focuses more on extractive facilitation methods designed to capture and harness the client's insights and organize them into new strategies together with the client team. Clients are asked to trust the process of OD consulting and are often surprised at the insights yielded from the group that once considered themselves too inexperienced or stuck in the current state of the business. And because the insights came from the client, they are more likely to buy into these new strategies.

Some OD consultants have developed highly effective methodologies for this type of consulting engagement, but if consultants are not well trained in these types of facilitation skills, they can quickly lose credibility with the client. OD consultants are often labeled as "wishy-washy" by clients who do not understand the OD approach. Others may be good facilitators but fail to effectively translate the client's insights into actual strategies. But who is to blame in these cases? Was the approach explained beforehand? Did the client vet the consultant and approach to ensure it would be a good fit for the organization? While there may be plenty of blame to go around, the OD approach can still be highly effective if conducted properly in the right environment.

The Hybrid Approach – As in any learning process, it best serves the learner to study all schools of thought on a given topic and to develop an approach that best suits the consultant's personal style and the client's specific need. I have found that combining the MC and OD approaches can be more effective than choosing one over the other. For example, let's look at the critical success factors of each approach and see where they can be used in the client engagement. One thing that management consultants bring to the table is outside experience and expertise. They have been exposed to many other companies and have developed their intellectual capital platform based on industry, process and functional area best practices. They also bring expertise in different areas of technology that are designed to "enable" these new strategies and streamline processes.

The OD approach offers much deeper interpersonal skills and facilitation methods. OD training methods are also less likely to be transactional, and start with the *awareness* of the individual, as it pertains to the change at hand, resulting in a more effective and sustainable learning experience for the recipient. MC and OD consultants can work together, forming more effective teams that can deliver results that are both cutting-edge and incorporate the unique insights and ideas of the client team. While facilitators work to extract the client's insights and knowledge, experts feed these new ideas with outside information that can contribute dramatically to the development of a powerful strategy. By working more collaboratively with the client, and staying on to see the company through the transformation phase, the consulting team will be more likely to see these newly generated ideas and strategies being successfully implemented.

Transformational Leadership

The term "leadership" construes many different images to different people. There are leaders who lead by example, some who lead as strong taskmasters and those who lead from behind. Either of these leadership styles, and others, have demonstrated success in business transformation initiatives. When we witness a successful consulting project, we look to see who led that engagement and associate that person's leadership style with success. However, the inverse is also true. Either one of these leadership styles can be associated with project failure. Therefore, I would argue that, while leadership style has something to do with business transformation success, it has more to do with preparation. The model below depicts a framework for Transformational Leadership that has been proven to help prepare and drive many large-scale business transformation efforts.

The integration of vision, strategy, alignment, momentum and celebration into an iterative planning and implementation cycle will not only serve as an effective augmentation to the standard project management methodology and tools, but will also foster a new culture of continuous change and transformation with our clients. The segments that follow describe the

Figure 14.1 The Transformational Leadership Model

important attributes of each step that have demonstrated success time and time again with regards to business transformation.

Vision

It is quite often that we hear of businesses developing and implementing new strategic plans, and you as a consultant may have even participated in this process a time or two in the past. And if you have, I invite you to ask yourself, what was the larger vision driving that strategy? If the strategy you implemented, for example, was to streamline the company's orders-to-cash process (i.e., the combined functions of order entry, sales, customer service, billing and accounts receivable), without a higher vision, then I would argue that this was a reactionary strategy that was driven by what the company's competitors are doing in that industry space. The strategy could have, on the other hand, been driven by a higher vision stated something like, "We will continue to revolutionize our business presence in the marketplace, maintaining our leadership position, and broadening our customer and market base." If that is the case, the strategy carries much more meaning and will likely span well beyond the bounds of the orders-to-cash process. That vision may also influence our clients to continuously improve their manufacturing processes, service delivery models and other functional areas and processes – all in an integrated fashion under a unified vision.

When US President John F. Kennedy announced his vision of "putting a man on the moon" he didn't articulate how that would be done. Rather, he drove that vision into all areas of government and industry across the United States, to the point that when a janitor working for NASA was asked by a reporter what his job was, he simply stated, "I am putting a man on the moon." This is the kind of vision that brings forth change, and every business transformation initiative must be aligned with a higher vision that *everyone* can get behind – a vision that inspires and motivates. A vision that will encourage every person in every role to do their part to achieve that vision. A vision that creates and sustains market leaders.

Strategy

As discussed earlier in this chapter, sustainable business transformation cannot result from a one-time strategy, also known as the "Five-Year Plan." These strategies create stagnation, and can put a company into a rut that will be very difficult to get out of over time, if change is not viewed and treated as the norm. A transformational strategic planning process begins by gathering leadership representatives from all areas of the business that will initiate, impact or be impacted by the change. For example, if the task is to accelerate the procurement process, and reduce costs and material flaws for a given product, then likely candidates to attend the planning session would be the heads of Engineering, Manufacturing and Supply Chain, because of the direct process implications such a change would have on each of these respective areas. Representatives from the company's HR, IT/IS and Regulatory organizations should also be involved, because of the anticipated changes that will occur with people's job functions, product quality, information systems and processes. Having the right people in the room at the time of the planning session will eliminate a lot of rework, resulting from unanticipated requirements and mid-project changes.

Once the appropriate organizational representation is gathered, the planning may begin by first articulating the broader vision that is driving the change, to ensure that everyone is aligned. When facilitating the planning session, the consultant may present several alternatives for the solution, articulating examples and best practices, keeping the group within the bounds of the stated goals and objectives, and then let the assembled leadership team make the final decisions. During the facilitation process, the consultant must be sure that the group is tracing each alternative change suggestion throughout the organization in a simulated fashion, to ensure that every entity impacted by the change is accounted for, and that those requirements are encapsulated in the overall plan.

For example, if one alternative were to implement a Product Lifecycle Management (PLM) software solution to enable a more streamlined product development process, then the question must be asked, what functional areas will be impacted by the change? Also, what areas could impact the new process, if not addressed? We would immediately see that, besides R&D, Procurement, Supply Chain, Engineering and Manufacturing would also be impacted. IT/IS would also need to weigh in on the direction of change, because it will be predominantly systems-driven. New standards, objectives and metrics would need to be modified for many personnel, ensuring their rewards systems and incentives are aligned with the actions that will result in the desired time reduction. As one can see, there is much more to the development of a successful, sustainable strategic plan than merely a simple decision made in isolation.

The new strategy resulting from the collaborative planning initiative may have a broad impact across the organization, with a great deal of complexity. There may also be a certain degree of risk associated with the change. In such cases, it is prudent to develop a plan that will not be based on an "all or nothing" approach. One alternative would be to pilot a small segment of the new change initiative in an area that would best represent the other areas to be impacted by the change (e.g., one product area), then after demonstrating success, the team would roll the change out to the rest of the organization (i.e., other product areas).

Another way to manage a complex rollout situation would be to roll out pieces of the functionality to different functional entities (e.g., Research, Development and Engineering) in a phased approach, ensuring that each area is fully stabilized before rolling it out to other functional areas (e.g., Supply Chain Planning, Procurement, etc.), until the implementation is complete. In either case, HR and other involved entities will have to ensure that peripheral requirements are being designed and implemented concurrently with each phase (e.g., training, change management, new personnel and team objectives, etc.). As a consultant, I have seen a few situations where such rollouts were met with multiple challenges, due to the lack of planning and coordination across the whole company.

Regardless of how many phases a project requires, there will be other strategic initiatives in the pipeline, and the company must be aware of its capacity for change. Depending on that capacity, the company may decide to prioritize and stagger the rollout of its strategic initiatives. Staggering strategic initiatives in a phased approach in not necessarily a flawed

Business Transformation and Innovation Consulting 327

alternative and may lead to greater success is the long run. In the spirit of continuous improvement, the organization may want to keep its pipeline full of value-generating change initiatives, which will help nurture and inspire a culture of continuous change. Parsing out the change initiatives will also help mitigate the risk of doing too much too fast, resulting in a loser-loses-all situation, which is, unfortunately, sometimes the case with so-called "big bang" implementations.

Alignment

Ensuring organizational alignment behind a strategic initiative can yield many positive results, but achieving alignment is all too often overlooked, or underplayed. There are two levels of alignment that should be achieved with any strategic initiative in order to achieve enterprise-wide understanding and buy-in, and these are *horizontal* and *vertical* alignment. In our previous example of product lifecycle time reduction, let's say, for example, that three entities were directly impacted by the change – R&D, Engineering and Manufacturing (Organizational Alignment Example below).

The leadership team behind the three functional areas impacted must be fully aligned (horizontal alignment), each attaining a complete understanding of the goals and objectives, required completion tasks and key performance indicators behind the change. Once this alignment is

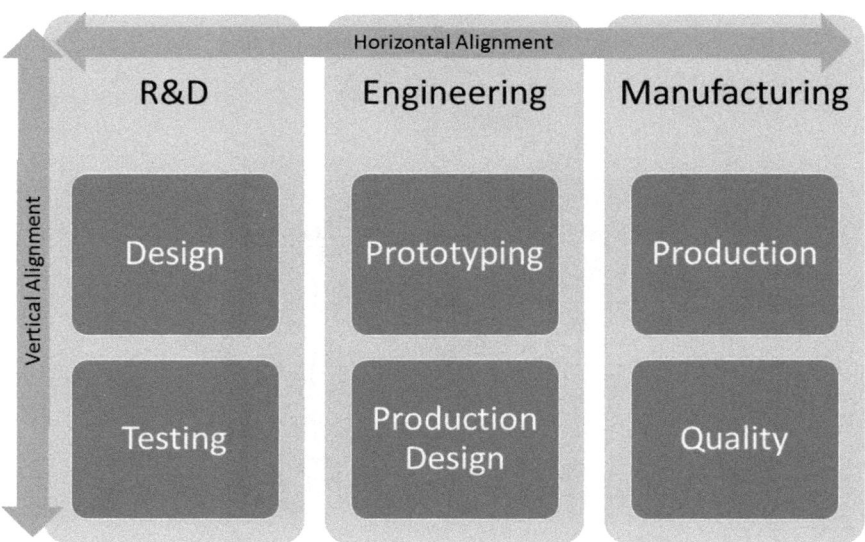

Figure 14.2 Organizational Alignment Example

attained the leader of each respective functional area must then ensure that the entities under their responsibility that are directly impacted are also aligned, and that the appropriate tasks are planned and assigned to those groups. For example, if the head of Engineering is aligned with the heads of R&D and Manufacturing, then the next step would be to bring that vision and strategy down to the Product Prototyping and Production Prototyping groups, so that they can design the necessary steps to make it happen.

In organizations where continuous change has become the norm, there are many moving parts. Keeping those parts moving under a simple model will prevent the interactive changes from becoming overly complex and difficult to manage. In the Transformational Alignment Model below, we can see how the vision and strategy influence executive alignment and action, and in turn, the executive alignment and action influence the operational alignment and action.

In the horizontal alignment process, the leader must ask, what does this new vision and strategy mean to my organization, and how will it be executed within each functional area? Also, what are the key performance indicators I will need to consider to ensure we are doing our part to meet the overall goals and objectives of the strategic initiative? The line managers responsible for those functional areas directly impacted

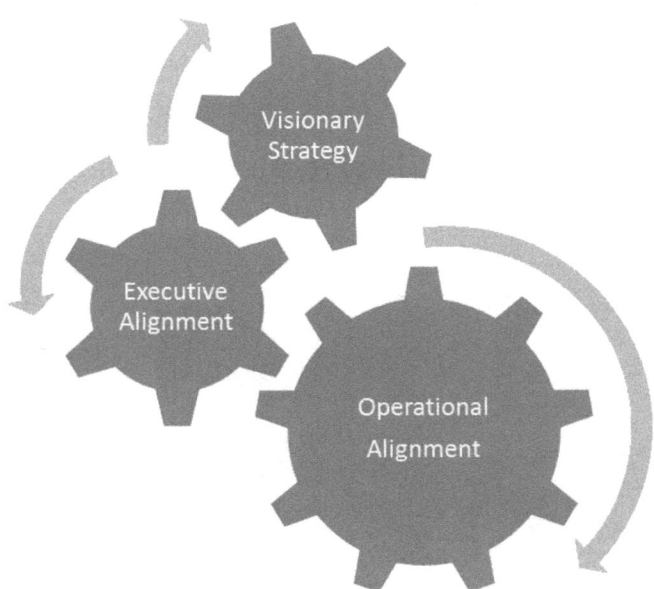

Figure 14.3 Transformational Alignment Model

by the change must ask, what changes need to occur within my team to ensure we are doing our part to meet those goals and objectives? What process, system and individual role-based metrics must I begin to consider to ensure alignment, and what job roles and descriptions will need to change? The consultant must ensure that all relevant answers to these questions are being captured and incorporated into the overall design of the change initiative.

During the alignment phase, it is not uncommon to see pockets of fear begin to emerge. This is a clear indicator of where the vision and strategy were not effectively communicated. Communication of the vision and strategy should be done with enthusiasm, stating all the benefits to the company, the department and the individual. The alignment process is a time to get everyone to thoroughly understand the changes and drivers, and most of all, to get the teams excited and bought into the new vision. The alignment phase is a good time to begin to identify the client project manager and those who will become members of the implementation team. Chosen client team members would include those not only able to achieve the objectives at hand, but also serve as an evangelist, spreading change and enthusiasm across the company. The following table contains key attributes to consider for selecting the right implementation team members.

Table 14.1 Key Consideration

Key Consideration	What does it mean?
Leadership	This person is respected by everyone, has proven leadership skills and is known to be well prepared for every situation.
Subject-Matter Knowledge	This person is well aware of the roles, responsibilities and processes within the area to be changed.
Systems Thinking	This person understands the impacts made to other parts of the organization and other parts of the organization that could potentially impact the area of change.
Critical Thinking	This person is not afraid to question a given design consideration if it has not been thoroughly thought through but will do so with tack and purpose.
Evangelism	This person shows lots of enthusiasm, is fully bought in to the change effort, and will likely spread that enthusiasm to other areas affected by the change.
Communication Skills	This person is articulate and has good writing skills. This person will not be hesitant to present to a larger group.
Project Management	This person understands project management, task assignment, critical path considerations and time management around key milestones.

If the consulting team responsible for implementation will be different than the team that facilitated the strategy session, then consideration should be given to the selection of appropriate team members. The consulting team members will need specific knowledge in the functional area in which they will be working, good facilitation skills, technical skills specific to any systems being implemented and client industry experience. The client team will be looking to the consultants for guidance and leadership, as they step into the unknown. A good consultant will have the ability to reassure the client with strong subject matter knowledge, change preparedness and, most of all, confidence.

When both the client and consulting teams have been chosen, it is a common practice to conduct one or more team building exercises, during which the new vision and strategy are introduced to the team, and team members are given the opportunity to align and bond under a new purpose. This could happen at the project kickoff event, but in many cases, it is done beforehand, to allow both teams to form a bond before starting the detailed planning phase of the project.

Momentum

As we enter the Momentum phase of the Transformational Leadership Model, the combined client-consultant team should be well prepared to kick off the project. During the project kickoff, the entire team is assembled and introduced to one another, and the executive sponsor conveys a motivational message to the team, outlining clear goals and objectives, as well as the strategic intent behind the project. Client and consulting project managers will then begin to outline the specific tasks required from each team member and present a preliminary project plan, with clear activities, milestones and critical path items to the rest of the team. Because there are so many proven project management methodologies, I will spare the reader of my presenting yet another one in this chapter. However, it is important to note that the preliminary project plan is just the starting point. As the teams complete their assessments of documenting the existing processes and organization (a.k.a. as-is assessment), and begin designing the new process, organization and systems design (a.k.a. to-be design), the new design requirements will begin to add much detail to the project plan, and the project management team must therefore stay current with each functional area.

During the transformational change initiative, each functional team will take their new designs back to the entities and departments that will be impacted and present the suggested change, soliciting feedback and gaining buy-in from each area. These sessions not only solicit feedback from those not on the team that may have unique skills, experiences and insights, it also gives these people some say in the design, which can lead to increased buy-in, and eliminate some of the fears and uncertainties that are likely brewing among those not assigned to the project at this point. And if the team is doing their job correctly, they will turn these fears and uncertainties into excitement, with the prospect of a clear improvement for all.

The project team will bring others into the team, as needed, to walk them through simulations of the change processes, adding new insights into the design. They will have to foster inter-process and inter-functional participation in these simulations to ensure that the appropriate handoffs are being designed, passing the appropriate information on at the right time, and in the right context. This type of inter-process design and simulation goes against the structures taught in many business schools around the world.

Business design and integration are taught mostly in a linear fashion, such as Michael Porter's Value Chain model, which depicts a linear transfer of materials, goods and information across the various business entities. To effectively optimize the design of new, more effective processes, one must often disregard existing paradigms and structures, and with the objectives in mind, allow a new system and process to emerge, regardless of previous organizational hierarchies and boundaries. Once these optimal process flows have been designed in direct correlation with the strategic objectives, new organizational boundaries can be created to govern them and better facilitate the flow of materials, goods and information. Non-linear approaches such as this one typically present many more design options and can lead to the most effective, efficient and transparent design results.

As the new process and system designs are being implemented, it is the responsibility of the consultant in each functional area to ensure the proper knowledge is being transferred at the right time. Knowledge transfer can include industry best practices, process integration skills and information systems configuration and navigation know-how. It is assumed that the consulting team will eventually leave after the implementation is completed, and all good consultants will work to ensure their role is obsolete by the end of the engagement. The following model highlights the concept of knowledge transfer over time.

In the beginning of the engagement the consultant will bring most of the knowledge and skills into the project activities. By the end of the

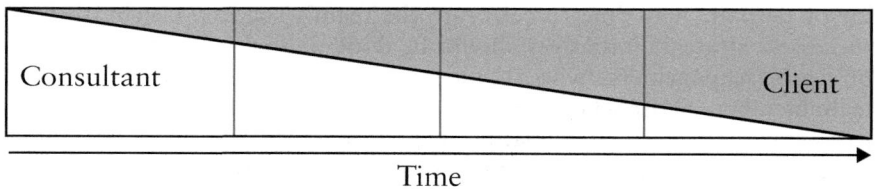

Figure 14.4 Knowledge Transfer Model

engagement, the consultant should strive to ensure that this knowledge has been successfully transferred to the client, as indicated by the increase of the shaded space over time, empowering the client to assume the new leadership role in its respective functional domain.

Towards the end of the implementation phase, the team will need to bring in the HR team responsible for the assignment of employee roles, objectives and metrics. They will need to closely examine the new roles created and develop job descriptions and appropriate reward systems for each. The HR team may also become involved in the design and implementation of new role-based and systems training at the end of the project. In order to create a transformative experience for the trainees, the team will ensure that training includes and articulates alignment with the vision, strategic goals and objectives, process and transactional systems training. This will ensure that trainees develop a full understanding of not only what to do, but also why they are doing it, what other functional areas will impact them, and what functional areas they will impact. Holistic training of this nature ensure a more productive worker, who is more likely to be able to determine the source of any issues that may arise during production.

Shortly after cutover to the new processes and systems, the team must remain in place to observe and react to any unanticipated issues that may arise with the new change. In many cases, the team will observe a shift – not only in the functional activities, but also in people's awareness. To see the "aha" moment that people experience after change can be very rewarding. On the other hand, some issues may present themselves that can suddenly shift the experience from exciting to fearful. This phase, when unforeseen issues arise unexpectedly, is known as the "valley of despair." With foreknowledge of this temporary phase, the project team can proactively communicate the likelihood of it occurring to the rest of the organization, explain that this is a temporary phase when the last minute issues are resolved, and indicate that they shouldn't be overly concerned. With proper post-implementation escalation procedures in place, any last minute issues will be quickly resolved, and the business transformation will be successfully completed.

Celebration

After finessing through the final transformation and navigating the valley of despair, it is time to celebrate the team's success. Celebration of successful strategic initiatives should be done publicly, in the attendance of senior management, who should recognize the achievements of each team member. Those who contributed to the project from outside the project team, i.e., those participating in process simulations and providing insights and feedback to the project, should also receive some level of recognition. The purpose of the celebration phase is not only to recognize the extra effort that each team member put in during the project, but also to publicly acknowledge the importance and prestige of being part of such a strategic change initiative.

The team celebration should be used to encourage others to participate in future strategic change efforts, demonstrating how they too can get involved, and in some cases, even enhance their careers. True transformation continues in the celebration phase, providing an opportunity for team members to experience self-actualization, or being part of something more than themselves, contributing to the greater good of the organization and its members. When others witness the transformation that occurs through a team experience of this sort, they will often be encouraged to become part of a future strategic change initiative, which could be happening again very soon. The first iteration of the continuous change effort has just been completed, and it is now time to begin planning the next phases and recruiting the next participants. In other words, strike while the iron is hot!

Compared to the old five-year cycle of strategic planning, implementation and stagnation, the new cycle doesn't rest. In a fractal-like pattern, the organization continues to blossom, launching new strategic changes that keep it in the leadership position. Each successful initiative further inspires the next, and people find that they are not getting burned out from such continuous change, but rather, being energized by it. If management can continue to feed the strategic change pipeline, and inspire its people with an awareness of the company's capacity for change (i.e., not compromising day to day operations), the company can realize a culture of continuous, positive change and innovation. And being able to observe and participate in this type of transformation as a consultant can be just as rewarding. But for us now, it's on to the next engagement!

Collaboration and Innovation

Corporate collaboration and innovation feed business transformation, and successful transformation efforts, in turn, contribute considerably to the attainment of an innovative culture. But collaboration was not always encouraged in businesses. In fact, until just 15 years ago, "closed" innovation was the norm, where corporate R&D centers were treated like Fort Knox, containing their product technology secrets in secure areas, and never letting anyone outside the company know their intentions. At the turn of the millennium, companies like Proctor & Gamble, General Mills and Unilever paved the way to a new concept called "open" or collaborative innovation, where they now look to the outside to inspire and find new technologies, processes and complementary products to better position their own products and services in the marketplace.

The mantra of these new cutting edge companies was, "why reinvent the wheel if someone else has the technology we need?" These companies have streamlined their product development processes so much, that they are no longer concerned about someone else seeing the vast majority of what they are developing (barring any highly strategic game-changing technologies that may be in the works). They post public online crowdsourcing challenges and requests for proposal (RFPs), encouraging the participation and collaboration of external resources towards the development of their new products. They are less concerned about other companies seeing most of what they are doing, because they are confident that these other companies will never catch up to the maturity of their products. And when they do, these companies will be ready to launch the next generation of that product, immediately rendering the copy cat's product obsolete.

The concept of collaborative innovation quickly became a disruptive event to those who were not on board. The innovation capacity of each individual in companies practicing in open, collaborative innovation has increased dramatically because of their access to vast external networks of collaborators, also known as "ecosystems," which can be deployed at their beck and call. It has also increased the speed of innovation, as these companies introduce new products to market at an accelerated pace. It also forced companies to rethink their internal processes, as they were not accustomed to having to bring in new partners and conducting smaller acquisitions on a regular basis. These companies now have to integrate other departments into the product development process, like Legal and Procurement, to complete the acquisition of the new capability before the collaborator becomes frustrated and walks away from the deal.

Let's take a closer look at why innovation is so important to a company's bottom line. A renowned professor from the University of Hertfordshire in the United Kingdom named Ralph Stacey looked at companies that introduced new products and services to the marketplace more frequently and found that they held a much higher position in what he calls the "Fitness Landscape." The fitness landscape (see below) consists of peaks and valleys, symbolizing the position that any product holds with regards to its success in the marketplace.

If a product was a market leader, it would be on a peak within the landscape but would not stay there for long without continuous innovation and refinement. Products found in valleys had less market share, struggling to maintain their position, let alone make it to the top. Stacey found that highly innovative companies were much more likely to land a product on a peak in the fitness landscape, and incremental innovators, on the other hand, would continuously attempt to climb the peak, only to be pushed down again and again by more innovative competitors in that same space.

When we think of innovation, many people automatically associate it with product innovation. But attaining and sustaining an innovative culture requires much more than that. A culture of innovation spans the entire organization, impacting areas like sales and marketing, supply chain, customer service, procurement and the leadership team. Innovation can emerge anywhere, and fostering a culture of innovation will help keep these virtuous conditions alive. As stated earlier, strategic change and innovation go

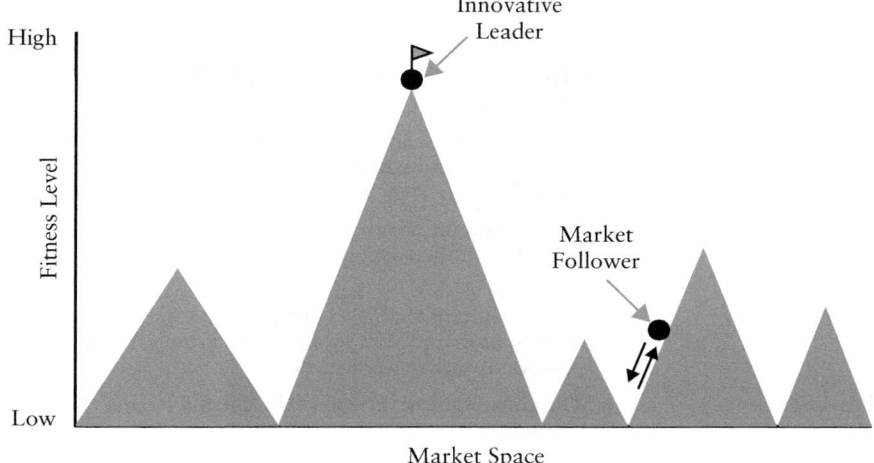

Figure 14.5 Ralph Stacey's Fitness Landscape

hand in hand. By presenting new strategic opportunities, and encouraging and rewarding strategic change, we inspire innovation in many areas. By establishing an iterative strategic planning process, these practices continue to permeate deep within the fabric of the organization and its culture.

The Business Transformation Consulting Experience

Simply put, business transformation is about getting a company from point A to point B. While that may look quite simple as stated above, there are many considerations that go into the transformation process. Consultants bring a vast arsenal of tools, methodologies, skill sets and experience (a.k.a. human capital) to the transformation effort. But there are other necessary traits that are not documented and are much more difficult to develop if a consultant doesn't possess them naturally. Those traits are explained in the table below.

During any business transformation effort there are two fundamental directions that either the client or the consultant can take. The first is "fear," and if we fall prey to that direction, we become consumed by the illusion it presents, stirring uncertainty and doubt. We begin to doubt the likelihood of delivering a successful project, and we even begin to doubt ourselves. Fear is also highly contagious, spreading from team member to team member, unless it is met by a stronger, more positive conviction. The alternative to fear in the transformation effort is "vision." When a team member fully understands the vision and is aligned with its purpose, their conviction or belief will transcend any occurrence of fear that emerges from within the team. I make these

Table 14.2 Transformational Traits

Transformational Traits	Explanation
Empathy	The consultant has the ability to step into the shoes of the client, seeing things from their perspective.
Presence	The consultant can shut down everything else on his or her mind and completely focus on the person in front of them. They are 100% present for that person.
Inspiration	The consultant has the ability to inspire others, spreading enthusiasm with those with whom they are working.
Adaptability	The consultant is able to quickly and rationally assess the situation and shift to a new position if the original position is met with obstacles.
Proactive	The consultant never leaves the client guessing. The consultant is well prepared for the next step and articulates it at the right time and place.
Leads with Vision	The consultant is always aware of the higher vision and value proposition driving the engagement and makes decision in alignment with that vision.
Confident	The consultant always shows confidence in the face of coworkers and client team members, as they are often looking up to that person to determine whether or not they feel confident themselves.
Communication Skills	The consultant has the ability to write effective and appropriate documentation and presentations and can verbally convey the message effectively and clearly.
Judgment	The consultant makes sound judgments based on facts and experience and will always seek other opinions if the decision criteria are not clear.
Interpersonal Skills	The consultant gets along with others and has favorable social and collaboration skills, fully participating in client events.

statements because fear is seen frequently in business transformation engagements like the ones discussed in this chapter. Our clients are undergoing vast changes and stepping into the unknown. It is not "if," but when fear will spring up within the team, and it is up to the consultant to hold to that higher vision and guide people back to the path of positive change.

Organizations are transformed only when people are transformed. Seasoned consultants can recognize the shift that occurs with the client, when they finally comprehend the purpose and value they are generating through a new strategic change. Consultants begin to develop a sixth sense around "feeling" when a project is successfully completed because of how the client is reacting. Consulting, therefore, can be a highly rewarding profession for this very reason. While the profession does come with frequent travel, late nights and occasional stressful on-the-spot situations, having the opportunity to facilitate change throughout an entire organization, and seeing the shift that occurs in individuals when they have successfully completed their mission, is a unique experience that many people will never have. When we see the transformation in others, we ourselves are transformed to a new state of awareness that goes much deeper than mere job experience.

Chapter Bibliography

1. Argyris, Chris. "Teaching Smart People How to Learn." *Harvard Business Review* (May/June 1991): 99–109.
2. Argyris, Chris, and Donald Schon. *Organizational Learning: A Theory of Action Perspective*. Reading, MA: Addison-Wesley, 1978.
3. Barbasi, Albert L. *Linked*. New York: Penguin Plume, 2003.
4. Burns, Tom, and G.M. Stalker. "Mechanistic and Organic Systems." *Classics of Organization Theory*, 4th Edition. J.M. Schafritz, and J.S. Ott, eds. Orlando, FL: Harcourt Brace, 1996.
5. Castells, Manuel. *The Rise of the Network Society*. Malden, MA: Blackwell Publishers, 1996.
6. Collins, James, and Jerry Porras. *Built to Last*. New York: Harper Business Books, 1997.
7. Daneke, Gregory. "Coming Full Circle: On the Return of Systems Thinking to Strategic Management." *Journal of Business and Management* (Fall 1994): 8–33.
8. Gardner, Howard. *Multiple Intelligences: The Theory in Practice*. New York: Basic Books, 1993.
9. Hamel, Gary. *Leading the Revolution*. Boston: Harvard Business School Press, 2000.
10. Heim, Matthew C. *Breaking the Musashi Code: Transcending Competition through Visionary Strategy*. Sonoma, CA: Visionary Partnership Press, 2007.
11. Jaworski, Joseph. *Synchronicity: The Inner Path of Leadership*. San Francisco: Barrett Koehler, 1996.
12. Katzenback, Jon R., and Douglas K. Smith. *The Wisdom of Teams: Creating the High-Performance Organization*. New York: Harper Perennial, 1999.
13. Kotter, John P.A. *A Force of Change: How Leadership Differs from Management*. New York: The Free Press, 1990.
14. Oshry, Barry. *Seeing Systems: Unlocking the Mysteries of Organizational Life*. San Francisco: Barrett Koehler, 1995.
15. Porter, Michael E. *Competitive Advantage: Creating and Sustaining Superior Performance*. New York: The Free Press, 1985.
16. Porter, Michael E. *Competitive Strategy*. New York: The Free Press, 1980.
17. Scharmer, C. Otto. *Theory U: Leading from the Future as it Emerges*. San Francisco: Barrett Koehler, 2009.
18. Senge, Peter M. *The Fifth Discipline: The Art and Practice of the Learning Organization*. New York: Currency Doubleday, 1990.
19. Senge, Peter M. *Presence: Human Purpose and the Field of the Future*. New York: Currency Doubleday, 2008.

20. Shaner, David. *The Seven Arts of Change: Leading Business Transformation that Lasts*. New York: Union Square Press, 2010.
21. Stacey, Ralph. *Complexity and Creativity in Organizations*. San Francisco: Barrett Koehler, 1996.
22. Tart, Charles T. *States of Consciousness*. Lincoln, NE: Blackinc.com, 2001.
23. Tichy, Noel M., and Eli Cohen. "The Teaching Organization." *Training and Development* (July 1998): 27–33.
24. Wheatley, Margaret. *Leadership and the New Science*. San Francisco: Barrett Koehler, 1992.
25. Youngblood, Mark D. *Life at the Edge of Chaos: Creating the Quantum Organization*. Dallas, TX: Perceval Publishing, 1997.

Part V

Managing and Growing the Consulting Firm

15 Managing Growth Stages in Consulting Firms 341
    (LARRY E. GREINER, UNIVERSITY OF SOUTHERN CALIFORNIA, AND
    JAMES K. MALERNEE, CONERSTONE RESEARCH)

16 High-Performance Consulting Firms 365
    (JAY W. LORSCH, HARVARD BUSINESS SCHOOL)

17 Knowledge Management in Consulting 379
    (MICHAEL A. MISCHE, UNIVERSITY OF SOUTHERN CALIFORNIA)

Introduction

Consultants are attracted to consulting careers because the work itself is interesting, and it often provides a career gateway and shortcut to securing a senior executive position upon leaving the consulting firm. Rarely are consultants interested in long-term careers in consulting or advancing to its senior executive ranks. Instead, they prefer to be out with clients, not staying in the office to hold meetings and manage expense reports. Moreover, they are quite aware that consultants are themselves quite difficult to manage because they typically have big egos and prefer autonomy over supervision. As a result, many consulting firms suffer from poor leadership, lack of coordination, and inability to change when confronted with competitive threats or strategic opportunities.

Ironically, today's highly competitive consulting environment requires that consulting firms be successfully led by capable senior management. Competition is fierce, clients are more demanding, and the structure of the industry is changing rapidly. The successful consulting firm leader will not only have to manage the firm's resources efficiently day to day but also inspire and motivate the staff to improve the firm's ability to compete. Without exceptional leadership, the firm is likely to falter and even fail.

This section examines the consulting firm from three different angles of effectiveness—Chapter 15 on managing growth stages of the firm, Chapter 16 on the characteristics of high performance firms, and Chapter 17 on creating and sharing knowledge within the firm—all three areas of concern are highly significant for mobilizing the intellectual capital of the firm and achieving greater competitive advantage in the marketplace.

Chapter 15, "Managing Growth Stages in Consulting Firms," focuses on how these firms cope with growth and why they either fail or succeed over their life cycle. The chapter presents four stages of growth, with each stage culminating in a major crisis that needs to be resolved by the firm's leadership before growth can be resumed. Each stage is different and requires a different management approach. Unfortunately, most consulting firms do not make it through all four stages of growth; instead, they bog down with disagreement among the senior partners, some of whom want to grow and others who do not. The chapter concludes with advice to senior partners about how they need to let go of past practices, even their own power, in order to facilitate growth of the firm.

Chapter 16, "High-Performance Consulting Firms," describes the "best practices" employed by highly successful consulting firms. The author builds on results from his research to offer evidence of common practices across high performing firms. These practices range from a shared strategic identity throughout the firm to the attraction and retention of consultant "stars." Also, the senior leadership challenge requires wearing three hats at once and equally well: those of producer, leader, and owner. In the end, if the firm is to be successful, strong alignment is required by the consulting firm across its strategy, goals, people, culture, governance, and leadership.

Chapter 17, "Knowledge Management in Consulting," explores the role of knowledge management consulting by addressing nine key questions. The chapter begins with a discussion of what knowledge is and how knowledge differs from data and information. Further, it discusses how consultants use knowledge, what management consulting knowledge is, and how knowledge can best be managed. Following this discussion the chapter focuses on how knowledge is created and gained by the consultant and how it is made available within the consulting firm. As a key in consulting is how knowledge is developed or captured for a specific assignment, this is then highlighted. The chapter ends by exploring how wisdom differs from knowledge, and what can be the potential future of knowledge.

15 Managing Growth Stages in Consulting Firms

Larry Greiner and James Malernee

From 1960 to 2000, the consulting industry experienced phenomenal growth, prompting many industry leaders and pundits to predict continued high rates of growth long into the future. The economic signs all seemed favorable; consulting firms were selling larger and larger contracts to clients; MBA recruits were receiving astronomical salaries and signing bonuses; and more and more firms were lining up to do IPOs with fast run-ups in market value.

Yet, as we all know with hindsight, this golden era of growth came to a rude and resounding slowdown, if not a complete halt for many firms, shortly after the start of the new millennium. Even as late as 2004, numerous firms in a stagnant economy were still struggling, trying to grow again but realizing that it may be more up to their management know-how and ingenuity than simply relying on the industry's coat tails.

The purpose of this chapter is to take a close look at how individual consulting firms cope with growth and either fail or succeed. While we all recognize that the industry's growth rate depends heavily on the general state of the economy, we are much less aware of how this growth takes place within individual consulting firms. It is common to think of a firm's growth as merely a performance outcome that is measured by revenues, profits, project size, and number of employees. Instead, as we shall point out in this chapter, growth is much more than a simple "outcome"; it is a deeper complex process that is continuously and privately at work inside each consulting firm. Furthermore, growth has to be managed and planned for on a daily basis; otherwise, regardless of the economy, a single firm can easily fall on hard times and become a tombstone in the already large graveyard of defunct consulting firms.

The consulting industry landscape is littered with the victims of bad growth management. While numerous reasons account for the success and failure of consulting firms, growth management issues have to be near the top of the list. Looking back just twenty years ago, who would have thought

> **Consulting Insights**
>
> **Case of Failed Growth**
>
> A notable case of failure occurred in 1997 for the once-promising strategy consulting firm Mitchell Madison Group (MMG), which in five years had expanded to fourteen offices around the world and 800 employees. Moreover, ex-McKinsey partners who presumably knew something about good management led it. The story of MMG's demise is extensively reported in the March 2001 issue of *Consulting*, but below is a telling quote from an ex-MMG partner about the numerous problems created by the firm's leadership and its obsession with growth:
>
>> Growth quickly became a divisive issue for the firm's board of directors, as well as for those partners who routinely asked the question: "Why not grow at a rate we can actually afford?" By early 1998, the push for growth had begun to take its toll on the firm in other ways. Distrust of the firm's compensation scheme had spread as more new partners were hurried into the firm using new perks and special arrangements. Moreover, as more partners were added to the payroll, a number of MMG's founding partners and directors sensed the board's powers decaying as well as its efficacy as a vehicle of governance.[1]

that Andersen Consulting, which was smaller than Arthur D. Little at the time, would today be one of the largest consulting firms in the world and renamed Accenture? Or that Arthur D. Little would enter bankruptcy? Or that in 2003, IBM's consulting arm, IBM Global Services, would be larger than its hardware business?

Growth Study

Given the difficulties experienced by so many firms in managing their growth, we decided a few years ago to begin a study to determine if professional services firms (PSFs) pass through discernable stages of growth. Our study examined a range of PSFs, including consulting, accounting, legal, advertising, and investment banking firms. Our interest in making this study grew out of Professor Greiner's earlier *Harvard Business Review* classic, "Evolution and Revolution as Organizations Grow,"[2] and Dr. Malernee's managerial background as cofounder and CEO of Cornerstone Research, a rapidly growing economic research consulting firm. Professor Greiner's earlier work had focused primarily on industrial firms, not professional services firms, which were only in their ascendancy at the time.

We will report here our findings on growth stages in consulting firms for the first time. During the course of our research, we performed an extensive examination of documents and articles written about many PSFs, including several consulting firms. We also conducted over 200 interviews with partners and staff from current firms and ones that had failed or been acquired. All of the current firms are well-established ones that have grown through their own wholly owned resources, full-time staff, and management; in other words, they were not franchises or networks of independent consultants, neither of which have grown to any substantial size. Our interviews covered each firm's history, the types of organization structure employed, major strategic decisions made, financial and marketing problems encountered, management systems and controls introduced, and changes in key leadership.[3]

Interestingly, our research results across all the PSFs appear strikingly similar, revealing clear discernable stages of growth. Of course, in this type of qualitative research with a relatively small sample, we caution that more research is needed. Readers of this chapter who work in consulting firms should match their own experience against our findings.

Growth Issues

Most consultants do not start or join a firm because they want to climb the firm's hierarchy to become CEO. Rather, their primary motivation is to practice consulting and perhaps eventually to become a partner, though usually they move on to executive positions. They often view participation in the consulting firm's management as a "necessary evil" that, in most instances, should be delegated to lesser-paid, "nonprofessional" administrators.

Unfortunately, these consulting professionals, when they eventually assume leadership positions in consulting firms, often fail in their attempts at managing the growth process. Only a few out of the thousands of start-up consulting firms actually become large, thriving organizations. The great majority of firms either fail or remain small "mom and pop" operations of five to fifteen employees. Even the few firms that grow very large frequently experience serious setbacks; for example, consider what happened to Arthur Andersen after the Enron scandal. Even the prestigious strategy consulting firm Bain and Co., in the early 1990s, faced the departure of top partners, followed by a business downturn. At the time, *Business Week* reported:

> Today Bain is the one that seems to need a consultant. The firm's workforce, about 1000 professionals and support staff is down 30 percent, thinned by two rounds of layoffs and by the defections of key

executives. "We were very good consultants, but not very good managers," says one executive.[4]

So why do leaders of consulting firms choose to grow their firms in the face of such difficulties? Clearly, one reason is to take advantage of the rising tide of a growing and expanding industry. Since 1983, the industry has grown from $3.5 billion to approximately $120 billion in revenues. Other reasons, all quite rational, include the need to broaden services in order to serve growing clients and to attract larger clients; to be able to take advantage of the leverage effect on profits by hiring junior professionals and billing them out at higher rates than their salary cost; and to reach a size where the firm can go public and secure growth capital, as well as shares to reward partners.

Growth Stages and Crises

Despite the advantages of growth, those consulting firms that launch themselves on a growth path are hardly assured of success. For the firm, growth creates significant strategic, marketing, and organizational challenges that have to be managed. Our research suggests that most surviving firms grow through a life cycle of four distinct stages, with each stage requiring a different strategic approach to its marketplace and a unique set of management practices.[5] In addition, each stage is followed by a crisis that needs to be resolved for the firm to advance into the next stage of growth. Below are the four stages and crises identified in our study, which are also depicted graphically in Exhibit 15.1.

- *Stage I: Exploring* the Market for Growth Opportunities
  Crisis: Need to Agree on Growth Vision and Targeted Market Segment
- *Stage II: Focusing* on a Specialized Market Niche
  Crisis: Need to Broaden Services and Develop Staff Capabilities
- *Stage III: Diversifying* into Multiple Offices and Related Services
  Crisis: Need for Common Approach to Clients and Sharing of Ownership
- *Stage IV: Institutionalizing* into a One-Firm Firm
  Crisis: Need to Enter New Domains and Increase Organizational Flexibility

Role of Crises

A consulting firm's passage through the four stages is not automatic; instead, toward the end of each stage, it encounters a major crisis that must be resolved for the firm to move forward. Few firms survive all the way through the four stages; instead, most do not grow beyond the first stage; others manage to grow through Stage II but then are sold or split-up when they fall victim to conflict among the partners.

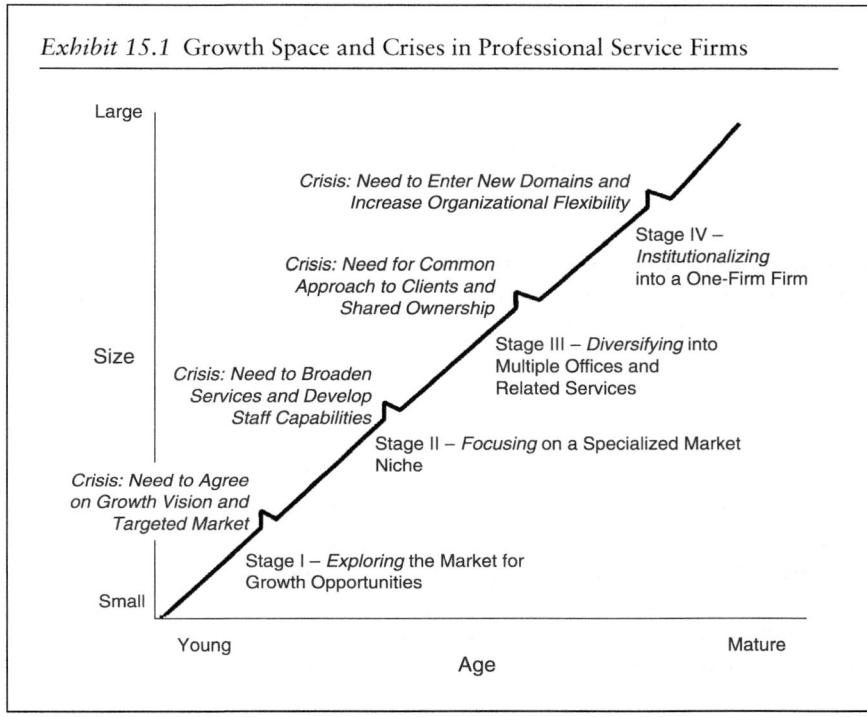

Exhibit 15.1 Growth Space and Crises in Professional Service Firms

The impetus for a crisis can be internal when one of the partners advocates a new growth path and the others disagree or external when there are signs of falling behind major competition. Crises can be short if a solution is found quickly or prolonged by continuous partner disagreement, thereby stopping growth and perhaps causing the sale of the firm.

The onslaught of a crisis, however, appears necessary to provoke the partners into action and change. Crises seem inevitable because resistance often arises when partners and employees are confronted with the necessity to introduce new practices required to move to the next stage. Reluctant partners and employees frequently oppose change because they are attached to past practices that they see as the source of success. So it is difficult for them to understand why these once successful practices cannot continue. They hang on to old habits and refuse to let go. Sometimes the crisis is mild if the partners have agreed upon and prepared a solution much earlier, or it can be severe if the partners continue to be in strong disagreement.

Management Practices

Exhibit 15.2 summarizes the different management practices that are characteristic of each stage in the growth life cycle. These practices are described in detail in the remainder of this chapter. They provide a "roadmap" for leaders of consulting firms and also for those who are currently working for or may aspire to work for a consulting firm, so they can understand better what lies ahead.

While the stages presented here are shown with distinct boundaries so as to illustrate more clearly their sequence and effects, in actual practice each stage and crisis is likely to overlap as new management practices are introduced and old ones are abandoned. The average length of a growth stage for firms in our study was approximately seven years, ranging between four and ten years, with the later stages lasting longer than the earlier stages. The crises lasted from a few months to one year, although the longer crises usually ended in the sale of a firm or its continued decline.

Stage I: Exploring the Market for Growth Opportunities

The origin of a new consulting firm typically begins when an experienced professional "hangs out his or her shingle," often after leaving the security of a larger firm. This entrepreneurial step is frequently taken in collaboration with one or two other partners who are colleagues from their former firm. They agree to share ownership, pool their efforts, and hope that revenues will cover modest draws and limited office expenses. (Throughout the remainder of this chapter, we will use the term "partner" to refer to the leading owners of a firm, even though the legal form of ownership may be either a partnership or a corporation.)

The founding partners typically go through an initial period of testing both the market and each other. Each partner attempts to attract clients who are receptive to his or her particular expertise. For example, one partner may pursue clients interested in compensation plans, while another may seek clients with production problems. It is unclear to the partners as to which specific service will succeed in the market, what types of clients will be attracted, or which partners may be more adept at selling. Here is how one partner described his firm's "shotgun" approach to the market during its start-up stage:

> Potential clients would ask us, "What do you do?" and we would say "What do you want?" We did all kinds of projects. We did business brokering . . . we did sales training . . . you name it.

Also confronting the partners is the difficult management challenge of learning to work together in making decisions. They gradually discover whether they share the same ideas on how the firm should be run, if their commitment to the venture is similarly high, and if their work styles are complementary. With little formal organization structure, the partners meet

Exhibit 15.2 Life-Cycle Model and Management Practices

	Stage I—Exploring	Stage II—Focusing
Strategy	Each partner sells his/her individual expertise to a diverse range of clients. Search for clients and market feedback.	Focus on single market niche, selling specialization to a targeted group of clients or industry.
Organization Structure	Centered around founders, their personalities, values, and practices.	Project team formed for each client. Partners act as project leaders, sharing junior professionals among them.
Systems and Rewards	Training is on the job; no policies. Founders split profits evenly. Firm is staffed with principals only and a few clerical employees. Minimal systems needed. Little development of people.	Office/Administrative Manager installed. Minimal training. Founders split profits and pay bonuses to select juniors—even one or two might be made junior partners.
Management Style	Authoritative but informal. Deference to founders' decisions.	Founders divide roles. One founder specializes in internal management, while others develop business.
Decision Process	Consensus among partners, but sometimes dominated by one founder with most clients.	Reliance on consensus among partners, after perhaps checking for input from top juniors.
Culture	Informal, family-like atmosphere, individualistic, and entrepreneurial.	Task oriented. Adherence to founders' values and their methodologies.
Sources of Conflict	Founders can easily have different visions of the firm. Will this venture work? Do we want to grow the firm or stay small? Should we focus on a particular market or take a more individualistic approach?	Should we expand services to meet client needs or continue to focus on our core competency? Some senior partners advocate expansion, while others resist diversification.
Strategy	Expansion into new offices and closely related practice areas, sometimes through acquisition. Begin international expansion.	Marketing the firm's image and cross-selling the firm's reputation in various areas of its expertise. More uniform services to clients. Major acquisitions. Strong overseas presence.

(*Continued*)

Exhibit 15.2 (Continued)

	Stage III—Diversifying	Stage IV—Institutionalizing
Organization Structure	Decentralized profit centers led by younger managers. Executive committee of senior partners—in addition, perhaps larger advisory council of office and practice managers.	Matrix structure with partners appointed to lead practice areas and regions/offices. Full-time Managing Director, often elected, manages the administrative side of the business.
Systems and Rewards	More complex information systems for reporting on each office and service. Policies codified and written. Business plans begin to appear. Bonuses for unit performance, especially to head of each sub-unit.	Training programs formalized to teach the "firm approach." Strategic plans are routinely drafted. Career tracks and performance evaluation become more standardized. Accounting, HR, and MIS formalized as staff functions. Rewards for both sub-unit and corporate performance. Broader ownership.
Management Style	Founders delegate increased responsibility for daily operations to leaders of offices and practice areas.	Collaborative management style in teams and committees.
Decision Process	Operating decisions made at sub-unit level. Promotion and policy decisions continue to be made by founding partners.	Founders step aside. New leaders take over. Strategy and capital decisions made at corporate headquarters.
Culture	Diverse units with each of the practices centering on values of their respective leaders.	Firm's values extol its history and reputation. Employees hired to fit a common profile that complements the culture. The culture becomes cohesive and monolithic.
Sources of Conflict	Rivalry between satellite offices and the head office. How do we prevent fragmentation? What should be the equity stake of key business developers in relation to the founders? Should we build this organization into an institution?	Are we becoming too depersonalized? Are we becoming bureaucratic? Is the firm becoming insulated from the market? How do we create innovation and more growth?

informally to decide various issues by consensus, whether it be the design of a brochure or the purchase of a computer.

In the firm's quest for economic survival, the partners set their billing rates lower than rates charged by their larger competitors. Overhead expenses are restricted to spartan offices and contracted services. The partners' wages are based on a minimal but livable salary, which usually remains fixed for the first year unless there are negative interim results. At the end of the year, profits are divided among the partners or reinvested in the firm. Growth will require more money going to reinvestment, and this will provide a test of partner commitment to further growth.

Most start-up firms never grow beyond this entrepreneurial stage. Instead, their partners choose to remain small, with their partners using the firm as an efficient overhead shelter while they go about their individual marketing efforts. They each manage to sell enough business to support themselves and make a contribution to overhead. Occasionally, one partner will obtain a project large enough to include another partner or assistant. They respond to workload problems by hiring a secretary and employing occasional subcontractors.

Those few firms that grow successfully beyond this start-up stage do so only after discovering a promising market niche for a particular service and only after all the partners agree to focus their energies on pursuing this specialized niche.

First Major Crisis: *Need to Agree on Growth Vision and Targeted Market Segment*

When a promising and profitable niche becomes evident, the founders must make a strategic choice. Do they continue as before with each partner pursuing his/her separate specialization and personal set of clients, or do they collectively focus their energies and resources on the more promising specialization that one or two of them have found while exploring the market?

At this point, open communication among the partners is essential to examining what each one wants the firm to become and in determining what each is prepared to contribute. They need to ask themselves: Is the promising specialized market niche large enough to support our further growth if we all agree to focus on it? Do all of us want the firm to grow larger? If so, how willing are we to let go of what we have been doing to focus on one major service (e.g., human resources consulting to financial services industry)? How should we work together? What roles should each of us play? Who will look out for administration? Who will sell business? Who will run projects? How many junior people should we hire, and what should be their skills?

As the partners address these difficult questions, underlying differences often emerge among them. They are often surprised to learn that they are not all in full agreement on whether to grow further or on what to specialize, as evident in this example from a small consulting firm:

> We didn't realize that there were problems because we all thought we were talking about the same thing. And then, a year later, it was very clear to me that our motives and goals were very different. One partner wanted to be the single person in-charge, while the other two wanted to run it by committee.

Consequently, many firms flounder and break up at this point, including the small consulting firm just mentioned, as its demise is recalled by one of its ex-partners:

> Robert began to feel like he was putting a lot more effort and revenues into the firm than the others. He knew there was a good market for his specialty, but he began to question our ability to support him, so he left. We then folded.

Those few firms whose partners do finally reach agreement and choose to grow larger will typically implement a highly focused strategy, which includes a new and very different set of management practices from the first stage.

Stage II: Focusing on a Specialized Market Niche

Stage II begins when the partners decide to join together in selling one unique service to a focal set of clients. They no longer go their separate ways to sell only their individual talents to a diverse list of clients. Thus, for example, a consulting firm in Stage II might decide to sell only training programs in information systems to the middle market in the retail industry, because this market opportunity was discovered to be most promising during Stage I. The CEO of a now large management consulting firm reflects back on how he and his partners made this strategic choice:

> We began by doing an array of projects, anything the client would buy. And then we came to a point where we had to decide if we were going to go anywhere, we needed to define some things. So the first big decision was: Who are we, what is our competence, and what should we become? We decided we would be the productivity people, and we honed in on the real estate industry. We attacked it through making speeches, writing articles, and joining trade associations. One of our partners left, and we had to recruit new people who knew more about real estate.

Having chosen to specialize, the firm also faces a challenge in developing a core competency in its area of expertise. The firm's staff and internal practices must be reoriented toward improving its capability to deliver the chosen specialization. To do so, the partners decide to hire and train several junior associates. This step allows the firm to take on larger projects with lower priced staff, thereby enhancing the economic leverage of the firm and freeing partners from the vicious "do-sell" cycle. Previously, partners felt compelled either to work on projects at the expense of developing new clients or to take time off to sell new business and thereby cause delays in project completion. Now they act more efficiently by assigning less expensive, junior employees to work on existing projects while they devote more time to developing new business.[6]

In moving ahead, it is necessary to introduce a new project-type organizational structure and more formal procedures to handle the growing client load and expanded workforce. Each partner now acts as a project leader while sharing junior professionals across projects. The partners also divide their roles; one partner handles administration, while the others concentrate on selling. Basic accounting and computer systems are installed for processing invoices, project costs, and payroll. An increased administrative load eventually prompts the partners to hire a full-time office manager. Additional clerical staff are added under the office manager for preparing proposals, typing reports, and maintaining the firm's information system.

Decision making continues to reside with the founding partners who rely on achieving consensus among them before acting. They occasionally check with younger associates for their input on major decisions, but they still retain sole responsibility for hiring, assigning, evaluating, and compensating all employees. At the end of the year, the partners allocate bonuses among themselves and to a few high performers in the staff.

Success in Stage II gradually sows the seeds for the firm's second major crisis involving the need to serve increased client demands and to reach out to new markets as a further stimulus to growth. Simply remaining a one-product company in one location is insufficient to fuel continued growth.

Second Major Crisis: *Need to Broaden Services and Develop Staff Capabilities*

This crisis often begins when the firm's larger clients ask to be served in new ways, either with additional services or in new locations. They may even threaten to take their business elsewhere if the firm does not respond. Some clients request services not currently being performed by the consulting firm, such as a client asking for training programs once the consulting firm has installed a new information system. Still others may want the same service delivered to their operations in other locales. This crisis often becomes severe because the firm does not possess the necessary range of services in-house for expansion, nor does it have a trained staff able to deliver new services or possessing the willingness to move to a new office.

In order to grow, the partners need to decide if they want to open a new office or if they want to add a new service or both. To do so, they must assess their internal capabilities, since, during Stage II, the large majority of staff has specialized on delivering a single type of service out of one location. This decision by the partners includes not only assessing the skills of the staff to provide a new service but determining if any partners are willing to move and open a new office.

The client mix of the firm has likely changed during Stage II as some of the firm's clients have grown larger and become more sophisticated in their demands. As a result, the firm's staff requires more advanced skills to perform larger and more complex projects. Frequently in short supply are competent managers and technically qualified staff.

So the central issue becomes one of not only how to broaden the services offerings but also to build capable staff. The partners' awareness for this need is usually late in coming. It typically happens when they find that they can't do everything themselves, which has included long hours of selling, managing, and performing projects. They have been so busy and task focused that they have neglected the developmental needs of their staff.

As a result, the partners find themselves in a difficult situation—to live with and retrain the current staff or go outside for new talent and run the risk of alienating the original staff. The original staff is likely not up to standard in handling newer, more complex types of clients. They were hired earlier for their willingness to assist the partners with minor assignments and to be technically focused. Rarely has any training been given to them; they have learned on the job. Unfortunately, not many of the staff know how to sell or manage projects, nor are they willing to relocate to a new office.

The partners must choose among three strategic alternatives: 1) remain the same and probably stop growth in their current location; or 2) continue to grow by diversifying the line of services while continuing to operate out of the same office; or 3) grow through opening new offices and delivering the same existing service. They worry that services diversification, even in the same locale, may dilute the firm's specialized focus and undermine its established efficiencies and competencies. On the other hand, the choice of opening new offices raises the troubling issue of staffing, especially in deciding which partner will have to uproot and move.

Some firms respond to this crisis by choosing the first alternative of remaining at their current size level in the same place, hoping that the future market for their existing specialized service is large enough to replace the loss of clients requiring broader services or the same service in other locales. Still other firms experience severe conflict, as their partners are unable to reconcile their differences about growth versus nongrowth, or to open new offices or to add new services, prompting some partners to depart or even forcing the sale of the firm. The partners become the critical stumbling block because none of them want to move, nor do they want to stop performing their current speciality and launch into a new one.

For those few remaining firms that choose to grow larger and take on the risk of diversifying into new practice areas or opening new offices, the next step requires another major shift in the firm's strategy and organization structure.

Stage III: Diversifying into Multiple Offices and Related Services

Most Stage III firms typically choose first to open additional offices for their existing service instead of diversifying into new product lines. Stage III firms tend to pursue the new office route and stick with their current specialty service because it is their core competence. The partners feel more comfortable and confident in being able to pull off this type of expansion. To begin an entirely new service area threatens the skills of the current staff and the existing culture. It is also easier for them to staff the new offices with current personnel than add a new service. But even this decision proves difficult because one of the partners will most likely have to move since they don't trust an unknown to run another office.

Only a very few consulting firms try to open both new offices and add services at the same time, because they risk diluting resources and overextending their staff. This step often fails as it creates significant management problems for senior partners who try to coordinate multiple services across multiple offices, to say nothing for finding qualified staff for both offices and practices. It is a challenge that most founding partners are not up to at this point. A better and more workable strategy is to proceed sequentially—opening an office or two and then gradually expanding services one at a time. This is the process we found in the more successful growth firms.

The partners are likely to decide to broaden the firm's line of services only after opening a few offices delivering their original service as a starting point. However, these firms cannot effectively provide all services that every client may desire, so most firms will select only services that are closer to their core competency. For example, we observed an information systems consulting firm that decided to add hardware selection and training programs to its existing systems design service, while avoiding something as diverse as strategic planning. Similarly, the location of new offices is usually determined by where the firm's major clients are located and where senior managers are willing to live. One mid-size IT consulting firm, Clarkston Consulting, has four established offices but allows its consultants to live in other cities while focusing on clients in three industries—life sciences, manufacturing, and high technology.

As the firm grows and becomes financially stronger, it may also begin to make acquisitions of smaller firms as a way of adding related services and additional offices. Later in Stage III, a few of these firms will begin to expand globally, usually through acquisitions. Right Management Consultants, a rapidly expanding human resources and outplacement consulting firm, has actively pursued this policy around the world, adding more than five international acquisitions a year in recent years. However, acquisitions present a further challenge to acquirers who must integrate new partners and diverse cultures. The preferred merger integration process in successful firms is to absorb the acquiree completely into the acquirer's systems and practices and to buy out any partners who do not seem to fit.

All senior employees at the management level in Stage III firms are expected to specialize, either by office or practice area. Younger members remain specialized but are usually shared across offices on larger projects. Training programs are introduced to develop junior staff members faster than might occur on the job. In addition, it often proves necessary to recruit experienced "lateral hires" from competitor firms, although this poses a risk because "outsiders" may not share the firm's values and goals. These hires are carefully screened for compatibility.

To support diversification, a decentralized organization structure is introduced to manage the greatly broadened scope of offices and services, as well as to open up career opportunities. The new offices become relatively self-contained sub-units managed by younger, high-potential employees desiring more responsibility. They act as profit center managers, accountable for obtaining new clients, managing their sub-units efficiently, and developing their unit's employees.[7]

In the firm's new decentralized structure, formal management systems are implemented to control and reward performance in each profit center. The various offices and service areas are each expected to develop a budget and profit plan, and the firm's information system is redesigned to record each unit's performance results. The reward system is changed to provide substantial incentive bonuses for the heads of each practice area and office. Eligibility for bonuses is gradually extended to the entire professional group. A senior committee is established at the firm's headquarters to evaluate performance and make compensation recommendations.

The managing partner of a large international consulting firm describes below how, during Stage III, he introduced a new budgeting system to fit with his firm's recently decentralized structure and new practice areas:

> We had formalized the practice areas but we still had a top-down planning and control system. I transformed revenue setting to a bottom-up method. Practice leaders would then have to think about how much business they are going to generate from existing and new clients. The process forced people to quantify what had previously been implicit in top-down annual goals.

However, in most Stage III firms, the partners only allow the younger leaders to make operating decisions at their sub-unit levels, excluding them from key firm-wide decisions about promotion, compensation, and expansion. Therein lies the next major crisis. The firm's diversification and decentralization efforts in Stage III eventually pose a major challenge for reuniting and coordinating the firm as "one firm" in its next growth stage.

Third Major Crisis: *Need for Common Approach to Clients and Sharing of Ownership*

Signs of this crisis begin to appear in competitive rivalries and parochialism among the decentralized sub-units spawned during Stage III. Local offices have been conditioned by the firm's reward and control system to behave separately as profit centers—to look out more for themselves than the firm as a whole. As a result, lack of cooperation between offices and practice areas eventually makes it difficult to cross-sell different services and to interchange personnel for staffing large projects. Increasingly, the various sub-units begin to ignore and resist directives from headquarters. The firm starts to fragment into a loosely disjointed organization of fiefdoms.

Large clients also begin to complain about the firm's uncoordinated practices across offices. They want assurance that the same level of service will be delivered consistently across all the client's operations domestically and world-wide. Unfortunately, this is difficult to achieve since each office and practice area have developed different cultures guided by leadership personalities who want to remain in control of their units. Some units were acquired and not fully absorbed and, therefore, retain their pre-acquisition practices.

A closely related challenge also involves the firm's junior leaders, who now expect to share in a "piece of the action" with the founding partners. These young leaders are the new "rainmakers" for the firm, having successfully managed new offices and practice areas, secured additional clients, and contributed significantly to profit growth. Yet they feel under-rewarded and excluded by the senior partners from making firm-wide strategic and personnel decisions. They become less willing to cooperate despite pleas for commonality from the "in-group" of senior partners. They want to be better rewarded with ownership and greater power for decisions affecting the firm as a whole. In their frustration with senior management, some junior partners decide to leave, accepting attractive offers from competitors and clients; still others split off to form their own firms. Our interviews revealed one such rebellion among junior partners, as recounted to us by one of its co-conspirators:

> A colleague of mine wanted a greater amount of equity, compensation, and recognition for his business development efforts. We agreed with

him, so he tried to orchestrate the notion of a name change for the firm, and then a change in the system where he would get rewarded by a higher annual bonus and more point allocations. This was met by enormous resentment from the older partners. So we tried to arrange a spin-off of a select group of consulting colleagues . . . and that caused the old partners to give-in.

This Stage III crisis poses a major dilemma for the founding partners—either they opt for growth through taking on more coordination responsibility to build a common approach toward clients, as well as sharing ownership and power with new leaders, or they choose to stop growth and retain exclusive control for themselves. These twin issues of coordination and ownership are closely related because the firm's senior leadership, without support from the younger leaders, lacks sufficient power to reunite the firm and coordinate its resources. Those firms that fail to come up with a solution are often sold to an acquiring firm as the original partners decide to cash in their equity. Still other firms may begin to decline as their partners stubbornly resist change, even as junior leaders depart with established clients.

The remaining firms, whose founders retain a vision of growth, choose to make the difficult transition to Stage IV. This effort to share and reunite the firm is not an easy decision for the founding partners to make. In deciding to share senior leadership and ownership, the founding partners must dilute their equity without substantial, monetary incentive to do so. They also realize that their retirement will likely occur before earning back sufficient income to offset their lost equity and that they will need to give up power and step back into the shadows as new senior leadership takes over.

Stage IV: Institutionalizing into a One-Firm Firm

To bring the firm together, the senior partners frequently turn to one of the younger, more respected leaders now running a practice area or an office, and they ask him or her to become the firm's new managing partner. This move, which we observed in several firms, helps to win over the younger leaders, who then join as a team in unifying the firm. The new senior "owner" managers of the firm move rapidly to orchestrate a transition from Stage III's loose confederation of offices and practices to a strong, highly coordinated entity with a worldwide reputation. They become the firm's senior management as the founders gradually step aside and retire. The dominant working styles of the new leaders are ones of collaboration and teamwork as they promote unity throughout the firm. Together, they subscribe to a "professional" and corporate form of management.

In Stage IV, the primary challenge is to pull the firm back together through uniting decentralized units and establishing a strong institutional image in the marketplace. These changes are demonstrated not just through external advertising but also by establishing consistent internal practices to create a "one-firm firm" with delivery of uniform services around the globe. The marketing emphasis shifts to promote the name and reputation of the firm itself, not the names and capabilities of individual partners or offices, as was the case in Stage III. The firm becomes a "brand name" recognizable worldwide; McKinsey is an outstanding example.

While some firms in prior stages may have launched marketing and advertising campaigns to promote themselves, Stage IV firms emphasize a deeper process of institutionalization to establish a strong "firm identity," including a core set of values and practices that unify employees under a common culture and delivery approach to clients. This new identity becomes pervasive throughout the firm, ranging from the types of people recruited, to training programs, and to consistent approaches toward clients. Here we see the emergence of the "Andersen Way" or the "Bainies."

Strategically, these large firms usually move to differentiate themselves from other firms by staking out a clear domain among one of five broad types of management consulting: IT, strategy and organization, marketing, operations, or human resources, which are then supplied to a wide variety of industries. Rarely do they become known as superior in more than one domain, though they may offer services in these other domains. Under its chosen domain, the firm also builds a range of closely related sub-services and delivers them in a uniform way wherever a client's operations may be located. Thus, a firm in the IT domain delivers systems design, hardware and software selection, training, and outsourcing services.

At this point in their evolution, most Stage IV firms have established themselves globally with offices in many countries. They assure large international clients that they can deliver the same service with the same quality worldwide. More acquisitions are made, including even mega-mergers, such as occurred between Cap Gemini and Ernst & Young. These mergers help to provide global scale, acquire a larger client base, weed out underperforming partners, and close redundant offices.

The organization is reshaped from its Stage III decentralized profit centers into a highly coordinated global matrix based on geography (e.g., North America, Europe, and Asia) and practice/industry areas (e.g., change management and financial services). Numerous offices are grouped under regional managers whose responsibility is to coordinate projects and personnel across local offices to assure a more uniform level of service. They are also likely to appoint regional and global practice leaders, especially for industries, who coordinate and develop resources for their special focus.

Sophisticated management systems are introduced to manage this complex matrix as well as to ensure consistent treatment of clients. Extensive employee training becomes essential for educating all consultants in the firm's preferred "approach" to serving clients, including Web-based virtual training and centralized face-to-face training. One such example is Accenture's central training facility in St. Charles, Illinois, which was described as follows to us by one Accenture partner:

> We have a centralized training facility—a university type campus for many more than 1,000 participants—and we use it to teach everyone our methods and approaches to clients. The partners do much of the teaching, and they communicate our values along with technical skills. Everyone is expected to practice the same approach worldwide.

Increased emphasis is given by the firm's senior management to strategic planning so as to allocate firm-wide resources toward the best opportunities and priorities. To coordinate and review strategic plans, an executive council of senior partners from offices and lines of service is appointed or elected. Various communication forums, such as annual partners' meetings and newsletters, are established to keep employees well informed. At headquarters, new staff groups are created in Human Resources, Information Technology, Marketing, and Accounting to serve the line operating units and promote uniform practices.

The human resources system is redesigned to encourage rapid career advancement for those individuals who not only perform at a high level but also subscribe to the firm's values and standardized approach toward clients. Clear and uniform policies are established for employee selection, promotion, performance evaluation, and ethical conduct. The recruitment of consultants is conducted worldwide. Year-end rewards are based on a combination of total firm, sub-unit, and individual performances. The array of awards includes cash bonuses and shares, along with promotion to partner and officer status. Planned turnover is used to weed out low performers and those who deviate from the firm's prescribed norms and standards.

In Stage IV, the sheer size of the firm and the magnitude of its overhead expenses cause it to pursue large projects with high fees and delivered to a limited range of global clients and government agencies. On the downside, this approach results in lost middle-market opportunities, leaving a niche to be filled by smaller regional firms. The firm's market orientation also suffers from having solidified its reputation within a particular consulting domain (e.g., IT consulting); however, this tends to limit the firm in making forays into other domains (e.g., strategy and organization consulting). Organizationally, the one-firm firm approach begins to create a great deal of conformity in consultant behavior as they adhere to the firm's preferred way of doing things.

Fourth Major Crisis: *Need to Enter New Domains and Increase Organizational Flexibility*

The uniformity of the one-firm firm market orientation in Stage IV eventually loses much of its competitive edge because it limits the range of services and restricts flexibility toward clients. The firm's monolithic organization and standardized approach to very large clients begins to inhibit the tailoring of proposals to fit unique client needs. Clients with worldwide operations also need specialized localization assistance. Furthermore, and likely most important, not all clients want a standardized consulting approach where they feel shoehorned into someone else's ill-fitting shoes. These clients have learned that to compete they need to be different from their competitors, not the same.

Another problem involves market limitations caused by the boundaries of the market domain that the firm has established for itself in Stage IV. In order to compete, the largest firms have stayed mainly within their market domains. Thus, many IT firms like KPMG (now BearingPoint) have created themselves as largely IT firms. Or the general management firms like McKinsey and Bain have mainly stayed within the strategy and organization domain.

This is not to say that large consulting firms haven't tried venturing out from their stated domains, but the evidence is that they have not been particularly successful in doing so. Even in these forays, the IT-oriented firms, for example, tend to launch strategy practices with an IT orientation. Clients also see the firm only for its main domain orientation and, therefore, don't consider them as qualified in other domains. Simply trying to become a one-firm firm within one particular domain has been an immense challenge in Stage IV, but becoming successful at it has also created a firm with a limited range of market breadth.

A large overhead structure has also been built up during Stage IV because of the firm's attempts to market and advertise its one-firm firm image as well as to invest in expensive marketing directed at specific clients. Some firms hire a sales force that begins to replace consultants as the principal marketing arm. An expensive office structure has also been created around the world, including complex control and administrative systems, and consultants' salaries have crept up in order to attract and retain a large workforce, numbering at this point in the thousands.

All of this means that fees to clients are high, causing some purchasing resistance, especially during down economic times. Marketplace and economic difficulties are also symptomatic of an even deeper problem in the firm's homogeneous culture. An organizational form of "hardening of the arteries" begins to set in to undermine the firm's effectiveness in the marketplace. A uniform "type" of partner has been developed and molded to fit the firm's universal values; this person is typically one who is loyal and hardworking but probably lacking in creativity and entrepreneurial instinct.

And at lower levels, newly recruited, bright, young professionals without a lengthy socialization process behind them begin to feel depersonalized in the sameness of a culture where everyone is expected to behave as one. Many of these employees will stay only long enough to enhance their resumes before making a career jump.

Solutions to this crisis require exploring uncharted waters that are not clear for even the largest consulting firms as they grapple with the relative clumsiness of their large size, overhead costs, distant global reach, and resistant cultures. It remains for these large firms to reinvent themselves to enter a fifth stage. Clearly, they need to reduce their overhead costs, but more important is a need to restore greater flexibility in both their internal practices and their approaches toward clients. But that is not easy.

Making radical changes is difficult because private consulting firms and even public ones typically elect (or express strong sentiments from below) their Managing Partners (CEOs), but they are unlikely to be replaced unless the firm's profits are in serious decline. Even then, hundreds of partners may not vote for or support a reform candidate who might well replace them tomorrow in a radical shakeup. For example, the CEO of Bain & Co., when speaking of the challenges facing McKinsey, said, "It's an open question as to what extent such large, complex multi-country institutions will be able to retain their partnership principles and operate efficiently."[8]

Fifth Stage and Resulting Crisis?

Only the very largest consulting firms are beginning to deal with a possible fifth stage. Their efforts will define it for researchers to write about later. Different routes are currently being pursued: One is to make the large firm feel and act smaller; another is to enter new domains of consulting through acquisitions, including even nonconsulting services; and a third is to create R&D units and separate start-up ventures—and perhaps all three.

The "small is beautiful" approach was related to us by the CEO of a $2 billion consulting firm:

> We used to grow offices up to eighty or ninety people, but then they would always fall back to about sixty. And so now we make sure that whenever they get too big, we split them apart.

This spin-off approach is similar to the successful strategy used by the pharmaceutical giant Johnson & Johnson, which has created over 190 separate companies with different names, many from internal spin-offs. J&J's various company general managers are rewarded for creating new companies and spinning them off as freestanding subsidiaries. Other large consulting firms are now pursuing spin-offs and even new venture strategies with start-ups, R&D incubators and acquisitions, some of which include Booz Allen's Aestix, CGE&Ys Bios Group and Net-Strike, Hewitt Associate's Sageo, and EDS's Ebreviate.

Another approach is for large firms to use major acquisitions and alliances to reposition themselves outside their established Stage IV domains. For example, one strategy consulting firm in our study, after entering into an alliance with an operations-oriented consulting firm, decided with its new partner to be acquired by a larger information systems software firm. Another example is Mercer Consulting, originally a human resources firm, which has acquired Delta Consulting, a strategy and organization consulting firm, and others.

Our prediction is that the next growth stage will likely involve further consolidation, resulting from major acquisitions and alliances, as key players seek greater scale and diversity of services along the value chain. It seems clear that these firms cannot reach their growth objectives solely through internal reliance on their own capabilities. For example, IT-oriented firms have recently sought growth through adding non-consulting services like outsourcing and software alliances. However, even these large consulting firms pale in their available capital resources for making acquisitions when compared to the large hardware firms, namely, IBM and HP. We may also see the software giants Microsoft and Cisco move to acquire a large IT consulting firm like Deloitte Consulting. The big IT consulting firms themselves may attempt to acquire a strategy consulting firm like Monitor or specialized software firms like SAP and PeopleSoft.

So this last stage may see current firms being absorbed into a few big mega-holding firms composed of several firms ranging from consulting services to nonconsulting enterprises—all positioned somewhere along the value chain. We may finally arrive at the long ago dream of "one-stop-shopping." But that has its own problems that will no doubt emerge.

Today's smaller firms that are still located back in earlier growth stages should continue to prosper. The giants are not likely to compete directly against them because of the relatively small size of projects involved. However, as these small firms become larger, they will become ripe acquisition targets. Their challenge is to prepare for this eventuality by managing effectively through their earlier stages and related growth issues.

Developmental Leadership

Developmental leadership depends on a firm's partners being willing to change within themselves if they are also to change their firm. They must possess strong leadership qualities of anticipation, confrontation, and choice. We see the growth of a firm as inseparable from the personal growth of its leadership. Each phase in a firm's life cycle requires key leaders to create a new strategic vision and risk their positions of power and ownership. These partners must continually reevaluate old practices in light of their evolving competitive environment and accept the challenge of introducing new practices and behaviors. Through farsighted acts of leadership and personal change, the firm itself is transformed.

Developmental Perspective

Leaders of firms, if they are to grow their firms effectively, must learn to manage from a developmental perspective. Too often they are quick to blame their firm's problems on market forces, employee mistakes, and bad luck. But today's problems frequently have roots in yesterday's management practices, while the solutions lay hidden in current tensions caused by the pull of the future and the hold of the past; for example, a young partner may want to open a new office but the senior partners prefer to stay put in their current location.

An irony difficult for many firm leaders to understand is that previously successful practices eventually serve to undermine the firm and restrict its growth. Each of the growth stages contains a paradox where the past solution becomes the future problem. For example, Stage I's emphasis on "exploring the market" allows each partner to have a key role and to aid in testing for various market opportunities; however, it also inhibits focused effort and the necessary channeling of resources essential to Stage II. Or there is the paradox of Stage III where we see a shift to diversification that greatly enhances growth but eventually creates a fragmented firm giving poor service to large clients.

In every firm, its leaders need to understand what stage they are in during its growth life cycle. If they do, then they can anticipate better what lies ahead and then prepare for the upcoming crisis and the new management demands of the next stage. For example, in Stage I, it is important for all the partners to understand early that if they "stumble" upon a strong growth market in one of their expertises they may well have to focus on that area if they want to grow, or they will have to opt out of the growth race. Also, during Stage II's intense specialization, the partners need to begin developing future managers who can lead offices and new practices in Stage III. And in the later stages, the senior partners must begin to share ownership with the younger leaders if the firm is to outlive the senior partners' retirements and departures. In any of these instances, the crisis is likely to become severe if the leaders wait too long to take action.

Stopping Growth

Each firm and its leadership must continuously confront the basic underlying strategic choice facing all firms—whether to grow or not. Growth is neither automatic nor assured, nor is it an absolute necessity. However, stopping growth becomes more difficult as the firm develops into its later stages. Getting off the growth path is easier when the firm is small and only the partners' ambitions are at stake. But, as the firm grows larger, a decision to stop growth, or even slow it down, runs the risk of causing high turnover from disappointed employees or the loss of major clients. Also, if the firm has gone public with an IPO, it will have to contend with investors and analysts constantly pressing for improved performance and further growth.

In wanting to stay small, the partners must guard against becoming complacent, which can cause employees to leave or the loss of proposals to more alert competition. They still must find other ways to grow, not in size and geography, but perhaps in the kinds of projects undertaken. One new source of stimulation might be forming a local alliance with other small consulting firms that specialize in different practice areas; that way, they can make referrals to each other and sponsor joint training or even share overhead. Another possibility is to use contract consultants to bid on and secure larger projects than could be undertaken by a small permanent staff, who are usually eager to work with others on larger projects. A number of independent consultants work in major cities. A third possibility is to manage the consulting firm differently, sharing jobs and rotating employees more frequently. It might also grow in profits, but not in employees, by taking on higher margin projects.

Letting Go

Deciding to grow larger implies for many partners a loss of power and control, which is often difficult for them to give up. As a result, many firms become paralyzed by inaction or internal conflict among the partners.

The psychological phenomenon of "letting go" is one of the hardest challenges that any partner will face during his/her professional career. Moving from one stage to another requires one or more partners to let go of something that is highly cherished, whether that be giving up attachment to running a practice area or moving to another city to open a new office, or withdrawing from full-time consulting to assume a top-level administrative job in the firm.

At some point, all the founding partners will eventually leave the firm. Some will choose to depart midstream because they don't like what lies ahead. Other partners will choose to stay because they are more flexible and intrigued by the challenge of moving on and growing with the firm. Finally, all the original partners must eventually depart for retirement, leaving the firm in the hands of the new leaders whom they have personally developed and mentored as their successors, thereby assuring the firm's growth into the future.

Notes

1 *Consulting Magazine* (March 2001).
2 Larry E. Greiner, "Evolution and Revolution as Organizations Grow," *Harvard Business Review* (November–December, 1972).
3 We also wish to thank Stephanie Kondik for her assistance in the research phase of this project.
4 *Business Week* (February 11, 1991): 52–53.
5 Other studies that identify life cycles in firms include: N. Churchill and V. Lewis, "The Five Stages of Small Business Growth," *Harvard Business Review* (May–June, 1983): 3–12; J. Kimberly and R. Miles, *The Organizational Life-cycle* (San Francisco, CA: Jossey-Bass, 1980); B. Scott, "Stages of Corporate Development," Harvard Business School, Boston, MA, (Unpublished Paper, 1973); L. Greiner, "Evolution and Revolution as Organizations Grow," *Harvard Business Review* (November–December, 1972): 37–46.
6 For an analysis of the benefits and calculation of economic leverage in firms, see D. Maister, "Balancing the Professional Service Firm," *Sloan Management Review* (Fall 1982): 5–19.
7 For a detailed discussion of professionals as managers in decentralized structures, see J. Lorsch, "When Professionals Have to Manage," *Harvard Business Review* (July–August, 1987): 78–83.
8 Jack Sweeney, "Marvin's Shoes, a Tale of Two Firms," *Consulting Magazine* (May 2002): 20.

16 High-Performance Consulting Firms

Jay W. Lorsch

Why do some consulting firms like McKinsey, Bain, and the Boston Consulting Group continue to prosper and survive, while others like the venerable Arthur D. Little decline and eventually disappear? Or why do organizations like Accenture, American Management Systems, or IBM grow successfully as IT consultants, while so many other firms struggle and fail? Whether you are a partner in a large firm or about to hang out your own shingle for the first time, such questions are critically important.

Each firm will obviously find its own way and no doubt appear quite different on the surface. However, the underlying roots of success appear to be the same, whether the firm is new or long established, or whether it is large or small. So in this chapter, I shall explain what makes for high-performing consulting firms. The research that underlies my explanation was conducted in successful professional firms of all types, and the findings have direct relevance to most consulting firms, both large and small.[1]

The basic key, as I will explain, is for a firm to accomplish two critical tasks: 1) to create an effective strategy to provide consulting services to clients; and 2) to align its structure, processes, leadership, culture, and people so that they support and reinforce each other and the firm's strategy as the firm grows.

Strategy, Goals, and People Success Factors

Designing Strategy First

Most top managers in any consulting firm would agree that the key to success is having the right strategy and financial model. That is indeed what our research has shown. Success, these managers would say, depends on providing services to chosen clients in a manner that is superior to what other competing firms can offer and is also superior to what clients can do on their own. Success also depends on providing the given services at a competitive fee and in a cost-effective way so that the firm reaps a healthy profit.

The basic strategy and business model of most successful consulting firms is about as simple as what I have just described, but my research has also shown that is not enough. The key lies in strategy execution, which includes both forming the strategy and making it happen in practice. As in so many business situations, the devil is in the details. For example, just consider the word "strategy." When I speak about a firm's strategy, I am not concerned with advocating some vague visionary plan or simplistic chart on the wall. Rather, I mean the actual and detailed design and content of the firm's strategy, including its market focus, the services to be delivered, financial objectives, and the required behavior of professionals to accomplish certain desired outcomes.

The firm's top management must decide just how they want to compete in specific ways that will allow the firm to win out against equally strong firms. Throughout this effort, a realistic assessment must be made about the firm's capabilities and how these can be channeled into a winning formula—and here I come to the specific goals that need to+be set as part of the firm's strategy.

Setting Focused Goals

Strategy is really about goals. What are the firm's goals? Many goals are, of course, financial—the returns the owners hope to achieve on their capital as well as for their personal efforts. But goals can and should include issues of size and durability. How big do the partners want their firm to become? Do they want to build a firm that will endure long after they've retired, or are they intending, at some point, to sell the firm or exit in some other way? On what clients is the firm focusing, and why? How much geography is it planning to cover and why? Should the firm concentrate on one region or strive for national reach or become global in scope? Should the firm become a specialist in one particular service arena, or does it want to offer a broad spectrum of services? And furthermore, what level and type of service does the firm offer to clients?

All of these are valid questions, but the specific answers are frequently different for each firm. What all successful firms have in common is that they have carefully thought through at the partner level their goals and the means to achieve them, and they have made clear choices to focus on certain ones. They don't try to be all things to all clients. For example, Bain and McKinsey each offer their clients a customized study of particular problems. But other firms, such as Accenture, offer a more standardized approach wherein clients know that the same service will be delivered worldwide. Both options clearly are effective for these firms, but they work in large part because their partners have not only chosen a defined strategy built on specific goals but they have communicated them widely to all employees—leading to a broader and deeper understanding about why their respective firms are offering a particular brand of service.

Forging a Strong Strategic Identity

Putting strategy and goals down in detail and on paper with the senior management is only a starting point. Much of this can be accomplished in discussion, but the issue of strategy goes deeper, even within this group of leaders. They must not just say the strategy but believe in and behave like it in their daily leadership behavior. This takes us to the need for creating a strong strategic identity to guide employees, which will be reflected in the behavior of *all* consultants and staff throughout the firm.

Let me explain in more detail what I mean by "strategic identity" because its definition further underscores why consensus around a firm's strategy—and also partner and associate behavior that reflects this consensus—is so important. Strategic identity for a consulting firm is analogous to the personal identity of an individual. It is what the firm wants to become, what it stands for in its beliefs and values, and how it behaves with clients. It gives all of the firm's members a clear sense of who they are and what they should do well in their work. It guides them in making choices about how they deal with and serve clients. It helps them resist the temptation to make a decision for short-term gains or personal recognition—because it is a constant reminder of the greater purpose of their day-to-day work.

A firm's strategic identity is also visible externally. Clients recognize it and use it as a way of judging a firm's capabilities. Competitors recognize it as well. If you consider any of the most successful consulting firms, chances are great that you'll be able to describe the firm's identity to a colleague, and that colleague would use similar descriptors in telling you about the same firm.

Strategic drift, which I mentioned above, blurs this understanding. It confuses the partners' and the clients' understanding of what a firm's core capabilities are. Successful firms thus work hard to preserve and reinforce their strategic identity. They focus on maintaining a strong internal consensus about the firm's strategy. Firm leaders at all levels understand their firm's strategic choices and its resulting identity. They recognize their obligation to not allow strategic drift.

Having a strong and widely shared strategic identity does not imply rigidity. New strategic innovations are not stifled in successful firms. Innovation is encouraged, but the critical "detail" here is that one's colleagues must sanction it as a legitimate experiment that promises to strengthen the firm's strategy and identity.

Creating Consensus and Commitment

Which brings me to another critical "detail." It is not enough for a firm's top leaders and partnership group to agree on a strategy, even one with specific goals and a clear statement of identity. In successful firms, *all* the professionals must reach a strong consensus about these strategic choices and the validity of the firm's business model. Put another way, in the most successful firms, *every* professional member of the firm is in agreement about the firm's future direction and also about the behaviors that are required to keep the firm on track. Next, everyone in the firm must be brought on board and behave the strategy in their daily activities.

Here's why such consensus is critical. Consultants, even those in highly successful firms, are individual operators to a great extent. They spend most of their time working in client locations with a dedicated, but temporary, team of colleagues. Even when they are in their firm's office, they work independently with others on a particular client team. The team leader, whether manager, partner, principal, or director, has wide latitude to make many decisions without checking with a "boss." Nobody is standing over him or her, or rarely is anyone expecting a detailed report on what the team is doing on a daily basis.

Under these autonomous circumstances, it is quite possible for consultants to deviate from their firm's strategic choices. In essence, they may easily choose a path outside the firm's strategy. This "strategic drift" is a constant danger, even in successful consulting firms, and the consequences can be quite harmful. First, the economic model can be undermined. Second, the firm's strategic identity can be weakened, and as a result, the firm can become dangerously fragmented, both internally and in the eyes of clients and other stakeholders.

Building a Galaxy of Stars

Making the right decisions about the firm's strategy and developing a strong consensus that supports this strategic direction is clearly important to high-performance firms. And without firm-wide agreement among the consultants about the kinds of behaviors that will support that strategy, they will likely operate all over the map in determining which clients to attract and serve, as well as how to serve them. But none of these ingredients will work unless the right group of talented and committed people is assembled to lead the firm.

Think about it this way—your firm has this great strategic idea. In theory, it will enable you to do a better job of serving clients than any competitor. But that's "in theory." Here's the rule—*nobody ever built a successful firm on theory alone*. Successful firms are built by attracting and developing outstanding professionals—what I call "stars."[2] By stars I mean professionals who have the necessary skills and knowledge to deliver on the firm's strategy while also providing the firm with the quality of leadership that success requires. Stars are the professionals who are, or are going to be, the most outstanding contributors to the firm.

At the start of this chapter, I mentioned that successful firms deliver superior service to clients in a cost-effective way that allows them to make a healthy profit. Here's another "detail" that turns the business model into reality: In consulting firms—as in any professional firm—*the people you pay are ultimately more important than the people who pay you.* Your strategy may be brilliant, but unless you attract, develop, and keep talented professionals who excel at delivering on your strategy, your firm will never perform up to its potential.

Take a moment to consider "new" or "potential" stars—those professionals who are someday expected to take up the mantel of leadership. Each firm's stars have unique qualities that make them suited to the firm's strategy and organization. And in the highest performing consulting firms, the recruitment and training process is explicitly focused on finding and honing that fit. Two examples from exemplary firms make this point:

1 Bain & Co., a strategy consulting firm, recruits mostly MBAs, as well as a few younger people with bachelor's degrees who are likely to go on to earn an MBA and return later to Bain. These young people are selected not only for their intellect and educational accomplishments, but also because they possess other qualities that fit the "Bain way" of doing things. That is, they seem to be hard workers, team players, and interested in hands-on work with clients, as opposed to being more interested in developing theories, or in taking a more distant, advisory role. They also appear to have the interpersonal skills necessary to work effectively with clients and have the potential to grow into firm leaders.
2 Accenture, the large IT consulting firm, instead looks for its new talent mainly on undergraduate campuses. Accenture seeks outstanding graduates with bachelor's degrees who have the right combination of intellect and other qualities to learn the Accenture approach to consulting. Once they are hired, they are enrolled in an intensive educational program at the firm's learning center in St. Charles, Illinois. Partners become the teachers in this program.

Where Bain wants most of its young consultants to have an advanced business education coming into the game, Accenture is less concerned about the prior training of its young recruits' education, believing instead that it can supplement raw talent with education in the "Accenture Way" of performing consulting. The point here is not the specifics of each firm's selection requirements, but that each firm has an approach that fits its own unique strategy and organization.

Requiring High Involvement from Partners

Outstanding firms share another detail with regard to recruiting new stars as well: Senior leaders are deeply involved in the process. In fact, in these firms, senior partners are expected to commit substantial amounts of time to the recruiting and selection process. No one can be selected to join one of these firms without having gone through an arduous set of interviews, mostly conducted by partners. Why? First, it is well understood throughout the firm that adding talent—any talent—is not enough. It's the input of the *right* talent that is critical to the firm's success. Second, the experienced partners have an internalized sense of the qualities required of new recruits to succeed. They know potential success when they meet it!

Once a potential "star" joins a successful consulting firm, the investment in his or her development begins in earnest. In some firms, such as the aforementioned Accenture, there is formal education. But in the majority of premier firms, the emphasis is on learning on the job. Young professionals join project teams and work alongside more experienced consultants and under the leadership of partner-level consultants.

Through a variety of such assignments, new recruits learn the craft of consulting as it is practiced in their firm. And again, experienced consultants invest a major amount of time working with these younger consultants. This takes place through teaching and coaching on the job, in explaining to a new recruit why the partner said "this" to the client at a meeting, but not "that." Or why the partner pursued a particular client aggressively but cut off negotiations with another potential customer early on. It also involves a careful process of formal performance evaluation. Young people receive extensive feedback, both formal and informal, about how they are doing and how they should think about advancing their careers. In successful firms, this practice of giving and receiving constant feedback is an addiction.

It is important to note that the partners' commitment to training is not a "soft" pledge; rather, at outstanding firms, the clear expectation is that senior partners will be engaged in a very real way in the recruiting process and in the training and development of associates. Partners are held accountable for this responsibility when setting formal performance goals and at the time of compensation review.

Supporting Those Who Leave

Some potential stars, over time, find that they are not suited to the firm that hired them. And some find that they are not suited to a career in consulting. Those who reach this conclusion often do so before one of their superiors tells them they are not suited for the firm or to consulting in general. Because these young consultants have succeeded at everything else they have undertaken—education, extracurricular activities, prior short-term jobs, etc.—"not succeeding" is a new experience for them. But they are generally quick to understand that it is more a matter of "fit" than personal flaws, and they decide to move on.

Successful firms provide a great deal of support to these career changes. They help those leaving to find other jobs that are better suited to their talents, often with clients. They make an effort to ensure that the soon-to-be former employees exit with their egos intact and with positive feelings about the firm. Thus, the firm gains a loyal alumnus, one who may well become an important source of new engagements down the road. Outstanding firms retain contact with and encourage their alumni. McKinsey, for example, has a one-inch thick alumni directory!

To sum up these special characteristics of people development in successful consulting firms, they put in place both the right people and a set of people-oriented systems that are aligned well with both the firm's strategy and the needs of its young talent. As a result, new consultants are motivated to contribute their efforts to the firm, to develop skills that are in alignment with the firm's strategic identity, and to make choices about their futures that will support the firm. At the same time, those who leave the firm do so with positive feelings about the firm and are likely to benefit the firm, in one way or another, over time.

Leadership and Partnership Behavior

The Three-Hat Challenge

In the early stages of their careers, stars learn the craft of consulting: how to lead project teams; how to deal with clients; and eventually, how to attract new clients. All of this work can be thought of as "producing." It is the core work of becoming a professional consultant.

But those stars who become proficient at "producing" generally have their eyes set on the "next tier;" they want to become partners. Even though some successful firms are no longer legally partnerships, those associates promoted into key leadership roles, usually with the understanding they have a long-term future with the firm, are referred to as "partners."

At successful firms, the decision to promote someone from associate to partner is undertaken with the utmost care for several reasons. First, the move sends a signal to the rest of the firm, thereby either enhancing or eroding the firm's strategic identity. Second, the promotion brings with it certain challenges that are almost impossible to prepare for in advance. If the soon-to-be former associate is not ready to handle the additional complexity, they will crash and burn quickly.

What are the challenges facing the new leaders? First, in addition to being "producers" (the first hat), they are suddenly expected to be "leaders" (the second hat). On the way to their new positions, they likely exercised some degree of team leadership, although that was integral to their work as consultants. But now they are expected to assume more significant and much broader leadership responsibilities, whether it is for heading up a practice area or a geographic entity or a firm-wide committee.

Suddenly their "free" time, already scarce, is almost nonexistent. Not only are they accountable for the performance of their part of the firm, but they are now among the group of people responsible for developing the young stars, which requires spending considerable time on recruiting, coaching, and evaluation.

And as if that weren't complicated enough, they are also asked to wear a third hat—that of "owner." To some extent this third hat also calls for a shift in psychological focus. It's their firm now. Both their psyches and economic well-being are closely tied to how well the firm does. Further, the ownership hat means they are expected to participate in the governance of the firm. This means serving on firm-wide committees or special task forces or perhaps taking on even greater leadership responsibilities by heading a new practice area or major office.

The "three-hat challenge" is incredibly complex and demanding. Outsiders might ask, "Why do consulting firms organize themselves in this strange way where the leaders are expected not only to lead but also to sell and perform consulting? Why don't these firms follow the advice they give to their clients; that is, to develop a hierarchical management structure where senior executives oversee those who are producing the results?"

The answer lies in the unique characteristics of the consulting business, at least as outstanding firms practice it. One factor is that clients want, even demand, continuous contact with partner-level consultants. Just because a consultant has been asked by the firm to lead a practice area, clients do not want to lose his or her services. Another reason for this curious arrangement of both leading and doing is that the long-term success of the firm depends on close contact with young consultants who must be groomed for future leadership roles.

Developing young people requires, among other things, working directly with them on client projects, and that includes staying "up-to-speed" on the substantive issues that concern young consultants in their work. Another reason is that those who have been elevated to the lofty heights of partnership actually enjoy their consulting work. They joined the firm to be consultants, and they enjoy working with clients, solving their problems, and receiving positive feedback. While they understand the necessity and obligation to play their leadership and owner's role, the act of doing good consulting work is still a great source of motivation, and they are unwilling to give it up!

The three-hat arrangement, with all its attendant problems of time management and the push-pull of personal interest versus firm interest, exists in all outstanding consulting firms. In fact, it exists in all kinds of professional service firms—accounting firms, law firms, and investment banks—for the reasons just cited. How do partners make the three-hat challenge work?

High-Performance Consulting Firms 373

At the partner level, it is impossible to understate the importance of being able to "self-manage." One needs to develop an explicit set of priorities, or what Kotter calls a "personal agenda."[3] It is also necessary to reach out to others in the firm for support. Younger associates and other partners all can help. They can follow up a new client lead or jump in to help a client team. In successful firms, it is generally accepted that to make this type of structure work, it requires a high degree of teamwork from all those involved.

Performance Evaluation and Rewards

Making the three-hat arrangement work also requires the development of a well-executed performance management and career development system at the partner level. In outstanding consulting firms, for example, performance assessment and personal development do not stop when one joins the ranks of the partnership. Partners also receive performance evaluations and suggestions for improving their skills. Usually, these evaluations are conducted either by a more senior partner or by a committee of partners.

In all successful firms, the partners are judged especially on how well they are doing in wearing all three hats. Their performance as a consultant, a leader, and an owner are all part of the evaluation mix. That's not to say that all partners are expected to be equally strong on all dimensions. For sure, some partners excel as rainmakers, while others may be more outstanding as star-makers. Still other partners may make a significant contribution to the firm's governance.

Regardless of where each partner's strengths lie, there are three important points to remember about partner evaluation in high-performing firms:

> First, it happens! Partners in outstanding firms are evaluated regularly. Nobody is permitted to rest on his or her laurels—to say, "Well, I've made it, now I can relax."
> Second, not all partners are expected to make equal contributions as owners, producers, and leaders. Each partner has his or her own mix of activities and his or her own strengths and weaknesses.
> Finally, though each partner is evaluated on how well he or she plays each role, the message is clear to all—you must wear all three hats! Success as a firm requires that the partnership as a whole place a high value on practicing all three roles effectively.

These three points must be strongly reinforced by the firm's compensation system. While the specifics of compensation arrangements differ across successful firms, two commonalities stand out among them. First, pay is used to reinforce the message that wearing all three hats is important. Second, pay arrangements for all partners are tied, to a large extent, to firm-wide results, not simply individual achievement. Whatever other goals the compensation scheme encourages partners to achieve, contribution to firm-wide results is highly rewarded. Being a strong collaborator in helping to build a unified firm is a shared value across all successful firms, and pay is tied to this end.

Participation in Governance

The third hat of an owner requires active involvement in the firm's governance process. Because most successful firms are considered to be partnerships, regardless of their legal ownership form, managing the governance process effectively is a significant factor in contributing to a successful firm. Governance in these firms includes decisions about: who is admitted to the partnership; distribution of firm profits and the related question of partner compensation; major strategic questions; and the selection of the firm's leader.

In all high-performing firms, the partners expect to be, and are, involved in all aspects of firm governance. They are expected to step back and, as an owner, consider what is best for the firm. As I have said, too strong a focus on one's personal interests is frowned upon in high-performing firms. Doing what is best for the whole firm and all its partners is the ultimate objective of all governance activities in these firms.

One common goal is to make the partner selection decision on a firm-wide basis. That is, the process is designed to prevent offices or practices from lobbying for their favorite candidates. The intent is to prevent competition from among the firm's various sectors to threaten the firm's overall cohesion and strategic identity. Engaging in politics for oneself or others is frowned upon.

Similarly, the process for selecting a firm's leader may be managed by a committee, but the ultimate decision typically involves all the partners and requires their vote. For example, a representative committee may solicit nominations from among the partners and then interview the possible candidates as well as those who nominated them so as to develop a limited slate of candidates to consider. But again, the goal in successful firms is to minimize conflict and tension between specific practice areas or geographic offices and to select a leader who will have the greatest level of acceptance and support from all partners.

The Managing Director

In a partnership-like environment, the job of taking responsibility for firm-wide leadership is an extremely complex task. What I have found in successful firms is that the managing director operates as if he or she is not a CEO sitting atop a management hierarchy. Rather, these leaders realize they are surrounded by other leaders who are also "owners."

These managing directors do not issue edicts. They lead from *within* the partnership, always striving to build consensus among their fellow owners regarding the firm's direction and governance.

They are on constant guard to ensure that each decision being advocated serves to strengthen the firm's overall strategic identity. They are also on constant guard to make sure that their fellow partners are not simply paying lip service to that identity but are, in fact, behaving in ways that explicitly support it. Often there are real conflicts, given each partner's personal situation. Consider these real examples: A senior partner who is about to retire decides to oppose a decision to invest the firm's resources in developing a new office in Asia, yet another younger partner wants to move to Asia to head up the office. Similarly, a successful partner interested in the technology sector wants to sign on a client in that field, but the firm as a whole has never agreed to invest in developing that particular sector and expertise.

The managing directors of high-performing firms are exceptional in finding ways to acknowledge and empathize with individual views, while at the same time encouraging colleagues to continue to put the firm's best interests first. It's a tall order—keeping a group of people with largely independent egos in close alignment.

This senior leadership position is a different sort of job from being the CEO of a client company. In many ways, it is more challenging. For the high-performance firms, the managing directors appear to possess a large quotient of what Goleman calls "emotional intelligence,"[4] which includes the capacity to understand one's self and others and to control one's emotions in achieving an effective dialogue with others. They do not sit in their offices and wait for people to come to them; rather, they are in continuous contact with many partners, asking for their views and hearing reactions to controversial decisions. Above all, they are good listeners and questioners.

The Firm's Culture: Cause and Consequences

At the outset, I emphasized that consultants in high-performance firms typically do not feel constrained by formal roles and that they spend their time working with clients without close supervision from their firm's senior leaders. This means there is always the risk that a consultant will move in directions that are inconsistent with their firm's strategic identity. Temptation is always present in the form of clients who offer more work and money—if only you will do this or that, even when it may be contrary to the firm's strategy.

In the face of such temptation and without the presence of a formal hierarchy or clear policy, it is the strong culture of high-performing firms that keeps everyone singing from the same hymnbook. Culture refers to the set of beliefs members hold about how they are expected to behave and what values they are to share with their fellow consultants.[5] By "strong," I mean that the belief systems are well understood and accepted by all the firm's members.

Consultants on the way up through these firms are inoculated with the values of their firm's culture. When they face the temptation to wander off in new directions, they have been so infused with their firm's culture that they understand that such deviation is unacceptable. My intent is not to imply that new ideas or innovations are impossible in these firms. Quite the contrary! What must happen, though, is new ideas must be acceptable to the partners. A consensus must be developed as to why embarking on a new direction makes sense for the firm.

While many differences exist among firms in their specific beliefs, a number of common themes are evident across successful firms. One is the importance of *focusing relentlessly on clients* and their needs, while simultaneously *building the firm's pool of star talent*. Another is a strong belief in the *importance of working in teams*. Ambitious consultants may exhibit competitive tendencies with their colleagues, but in successful firms not only the leaders but also one's peers frown upon such behavior. Rather, emphasis is placed on working collaboratively in teams.

Another belief shared by successful consulting firms is that the *firm is a unified community*, one entity. It is what Maister has labeled as the "one-firm firm."[6] Connected to this is a strong belief in the importance of *perpetuating the firm for the long term*. The current generation of partners is expected to worry not just about their own well-being but also about building a firm that will be successful for future generations. A final belief characteristic of successful firms is that they are and must function as a *unified partnership*. Decisions must be agreed to and be accepted by the partners. It is their firm, and they are its leaders and ultimate decision makers.

In the successful firms, their leaders preach about culture and its beliefs in their informal and formal talks and speeches. They, too, shape it on a daily basis with their behavior and decisions. They understand that the firm's cultural values must be constantly articulated in words and actions. Not only do they reinforce it, they actively manage it. If they think the beliefs around which the firm is run need to change, they work to develop a consensus among their fellow partners about the need for change. Once agreement is reached, they become vocal advocates of the firm's new beliefs and provide explanations for them.

Overall, a strong culture in successful firms serves to reinforce the alignment of strategy and internal practices with the needs of the firm's professionals. Culture, in this sense, is like the superglue that holds the firm in close alignment. However, unlike real superglue, effective leadership can reduce its "stickiness" if change is needed, allowing the firm to create a new alignment for moving in a new direction.

Alignment and Firm Size

The leaders of high-performance firms see their overall responsibility as one of achieving and managing alignment in the firm's different growth stages (see Chapter 15). All other decisions—whether to accept or reject an individual client, where to place resources, which associates to promote to the partnership—are ultimately part of the job of building and sustaining alignment. It is obviously a daunting task in a large, global consulting firm with dozens, or maybe even hundreds, of partners. Yet, leaders of successful firms have been accomplishing this responsibility since the creation of the first major consulting firm fifty years ago. It is a complicated leadership job, but with determination and skill, it gets done.

For those who are involved in leading and building smaller firms, there is good news! While I believe the lessons that I have drawn from the "powerhouses" of consulting and described here have relevance for most firms, I also believe, as I said earlier, that the tasks of leadership are much easier in smaller firms, though nevertheless essential. In small firms, consensus must be achieved among fewer partners. It is possible to get everyone in the same meeting room and to reach joint decisions, whether about strategic direction, partner compensation, or the future of younger professionals. It is also easier to carefully select new talent, to tend to their development, and to shape their careers while simultaneously wearing their producer and owner hats.

Obviously, all this gets more complicated as a consulting firm succeeds and grows in size and complexity. All consultants and all firms should worry about alignment from the moment their first business cards are printed. Alignment is a complicated state that evolves over time and size, and it is a goal to work toward that will never be fully achieved. However, it is easier when you have a clean slate and a small firm. If you start in the wrong direction, making changes later will be much more difficult.

In the end, for all firms, becoming successful requires a mix of strategic, organizational, and leadership attributes that are carefully put in place over the years, while keeping a close eye on alignment. Success cannot be reduced simply to a firm's leadership or its product line or its culture. I have outlined many of the necessary attributes here, as identified in my research on high-performing firms. Still, as firms move into the future, other successful practices will be invented by firms and their leaders and then written about by researchers. It will be interesting to read about high-performance firms ten years from now.

Notes

1 Jay W. Lorsch and Thomas J. Tierney, *Aligning the Stars: How to Succeed When Professionals Drive Results* (Boston: Harvard Business Press, 2002).
2 Lorsch and Tierney, op. cit.
3 John P. Kotter, *The General Managers* (New York: Free Press, 1982).
4 Daniel Goleman, "What Makes a Leader," *Harvard Business Review*, 76, no. 6 (November–December, 1998). Also, Daniel Goleman, *Emotional Intelligence: Why It Can Matter More Than IQ, for Character, Health, and Lifelong Achievement* (New York: Bantam, 1998).

5 Edgar H. Schein, *Organizational Culture and Leadership* (San Francisco: Jossey-Bass, 1985) and John P. Kotter and James L. Heskett, *Corporate Culture and Performance* (New York: Free Press, 1992) are two books that explore the definition and importance of culture in a broad array of companies.
6 David H. Maister, *Managing the Professional Service Firm* (New York: Free Press, 1993).

17 Knowledge Management in Consulting

Michael A. Mische

1.0 Introduction

For any management consultancy, human capital is its most unique and strategic asset. Without human capital the consulting firm is devoid of energy, creativity, perspective and empathy. Energy, perspective and empathy are very human qualities that manifest themselves in many ways. Consultants demonstrate energy through their performance, dedication to the profession, constant learning and competing for clients. But how consultants go about doing those things is reflective and incorporative of how the consultant learns, creates and applies both institutional and individual *knowledge* and ultimately, *wisdom*.

Knowledge is the creation of the human experience, and wisdom is the personification of knowledge. Both are essential assets to competing successfully in a notoriously intense and rival rich industry. It's not difficult for consultants to amass experience, but the ability to generate, manage and disseminate knowledge and create wisdom are very different from mere experience. For the firm that creates and possesses it, *knowledge* is a formidable weapon that can create a sizable competitive advantage. However, it is *wisdom* that creates separation and distinction for a "wise" firm from its competitors.

In this chapter we will explore the role of knowledge and wisdom in management consulting and address nine key questions:

1 What is knowledge, and how is knowledge distinguished from data and information?
2 How do consultants and consultancy firms compete using knowledge?
3 What is management consulting knowledge?
4 How can knowledge be best managed in a large management consultancy?
5 How is knowledge created or acquired by a consultancy?
6 How is knowledge dispersed through a consultancy organization?
7 How can the knowledge developed or captured on a particular project and client be learned and applied to other client situations, without violating any contractual provisions for intellectual property and confidentiality or professional ethical standards?

380 Michael A. Mische

8   What is wisdom, and how does wisdom differ from knowledge?
9   What is the future of knowledge?

The chapter addresses examines the subject and practice of knowledge in management consulting. In particular, the challenges of creating and distributing knowledge, managing knowledge and using knowledge and *wisdom* for competitive advantage and client benefit are explored.

This chapter is organized into five sections:

1.0   Introduction
    1.1   We Think . . . Consultants and Knowledge
    1.2   Defining Knowledge
    1.3   Defining Management Consulting Knowledge
2.0   Competing on Knowledge
3.0   Learning and Knowledge Transfer in Management Consulting
4.0   Knowledge Management Systems in Consulting (KMX)
5.0   Conclusion . . .: Thinking About the Future of Knowledge
6.0   Key Words

    Knowledge
    Knowledge Management
    Relevant Knowledge
    Explicit Knowledge
    Tacit Knowledge
    Apprentice Model
    Master
    Knowledge Management Exchange (KMX)
    Embedded Knowledge
    Encoded Knowledge
    Communities of Practice

The chapter contains three exhibits in support of the topics and subjects. Additionally, there are 39 endnotes to guide the reader to the sources used in this chapter and additional materials and resources. The list of exhibits include:

Number	Title
17.1	**Five Stages of Knowledge**
17.2	**Objectives/Benefits of Knowledge Management in PSFs**
17.3	**Knowledge Development Cycle**

At the completion of this chapter the reader should have a thorough understanding of knowledge in management consulting, how consultants create and manage knowledge and how knowledge and wisdom combine to create competitive advantage and separation amongst the Elite-8 consulting and other consulting firms.

1.1 We Think . . . *Consultants and Knowledge*

As a young consultant I sat quietly before a meeting listening to an esteemed consulting partner casually talk with a potential client. With over 30 years of consulting experience, the partner had a CPA and MBA and was well published and highly respected throughout the firm. "Ray" was a patient man who prided himself on knowing his business, his clients and building long-term relationships with both clients and young professionals aspiring to be partners. As a partner, there were none finer. He always took the time to talk to you, always wanted to know what you were working on and what you were learning. I was fortunate to be working for him . . . everyday was a learning experience.

On that day so many years ago, our consulting firm had been invited to discuss business process reengineering (BPR) with the CEO of a major manufacturing company. BPR was a major topic among business as well as a "cash-competency" of consulting firms. As the CEO was running a little late, we were invited to wait in the conference room and were soon joined by the executive vice president of manufacturing. His name was "Bill." Bill was an imposing figure with stellar credentials. He was an engineer by education with a degree from a Big-10 school and an MBA from a top-25 business school. But he was strikingly cynical and satirical in his approach to the conversation.

By the abject nature of his tone it was clear that Bill had little respect for management consultants and a disdain for consulting. He began the conversation by asking Ray whether he had heard the joke about the consultant and client's watch. Ray smiled, laughed and acknowledged that he had and then lightly asked whether Bill had heard the one about the client and the fees? Bill didn't smile and didn't laugh. And so went the next twenty minutes.

But what has resonated with me about that day was when Bill cynically challenged Ray by asking, *"So what do consultants really do?* I mean, how do you guys earn a living? I build things here that people buy. What do you do?" In the course of the conversation Ray had already discussed services and the value of using a consultant. Ray took in a deep breath, and I could see a bit of frustration creeping into his face, but I also saw a bit of anticipation and almost a smile. It was as if Ray knew exactly when that question was coming. Squaring his shoulders, Ray replied, "Well, Bill, *we think*. While you are fully absorbed with building your quality products and managing your customers, *we think* a lot about you, your business and your competition. In fact, we think about you all of the time." No sooner had Ray said those words that CEO had entered the room. He warmly embraced Ray with a handshake and hug and then he turned and greeted me. The CEO had said that he had read one of my articles on BPR and IT and was pleased to meet me. As Ray and the CEO caught up, Bill was clearly taken aback by the reception and dialogue between Ray and the CEO. Frankly, I don't remember much of Bill after that; other than for the rest of the meeting he sat stoically and said absolutely . . . *nothing* . . . perhaps he too was thinking.

"*We think,*" those two words have remained with me my entire consulting and academic career. *Thinking* does describe and is a large part of the management consultant's role with clients. Management consultants may not be any smarter, or intelligently gifted, or better educated than their clients. Those days of consulting aristocracy are long gone. But contemplative analysis and *thinking* with clarity, objectivity and independence are what management consultants *must* do and should do better than their clients. Clients may have the explicit knowledge and deep expertise on how to build a product and manage customers, but consultants must be able to bring the proper experience and the relevant perspective and wisdom to the client. In doing so, the consultant *must* successfully integrate both consultant and client knowledge for client advancement and betterment.

As the years would pass, I would continue to ponder the impact that those two words had on me both professionally and personally. The lessons that I learned that day were relatively easy, but the amount of knowledge that was transferred to me about the subtleties of client management, how to interact with adverse clients and how to maintain a sense of control, without exerting control, took years to coalesce and form.

1.2 Defining Knowledge

As in any profession, society and endeavor, knowledge is multi-dimensional. Knowledge is "fun" in that once learned and applied, it changes and it evolves. The speed at which it evolves is contingent on and reflective of many factors, including the importance or relevancy of the knowledge, the intellectual capabilities of those creating or using it, technology and the social construct. Our personal experiences and interpretations influence how we learn, apply and adapt knowledge to a set of circumstances. As in any endeavor and profession involving knowledge, we must ask five seminal questions about management consulting knowledge:

- *What is knowledge?*
- *What is consulting knowledge?*
- *How is knowledge used in consulting?*
- *How is consulting knowledge acquired?*
- *How is consulting knowledge managed?*

As a starting point, let's explore some various definitions of knowledge:

- *Webster's Dictionary* defines knowledge as: "a (1) : the fact or condition of knowing something with familiarity gained through experience or association (2) : acquaintance with or understanding of a science, art, or technique, b (1) : the fact or condition of being aware of something (2) : the range of one's information or understanding, c : the circumstance or condition of apprehending truth or fact through reasoning : cognition, d : the fact or condition of having information or of being learned."[1]

- In their 2010 work, researchers Wang and Noe define knowledge as: "information processed by individuals including ideas, facts, expertise and judgment relevant for individual, team and organizational performance."[2]
- Finally, Davenport and Pusek in 1998 defined knowledge as: "A fluid mix of framed experience, values, contextual information, and expert insight that provides a framework for evaluating and incorporating new experiences and information."[3]

In *Webster's* basic definition, knowledge is *"knowing"* something that has been learned or acquired. An essential consideration of *Webster's* definition is that knowledge, whether learned or acquired, has components of self-awareness, cognition, awareness and association . . . all elements of a social construct and all of which require some type of personal synthesis. This theme of knowing something resonates throughout the literature and institutional importance of knowledge. Stated differently, Funmilola Olubunmi Omotayo describes, "Knowledge is the insights, understandings, and practical know-how that people possess. It can then be stated that knowledge is an invisible or intangible asset, in which its acquisition involves complex cognitive processes of perception, learning, communication, association and reasoning."[4] Thus, knowledge is not only learned, it is experienced and as such it incorporates and reflects personal bias, perceptions, values and cognitive abilities, as well as social construct. These elements are essential to consulting and how the consultant and consultancy goes about the process of crafting and delivering services to clients.

Early knowledge researchers identified five types of knowledge forms: embedded, embodied, embrained, encultured and encoded.[5] Although useful as distinguishing characteristics, it's how that knowledge is created, captured, interpreted and classified that is of importance to the consultant and consultancy.

In general, knowledge consists of two broad types: *Tacit* and *Explicit*. For the professional management consultant and consultancy, it is the interactions and the juxtapositions between tacit and explicit knowledge, along with discovery, learning, social construct and personal synthesis, that create the greatest value for the client and competitive advantages for the firm.[6] Specifically:

- *Tacit* knowledge is predominantly experiential in nature. That is, it is created and acquired through a combination of formal learning and life's tribulations and interactions. As it is tacit, this form of knowledge is always incorporative of personal bias, beliefs, values, impressions and standards. Tacit knowledge is reflective of the social construct in which it was formed. Tacit knowledge can be "passed" on through memorialization of thoughts and feelings. A chef passing *hints* about where to source the finest ingredients for a receipt and how to vary the cooking times in a certain type of oven using a certain type of cookery and at a certain altitude is an example of tacit knowledge.[7] Tacit knowledge is:

- Highly personalized and is *embrained* in the individual and may be difficult to express or pass along.[8] For example, it is not uncommon for superstar athletes to find it extraordinarily difficult to transition into coaching, or for a CEO to find it far more challenging to become a professor in an MBA program.
- *Encultured* and *embodied* in the culture, norms and social construct of the firm and the behaviors of its professionals.

- *Explicit* knowledge is that which is codified, taught, learned and practiced. Either formally or through trial and error and/or probing and learning, explicit knowledge is generally taught and learned. We find this form of knowledge codified or memorialized in books, electronic data files, curricula, software and training programs. Knowledge of the U.S. Internal Revenue Code is explicit knowledge.[9] Explicit knowledge is:

  - *Encoded* in procedures, operations, measurements and standards of performance. They are taught and learned, and competency of that particular knowledge is often measured. Encoded knowledge is also knowledge that is enforced. Knowing the chain of command for decision-making (not how a decision is made) and knowing the procedures for communicating those decisions are forms of encoded knowledge. Procedures manuals, the U.S. Internal Revenue Code and the AICAP's Generally Accepted Accounting Principles (GAAP) are examples of encoded knowledge.
  - *Embedded* in the daily operations, communications, interactions and vocabulary of the organization.[10] Embedded knowledge is routine knowledge and spans a broad spectrum of knowledge, including from "knowing" what forms to use to get reimbursed for travel expenses to applying for security clearance and authorization to move intellectual property. Embedded knowledge is integral to practicing the knowledge, therefore it is difficult to separate or bifurcate from the *behavior* of performing the practice.[11]

As knowledge is "developed" it navigates through an endless cycle of changes in form, functions, features, definition and utility. Specifically:

- Raw data represents data in its most primitive form. Unstructured and unformed, raw data can also be incomplete and in need of further development, verification or definition. Raw data is the "first order" data that must be verified, refined and formed into consistent data.

Knowledge Management in Consulting 385

- Formed data is data that has been placed into some type of logical structure. This data is formal, complete, defined and has been formed into a logical structure.
- Information is data that has meaning, form and definition. Researchers Tom Davenport and Larry Prusak note that information *"gives shape to data."*[12] In this sense, information gives or places context and purpose to the data along with the various relationships in and among data the form of causality, correlation or randomness of occurrence or relationship.
- Knowledge is the final product of data and information. Knowledge represents the synthesis, consolidation and conditioning of data and information to create intellectual capital, individual and institutional information, doctrine, codification and perspective.
- Wisdom is created through life's experiences and the continuous synthesis of learning, applying, adapting and learning again. With wisdom, knowledge is given a personal context and perspective of what worked, what failed, how things worked or failed, how things failed and why. Wisdom invokes personal beliefs and biases, as well as hopes and dreams. Above all, wisdom reflects or injects into knowledge the context and perspective of life.

Exhibit 17.1 provides an illustration of how knowledge in a PSF is created and evolves. These five steps, in turn, help to craft escalating framework for what I defined in 1995 as the:

Exhibit 17.1 Five Stages of Knowledge

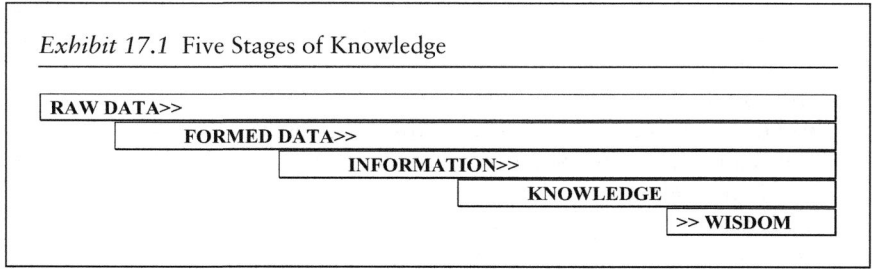

As management consulting is both a profession and process, it has unique knowledge that express and profile some unique characteristics with specific definition.

1.3 Defining Management Consulting Knowledge

As consulting is both professional and process-centric, consulting knowledge not only incorporates the five elements of knowledge, it most certainly must include a *significant* amount of personal perspective as characterized by both *tacit* knowledge and *wisdom*. Like medicine and law, consulting knowledge is very specific and has specific meaning to the community of professional consulting practitioners. I define management consulting knowledge as:

> **Management Consulting Knowledge Defined**
>
> *Knowledge is any relevant intellectual capital, information, learning and personal perspective of a situation, environment, process, doctrine, method or codification of data and information.*

Central to the definition of consulting knowledge is the concept of *relevancy* of knowledge. I define *relevant consulting knowledge* as knowledge that has direct and specific meaning, form and substance that is *applicable* to the particular consulting situation, data and circumstances. Relevant knowledge is meaningful knowledge. Relevant knowledge always embodies and personifies subject matter expertise, perspective and experience. As such, relevant knowledge is analogous by design in that there is continuous matching of prior learning and experiences with current and anticipated conditions. Relevant *consulting* knowledge generates a number of benefits for both the client and consultancy:

- Deployed affectively, relevant knowledge can and will differentiate a consulting firm from its competitors and distinguish it among clients and potential clients.
- Clients who perceive consultants with knowledge generally gravitate to those consultants for services. Applied properly, consulting knowledge can accelerate benefits for clients and generate greater value for clients relative to the client's financial investment in consulting services.
- Dispersed properly, knowledge can contribute to the enhanced learning and more robust development of individual management consulting professionals.
- Managed effectively, knowledge can lead to accelerated and enhanced performance by the consultancy in the delivery of services, as well as improved client perceptions.

The knowledge that a consultancy possesses is essential to its ability to compete and differentiate itself from other consultancies. In this regard, the ability of the consultancy to generate, capture and manage both explicit and tacit knowledge is an essential core competency of management consultancies. A consulting firm that is highly competent and proficient in its generation and management of knowledge will create separation from those that are less effective. However, that knowledge is only essential and strategic if it is *relevant* to the needs of the paying clients and the consulting process. Relevancy means that the knowledge has an alignment with the strategies, operations and competencies of the consultancy and that the knowledge is supportive of the consultancy's business model and client demands. It does a firm little value if the knowledge is misaligned or inappropriate with its strategies and the needs of its clients.

From a client's perspective, it's not the knowledge that is the most coveted asset that it is trying to acquire from the consultant . . . it's the relevant knowledge and *wisdom*. Wisdom embodies knowledge and when applied it incorporates both institutional and individual perspectives, experiences and - interpretations. Wisdom contains the informal knowledge in the form of intuition as well as the formal knowledge learned through education and application. This perspective is usually gained through life's experiences, formal and informal learning environments and direct application of learning to situations, processes, methods and doctrine and has references to one's cultural origins and current cultural situation. In Professional Service Firms (PSFs) the application of knowledge to the codification of data and information is important since many professional firms, such as law firms and the Big-4 advisory firms, must adhere to formal standards of professionally prescribed behaviors and practices. Furthermore, these firms often must operate within the parameters of legal licensing standards, regulatory agencies and professional pronouncements.

As discussed, all professions possess knowledge. Like other professions and trades, consulting knowledge is specific in nature. Although there are many forms, *specific* management consulting knowledge can be characterized into *five* domains:

1 **Consulting Process Knowledge (CPK).** This is *tacit* knowledge that is specific to the consulting process of marketing, performing and delivering professional services. This knowledge is largely explicit with respect to the standards and practices of fieldwork, professional ethics and client interactions. This knowledge includes, for example, how to write proposals consistent with firm standards, how to document work performed, billing practices and how to prepare client deliverables. Tacit knowledge is developed through learning. Consulting learning is composed of both formal development and informal practices. A large part of the tacit knowledge is acquired through the apprentice-master model described below. Transferring this knowledge is generally accomplished on a personal basic—that is, from one person to another person. However, as this form of transfer is social, barriers are present to impede the transfer. These barriers span the range from cultural, physical, personal bias, personal animosity, professional insecurities, as well as lack of incentives.[13]
2 **Experiential and Referential Industry, Economy, Nation and Cultural Knowledge (ERK).** This is knowledge that is acquired through years of working in, researching and studying a particular industry,

economy, culture and/or nation. Much of this knowledge is tacit, as this type of expertise is best acquired and benefits from actual experience, immersion and "doing." Tacit knowledge of an industry or economy is gained through years of learning and perfecting a craft and profession. Generally, tacit knowledge is first learned/acquired through explicit methods and then put into practice and used in actual situations. Once used, experiential references are amassed, and over time relevant tacit knowledge is created. Explicit knowledge of an industry, economy, culture or nation can first be acquired through formal learning methods. Skills in research, case readings, industry structural analysis, nation and cultural studies can all be acquired and massed through formal knowledge transfer methods, such as higher education.

3 **Subject Matter Expertise (SME).** Members of professions such as law, medicine and consulting are considered subject matter experts. Subject matter expertise is gained through formal training, on-the-job training and years of practicing a profession (doing). For recognized and regulated professions, academic preparation is a prerequisite for SME. Early development of an SME is heavily biased towards explicit knowledge. Later, as one's career progresses and develops, SME is augmented and shaped by tacit knowledge and one's direct experience with the subject matter. SME requires years of development and practice within an industry or several industries.

4 **Client Specific Knowledge (CSK).** In management consulting, having extensive knowledge of a client, its behavior patterns, its history and its industry is essential for delivering responsive services. CSK is predominantly tacit in nature and is acquired through years of involvement with the client and its industry.

5 **Professional Practice and Behavior Knowledge (PPK).** In the major professions, professional practices, ethics and protocols are established by three standards: regulatory authority such as a government agency upon satisfying requirements, professional associations that grant competency to practice upon examination and generally accepted professional guidelines for behavior. For the regulated and licensed industries such as law and medicine, for the Big-4 accounting firms with advisory practices, these standards are regulatory in nature. Therefore, knowledge of PPK in these firms is explicit in form and substance. It is learned, tested and reinforced. The application of the learned (explicit) knowledge is subject to tacit knowledge interpretation and application.

In management consulting, a practitioner must be competent in all five of these knowledge domains. In some instances, it is clear that the knowledge is acquired through explicit means, usually in the form of education. In other situations, it is acquired through tacit methods.

Reflecting back on my meeting with Ray, the partner and the CEO and Bill, the knowledge acquired during those two hours was purely tacit in form and substance. Consultants *learn* by doing and experiencing the moment. Subsequently, consultants reflect and contemplate on what they have learned and then *adopt* those lessons as *knowledge*. Once that knowledge is created the consultant begins to amass a *referential* base of experience. The referential experience base is constantly accessed, applied and *adapted* to new situations. Over the years and many, many client situations and countless interactions, the consultant should have, just as Ray had, a highly developed sense of situational awareness, an appreciation of the moment and, as a result, *wisdom*.

2.0 Competing on Knowledge

Peter Drucker's early work identified knowledge as a necessary competency and one of strategic value.[14] More recent work confirmed what most consultancies and organizations intuitively or explicitly knew: relevant knowledge can create competitive advantage and greater profitability.[15] Furthermore, the ability to manage knowledge to create competitive advantage and improved revenues and profits is not restricted merely to the consultancy profession; other industries can also benefit from knowledge management.[16]

Human capital and knowledge are the essential atributes of the industry. The most successful consultants integrate the appropriate academic training, deep subject matter and industry expertise, professional experience and business and personal acumen to craft creative and responsive solutions for their clients. The consultant and consultancy firm that can bring the most depth of knowledge, engaged professionals and responsive process can or should be in a superior position to provide the highest level of services to the client. Researchers Robert Eccles, Ana Kreacic and Penelope Rossano have summarized the benefits of knowledge and management in Exhibit 17.2 as eight objectives:

Exhibit 17.2 Objectives/Benefits of Knowledge Management in PSFs

---

Greater efficiency and professional productivity
Improving client service delivery and value
Increasing commercialization and sales
People development
Improving collaboration among staff and experts
Competitive differentiation
Minimizing risk

Source: Eccles, Robert G,; Kreacic, Ana; Rossano, Penelope, "A Note on Knowledge Management in Professional Service Firms," Harvard Business School Publishing. August 2013. (Prod. #9-314-034)

Through the centuries, and certainly in modern times, clients have turned to management consultants to gain specific insights into conditions or situations, solve problems or create or capitalize upon opportunities. Management consultants have responded to their clients by hiring some of the best and brightest talent from the top business schools and industry. The historical model of hiring the best and brightest and industry experience have served both the client and consulting industry well. But, times have changed.

Management consulting firms are *knowledge centric*. Unlike a manufacturing concern, a retail operation, a distribution company or high-tech firm, a consultancy is primarily composed of one asset and productive resource... *people*. The consultancy may have methods, technologies and practices, but those are expressed through people and its services to clients delivered through human performance. Unlike a manufacturer or retailer, a consultancy has no (or very few) physical products to sell. There is no physical inventory to account for or price. There are no yearend products to push to make way for the new season or model year. There are no warehouses or distribution centers, and consultants go to where the client is; the client rarely visits the consultant. Advertising may help (a little) in brand awareness but, unlike the many other industries, will not drive demand for consulting services. And since, for the most part, consulting rates are inelastic to demand, discounting fees will not yield increased sales of any magnitude.

In management consulting, there are five critically strategic axioms of knowledge and competing on knowledge:

1 Human capital is the only truly unique asset that consultancy firms have. With human capital comes individual knowledge and judgment. That knowledge is the form of tacit and explicit, which over time transforms into wisdom. Since its services, processes and methods are replicable by other firms and clients, knowledge alone is wholly and uniquely strategic. Thus, it's essential for a consultancy firm to create, capture and manage both individual and institutional knowledge.
2 The knowledge that a firm creates and captures ultimately becomes relevant institutional knowledge that positions it to compete differently and, ostensibly, more effectively. Knowledge enables the consultancy to evaluate changes in its environment and adapt to the demands of clients, as well as to its competitors.
3 The consulting process and the results of that process, including service delivery, create unique and valuable insights in the form of knowledge. Aspects of consulting team behavior, client behavior and values, client perceptions of value and benefits will all yield valuable lessons to the consultant and firm. How a consultancy elects to incorporate those lessons to create knowledge for its service models, service delivery processes and behavior impacts, to a large part, how the client and competitors view that firm.

4   The most effective consultancies must be highly flexible, energetic and capable of extensive knowledge sharing and creation. The ability of a consultant to capture and institutionalize knowledge can create or inhibit its competiveness and ability to deliver services efficiently and effectively to clients. How the firm designs its basic organization and construct for delivering services to clients has a direct impact on its ability to fully leverage its knowledge for clients.

5   How a consultancy goes about learning, creating, acquiring and managing knowledge is strategic to its capability of delivering that knowledge to its clients. In this sense, how a consultancy learns and how it *converts* that learning into knowledge are inextricably linked.

In today's consulting arena, clients no longer have to run to consultants to solve complex problems or conduct sophisticated research or studies. As technology evolved, so has client access to information and "knowledge." Higher education has produced an endless stream of MBAs, all of whom have the requisite analytical skills that historically only consultants possessed. The consulting profession itself contributed, indeed, created systemic changes in the dynamics and behavior of the industry. As the consulting profession grew and contracted, highly competent and trained professionals enterd and exited the profession to find employment with clients. The combination of technology and employee defections from the traditional consulting firms to clients created "in-sourcing" consulting capabilities that permanently changed the dynamics of the consulting industry.

For much of the 1925 to 1990 period, management consulting was demarcated among three lines: the Big-3,[17] the Big-4[18] and all others. With the proliferation of technology, the emergence of the Internet and a steady stream of MBAs being produced every year, the demarcation and differentiation along those traditional lines and firms has faded. The once well-demarcated boundaries between what was traditional Big-3 management consultancy firms and the Big-4 accounting firms providing consulting services has dissipated to the point of being almost non-recognizable and non-existent. With the degradation of differentiation and the widespread availability of high quality talent, other firms such as Accenture evolved to become single-service providers (SSPs)—a sort of a one-stop department store for all consulting needs. What was once called the Big-3 and Big-4 are now what I call the Elite-8.[19] The Elite-8 have similar services and homogeneity of talent and access to talent. However, the sheer size in personnel, number of offices, resources and financial results of the former Big-4 and Accenture dwarf and dominate the legacy consultancy Big-3 firms. As a result, client perceptions of management consultants have become more homongenized and relatively undifferentiated, and as client access to knowledge and talent has become uniformly easier and unrestricted, brand distinction and separation among the Elite-8 firms are far more difficult to achieve.

Although there are many factors that influence a client's selection of a management consultant, understanding the competitive value of knowledge and intelligence is gaining commercial momentum. In general, major consultancy firms compete amongst themselves and for clients based primarily on ten factors:

1. Reputation and stature of the firm.
2. Size and scope of the firm, such as global reach.
3. Practice specialty and subject matter expertise of the firm.
4. Social pedigree of the firm, including its professionals.
5. Industry presence and experience of the firm.
6. Professional standards, methods and practices of the firm.
7. Delivery capabilities of the firm.
8. Personal professional qualities (likeability, affinity and trust) of the personnel.
9. Legal capacity and financial resources to support major work and legal obligations.
10. Knowledge.

The actual criteria employed by a client in the selection of a consultant will be biased on any one or several of the above depending on client situation, preference or need. Nonetheless, competing on those ten factors requires the consultancy to commit considerable resources to the management of five major *processes*: (1) management of time, (2) management of talent, (3) creation of methods, (4) application of processes and (5) acquisition and management of *knowledge*. The most essential "asset" of a consultancy is its people . . . and the most essential process is knowledge management. Since knowledge is a uniquely human quality, creating, capturing, managing and disseminating knowledge are critical and essential *competitive* competencies of the consultancy firm.

A fundamental prerequisite for any knowledge management activity is the capture of the knowledge. Capturing *explicit* knowledge has its challenges, but because it is explicit, it's relatively straightforward. Everyday explicit knowledge of a subject is created, captured, disseminated and taught throughout organizations in various ways, including formal training, online forums and traditional educational and learning methods. However, capturing the appropriate and relevant *tacit* knowledge presents a different set of challenges. Tacit knowledge is far more personal in nature. As such, it is generally protected by those who have it and coveted by those who do not. The early research indicated that knowledge, especially in its tacit form, is asymmetrical and those who possess it are reluctant to share it without an expectation of reward or reciprocity.[20] Knowledge, as the saying goes is *power*, so it's not surprising that subsequent work suggests that "knowledge sharing hostility" is present in many organizations.[21] For any organization, such as a management consultancy that relies on knowledge, the reluctance and phenomenon of hostility can potentially be debilitating.[22]

The four major professions comprising accounting, consulting, law and medicine have long practiced the capture and distribution of both explicit and tacit knowledge. A young physician is "apprenticed" as an intern and then as a resident before being released on her own to treat patients. An accountant or lawyer who successfully passes the rigorous CPA or BAR exams becomes a staff accountant or lawyer who is then qualified to develop his professional skills under the structure of a firm and its experienced partners. Although no entrance or requisite examinations exist in the general profession of management consulting, the dynamics of working for more experienced personnel are the same.

Management consulting is a complex business and process, and there is an inherent ambiguity to it. Measuring the results of management consulting and client satisfaction is often imprecise. For example, "How does a client really measure the *'We think'* factor of consulting?" More fundamentally, fundamental to that question is, "How does a consultancy firm express its knowledge?"

In consulting there are four conditions that are uniformly present:

- In any client situation, the management consultant must work and *think* with imperfect, incomplete, inaccurate and unstructured data that may be inaccurate.
- The consultant generally must work and *think* in the context of the client and the client's environment.
- As a *process*, must deliver services in a manner that satisfies not only the contractual obligations and responsibilities of the consultant, but also meet the "emotional" needs of the client.
- In performing services the consultant must *demonstrate* objectivity, impartiality and the practical application of knowledge and wisdom.

Demonstrating knowledge and intellectual capital are challenging for any firm. In fact, the long-term viability and success of the top firms, especially the Elite-8, has created a "deserved" *presumption* of intellectual capital and knowledge. The difficulty is how to best express that to the market. Consultancy firms can best demonstrate and express their institutional capital and knowledge through four methods:

- **Publication of Knowledge.** Consultancy firms that conduct verifiable research and publish that research in commercial form can position themselves as "thought leaders" in a particular subject or industry. The key to strategically positioning knowledge as *differentiating* thought leadership is the knowledge itself. That is, the knowledge must be relevant and responsive to the client and provide value and insight to the client.
- **Demonstration of Knowledge.** Consultancy firms can enhance the perceptions of their competitiveness and thought leadership through the creation of "Knowledge Centers." Knowledge Centers are organizational units specifically dedicated to the creation, capturing and managing of relevant intellectual capital. A Knowledge Center can be created

and organized around an industry, subject matter, technology or business process.
- **Collaborative Relationships.** Creating knowledge can be a time-consuming and costly process. Consultancy firms can reduce the costs, time and risks of creating and capturing relevant and specific knowledge through formal collaborative relationships. Typically, these relationships can be built with and among schools of higher learning, specialized institutes and centers and credentialed and recognized individuals.
- **Knowledge Management Systems (KMX).** All major consultancy firms, certainly those belonging to the Elite-8, all employ technologies that provide for the capture and management of institutional knowledge. The purpose of these "systems" is to help disperse relevant knowledge and practices throughout the organization. Ultimately, these systems are designed to provide efficiency and insight into a consulting process, project or situation. The concept of KMX will be discussed more thoroughly in Section 4.0 of this chapter.

How a management consultant *thinks* and how the consultancy applies its relevant institional *knowledge* to a client have a direct and profound impact on the analysis, judgment and conclusions that the consultancy formulates for and behalf of the client. Those "outcomes" and behaviors should be clear manifestations of the management consulting process and application of knowledge and wisdom. In this context and to be responsive to the client's needs, the work performed by the consultant must demonstrate the appropriate strategic, operational and financial relevancy for the client. Concurrent with its work, a highly effective consultant and consultancy learns from its clients while simultaneously transferring knowledge to its clients. Accordingly, a major obligation of the consultant is to leave the client in the best possible position of self-sufficiency and sustainability through the transfer of appropriate knowledge.

3.0 Learning and Knowledge Transfer in Management Consulting

Having established the components of knowledge and the significance of tacit and explicit knowledge in the consulting process, it is important to understand how consultants learn. Knowledge is developed through a continuous learning process until it becomes a de facto standard and wisdom. Learning is a personal process that involves a complex combination of formal, informal, experiential and existential methods. How both tacit and explicit knowledge is formed and learned are of significant concern to any organization or culture, especially PSFs. As illustrated in Exhibit 17.3, the development process of *knowledge* is reflective of a continuous cycle of five steps.

At each step of the cycle, tacit and explicit knowledge is learned. Indeed, explicit methods such as classroom or online training may be used, case teaching may be invoked, testing and comprehensive examinations may be

> Exhibit 17.3 Knowledge Development Cycle
>
> *(1) Discovering > (2) Learning & Synthesizing > (3) Applying & Synthesizing > (4) Adapting & Synthesizing > (5) Modifying, Adopting & Owning (Personalization)*

employed, as well as experiential and virtual learning technologies. Procedural knowledge of quality assurance practices, firm requirements of senior personnel, client review and service delivery standards are just a few examples of explicit learning methods for a consultancy. Explicit knowledge is more direct and more easily attained and learned than tacit knowledge.

Tacit knowledge, on the other hand, is more difficult and, sometimes, more ambiguous than explicit. Tacit knowledge is generally what clients covet the most. Tacit knowledge is that knowledge that is learned through trial and error, life's lessons and extensive experience. In management consulting there should always be a symbiotic and synergistic relationship between the consultant and client. Tacit knowledge is difficult to acquire because it is *shared* knowledge. The person who possesses the knowledge must be motivated and incentivized to want to share that knowledge and that is problematic.

- A fundamental test is whether the work performed by the consultant is responsive to the needs of the client. Responsiveness to client needs is a given and necessary outcome. Clients expect great work that satisfies their needs. Hence, simply doing "great" work is the minimum threshold for consultant performance. Clients generally seek insights from the tacit knowledge.
- A second test is whether the client enjoyed and benefited from the processes used by the management consultant in performing the work. That is, was the experience favorable and was the behavior of the consultant exemplary? Clients expect a professional relationship and well-organized and managed consulting process. Clients expect the work to be responsive and performed "on-time," "in budget" and to a high standard. Those criteria are the givens. But what is more enduring is the process that the consultant used. Clients remember the process and experience with the consultant long after the results and deliverables are forgotten. Clients equate tacit knowledge with the lessons learned from the consultant related to structure, organization and process.
- A third test is whether knowledge itself is created and shared. Clients engage management consultants for a variety of reasons that span the spectrum from the need for a specific SME or industry insight to shifting the burden of risk and hazards of litigation onto the shoulders of a major consultancy. Thus, the issue for most clients is not only of performance, as indicated above, but whether the consultant has utilized its institutional knowledge for the benefit of the client. The

incorporation of tacit knowledge into the client service and delivery model and process is a key determinant of client's ability to sustain work after the consultant departs.

Research by McIver and Wang supports the long held empirical sentiment that different types of work and environments that the work is performed in have fundamentally different knowledge characteristics, learning dynamics and therefore measurements.[23] In consulting, knowledge and learning are clearly correlated with the environment, community of practice and individual abilities.

To compete successfully and sustain itself in an ever-escalating intensive environment, the consultancy firm's future rests on its ability to attract and retain exceptional talent and monetize its intellectual property . . . its knowledge of process and subject matter and its wisdom of clients. It is the *wisdom* that clients demand and pay for. The wisdom is the synthesis of a continuous process of learning, adaptation and applying and generating knowledge in the context of a life and career.

In management consulting the explicit knowledge is a relatively straightforward process. First, the firms hire well-educated and talented graduates from top MBA programs. Second, the firms invest in those individuals through training and development programs. Third, and most importantly, once hired and trained, new consultants are placed on projects with experienced consultants. Knowledge is transferred from the experienced consultant to the less experienced consultant. In management consulting, tacit knowledge development involving the nuances of consulting, client relations, consulting team management and the subtle behaviors of the consulting process is generally accomplished through the traditional Master-Apprentice Model.[24]

The master-apprentice has been long established as a means of creating and transferring both explicit and tacit knowledge. The model has its historical lineage in the twelfth century when craftsman guilds began to appear in Medieval Europe. Prior to the formation of the guilds, stone masons formed societies for the training of future masons. Researchers Nielsen and Kvale have identified four characteristics common to the master-apprentice model:

1 **Participation in a Community of Practice.** In consulting the community is composed of the consultancy firm, a practice specialization within the firm and subject specialization.
2 **Professional Identity.** Clearly professional identity is critical to any specialized field of endeavor. Members of consulting firms are associated with being professionals. Members of the Big-4 accounting firms who are consultants are governed by the professional practices of the AICPA and other regulatory and sanctioning agencies.
3 **Learning through Imitation of the Master.** Although classroom and online training is beneficial, consulting cannot be learned through

academic preparation only. Consulting is best learned by performing the work using a structure and participating on a team (community) under the management and direction of a highly experienced consultant. In large firms, the "master" takes the form of the institution and the individual experienced consultant (usually the partners of the firm). The institution will have its own standards and practices for performing the work and ensuring consistency.

4   **Quality of Work Is Assessed through the Community of Practice.**[25] Evaluating the work of a professional service provider, especially a consultant, is difficult. Often the work assessment process is subjective. For consulting and notwithstanding the constant focus on work generation, determining quality is achieved through an assessment of six criteria: (1) responsiveness to client needs and scope, (2) adherence to institutional standards and practices, (3) comparison to competitor products, (4) generation of desired results and benefits, (5) satisfaction of client and likeliness of recurring business and (6) generation of new or updated knowledge.

In the master-apprentice model, learning is accomplished through verbal instructions, examples, emulation and a long process of *doing*. In the course of performing work, knowledge was transferred from the "master craftsman" to the "apprentice." The master craftsman possesses the *wisdom* of the trade or profession. *Webster's Dictionary* defines "apprentice" as "one who is learning by practical experience under skilled workers a trade, art, or calling."[26] Another "important distinction is that the apprentice does not have sufficient training in his chosen field to work independently."[27]

After the requisite number of years of learning by *doing*, the apprentice would earn the right to become a "journeyman." A journeyman was a fully trained and competent craftsman, but not yet experienced enough to be considered a craftsman. The journeyman would possess the explicit knowledge and would be amassing more comprehensive and sophisticated tacit knowledge as well. Because a journeyman was fully trained he or she may have been the original independent contractor and 1099 worker since he or she could work without supervision and could work for any employer or client.

Although the master-apprentice model is generally associated with the skilled arts and vocations, such as electrical and plumbing trades, much is similar to management consulting. A new consultant may have extensive academic training or even direct industry experience, but those qualifications notwithstanding do not necessarily equate to tacit knowledge of the consulting process. In management consulting, as in the master-apprentice model, there is a progression of learning and knowledge. At each organizational level in consulting, responsibilities change, as do explicit and tacit knowledge. Ultimately, it is the tacit knowledge, combined with deep subject matter expertise, that is the most important at the highest levels of the profession.

Tacit knowledge is passed from the more experienced to the less experienced. In addition to the explicit knowledge of a subject or industry, a "master" consultant (for example, a partner in a Big-4 firm) who is highly experienced *knows* how the work must be done and how it can be best accomplished. Generally, a "master" is a member of and resident (immersed) in a community of practice (CoP). A CoP is a group of professionals who share common interests, subject matter expertise, industry expertise and knowledge. As a professional performs or practices her profession, knowledge is amassed through doing and learning from those around her. Learning and knowledge is individual, immersion-based and integrative.[28] As an experienced professional, the master and members of the CoP *know* how to best interact with clients and what management techniques can best motivate and position the consulting team for exemplary performance. This experience is largely tacit in form and substance and highly personalized.

In the master-apprentice relationship, it is incumbent on the experienced consultant to teach and transfer skills to the less experienced. Understanding that the master-apprentice model is highly asymmetrical in form and function and contingent on the skills of the "master" to transfer knowledge, consultancy are confronted with the daunting task of how to best *capture* and represent the tacit knowledge for continued use. That is, the challenge for the consultancy is how to best: (1) identify relevant tacit knowledge, (2) capture relevant tacit knowledge for institution use and (3) disperse and replicate the use of relevant tacit knowledge for institutional advantage and client benefit.

4.0 Knowledge Management Systems in Consulting

Major consultancy firms were early adopters of IT and implementers of Knowledge Management Exchanges (KMX) systems.[29] But what is knowledge management without sufficient and relevant content? As in defining knowledge, there are many, many definitions for Knowledge Management. For example:

- Donald Hislop defines knowledge management as: "an umbrella term which refers to any deliberate efforts to manage knowledge of an organisation's workforce via the use of . . . a particular culture and people management practices."[30]

There are many other others, but most miss the mark with repsect to management consulting. Knowledge management is a *process*. Culture, management practices, technology and software can certainly help and support knowledge management, but in and of themselves, they are *not* knowledge management. The *process* of knowledge management must have purpose, a clear alignment with the strategy of the institution, a process and integrative facility that is relevant and useful. I define a knowledge management system as:

> **Knowledge Management System (KMX)**
>
> An integrated *process* and *system* of creating, discovering, capturing, codifying and delivering relevant explicit and tacit knowledge for institutional and individual use.

Prior to the IT-based solutions that began to emerge in the mid-1980's, KMX within the major consultancies was somewhat problematic. If the consultant resided in a large office, she would have access to resources and "knowledge." For example, a large city office, say New York or San Francisco, might have physical "libraries" full of previous consulting assignments. Furthermore, in the large offices there was a greater concentration of talent and most likely, access to more professionals with experience. In contrast, consultants who were physically removed from the mainstream offices or were in smaller offices had a much more challenging path to navigate to access knowledge. Essentially these early, pre-1985 KMXs were of five basic architectures, each of which shared some common features. Specifically:

- **Social Roadmap.** This form of KMX is highly decentralized and dynamic in form and application. The roadmap is largely informal and is designed to direct and connect less experienced professionals to more experienced subject matter and industry experts. The idea is to help create a higher level of social interaction among professions, a greater sense of unity and enhancement and extension of "communities of practice."
- **Designated Subject Matter Expert Guide.** This form of KMX is generally centralized and is based on organizational title and responsibility. The subject matter expert guide is similar to the social roadmap, but has more formality and structure. Under this design, certain experienced individuals are designated experts, leaders and authorities. Formal processes and procedures are installed to communicate and coordinate among the designated experts and the consultant in the field actually doing the work.
- **Knowledge Mapping.** Knowledge mapping combines elements of the social roadmap with designated subject matter expert models. In this model, subject matter experts are mapped within the organizational and process design of the consultancy. However, as this architecture is highly personalized, it is susceptible to many inhibitors to effectiveness of information flow and knowledge exchange.[31]
- **Central Repository.** Depending on the technology and IT architecture, this form of KMX can be either centralized or decentralized. Almost all of the major firms, certainly the Big-4 (-formally Big-8 and -Big-6), had

central repositories of prior work. Under this design all consulting projects performed above a minimum threshold would be sent to a central repository for codification and collection purposes. The central repository would library the work for future reference and use.
- **Work Papers.** This approach to KMX is highly decentralized and susceptible to informal practices and fragmentation. Another method of knowledge capture and retention are the work papers that a consultancy generated while performing the work. In the accounting firms, work papers are highly structured, organized to a particular standard and are also periodically reviewed by the partners and peer groups. Work papers in the pre-1985 consulting environment were a terrific source of both explicit and tacit knowledge but since they were resident in the local offices or with the local community of practice, they were highly decentralized and sometimes difficult to obtain.

Among the premier consultancy firms the concepts of institutional knowledge and individual practitioner knowledge are not new and have long been considered as essential to the sustainability of the firm and its competitive position. Examples of professional knowledge codification, at least in the U.S., date back to the 1920's. Firms such as Peat, Marwick & Mitchell (KPMG), Price Waterhouse (PWC) and McKinsey were all pioneers in the early codification of both explicit and tacit knowledge. This knowledge was captured and disseminated in the form of hardcopy manuals and reference guides. In the 1970's firms such as Andersen Consulting (Accenture) and McKinsey would develop specific knowledge in the form of methodologies (Method 1) and MECE,[32] respectively, as expressions of formal knowledge capture and management. By the mid-1980's, and into the 1990's, these early forms of knowledge management would evolve into massive databases of client and project information in the form of Andersen's Knowledge Management System (KMX) and McKinsey's Firm Practice Information System (FPIS).[33]

The advent of information technology (IT), especially during the 1980's when the cost of technology was falling and advances in IT were made daily, created a shift in the way knowledge management was operated within consultancy. In the 1990's virtually all of the major consultancies embraced KMX in some form or another. Indeed, many firms made an attempt to move beyond the rigidity and limitations of the early KMX designs.

The initial generation of IT-enabled KMX concentrated on making the central repository more relevant and accessible and automating the work papers as a primary mehtod of capturing knowledge. The presence of electronic mail systems and ultimately the Internet provided for the broad distribution of knowledge. In particular:

- In the later 1980's and early 1990's, KPMG attempted to leverage its firm-wide knowledge using a uniform platform. Christened the "Shadow Partner" the ill-fated KPMG attempt at KMX was intended to leverage individual tacit and institutional knowledge for the betterment of client

service. However noble the effort, the architecture was flawed and the investment was poorly justified.
- As the 1990's moved on, firms such as Ernst & Ernst (now Ernst & Young) and Andersen Consulting (now Accenture) implemented firm-wide KMX systems.[34] But many of these early adopters experienced difficulties not only in the technical application of KMX, but also the human use of the technology and application of the knowledge content. For example, Andersen Consulting's KMX of the early and mid-1990's was composed of thousands of repositories built on Lotus Notes. The existence of so many databases and thousands of consultants made the process of KMX extremely challenging.

Today, all major consulting firms have some form of technology-enabled KMX in place. KMX is a necessary condition to competing effectively in the consulting industry. With search technologies such as Google and infrastructure technologies such as the Internet, Internet 2.0 and the Internet of Things (IoT), the creation of KMX architectures and capabilities for consultancy firms are easier to implement. Modern KMX are composed of advanced search facilities, multi-relational databases, blogs, chat rooms, idea jams,[35] structured and unstructured query facilities, social media components, social collaboration facilitation tools, tagging, data analytic tools and specialized KMX software. A modern design may also include explicit learning and testing features, as well as highly advanced *tacit* knowledge transfer features using gamification,[36] artificial intelligence (AI), virtual reality and experiential learning facilities.[37]

Creating a robust KMX for consulting purposes requires significant capital investment, extensive time and resources, cultural participation and change, if necessary, and strategy. Make a mistake and the KMX effort may suffer badly, and switching costs or back-out costs may not be just high, but prohibitive. The top challenges for any consultancy firm using KMX, or any firm for that matter, include:

1. Creating a strategy for knowledge.
2. Knowing what knowledge to populate the KMX . . . relevancy and purpose of knowledge.
3. Providing for the continuous updating, replenishing and editing of both explicit and tacit knowledge.
4. Incentivizing professionals to contribute knowledge.
5. Providing for the mass deployment, use and leverage (exploitation) of the knowledge by the practicing consultants.
6. Providing for alignment of the KMX and its content to the firm's strategy and business model.
7. Managing and protecting internally generated intellectual property (IP).
8. Ensuring security and privacy.
9. Enabling for the appropriate and effective transfer of both explicit and tacit knowledge to clients.
10. Ensuring proper governance, organizational placement and leadership.

To be effective *with* KMX, the consultancy must have a strategy for KMX. Mapping out the strategic intent, objectives and parameters for knowledge, how to capture and deploy knowledge and how to best optimize knowledge for client benefit and firm differentiation require the firm to make a series of commitments. These commitments include procedural, cultural, financial, organizational and strategic, as well as technical. Some of the critical success factors in KMX for consultancy firms include:

- Organizational placement and leadership are essential. Firms that profile KMX and lead the function with C-suite executives, such as Chief Knowledge Officer or Chief Learning Officer, send a strong message to both employees and clients of the firm's commitment to knowledge.
- Creating a method and the mechanics for capturing knowledge including how to:
  - Cultivate > Memorialize > Classify > Codify Knowledge
- Implementing relevancy filters to ensure that the proper knowledge is captured:
  - Alignment to firm strategy
  - Recognition of what is new and creating new value versus updating and adding value
  - Client value and benefits
  - Firm differentiation and operational value
- Incentivizing managers and leadership to contribute tacit knowledge of people, processes, subjects, industries and client behaviors.
- Creating a knowledge-centric culture where knowledge is perceived as strategic and differentiating.

5.0 Conclusion: Thinking About the Future of Knowledge

In this chapter we have examined and discussed the role of knowledge in management consulting, how consultants learn and how consultancies can use knowledge to its strategic advantage. With those accomplished . . . let's *think* about the future of knowledge in management consulting.

No doubt, consulting is one of the ultimate knowledge businesses and professions, and KMX has evolved far beyond simple archiving. Across all industries and subjects, explicit knowledge is growing exponentially. So there is little doubt that explicit technologies and methods will continue to evolve to accommodate the changes and sheer size and quantity of knowledge. However, it's the future of tacit knowledge that's most interesting.

As we think about the future of tacit knowledge, the possibilities become increasingly exciting. Let's conclude this chapter with five thoughts!

- First, consultancy firms will place greater emphasis on capturing tacit knowledge and institutionalizing that knowledge into wisdom.
- Second, consultancy firms will differentiate themselves on knowledge . . . more specifically how clients perceive that tacit knowledge and how they, the clients, can benefit from that tacit knowledge. The consultancy that can best profile that knowledge will create separation from its competitors.
- Third, the capturing and socialization of tacit knowledge within the consultancy should accelerate and enhance the development of younger consultants. This transfer of tacit knowledge will have a profound influence on how the younger consultants interact with clients and with the more experienced leaders of the firm and will permanently alter the traditional master-apprentice type of knowledge transfer. No doubt, knowledge development within the firm will be escalated and accelerated at unprecedented rates. At some point, the convergence of tacit and explicit knowledge will form the basis for using Artificial Intelligence (AI) in the consulting process.
- Fourth, as more and more tacit knowledge is captured and deployed, more accurate measurements will need to be created and implemented to better assess the effectiveness and impact of tacit knowledge on individual project performance and ultimately, client results.
- Finally, with technology and greater transparency of the consulting process,[38] consultancies will face more complex decisions, and correspondingly, more opportunities to transfer knowledge back and forth to their clients. Ultimately, the emergence and use of AI based KMX will aid in the delivery of client services and consulting project team performance. This interconnectivity of knowledge will create different client management skills and will alter the client/consultant relationship.

We now come full circle and back to Ray, the partner who so many years ago simply described consulting with two words . . . "*We think.*" Reflecting on those words, Ray was right. In the twenty-first century, we think faster, with more synthesis, more connectivity, greater access to knowledge and with greater tools . . . but despite all of the tools and technology, in the end, "*We Think!*" and hopefully we do so contemplatively and with greater purpose and clarity.

Notes

1 See, http://www.merriam-webster.com/dictionary/knowledge. Merriam-Webster Dictionaries. (1915). *School Science and Mathematics*, 15(6), pp.538. doi:10.1111/j.1949-8594.1915.tb13977.x.
2 Wang, S. and Noe, R. A. (2010). "Knowledge Sharing: A Review and Directions for Future Research." *Human Resource Management Review*, 20(2), pp. 115–31. doi:10.1016/j.hrmr.2009.10.001.

3 See, Davenport, T. and Prusak, L. (1998). *Working Knowledge: How Organizations Manage What They Know* (Boston: Harvard Business School Press).
4 Omotayo, F. O. (2015). "Knowledge Management as an Important Tool in Organisational Management: A Review of Literature." *Library Philosophy and Practice*, University of Nebraska at: http://digitalcommons.unl.edu/libphilprac/1238.
5 Blackler, F. (1995). "Knowledge, knowledge work and organisations: An overview and interpretation." *Organisation Studies*, 16(6), pp. 1021–46. doi:10.1177/017084069501600605, as cited by Funmilola Olubunmi Omotayo.
6 See Nonaka, I. and Takeuchi, H. (1996). "The Knowledge-Creating Company: How Japanese Companies Create the Dynamics of Innovation." *Long Range Planning* 29(4), pp.592. doi:10.1016/0024-6301(96)81509-3.
7 See also Michael Polanyi at: http://infed.org/mobi/michael-polanyi-and-tacit-knowledge/.
8 Hislop, D. (2010). "Knowledge management as an ephemeral management fashion?" *Journal of Knowledge Management*, 14(6), pp.779–790 at: http://www.emeraldinsight.com/doi/abs/10.1108/13673271011084853.
9 For additional discussion of explicit knowledge, see http://ww.basicknowledge101.com/pdf/KM_roles.pdf. See also: Smith, E. A. (2001). "The Role of Tacit and Explicit Knowledge in the Workplace." *Journal of Knowledge Management*, 5(4) at: http://ww.basicknowledge101.com/pdf/KM_roles.pdf.
10 Hislop, D. (2013). *Knowledge Management in Organisations: A Critical Introduction*, 3rd Ed. (UK: Oxford University Press). See also: Hislop, D. (2010). "Knowledge management as an ephemeral management fashion?" *Journal of Knowledge Management*, 14(6), pp. 779–790 at: http://www.emeraldinsight.com/doi/abs/10.1108/13673271011084853.
11 Yakhlef, A. (2010). "The Corporeality of Practice-based Learning." *Organisational Studies*, 31(4).
12 See Davenport and Prusak, op. cit.
13 Sun, P.Y. and Scott, J. L. (2005). "An Investigation of Barriers to Knowledge Transfer." *Journal of Knowledge Management*, 9(2), at: http://dx.doi.org/10.1108/13673270510590236.
14 Drucker, P. (1994). "The Age of Social Transformation," *The Atlantic Monthly*, November.
15 Bosua, R. and Venkitachalam, K. (2013). "Aligning strategies and processes in knowledge management: A framework." *Journal of Knowledge Management*, 17, at: http://www.emeraldinsight.com/doi/abs/10.1108/JKM-10-2012-0323.
16 Teng, J.T.C. and Song, S. (2011). "An exploratory examination of knowledge-sharing behaviors: Solicited and voluntary." *Journal of Knowledge Management*, 15(1), pp. 104–117, as cited by Omoytayo.
17 Historically the Big-3 consulting firms were BCG, Bain and McKinsey.
18 The historical Big-8 accounting firms consolidated into the Big-6. Further consolidation followed to create the current Big-4: Deloitte, Ernst & Young, KPMG and PriceWaterhouseCoopers. In 2002, Arthur Andersen ceased operations as an accountancy firm.
19 The Elite-8 as defined by author: Accenture, BCG, Bain, Deloitte, Ernst & Young, KPMG, McKinsey and PriceWaterhouseCoopers.
20 See Davenport and Prusak, op. cit.
21 Husted, K. and Michailova, S. (2002). "Diagnosing and Fighting Knowledge based Sharing." *Organizational Dynamics*, 31(1), at: https://www.researchgate.

net/publication/247142520_Diagnosing_and_Fighting_Knowledge-Sharing_Hostility.
22 Husted, K., Michailova, S., Minbaeva, D.B. and Pedersen, T. (2012). "Knowledge-sharing hostility and governance mechanisms: an empirical test." *Journal of Knowledge Management*, 16(5), pp. 754–773.
23 McIver, D. and Wang, X. (2016). "Measuring knowledge in organizations: A knowledge-in-practice approach." *Journal of Knowledge Management*, 20(4), at: http://www.emeraldinsight.com/doi/pdfplus/10.1108/JKM-11-2015-0478.
24 For additional perspective on the master-apprentice model of learning and knowledge transfer, see: Brandt, B.L., Farmer Jr., J.A. and Buckmaster, A. (1993). *Cognitive apprenticeship approach to helping adults learn. New Directions for Adult and Continuing Education*, 59, pp. 69–78. See also, Pratt, D.D. (1998). *Five Perspectives on Teaching in Adult and Higher Education* (Malabar, FL: Krieger Publishing Company).
25 See Klaus og Steinar Kvale, N. (1999). *Mesterlære: læring som sosial praksis* (Oslo: Ad Notam Gyldendal).
26 See http://www.merriam-webster.com/dictionary/apprentice.
27 See http://work.chron.com/difference-between-journeyman-apprentice-15642.html.
28 Jeon, S., Kim, Y. and Koh, J. (2011). "An Integrative Model for Knowledge Sharing in Communities-of-Practice." *Journal of Knowledge Management*, 15(2), at: http://dx.doi.org/10.1108/13673271111119682.
29 See Sarvary, M. (1999). "Knowledge Management and Competition in the Consulting Industry." *California Management Review* 41(2), Winter 1999, at: http://cmr.berkeley.edu/search/articleDetail.aspx?article=4471.
30 See Hislop, op. cit.
31 Lee, J. and Fink, D. (2013). "Knowledge Mapping" Encouragements and Impediments to Adoption." *Journal of Knowledge Management*, 17(1), at: http://dx.doi.org/10.1108/13673271311300714.
32 McKinsey's Mutually Exclusive-Collectively Exhaustive (MECE) proprietary methodology.
33 See Indu, P. and Gupta, V. (2007). "McKinsey's Knowledge Management Practices." ICMR, at: www.icmrindia.org.
34 See Meister, D. and Davenport, T. (2005). "Knowledge Management at Accenture." Richard Ivey School of Business, Ivey Management Services, *Harvard Business Review*, October 11, at: https://hbr.org/product/knowledge-management-at-accenture/905E18-PDF-ENG.
35 Developed by IBM. See http://www-03.ibm.com/ibm/history/ibm100/us/en/icons/innovationjam/. See also http://timkastelle.org/blog/2010/01/using-jams-to-select-ideas/.
36 For more information on "Gamification," see https://en.wikipedia.org/wiki/Gamification. See also https://www.coursera.org/learn/gamification. See also http://www.theatlantic.com/technology/archive/2011/08/gamification-is-bullshit/243338/.
37 See Burke, B. (2013). "The Gamification of Business." *Forbes*, January 21, at: http://www.forbes.com/sites/gartnergroup/2013/01/21/the-gamification-of-business/.
38 See Christensen, C. (2013). "Consulting on the Cusp of Disruption." *Harvard Business Review*, October, at: https://hbr.org/2013/10/consulting-on-the-cusp-of-disruption.

Part VI

Looking Ahead at Management Consulting

18 Ethics and the Trusted Advisor   411
    (CHARLES H. GREEN, CEO TRUSTED ADVISOR ASSOCIATES)

19 Consulting in Entrepreneurship: Essential
    Foundations for Consultants   423
    (RICKIE A. MOORE, EMLYON BUSINESS SCHOOL)

Introduction

Several major trends in the consulting industry, previously discussed in Chapter 1, are causing major changes. In addition, each chapter in this book has also raised additional questions about the future of consulting in its particular area of concern. In this section, two new concerns are considered that bear significantly on what will happen to management consulting.

First, the ethical challenges and needs to develop a "trusted advisor client relationship," and second, the need to establish a stronger entrepreneurial perspective to better understand a client's issues, needs, and approaches to build best solutions.

For Chapter 18, "Ethics and the Trusted Advisor," the author describes ethical problems in consulting firms as much more adverse consequences of values rather than virtues. There are several problems described in some detail. These include: 1) the lack of transparency, 2) misguided professionalism, and 3) misconceived goals and objectives.

With respect to transparency it is posited that it needs to be virtually 100 percent. Shared and clear understanding is paramount. There is no real viable reason to withhold information; trust is argued to be a (if not the) positive value that creates client trust, and without it, there will be significant (adverse) issues.

As for misguided professionalism, behaving inappropriately does adversely affect the relationship and the consultancy. Specific and constructive behaviors are key. And following professional and societal "etiquette" is required.

Regarding misconceived goals and objectives, the author observes how consultants often can become more focused on the "metrics" of "success" and mistake "ends" for "means." This is often manifest in a "winning attitude" that interferes with the engagement and long-term perspective the consultant should have with the client.

The author uses these three areas of misalignment to lead the reader to understanding the true need for a "trusted advisor" relationship. And helping us understand this need, the reader is presented with discussions and arguments so as to better learn how to create respect and behave with good ethics in a trusted advisor relationship.

For Chapter 19 the author posits that there is a substantial opportunity and need for greater consulting to entrepreneurs and entrepreneurialism ventures. This is a product of the enormous effects of innovation/creative thinking and the role of the VC or like consultant/entrepreneur in today's marketplace. Thus, the text concludes with the subject and focus of "Consulting in Entrepreneurship: Essential Foundations for Consultants."

Herein, the author provides insight and perspectives for a potential high-growth, yet largely and currently untapped "market" for entrepreneur consulting. As more and more entrepreneurial ventures have become more prominently known, used, and valued, the practice of Consulting to Entrepreneurs has gained greater notice, interest, and attraction. Very notable examples over the past decade plus include the formation of Facebook in 2004, Twitter in 2006, and Snapchat in 2011. (See data below.)

And as more persons are now being drawn to this more developing field of consulting, the author provides us with insight and perspective—especially regarding the creation of value primarily for the Entrepreneur and consequently for the multiple stakeholders that would/could benefit.

It is observed that the entrepreneur's (and the consultant's) ability to detect, understand, interpret, organize, and convert information related to value creation is paramount. And it is the consultant's and the entrepreneur's challenge to effectively and efficiently transform that information into valuable and viable commercial outcomes. As such, the creativity and inventiveness of the Entrepreneur (and consultant, thereto) will directly determine the quality and differentiation of the product or service that would be launched on the market to satisfy the customers' needs.

This process of value creation requires intuition, articulate conception, and effective construction and implementation. The principal focus of Chapter 19 is to explore this "process" and significant opportunity for consultancy.

Supplementary notes related to three specific examples of Facebook, Twitter, and Snapchat may well be quite interesting in "setting the stage" for the reader of this chapter.

For Facebook:

Slightly more than a decade past its origin, Facebook, on July 13, 2015, was noted as the fastest company in the Standard & Poor's 500 Index to reach a

Looking Ahead at Management Consulting 409

market cap of $250 billion. (Michelle F. Davis (July 13, 2015) and "Facebook Close Sets Speed Record for $250 Billion Market Cap". Bloomberg.com)

Further, Facebook has more than 1.65 billion monthly active users as of March 31, 2016. ("Company Info — Facebook Newsroom". Facebook)

For Twitter:

Just ten years after launch, Twitter, as of March 2016, had more than 310 million monthly active users. ("About Twitter, Inc.". Twitter)

For Snapchat:

The application that we know as Snapchat was "initially" launched in May 2011 and then relaunched two months later in July 2011. (J.J. Colao, "The Inside Story of Snapchat: The World's Hottest App or a $3 Billion Disappearing Act?". *Forbes*, January 6, 2014)

Further, Snapchat evolved into a mix of private messaging and public content, including brand networks, publications, and live events such as sports and music. Nevertheless, according to survey (value) studies conducted in March 2016, Snapchat was still being accessed by users. (Andrew Wallenstein, Susanne Ault, "Snapchat Content Survey: How Much Millennials Actually Use Live Stories, Discover and More". *Variety*, March 24, 2016)

18 Ethics and the Trusted Advisor

Charles H. Green

One way to think about ethics in the consulting profession is to start with a paradigm relationship – that of the "Trusted Advisor."[1] It's a concept that most consultants respect and aspire to (even if they may be a little imprecise on the definition). The term "trusted advisor" intuitively resonates with "ethical" for most consultants – an "unethical trusted advisor" is almost an oxymoron.

In fact, exploring the connection helps clarify both concepts – "trusted advisor" and "consulting ethics."

Ethics, Virtues, and Values

Both ethics and trust have to do with relationships – a trivial-sounding observation that is in fact fundamental.

Much discussion of "ethics" is discussion about personal virtues – and not about relationships per se. Consulting firms frequently cite concepts like "integrity," "pursuit of excellence," "client service," or "passion" in their values statements; those particular qualities are individual traits. They do not have to do with the way consultants interact with their clients – or with their employees, for that matter.

The same is true in some discussions of trust. Discussions of trust in terms of expertise, or reliability, or work ethic, or mastery are discussions about individual traits. Those particular traits do not speak directly to how those individuals relate to their clients. In this chapter, I'll use the term "virtues" to refer to these individual qualities. They are undoubtedly important and have a critical place in consulting firms. But they do not, in the terms of this chapter, speak to relationships.

The attributes affecting relationships are different – they specifically refer to the ways consultants interact with clients and staff and the way clients in turn engage with consultants. In this chapter I'll use the term "values" to describe attributes that have to do with relationships, as opposed to individual traits.[2]

What is included in the "values" group? Here's a short list:

- Collaboration
- Client focus (for the sake of the client)
- Relationship orientation (not project or transactional orientation)
- Transparency
- Empathy
- Vulnerability

Unlike the virtues of excellence or integrity, the values list by definition deals with relationships. Collaboration, by definition, requires a partner. Client focus, by definition, requires both a client and an entity doing the focusing. One cannot empathize without an object of one's empathy, and so forth.

This distinction between individual virtues and relationship values has evident practical consequences. On the ethics side, we've all seen firms with super-smart consultants who are abusive to internal staff,[3] yet who are forgiven because they deliver excellent quality, or have integrity (though often these are cover for "he sells a lot," or "clients love the result"). But can you be abusive and still be ethical? Not by the standards of values outlined above – an abusive relationship is intuitively unethical.

The same is true for trust. Part of being a trusted advisor is being trustworthy, in the sense of the virtues – we need to be credible, competent, and reliable. But those virtues are not sufficient to create a trusted advisor relationship. For that to be the case, we have to relate to our clients in certain ways – the ways of the values listed above.

> By this view, ethics in consulting has to be about more than just virtues – it must address values-based relationships. Similarly, if one is to be a trusted advisor, it is not enough to achieve personal excellence; we must also address personal relationships – client relationships in particular.[4]

So what? What are some practical implications? They fall into three areas:

- How do trusted advisors behave? How do ethical consultants and an ethical firm appear? And what are common ethical and trust violations?
- How can we create ethical firms of trusted advisors?
- How can you evaluate success as a trusted advisor and as an ethical firm?

How Do Trusted Advisors Behave?

Trusted Advisor Associates created the TQ Trust Quotient, a self-assessment instrument based on the Trust Equation,[5] from the book *The Trusted*

Advisor.[6] Both express the elements of personal trustworthiness, in the form of an equation:

$$\frac{(\text{Credibility} + \text{Reliability} + \text{Intimacy})}{\text{Self-Orientation}}$$

This definition blends what I called "virtues" above – Credibility and Reliability – with two elements that fit more in the "values" list – Intimacy (the ability to be vulnerable and convey safety in engagement with another party) and Self-Orientation (the degree to which we are focused on ourselves, vs. on others, either through selfishness or neurotic self-obsession).

The TQ has collected over 70,000 online takers since its introduction in 2010. There are several findings,[7] including:

- Women are statistically significantly more trustworthy than men
- Almost all of the higher scores for women is due to the Intimacy factor

This finding correlates strongly with occupational surveys of trustworthiness by major organizations like Pew Research[8] and Gallup,[9] who consistently find that lawyers rank near the bottom of such lists – and that nurses rank at the top.

Lawyers are a largely male profession – and score extremely highly on the C and R factors on the TQ. Nursing, of course, is a largely female profession, one we associate more highly with the values of Intimacy and low self-orientation.

The other finding from the TQ research is that, of the four factors, the Intimacy component is statistically more powerful than the others. That is, based both on multiple regression analysis and on incidence of paired correlations with TQ scores, it is intimacy that most drives trustworthiness.

Which means – when we ask how trusted advisors behave, the single most important answer is:

Trusted advisors put more emphasis on the values, as opposed to the virtues, than do non-trusted advisors.

The parallel with ethical consultants and ethical firms seems strong. Certainly ethical consultants and firms have a strong grounding in virtues – they're rigorous, disciplined, honest, and have integrity. But when it comes to ethical behavior, those virtues are table stakes, jacks for openers. They are, in other words, necessary but not sufficient conditions. Being virtuous may be necessary to be ethical – but it is not, by itself, enough.

Indeed, the ethical problems that consulting firms find themselves in are much more often failures of values than of virtues – for example, conflicts of interest.[10] (There are of course major exceptions, like the insider trading case of McKinsey CEO Raj Gupta,[11] a clear virtues violation).

Interestingly, values problems like conflicts of interest are also failures to operate as a trusted advisor.

There are several such problems of ethics and trust.

a. *Lack of transparency.* For dozens of reasons (most of which boil down to fear), consultants fear sharing information with clients.

    - At the most elemental level, they think they must convey expertise at all times – the basic fundamental "sin" of a consultant is to admit ignorance. From a trust perspective, this tendency flies in the face of transparency; consultants forget that probably the *most* credible thing you can say is, "I don't know."
    - Consultants also fear transparency regarding their firm's rate structure. They've usually been told, either directly or indirectly, not to share such information with clients. Since they're already overly concerned with being perceived "worth" their daily or hourly rates, it's an easy step to trying to conceal rates.
    - Some firms misconstrue the business development process, thinking that they can't "give away" value content without being paid; they ignore the powerful role of "sample selling" in intangible services, and again keep information close to the vest.
    - Most firms are fearful of sharing content. Stated reasons include competitive advantage, intellectual property, or client desires for secrecy. While some businesses do have legitimate IP concerns (software patents, for example) and some clients indeed want secrecy, the well-known secret is that most value lies in execution. Some firms joke that they could be given a competitor's entire strategy book and wouldn't know what to do with it, because they are hard-wired to do things their own way.
    - Finally, most firms are uncomfortable being transparent internally about issues of compensation and promote criteria; those that are transparent end up spending considerable energy trying to define detailed behavioral rationales, which can often still be unsatisfying.

The trusted advisor answer, which is also the ethical answer, is to set a path that is virtually 100 percent transparent. When faced with a decision to share or not to share a piece of information, consultants should ask themselves, and leaders should ask consultants, over and over – what is the rationale for *withholding* this information from clients? And, with equal rigor, what would be *gained* if we were to share this information?

Yet admission of the truth – transparency – is itself a positive value that creates client trust. Absent transparent truth telling, clients will easily create fantasy stories with more negativity than the real situation. They will ascribe motives which may or may not be true, but which are rarely positive. Increasingly, in the digital age, the truth has a way of ending up on the front page of the medium du jour despite best efforts to control it. Better to come to terms with the truth, and live a professional life of transparency.

Transparency is a value in the way I have defined it at the outset in this paper, in that it is about relationships. The absence of transparency is a negative for ethics; "sunlight is the best disinfectant." Not surprisingly, transparency is a cornerstone value of being a trusted advisor. For an artful trusted advisor, there is no aspect of reality or truth that cannot be shared with a client in a sensitive, socially acceptable, client-centric mode. Anything else creates a barrier which is incompatible with trust-based relationships.

b. *Misguided professionalism.* Consultants are, quite appropriately, concerned with "behaving professionally." Unfortunately, that concern can itself create ethical and trust barriers. Consultants are frequently told to maintain behaviors of professionalism with their clients. Some of these make good sense – dress codes, airline travel policies, and discretion in public places. But others don't.

- Most firms define professionalism as the opposite of informal, personal, or direct conversations about private lives. This fits very well with most consultants, who often don't have high EQ skills and prefer to operate in a content-based meritocracy anyway, but it's harmful nonetheless. The rules of etiquette in society at large apply in business: don't get too *private* too soon. At the same time, consultants must become comfortable with being *personal* very soon.

By "private," I mean sharing children's pictures, or chatting about life outside work. That is up to individuals, governed by the norms that govern all of us. By "personal," I mean the ability to become intimate with others – to speak directly, with respect and concern, about personal themes like pride, fear, concern, values, problems, status, organizational dynamics, and a hundred other "touchy" items. A consultant who doesn't know how to get personal quickly will be left dealing only with symptoms.

A trusted advisor knows how to get personal – with respect, but quickly. And an ethical consultant is one who is able to operate in the real world, to function as more than a sentient database, all the while being sensitive to personal and social norms. Such a consultant has to take risks – the critical half of a trust-based relationship. Risk is key to trust: consultants who wait for their client to create trust are passively at effect of their clients, and will miss many opportunities.

A misguided sense of "professionalism" is the biggest inhibitor to risk-taking, therefore to intimacy creation, and therefore to trusted advisor-ship. And without relationships, the ethical realm is seriously diminished; without relationships, we are left only with personal virtues.

c. *Misconceived goals and objectives.* Ironically, it is largely the fault of consultants that modern business has become obsessed with behaviorally decomposing initiatives into smaller and smaller pieces, and with metrics that are associated with them. "If you can't measure it you can't manage it" has become a meme, variously attributed to[12] Peter Drucker, Andy Grove, Robert Kaplan, and others. Despite being false on the face of it, the sentiment is a common one.

Consultancies themselves have pursued the meme and are tempted to manage by their own medicine – with ill effects for both trust and ethics.

- When faced with lots of metrics, it is easy to mistake the ends for the means. The project budget, the monthly quota, the utilization target, the number of spreadsheets in the deck all easily become front-of-mind for pressured consultants. When a consultant tries to meet his or her metrics in ways that aren't obviously client-driven, clients can frequently sense it. The phenomenon reduces trust. And because it is one-sided, self-centered – not relationship-centered – it is also largely unethical.
- Most consultants dislike "sales." It's why they prefer "business development," perhaps because of the passive voice phrasing. Yet deep down, they feel they must do just that. Most firms, because of their dislike for sales, haven't evolved their thinking past the mentality of general industry – a mentality of competitive strategy, pitting seller against buyer, focusing on closing, gaining power, and ultimately "winning."

This "winning" attitude is antithetical to a long-term collaborative client focus. A trusted advisor always and only wants what is right for the client, secure in the knowledge that that focus is precisely what will also serve the firm well. The problem of incompatible interests, so central to most business ethical issues, is largely unnecessary in consulting. Properly conceived, a trusted advisor relationship is all about synergy and win-win; the attitude benefits both consultant and client. An immature attitude about "sales" goals and objectives infects both trust and ethics.

These three areas of misalignment – lack of transparency, misguided professionalism, and misconceived goals and objectives – pervasively mitigate both trusted advisor relationships and ethical relationships.

How Can We Create Ethical Firms of Trusted Advisors?

What is the relationship between individuals and firms, with respect to both ethics and trusted advisor-ship? In a consulting firm, the relationship is relatively straightforward: a firm of ethical consultants is, pretty much, an ethical firm. A firm of trusted advisors is, pretty much, a firm you can trust.

This is because in consulting, the whole is largely the sum of its parts. That is decidedly not the case in other industries, e.g. pharmaceuticals.[13]

In pharma, there are serious structural conflicts of interest built into the system – issues of medical school researchers and faculty and their relationships to drug trials, medical industry publications, physicians and their relationships to marketing teams from pharma companies, and so forth. Nearly all employees in the pharmaceutical industry consider themselves to be highly ethical *individuals* – but the industry nonetheless ranks very low in perceived trustworthiness.

There are similar structural issues in financial services.[14] And as a result, ethical guidelines in those industries have become inextricably intertwined with legal compliance, to the point where employees talk about the "ethics-and-compliance" department. This drives "ethical" discussion *toward* behavioral, legal, and "virtuous" definitions, and *away* from "values" definitions, in the sense I am using in this article.

That is a very bad model for consulting – and fortunately, it's a model consulting doesn't need. For the most part, if everyone in a consulting firm is an ethical trusted advisor, there are few firm-wide ethical issues left to speak of.

This suggests that the second question – how to create ethical firms of trusted advisors – is more about social engineering and values transmission than it is about behaviors, checklists, or structural solutions.

Consulting (and other professional services, for the most part) are equal to the sum of their parts. Laws, structural considerations, or social restrictions do not heavily determine their behaviors; they are more the product of internal values, culture, and habits.

Put this way, the job of creating ethical firms of trusted advisors sounds relatively simple – preach the gospel of values, develop the culture, train people in the values (and virtues), and role model. Unfortunately, the methods of organizational change the profession recommends for its own larger-scale clientele often seduce the profession itself. "If it's good for our clients, we ought to be practicing what we preach," goes the logic.

It sounds good, but – consulting firms are very different from banks, IT organizations, and manufacturing or services businesses. The tools for instilling an ethos of trusted advisor and ethical behavior should be different.

The two biggest relevant differences are that consultancies are 99 percent about people, and that the paradigm for success is relationship-based, not competitive-based.

a. *People-based.* Consultants in nearly every firm when asked, "What differentiates you from other firms?" will answer, "the people." The answer is both vacuous and profound. Vacuous because if everyone has the same answer, there's no apparent differentiation.

But profound, because in fact, individuals are the ultimate differentiators. The people at one firm really do look and act differently from those at another firm. Consultants find their own "tribes" and find meaning in them.

While nearly everyone will agree with the above statements, in fact firms act in more "corporate" ways all the time – ways that are destructive of the core personal-ness at the heart of the firm.

- "Sell the firm, not the consultant" is something frequently told to young consultants; "the firm is bigger than one individual." True – but that means the individual is no longer at the heart of this expressed value. Which means relationships aren't at the heart of the value.

The subjective power of trust is such that people, including clients, don't trust firms – they trust people. A McKinsey-like brand name is powerful for getting a foot in the door – but it doesn't automatically get the sale. That means relationships have to be people-based. In a business as complex and situational as consulting, the real ethical issues are also personal issues, and if personal issues aren't front and center, then the issues are viewed as less ethical to that same extent.

b. *Relationship-based, not competitive-based.* Since Michael Porter and BCG[15] in the 1970s established Competitive Strategy[16] as the driver of business success, Porter's Five Forces model has commanded huge influence in consulting, consciously or unconsciously. The model posits five forces of competition for any business – two of which are suppliers and customers. By this view – still the dominant view of business at large – we are *essentially* at war with our clients.

- This is a view that cannot stand scrutiny *in* consulting (despite its validity as a subject matter *for* consulting). If the firm's objectives are at odds with the client's – much less *fundamentally* in conflict – then the firm and its consultants can never be fully trusted. Nor can there be much of an ethical relationship with a party whose interests *by definition* are at odds with the client's. Industry at large can arguably live with this view – think Adam Smith's Invisible Hand, and benevolent regulation – but consulting cannot.

Consultants live and die by their ability to live out the values of collaboration, client focus for the sake of the client, and total goal congruence. They must believe that they will do well as a function of doing right by their clients – not all at once, not on every project, not even on every client, but certainly in the long run across all clients.

By this view, an ethical relationship is fundamental to consulting in a way that is not true for industry at large. The same is true for trusted advisor relationships – the term, after all, was invented to describe advisory services of various types, and for the same reasons.

Since consultancies are about people and are relationship-based, not competitively based, the ways in which they can inculcate ethical and trusted advisor behavior are distinctive. They boil down to three:

- A common vocabulary
- A constant dialogue about values (not so much about virtues)
- Conspicuous role-modeling

Common vocabulary. Most consultancies, when they hear the word "scale," hear what IT firms hear – technological platforms, business processes, rollouts of change management plans, metrics, and incentives. But in consulting, the most powerful tool for scaling is simply a common vocabulary, consisting mainly of less than a half-dozen terms.

- Rules and guidelines in consulting are nearly impossible to create for all situations. It is an inherently creative and complex business. Core concepts, which can be heard, understood, and creatively interpreted, are critical to success. The handmaiden of those concepts is a small set of carefully selected words. Typically, the words chosen will heavily reflect the set of values mentioned earlier in this article – and not so much the virtues.

Constant dialogue about values. Because of the complexity of consulting organizations and the situations they face, covering all the eventualities (like one might do in a manufacturing plant) is an effort undertaken in vain. Instead, the firm has to rely on people correctly "deducing" what to do in a given situation, given the general principles, and the selected vocabulary, that leadership unfailingly puts out.

- I do not mean "deduction" with the rigor of geometry. But concepts like "think client first, incentives second" requires some careful thought. Are there exceptions? Are there ranges? Are there mitigating circumstances? Competing principles to be taken into account?
- Values questions aren't answered in a policy manual. Instead, consultants are taught how to deduce them by observing and experiencing more senior leaders work through them. The acquisition of ethical values, it has been written,[17] much resembles the acquisition of a trade; we learn it from those who have mastered it, by observing, guessing, observing consequences, and guessing again.
- A firm interested in pursuing ethical behavior, and in becoming trusted advisors, will vigorously pursue discussions about ethical and trust-based conundrums and dilemmas. Senior people will seize the opportunity, in office meetings, client projects, and shared road-trips, to discuss precisely these dilemmas with junior people. The point is not to inculcate them in fixed policies or mindless rules, but to teach them practical moral reasoning. And to avoid the teaching role is to avoid a key leadership role in the development of the successful firm.

Conspicuous Role-Modeling. Corporate change management initiatives typically end up stressing the importance of "leading with the CEO's office." CEOs probably don't have the time to do all the initiatives they are urged to do by consultancies. But the case of consultancies themselves is a little different: the leading is even more critical, and it has to involve more than just the CEO.

- It's one thing to preach a virtue, like hard work, or accuracy – and to occasionally slip up, or under-perform. We're all human, we reason, we can cut each other slack. But a leader who preaches transparency or collaboration – and who then hides information or acts out of self-interest – is immediately seen as hypocritical. A values violation is far worse than a virtues violation. It goes to the heart of relationships – between leader and consultant, firm and client. And because of the unique importance of trust and relationships in the consulting business, it is a form of unethical behavior that is uniquely upsetting.
- As noted above, consultancies are somewhat like trades, and not just in the formation of values. Consultants also learn the tools of the trade from their seniors. They are truly role models, across every dimension of success in business. And because the craft is so varied and situational, the learning of the craft is very much apprenticeship-based. Such relationships engender respect, and curiosity. The way the top leaders in a firm behave sends extremely powerful messages – particularly around the relative importance of virtues and values, and of which values really dominate.

Evaluating Success as a Trusted Advisor and as an Ethical Firm

I have argued that consultancies are prone to the error of thinking that the right answer for the clients' organizations ought to be the answer for their own firms. Yet, consultancies are different.

Trust-based, ethical relationships, I have argued, are at the *essential heart* of a successful consulting organization. That is not the case for industry at large, or is at least less clearly so. That means inconsistent, unethical, nontrust-based behavior is inherently unstable. On the other hand, consistent, ethical, trusted advisor-based behavior is conspicuously evident.

Simply put, it is not hard to recognize an ethical, trusted advisor-based firm. It is, in fact, remarkably easy. This is not like industries where checkbox compliance tools are required to measure progress. Nor is it like issues of employee satisfaction, where an annual survey might be required to track improvement on components of satisfaction.

When it comes to trust and ethics, there is a virtuous circle.

- Financially, it manifests very evidently in top-line revenue and in firm-wide gross margins (not necessarily in project margins). Clients vastly prefer to do business with trusted, ethical firms; that drives repeat business, cross-selling, and referral business – all of which drive down the cost of sales, which is the single biggest profit factor affecting profitability at the firm level for a consultancy.
- Culturally, it manifests as an absence of tension. An ethical, trust-based firm does not shy away from conflict – in fact, it welcomes confrontation, because it means real issues are being dealt with. Because issues

are spoken about openly and truthfully, few secrets are kept. Emotional intelligence is high. Clients know they can confide in consultants. All these result in consultants who are less neurotic, more self-assured, and more other-oriented than in other firms.

- On the client side, it manifests not only in repeat and referral business, but in personal relationships. Clients appreciate ethical trusted advisor firms because they can confide in them; be secure that they won't abuse privileges; know that the firm "has their back," that issues which inevitably arise will be dealt with fairly; and that the consultants they relate to genuinely have their personal as well as their firm interests at heart. Why would a client want to do business with anyone else?

Notes

1 A term that has been in the public domain for decades, first discussed at length in *The Trusted Advisor*, Maister, Green & Galford, Free Press Simon & Schuster, 2001.
2 For a very different approach to the same distinction, see "Values and Virtues: A Modern Confusion," by Canadian legal philosopher Iain T. Benson, http://www.catholiceducation.org/en/culture/catholic-contributions/values-and-virtues-a-modern-confusion.html.
3 See, for example, "Are You Abusive, Cynical, or Exciting?", David Maister, 2005, http://davidmaister.com/articles/are-you-abusive-cynical-or-exciting/.
4 The Code of Ethics of the Institute of Management Consultants USA is instructive, containing examples of both "values" and "virtues" as defined here. See http://c.ymcdn.com/sites/www.imcusa.org/resource/collection/FF4D824A-2E4D-4199-9263-63C5FD63D135/IMC_USA_Code_of_Ethics_(2005).pdf.
5 See http://trustedadvisor.com/why-trust-matters/understanding-trust/understanding-the-trust-equation.
6 Ibid.
7 White Paper, "Think Expertise Will Make You More Trusted? Think Again," Trusted Advisor Associates, http://trustedadvisor.com/public/files/pdf/2010_TA_Whitepaper_Think_Again_Special.pdf.
8 "Public Esteem for Military Still High," Pew Research Center, July 11, 2013, http://www.pewforum.org/2013/07/11/public-esteem-for-military-still-high/.
9 "Congress Retains Low Honesty Rating," Gallup, December 3, 2012, http://www.gallup.com/poll/159035/congress-retains-low-honesty-rating.aspx.
10 Consider Booz Allen Hamilton and the Edward Snowden case, described in "Investigate Booz Allen Hamilton, not Edward Snowden," *The Guardian*, June 14, 2013, http://www.theguardian.com/commentisfree/2013/jun/14/edward-snowden-investigate-booz-allen.
11 "Ex-McKinsey Boss, Rajat Gupta, Sentenced to 2 Years in Federal Prison," *Forbes*, October 24, 2012.
12 See this Google Questions and Answers thread for a complete discussion of the source, http://answers.google.com/answers/threadview?id=139473.
13 See for example, "Restoring the Pharmaceutical Industry's Reputation," Mark Kessel, *Mature Biotechnology*, 32, 983–990 (2014), October 9, 2014, http://www.nature.com/nbt/journal/v32/n10/full/nbt.3036.html.

14 See for example, "Trust in Financial Services," Edelman Trust Barometer, 2014, http://www.edelman.com/insights/intellectual-property/2014-edelman-trust-barometer/trust-in-business/trust-in-financial-services/.
15 See *The Boston Consulting Group on Strategy: Classic Concepts and New Perspectives*, John Wiley, 2006.
16 See *Competitive Strategy: Techniques for Analyzing Industries and Competitors*, Michael Porter, New York, Free Press, 1980.
17 *Voices: The Educational Formation of Conscience*, Thomas F. Green, Notre Dame, IN, University of Notre Dame Press, 1999.

Bibliography of Sources

"Are You Abusive, Cynical, or Exciting?" David Maister, 2005, http://davidmaister.com/articles/are-you-abusive-cynical-or-exciting/

The Boston Consulting Group on Strategy: Classic Concepts and New Perspectives, John Wiley, 2006.

Code of Ethics of Institute of Management Consultants USA, examples of both "values" and "virtues" as defined here. See http://c.ymcdn.com/sites/www.imcusa.org/resource/collection/FF4D824A-2E4D-4199-9263-63C5FD63D135/IMC_USA_Code_of_Ethics_(2005).pdf

Competitive Strategy: Techniques for Analyzing Industries and Competitors, Michael Porter, New York, Free Press, 1980.

"Congress Retains Low Honesty Rating," Gallup, December 3, 2012, http://www.gallup.com/poll/159035/congress-retains-low-honesty-rating.aspx

"Ex-McKinsey Boss, Rajat Gupta, Sentenced to 2 years in Federal Prison," *Forbes*, October 24, 2012.

"Investigate Booz Allen Hamilton, not Edward Snowden," *The Guardian*, June 14, 2013, http://www.theguardian.com/commentisfree/2013/jun/14/edward-snowden-investigate-booz-allen

"Public Esteem for Military Still High," PewResearchCenter, July 11, 2013, http://www.pewforum.org/2013/07/11/public-esteem-for-military-still-high/

"Restoring the Pharmaceutical Industry's Reputation," Mark Kessel, *Mature Biotechnology*, 32, 983–990, October 9, 2014, http://www.nature.com/nbt/journal/v32/n10/full/nbt.3036.html

"Trust in Financial Services," Edelman Trust Barometer, 2014, http://www.edelman.com/insights/intellectual-property/2014-edelman-trust-barometer/trust-in-business/trust-in-financial-services/

The Trusted Advisor, Maister, Green & Galford, Free Press Simon & Schuster, 2001.

"Values and Virtues: A Modern Confusion," Iain T. Benson, http://www.catholiceducation.org/en/culture/catholic-contributions/values-and-virtues-a-modern-confusion.html

Voices: The Educational Formation of Conscience, Thomas F. Green, Notre Dame, IN, University of Notre Dame Press, 1999.

19 Consulting in Entrepreneurship
Essential Foundations for Consultants

Rickie A. Moore

Entrepreneurship as an activity, a field or a discipline has transitioned and is still transitioning. It is increasingly a subject of much admiration, debate and controversy around the world. With an abundance of definitions and descriptions about the Entrepreneur and the notion of Entrepreneurship, along with its numerous, diverse and complex components, and multiple complementary dimensions, Entrepreneurship has been observed and analyzed by specialists including sociologists, historians, psychologists, behavioral scientists, strategists, etc.

Today, Entrepreneurship as a social and economic phenomenon is globally, a subject of high stakes – governments are hoping that it will reinvigorate society and the economy, create new economic structures and ventures and much needed jobs and employment. On the academic front, Entrepreneurship is a discipline that is increasingly being taught and a field that is extensively being researched in educational establishments around the world.[1,2,3] Observatories of entrepreneurial practices and phenomena are increasingly becoming permanent fixtures in many major cities.

In most countries, whether developed or developing, the practice of Entrepreneurship has become of source of liberty and economic freedom. However, with an extremely rich array of initiatives and diversity of implementation, Entrepreneurship represents a novel challenge for consultants as it can be very paradoxical, follow both orthodox and unorthodox rules, and can often be very controversial. Success is not necessarily the result of the best venture idea, and if anything, failure is often the prerequisite for succeeding.

As Entrepreneurs seek professional advice and assistance, consultants are finding out that Consulting in Entrepreneurship is a very risky journey into the "unknown". Management consulting in the fields of Strategy and Organization has been practiced for decades and most Business School graduates have traditionally looked to the consulting industry to start their careers.[4,5] However, despite the numerous turmoil and scandals that have rocked the profession over the last decade,[6,7] Management Consulting has resisted the downturns and has been progressively renewing itself. Strategy consulting has largely followed established strategy principles that were long taught and well-known, and which tended to guarantee predictability of outcomes.

Today however, consultants are being asked to exercise their skills in Entrepreneurship – a "new yet very different field" that is still emerging, and – one characterized by high unpredictability, high volatility, high uncertainty, and high ambiguity. Entrepreneurship is a field where start-ups can dethrone long established players, where incumbents are forced to compete for market share where they once dominated, where investors flock to ventures that have not yet proven their success, and where all the rules of the game are being rewritten constantly. Where traditional players took years to become global, firms are being born globally instantly in the entrepreneurial world. Where established players sought to own massive assets in order to control their competitive advantage, new Entrepreneurs are succeeding by owning little or no inventories. Traditional financiers such as banks, investment funds and private equity investors who were the exclusive backers of choice for new firms and entrepreneurial ventures are being replaced by widespread, unknown, individual, non-traditional investors who crowd-fund new ventures. Repeatability is not necessarily a guarantee of success, and strategies and approaches that were successful in one instance can lead to a total disaster in another.

How can consultants help their clients to compete in such a highly complex environment of Entrepreneurship? How can consultants facilitate the practice of Entrepreneurship and the development of Entrepreneurs in the new economy? How can consultants assist their clients to develop more successful entrepreneurial strategies in order to create new and sustainable economic opportunities in instances of such high uncertainty? What are the perspectives for the future of Consulting in Entrepreneurship?

The questions are numerous and the challenge is daunting. Entrepreneurship is a multidimensional, richly diverse, paradoxically complex subject that can be approached from several angles. Whichever angle is chosen there will most likely be enough to write an entire book on all the notions and components. However, in this chapter, I propose to provide consultants with an overview of some of the key foundations of the phenomenon and explain one of Entrepreneurship's core tenets and critical dimensions – value creation and its dynamic nature. With this backdrop, I then elucidate the evolution of the entrepreneurial role and profile and outline the need for an entrepreneurial mindset. My hope is that consultants will be able to more effectively craft their intervention strategies and assist their clients in their entrepreneurial endeavors as they navigate the various transitions involved in the phenomenon.

The Entrepreneurial Revolution

In the 1950s when Joseph Schumpeter coined the term Creative Destruction to explain the interplay of economic innovation and business cycles, he had been largely inspired by the works of Marx and his explanations about how economic phenomenon can perpetually create and facilitate the distribution of new value and wealth while destroying older ones.[8,9]

In the US, the creation of new businesses was championed as the key factor of the economic growth that began in the 1970s. Virgin was started in 1972, Bill Gates incorporated Microsoft in 1975 and Jobs launched Apple in 1976 same year as Anita Roddick founded the Body Shop, Dyson became a global name in 1979, and Dell followed in 1984. By the late 1980s, the established and large industrial giants were sharing GDP with brand new startups such as Google (1986) and small businesses that were considered to be creating more wealth than firms at any time before. It has been commonly reported that 95 percent of the wealth of the US has been created since 1980, and that small business generate half of the GDP, and half of the exports come from firms that employ fewer than twenty people.

The Entrepreneurial Revolution had begun. Four decades after Schumpeter, Jeffery Timmons, a long time mentor, colleague and friend, and internationally recognized scholar in Entrepreneurship, wrote in his 1999 *New Venture Creation: Entrepreneurship for the 21st Century*: "The Entrepreneurial Revolution is here to stay, having set the genetic code of the US and global economy for the twenty-first century and having sounded the death knell for Brontosaurus Capitalism of yesteryear. Entrepreneurs are the creators, the innovators, and the leaders who give back to society . . . and who, more than any others, change the way people live, work, learn, play and lead. Entrepreneurs create new technologies, products, processes and services that become the next wave of new industries. Entrepreneurs create value with high potential, high growth companies which are the job creation engines of the US economy."

As the entrepreneurial phenomenon rippled across sectors, industries, communities and geographies, globally, innovation and disruption increasingly became essential drivers of strategic differentiation and competitive advantage. While the environment of Entrepreneurship is already characterized by its complexity and uncertainty, technology is enabling the competitive landscape to be constantly redrawn. Due to the global interconnectedness and instant communications, changes in one market could trigger unintended and unexpected consequences in several others around the globe. As a result, there has been a marked escalation in the volatility in all spheres – markets, suppliers, customers, etc. Although many traditional players find this new context to be extremely unsettling and devastating, numerous Entrepreneurs are excited by the opportunities it offers.

Undoubtedly today, Entrepreneurs have been globally acclaimed as the new incubators and generators of wealth. They have attracted unprecedented attention as governments and educational establishments seek to comprehend the phenomenon, and replicate and amplify their impact. Entrepreneurship is now driving a global socio-economic and societal shift.

Creation or Discovery? Are Business Opportunities Created or Discovered?

Broadly, entrepreneurial initiatives can be classified as either necessity based or opportunity based. Though not mutually exclusive, they are often intertwined and codependent. If someone needs income to survive, he or she may be forced to identify new opportunities for generating revenue.

In necessity-based Entrepreneurship, the Entrepreneur is forced into Entrepreneurship as a means of survival. Confronted with severe economic difficulty, and with little or no prospect of obtaining gainful employment, the needs-based Entrepreneur has little choice but to create his/her own employment out of need. As a recognized means of resisting and combatting social exclusion, necessity-based Entrepreneurship narrows the gap of social inequities.

Opportunity based Entrepreneurship, on the other hand, is the Entrepreneurship of choice. Entrepreneurs are able to scan their environments and scout potential opportunities which they feel they can exploit for profit. Empowered and enabled to identify deficiencies in the economy and economic environment, opportunity-based Entrepreneurs can leverage their passion while pursuing the opportunity.

Academic scholars frequently debate these notions. Peter Drucker and Howard Stevenson are on record with challenging the Schumpeterian belief that Entrepreneurs create change through the creative-destruction cycles. Instead, they argue that in fact, Entrepreneurs exploit the opportunities that are caused by the cyclic change.

The Entrepreneurial Journey

As the Entrepreneur navigates the entrepreneurial landscape to identify the entrepreneurial opportunity, he/she embarks on a journey which may

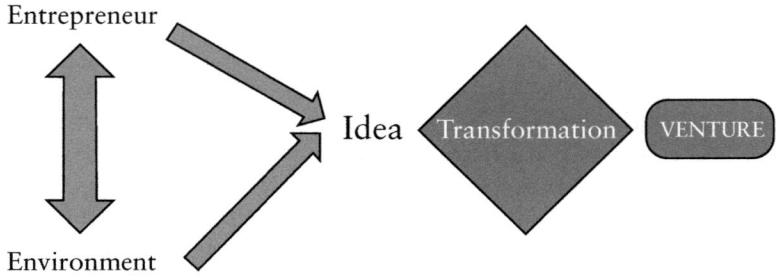

Figure 19.0

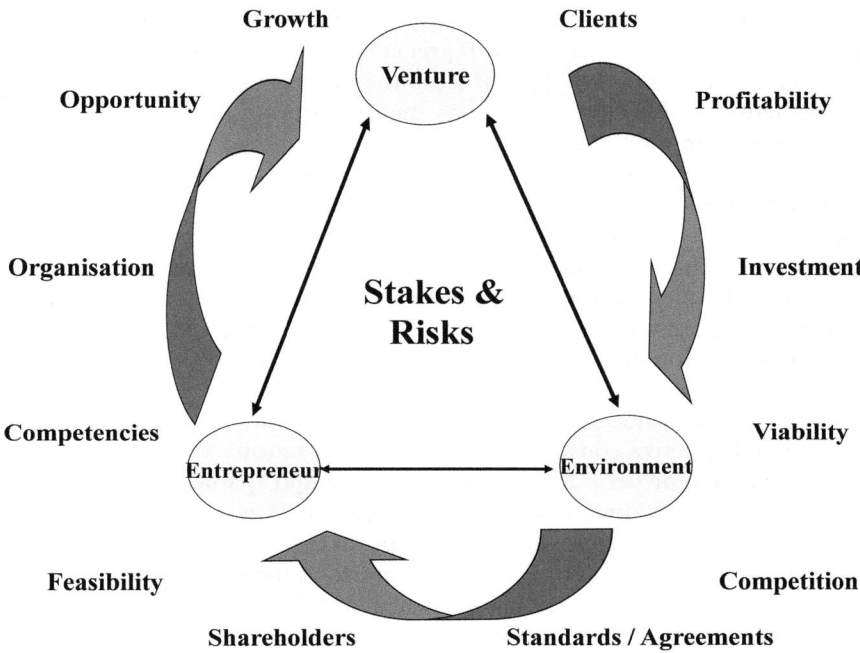

Figure 19.1 Entrepreneurial Journey

culminate with either an abandonment or implementation of intended venture (identified value). Though it may be considered as a linear transformation, it is much more continuous/discontinuous, sequential, cyclical, sporadic and iterative as a process. As the intended venture takes shape, the entrepreneurial journey may in essence resemble a rollercoaster ride. Throughout it all, there is the critical need to evaluate the stakes while seeking to mitigate the risks involved.

Concomitantly, the psychological state of the Entrepreneur also evolves with the maturation state and emerging/unfolding trajectory of the journey. With the diverse emotional and psychological stimulations, the focus and performance of the Entrepreneur will vary and so too will the value conception, value construction and value configuration of the intended venture.

Dynamic Value Creation in Entrepreneurship

Fundamentally, the practice of Entrepreneurship is the creation of economic value primarily for the Entrepreneur and consequently for the multiple stakeholders that will benefit from the process. This notion is pivotal to the action of Entrepreneurship as the opportunity-based Entrepreneur would have identified or heard the desire of the market and his/her environment and have responded appropriately. Therefore, the Entrepreneur's ability to detect, understand, interpret, organize and convert the information received in order to provide an adequate commercial response demonstrates the Entrepreneur's capacity to effectively and efficiently transform information into valuable and viable commercial outcomes. As such the creativity and inventiveness of the Entrepreneur will directly determine the quality and differentiation of the product or service that would be launched on the market to satisfy the customers' needs.

The process of value creation is one that requires intuition, articulate conception and effective construction and implementation. As customer needs can be punctual or periodic, conjunctural or tempo-spatial, the creation of value can be and is often fluid and dynamic. This transient nature of value creation directly correlates with the concepts of the Window of Opportunity and Time to Market. Therefore, it is incumbent on the Entrepreneur and his/her advisors to correctly ascertain or calculate the durability of the customer's need in order to better mitigate and minimize the risk and optimize the value creation. Value creation in Entrepreneurship is also multi-dimensional. It is first of all contemplated, constructed and configured . . . and could be either temporary or evolve over time. Secondly, the value can interchangeably be either in the product or service, or the access to or availability of the product or service, its delivery, its evolution, etc. With each dimension, the value configuration and proposition can change.

At its core, the act of Entrepreneurship consists of an individual or group of individuals, a venture idea or initiative and the environment. The articulation of the Entrepreneur and his/her idea and the interplay with the environment lays the foundation for the identification of the entrepreneurial idea. In starting a venture, the Entrepreneur will create an economic organization through which he or she will establish his/her legitimacy while creating economic value in the pursuit of the opportunity.

In creating the economic entity of the organization, the Entrepreneur has to marshal his/her resources and integrate them into a coherent organization in order to deliver the intended economic value. The final outcome of the organization is the result of several iterations, negotiations and compromises as the various resources are obtained, structured and implemented.

With the dynamic nature of value conception, value configuration and value creation comes the entrepreneurial trajectory. As the Entrepreneur crisscrosses between divergent stakeholders in the value creation effort, he/she can find himself or herself walking many tight ropes as he/she negotiates his/her way along the trajectory. Ultimately, is it critical that there is

Figure 19.2 Dynamics of Value Creation

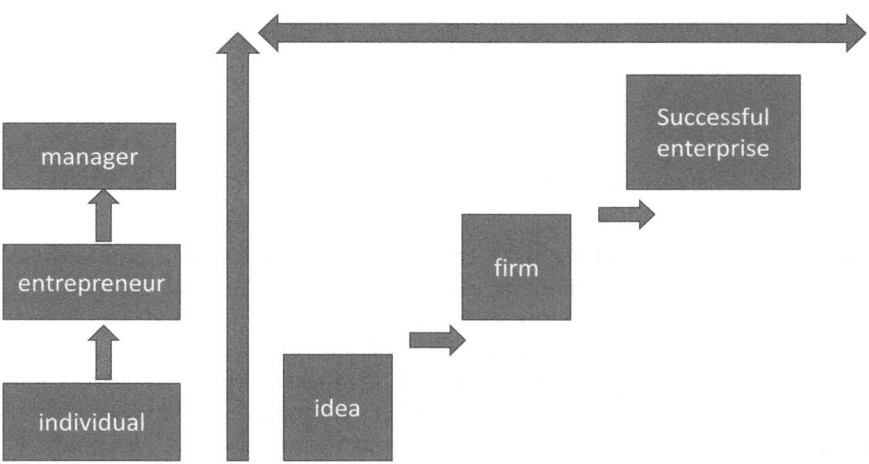

Figure 19.3 Evolution of Entrepreneur and Maturation of Venture

a high degree of coherence in the value configuration if the entrepreneurial action is to be effective.

The combined value creation firm creation process is an extremely important component in Entrepreneurship as it embodies an all-important dialogue between the Entrepreneur and the emergence of the organization. In a very intricate and complex manner, several competing, complementary and contradictory logics are intertwined as the dialogue takes place. As the entrepreneurial intention evolves into an entrepreneurial decision then an entrepreneurial action, the Entrepreneur needs to integrate and process the external elements and inputs while rationalizing and formalizing his/her own instincts and intuition. The transition then becomes from Individual to Entrepreneur and from an idea to a successful enterprise.

Evolution of Roles and Skillsets

Ventures that survive and thrive tend to evolve through five main stages:

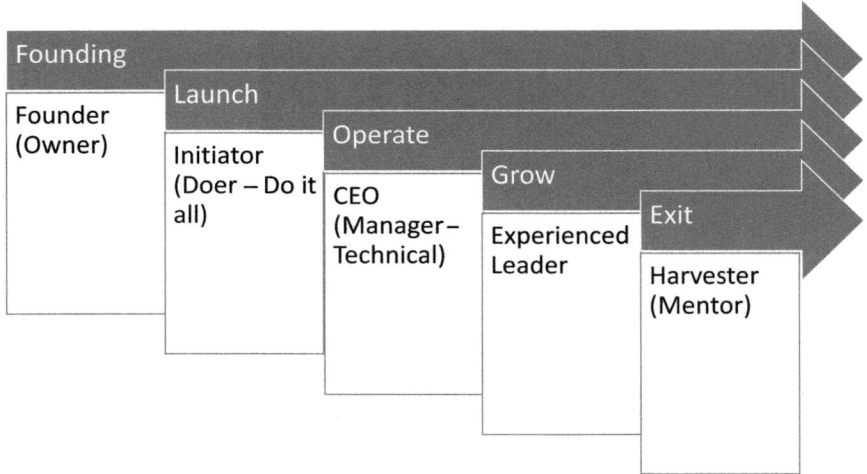

Figure 19.4 Venture Stage Evolution and Entrepreneuerial Skill Sets and Profiles

At each stage of the evolution, there are different expectations and requirements of the Entrepreneur in terms of his/her role and assorted skillsets. Very often, as the firm matures, the founder/owner may find him/herself in a situation where the role expectations and his/her preference and competencies can be inappropriate or at odds with the needs of the firm. There are numerous examples of situations where the founder is not necessarily the person who is best suited to manage it at the given stage. The Board of Directors can also play a critical role in influencing, shaping and spearheading the leadership evolution of the firm. Clearly one of the most important transitions in Entrepreneurship, it is often a source of anguish, controversy and conflict.

The Entrepreneurial Mindset

The ability to see entrepreneurial opportunities where others see problems is one of the hallmarks of the entrepreneurial mind. Driven by passion, Entrepreneurs are able to see opportunities in almost all instances and circumstances – situations of inefficiencies or deficiencies, lack of control, inadequate, ineffective or excessive control, inconsistencies, lack of structure, lack of organization, etc. Fundamentally, Entrepreneurs will be able to "connect the dots" and create new business models and approaches to redesigning industries and markets and exploiting market share by seeking to better respond to identified customers' needs. Actively vigilant and scouting for opportunities, Entrepreneurs are able to anticipate and predict future and emergent needs. Skilled Entrepreneurs take calculated risk in pursuing the chosen opportunities, knowing very well that success is never guaranteed. While numerous opportunities may be available, it is critical that the Entrepreneur focuses and not become distracted or dilute his/her attention by tackling/pursuing several opportunities at once. Knowing that not every element of their plan or intention has been fully analyzed and evaluated before acting, Entrepreneurs are also able to concentrate on the execution and implementation of their initiatives as they seek to gain impact and traction on the market.

For consultants, it is critical that they understand the entrepreneurial mind and its approach to risk. Where common sense and business logic might suggest no action, entrepreneurial logic would defy common sense and business logic by taking bold action. As such, consultants run the risk of being "wrong" if they had recommended no action and the Entrepreneur persevered and it turned out to be a success. If they recommended action and the result is not in keeping with expectations, the reliability, credibility and value of the advice will quickly be called into question as the consultant is expected to be the "expert", and trustworthy. And experts are expected to provide expertise which is supposed to be accurate and guarantee success.

Innovation and Disruptions – Evolution and Revolution

In today's world, innovation and, more importantly, technological innovation is helping Entrepreneurs disrupt existing industries and markets as they provide innovative good and services. Through the effective use of innovation, Entrepreneurs are able to redesign existing products and services and offer new forms of differentiation. In addition the combination of the creative entrepreneurial mind and effective use of technological innovations is paving the way for new and disruptive business models as markets and industries are being reconfigured. Value chains are being redesigned, markets are being resegmented and industry clusters are being reconfigured. In short, business as it is known is being redefined.

At the core of this transformation is the focus on customers – their behavior, their needs and their perceptions. If anything, the more successful Entrepreneurs have understood that focusing on and knowing their customers in a very intimate manner is key to facilitating the disruption. Inevitably, established firms in traditional industry segments compete on price as they seek to gain and maintain market share. With a finely honed entrepreneurial mindset, Entrepreneurs have realized that by focusing on customer behavior, they are enabled to identify new patterns, new links, new needs, and as such offer either new products and services to meet these new needs, or new ways to access the desired products and services. Disruptive entrepreneurial thinking can turn conventional logic and behavior into unconventional opportunity.

Using a variety of techniques such as combining previously uncombined and separate attributes or segments, integrating existing attributes in new clusters or abandoning unpopular, negative or unsatisfactory ones, Entrepreneurs can provide disruptive and innovative products and services with less hassle and greater attraction and desirability. Traditional barriers – technological, legislative, regulatory, organizational, financial, etc. – are either being circumvented, overcome or removed as new disruptions bring new value for customers and stakeholders.

Implications for Consultants

As the entrepreneurial phenomenon continues to accelerate and expand globally, so too will be the need for entrepreneurial consulting. The consulting industry will experience further evolution and revolution as consulting firms grapple to keep abreast with the rapidly changing global marketplace, disruptive business models and emerging innovation. While there will always be those consulting firms that will continue to specialize in fields such as back-office software, corporate strategy, HR, IT, etc., they will be challenged by the newer ones that offer more entrepreneurial services and desires such as breakthrough ideas, optimizing market launch and time-to-market strategies.

One of the first objectives of a consultant is to ensure that he/she has developed a clear understanding of Entrepreneurship and its complex myriad of notions, dimensions and characteristics. Without this foundation, they risk failing to grasp the potential of the phenomenon and the essence of the transitions. As the notion of value creation can be very dynamic, it is important for consultants to have the appropriate framework(s) for detecting, interpreting and understanding the signals that will be converted into a value proposition. Comprehending the multiple transitions that form the basis of the evolution and revolution in the phenomenon is thus critical if the consultant is to craft his/her intervention strategies and increase their pertinence.

We can also expect an increased shift in portfolio strategies as many consulting firms seek to embrace and expand their entrepreneurial operations and profiles, whether mentoring Entrepreneurs, operating their own investment funds, owning equity stakes or even initiating entrepreneurial ventures. These shifts would be confronted with the dilemmas and conflicts of interests that will inevitably arise.

As entrepreneurial firms mature and evolve, the roles and responsibilities of the Entrepreneurs also evolve. Demonstrating a variety of traits, competencies, qualities and behaviors, Entrepreneurs as a population have been compared to sprinters, marathoners, conductors, bowlers, golfers, market place and industry heroes, etc. With the disruptive approach, in situations of chaos or in times of consolidation, unorthodoxy becomes orthodoxy, and the unconventional becomes conventional. Entrepreneurs will see opportunities where others see problems. Consultants in order to facilitate more effective interventions, therefore need to fully understand the entrepreneurial mindset, be conversant with the advantages and disadvantages of each entrepreneurial profile, and accept and integrate the tensions inherent with each of them and that result from their interaction. Much like the skill sets which the Entrepreneurs must develop, consultants need to develop their toolsets in order to better advise and assist their entrepreneurial clients.

With the high social, psychological, emotional and sometimes economic costs of initiating entrepreneurial ventures, consultants as business advisors will be able to leverage their experience with their clients – project planning, implementation, business analysis, etc. – but many would find themselves in unknown terrains as the Entrepreneurs embark on totally disruptive ideas and business models. If in the former context, the consultant can bring his/her expertise to bear on a project, in the latter, he or she could find himself or herself out of his/her depths as the Entrepreneurs will be implementing bold, radical, never-been-done-before ideas. We often teach the FedEx case example where Fred Smith, the founder of the Fedex company, while a student, proposed the idea of starting a new venture delivering high-priority packages. His professor thought it was a bad business idea and supposedly, Smith received a poor grade for his work. Committed and motivated by his idea, in spite of the disagreement and disappointment of his grade, Smith continued to refine his idea and successfully launched the FedEx company we know so well. With the acclamation of the new service, along came the competition and a new industry was born. In 2016, according to Forbes, Smith is currently worth $2.3 billion, and FedEx ships more than 10.2 million packages daily in 220 countries.

With this new global entrepreneurial shift, consultants and the consulting industry are at a new crossroad. There are numerous questions to be answered – Can consulting firms be more entrepreneurial? What areas, what opportunities? How can consultants and consulting firms best engage with entrepreneurial clients? How should consultants and consulting firms embrace the risks associated with consulting in Entrepreneurship? However, the future holds untold opportunities for consultants:

- The collaborative economy is making inroads into traditional industries and is changing the way business is conducted
- New forms of Entrepreneurship will emerge and existing ones will mature – social Entrepreneurship, not-for-profit Entrepreneurship, etc.
- Governments are rapidly trying to accelerate the transformation of their traditional economies into entrepreneurial ones – they need to provide appropriate infrastructure and create financial and fiscal incentives that stimulate and promote Entrepreneurship
- Governments as legislators are forced to play catch-up as they come to grips with the new business models and approaches, and their consequences on both existing and intended legislation, and the regulation and stimulation of their economies and societies
- Traditional firms and establishments are seeking to embrace and develop more entrepreneurial strategies (corporate Entrepreneurship)

- With digitalization offering new forms of disruption, consultants can find themselves thrust into the foray as their clients seek advice on developing digital entrepreneurial strategies
- Entrepreneurs will be more creative and imaginative in their approaches (critical thinking)
- Innovation will continue to be enabled by technology
- Entrepreneurs will continue to seek and identify new entrepreneurial opportunities as they become more familiar with the contributions and potential of big data analytics

Consultants can thus expect to play the role of entrepreneurial facilitators more than initiators whether it is in business modeling, entrepreneurial marketing, seeding, funding or harvesting. Consultants can expect to be increasingly confronted with ethical issues in Entrepreneurship and entrepreneurial endeavors, as well as developing assessment frameworks and evaluation protocols to help clients better screen for viable entrepreneurial opportunities. From learning to ask the right questions to developing appropriate feasibility mechanisms, consultants will be required to help their clients avoid the entrepreneurial pitfalls and traps. Consultants too will face evolution and revolution as their clients and their fields of interventions grow.

Much as many would prefer to be on the right side of a failed initiative, consultants also risk finding themselves on the wrong side of success if the Entrepreneur is more risk-prone and the consultant more risk-averse. It is not that the consultant has to be indifferent when it comes to risk, but the paradoxical and bewildering nature of Entrepreneurship often proves rational logic and common sense to be a roadblock to success. With Entrepreneurship and entrepreneurial risk, the normative approach and rationality are often abandoned for intuitive, disruptive and sometimes seemingly irrational actions. When investing a client's future and perhaps continued existence, the risk of being wrong can prove to be extremely costly. Consultants would be existentially, psychologically and extensively challenged, if they are saddled with regrets, especially if the regrets have proven to be very costly.

Realizing that not many traditional consultants are able to understand and embrace the entrepreneurial psyche and mindset, very few Entrepreneurs turn to traditional consultants for entrepreneurial guidance. Instead, Entrepreneurs often turn to each other for their consulting advice. Much like a support group, Entrepreneurs revel in the opportunity to learn from the successes and setbacks of their peers. Nothing teaches Entrepreneurship like entrepreneurial experience. Consultants would be hard pressed to explain how many ventures they have started personally, and how they would advise entrepreneurs or their peers to proceed with their own ventures.

One area where there could be some leveraging of experience in consulting is the cost of procurement of services. While a large number of consulting firms continue to invoice by consulting time (days, hours and projects), some have adopted the practice of performance pricing where they negotiate a percentage of the revenue gain or outcome of their intervention. This performance practice is clearly driven by the consultant's stake in achieving the predicted or anticipated outcome of his/her intervention. In the entrepreneurial realm, such a practice can be likened unto equity performance where the consultant's fees will be determined by the financial performance or outcome of the venture. Clearly motivated by a very personal stake in the anticipated successful outcome of the client's operations, consultants run the risk of being less than objective and could even embark on controversial and debatable actions that would ensure the anticipated financial outcome so as to achieve their performance bonus. Consultants therefore risk finding themselves in the middle of an ethical firestorm as independent stakeholders question their moral and professional values and motivations. There are examples where financial consulting firms were hired to assist their clients to improve their financial performance and quickly realized that the client would never be able to succeed in the undertaking. Rather than being upfront and honest about the likely outcome, even though the client may disagree, the consultants then hedged bets on the collapse and failure of the client's enterprise. It has even been reported that some advisors had knowingly engineered their clients' performance, causing them to fail, so that they can be acquired.

Business angels are supposedly less aggressive than VC when it comes to assisting and mentioning new ventures. In "kind" services (personal experience and networks) more than cash and bringing their expertise more than their financial investments to the firms, Business Angels are able to engage with the founders to help bring the venture to reality and often serve as "internal consultants" to the ventures because of their past entrepreneurial experience which underscores their legitimacy and their roles.

The reality is that large consulting firms are increasingly finding themselves relatively unsuitable and out of price range for Entrepreneurs, many of whom bootstrap their ventures. Boutique consultants who are more affordable are better placed to leverage the opportunities on the market, as larger players would find themselves at odds with their brand value defense strategies should they engage with start-up Entrepreneurs who are unable to pay high fees. Large consulting firms can overcome the dilemma by adopting a VC-type profile where they will equity invest in their clients, and hence develop a significant portfolio of entrepreneurial ventures. However, there is need for caution. With such an approach, the consulting firms will also shift from being business advisors to becoming venture portfolio managers. This sounds like role reversal and a changing of the guards!

Notes

1 Gibb, A.A., 1992, "The Enterprise Culture and Education – Understanding Enterprise Education and Its Links with Small Business, Entrepreneurial and Wider Educational Goals", *International Small Business Journal*, 11(3), pp. 24.

2 Vesper, K., 1982, "Research on education for entrepreneurship". In: *Encyclopedia of Entrepreneurship*. Edited by Kent, C.A., Sexton, D.L. & Vesper, K. Englewood Cliffs: Prentice Hall, pp. 321.
3 Venkatamaran, S., 1997, *The Distinctive Domain of Entrepreneurship Research, Advances in Entrepreneurship, Firm Emergence and Growth*, Volume 3, pp. 119–138; Aldrich, H., Martinez, M., 2001, "Many are called but few are chosen: an evolutionary perspective for the study of Entrepreneurship", *Entrepreneurship Theory and Practice*, 25(4), pp. 41–56.
4 Kipping, M. & Engwall, L., 2002, Management Consulting, Emergence and Dynamics of a Knowledge Industry.
5 Greiner, L. & Poulfelt, F., 2005, The Contemporary Consultant.
6 Stewart, M., 2009, "The Management Myth: Why the Experts Keep Getting it Wrong", Norton.
7 Kihn, M., 2005, "House of Lies: How Management Consultant Steal Your Watch and Then Tell You The Time".
8 Schumpeter, J., 1942, Capitalism, Socialism and Democracy.
9 Schumpeter, J., 1942, Theory of Economic Development.

Bibliography

Christiansen, C., 2009, The Innovator's Dilemma.
Downes, L., 2009, The Laws of Disruption: Harnessing the New Forces That Govern Life and Business in the Digital Age.
Gartner, W., 1988, "Who Is an Entrepreneur? Is the Wrong Question", *American Journal of Small Business*, 12(4), pp. 11–31.
Greiner, L., 1972, "Evolution and Revolution as Organization Grow", *Harvard Business Review*.
Hernandez, E., 2001, *Le Processus entrepreneurial, Vers un modèle stratégique d'entrepreneuriat*, Paris: Le Harmattan, pp. 256.
McGrath, R. & MacMillian, I., 2000, *The Entrepreneurial Mindset*, Harvard Business School Press.
Moore, R., 2012, Why High-Level Entrepreneurs Go to Business School.
Moore, R., 2014, Crossing the Chasm: Marketing and Selling High-Tech Products to Mainstream Customers.
Moore, R., 2014, Uncertainty and The Entrepreneurial Mindset.
Moore, R., 2015, Why Entrepreneurs Aare Heading to France.
Nunes, P. & Downes, L., 2014, Bing Bang Disruption, Business Survival in the Age of Constant Innovation.
Shane, S. & Venkataraman, S., 2000, "The Promise of Entrepreneurship as a Field of Research", *Academy of Management Review*, 25(1), pp. 217–226.
Timmons, J., 1999, *New Venture Creation: Entrepreneurship for the 21st Century*. Boston: Irwin/McGraw-Hill.

Literature on Management Consulting

Adams, Susan & Zanzi, Alberto. *Preparing Better Consultants.* Charlotte, North Carolina. Information Age Publishing. 2011.
Anastasi, Shane. *The Seven Principles of Professional Services: A field guide for successfully walking the consulting tightrope.* Chicago. PS Principles. 2014.
Andler, Nicolai. *Tools for Project Management, Workshops and Consulting: A Must-Have Compendium of Essential Tools and Techniques.* Erlangen. Publicis. 2011.
Bens, Ingrid. *Facilitating with Ease! Core Skills for Facilitators, Team Leaders and Members, Managers, Consultants, and Trainers.* San Francisco. Jossey-Bass. 2012.
Biech, Elaine. *The Consultant's Quick Start Guide: An Action Plan for Your First Year in Business.* San Francisco. Pfeiffer. 2008.
Biggs, David. *Management Consulting: A Guide for Students.* South Western Educational Publishing. 2010.
Biswas, Sugata & Twitchell, Daryl. *Management Consulting: A Complete Guide to the Industry.* New York. Wiley. 2008.
Bjartveit, Steinar & Roos, Göran (eds.). *Scandinavian Perspectives on Management Consulting.* Oslo. Cappelen. Akademisk Forlag 2005.
Block, Peter. *Flawless Consulting: A Guide to Getting Your Expertise Used.* San Francisco. Pfeiffer. 2011.
Bressard, Jean-Luc. *The Management Consultant.* 2016. (Kindle)
Buono, Anthony F., de Caluwé, Léon & Stoppelenburg, Annemieke. *Exploring the Professional Identity of Management Consultants.* Charlotte, North Carolina. Information Age Publishing. 2013.
Buono, Anthony F. *An Evolving Paradigm: Integrative Perspectives on Organizational Development, Change, Strategic Management, and Ethics.* Charlotte, North Carolina. Information Age Publishing. 2012.
Buono, Anthony F. & Grossmann, Ralph& Lobnig, Hubert& Mayer, Kurt. *The Changing Paradigm of Consulting: Adjusting to the Fast-Paced World.* Charlotte, North Carolina. Information Age Publishing. 2011.
Buono, Anthony F. & Jamieson, David W. *Consultation for Organizational Change.* Charlotte, North Carolina. Information Age Publishing. 2010.
Buono, Anthony F.& Poulfelt, Flemming. *Client-Consultant Collaboration: Coping with Complexity and Change.* Charlotte, North Carolina. Information Age Publishing. 2009.

Buono, Anthony F. *Emerging Trends and Issues in Management Consulting: Consulting as a Janus-Faced Reality*. Charlotte, North Carolina. Information Age Publishing. 2009.
Buono, Anthony F. & Savall, Henri. Socio-Economic *Intervention in Organizations*. Charlotte, North Carolina. Information Age Publishing. 2007.
Buono, Anthony F. *Creative Consulting Innovative Perspectives on Management Consulting*. Charlotte, North Carolina. Information Age Publishing. 2006.
Buono, Anthony F. & Poulfelt, Flemming. *Challenges and Issues in Knowledge Management*. Charlotte, North Carolina. Information Age Publishing. 2005.
Cheng, Victor. *Case Interview Secrets: A Former McKinsey Interviewer Reveals How to Get Multiple Job Offers in Consulting*. Seattle. Innovation Press. 2012.
Edersheim, Elizabeth Haas. *McKinsey's Marvin Bower: Vision, Leadership, and the Creation of Management Consulting*. Hoboken. Wiley. 2006.
Friga, Paul N. *The McKinsey Engagement: A Powerful Toolkit For More Efficient and Effective Team Problem Solving*. McGraw-Hill Education. 2008.
Garner, Ronald A & Garner, C. William. *The Service Consultant: Principles of Service Management and Ownership*. New York. Delmar Cengage Learning. 2013.
Gausel, Erik. *The Consulting Way: A Guide to Becoming a Successful Management Consultant*. Bloomington. iUniverse. 2013.
Hale, Judith. *The Performance Consultant's Fieldbook: Tools and Techniques for Improving Organizations and People*. San Francisco. Pfeiffer. 2006.
Haroun, Chris. *Management Consulting Introduction: What Does A Consultant Do & Consulting Best Practices*. www.BusinessCareerCoaching.com. 2016.
Hattori, Shu. *The McKinsey Edge: Success Principles from the World's Most Powerful Consulting Firm*. Columbus. McGraw-Hill Education. 2015.
Kamat, Sameer. *Business Doctors – Management Consulting Gone Wild*. Booksoarus. 2016. (Kindle)
Katcher, Bruce L. & Snyder, Adam. *An Insider's Guide to Building a Successful Consulting Practice*. New York. AMACOM. 2010.
Kiechel, Walter. *The Lords of Strategy: The Secret Intellectual History of the New Corporate World*. Boston. Harvard Business Review Press. 2010.
Kihn, Martin. *House of Lies: How Management Consultants Steal Your Watch and Then Tell You the Time*. New York. Business Plus. 2006.
Kipping, Matthias & Clark, Timothy. *The Oxford Handbook of Management Consulting (Oxford Handbooks)*. New York. Oxford University Press. 2013.
Kubr, Milan. *Management Consulting: A Guide to the Profession*. New Delhi. Bookwell Publications. 2005.
McKenna, Christopher D. *The World's Newest Profession: Management Consulting in the Twentieth Century (Cambridge Studies in the Emergence of Global Enterprise)*. New York. Cambridge University Press. 2006.
McLaughlin, Michael W. *Winning the Professional Services Sale: Unconventional Strategies to Reach More Clients, Land Profitable Work, and Maintain Your Sanity*. Hoboken. Wiley. 2009.
Morrison, Janie. *How to Get a Job and Succeed as a Management Consultant*. Durham. Bull City Publishing. 2016. (Kindle)

Nelson, Bob & Economy, Peter. *Consulting For Dummies*. Hoboken. For Dummies. 2008.
Newton, Richard. *The Management Consultant: Mastering the Art of Consultancy (Financial Times Series)*. Harlow. FT Press. 2010.
Phelan, Karen. *I'm Sorry I Broke Your Company: When Management Consultants Are the Problem, Not the Solution*. San Francisco. Berrett-Koehler Publishers. 2013.
Poulfelt, Flemming. *Thought Consultancy – In action*. In Bjartveit, Steinar & Roos, Göran (eds.). *Scandinavian Perspectives on Management Consulting*. 2005.
Sandlin, Eileen Figure. *Start Your Own Consulting Business: Your Step-By-Step Guide to Success (StartUp Series)*. Entrepreneur Press. 2014.
Sauder, Lew. *Consulting 101, 2nd Edition: 101 Tips for Success in Consulting*. Lew Sauder. 2014.
Schein, Edgar H. *Humble Consulting: How to Provide Real Help Faster*. Oakland. Berrett-Koehler Publishers. 2016.
Schwarz, Roger M. *The Skilled Facilitator: A Comprehensive Resource for Consultants, Facilitators, Coaches, and Trainers*. San Francisco. Jossey-Bass. 2016.
Scott Sr., Nicolas L. *12 Habits of Great Apartment Leasing Consultants: The Ultimate Apartment Leasing Guide for Leasing Consultants Everywhere!*. Hustle University. 2014.
Scott, Beverly & Barnes, B. Kim. *Consulting on the Inside: A Practical Guide for Internal Consultants*. Alexandria, Virginia. Association for Talent Development. 2011.
Silberman, Mel. *The Consultant's Toolkit: High-Impact Questionnaires, Activities and How-to Guides for Diagnosing and Solving Client Problems*. Columbus. New York. McGraw-Hill Education. 2000.
Stern, Carl W. & Deimler, Michael S.. *The Boston Consulting Group on Strategy: Classic Concepts and New Perspectives*. Wiley. 2006.
Stroh, Linda H. & Johnson, Homer H.. *The Basic Principles of Effective Consulting*. Psychology Press. 2005.
Verlander, Edward G. *The Practice of Professional Consulting*. San Francisco. Pfeiffer. 2012.
Warfield, Taylor. *Hacking the Case Interview: Your Shortcut Guide to Mastering Consulting Interviews*. 2016. (Kindle)
Weiss, Alan. *The Consulting Bible: Everything You Need to Know to Create and Expand a Seven-Figure Consulting Practice*. Hoboken. Wiley. 2011.
Weiss, Alan. *Getting Started in Consulting*. Hoboken, New Jersey. Wiley. 2009.
Weiss, Alan. *Million Dollar Consulting Proposals: How to Write a Proposal That's Accepted Every Time*. Hoboken. Wiley. 2011.
Weiss, Alan. *Million Dollar Consulting: The Professional's Guide to Growing a Practice, Fifth Edition*. McGraw-Hill Education. 2016.
Whitehurst, Destin & Robinson, Erin. *The Case Interview: 20 Days to Ace the Case: Your Day-by-Day Prep Course to Land a Job in Management Consulting*. Berkeley. Tycho Press. 2016.
Wickham, Louise & Wilcock, Jeremy. *Management Consulting 5th edn: Delivering an Effective Project*. Harlow. Pearson. 2016.

Wickham, Louise. *Management Consulting Delivering an Effective Project.* Harlow. Pearson Custom Publishing. 2012.

Wickham, Philip A. & Wickham, Louise. *Management Consulting: Delivering an Effective Project (3rd Edition).* Harlow. Prentice Hall. 2008.

Zhao, Jonathan. *What They Teach You Inside Management Consulting: Lessons You Need to Know to Succeed Anywhere.* 2015. (Kindle)

Index

Note: Information in tables and figures is indicated by page numbers in *italics*.

Accenture 66
accounting firms 15
adaptability *332*
ADL *see* Arthur D. Little (ADL)
advertising 66–8; *see also* marketing
AIDA model 138
alignment: in business transformation and innovation consulting 323–6, *324*, *325*; in high-performance consulting firms 372–3; organizational *324*; transformational *324*
analysis: facilitation billing vs. 35
Andersen Consulting 66–7
Ansoff, Igor 117
anxiety: in change management 128
Apple Macintosh 84
application software providers 100–1
apprenticeship 392–3
Argyris, Chris 122
Arthur Andersen & Company 61–2
Arthur D. Little (ADL) 16–18
Asia, bowing in *214*
attitudes: professionalism and 38–41
audits: manufacturing 163; social 280
authority: as cultural nuance *215*
automotive industry: emerging technologies in 110

BAA *see* Broad Agency Announcements (BAA)
banking: emerging technologies in 110; as IT sector 92–3
Barnes Reports 172
BCG *see* Boston Consulting Group (BCG)
BearingPoint 26
Beckhard, Dick 128

benchmarking: in Operations Management consulting 163
Bennis, Warren 122
Big-3 387
Big-4 387
billing: analysis vs. facilitation 35
board consulting: board composition in 198; building blueprint in 197–200; CEO consulting and 202–3; conflicts of interest in 203; content of 195–6; culture in 199; focus in 198; leadership evaluation in 198–9; process issues in 196–7; scope of engagement in 198; stock-taking in 198; strategy in 199–200; value creation in 199–200; work processes in 198
boards of directors: accountability of 194; as active collaborators 195; as active monitors 194; as activists 195; as cosmetic appendage 194; historical phases of 194–5; independence of 194; as passive observers 194; role of 194; teams vs. 197
Boeing 245, 256–7
Booz Allen 29
Booz Allen Hamilton 18
Boston Consulting Group (BCG) 18, 41
Bower, Marvin 115
bowing *214*
BPR *see* business process reengineering (BPR)
branding 56–8
Broad Agency Announcements (BAA) 232–3
business design innovation 119–20
business models 7–8
business process reengineering (BPR) 377

442 Index

business schools *see* education
business transformation: defined 316–17
business transformation and innovation consulting: alignment in 323–6, *324, 325*; celebration in 328–9; collaboration in 329–32; experience 331–3, *332*; forcing strategy in *320*; human resources in 328; hybrid approach in 319; innovation in 329–32; knowledge transfer model in 327, *327*; leadership in 319–29, *320, 324, 325, 327*; management consulting approach in 317–18; momentum in 326–8, *327*; organizational development in 318; participative strategy in *320*; roles in 317–19; strategy in 321–3; telling strategy in *320*; transformational strategy in *320*; vision in 321
buyer-seller relationship 138
buyer values 60–2

Canback, Staffan 16
Capacity Analysis: in Operations Management consulting 163–4
casual dining: emerging technologies in 110
celebration: in business transformation and innovation consulting 328–9
"celebrity CEO" 184
central repository: in knowledge management system 395–6
CEO consulting: assessment of people in 193; audiences in 201; backstairs channel in 193; balance in 201; board consulting and 202–3; clientship in 192; client understanding in 201–2; coach role in 189; conflicts of interest in 203; content expert role in 189; content in 191; crisis management in 200; dilemmas in 192–4; ego inflation in 193; employee stakeholders in 184; executive succession in 200; expertise in 201; facilitation in 201; guru role in 189; high-quality work in 190; ideas vs. actions in 188; influence balance in 193; insulation in 192; listening in 191; over-identification in 193; performance evaluation in 200; positive personal engagement in 190–1; prescriptive vs. facilitative 188; process facilitator role in 189; process in 191; relationship development in 190–1; risk assessment in 200; roles 188–90; sage role in 189; shareholder investor in 184–5; stakeholder groups in 184–5; technician role in 188; tone in 190; trusted advisor role in 190; trust in 190; value chain constituencies in 184; value provision in 186
CEO(s): as attractive clients 186–8; "celebrity" 184; frustrated sophomore 187; "imperial" 183; isolation of 185–6, 192; perplexed new 187; reflective late-term 187–8; as role model 415–16; roles of 185; "second act" of 188; worried mid-term 187
Certified Management Consultant (CMC) 38
change: culture of 315; discontinuous 125; keeping up with 23; nature of 130
change management: best practices 129; consulting 127–8; in "fit models" notion 123; in global information systems rollout 219; history of 127–8
China 26
Christensen, Clayton 8
CICA *see* Competition in Contracting Act (CICA)
Citibank 18–19
Clarke, Scott 168
client needs 23–5
client professionalism 9–10
clients, skills with 41–2
client specific knowledge (CSK) 384
closing: in trust-based sales 144
Cloud computing 86–8
CMC (Certified Management Consultant) 38
Cold War 79
collaboration: in business transformation and innovation consulting 329–32
Colossus 77
commoditization 7
common vocabulary 415
communications: as cultural nuance 215; internal and external, linking of 58–60; as IT sector 92–3; messaging alignment in 59–60; in sales and marketing 58–60

Index 443

communication skills *332*
community of practice: participation in 392
compartmentalized approach 116–17
compensation 64–5
competition: in IT industry 94–5; in IT management consulting 103; knowledge and 385–90
Competition in Contracting Act (CICA) 232
Computer: birth of 78; mainframe 78–80, 80–1; personal 83–5
Computer Sciences Corporation (CSC) 9
concurrent enterprise design 131–3
confidence *332*
Congruence Model of Organizational Behavior 123–4
consolidation, market 9
constraints, theory of 157, 170n7
consulting, defining 33–4
consulting industry: early model of 115–16; financial crisis and 6; history of 16–23, 115–18; restructuring 15–16, 31–2; transformation 14–15; turbulence in 5–6; turnaround of 6–7
consulting process knowledge (CPK) 383
control: in change management 128
corporate profits: GDP vs. 92; IT spending vs. 92
Cost Accounting Standards 238
cost reduction 23–4
courage 46
CPK *see* consulting process knowledge (CPK)
Creative Destruction 420
Cresap, McCormack & Paget 18–19
crises: in growth management 340–2
cross-selling: in trust-based sales 145–6
cruisers 48–9
CSC 20
CSRA 9
cultural audits 280
culture: in board consulting 199; of change 315; in global consulting 213–15, *214–15*; in high-performance consulting firms 371–2; in mergers and acquisitions (M&A) consulting 308–9
customization: in Operations Management consulting 158, 169

data analytics 109
data protection laws 210, 218
delivery: emerging technologies in 110
Deloitte 9, 15
Deloitte & Touche 19
deregulation: Operations Management consulting and 167–8
developmental leadership 357–9
digital enterprise business model 108
digital transformation 8–9
disruption 11–12
diversity: homogeneity vs. 35–6
Dodd-Frank rules 194
dot.com 85–6
dot.com bust 14
drink: as cultural nuance *215*
Drucker, Peter 115, 422
Dudoff, Robert 51
due diligence: in mergers and acquisitions (M&A) consulting 298
dynamo 48

E-Curve 118
EDS 20, 46–7
education: emerging technologies in 110; formal vs. on the job 34–5; professionalism and 38–40
Elite-8 387
empathy *332*
employee groups: in CEO consulting 184
employee recognition programs 174–5
encounter design: in Operations Management consulting 165–6
ENIAC 77
enterprise design 131–3
Enterprise Resource Planning (ERP) 208, 315–16
entertainment: emerging technologies in 110
entrepreneurialism 10
Entrepreneurial Revolution 420–1
Entrepreneurship: as creation vs. discovery 421–2; disruption in 427–8; dynamic value creation in 423–5, *425*; innovation in 427–8; journey of *422*, 422–3; mindset in 426–7; necessity based 422; opportunity based 422; roles in 426; skillsets in 426; stages of *426*
Entrepreneurship consultation: implications for 428–31; as new field 419–20

444 *Index*

environment: aggressive, proactive approach to 132; as organizational system input 124
ERK *see* experiential and referential knowledge (ERK)
Ernst & Young 29, 59
ERP *see* Enterprise Resource Planning (ERP)
ethics: evaluation of success in 416–17; pressure for results vs. 34; values and 407–8
events: as cultural nuance *214*
execution gap 269
expectations: performance and 62–3
experiential and referential knowledge (ERK) 383–4
expertise: -based intervention strategy 277–9; in buying 139; professionalism vs. 39; shared 138; subject matter 384
explicit knowledge 380

Facebook 404–5
facilitate and learn delivery mode 272, 273–4
Facilitated Network business model 8
facilitated network provider (FNP) 111
facilitation billing 35
FAR *see* Federal Acquisition Regulation (FAR)
fast food 110; emerging technologies in 110
fear 46, 331
Federal Acquisition Regulation (FAR) 230–1, 238, 251–5
feedback loops 132
financial crisis 6
fit: as cultural nuance *214*
"fit models" 123
Fitness Landscape 330, *331*
Five Forces 118, 138
Five P's 154–6
FNP *see* facilitated network provider (FNP)
food: as cultural nuance *215*
forcing strategy *320*
future value space mapping 121

Galbraith, Jay 122, 123
Gantt, H. L. 153
gap analysis 163
GD *see* General Dynamics (GD)

gender communication: as cultural nuance *215*
General Dynamics (GD) 247
Gilbreth, Frank 153
Gilbreth, Lillian 153
Glen, Paul 42
global consulting: client organization in 208–9; cultural nuances in 213–15, *214–15*; data protection laws and 210, 218; experience 222–3; information systems rollout in 217–19; language and 214; local customers in 211–12; local laws and regulations in 209–10, 220–1; local markets in 211–12; local skills and practices in 210–11; multi-national acquisitions in 216–17; pre-engagement considerations in 206–15, *207*, *209*, *214–15*; state-run enterprise transformation in 219–21; supply chain in 212–13; variations in 205
Global Consulting Approach 206, *207*, 216–21
global imperative 25
globalization: Public Sector consulting and 226–7
global supply chains: in global consulting 212–13; in Operations Management consulting 167
Goldratt, Eliyahu 170n7
government, as IT sector 92–3; *see also* Public Sector consulting
Great Recession 6
greed 45
Greengard, Samuel 168
Growth Share Matrix 118
growth stage management, in consulting firms: common approach to clients in 351–2; crises and 340–2; developmental leadership in 357–9; diversification stage in 344, 349–52; failed 338–9; focusing stage in 343, 346–9; growth issues in 339–40; growth opportunities in 342–6; growth study in 339; institutionalization stage in 344, 352–6; management practices in 342; market exploration in 342–6; organizational flexibility in 355–6; ownership sharing in 351–2; service broadening in 348–9; staff development in 348–9; stages in

Index 445

340–57; stopping growth in 358–9; targeted market segments in 345–6; victims of bad 338–9; vision in 345–6
"guru consulting" 171–2

harbor freight: emerging technologies in 110
hardware-software integration 123
Harrah's 166
Hawthorne studies 122
healthcare: emerging technologies in 110
Henderson, Bruce 18, 117, 118
Hewlett-Packard 308–9
high-performance consulting firms: alignment in 372–3; commitment creation in 364; consensus creation in 364; culture in 371–2; firm size in 372–3; goal-setting in 362–3; governance participation in 370; leadership in 367–71; managing director in 370–1; partner involvement in 366; partnership behavior in 367–71; performance evaluation in 369–70; rewards in 369–70; strategic identity in 363–4; strategy first in 362; support of those who leave 366–7; talent in 364–6; three-hat challenge in 367–9
HII see Huntington Ingalls Industries (HII)
Hislop, Donald 394
history: of consulting industry 16–23, 115–18; as organizational system input 124
homogeneity: diversity vs. 35–6
Hughes Electronics Corporation 259–64
human capital: knowledge and 386; strategy 174, *177*
human interactive skills 39–40
human resources consulting: in Barnes Reports 172; buyers of 176; characteristics of 172–3; consultants in 174–6; defined 171; employee recognition programs in 174–5; field overview 176–8, *177*; "guru consulting" in 171–2; human capital strategy in 174, *177*; human resources outsourcing in 174, *177*; in IBISWorld 172–3; market segments in 173; market size in 172–3; technology consulting in 174, *177*; types of 173–4
human resources management: defined 171
human resources outsourcing 174, *177*
human resources process improvement and reengineering *177*
human resources program design and execution *177*
human resources technology consulting 174, *177*
Huntington Ingalls Industries (HII) 9, 248–9

IBISWorld 172–3
IBM 78, 79, 86
IBM 360 80–1
IBM 370 80–1
IBM Global Services 20
IDA see intelligent data analytics (IDA)
"imperial CEO" 183
implementation, accelerated 121
incentive-based pricing 52–3
information systems rollout: in global consulting 217–19
innovation: in business transformation and innovation consulting 329–32
innovation cycle 11
inspiration *332*
integrated enterprise design 131–3
integrated service provider (ISP) 111
integration: in mergers and acquisitions consulting 292–3; see also mergers and acquisitions (M&A) consulting
integrity 42–6
intelligent data analytics (IDA) 109
Internet 85–6, 126; see also IT management consulting
interpersonal skills 39–40, *332*
"intervention myopia" 285
intervention strategies: alternative 276–85; blending of 286–7; client implications of 287; consultant implications of 285–7; content focus in 270, 274–6; delivery mode in 270, 271–4; execution gap and 269; expertise-based 277–9; facilitate and learn delivery mode in 272, 273–4; importance of 269–70; industry implications of 287–8; key dimensions in 270–6; in mergers and acquisitions (M&A) consulting

446 *Index*

302–10; organization-based 279–80; organization development and 276; process-based 283–5; social systems content focus in 276; study and recommend delivery mode in 271–3; teaching-based 280–3; technical systems content focus in 274–6
intuition 115–16
isolation: of CEOs 185–6, 192
ISP *see* integrated service provider (ISP)
iterative approach 132
IT industry: banking in 92–3; communications in 92–3; competitive dynamics of 94–5; corporate profits and 92; defining 90–5; description of 90; dimensions 90–2; by function 94; government in 92–3; major markets in 92–4; manufacturing in 92–3; segments 92–4; size of 90–2; spending in 91; by technology 94
IT management consultant 95–7
IT management consulting: cloud computing and 86–8; competitive dynamics in 103; contractors in 99; defining 95–107; digital enterprise business model and transformation in 108; emergence of 81–3; emerging technologies in 110; evolution of 88–9; firms 97–102; future of 107–12; history of 76–89; intelligent data analytics in 109; Internet in history of 85–6; IT research providers in 101–2; market 98; organizational compression integration in 108; packaged software and 81–3; self-learning systems in 109; services 103–7; specialized IT service providers in 102; strategic IT consulting providers in 101, 104; technology and application software providers in 100–1; virtual enterprise and 86–8; virtual reality in 108–9
IT research providers 101–2

JIT *see* Just-in-Time (JIT)
judgment 115–16, *332*
Just-in-Time (JIT) 153, 160

Kaiser, Henry 153
Kennedy, John F. 321
KMX *see* knowledge management systems (KMX)
knowledge: benefits of 382; capture 388; -centric 386; client specific 384; competing on 385–90; consultants and 376–8; consulting process 383; defining 378–81; demonstration of 389–90; development 380–1; development cycle 391; experiential and referential 383–4; explicit 380; human capital and 386; management consulting 381–5; in master-apprentice model 392–3; professional practice and behavior 384; publication of 389; sharing hostility 388; stages of 381; subject matter expertise as 384; tacit 379–80; transfer 390–4; wisdom vs. 375
knowledge management: benefits of 385; central repository in 395–6; objectives 385; social roadmap in 395
knowledge management systems (KMX) 390, 394–8
knowledge mapping 395
knowledge transfer 327, *327*
KPMG 19

language: as cultural nuance 214, *215*; formal vs. informal *215*; global consulting and 214
laws: in global consulting 209–10, 220–1; state-run enterprises and 220–1
leadership 30–1; in business transformation and innovation consulting 319–29, *320*, *324*, *325*, *327*; developmental 357–9; in high-performance consulting firms 367–71; Operations Management consulting and 152–3; partners' failed 48–9
leading practices 12–13
lead qualification: in trust-based sales 145
lean operations: in Operations Management consulting 157
Leavitt, Harold 123
LEG Inc. 270
Leidos Holdings 248, 264–6
Lewin, Kurt 122
Liddy, Ed 308
listening: in mergers and acquisitions (M&A) consulting 303–4
LMC *see* Lockheed Martin Corporation (LMC)
Lockheed Martin Corporation (LMC) 244–5, 255–6

Lodish, Len 64
logistics: in Operations Management consulting 152
losers 49
Loughead, Allan 244
Loveman, Gary 166

MacDonald O'Leary, Julie 38
MacGregor, Douglas 122
Mainframe 78–80, 80–1
Maister, David 56, 66, 140
Managerial Grid 128
managing director: in high-performance consulting firms 370–1
manufacturing: global consulting and 210; as IT sector 92–3
manufacturing audits 163
market consolidation 9
market development 24
marketing: advertising in 66–8; aggressive 28; balance of, with sales 54–5; branding and 56–8; buyer values and 60–2; challenge of 52–3; communications in 58–60; compensation and 64–5; cycle 53; defined 51; effectiveness in 56–65, 57; expectations-performance match in 62–3; internal 59; launching initiative for 57; measurement and 63–4; media management in 66–8; monitoring and 63–4; pricing in 52–3; public relations in 66–8; recruiting and 59–60; relationship 65–6; research 61; rewards and 64–5; sales and, consistency between 51; in Sales and Marketing Matrix 54–5; sales vs. 52; selection in 54; in solo practices 68–9; stages in 53; strategy of firm in 56–8
Marsh & McLennan 19–20
Martin, Glenn 244
mass customization: in Operations Management consulting 158, 169
master-apprentice model 392–3
Materials Requirements Planning (MRP) 153
McKinsey & Co. 18, 40–1, 67
media management 66–8
Mercer Management Consulting 67
mergers and acquisitions (M&A): in consulting industry 9; in global consulting 216–17; stages of 294–6; as value creation strategy 290

mergers and acquisitions (M&A) consulting: with acquired firm as client 309–10; clarification of strategic intent in 304–5; common issues in 297–301; cost reduction in 299; culture in 308–9; decision facilitation in 305–6; due diligence in 298; dynamics of 291–7; in early integration 294, 295; emotions in 302–3; financial engineering in 299; focus of 295–6; future of 310–11; integration consulting in 291–2; integration in 292–3; integration managers in 306–7; intervention strategies in 302–10; lack of preparation in 293; listening in 303–4; morale auditor role in 307–8; in planning phase 294, 295; in post-combination period 294, 295; process improvement in 299; revenue enhancement in 299; roles in 294–6; synergy capture in 298–300; talent retention in 301; temporal constraints in 296–7; transaction advising in 291–2; trust in 302–3
messaging alignment 59–60
metaphor: as cultural nuance *214*
Millar, Victor E. 61–2
Mitchell Madison Group (MMG) 338
MMG *see* Mitchell Madison Group (MMG)
momentum: in business transformation and innovation consulting 326–8, *327*
Monitor 9
"morale auditor" role, in mergers and acquisitions (M&A) consulting 307–8
moving: emerging technologies in 110
MRP *see* Materials Requirements Planning (MRP)
multi-service operations consultants 153–4

Nadler, David 122, 123
needs, client 23–5
networks 28
network structure, virtual 126
"no-profit zones" 119
Northrop Grumman 9, 246–7, 257–9

objections: handling of, in trust-based sales 142–3
OD *see* organizational development (OD)

448 *Index*

onboarding: socialization and 40–1
open systems 123
open systems theory 122–3
Operations Management (OM) consulting: analytical tools in 162–4; benchmarking in 163; Capacity Analysis in 163–4; challenge of 169; contexts for 158–62; data gathering in 164; defining 151–3; deregulation and 167–8; documentation in 164–5; domestic issues in 159–60, 161; Five P's of 154–6; focused operations in 158; future issues in 165–9; gap analysis in 163; global issues in 159, 161–2; historical foundations of 153; independent operations consultants in 154; internal consulting groups in 154; key concepts in 156–8; leadership and 152–3; lean operations in 157; logistics in 152; manufacturing audits in 163; in manufacturing vs. services operations 155–6; mass customization in 158, 169; multiple facilities issues in 161–2; multi-service 153–4; outsourcing and 167; as overlooked 151; plant tours in 163; practical problems in 164–5; privatization and 167–8; Process Analysis in 163–4; productivity in 159, 165; quality in 159; real-time technology and 168; reward of 169; service encounter design in 165–6; single facility issues in 159–60; specialized operations consultants in 154; supply chain globalization and 167; supply chain management in 157; theory of constraints and 157; Total Quality Management in 156–7; virtual integration in 167; waste reduction in 152; worker resistance in 165
organization: as pillar of management consulting 114
organizational alignment *324*
organizational compression integration 108
organizational development (OD): in business transformation and innovation consulting 318
organizational diagnosis 123
organizational dynamics 123
organizational transformation process 125

organization-based intervention strategy 279–80
organization design 122, *177*
organization development 122, 276
outsourcing: as disturbing force 126; human resources 174, *177*; in Operations Management consulting 167; revenue 27–8

participative strategy *320*
partners, failed leadership of 48–9
performance: expectations and 62–3
performance evaluation: in high-performance consulting firms 369–70
pharmacy: emerging technologies in 110
PIMS *see* Profit Impact of Market Strategy (PIMS)
"pitch": in trust-based sales 143–4
Poggenpohl, Teresa 66–7
Pollino, Pat 67
Porter, Michael 118–19, 414
positioning: in trust-based sales 141
power: in change management 128
PPK *see* professional practice and behavior knowledge (PPK)
presence *332*
PricewaterhouseCoopers 19
pricing: incentive-based 52–3; in requests for proposal 237–8; in sales and marketing 52–3; trust and 141–2
Private Sector: splitting of, with Pubic Sector 7
privatization: Operations Management consulting and 167–8
proactive *332*
problem definition: in sales 147–8
Process Analysis: in Operations Management consulting 163–4
process-based intervention strategy 283–5
product development 24
productivity: in Operations Management consulting 159, 165
professional identity 392
professionalism: attitudes and 38–41; B-school problem and 38–40; client 9–10; downsides of 39; education and 38–40; elements of 37; enforcement problems and 46–9; expertise vs. 39; integrity and 42–6; interpersonal skills and 39–40; misguided 411; partner leadership

and 48–9; and skills with clients 41–2; success and 44–5
professional organizations: Public Sector consulting and 230
professional practice and behavior knowledge (PPK) 384
Profit Impact of Market Strategy (PIMS) 118
profits, corporate: GDP vs. 92; IT spending vs. 92
proposal writing: in trust-based sales 146–8
public ownership 28–9
public relations 66–8
Public Sector: splitting of, with Private Sector 7
Public Sector consulting: Boeing in 245, 256–7; Broad Agency Announcements in 232–3; client knowledge in 236; commencement of engagements in 233, 234; company size in 236; competition in 234–5; Competition in Contracting Act in 232; context 228; Cost Accounting Standards in 238; defined 224–9; Federal Acquisition Regulation in 230–1, 238, 251–5; federal vs. state/local/educational 227–8; future of 249; General Dynamics in 247; globalization and 226–7; Huntington Ingalls Industries in 248–9; industry size 228; largest consultants in 228–9, 244–9; Leidos Holdings in 248, 264–6; Lockheed Martin in 244–5, 255–6; Northrop Grumman in 246–7, 257–9; pricing in 237–8; private sector vs. 224–5; professional organizations in 230; Raytheon in 247–8, 259–64; relationship building in 229–30; requests for proposal in 229–31, 234–5, 237–43, 239–41; Small Business Administration and 234; socioeconomic requirements in 234; in United States vs. other countries 225–7; winning proposals in 230–1
public service: emerging technologies in 110
public utilities: emerging technologies in 110

quality: in Operations Management consulting 159

Rackham, Neil 140
Ramo, Simon 246
Raytheon 247–8, 259–64
recruiting: marketing and 59–60
regulations: in global consulting 209–10
relationship marketing 65–6
relationships 29–30
requests for proposal (RFPs) 229–30, 234–5, 237–43, 239–41
research, marketing 61
research providers 101–2
resistance, worker: in Operations Management consulting 165
resources: as organizational system input 124
restructuring: industry 15–16, 31–2; role 32–3
revenue: outsourcing 27–8; by practice area 20–1, 22
rewards 64–5; in high-performance consulting firms 369–70
RFPs see requests for proposal (RFPs)
rituals: as cultural nuance 214
Rockwell International 256–7
role-modeling 415–16
role restructuring 32–3
"Rule of Three" 31
Rules of Romance 147–8

Saatchi 19
SAIC see Science Applications International Corporation (SAIC)
sales: advertising in 66–8; balance of, with marketing 54–5; buyer values and 60–2; challenge of 52–3; communications in 58–60; compensation and 64–5; in consulting industry vs. industry at large 138–9; cycle 53; expectations-performance match and 62–3; marketing and, consistency between 51; marketing vs. 52; measurement and 63–4; media management in 66–8; monitoring and 63–4; paradox of 137–40; pricing in 52–3; problem definition in 147–8; public relations in 66–8; rewards and 64–5; screening phase in 138, 139; selection in 54, 139; self-sabotage in 139–40; in solo practices 68–9; stages in 53; strategy of firm in 56–8; see also trust-based sales
Sales and Marketing Matrix 54–5

Sarbanes-Oxley legislation 194
schools *see* education
Schumpeter, Joseph 420
Science Applications International Corporation (SAIC) 9
scientific management 16–18
Scitor Corporation 225–6
screening phase: in sales 138, 139
selection 54, 139
selfishness 45
self-learning systems (SLS) 109
self-sabotage: in sales 139–40
seller as agent 138
service encounter design: in Operations Management consulting 165–6
shareholder investor: in CEO consulting 184–5
Sheth, Jag 66
short-termism 45
simplicity 12
Singapore Airlines 58
Sloan, Alfred P. 118
SLS *see* self-learning systems (SLS)
Small Business Administration 234
SME *see* subject matter expertise (SME)
Snapchat 405
social audits 280
socialization 40–1
social roadmap 395
software: -hardware integration 123; packaged 81–3; providers 100–1
Sogetti 19
solo practices: sales and marketing in 68–9
solution shop business model 8
Southwest Airlines 58
specialization 285
specialized IT service providers 102
specialized operations consultants 154; *see also* Operations Management (OM) consulting
specialty service provider (SSP) 111
SRA 9
SSP *see* specialty service provider (SSP)
Stacey, Ralph 330, *331*
state-run enterprises: in global consulting 219–21
Stevenson, Howard 422
"strategic drift" 364
strategic IT consulting providers 101, 104
strategy: in board consulting 199–200; in business transformation and innovation consulting 321–3; elements of 120; as pillar of management consulting 114; in sales and marketing 56–8
study and recommend delivery mode 271–3
subject matter expertise (SME) 384, 395
supply chain management: in Operations Management consulting 157
supply chains, global: in global consulting 212–13; in Operations Management consulting 167

tacit knowledge 379–80
talent retention: in mergers and acquisitions (M&A) consulting 301
Taylor, Frederick W. 153, 274, 317
teaching-based intervention strategy 280–3
teams: boards of directors vs. 197
technology: Operations Management consulting and 168
technology and application software providers 100–1
technology shifts: coping with 24–5; *see also* IT management consulting
telling strategy *320*
theory of constraints 157, 170n7
three-hat challenge 367–9
Timmons, Jeffery 421
Total Quality Management (TQM) 153, 156–7, 160
Towers Perrin 18
TQM *see* Total Quality Management (TQM)
transformational alignment *324*
transformational strategy *320*
transformational traits *332*
transparency 140, 410–11
transportation: emerging technologies in 110
travel: emerging technologies in 110
trends 23–31
Trianz 16
trust-based sales: client relationships in 140–1; closing in 144; cross-selling in 145–6; handling objections in 142–3; lead qualification in 145; and paradox of traditional sales 137–40; "pitch" in 143–4; positioning in 141; pricing and 141–2; problem

definition in 147–8; proposal writing in 146–8; transparency in 140; *see also* sales
trusted advisor(s): behavior of 408–12; in CEO consulting 190; evaluation of 416–17; firms consisting of 412–16
Trust Equation 139
TRW 9, 246–7, 257–9
Tushman, Michael 122, 123
Twitter 405

UI *see* User Interface (UI)
USAir 300
User Interface (UI): as cultural nuance 215

value-added process business business model 8
value chain constituencies 184
value creation 10–11
Value-Driven Business Design 120–2
value migration 121
values: buyer 60–2; dialogue on 415; ethics and 407–8
value space mapping 121
value system 40–1
Virtual enterprise 86–8
virtual integration: in Operations Management consulting 167
virtual network structure 126
virtual reality (VR) 108–9
virtual service provider (VSP) 111
virtues 407–8
vision 331, *332*; in business transformation and innovation consulting 321; in growth management 345–6
vocabulary, common 415
VR *see* virtual reality (VR)
VSP *see* virtual service provider (VSP)

warehousing: emerging technologies in 110
waste reduction 152
Watson, Thomas J. 78
wisdom: knowledge vs. 375
Woolridge, Dean 246
worker resistance: in Operations Management consulting 165
work papers: in knowledge management system 396
World War II 77
Wright, Oliver 82

Xerox Sales program 144

Y2K 85–6

PGMO 05/28/2018